The Random House Basic Dictionary

Spanish-English
English-Spanish

S0-ACR-644

The Random House Basic Dictionary

Spanish-English
English-Spanish

Edited by
Donald F. Solá
Cornell University

Under the General Editorship of
Professor Frederick B. Agard
Cornell University

The Ballantine Reference Library
Ballantine Books · New York

Copyright © 1981, 1967, 1954 by Random House, Inc.

All rights reserved under International and Pan-American
Copyright Conventions. Published in the United States by
Ballantine Books, a division of Random House, Inc., New
York, and simultaneously in Canada by Random House of
Canada Limited, Toronto.

Library of Congress Catalog Card Number: 67-20648

ISBN 0-345-38708-2

This edition published by arrangement with Random House,
Inc.

Previously published as *The Spanish Vest Pocket Dictionary*
and *The Random House Spanish Dictionary*.

Manufactured in the United States of America

First Ballantine Books Edition: August 1981
Twentieth Printing: August 1993

First Special Edition: August 1981
Second Special Edition: October 1981

Concise Pronunciation Guide

Spanish Letter	Pronunciation
a	Like English *a* in *father*.
b, v	At beginning of word group and after *m* or *n* like English *b*. Elsewhere, like English *v*, but pronounced with both lips instead of upper teeth and lower lip.
c	Before *e* or *i*, like English *th* in *thin* (in Northern Spain); like Spanish *s* (in Southern Spain and the Americas); elsewhere, like English *k* in *key*.
ch	Like English *ch* in *child*.
d	At beginning of word group and after *n* or *l*, like English *d*. Elsewhere, like English *th* in *either*.
e	Like English *e* in *bet*.
f	As in English.
g	Before *e* or *i*, the same as Spanish *j*. Elsewhere, like English *g* in *get*.
gu	Before *e* or *i*, like English *g* in *get*. Elsewhere, like English *gw* in *Gwynn*.
gü	Like English *gw* in *Gwynn*.
h	Silent.
i	Like English *i* in *machine*, but more clipped. Before or after another vowel, like English *y* (except when accented.)
j	Like English *h*, but more rasping.
k	Like English *k*.

Spanish Letter	Pronunciation
l	Like English *l* in *like*, but with the tongue behind the upper front teeth.
ll	Like English *lli* in *million* (in Northern Spain); like Spanish *y* (in Southern Spain and the Americas).
m	As in English.
n	As in English.
ñ	Like English *ny* in *canyon*.
o	Approximately like English *o* in *vote*, but more clipped.
p	As in English.
qu	Like English *k*.
r	Not at all like American English *r*; a quick flap of the tongue-tip on the roof of the mouth.
rr	A strongly "rolled" or trilled version of Spanish *r*.
s	Like English *s* in *lease*.
t	As in English.
u	Like English *oo* in *boot*, but more clipped. Before *e* or after another vowel, like English *w* (except when accented).
v	See *b* above.
x	Like English *x*; although before consonants many speakers pronounce it like Spanish *s*; like Spanish *j* (in Mexican Indian words).
y	Approximately like English *y* in yes.
z	Like English *th* in *thin* (in Northern Spain); like English *s* in *lease* (in Southern Spain and the Americas).

Spanish Accentuation

In a number of words spoken stress is marked by an accent ('): *nación*, *país*, *médico*, *día*.

Words which are not so marked are, generally speaking, stressed on the next-to-the-last syllable if they end in a vowel, *n*, or *s*; and on the last syllable if they end in a consonant other than *n* or *s*.

Note: An accent is placed over some words to distinguish them from others having the same spelling and pronunciation but differing in meaning.

Irregular Verbs

Infinitive	Present	Future	Preterit	Past Part.
andar	ando	andaré	anduve	andado
caber	quepo	cabré	cupe	cabido
caer	caigo	caeré	caí	caído
conducir	conduzco	conduciré	conduje	conducido
dar	doy	daré	dí	dado
decir	digo	diré	dije	dicho
estar	estoy	estaré	estuve	estado
haber	he	habré	hube	habido
hacer	hago	haré	hice	hecho
ir	voy	iré	fuí	ido
jugar	juego	jugaré	jugué	jugado
morir	muero	moriré	morí	muerto
oír	oigo	oiré	oí	oído
poder	puedo	podré	pude	podido
poner	pongo	pondré	puse	puesto
querer	quiero	querré	quise	querido
saber	sé	sabré	supe	sabido
salir	salgo	saldré	salí	salido
ser	soy	seré	fuí	sido
tener	tengo	tendré	tuve	tenido
traer	traigo	traeré	traje	traído
valer	valgo	valdré	valí	valido
venir	vengo	vendré	vine	venido
ver	veo	veré	ví	visto

Abbreviations

a.	adjective
abbr.	abbreviation
adv.	adverb
aero.	aeronautical
agr.	agriculture
anat.	anatomy
art.	article
bot.	botany
chem.	chemistry
coll.	colloquial
com.	commercial
conj.	conjunction
dem.	demonstrative
f.	feminine
fin.	finance
geog.	geography
govt.	government
gram.	grammar
interj.	interjection
interrog.	interrogative
leg.	legal
m.	masculine
mech.	mechanics
med.	medicine
Mex.	Mexico
mus.	musical
n.	noun
naut.	nautical
pl.	plural
prep.	preposition
pron.	pronoun
punct.	punctuation
rel.	relative, religion
S.A.	Spanish American
v.	verb

Useful Phrases

Good day, Good morning.   Buenos días.
Good afternoon.   Buenas tardes.
Good night, Good evening.   Buenas noches.
Hello.   ¡Hola!
See you later.   Hasta luego.
Goodbye.   ¡Adiós!
How are you?   ¿Cómo está usted?
I am fine, thank you.   Estoy bien, gracias.
I am pleased to meet you.   Mucho gusto en conocerle.
Thank you very much.   Muchas gracias.
You're welcome.   De nada.
Please.   Por favor.
Good luck.   ¡Buena suerte!
To your health.   ¡Salud!

Please help me.   Ayúdeme, por favor.
I don't know.   No sé.
I don't understand.   No entiendo.
Do you understand?   ¿Entiende usted?
I don't speak Spanish.   No hablo español.
Do you speak English?   ¿Habla usted inglés?
How do you say...in Spanish?   ¿Cómo se dice...en español?
Speak slowly, please.   Hable despacio, por favor.
Please repeat.   Repita, por favor.
I don't like it.   No me gusta.

What is your name?   ¿Cómo se llama usted?
My name is...   Me llamo...
I am an American.   Soy norteamericano.

How is the weather?   ¿Qué tiempo hace?
It's cold (hot) today.   Hace frío (calor) hoy.
What time is it?   ¿Qué hora es?

How much is it?   ¿Cuánto es?
It is too much.   Es demasiado.
What do you wish?   ¿Qué desea usted?
I want to buy...   Quiero comprar...

I am hungry.   Tengo hambre.

I am thirsty.   Tengo sed.

Where is there a restaurant?   ¿Dónde hay un restaurante?

The bill, please.   La cuenta, por favor.

Where is there a hotel?   ¿Donde hay un hotel?

Where is the post office?   ¿Dónde está el correo?

Take me to...   Lléveme a...

I believe I am ill.   Creo que estoy enfermo.

Please call a doctor.   Por favor, llame al médico.

I want to send a telegram.   Quiero poner un telegrama.

As soon as possible.   Cuanto antes.

Round trip   Ida y vuelta.

Where can I change my money?   ¿Dónde puedo cambiar mi dinero?

Can you accept my check?   ¿Puede aceptar usted mi cheque?

What is the postage?   ¿Cuánto es el franqueo?

Right away.   ¡Pronto!

Help.   ¡Socorro!

Come in.   ¡Pase usted!

Pardon me.   Dispense usted.

Stop.   ¡Pare!

Look out.   ¡Cuidado!

Hurry.   ¡De prisa!

Go on.   ¡Siga!

To (on, at) the right   A la derecha.

To (on, at) the left   A la izquierda.

Straight ahead   Adelante.

Signs

Caution   Precaución

Danger   Peligro

Exit   Salida

Entrance   Entrada

Stop   Alto

Closed   Cerrado

Open   Abierto

Slow   Despacio

No smoking   Prohibido fumar

No admittance   Prohibida la entrada

One way   una vía

Women   Señoras, Mujeres, Damas

Men   Señores, Hombres, Caballeros

Ladies' Room   El cuarto de damas

Men's Room   El servicio

Weights and Measures

The Spanish use the *Metric System* of weights and measures, which is a decimal system in which multiples are shown by the prefixes: deci- (one tenth); centi- (one hundredth); mili- (one thousandth); deca- (ten); hecto- (hundred); kilo- (thousand).

1 centímetro	=	.3937 inches
1 metro	=	39.37 inches
1 kilómetro	=	.621 mile
1 centigramo	=	.1543 grain
1 gramo	=	15.432 grains
1 kilogramo	=	2.2046 pounds
1 tonelada	=	2,204 pounds
1 centilitro	=	.338 ounces
1 litro	=	1.0567 quart (liquid);
		.908 quart (dry)
1 kilolitro	=	264.18 gallons

Money

	Monetary Unit		Monetary Unit
Spain	peseta	El Salvador	colón
Argentina	peso	Guatemala	quetzal
Bolivia	peso	Haiti	gourde
Brazil	cruzeiro	Honduras	lempira
Chile	escudo	Mexico	peso
Colombia	peso	Nicaragua	córdoba
Costa Rica	colón	Panama	balboa
Cuba	peso	Paraguay	guaraní
Dominican		Peru	sol
Republic	peso	Uruguay	peso
Ecuador	sucre	Venezuela	bolívar

Numerals

Cardinal

1	uno, una	30	treinta
2	dos	31	treinta y uno
3	tres	32	treinta y dos
4	cuatro	40	cuarenta
5	cinco	50	cincuenta
6	seis	60	sesenta
7	siete	70	setenta
8	ocho	80	ochenta
9	nueve	90	noventa
10	diez	100	cien
11	once	101	ciento uno
12	doce	102	ciento dos
13	trece	200	doscientos, -as
14	catorce	300	trescientos, -as
15	quince	400	cuatrocientos, -as
16	dieciséis	500	quinientos, -as
17	diecisiete	600	seiscientos, -as
18	dieciocho	700	setecientos, -as
19	diecinueve	800	ochocientos, -as
20	veinte	900	novecientos, -as
21	veinte y uno (or veintiuno)	1.000	mil
		2.000	dos mil
22	veinte y dos (or veintidos)	100.000	cien mil
		1.000.000	un millón
		2.000.000	dos millones

Ordinal

1st	primero	6th	sexto
2nd	segundo	7th	séptimo
3rd	tercero	8th	octavo
4th	cuarto	9th	noveno
5th	quinto	10th	décimo

Days of the Week

Sunday	domingo
Monday	lunes
Tuesday	martes
Wednesday	miércoles
Thursday	jueves
Friday	viernes
Saturday	sábado

Months

January	enero	**July**	julio
February	febrero	**August**	agosto
March	marzo	**September**	septiembre
April	abril	**October**	octubre
May	mayo	**November**	noviembre
June	junio	**December**	diciembre

Spanish-English

A

a, *prep.* to; at.
abacero, *m.* grocer.
abad, *m.* abbot.
abadía, *f.* abbey.
abajo, *adv.* down; downstairs.
abandonar, *v.* abandon.
abanico, *m.* fan. —abanicar, *v.*
abaratar, *v.* cheapen.
abarcar, *v.* comprise; clasp.
abastecer, *v.* supply, provision.
abatido, *a.* dejected, despondent.
abatir, *v.* depress, dishearten.
abdicar, *v.* abdicate.
abdomen, *m.* abdomen.
abeja, *f.* bee.
abejarrón, *m.* bumblebee.
abertura, *f.* opening, aperture, slit.
abeto, *m.* fir.
abierto, *a.* open; overt.
abismo, *m.* abyss, chasm.
ablandar, *v.* soften.
abochornar, *v.* embarrass.
abogado, *m.* lawyer, attorney.
abolengo, *m.* ancestry.
abolición, *f.* abolition.
abolladura, *f.* dent. —abollar, *v.*
abominable, *a.* abominable.
abominar, *v.* abhor.
abonar, *v.* pay; fertilize.
abonarse, *v.* subscribe.
abono, *m.* fertilizer; subscription.
aborrecer, *v.* hate, loathe, abhor.
aborto, *m.* abortion.
abovedar, *v.* vault.
abrasar, *v.* burn.
abrazar, *v.* embrace; clasp.
abrazo, *m.* embrace.
abreviar, *v.* abbreviate, abridge, shorten.
abreviatura, *f.* abbreviation.
abrigar, *v.* harbor, shelter.
abrigarse, *v.* bundle up.
abrigo, *m.* overcoat; shelter; (*pl.*) wraps.
abril, *m.* April.
abrir, *v.* open; (med.) lance.
abrochar, *v.* clasp.
abrojo, *m.* thorn.
abrumar, *v.* overwhelm, crush, swamp.
absceso, *m.* abscess.
absolución, *f.* absolution; acquittal.
absoluto, *a.* absolute; downright.
absolver, *v.* absolve, pardon.
absorbente, *a.* absorbent.
absorber, *v.* absorb.
absorción, *f.* absorption.
abstenerse, *v.* abstain; refrain.
abstinencia, *f.* abstinence.
abstracción, *f.* abstraction.
abstraer, *v.* abstract.
absurdo, 1. *a.* absurd. 2. *m.* absurdity.

abuela, *f.* grandmother.
abuelo, *m.* grandfather; (*pl.*) grandparents.
abultado, *a.* bulky.
abultamiento, *m.* bulge. —abultar, *v.*
abundancia, *f.* abundance, plenty.
abundante, *a.* abundant, plentiful.
abundar, *v.* abound.
aburrido, *a.* boring, tedious.
aburrimiento, *m.* boredom.
aburrir, *v.* bore.
abusar, *v.* abuse, misuse.
abusivo, *a.* abusive.
abuso, *m.* abuse.
abyecto, *a.* abject, low.
acá, *adv.* here.
acabar, *v.* finish. a. de . . ., to have just . . . .
academia, *f.* academy.
académico, *a.* academic.
acaecer, *v.* happen.
acanalar, *v.* groove.
acaparar, *v.* hoard; monopolize.
acariciar, *v.* caress, stroke.
acaso, *m.* chance. por si a., just in case.
acceder, *v.* accede.
accesible, *a.* accessible.
acceso, *m.* access, approach.
accesorio, *a.* accessory.
accidental, *a.* accidental.
accidente, *m.* accident, wreck.
acción, *f.* action; act; (com.) share of stock.
acechar, *v.* ambush, spy on.
aceite, *m.* oil.
aceitoso, *a.* oily.
aceituna, *f.* olive.
aceleración, *f.* acceleration.
acelerar, *v.* accelerate, speed up.
acento, *m.* accent.
acentuar, *v.* accent, accentuate, stress.
acepillar, *v.* brush; plane (wood).
aceptable, *a.* acceptable.
aceptación, *f.* acceptance.
aceptar, *v.* accept.
acequia, *f.* ditch.
acera, *f.* sidewalk.
acerca de, *prep.* about, concerning.
acercar, *v.* bring near.
acercarse, *v.* approach, come near, go near.
acero, *m.* steel.
acertar, *v.* guess right. a. en, hit (a mark).
acertijo, *m.* puzzle, riddle.
acidez, *f.* acidity.
ácido, 1. *a.* sour. 2. *m.* acid.
aclamación, *f.* acclamation.
aclamar, *v.* acclaim.
aclarar, *v.* brighten; clarify, clear up.
acoger, *v.* welcome, receive.
acogida, *f.* welcome, reception.
acometer, *v.* attack.

acomodador, *m.* usher.
acomodar, *v.* accommodate, fix up.
acompañamiento, *m.* accompaniment; following.
acompañar, *v.* accompany.
acondicionar, *v.* condition.
aconsejable, *a.* advisable.
aconsejar, *v.* advise.
acontecer, *v.* happen.
acontecimiento, *m.* event, happening.
acorazado, *m.* battleship.
acordarse, *v.* remember, recollect.
acortar, *v.* shorten.
acosar, *v.* beset, harry.
acostar, *v.* lay down; put to bed.
acostarse, *v.* lie down; go to bed.
acostumbrado, *a.* accustomed; customary.
acostumbrar, *v.* accustom.
acrecentar, *v.* increase.
acreditar, *v.* accredit.
acreedor -ra, *n.* creditor.
acróbata, *m.* acrobat.
actitud, *f.* attitude.
actividad, *f.* activity.
activista, *a.* & *n.* activist.
activo, *a.* active.
acto, *m.* act.
actor, *m.* actor.
actriz, *f.* actress.
actual, *a.* present.
actuar, *v.* act.
acuarela, *f.* watercolor.
acuario, *m.* aquarium.
acuático, *a.* aquatic.
acuchillar, *v.* slash, knife.
acudir, *v.* rally; hasten; be present.
acuerdo, *m.* accord, agreement; settlement. de a., in agreement, agreed.
acumulación, *f.* accumulation.
acumular, *v.* accumulate.
acuñar, *v.* coin, mint.
acupuntura, *f.* acupuncture.
acusación, *f.* accusation, charge.
acusado -da, *a.* & *n.* accused; defendant.
acusador -ra, *n.* accuser.
acusar, *v.* accuse; acknowledge.
acústica, *f.* acoustics.
achicar, *v.* diminish, dwarf; humble.
adaptación, *f.* adaptation.
adaptar, *v.* adapt.
adecuado, *a.* adequate.
adelantado, *a.* advanced; fast (clock).
adelantamiento, *m.* advancement, promotion.
adelantar, *v.* advance.
adelante, *adv.* ahead, forward, onward, on.
adelanto, *m.* advancement, progress, improvement.
adelgazar, *v.* make thin.

ademán, *m.* attitude; gesture.

además, *adv.* in addition, besides, also.

adentro, *adv.* in, inside.

adepto, *a.* adept.

aderezar, *v.* prepare; trim.

adherirse, *v.* adhere, stick.

adhesivo, *a.* adhesive.

adición, *f.* addition.

adicional, *a.* additional, extra.

adicto, *a. & m.* addicted; addict.

adiós, *m. & interj.* good-bye, farewell.

adivinar, *v.* guess.

adjetivo, *m.* adjective.

adjunto, *a.* enclosed.

administración, *f.* administration.

administrador, *m.* administrator.

administrar, *v.* administer; manage.

administrativo, *a.* administrative.

admirable, *a.* admirable.

admiración, *f.* admiration; wonder.

admirar, *v.* admire.

admisión, *f.* admission.

admitir, *v.* admit, acknowledge.

adolescencia, *f.* adolescence, youth.

adolescente, *a.* adolescent.

adónde, *adv.* where.

adondequiera, *conj.* wherever.

adopción, *f.* adoption.

adoptar, *v.* adopt.

adoración, *f.* worship, love, adoration. —adorar, *v.*

adormecer, *v.* drowse.

adornar, *v.* adorn; decorate.

adorno, *m.* adornment, trimming.

adquirir, *v.* acquire, obtain.

adquisición, *f.* acquisition, attainment.

aduana, *f.* custom house, customs.

aducto. *m.* input.

adujada, *f.* (naut.) coil of rope.

adulación, *f.* flattery.

adular, *v.* flatter.

adulterar, *v.* adulterate.

adulterio, *m.* adultery.

adulto, *a. & m.* adult.

adusto, *a.* gloomy, austere.

adverbio, *m.* adverb.

adversario, *m.* adversary.

adversidad, *f.* adversity.

adverso, *a.* adverse.

advertencia, *f.* warning.

advertir, *v.* warn; notice.

adyacente, *a.* adjacent.

aéreo, *a.* aerial; air.

aeromoza, *f.* stewardess, flight attendant.

aeroplano, *m.* airplane.

aeropuerto, *m.* airport.

aerosol, *m.* aerosol, spray.

afable, *a.* affable, pleasant.

afanarse, *v.* toil.

afear, *v.* deface, mar, deform.

afectación, *f.* affectation.

afectar, *v.* affect.

afecto, *m.* affection, attachment.

afeitada, *f.* shave. —afeitarse, *v.*

afeminado, *a.* effeminate.

afición, *f.* fondness; liking; hobby.

aficionado, *a.* fond.

aficionado -da, *n.* fan, devotee; amateur.

aficionarse a, *v.* become fond of.

afilado, *a.* sharp.

afilar, *v.* sharpen.

afiliación, *f.* affiliation.

afiliado, *m.* affiliate. —afiliar, *v.*

afinar, *v.* polish, tune up.

afinidad, *f.* relationship.

afirmación, *f.* affirmation, statement.

afirmar, *v.* affirm, assert.

afirmativa, *f.* affirmative. — afirmativo, *a.*

aflicción, *f.* affliction; sorrow, grief.

afligido, *a.* sorrowful, grieved.

afligir, *v.* grieve, distress.

aflojar, *v.* loosen.

afortunado, *a.* fortunate, successful, lucky.

afrenta, *f.* insult, outrage, affront. —afrentar, *v.*

afrentoso, *a.* shameful.

africano -na, *a. & n.* African.

afuera, *adv.* out, outside.

afueras, *f.pl.* suburbs.

agacharse, *v.* squat, crouch; cower.

agarrar, *v.* seize, grasp, clutch.

agarro, *m.* clutch, grasp.

agencia, *f.* agency.

agente, *m.* agent, representative.

ágil, *a.* agile, spry.

agitación, *f.* agitation, ferment.

agitado, *a.* agitated; excited.

agitador, *m.* agitator.

agitar, *v.* shake, agitate, excite.

agobiar, *v.* oppress, burden.

agosto, *m.* August.

agotamiento, *m.* exhaustion.

agotar, *v.* exhaust, use up, sap.

agradable, *a.* agreeable, pleasant.

agradar, *v.* please.

agradecer, *v.* thank; appreciate, be grateful for.

agradecido, *a.* grateful, thankful.

agradecimiento, *m.* gratitude, thanks.

agravar, *v.* aggravate, make worse.

agravio, *m.* wrong. —agraviar, *v.*

agregado, *a. & m.* aggregate.

agregar, *v.* add; gather.

agresión, *f.* aggression; (leg.) battery.

agresivo, *a.* aggressive.

agresor, *m.* aggressor.

agrícola, *a.* agricultural.

agricultor, *m.* farmer.

agricultura, *f.* agriculture, farming.

agrio, *a.* sour.

agrupar, *v.* group.

agua, *f.* water. —aguar, *v.*

aguacate, *m.* avocado, alligator pear.

aguantar, *v.* endure, stand, put up with.

aguardar, *v.* await; expect.

aguardiente, *m.* brandy.

agudo, *a.* sharp, keen, shrill, acute.

agüero, *m.* omen.

águila, *f.* eagle.

aguja, *f.* needle.

agujero, *m.* hole.

aguzar, *v.* sharpen.

ahí, *adv.* there.

ahogar, *v.* drown; choke; suffocate.

ahondar, *v.* deepen.

ahora, *adv.* now.

ahorcar, *v.* hang (execute).

ahorrar, *v.* save, save up; spare.

ahorros, *m.pl.* savings.

ahumar, *v.* smoke.

airado, *a.* angry, indignant.

aire, *m.* air. —airear, *v.*

aislamiento, *m.* isolation.

aislar, *v.* isolate.

ajedrez, *m.* chess.

ajeno, *a.* alien; someone else's.

ají, *m.* chili.

ajo, *m.* garlic.

ajustado, *a.* adjusted; trim; exact.

ajustar, *v.* adjust.

ajuste, *m.* adjustment, settlement.

al, *contr.* of a + el.

ala, *f.* wing; brim (of hat).

alabanza, *f.* praise. —alabar, *v.*

alabear, *v.* warp.

alambique, *m.* still.

alambre, *m.* wire. a. de púas, barbed wire.

alarde, *m.* boasting, ostentation.

alargar, *v.* lengthen; stretch out.

alarma, *f.* alarm. —alarmar, *v.*

alba, *f.* daybreak, dawn.

albanega, *f.* hair net.

albañil, *m.* bricklayer; mason.

albaricoque, *m.* apricot.

albergue, *m.* shelter. —albergar, *v.*

alborotar, *v.* disturb, make noise, brawl, riot.

alboroto, *m.* brawl, disturbance, din, tumult.

álbum, *m.* album.

alcachofa, *f.* artichoke.

alcalde, *m.* mayor.

alcance, *m.* reach; range; scope.

alcanfor, *m.* camphor.

alcanzar, *v.* reach, overtake, catch.

alcayata, *f.* spike.

alce, *m.* elk.

alcoba, *f.* bedroom; alcove.

alcohol, *m.* alcohol.

alcohólico, a. alcoholic.

aldaba, f. latch.

aldea, f. village.

alegación, f. allegation.

alegar, v. allege.

alegrar, v. make happy, brighten.

alegrarse, v. be glad.

alegre, a. gay, cheerful, merry.

alegría, f. gaiety, cheer.

alejarse, v. move away, off.

alemán -ana, a. & n. German.

Alemania, f. Germany.

alentar, v. cheer up, encourage.

alergia, f. allergy.

alerta, adv. on the alert.

aleve, alevoso, a. treacherous.

alfabeto, m. alphabet.

alfalfa, f. alfalfa.

alfarería, f. pottery.

alférez, m. (naval) ensign.

alfil, m. (chess) bishop.

alfiler, m. pin.

alfombra, f. carpet, rug.

alforja, f. knapsack; saddle-bag.

algarabía, f. jargon; din.

álgebra, f. algebra.

algo, pron. & adv. something, somewhat; anything.

algodón, m. cotton.

alguien, pron. somebody, someone; anybody, anyone.

algún -no -na, a. & pron. some; any.

alhaja, f. jewel.

aliado, a. & m. allied; ally. — aliar, v.

alianza, f. alliance.

alicates, m.pl. pliers.

aliento, m. breath. dar a., encourage.

aligerar, v. lighten.

alimentar, v. feed, nourish.

alimento, m. nourishment, food.

alinear, v. line up; (pol.) align.

alisar, v. smooth.

alistamiento, m. enlistment.

alistar, v. make ready, prime.

alistarse, v. get ready; (mil.) enlist.

aliviar, v. alleviate, relieve, ease.

alivio, m. relief.

alma, f. soul.

almacén, m. department store; storehouse.

almacenaje, m. storage.

almacenar, v. store.

almanaque, m. almanac.

almeja, f. clam.

almendra, f. almond.

almíbar, m. syrup.

almidón, m. starch. —almidonar, v.

almirante, m. admiral.

almohada, f. pillow.

almuerzo, m. lunch. —almorzar, v.

alojamiento, m. lodging, accommodations.

alojar, v. lodge, house.

alojarse, v. stay, room.

alquiler, m. rent. —alquilar, v.

alrededor, adv. around.

alrededores, m.pl. environs.

altanero, a. haughty.

altar, m. altar.

altavoz, m. loudspeaker.

alteración, f. alteration.

alterar, v. alter.

alternativa, f. alternative. — alternativo, a.

alterno, a. alternate. —alternar, v.

alteza, f. highness.

altivo, a. proud, haughty; lofty.

alto, 1. a. high, tall; loud. 2. m. height, story (house).

altura, f. height, altitude.

alud, m. avalanche.

aludir, v. allude.

alumbrado, m. lighting.

alumbrar, v. light.

aluminio, m. aluminum.

alumno -na, m. student, pupil.

alusión, f. allusion.

alza, f. rise; boost.

alzar, v. raise, lift.

allá, adv. there. más a., beyond, farther on.

allanar, v. flatten, smooth, plane.

allí, adv. there. por a., that way.

ama, f. housewife, mistress (of house). a. de llaves, housekeeper.

amable, a. kind; pleasant, sweet.

amalgamar, v. amalgamate.

amamantar, v. suckle, nurse.

amanecer, 1. m. dawn, daybreak. 2. v. dawn; awaken.

amante, m. lover.

amar, v. love.

amargo, a. bitter.

amargón, m. dandelion.

amargura, f. bitterness.

amarillo, a. yellow.

amarradero, m. mooring.

amarrar, v. hitch, moor, tie up.

amartillar, v. hammer; cock (a gun).

amasar, v. knead, mold.

ámbar, m. amber.

ambarino, a. amber.

ambición, f. ambition.

ambicionar, v. aspire to.

ambicioso, a. ambitious.

ambiente, m. environment, atmosphere.

ambigüedad, f. ambiguity.

ambiguo, a. ambiguous.

ambos, a. & pron. both.

ambulancia, f. ambulance.

amenaza, f. threat, menace.

amenazar, v. threaten, menace.

ameno, a. pleasant.

americana, f. suit coat.

americano -na, a. & n. American.

ametralladora, f. machine gun.

amigable, a. amicable, friendly.

amígdala, f. tonsil.

amigo -ga, n. friend.

amistad, f. friendship.

amistoso, a. friendly.

amniocéntesis, m. amniocentesis.

amo, m. master.

amonestaciones, f.pl. banns.

amonestar, v. admonish.

amoníaco, m. ammonia.

amontonar, v. amass, pile up.

amor, m. love. a. propio, self-esteem.

amorío, m. romance, love affair.

amoroso, a. amorous; loving.

amortecer, v. deaden.

amparar, v. aid, befriend; protect, shield.

amparo, m. protection.

ampliar, v. enlarge; elaborate.

amplificar, v. amplify.

amplio, a. ample, roomy.

ampolla, f. bubble; bulb; blister.

amputar, v. amputate.

amueblar, v. furnish.

analfabeto, a. & m. illiterate.

análisis, m. or f. analysis.

analizar, v. analyze.

analogía, f. analogy.

análogo, a. similar, analogous.

anarquía, f. anarchy.

anatomía, f. anatomy.

ancho, a. wide, broad.

anchoa, f. anchovy.

anchura, f. width, breadth.

anciano -na, a. & m. old, aged (person).

ancla, f. anchor. —anclar, v.

anclaje, m. anchorage.

andamio, m. scaffold.

andar, v. walk; move, go.

andén, m. (railroad) platform.

andrajoso, a. ragged, uneven.

anécdota, f. anecdote.

anegar, v. flood, drown.

anestesia, f. anesthetic.

anexar, v. annex.

anexión, f. annexation.

anfitrión, m. host.

ángel, m. angel.

angosto, a. narrow.

anguila, f. eel.

angular, a. angular.

ángulo, m. angle.

angustia, f. anguish, agony.

angustiar, v. distress.

anhelar, v. long for.

anidar, v. nest, nestle.

anillo, m. ring; circle.

animación, f. animation; bustle.

animado, a. animated, lively; animate.

animal, a. & m. animal.

ánimo, m. state of mind, spirits; courage.

aniquilar, v. annihilate, destroy.

aniversario, m. anniversary.

anoche, adv. last night.

anochecer, 1. m. twilight, nightfall. 2. v. get dark.

anónimo, a. anonymous.

anormal, a. abnormal.

anotación, f. annotation.

anotar, v. annotate.

ansia, ansiedad, f. anxiety.

ansioso, a. anxious.

antagonismo, m. antagonism.

antagonista, m. & f. antagonist, opponent.

anteayer, adv. day before yesterday.

antebrazo, m. forearm.

antecedente, a. & m. antecedent.

anteceder, v. precede.

antecesor, m. ancestor.

antemano, de a., in advance.

antena, f. antenna.

anteojos, m.pl. eyeglasses.

antepasado, m. ancestor, forefather.

anterior, a. previous, former.

antes, adv. before; formerly.

anticipación, f. anticipation.

anticipar, v. anticipate; advance.

anticuado, a. antiquated, obsolete.

antídoto, m. antidote.

antigüedad, f. antiquity; antique.

antiguo, a. former; old; ancient, antique.

antílope, m. antelope.

antinuclear, a. antinuclear.

antipatía, f. antipathy.

antipático, a. disagreeable, nasty.

antiséptico, a. & m. antiseptic.

antojarse, v. se me antoja ..., etc., I desire ..., take a fancy to ..., etc.

antojo, m. whim, fancy.

antorcha, f. torch.

antracita, f. anthracite.

anual, a. annual, yearly.

anudar, v. knot; tie.

anular, v. annul, void.

anunciar, v. announce; proclaim, advertise.

anuncio, m. announcement; advertisement.

añadir, v. add.

añil, m. bluing.

año, m. year.

apacible, a. peaceful, peaceable.

apaciguamiento, m. appeasement.

apaciguar, v. appease; placate.

apagado, a. dull.

apagar, v. extinguish, quench, put out.

aparador, m. buffet, cupboard.

aparato, m. apparatus; machine; appliance, set.

aparecer, v. appear, show up.

aparejo, m. rig. —aparejar, v.

aparentar, v. pretend; profess.

aparente, a. apparent.

apariencia, aparición, f. appearance.

apartado, 1. a. aloof; separate. 2. m. post-office box.

apartamento, m. apartment. a. en propiedad, condominium.

apartar, v. separate; remove.

aparte, adv. apart; aside.

apartheid, m. apartheid.

apasionado, a. passionate.

apatía, f. apathy.

apearse, v. get off, alight.

apedrear, v. stone.

apelación, f. appeal. —apelar, v.

apellido, m. family name.

apenas, adv. scarcely, hardly.

apéndice, m. appendix.

apercibir, v. prepare, warn.

aperitivo, m. appetizer.

aperos, m.pl. implements.

apetecer, v. desire, have appetite for.

apetito, m. appetite.

ápice, m. apex.

apilar, v. stack.

apio, m. celery.

aplacar, v. appease; placate.

aplastar, v. crush, flatten.

aplaudir, v. applaud, cheer.

aplauso, m. applause.

aplazar, v. postpone, put off.

aplicable, a. applicable.

aplicado, a. industrious, diligent.

aplicar, v. apply.

aplomo, m. aplomb, poise.

apoderado, m. attorney.

apoderarse de, v. get hold of, seize.

apodo, m. nickname. —apodar, v.

apologético, a. apologetic.

apoplejía, f. apoplexy.

aposento, m. room, flat.

apostar, v. bet, wager.

apóstol, m. apostle.

apoyar, v. support, prop; lean.

apoyo, m. support; prop; aid; approval.

apreciable, a. appreciable.

apreciar, v. appreciate, prize.

aprecio, m. appreciation, regard.

apremio, m. pressure, compulsion.

aprender, v. learn.

aprendiz, m. apprentice.

aprensión, f. apprehension.

aprensivo, a. apprehensive.

apresurado, a. hasty, fast.

apresurar, v. hurry, speed up.

apretado, a. tight.

apretar, v. squeeze, press; tighten.

apretón, m. squeeze.

aprieto, m. plight, predicament.

aprobación, f. approbation, approval.

aprobar, v. approve.

apropiación, f. appropriation.

apropiado, a. appropriate. —apropiar, v.

aprovechar, v. profit by.

aprovecharse, v. take advantage.

aproximado, a. approximate.

aproximarse a, v. approach.

aptitud, f. aptitude.

apto, a. apt.

apuesta, f. bet, wager, stake.

apuntar, v. point, aim; prompt; write down.

apunte, m. annotation, note; promptings, cue.

apuñalar, v. stab.

apurar, v. hurry; worry.

apuro, m. predicament, scrape, trouble.

aquel, aquella, dem. a. that.

aquél, aquélla, dem. pron. that (one); the former.

aquello, dem. pron. that.

aquí, adv. here. por a., this way.

aquietar, v. allay; lull, pacify.

ara, f. altar.

árabe, a. & n. Arab, Arabic.

arado, m. plow. —arar, v.

arándano, m. cranberry.

araña, f. spider. a. de luces, chandelier.

arbitración, f. arbitration.

arbitrador -ra, n. arbitrator.

arbitraje, m. arbitration.

arbitrar, v. arbitrate.

arbitrario, a. arbitrary.

árbitro, m. arbiter, umpire, referee.

árbol, m. tree; mast.

arbusto, m. bush, shrub.

arca, f. chest; ark.

arcada, f. arcade.

arcaico, a. archaic.

arce, m. maple.

arcilla, f. clay.

arco, m. arc; arch; (archer's) bow. a. iris, rainbow.

archipiélago, m. archipelago.

archivo, m. archive; file. —archivar, v.

arder, v. burn.

ardid, m. stratagem, cunning.

ardiente, a. ardent, burning, fiery.

ardilla, f. squirrel.

ardor, m. ardor, fervor.

arduo, a. arduous.

área, f. area.

arena, f. sand; arena.

arenoso, a. sandy.

arenque, m. herring.

arete, m. earring.

argentino -na, a. & n. Argentine.

argüir, v. dispute, argue.

árido, a. arid.

aristocracia, f. aristocracy.

aristócrata, f. aristocrat.

aristocrático, a. aristocratic.

aritmética, f. arithmetic.

arma, f. weapon, arm.

armadura, f. armor; reinforcement; framework.

armamento, m. armament.

armar, v. arm.

armario, m. cabinet, bureau, wardrobe.

armazón, m. framework, frame.

armería, f. armory.

armisticio, m. armistice.

armonía, f. harmony.

armonioso, a. harmonious.

armonizar, v. harmonize.

arnés, m. harness.

aroma, *f.* aroma, fragrance.
aromático, *a.* aromatic.
arpa, *f.* harp.
arquear, *v.* arch.
arquitecto, *m.* architect.
arquitectura, *f.* architecture.
arquitectural, *a.* architectural.
arrabal, *m.* suburb.
arraigar, *v.* take root, settle.
arrancar, *v.* pull out, tear out; start up.
arranque, *m.* dash, sudden start; fit of anger.
arrastrar, *v.* drag.
arrebatar, *v.* snatch, grab.
arrebato, *m.* sudden attack, fit of anger.
arrecife, *m.* reef.
arreglar, *v.* arrange; repair, fix; adjust, settle.
arreglárselas, *v.* manage, shift for oneself.
arreglo, *m.* arrangement, settlement.
arremeter, *v.* attack.
arrendar, *v.* rent.
arrepentimiento, *m.* repentance.
arrepentirse, *v.* repent.
arrestar, *v.* arrest.
arriba, *adv.* up; upstairs.
arriendo, *m.* lease.
arriero, *m.* muleteer.
arriesgar, *v.* risk.
arrimarse, *v.* lean.
arrodillarse, *v.* kneel.
arrogancia, *f.* arrogance.
arrogante, *a.* arrogant.
arrojar, *v.* throw, hurl; shed.
arrollar, *v.* roll, coil.
arroyo, *m.* brook; gully; gutter.
arroz, *m.* rice.
arruga, *f.* ridge; wrinkle.
arrugar, *v.* wrinkle, crumple.
arruinar, *v.* ruin, destroy, wreck.
arsenal, *m.* arsenal; armory.
arsénico, *m.* arsenic.
arte, *m.* (*f.* in *pl.*) art, craft; wiliness.
arteria, *f.* artery.
artesa, *f.* trough.
artesano, *m.* artisan, craftsman.
ártico, *a.* arctic.
articulación, *f.* articulation; joint.
articular, *v.* articulate.
artículo, *m.* article.
artífice, *m. & f.* artisan.
artificial, *a.* artificial.
artificio, *m.* artifice, device.
artificioso, *a.* affected.
artillería, *f.* artillery.
artista, *m. & f.* artist.
artístico, *a.* artistic.
arzobispo, *m.* archbishop.
as, *m.* ace.
asado, *m.* roast.
asaltador, *m.* assailant.
asaltar, *v.* assail, attack.
asalto, *m.* assault. —**asaltar**, *v.*
asamblea, *f.* assembly.

asar, *v.* roast; broil, cook (meat).
asaz, *adv.* enough; quite.
ascender, *v.* ascend, go up; amount.
ascenso, *m.* ascent.
ascensor, *m.* elevator.
ascensorista, *m. & f.* (elevator) operator.
asco, *m.* nausea; disgusting thing. **qué a.**, how disgusting.
aseado, *a.* tidy. —**asear**, *v.*
asediar, *v.* besiege.
asedio, *m.* siege.
asegurar, *v.* assure; secure.
asegurarse, *v.* make sure.
asemejarse a, *v.* resemble.
asentar, *v.* settle; seat.
asentimiento, *m.* assent. — **asentir**, *v.*
aseo, *m.* neatness, tidiness.
aserción, *f.* assertion.
aserrar, *v.* saw.
asesinar, *v.* assassinate; murder, slay.
asesinato, *m.* assassination, murder.
asesino -na, *n.* murderer, assassin.
aseveración, *f.* assertion.
aseverar, *v.* assert.
asfalto, *m.* asphalt.
así, *adv.* so, thus, this way, that way. **a. como**, as well as. **a. que**, as soon as.
asiático -ca, *a. & n.* Asiatic.
asiduo, *a.* assiduous.
asiento, *m.* seat; chair; site.
asignar, *v.* assign; allot.
asilo, *m.* asylum; sanctuary.
asimilar, *v.* assimilate.
asir, *v.* grasp.
asistencia, *f.* attendance, presence.
asistir, *v.* be present, attend.
asno, *m.* donkey.
asociación, *f.* association.
asociado, *m.* associate, partner.
asociar, *v.* associate.
asolar, *v.* desolate; burn, parch.
asoleado, *a.* sunny.
asomar, *v.* appear, loom up, show up.
asombrar, *v.* astonish, amaze.
asombro, *m.* amazement, astonishment.
aspa, *f.* reel. —**aspar**, *v.*
aspecto, *m.* aspect.
aspereza, *f.* harshness.
áspero, *a.* rough, harsh.
aspiración, *f.* aspiration.
aspirador, *m.* vacuum cleaner.
aspirar, *v.* aspire.
aspirina, *f.* aspirin.
asqueroso, *a.* dirty, nasty, filthy.
asta, *f.* shaft.
asterisco, *m.* asterisk.
astilla, *f.* splinter, chip. —**astillar**, *v.*
astillero, *m.* dry dock.
astro, *m.* star.
astronauta, *m.* astronaut.

astronomía, *f.* astronomy.
astucia, *f.* cunning.
astuto, *a.* astute, sly, shrewd.
asumir, *v.* assume.
asunto, *m.* matter, affair, business; subject.
asustar, *v.* frighten, scare, startle.
atacar, *v.* attack, charge.
atajo, *m.* shortcut.
ataque, *m.* attack, charge; spell, stroke.
atar, *v.* tie, bind, fasten.
atareado, *a.* busy.
atascar, *v.* stall, stop, obstruct.
ataúd, *m.* casket, coffin.
atavío, *m.* dress; gear, equipment.
atemorizar, *v.* frighten.
atención, *f.* attention.
atender, *v.* heed; attend to, wait on.
atenerse a, *v.* count on, depend on.
atentado, *m.* crime, offense.
atento, *a.* attentive, courteous.
ateo, *m.* atheist.
aterrizar, *v.* land.
atesorar, *v.* hoard.
atestar, *v.* witness.
atestiguar, *v.* attest, testify.
atinar, *v.* hit upon.
atisbar, *v.* scrutinize, pry.
Atlántico, *m.* Atlantic.
atlántico, *a.* Atlantic.
atlas, *m.* atlas.
atleta, *m.* athlete.
atlético, *a.* athletic.
atletismo, *m.* athletics.
atmósfera, *f.* atmosphere.
atmosférico, *a.* atmospheric.
atómico, *a.* atomic.
átomo, *m.* atom.
atormentar, *v.* torment, plague.
atornillar, *v.* screw.
atracción, *f.* attraction.
atractivo, **1.** *a.* attractive. **2.** *m.* attraction.
atraer, *v.* attract; lure.
atrapar, *v.* trap, catch.
atrás, *adv.* back; behind.
atrasado, *a.* belated; backward; slow (clock).
atrasar, *v.* delay, retard; be slow.
atraso, *m.* delay; backwardness; (*pl.*) arrears.
atravesar, *v.* cross.
atreverse, *v.* dare.
atrevido, *a.* daring, bold.
atrevimiento, *m.* boldness.
atribuir, *v.* attribute, ascribe.
atributo, *m.* attribute.
atrincherar, *v.* entrench.
atrocidad, *f.* atrocity, outrage.
atronar, *v.* deafen.
atropellar, *v.* trample; fell.
atroz, *a.* atrocious.
aturdir, *v.* daze, stun, bewilder.
audacia, *f.* audacity.
audaz, *a.* audacious, bold.
audible, *a.* audible.
audiovisual, *a.* audiovisual.
auditorio, *m.* audience.
aula, *f.* classroom, hall.

aullar, v. howl, bay.

aullido, m. howl.

aumentar, v. augment; increase, swell.

aun, aún, adv. still; even. a. cuando, even though, even if.

aunque, conj. although, though.

áureo, a. golden.

aureola, f. halo.

aurora, f. dawn.

ausencia, f. absence.

ausentarse, v. stay away.

ausente, a. absent.

auspicio, m. auspice.

austeridad, f. austerity.

austero, a. austere.

austriaco -ca, a. & n. Austrian.

auténtico, a. authentic.

auto, automóvil, m. auto, automobile.

autobús, m. bus.

automático, a. automatic.

autonomía, f. autonomy.

autor, m. author.

autoridad, f. authority.

autoritario, a. authoritative.

autorizar, v. authorize.

auxiliar, 1. a. auxiliary. **2.** v. assist, aid.

auxilio, m. aid, assistance.

avaluar, v. evaluate, appraise.

avance, m. advance. **—avanzar,** v.

avaricia, f. avarice.

avariento, a. miserly, greedy.

avaro -ra, a. & m. miser; miserly.

ave, f. bird.

avena, f. oat.

avenida, f. avenue; flood.

avenirse, v. compromise; agree.

aventajar, v. surpass, get ahead of.

aventar, v. fan; scatter.

aventura, f. adventure.

aventurar, v. venture, risk, gamble.

aventurero, a. & m. adventurous; adventurer.

avergonzado, a. ashamed, abashed.

avergonzar, v. shame, abash.

avería, f. damage. **—averiar,** v.

averiguar, v. ascertain, find out.

aversión, f. aversion.

avestruz, m. ostrich.

aviación, f. aviation.

aviador -ra, n. aviator.

ávido, a. avid; eager.

avión, m. airplane.

avisar, v. notify, let know; warn, advise.

aviso, m. notice, announcement; advertisement; warning.

avispa, f. wasp.

avivar, v. enliven, revive.

aya, f. governess.

ayatola, m. ayatollah.

ayer, adv. yesterday.

ayuda, f. help, aid. **—ayudar,** v.

ayudante, a. assistant, helper; adjutant.

ayuno, m. fast. **—ayunar,** v.

ayuntamiento, m. city hall.

azada, f., **azadón,** m. hoe.

azafata, f. stewardess, flight attendant.

azar, m. hazard, chance. **al a.,** at random.

azotar, v. whip, flog; belabor.

azote, m. scourge, lash.

azúcar, m. sugar.

azul, a. blue.

azulado, a. azure.

azulejo, m. tile; bluebird.

B

baba, f. drivel, **—babear,** v.

babador, m. bib.

babucha, f. slipper.

bacalao, m. codfish.

bacía, f. washbasin.

bacterias, f.pl. bacteria.

bacteriología, f. bacteriology.

bachiller -ra, n. bachelor (degree).

bahía, f. bay.

bailador -ra, n. dancer.

bailar, v. dance.

bailarín -ina, n. dancer.

baile, m. dancing, dance.

baja, f. fall (in price); (mil.) casualty.

bajar, v. lower; descend.

bajeza, f. baseness.

bajo, 1. prep. under, below. **2.** a. low; short; base.

bala, f. bullet; ball; bale.

balada, f. ballad.

balancear, v. balance; roll, swing, sway.

balanza, f. balance; scales.

balbuceo, m. stammer; babble. **—balbucear,** v.

balcón, m. balcony.

balde, m. bucket, pail. **de b.,** gratis. **en b.,** in vain.

balística, f. ballistics.

balompié, m. football.

balón, m. football; (auto.) balloon tire.

baloncesto, m. basketball.

balota, f. ballot, vote, **—balotar,** v.

balsa, f. raft.

bálsamo, m. balm.

baluarte, m. bulwark.

ballena, f. whale.

bambolearse, v. sway.

bambú, m. bamboo.

banal, a. banal, trite.

banana, f. banana.

banano, m. banana tree.

bancarrota, f. bankruptcy.

banco, m. bank; bench; school of fish.

banda, f. band.

bandada, f. covey; flock.

bandeja, f. tray.

bandera, f. flag; banner; ensign.

bandido, m. bandit.

bando, m. faction.

bandolero, m. bandit, robber.

banquero, m. banker.

banqueta, f. stool; (Mex.) sidewalk.

banquete, m. feast, banquet.

banquillo, m. stool.

bañera, f. bathtub.

baño, m. bath; bathroom.

bañar, v. bathe.

baraja, f. pack of cards; game of cards.

baranda, f. railing, banister.

barato, a. cheap.

barba, f. beard; chin.

barbacoa, f. barbecue; stretcher.

barbaridad, f. barbarity; (Am.) excess (in anything).

bárbaro, a. barbarous; crude.

barbería, f. barbershop.

barbero, m. barber.

barca, f. (small) boat.

barcaza, f. barge.

barco, m. ship, boat.

barniz, m. varnish. **—barnizar,** v.

barómetro, m. barometer.

barón, m. baron.

barquilla, f. (naut.) log.

barra, f. bar.

barraca, f. hut, shed.

barrear, v. bar, barricade.

barreno, m. blast, blasting. **—barrenar,** v.

barrer, v. sweep.

barrera, f. barrier.

barricada, f. barricade.

barriga, f. belly.

barril, m. barrel; cask.

barrio, m. district, ward, quarter.

barro, m. clay, mud.

base, f. base; basis. **—basar,** v.

bastante, 1. a. enough, plenty of. **2.** adv. enough; rather, quite.

bastar, v. suffice, be enough.

bastardo -a, a. & n. bastard.

bastear, v. baste.

bastidor, m. wing (in theater).

bastón, m. (walking) cane.

bastos, m.pl. clubs (cards).

basura, f. refuse, dirt; garbage; junk.

basurero, m. scavenger.

batalla, f. battle. **—batallar,** v.

batallón, m. batallion.

batata, f. sweet potato.

bate, m. bat. **—batear,** v.

batería, f. battery.

batido, m. (cooking) batter.

batir, v. beat; demolish; conquer.

baúl, m. trunk.

bautismo, m. baptism.

bautista, m. & f. Baptist.

bautizar, v. Christen, baptize.

bautizo, m. baptism.

baya, f. berry.

bayoneta, f. bayonet.

beato, a. blessed.

bebé, m. baby.

beber, v. drink.

bebible, a. drinkable.

bebida, f. drink, beverage.

beca, f. grant, scholarship.
becado -da, n. scholar.
becerro, m. calf; calfskin.
beldad, f. beauty.
belga, a. & n. Belgian.
Bélgica, f. Belgium.
belicoso, a. warlike.
beligerante, a. & n. belligerent.
bellaco, 1. a. sly, roguish. 2. m. rogue.
belleza, f. beauty.
bello, a. beautiful.
bellota, f. acorn.
bendecir, v. bless.
bendición, f. blessing, benediction.
bendito, a. blessed.
beneficio, m. benefit. —beneficiar, v.
beneficioso, a. beneficial.
benevolencia, f. benevolence.
benévolo, a. benevolent.
benigno, a. benign.
beodo, a. drunk.
berenjena, f. eggplant.
beso, m. kiss. —besar, v.
bestia, f. beast, brute.
betabel, m. beet.
Biblia, f. Bible.
bíblico, a. Biblical.
biblioteca, f. library.
bicarbonato, m. bicarbonate.
bicicleta, f. bicycle.
bien, 1. adv. well. 2. n. good; (pl.) possessions.
bienestar, m. well-being, welfare.
bienhechor -ra, n. benefactor.
bienvenida, f. welcome.
bienvenido, a. welcome.
biftec, m. steak.
bifurcación, f. fork. —bifurcar, v.
bigamía, f. bigamy.
bígamo -a, n. bigamist.
bigotes, m.pl. mustache.
bilis, f. bile.
billar, m. billiards.
billete, m. ticket; bank note, bill.
billón, m. billion.
biodegradable, a. biodegradable.
biografía, f. biography.
biología, f. biology.
biombo, m. screen.
bisel, m. bevel. —biselar, v.
bisonte, m. bison.
bisté, bistec, m. steak.
bizarro, a. brave; generous; smart.
bizcocho, m. biscuit, cake.
blanco, 1. a. white; blank. 2. m. white; target.
blandir, v. brandish, flourish.
blando, a. soft.
blanquear, v. whiten; bleach.
blasfemar, v. blaspheme, curse.
blasfemia, f. blasphemy.
blindado, a. armored.
blindaje, m. armor.
bloque, m. block. —bloquear, v.
bloqueo, m. blockade. —bloquear, v.

blusa, f. blouse.
bobo -ba, a. & n. fool; foolish.
boca, f. mouth.
bocado, m. bit; bite, mouthful, morsel.
bocanada, f. puff (of smoke); mouthful (of liquor).
bocina, f. horn.
bochorno, m. sultry weather; embarrassment.
boda, f. wedding.
bodega, f. wine cellar; (naut.) hold; grocery store.
bofetada, f. bofetón, m. slap.
boga, f. vogue; fad.
bogar, v. row (a boat).
bohemio -a, a. & n. Bohemian.
boicoteo, m. boycott. —boicotear, v.
boina, f. beret.
bola, f. ball.
bolera, f. bowling alley.
boletín, m. bulletin.
boleto, m. ticket.
boliche, m. bowling alley.
boliviano -a, a. & n. Bolivian.
bolos, m.pl. bowling.
bolsa, f. purse; stock exchange.
bolsillo, m. pocket.
bollo, m. bun, loaf.
bomba, f. pump; bomb; gas station.
bombardear, v. bomb; bombard, shell.
bombear, v. pump.
bombero, m. fireman.
bombilla, f. (light) bulb.
bonanza, f. prosperity; fair weather.
bondad, f. kindness; goodness.
bondadoso, a. kind, kindly.
bonito, a. pretty.
bono, m. bonus; (fin.) bond.
boqueada, f. gasp; gape. —boquear, v.
boquilla, f. cigarette holder.
bordado, m., bordadura, f. embroidery.
bordar, v. embroider.
borde, m. border, rim, edge, brink, ledge.
borla, f. tassel.
borracho, a. drunk.
borrachón, m. drunkard.
borrador, m. eraser.
borradura, f. erasure.
borrar, v. erase, rub out.
borrasca, f. squall, storm.
borrico, m. donkey.
bosque, m. forest, wood.
bostezo, m. yawn. —bostezar, v.
bota, f. boot.
botalón, m. (naut.) boom.
botánica, f. botany.
botar, v. throw out, throw away.
bote, m. boat; can, box.
botica, f. pharmacy, drugstore.
boticario, m. pharmacist, druggist.
botín, m. booty, plunder, spoils.
boto, a. dull, stupid.

botón, m. button.
botones, m. bellboy (in a hotel).
bóveda, f. vault.
boxeador, m. boxer.
boxeo, m. boxing. —boxear, v.
boya, f. buoy.
boyante, a. buoyant.
bozal, m. muzzle.
bramido, m. roar, bellow. —bramar, v.
brasileño -ña, a. & n. Brazilian.
bravata, f. bravado.
bravear, v. bully.
braza, f. fathom.
brazada, f. (swimming) stroke.
brazalete, m. bracelet.
brazo, m. arm.
brea, f. tar, pitch.
brecha, f. gap, breach.
bregar, v. scramble.
breña, f. rough country with brambly shrubs.
Bretaña, f. Britain.
breve, a. brief, short. en b., shortly, soon.
brevedad, f. brevity.
bribón, m. rogue, rascal.
brida, f. bridle.
brigada, f. brigade.
brillante, 1. a. brilliant, shiny. 2. m. diamond.
brillo, m. shine, glitter. —brillar, v.
brinco, m. jump; bounce, skip. —brincar, v.
brindis, m. toast. —brindar, v.
brío, m. vigor.
brioso, a. vigorous, spirited.
brisa, f. breeze.
británico, a. British.
brocado, m. brocade.
brocha, f. brush.
broche, m. brooch, clasp, pin.
broma, f. joke. —bromear, v.
bronce, m. bronze; brass.
bronquitis, f. bronchitis.
brotar, v. gush; sprout; bud.
brote, m. bud, shoot.
bruja, f. witch.
brújula, f. compass.
bruma, f. mist.
brumoso, a. misty.
brusco, a. brusque; abrupt, curt.
brutal, a. savage, brutal.
brutalidad, f. brutality.
bruto, 1. a. brutish; ignorant. 2. m. blockhead.
bucear, v. dive.
bueno, a. good, fair; well (in health).
buey, m. ox, steer.
búfalo, m. buffalo.
bufanda, f. scarf.
bufón -ona, n. fool, buffoon, clown.
buho, m. owl.
buhonero, m. peddler, vender.
bujía, f. spark plug.
bulevar, m. boulevard.
bulto, m. bundle; lump.
bullicio, m. bustle, noise.
bullicioso, a. boisterous, noisy.
buñuelo, m. bun.

buque, *m.* ship.
burdo, *a.* coarse.
burgués -esa, *a.* & *n.* bourgeois.
burla, *f.* mockery; fun.
burlador, *m.* trickster, jokester.
burlar, *v.* mock, deride.
burlarse de, *v.* scoff at; make fun of.
burro, *m.* donkey.
busca, *f.* search, pursuit, quest.
buscar, *v.* seek, look for; look up.
busto, *m.* bust.
butaca, *f.* armchair; (theat.) orchestra seat.
buzo, *m.* diver.
buzón, *m.* mailbox.

C

cabal, *a.* exact; thorough.
cabalgar, *v.* ride horseback.
caballeresco, *a.* gentlemanly, chivalrous.
caballería, *f.* cavalry; chivalry.
caballeriza, *f.* stable.
caballero, *m.* gentleman; knight.
caballete, *m.* sawhorse; easel; ridge (of roof).
caballo, *m.* horse.
cabaña, *f.* cabin; booth.
cabecear, *v.* pitch (as a ship).
cabecera, *f.* head (of bed, table).
cabello, *m.* hair.
caber, *v.* fit into, be contained in. **no cabe duda,** there is no doubt.
cabeza, *f.* head; warhead.
cabildo, *m.* city hall.
cabizbajo, *a.* downcast.
cablegrama, *m.* cablegram.
cabo, *m.* end; (geog.) cape; (mil.) corporal. **llevar a c.,** carry out, accomplish.
cabra, *f.* goat.
cacahuete, *m.* peanut.
cacao, *m.* cocoa; chocolate.
cacerola, *f.* pan, casserole.
cachorro, *m.* cub; puppy.
cada, *a.* each, every.
cadáver, *m.* corpse.
cadena, *f.* chain.
cadera, *f.* hip.
cadete, *m.* cadet.
caer, *v.* fall.
café, *m.* coffee; café.
cafetal, *m.* coffee plantation.
cafetera, *f.* coffee pot.
caída, *f.* fall, drop; collapse.
caimán, *m.* alligator.
caja, *f.* box, case.
cajero -ra, *n.* cashier.
cajón, *m.* drawer.
cal, *f.* lime.
calabaza, *f.* calabash, pumpkin.
calabozo, *m.* jail, cell.
calambre, *m.* cramp.
calamidad, *f.* calamity, disaster.
calcetín, *m.* sock.
calcio, *m.* calcium.

calcular, *v.* calculate, figure.
cálculo, *m.* calculation, estimate.
caldera, *f.* kettle, caldron; boiler.
caldo, *m.* broth.
calefacción, *f.* heat, heating.
calendario, *m.* calendar.
calentar, *v.* heat, warm.
calidad, *f.* quality, grade.
caliente, *a.* hot, warm.
calificar, *v.* qualify.
calma, *f.* calm, quiet.
calmado, *a.* calm.
calmante, *a.* soothing, calming.
calmar, *v.* calm, quiet, lull, soothe.
calor, *n.* heat, warmth. **tener c.,** to be hot, warm; feel hot, warm. **hacer c.,** to be hot, warm (weather).
calorífero, *m.* radiator.
calumnia, *f.* slander. **—calumniar,** *v.*
caluroso, *a.* warm, hot.
calvario, *m.* Calvary.
calvo, *a.* bald.
calzado, *m.* footwear.
calzar, *v.* wear (as shoes).
calzoncillos, *m.pl.* shorts.
calzones, *m.pl.* trousers.
callado, *a.* silent, quiet.
callarse, *v.* quiet down; keep still; stop talking.
calle, *f.* street.
callejón, *m.* alley.
callo, *m.* callus, corn.
cama, *f.* bed.
cámara, *f.* chamber; camera.
camarada, *m.* & *f.* comrade.
camarera, *f.* chambermaid; waitress.
camarero, *m.* steward; waiter.
camarón, *m.* shrimp.
camarote, *m.* stateroom, berth.
cambiar, *v.* exchange, change, trade; cash.
cambio, *m.* change, exchange. **en c.,** on the other hand.
cambista, *m.* banker, broker.
cambur, *m.* banana.
camello, *m.* camel.
camilla, *f.* stretcher.
caminar, *v.* walk.
camino, *m.* road; way.
caminata, *f.* tramp, hike.
camión, *m.* truck.
camisa, *f.* shirt.
camisería, *f.* haberdashery.
camiseta, *f.* undershirt; T-shirt.
campamento, *m.* camp.
campana, *f.* bell.
campanario, *m.* bell tower, steeple.
campaneo, *m.* chime.
campaña, *f.* campaign.
campeón, *m.* champion.
campeonato, *m.* championship.
campesino -na, *n.* peasant.
campestre, *a.* country, rural.
campo, *m.* field; (the) country.
Canadá, *m.* Canada.

canadiense, *a.* & *n.* Canadian.
canal, *m.* canal; channel.
canalla, *f.* rabble.
canario, *m.* canary.
canasta, *f.* basket.
cáncer, *m.* cancer.
canciller, *m.* chancellor.
canción, *f.* song.
candado, *m.* padlock.
candela, *f.* fire; light; candle.
candelero, *m.* candlestick.
candidato -ta, *n.* candidate; applicant.
candidatura, *f.* candidacy.
canela, *f.* cinnamon.
cangrejo, *m.* crab.
caníbal, *m.* cannibal.
canje, *m.* exchange, trade. **—canjear,** *v.*
cano, *a.* gray.
canoa, *f.* canoe.
cansado, *a.* tired, weary.
cansancio, *m.* fatigue.
cansar, *v.* tire, fatigue, wear out.
cantante, *m.* & *f.* singer.
cantar, 1. *m.* song. 2. *v.* sing.
cántaro, *m.* pitcher.
cantera, *f.* (stone) quarry.
cantidad, *f.* quantity, amount.
cantina, *f.* bar, tavern; restaurant.
canto, *m.* chant, song, singing; edge.
caña, *f.* cane, reed; sugar cane.
cañón, *m.* canyon; cannon; gun barrel.
caoba, *f.* mahogany.
caos, *m.* chaos.
caótico, *a.* chaotic.
capa, *f.* cape, cloak; coat (of paint).
capacidad, *f.* capacity; capability.
capacitar, *v.* enable.
capataz, *m.* foreman.
capaz, *a.* capable, able.
capellán, *m.* chaplain.
caperuza, *f.* hood.
capilla, *f.* chapel.
capital, *m.* capital. *f.* capital (city).
capitalista, *a.* & *n.* capitalist.
capitán, *m.* captain.
capitular, *v.* yield.
capítulo, *m.* chapter.
capota, *f.* hood.
capricho, *m.* caprice; fancy, whim.
caprichoso, *a.* capricious.
cápsula, *f.* capsule.
capturar, *v.* capture.
capucha, *f.* hood.
capullo, *m.* cocoon.
cara, *f.* face.
caracol, *m.* snail.
carácter, *m.* character.
característica, *f.* characteristic.
característico, *a.* characteristic.
caramba, mild exclamation.
caramelo, *m.* caramel; candy.
carátula, *f.* dial.
caravana, *f.* caravan.
carbón, *m.* carbon; coal.

carbonizar, v. char.
carburador, m. carburetor.
carcajada, f. burst of laughter.
cárcel, f. prison, jail.
carcelero, m. jailer.
carcinogénico, a. carcinogenic.
cardenal, m. cardinal.
carecer, v. lack.
carestía, f. scarcity; famine.
carga, f. cargo; load, burden; freight.
cargar, v. carry; load; charge.
cargo, m. load; charge, office.
caricia, f. caress.
caridad, f. charity.
cariño, m. affection, fondness.
cariñoso, a. affectionate, fond.
carisma, m. charisma.
caritativo, a. charitable.
carmesí, a. & m. crimson.
carnaval, m. carnival.
carne, f. meat, flesh; pulp.
carnero, m. ram; mutton.
carnicería, f. meat market; massacre.
carnicero, m. butcher.
carnívoro, a. carnivorous.
caro, a. dear, costly, expensive.
carpa, f. tent.
carpeta, f. folder; briefcase.
carpintero, m. carpenter.
carrera, f. race; career.
carreta, f. wagon, cart.
carrete, m. reel, spool.
carretera, f. road, highway.
carril, m. rail.
carrillo, m. cart (for baggage or shopping).
carro, m. car, automobile; cart.
carroza, f. chariot.
carruaje, m. carriage.
carta, f. letter; (pl.) cards.
cartel, m. placard, poster; cartel.
cartera, f. pocketbook, handbag, wallet; portfolio.
cartero, m. mailman, postman.
cartón, m. cardboard.
cartucho, m. cartridge; cassette.
casa, f. house, dwelling; home.
casaca, f. dress coat.
casado, a. married.
casamiento, m. marriage.
casar, v. marry, marry off.
casarse, v. get married. c. con, marry.
cascabel, m. jingle bell.
cascada, f. waterfall, cascade.
cascajo, m. gravel.
cascanueces, m. nutcracker.
cascar, v. crack, break, burst.
cáscara, f. shell, rind, husk.
casco, m. helmet; hull.
casera, f. landlady; housekeeper.
caserío, m. settlement.
casero, 1. a. homemade. 2. m. landlord, superintendent.
caseta, f. cottage, hut.
casi, adv. almost, nearly.
casilla, f. booth; ticket office; pigeonhole.
casino, m. club; clubhouse.

caso, m. case. hacer c. a, pay attention to.
casorio, m. informal wedding.
caspa, f. dandruff.
casta, f. caste.
castaña, f. chestnut.
castaño, 1. a. brown. 2. m. chestnut tree.
castañuela, f. castanet.
castellano, a. & m. Castillian.
castidad, f. chastity.
castigar, v. punish.
castigo, m. punishment.
castillo, m. castle.
castizo, a. pure, genuine; noble.
casto, a. chaste.
castor, m. beaver.
casual, adj. accidental, coincidental.
casualidad, f. coincidence. por c., by chance.
casuca, f. hut, shanty, hovel.
catadura, f. act of tasting; appearance.
catalán, a. & m. Catalonian.
catálogo, m. catalogue. —catalogar, v.
catar, v. taste; examine, try; bear in mind.
catarata, f. cataract, waterfall.
catarro, m. head cold.
catástrofe, f. catastrophe.
catecismo, m. catechism.
cátedra, f. professorship.
catedral, f. cathedral.
catedrático, m. professor.
categoría, f. category.
categórico, a. categorical.
catequizar, v. catechize.
catolicismo, m. Catholicism.
católico -ca, a. & n. Catholic.
catorce, a. & pron. fourteen.
catre, m. cot.
cauce, m. riverbed; ditch.
caución, f. precaution; security, guarantee.
cauchal, m. rubber plantation.
caucho, m. rubber.
caudal, m. means, fortune; (pl.) holdings.
caudaloso, a. prosperous, rich.
caudillaje, m. leadership; tyranny.
caudillo, m. leader, chief.
causa, f. cause. —causar, v.
cautela, f. caution.
cauteloso, a. cautious.
cautivar, v. captivate.
cautiverio, m. captivity.
cautividad, f. captivity.
cautivo -va, a. & n. captive.
cauto, a. cautious.
cavar, v. dig.
caverna, f. cavern, cave.
cavernoso, a. cavernous.
cavidad, f. cavity, hollow.
cavilar, v. criticize, cavil.
cayado, m. shepherd's staff.
cayo, m. small rocky islet, key.
caza, f. hunting, pursuit, game.
cazador, m. hunter.
cazar, v. hunt.
cazatorpedero, m. destroyer.
cazo, m. ladle, dipper; pot.

cazuela, f. crock.
cebada, f. barley.
cebo, m. bait. —cebar, v.
cebolla, f. onion.
ceceo, m. lisp. —cecear, v.
cecina, f. dried beef.
cedazo, m. sieve, sifter.
ceder, v. cede; transfer; yield.
cedro, m. cedar.
cédula, f. decree. c. personal, identification card.
céfiro, m. zephyr.
cegar, v. blind.
ceguedad, ceguera, f. blindness.
ceja, f. eyebrow.
cejar, v. go backwards; yield; retreat.
celada, f. trap; ambush.
celaje, m. appearance of the sky.
celar, v. watch carefully, guard.
celda, f. cell.
celebración, f. celebration.
celebrante, m. officiating priest.
celebrar, v. celebrate, observe.
célebre, a. celebrated, noted, famous.
celebridad, f. fame; celebrity; pageant.
celeridad, f. speed, rapidity.
celeste, a. celestial.
celestial, a. heavenly.
célibe, 1. a. unmarried. 2. m. & f. unmarried person.
celo, m. zeal; (pl.) jealousy.
celosía, f. Venetian blind.
celoso, a. jealous; zealous.
céltico, a. Celtic.
célula, f. (biol.) cell.
celuloide, m. celluloid.
celulosa, f. cellulose.
cellisca, f. sleet. —cellisquear, v.
cementar, v. cement.
cementerio, m. cemetery.
cemento, m. cement.
cena, f. supper.
cenagal, m. swamp, marsh.
cenagoso, a. swampy, marshy, muddy.
cenar, v. dine, eat.
cencerro, m. cowbell.
cendal, m. thin, light cloth; gauze.
cenicero, m. ashtray.
ceniciento, a. ashen.
cenit, m. zenith.
ceniza, f. ash, ashes.
censo, m. census.
censor, m. critic.
censura, f. reproof, censure; censorship.
censurable, a. objectionable.
censurar, v. censure, criticize.
centavo, m. cent.
centella, f. thunderbolt, lightning.
centellear, v. twinkle, sparkle.
centelleo, m. sparkle.
centenar, m. (a) hundred.
centenario, m. centennial, centenary.
centeno, m. rye.

centigrado, *a.* centigrade.
centimetro, *m.* centimeter.
céntimo, *m.* cent.
centinela, *m.* sentry, guard.
central, *a.* central.
centrar, *v.* center.
céntrico, *a.* central.
centro, *m.* center.
centroamericano -na, *a. & n.* Central American.
ceñidor, *m.* belt, sash; girdle.
ceñir, *v.* gird.
ceño, *m.* frown.
ceñudo, *a.* frowning, grim.
cepa, *f.* stump.
cepillo, *m.* brush; plane. — **cepillar**, *v.*
cera, *f.* wax.
cerámica, *m.* ceramics.
cerca, **1.** *adv.* near. **2.** *f.* fence, hedge.
cercado, *m.* enclosure; garden.
cercamiento, *m.* enclosure.
cercanía, *f.* proximity.
cercano, *a.* near, nearby.
cercar, *v.* surround.
cercenar, *v.* clip; lessen, reduce.
cerciorar, *v.* make sure; affirm.
cerco, *m.* hoop; siege.
cerda, *f.* bristle.
cerdo, *m.* hog.
cerdoso, *a.* bristly.
cereal, *a. & m.* cereal.
cerebro, *m.* brain.
ceremonia, *f.* ceremony.
ceremonial, *a. & m.* ceremonial, ritual.
ceremonioso, *a.* ceremonious.
cereza, *f.* cherry.
cerilla, *f.*, **cerillo**, *m.* match.
cerner, *v.* sift.
cero, *m.* zero.
cerrado, *a.* cloudy; obscure; stupid.
cerradura, *f.* lock.
cerrajero, *m.* locksmith.
cerrar, *v.* close, shut.
cerro, *m.* hill.
cerrojo, *m.* latch, bolt.
certamen, *m.* contest; competition.
certero, *a.* accurate, exact; certain, sure.
certeza, *f.* certainty.
certidumbre, *f.* certainty.
certificado, *m.* certificate.
certificar, *v.* certify; register (a letter).
cerúleo, *a.* cerulean, sky-blue.
cervecería, *f.* brewery; beer saloon.
cervecero, *m.* brewer.
cerveza, *f.* beer.
cesante, *a.* unemployed.
cesar, *v.* cease.
césped, *m.* sod, lawn.
cesta, *f.*, **cesto**, *m.* basket.
cetrino, *a.* yellow, lemon-colored.
cetro, *m.* scepter.
cicatero, *a.* stingy.
cicatriz, *f.* scar.
cicatrizar, *v.* heal.
ciclamato, *m.* cyclamate.

ciclo, *m.* cycle.
ciclón, *m.* cyclone.
ciego -ga, **1.** *a.* blind. **2.** *n.* blind person.
cielo, *m.* heaven; sky, heavens; ceiling.
ciempiés, *m.* centipede.
cien, **ciento**, *a. & pron.* hundred. **por c.**, per cent.
ciénaga, *f.* swamp, marsh.
ciencia, *f.* science.
cieno, *m.* mud.
científico, **1.** *a.* scientific. **2.** *n.* scientist.
cierre, *m.* fastener, snap, clasp.
cierto, *a.* certain, sure, true.
ciervo, *m.* deer.
cierzo, *m.* northerly wind.
cifra, *f.* cipher, number. — **cifrar**, *v.*
cigarra, *f.* locust.
cigarrera, **cigarrillera**, *f.* cigarette case.
cigarrillo, *m.* cigarette.
cigarro, *m.* cigar; cigarette.
cilíndrico, *a.* cylindrical.
cilindro, *m.* cylinder.
cima, *f.* summit, peak.
cimarrón, **1.** *a.* wild, untamed. **2.** *m.* runaway slave.
címbalo, *m.* cymbal.
cimbrar, *v.* shake, brandish.
cimientos, *m.pl.* foundation.
cinc, *m.* zinc.
cincel, *m.* chisel. — **cincelar**, *v.*
cinco, *a. & pron.* five.
cincuenta, *a. & pron.* fifty.
cincha, *f.* (harness) cinch. — **cinchar**, *v.*
cine, *m.* movies; movie theater.
cíngulo, *m.* girdle.
cínico, *a. & n.* cynical; cynic.
cinta, *f.* ribbon, tape; (movie) film.
cintilar, *v.* glitter, sparkle.
cinto, *m.* belt; girdle.
cintura, *f.* waist.
cinturón, *m.* belt.
ciprés, *m.* cypress.
circo, *m.* circus.
circuito, *m.* circuit.
circulación, *f.* circulation.
circular, **1.** *a. & m.* circular. **2.** *v.* circulate.
círculo *m.* circle, club.
circundante, *a.* surrounding.
circundar, *v.* encircle, surround.
circunferencia, *f.* circumference.
circunlocución, *n.* circumlocution.
circunscribir, *v.* circumscribe.
circunspección, *n.* decorum, propriety.
circunspecto, *a.* circumspect.
circunstancia, *f.* circumstance.
circunstante, *m.* bystander.
circunvecino, *a.* neighboring, adjacent.
cirio, *m.* candle.
ciruela, *f.* plum; prune.
cirugía, *f.* surgery.
cirujano, *m.* surgeon.

cisne, *m.* swan.
cisterna, *f.* cistern.
cita, *f.* citation; appointment, date.
citación, *f.* citation; (legal) summons.
citar, *v.* cite, quote; summon; make an appointment with.
ciudad, *f.* city.
ciudadanía, *f.* citizenship.
ciudadano -na, *n.* citizen.
ciudadela, *f.* fortress, citadel.
cívico, *a.* civic.
civil, *a. & n.* civil; civilian.
civilidad, *f.* politeness, civility.
civilización, *f.* civilization.
civilizador, *a.* civilizing.
civilizar, *v.* civilize.
cizallas, *f.pl.* shears. — **cizallar**, *v.*
cizaña, *f.* weed; vice.
clamar, *v.* clamor.
clamor, *m.* clamor.
clamoreo, *m.* persistent clamor.
clamoroso, *a.* clamorous.
clandestino, *a.* secret, clandestine.
clara, *f.* white (of egg).
claraboya, *m.* skylight; bull's-eye.
clarear, *v.* clarify; become light, dawn.
claridad, *f.* clarity.
clarificar, *v.* clarify.
clarín, *m.* bugle, trumpet.
clarinete, *m.* clarinet.
clarividencia, *f.* clairvoyance.
claro, *a.* clear; bright; light (in color); of course.
clase, *f.* class; classroom; kind, sort.
clásico, *a.* classic, classical.
clasificar, *v.* classify, rank.
claustro, *m.* cloister.
cláusula, *f.* clause.
clausura, *f.* cloister; inner sanctum.
clavado, *m.* dive.
clavar, *v.* nail, peg, pin.
clave, *f.* code; (mus.) key.
clavel, *m.* carnation.
clavetear, *v.* nail.
clavija, *f.* pin, peg.
clavijero, *m.* hatrack.
clavo, *m.* nail, spike.
clemencia, *f.* clemency.
clemente, *a.* merciful.
clerecía, *f.* clergy.
clerical, *a.* clerical.
clérigo, *m.* clergyman.
clero, *m.* clergy.
cliente, *m. & f.* customer, client.
clientela, *f.* clientele, practice.
clima, *m.* climate.
clímax, *m.* climax.
clínica, *f.* clinic.
clíper, *m.* clipper ship.
cloaca, *f.* sewer.
cloquear, *v.* cluck, cackle.
cloqueo, *m.* cluck.
cloro, *m.* chlorine.
club, *m.* club, association.
clueca, *f.* brooding hen.

coacción, *n.* compulsion.

coagular, *v.* coagulate, clot.

coágulo, *m.* clot.

coalición, *f.* coalition.

coartar, *v.* limit.

cobarde, *a. & n.* cowardly; coward.

cobardía, *f.* cowardice.

cobertizo, *m.* shed.

cobertor, *m.,* **cobija,** *f.* blanket.

cobertura, *f.* cover, wrapping.

cobijar, *v.* cover; protect.

cobrador, *m.* collector.

cobranza, *f.* collection or recovery of money.

cobrar, *v.* collect; charge; cash.

cobre, *m.* copper.

cobrizo, *a.* coppery.

cobro, *m.* collection or recovery of money.

coca, *f.* coca leaves.

cocaína, *f.* cocaine.

cocal, *m.* coconut plantation.

cocear, *v.* kick; resist.

cocer, *v.* cook, boil, bake.

cocido, *m.* stew.

cociente, *m.* quotient.

cocimiento, *m.* cooking.

cocina, *f.* kitchen.

cocinar, *v.* cook.

cocinero -ra, *n.* cook.

coco, *m.* coconut; coconut tree.

cocodrilo, *m.* crocodile.

coctel, *m.* cocktail.

coche, *m.* coach; car, automobile.

cochera, *f.* garage.

cochero, *m.* coachman; cab driver.

cochinada, *f.* filth; herd of swine.

cochino, *m.* pig, swine.

codazo, *m.* nudge with the elbow.

codicia, *f.* avarice, greed; lust.

codiciar, *v.* covet.

codicioso, *a.* covetous; greedy.

código, *m.* (law) code.

codo, *m.* elbow.

codorniz, *f.* quail.

coetáneo, *a.* contemporary.

cofrade, *m.* fellow member of a club, etc.

cofre, *m.* coffer; chest; trunk.

coger, *v.* catch; pick; take.

cogote, *m.* nape.

cohecho, *m.* bribe. —**cohechar,** *v.*

coheredero, *m.* co-heir.

coherente, *a.* coherent.

cohesión, *f.* cohesion.

cohete, *m.* fire cracker, rocket.

cohibición, *n.* restraint; repression.

cohibir, *v.* restrain; repress.

coincidencia, *f.* coincidence.

coincidir, *v.* coincide.

cojear, *v.* limp.

cojera, *m.* limp.

cojín, *m.* cushion.

cojinete, *m.* small cushion, pad.

cojo, *a.* lame.

col, *f.* cabbage.

cola, *f.* tail; glue; line, queue. **hacer c.,** stand in line.

colaboración, *f.* collaboration.

colaborar, *v.* collaborate.

coladera, *f.* strainer.

colador, *m.* colander, strainer.

colapso, *m.* collapse, prostration.

colar, *v.* strain; drain.

colateral, *a.* collateral.

colcha, *f.* bedspread, quilt.

colchón, *m.* mattress.

colear, *v.* wag the tail.

colección, *f.* collection, set.

coleccionar, *v.* collect.

colecta, *f.* collection (a prayer).

colectivo, *a.* collective.

colector, *m.* collector.

colega, *m. & f.* colleague.

colegial, *m.* college student.

colegiatura, *f.* college scholarship.

colegio, *m.* (private) school, college.

colegir, *v.* infer, deduce.

cólera, *f.* rage, wrath.

colérico, *adj.* angry, irritated.

coleto, *m.* leather jacket.

colgador, *m.* rack, hanger.

colgaduras, *f.pl.* drapery.

colgante, *a.* hanging.

colgar, *v.* hang up, suspend.

colibrí, *m.* hummingbird.

coliflor, *m.* cauliflower.

coligarse, *v.* band together, unite.

colilla, *f.* butt of a cigar or cigarette.

colina, *f.* hill, hillock.

colinabo, *m.* turnip.

colindante, *a.* neighboring, adjacent.

colindar, *v.* neighbor, abut.

coliseo, *m.* theater; coliseum.

colisión, *f.* collision.

colmar, *v.* heap up, fill liberally.

colmena, *f.* hive.

colmillo, *m.* eyetooth; tusk; fang.

colmo, *m.* height, peak, extreme.

colocación, *f.* place, position; employment, job; arrangement.

colocar, *v.* place, locate, put, set.

colombiano -na, *a. & n.* Colombian.

colon, *m.* colon (of intestines).

colonia, *f.* colony.

colonial, *a.* colonial.

colonización, *f.* colonization.

colonizador, *m.* colonizer.

colonizar, *v.* colonize.

colono, *m.* colonist; tenant farmer.

coloquio, *m.* conversation, talk.

color, *m.* color. —**colorar,** *v.*

coloración, *f.* coloring.

colorado, *a.* red, ruddy.

colorar, *v.* color, paint; dye.

colorete, *m.* rouge.

colorido, *m.* color, coloring. —**colorir,** *v.*

colosal, *a.* colossal.

columbrar, *v.* discern.

columna, *f.* column, pillar, shaft.

columpiar, *v.* swing.

columpio, *m.* swing.

collado, *m.* hillock.

collar, *m.* necklace; collar.

coma, *f.* coma; comma.

comadre, *f.* midwife; gossip; close friend.

comadreja, *m.* weasel.

comandancia, *m.* command; command post.

comandante, *m.* commandant; commander; major.

comandar, *v.* command.

comandita, *f.* silent partnership.

comanditario, *m.* silent partner.

comando, *m.* command.

comarca, *f.* region; border, boundary.

comba, *f.* bulge.

combar, *v.* bend; bulge.

combate, *m.* combat. —**combatir,** *v.*

combatiente, *a. & m.* combatant.

combinación, *f.* combination; (lady's) slip.

combinar, *v.* combine.

combustible, 1. *a.* combustible. **2.** *m.* fuel.

combustión, *f.* combustion.

comedero, *m.* trough.

comedia, *f.* comedy; play.

comediante, *m.* actor; comedian.

comedido, *a.* polite, courteous, obliging.

comedirse, *v.* to be polite or obliging.

comedor, *m.* dining room. **coche c.,** dining car.

comendador, *m.* commander.

comensal, *m.* member of a household.

comentador, *m.* commentator.

comentario, *m.* commentary.

comente, *m.* comment. —**comentar,** *v.*

comenzar, *v.* begin, start, commence.

comer, *v.* eat, dine.

comercial, *a.* commercial.

comerciante, *m.* merchant, trader, businessman.

comerciar, *v.* trade, deal, do business.

comercio, *m.* commerce, trade, business.

comestible, 1. *a.* edible. **2.** *m.* (*pl.*) groceries, provisions.

cometa, *m.* comet. *f.* kite.

cometer, *v.* commit.

cometido, *m.* commission; duty; task.

comezón, *f.* itch.

comicios, *m.pl.* primary elections.

cómico -ca, *a. & n.* comic, comical; comedian.

comida, *f.* food; dinner; meal.

comidilla, *f.* light meal; gossip.

comienzo, *m.* beginning.

comilitona, *f.* banquet.

comilón, *m.* glutton; heavy eater.

comillas, *f.pl.* quotation marks.

comisario, *m.* commissary.

comisión, *f.* commission. — **comisionar**, *v.*

comisionado, *m.* agent, commissioner.

comisionar, *v.* commission.

comiso, *m.* (law) confiscation of illegal goods.

comistrajo, *m.* mess, hodge-podge.

comité, *m.* committee.

comitiva, *f.* retinue.

como, *conj. & adv.* like, as.

cómo, *adv.* how.

cómoda, *f.* bureau, chest (of drawers).

cómodamente, *adv.* conveniently.

comodatario, *m.* pawnbroker.

comodato, *m.* loan.

comodidad, *f.* convenience, comfort; commodity.

cómodo, *a.* comfortable; convenient.

comodoro, *m.* commodore.

compacto, *a.* compact.

compadecer, *v.* be sorry for, pity.

compadraje, *m.* clique.

compadre, *m.* close friend.

compaginar, *v.* put in order; arrange.

companaje, *m.* cold lunch.

compañerismo, *m.* companionship.

compañero -ra, *n.* companion, partner.

compañía, *f.* company.

comparable, *a.* comparable.

comparación, *f.* comparison.

comparar, *v.* compare.

comparativamente, *adv.* comparatively.

comparativo, *a.* comparative.

comparecer, *v.* appear.

comparendo, *m.* summons.

comparsa, *f.* carnival masquerade; retinue.

compartimiento, *m.* compartment.

compartir, *v.* share.

compás, *m.* compass; beat, rhythm.

compasar, *v.* measure exactly.

compasible, *a.* compassionate.

compasión, *f.* compassion.

compasivo, *a.* compassionate.

compatibilidad, *f.* compatibility.

compatible, *a.* compatible.

compatriota, *m. & f.* compatriot.

compeler, *v.* compel.

compendiar, *v.* summarize; abridge.

compendiariamente, *adv.* briefly.

compendio, *m.* summary; abridgment.

compendiosamente, *adv.* briefly.

compensación, *f.* compensation.

compensar, *v.* compensate.

competencia, *f.* competence; competition.

competente, *a.* competent.

competentemente, *adv.* competently.

competición, *f.* competition.

competidor, *a. & n.* competitive; competitor.

competir, *v.* compete.

compilación, *f.* compilation.

compilar, *v.* compile.

compinche, *m.* pal.

complacencia, *f.* complacency.

complacer, *v.* please, oblige, humor.

complaciente, *a.* pleasing, obliging.

complejidad, *f.* complexity.

complejo, *a. & n.* complex.

complemento, *m.* complement; (gram.) object.

completamente, *adv.* completely.

completamiento, *m.* completion, finish.

completar, *v.* complete.

completo, *a.* complete, full, perfect.

complexidad, *f.* complexity.

complexión, *f.* nature, temperament.

complexo, *a.* complex, intricate.

complicación, *f.* complication.

complicado, *a.* complicated.

complicar, *v.* complicate.

cómplice, *m. & f.* accomplice, accessory.

complicidad, *f.* complicity.

complot, *m.* conspiracy.

componedor, *m.* typesetter.

componenda, *f.* compromise; settlement.

componente, *a. & m.* component.

componer, *v.* compose; fix, repair.

componible, *a.* reparable.

comportable, *a.* endurable.

comportamiento, *m.* behavior.

comportarse, *v.* behave.

comporte, *m.* behavior.

composición, *f.* composition.

compositivo, *a.* synthetic; composite.

compositor -ra, *n.* composer.

compostura, *f.* composure; repair; neatness.

compota, *f.* (fruit) sauce.

compra, *f.* purchase. **ir de compras**, to go shopping.

comprador -ra, *n.* buyer, purchaser.

comprar, *v.* buy, purchase.

comprehensivo, *a.* comprehensive.

comprender, *v.* comprehend, understand; include, comprise.

comprensibilidad, *f.* comprehensibility.

comprensible, *a.* understandable.

comprensión, *f.* comprehension, understanding.

comprensivo, *m.* comprehensive.

compresa, *f.* medical compress.

compresión, *f.* compression.

comprimir, *v.* compress.

comprobación, *f.* proof.

comprobante, **1.** *a.* proving. **2.** *m.* proof.

comprobar, *v.* prove; verify, check.

comprometer, *v.* compromise.

comprometerse, *v.* become engaged.

compromiso, *m.* compromise; engagement.

copropietario, *m.* co-owner.

compuerta, *f.* floodgate.

compuesto, *m.* composition; compound.

compulsión, *f.* compulsion.

compulsivo, *a.* compulsive.

compunción, *f.* compunction.

compungirse, *v.* regret, feel remorse.

computación, *f.* computation.

computador, *m.* computer.

computar, *v.* compute.

cómputo, *m.* computation.

comulación, *f.* cumulation.

comulgar, *v.* take communion.

comulgatorio, *m.* communion altar.

común, *a.* common, usual.

comunal, *m.* common people.

comunero, *m.* commoner.

comunicable, *a.* communicable.

comunicación, *f.* communication.

comunicante, *m. & f.* communicant.

comunicar, *v.* communicate; convey.

comunicativo, *a.* communicative.

comunidad, *f.* community.

comunión, *f.* communion.

comunismo, *m.* communism.

comunista, *a. & n.* communistic; communist.

comúnmente, *adv.* commonly; usually; often.

con, *prep.* with.

concavidad, *f.* concavity.

cóncavo, **1.** *a.* concave. **2.** *m.* concavity.

concebible, *a.* conceivable.

concebir, *v.* conceive.

conceder, *v.* concede.

concejal, *m.* councilman.

concejo, *m.* city council.

concento, *m.* harmony.

concentración, *f.* concentration.

concentrar, *v.* concentrate.

concepción, f. conception.

conceptible, a. conceivable.

concepto, m. concept; opinion.

concerniente, a. concerning.

concernir, v. concern.

concertar, v. arrange.

concertina, f. concertina.

concesión, f. concession.

conciencia, f. conscience; consciousness; conscientiousness.

concienzudo, a. conscientious.

concierto, m. concert.

conciliación, f. conciliation.

conciliador, m. conciliator.

conciliar, v. conciliate.

concilio, m. council.

concisión, f. conciseness.

conciso, a. concise.

concitar, v. instigate, stir up.

conciudadano, m. fellow citizen.

concluir, v. conclude.

conclusión, f. conclusion.

conclusivo, a. conclusive.

concluso, a. concluded; closed.

concluyentemente, adv. conclusively.

concomitante, a. concomitant, attendant.

concordador, m. moderator; conciliator.

concordancia, f. agreement, concord.

concordar, v. agree; put or be in accord.

concordia, f. concord, agreement.

concretamente, adv. concretely.

concretar, v. summarize.

concretarse, v. limit oneself to.

concreto, a. & m. concrete.

concubina, f. concubine, mistress.

concupiscente, a. lustful.

concurrencia, f. assembly; attendance; competition.

concurrente, a. concurrent.

concurrido, a. heavily attended or patronized.

concurrir, v. concur; attend.

concurso, m. contest, competition; meeting.

concha, f. (sea) shell.

conde, m. (title) count.

condecente, a. appropriate, proper.

condecoración, f. decoration; medal; badge.

condecorar, v. decorate with a medal.

condena, f. prison sentence.

condenación, f. condemnation.

condenar, v. condemn; damn; sentence.

condensación, f. condensation.

condensar, v. condense.

condesa, f. countess.

condescendencia, f. condescension.

condescender, v. condescend, deign.

condescendiente, a. condescending.

condición, f. condition.

condicional, a. conditional.

condicionalmente, adv. conditionally.

condimentar, v. season, flavor.

condimento, m. condiment, seasoning, dressing.

condiscípulo, m. schoolmate.

condolencia, f. condolence, sympathy.

condolerse de, v. sympathize with.

condómino, m. co-owner.

condonar, v. condone.

cóndor, m. condor (bird).

conducción, f. conveyance.

conducente, a. conducive.

conducir, v. conduct, escort, lead; drive.

conducta, f. conduct, behavior.

conducto, m. pipe, conduit; sewer.

conductor, m. driver; conductor.

conectar, v. connect.

conejera, f. rabbit warren; place of ill repute.

conejo, m. rabbit.

conexión, f. connection; coupling.

conexivo, a. connective.

conexo, a. connected, united.

confalón, m. ensign, standard.

confección, f. workmanship; ready-made article; concoction.

confeccionar, v. concoct.

confederación, f. confederation.

confederado, a. & m. confederate.

confederar, v. confederate, unite, ally.

conferencia, f. lecture; conference.

conferenciante, m. & f. lecturer, speaker.

conferenciar, v. confer.

conferencista, m. & f. lecturer, speaker.

conferir, v. confer.

confesar, v. confess.

confesión, f. confession.

confesionario, m. confessional.

confesor, m. confessor.

confetti, m. pl. confetti.

confiable, a. dependable.

confiado, a. confident; trusting.

confianza, f. confidence, trust, faith.

confiar, v. entrust; trust, rely.

confidencia, f. confidence, secret.

confidencial, a. confidential.

confidente, m. & f. confidant.

confidentemente, adv. confidently.

confín, m. confine.

confinamiento, m. confinement.

confinar, v. confine, imprison; border on.

confirmación, f. confirmation.

confirmar, v. confirm.

confiscación, f. confiscation.

confiscar, v. confiscate.

confitar, v. sweeten; make into candy or jam.

confite, m. candy.

confitería, f. confectionery; candy store.

confitura, f. confection.

conflagración, f. conflagration.

conflicto, m. conflict.

confluencia, f. confluence, junction.

confluir, v. flow into each other.

conformación, f. conformation.

conformar, v. conform.

conforme, 1. a. acceptable, right, as agreed; in accordance, in agreement. 2. conj. according as.

conformidad, f. conformity; agreement.

conformismo, m. conformism.

conformista, m. conformist.

confortar, v. comfort.

confraternidad, m. brotherhood, fraternity.

confricar, v. rub.

confrontación, f. confrontation.

confrontar, v. confront.

confucianismo, m. Confucianism.

confundir, v. confuse; puzzle, mix up.

confusamente, adv. confusedly.

confusión, f. confusion, mix-up; clutter.

confuso, a. confused; confusing.

confutación, n. disproof.

confutar, v. refute, disprove.

congelable, a. congealable.

congelación, f. congealment; deep freeze.

congelado, a. frozen, congealed.

congelar, v. congeal, freeze.

congenial, a. congenial; analogous.

congeniar, v. be congenial.

congestión, f. congestion.

conglomeración, f. conglomeration.

congoja, f. grief, anguish.

congraciamiento, m. flattery; ingratiation.

congraciar, v. flatter; ingratiate oneself.

congratulación, f. congratulation.

congratular, v. congratulate.

congregación, f. congregation.

congregar, v. congregate.

congresista, m. & f. congressional representative.

congreso, m. congress; conference.

conjetura, f. conjecture. —conjeturar, v.

conjetural, a. conjectural.

conjugación, f. conjugation.

conjugar, v. conjugate.

conjunción, *f.* union; conjunction.

conjuntamente, *adv.* together, jointly.

conjunto. 1. *a.* joint, unified. **2.** *m.* whole.

conjuración, *f.* conspiracy, plot.

conjurado, *m.* conspirator, plotter.

conjurar, *v.* conjure.

conllevador, *m.* helper, aide.

conmemoración, *f.* commemoration; remembrance.

conmemorar, *v.* commemorate.

conmemorativo, *a.* commemorative, memorial.

conmensal, *m.* messmate.

conmigo, *adv.* with me.

conmilitón, *m.* fellow soldier.

conminación, *f.* threat, warning.

conminar, *v.* threaten.

conminatorio, *a.* threatening, warning.

conmiseración, *f.* sympathy.

conmoción, *f.* commotion, stir.

conmovedor, *a.* moving, touching.

conmover, *v.* move, affect, touch.

conmutación, *f.* commutation.

conmutador, *m.* electric switch.

conmutar, *v.* exchange.

connotación, *f.* connotation.

connotar, *v.* connote.

connubial, *a.* connubial.

connubio, *a.* matrimony.

cono, *m.* cone.

conocedor -ra, *n.* expert, connoisseur.

conocer, *v.* know, be acquainted with; meet, make the acquaintance of.

conocible, *a.* knowable.

conocido -da, 1. *a.* familiar, well known. **2.** *n.* acquaintance, person known.

conocimiento, *m.* knowledge, acquaintance; consciousness.

conque, *conj.* so then; and so.

conquista, *f.* conquest.

conquistador, *m.* conqueror.

conquistar, *v.* conquer.

consabido, *a.* aforesaid.

consagración, *f.* consecration.

consagrado, *a.* consecrated.

consagrar, *v.* consecrate, dedicate, devote.

consanguinidad, *f.* consanguinity.

consciente, *a.* conscious, aware.

conscientemente, *adv.* consciously.

conscripción, *f.* conscription for military service.

consecución, *f.* attainment.

consecuencia, *f.* consequence.

consecuente, *a.* consequent; consistent.

consecuentemente, *adv.* consequently.

consecutivamente, *adv.* consecutively.

consecutivo, *a.* consecutive.

conseguir, *v.* obtain, get, secure; succeed in, manage to.

conseja, *n.* fable.

consejero -ra, *n.* adviser, counselor.

consejo, *m.* council; counsel (piece of) advice.

consenso, *m.* consensus.

consentido, *a.* spoiled, bratty.

consentimiento, *m.* consent.

consentir, *v.* allow, permit.

conserje, *m.* superintendent, keeper.

conserva, *f.* conserve, preserve.

conservación, *f.* conservation.

conservador, *a. & m.* conservative.

conservar, *v.* conserve.

conservativo, *a.* conservative, preservative.

conservatorio, *m.* conservatory.

considerable, *a.* considerable, substantial.

considerablemente, *adv.* considerably.

consideración, *f.* consideration.

consideradamente, *adv.* considerably.

considerado, *a.* considerate.

considerando, *conj.* whereas.

considerar, *v.* consider.

consigna, *f.* watchword.

consignación, *f.* consignment.

consignar, *v.* consign.

consignatorio, *m.* consignee; trustee.

consigo, *adv.* with herself, with himself, with oneself, with themselves, with yourself, with yourselves.

consiguiente, 1. *a.* consequent. **2.** *m.* consequence.

consiguientemente, *adv.* consequently.

consistencia, *f.* consistency.

consistente, *a.* consistent.

consistir, *v.* consist.

consistorio, *m.* consistory.

consocio, *m.* associate; partner; comrade.

consola, *f.* console.

consolación, *f.* consolation.

consolar, *v.* console.

consolativo, *a.* consolatory.

consolidación, *n.* consolidation.

consolidado, *a.* consolidated.

consolidar, *v.* consolidate.

consonancia, *f.* agreement, accord, harmony.

consonante, *a. & n.* consonant.

consonar, *v.* rhyme.

consorte, *m. & f.* consort, mate.

conspicuo, *a.* conspicuous.

conspiración, *f.* conspiracy, plot.

conspirador -ra, *n.* conspirator.

conspirar, *v.* conspire, plot.

constancia, *f.* perseverance; record.

constante, *a.* constant.

constantemente, *adv.* constantly.

constar, *v.* consist; be clear, be on record.

constelación, *f.* constellation.

consternación, *f.* consternation.

consternar, *v.* dismay.

constipación, *f.* head cold.

constipado, *a.* having a head cold.

constitución, *f.* constitution.

constitucional, *a.* constitutional.

constitucionalidad, *f.* constitutionality.

constituir, *v.* constitute.

constitutivo, *m.* constituent.

constituyente, *a.* constituent.

constreñidamente, *adv.* compulsively; with constraint.

constreñimiento, *m.* compulsion; constraint.

constreñir, *v.* constrain.

constricción, *f.* constriction.

construcción, *f.* construction.

constructivo, *a.* constructive.

constructor, *m.* builder.

construir, *v.* construct, build.

consuelo, *m.* consolation.

cónsul, *m.* consul.

consulado, *m.* consulate.

consular, *a.* consular.

consulta, *f.* consultation.

consultación, *f.* consultation.

consultante, *m. & f.* consultant.

consultar, *v.* consult.

consultivo, *a.* consultative.

consultor, *m.* adviser.

consumación, *f.* consummation; end.

consumado, *a.* consummate, downright.

consumar, *v.* consummate.

consumidor, *m.* consumer.

consumir, *v.* consume.

consumo, *m.* consumption.

consunción, *m.* consumption, tuberculosis.

contabilidad, *f.* accounting, bookkeeping.

contabilista, contable, *m. & f.* accountant.

contacto, *m.* contact.

contado, *m.* **al c.,** (for) cash.

contador -ra, *n.* accountant, bookkeeper.

contagiar, *v.* infect.

contagio, *m.* contagion.

contagioso, *a.* contagious.

contaminación, *f.* contamination, pollution.

contaminar, *v.* contaminate, pollute.

contar, *v.* count; relate, recount, tell. **c. con,** count on.

contemperar, *v.* moderate.

contemplación, *f.* contemplation.

contemplador -ra, *n.* thinker.

contemplar, *v.* contemplate.

contemplativamente, *adv.* thoughtfully.

contemplativo, *a.* contemplative.

contemporáneo -nea, *a. & n.* contemporary.

contención, *f.* contention.

contencioso, *a.* quarrelsome; argumentative.

contender, *v.* cope, contend; conflict.

contendiente, *m. & f.* contender.

contenedor -ra, *n.* tenant.

contener, *v.* contain; curb, control.

contenido, *m.* contents.

contenta, *f.* endorsement.

contentamiento, *m.* contentment.

contentar, *v.* content, satisfy.

contentible, *a.* contemptible.

contento, 1. *a.* contented, happy. 2. *m.* contentment, satisfaction, pleasure.

contérmino, *a.* adjacent, abutting.

contestable, *a.* disputable.

contestación, *f.* answer. —contestar, *v.*

contextura, *f.* texture.

contienda, *f.* combat; match; strife.

contigo, *adv.* with you.

contiguamente, *adv.* closely.

contiguo, *a.* adjoining, next.

continencia, *f.* continence, moderation.

continental, *a.* continental.

continente, *m.* continent; mainland.

continentemente, *adv.* in moderation.

contingencia, *f.* contingency.

contingente, *a.* contingent; incidental.

continuación, *f.* continuation. a c., thereupon, hereupon.

continuamente, *adv.* continuously.

continuar, *v.* continue, keep on.

continuidad, *f.* continuity.

continuo, *a.* continual; continuous.

contorcerse, *v.* writhe, twist.

contorción, *f.* contortion.

contorno, *m.* contour; profile, outline; neighborhood.

contra, *prep.* against.

contraalmirante, *m.* rear admiral.

contraataque, *m.* counterattack.

contrabalancear, *v.* counterbalance.

contrabandear, *v.* smuggle.

contrabandista, *m.* smuggler.

contrabando, *m.* contraband, smuggling.

contracción, *f.* contraction.

contracepción, *f.* contraception, birth control.

contractual, *a.* contractual.

contradecir, *v.* contradict.

contradicción, *f.* contradiction.

contradictorio, *adj.* contradictory.

contraer, *v.* contract; shrink.

contrahacedor -ra, *n.* imitator.

contrahacer, *v.* forge.

contralor, *m.* comptroller.

contramandar, *v.* countermand.

contraorden, *f.* countermand.

contraparte, *f.* counterpart.

contrapesar, *v.* counterbalance, offset.

contrapeso, *m.* counterweight.

contrapunto, *m.* counterpoint.

contrariamente, *adv.* contrarily.

contrariar, *v.* contradict; vex; antagonize; counteract.

contrariedad, *f.* contrariness; opposition; contradiction; disappointment; trouble.

contrario, *a. & m.* contrary, opposite.

contrarrestar, *v.* resist; counteract.

contrasol, *m.* sunshade.

contraste, *m.* contrast. —contrastar, *v.*

contratar, *v.* engage, contract.

contratiempo, *m.* accident; misfortune.

contratista, *m.* contractor.

contrato, *m.* contract.

contribución, *f.* contribution; tax.

contribuir, *v.* contribute.

contribuyente, *m.* contributor; taxpayer.

contrición, *f.* contrition.

contristar, *v.* afflict.

contrito, *a.* contrite, remorseful.

control, *m.* control. —controlar, *v.*

controversia, *f.* controversy.

controversista, *m.* disputant.

controvertir, *v.* dispute.

contumacia, *f.* stubbornness.

contumaz, *adj.* stubborn.

contumelia, *f.* contumely; abuse.

conturbar, *v.* trouble, disturb.

contusión, *f.* contusion; bruise.

convalecencia, *f.* convalescence.

convalecer, *v.* convalesce.

convaleciente, *a.* convalescent.

convecino, *a.* near, close.

convencedor, *adj.* convincing.

convencer, *v.* convince.

convencimiento, *m.* conviction, firm belief.

convención, *f.* convention.

convencional, *a.* conventional.

conveniencia, *f.* suitability; advantage, interest.

conveniente, *a.* suitable; advantageous, opportune.

convenio, *m.* pact, treaty; agreement.

convenir, *v.* assent, agree, concur; be suitable, fitting, convenient.

convento, *m.* convent.

convergencia, *f.* convergence.

convergir, *v.* converge.

conversación, *f.* conversation.

conversar, *v.* converse.

conversión, *f.* conversion.

convertible, *a.* convertible.

convertir, *v.* convert.

convexidad, *f.* convexity.

convexo, *a.* convex.

convicción, *f.* conviction.

convicto, *adj.* guilty.

convidado -da, *n.* guest.

convidar, *v.* invite.

convincente, *a.* convincing.

convite, *m.* invitation, treat.

convocación, *f.* convocation.

convocar, *v.* convoke, assemble.

convoy, *m.* convoy, escort.

convoyar, *v.* convey; escort.

convulsión, *f.* convulsion.

convulsivo, *adj.* convulsive.

conyugal, *adj.* conjugal.

cónyuge, *n.* spouse, mate.

coñac, *m.* cognac, brandy.

cooperación, *f.* cooperation.

cooperador, *adj.* cooperative.

cooperar, *v.* cooperate.

cooperativo, *a.* cooperative.

coordinación, *f.* coordination.

coordinar, *v.* coordinate.

copa, *f.* goblet.

copartícipe, *m.* partner.

copete, *m.* tuft; toupee.

copia, *f.* copy. —copiar, *v.*

copiadora, *f.* copier.

copioso, *a.* copious.

copista, *m.* copyist.

copla, *f.* popular song.

coplero, *m.* poetaster.

cópula, *f.* connection.

coqueta, *f.* flirt. —coquetear, *v.*

coraje, *m.* courage, bravery; anger.

coral, 1. *a.* choral. 2. *m.* coral.

coralino, *a.* coral.

corazón, *m.* heart.

corazonada, *f.* foreboding.

corbata, *f.* necktie.

corbeta, *f.* corvette.

corcova, *f.* hump, hunch.

corcovado, *a.* hunchback.

corcho, *m.* cork.

cordaje, *m.* rigging.

cordel, *m.* string, cord.

cordero, *m.* lamb.

cordial, *a.* cordial, hearty.

cordialidad, *f.* cordiality.

cordillera, *f.* mountain range.

cordón, *m.* cord; (shoe) lace.

cordura, *f.* sanity.

coreografía, *f.* choreography.

corista, *f.* chorus girl.

corneja, *f.* crow.

córneo, *a.* horny.

corneta, *f.* bugle, horn, cornet.

corniforme, *a.* horn-shaped.

cornisa, *f.* cornice.

cornucopia, *f.* cornucopia.

coro, *m.* chorus; choir.

corola, *f.* corolla.

corolario, *m.* corollary.

corona, *f.* crown, halo, wreath.

coronación, *f.* coronation.

coronamiento, *f.* completion of a task.

coronar, v. crown.

coronel, m. colonel.

coronilla, f. small crown.

corporación, f. corporation.

corporal, adj. corporeal, bodily.

corpóreo, a. corporeal.

corpulencia, f. corpulence.

corpulento, a. corpulent, stout.

corpuscular, a. corpuscular.

corpúsculo, m. corpuscle.

corral, m. corral, pen, yard.

correa, f. belt, strap.

corrección, f. correction.

correcto, a. correct, proper, right.

corrector, m. corrector, proofreader.

corredera, f. race course.

corredizo, a. easily untied.

corredor, m. corridor; runner.

corregible, a. corrigible.

corregidor, m. corrector; magistrate, mayor.

corregir, v. correct.

correlación, f. correlation.

correlacionar, v. correlate.

correlativo, a. correlative.

correo, m. mail.

correoso, a. leathery.

correr, v. run.

correría, f. raid; escapade.

correspondencia, f. correspondence.

corresponder, v. correspond.

correspondiente, a. & m. corresponding; correspondent.

corresponsal, m. correspondent.

corretaje, m. brokerage.

correvedile, m. tale bearer; gossip.

corrida, f. race. c. (de toros), bullfight.

corrido, a. abashed; expert.

corriente, 1. a. current, standard. 2. f. current, stream. m. al c., informed, up to date.

corroboración, f. corroboration.

corroborar, v. corroborate.

corroer, v. corrode.

corromper, v. corrupt.

corrompido, adj. corrupt.

corrupción, f. corruption.

corruptela, f. corruption, vice.

corruptibilidad, f. corruptibility.

corruptor, m. corrupter.

corsario, m. corsair.

corsé, m. corset.

corso, m. piracy.

cortadillo, m. small glass.

cortado, a. cut.

cortadura, f. cut.

cortante, a. cutting, sharp, keen.

cortapisa, f. obstacle.

cortaplumas, m. penknife.

cortar, v. cut, cut off, cut out.

corte, f. court. m. cut.

cortedad, f. smallness; shyness.

cortejar, v. pay court to, woo.

cortejo, m. court, courtship; sweetheart.

cortés, a. civil, courteous, polite.

cortesana, f. courtesan.

cortesano. 1. a. courtly, courteous. 2. m. courtier.

cortesía, f. courtesy.

corteza, f. bark; rind; crust.

cortijo, m. farmhouse.

cortina, f. curtain.

corto, a. short.

corva, f. bend of the knee.

cosa, f. thing. c. de, a matter of, roughly.

cosecha, f. crop, harvest. —cosechar, v.

coser, v. sew, stitch.

cosmético, a. & m. cosmetic.

cosmopolita, a. & n. cosmopolitan.

coso, m. arena for bull fights.

cosquilla, f. tickle. —cosquillar, v.

cosquilloso, a. ticklish.

costa, f. coast; cost, expense.

costado, m. side.

costal, m. sack, bag.

costanero, a. coastal.

costar, v. cost.

costarricense, a. & n. Costa Rican.

coste, m. cost, price.

costear, v. defray, sponsor; sail along the coast of.

costilla, f. rib; chop.

costo, m. cost, price.

costoso, a. costly.

costra, f. crust.

costumbre, f. custom, practice, habit.

costura, f. sewing; seam.

costurera, f. seamstress, dressmaker.

cota de malla, coat of mail.

cotejar, v. compare.

coteleta, f. cutlet.

cotidiano, a. daily; everyday.

cotillón, m. cotillion.

cotización, f. quotation.

cotizar, v. quote (a price).

coto, m. enclosure; boundary.

cotón, m. printed cotton cloth.

cotufa, f. Jerusalem artichoke.

coturno, m. buskin.

covacha, f. small cave.

coxal, a. of the hip.

coy, m. hammock.

coyote, m. coyote.

coyuntura, f. joint; juncture.

coz, f. kick.

crac, f. failure.

cráneo, m. skull.

craniano, a. cranial.

crapuloso, a. drunken.

crasiento, a. greasy, oily.

craso, a. fat; gross.

cráter, m. crater.

craza, f. crucible.

creación, f. creation.

creador -ra, a. & n. creative; creator.

crear, v. create.

creativo, a. creative.

crébol, m. holly tree.

crecer, v. grow, grow up; increase.

creces, f.pl. increase, addition.

crecidamente, adv. abundantly.

crecido, a. increased, enlarged; swollen.

creciente, 1. a. growing. 2. f. crescent.

crecimiento, m. growth.

credenciales, f.pl. credentials.

credibilidad, f. credibility.

crédito, m. credit.

credo, m. creed, belief.

credulamente, adv. credulously, gullibly.

credulidad, f. credulity.

crédulo, a. credulous.

creedero, a. credible.

creedor, a. credulous, believing.

creencia, f. belief.

creer, v. believe; think.

creíble, a. credible, believable.

crema, f. cream.

cremación, f. cremation.

cremar, v. cremate.

crémor tártaro, cream of tartar.

creosota, f. creosote.

crepitar, v. crackle.

crepuscular, a. of or like the dawn or dusk.

crepúsculo, m. dusk, twilight.

crescendo, m. crescendo.

crespo, a. crisp; curly.

crespón, m. crepe.

cresta, f. crest.

crestado, a. crested.

creta, f. chalk.

cretáceo, a. chalky.

cretinismo, m. cretinism.

cretino, n. & a. cretin.

cretona, f. cretonne.

creyente, 1. a. believing. 2. n. believer.

creyón, m. crayon.

cría, f. (stock) breeding; young (of an animal), litter.

criada, f. girl servant, maid.

criadero, m. (agr.) nursery.

criado -da, m. servant.

criador, a. fruitful, prolific.

crianza, f. breeding; upbringing.

criar, v. raise, rear, bring up; breed.

criatura, f. creature; infant.

criba, f. sieve; crib.

cribado, a. sifted.

cribar, v. sift.

crimen, m. crime.

criminal, a. & m. criminal.

criminalidad, f. criminality.

criminalmente, adv. criminally.

criminoso, a. criminal.

crin, f. mane of a horse.

crinolina, f. crinoline.

criocirugía, f. cryosurgery.

criollo -lla, a. & n. native; creole.

cripta, f. crypt.

criptografía, f. cryptography.

crisantemo, m. chrysanthemum.

crisis, f. crisis.

crisma, m. chrism.

crisol, *m.* crucible.

crispamiento, *m.* twitch, contraction.

crispar, *v.* contract (the muscles); twitch.

crista, *f.* heraldic crest.

cristal, *m.* crystal; lens.

cristalería, *f.* glassware.

cristalino, *a.* crystalline.

cristalización, *f.* crystallization.

cristalizar, *v.* crystallize.

cristianar, *v.* baptize.

cristiandad, *f.* Christendom.

cristianismo, *m.* Christianity.

cristiano -na, *a. & n.* Christian.

Cristo, *m.* Christ.

criterio, *m.* criterion; judgment.

crítica, *f.* criticism; critique.

criticable, *a.* blameworthy.

criticador, *a.* critical.

criticar, *v.* criticize.

crítico, *a. & m.* critical; critic.

croar, *v.* croak.

crocante, *m.* peanut brittle.

crocitar, *v.* crow.

crocodilo, *m.* crocodile.

cromático, *a.* chromatic.

cromo, *m.* chromium.

cromotipia, *f.* color printing.

crónica, *f.* chronicle.

crónico, *a.* chronic.

cronión, *m.* concise chronicle.

cronista, *m.* chronicler.

cronología, *f.* chronology.

cronológicamente, *adv.* chronologically.

cronológico, *a.* chronologic.

cronómetro, *m.* chronometer.

croqueta, *f.* croquette.

croquis, *m.* sketch; rough outline.

crótalo, *m.* rattlesnake; castanet.

cruce, *m.* crossing, crossroads, junction.

crucero, *m.* cruiser.

crucífero, *a.* cross-shaped.

crucificado, *a.* crucified.

crucificar, *v.* crucify.

crucifijo, *m.* crucifix.

crucifixión, *f.* crucifixion.

crudamente, *adv.* crudely.

crudeza, *f.* crudeness.

crudo, *a.* crude, raw.

cruel, *a.* cruel.

crueldad, *f.* cruelty.

cruelmente, *adv.* cruelly.

cruentamente, *adv.* bloodily.

cruento, *a.* bloody.

crujía, *f.* corridor.

crujido, *m.* creak.

crujir, *v.* crackle, creak; rustle.

cruórico, *a.* bloody.

crup, *m.* croup.

crustáceo, *m. & a.* crustacean.

cruz, *f.* cross.

cruzada, *f.* crusade.

cruzado -da, *n.* crusader.

cruzamiento, *m.* crossing.

cruzar, *v.* cross.

cruzarse con, *v.* to (meet and) pass.

cuaderno, *m.* notebook.

cuadra, *f.* block; (hospital) ward.

cuadradamente, *adv.* exactly, precisely; completely, in full.

cuadradillo, *m.* lump of sugar.

cuadrado, *a. & m.* square.

cuadrafónico, *a.* quadraphonic.

cuadragésima, *f.* Lent.

cuadragesimal, *a.* Lenten.

cuadrángulo, *m.* quadrangle.

cuadrante, *m.* quadrant; dial.

cuadrar, *v.* square; suit.

cuadricular, *a.* in squares.

cuadrilátero, *a.* quadrilateral.

cuadrilla, *f.* band, troop, gang.

cuadrinieto, *n.* great-grandchild.

cuadro, *m.* picture; painting; frame. **a cuadros,** checked, plaid.

cuadro de servicio, timetable.

cuadrupedal, *a.* quadruped.

cuádruplo, *a.* fourfold.

cuajada, *f.* curd.

cuajamiento, *m.* coagulation.

cuajar, *v.* coagulate; overdecorate.

cuajo, *m.* rennet; coagulation.

cuakerismo, *m.* Quakerism.

cuákero, *n. & a.* Quaker.

cual, *rel. pron.* which.

cuál, *a. & pron.* what, which.

cualidad, *f.* quality.

cualitativo, *a.* qualitative.

cualquiera, *a. & pron.* whatever, any; anyone.

cuando, *conj.* when.

cuando, *adv.* when. **de cuando en cuando,** from time to time.

cuantía, *f.* quantity; amount.

cuantiar, *v.* estimate.

cuantidad, *f.* quantity.

cuantiosamente, *adv.* abundantly.

cuantioso, *a.* abundant.

cuantitativo, *a.* quantitative.

cuanto, *a., adv. & pron.* as much as, as many as; all that which. **en c.,** as soon as. **en c. a,** for. **c. antes,** as soon as possible. **c. más . . . tanto más,** the more . . . the more. **unos cuantos,** a few.

cuánto, *a. & adv.* how much, how many.

cuaquerismo, *m.* Quakerism.

cuáquero, *n. & a.* Quaker.

cuarenta, *a. & pron.* forty.

cuarentena, *f.* quarantine.

cuaresma, *f.* Lent.

cuaresmal, *a.* Lenten.

cuarta, *f.* quarter; quadrant; quart.

cuartana, *f.* ague.

cuartear, *v.* divide into quarters.

cuartel, *m.* (mil.) quarters; barracks; (naut.) hatch. **c. general,** headquarters. **sin c.,** giving no quarter.

cuartelada, *f.* military uprising.

cuarterón, *n. & a.* quadroon.

cuarteto, *m.* quartet.

cuartillo, *m.* pint.

cuarto, 1. *a.* fourth. 2. *m.* quarter; room.

cuarto de baño, bathroom.

cuarto de dormir, bedroom.

cuarzo, *m.* quartz.

cuasi, *adv.* almost, nearly.

cuate, *a. & n.* twin.

cuatrero, *m.* cattle rustler.

cuatrillón, *m.* quadrillion.

cuatro, *a. & pron.* four.

cuatrocientos, *a. & pron.* four hundred.

cuba, *f.* cask, tub, vat.

cubano -na, *a. & n.* Cuban.

cubero, *m.* cooper.

cubertura, *f.* cover.

cubeta, *f.* small barrel, keg.

cúbico, *a.* cubic.

cubierta, *f.* cover; envelope; wrapping; tread (of a tire); deck.

cubiertamente, *adv.* secretly, stealthily.

cubierto, *m.* place (at table).

cubil, *m.* lair.

cubo, *m.* cube; bucket.

cubrecama, *f.* bedspread.

cubrir, *v.* cover.

cubrirse, *v.* put on one's hat.

cucaracha, *f.* cockroach.

cuclillo, *m.* cuckoo.

cuco, *a.* sly.

cuculla, *f.* hood, cowl.

cuchara, *f.* spoon, tablespoon.

cucharada, *f.* spoonful.

cucharita, cucharilla, *f.* teaspoon.

cucharón, *m.* dipper, ladle.

cuchicheo, *m.* whisper. —cuchichear, *v.*

cuchilla, *f.* cleaver.

cuchillada, *f.* slash.

cuchillería, *f.* cutlery.

cuchillo, *m.* knife.

cucho, *m.* fertilizer.

cuchufleta, *f.* jest.

cuelga, *f.* cluster, bunch.

cuelgacapas, *m.* coat rack.

cuello, *m.* neck; collar.

cuenca, *f.* socket; (river) basin; wooden bowl.

cuenco, *m.* earthen bowl.

cuenta, *f.* account; bill. **darse c.,** to realize. **tener en c.,** to keep in mind.

cuentagotas, *m.* dropper (for medicine).

cuentista, *m.* informer.

cuento, *m.* story, tale.

cuerda, *f.* cord; chord; rope; string; spring (of clock). **dar c. a,** to wind (clock).

cuerdamente, *adv.* sanely; prudently.

cuerdo, *a.* sane; prudent.

cuerno, *m.* horn.

cuero, *m.* leather; hide.

cuerpo, *m.* body; corps.

cuervo, *m.* crow, raven.

cuesco, *m.* pit, stone (of fruit).

cuesta, *f.* hill, slope. **llevar a cuestas,** to carry on one's back.

cuestación, *f.* solicitation for charity.

cuestión, f. question; affair; argument.

cuestionable, a. questionable.

cuestionar, v. question; discuss; argue.

cuestionario, m. questionnaire.

cuete, m. firecracker.

cuetzale, m. quetzal.

cueva, f. cave; cellar.

cugujada, f. lark.

cuidado, m. care, caution, worry. tener c., to be careful.

cuidadosamente, adv. carefully.

cuidadoso, a. careful, painstaking.

cuidante, n. caretaker, custodian.

cuidar, v. take care of.

cuita, f. trouble, care, grief.

cuitado, a. unfortunate; shy, timid.

culatamiento, m. timidity.

culata, f. haunch, buttock; butt of a gun.

culatada, f. recoil.

culatazo, m. blow with the butt of a gun; recoil.

culebra, f. snake.

culero, a. lazy, indolent.

culinario, a. culinary.

culminación, f. culmination.

culminar, v. culminate.

culpa, f. fault, guilt, blame. tener la c., to be at fault. echar la culpa a, to blame.

culpabilidad, f. guilt, fault, blame.

culpable, a. at fault, guilty, to blame.

culpar, v. blame, accuse.

cultamente, adv. politely, elegantly.

cultivable, a. arable.

cultivación, f. cultivation.

cultivador, m. cultivator.

cultivar, v. cultivate.

cultivo, m. cultivation; (growing) crop.

culto, 1. a. cultured, cultivated. 2. m. cult; worship.

cultura, f. culture; refinement.

cultural, a. cultural.

culturar, v. cultivate.

cumbre, f. summit, peak.

cumpleaños, m.pl. birthday.

cumplidamente, adv. completely.

cumplido, a. polite, polished.

cumplimentar, v. compliment.

cumplimiento, m. fulfillment; compliment.

cumplir, v. comply; carry out, fulfill; reach (years of age).

cumular, v. accumulate.

cumulativo, a. cumulative.

cúmulo, m. heap, pile.

cuna, f. cradle.

cundir, v. spread; expand; propagate.

cuneiforme, a. cuneiform, wedge-shaped.

cuneo, m. rocking.

cuña, f. wedge.

cuñada, f. sister-in-law.

cuñado, m. brother-in-law.

cuñete, m. keg.

cuociente, m. quotient.

cuota, f. quota; dues.

cuotidiano, a. daily.

cupé, m. coupé.

cúpido, m. lover.

cupo, m. share; assigned quota.

cupón, m. coupon.

cúpula, f. dome.

cura, m. priest. f. treatment, (medical) care. c. de urgencia, first aid.

curable, a. curable.

curación, f. healing; cure; (surgical) dressing.

curado, a. cured, healed.

curador, m. custodian; curator.

curandero, m. healer, medicine man.

curar, v. cure, heal, treat.

curativo, a. curative, healing.

curia, f. ecclesiastical court.

curiosear, v. snoop, pry, meddle.

curiosidad, f. curiosity.

curioso, a. curious.

curro, a. showy, loud, flashy.

cursante, n. student.

cursar, v. frequent; attend to.

cursi, a. vulgar, shoddy, in bad taste.

curso, m. course.

curtidor, m. tanner.

curtir, v. tan.

curva, f. curve; bend.

curvatura, f. curvature.

cúspide, f. top, peak.

custodia, f. custody.

custodiar, v. guard, watch.

custodio, m. custodian.

cutáneo, a. cutaneous.

cutícula, f. cuticle.

cutis, m. or f. skin, complexion.

cuyo, a. whose.

CH

chabacano, a. clumsy.

chacal, m. jackal.

chacó, m. shako.

chacona, f. chaconne.

chacota, f. fun, mirth.

chacotear, v. joke.

chacra, f. small farm.

chafallar, v. mend badly.

chagra, m. rustic; rural person.

chal, m. shawl.

chalán, m. horse trader.

chaleco, m. vest.

chalet, m. chalet.

challí, m. challis.

chamada, f. brushwood.

chamarillero, m. gambler.

chamarra, f. coarse linen jacket.

chambelán, m. chamberlain.

champaña, m. champagne.

champú, m. shampoo.

chamuscar, v. scorch.

chancaco, a. brown.

chancear, v. jest, joke.

chanciller, m. chancellor.

chancillería, f. chancery.

chancla, f. old shoe.

chancleta, f. slipper.

chanclos, m.pl. galoshes.

chancro, m. chancre.

changador, m. porter, handyman.

chantaje, m. blackmail.

chantajista, n. blackmailer.

chanto, m. flagstone.

chantre, m. precentor.

chanza, f. joke, jest. —chancear, v.

chanzoneta, f. chansonette.

chapa, f. (metal) sheet, plate; lock.

chaparrada, f. shower.

chaparral, m. chaparral.

chaparreras, f.pl. chaps.

chaparrón, m. downpour.

chapear, v. veneer.

chapeo, m. hat.

chapitel, m. spire, steeple; (architecture) capital.

chapodar, v. lop.

chapón, m. inkblot.

chapotear, v. paddle or splash in the water.

chapoteo, m. splash.

chapucear, v. fumble, bungle.

chapucero, a. sloppy, bungling.

chapurrear, v. speak (a language) brokenly.

chapuz, m. dive; ducking.

chapuzar, v. dive, duck.

chaqueta, f. jacket, coat.

charada, f. charade.

charamusca, f. twisted candy stick.

charanga, f. military band.

charanguero, m. peddler.

charca, f. pool, pond.

charco, m. pool, puddle.

charla, f. chat; chatter, prattle. —charlar, v.

charladuría, f. chatter.

charlatán, m. charlatan.

charlatanismo, m. charlatanism.

charol, m. varnish.

charolar, v. varnish; polish.

charquear, v. jerk (beef).

charquí, m. jerked beef.

charrán, a. roguish.

chascarrillo, m. risqué story.

chasco, m. disappointment, blow; practical joke.

chasis, m. chassis.

chasquear, v. fool, trick; disappoint; crack (a whip).

chasquido, m. crack (sound).

chata, f. bedpan.

chato, a. flat-nosed, pug-nosed.

chauvinismo, m. chauvinism.

chauvinista, n. & a. chauvinist.

chelín, m. shilling.

cheque, m. (bank) check.

chica, f. girl.

chicana, f. chicanery.

chicle, m. chewing gum.

chico, 1. a. little. 2. m. boy.

chicote, *m.* cigar; cigar butt.
chicotear, *v.* whip, flog.
chicha, *f.* an alcoholic drink.
chícharo, *f.* pea.
chicharra, *f.* cicada; talkative person.
chicharrón, *m.* crisp fried scrap of meat.
chichear, *v.* hiss in disapproval.
chichón, *m.* bump, bruise, lump.
chifladura, *f.* mania; whim; jest.
chiflar, *v.* whistle; become insane.
chiflido, *m.* shrill whistle.
chile, *m.* chili.
chileno -na, *a.* & *n.* Chilean.
chillido, *m.* shriek, scream, screech. —**chillar**, *v.*
chillón, *a.* shrill.
chimenea, *f.* chimney, smokestack; fireplace.
china, *f.* pebble; maid; Chinese woman.
chinarro, *m.* large pebble, stone.
chinche, *f.* bedbug; thumbtack.
chinchilla, *f.* chinchilla.
chinchorro, *m.* fishing net.
chinela, *f.* slipper.
chinero, *m.* china closet.
chino -na, *a.* & *n.* Chinese.
chiquero, *m.* pen for pigs, goats, etc.
chiquito, 1. *a.* small, tiny. 2. *n.* small child.
chiribitil, *m.* small room, den.
chirimía, *f.* flageolet.
chiripa, *f.* stroke of good luck.
chirla, *f.* mussel.
chirle, *a.* insipid.
chirona, *f.* prison, jail.
chirrido, *m.* squeak, chirp. —**chirriar**, *v.*
chis, *interj.* hush!
chisgarabís, *n.* meddler; unimportant person.
chisguete, *m.* squirt, splash.
chisme, *m.* gossip. —**chismear**, *v.*
chismero, *m.* gossiper.
chismoso, *adj.* gossiping.
chispa, *f.* spark.
chispeante, *a.* sparkling.
chispear, *v.* sparkle.
chisporrotear, *v.* emit sparks.
chistar, *v.* mumble.
chiste, *m.* joke, gag; witty saying.
chistera, *f.* fish basket; top hat.
chistoso, *a.* funny, comic, amusing.
chito, *interj.* hush!
chiva, *f.* female goat.
chivato, *m.* kid, young goat.
chivo, *m.* male goat.
chocante, *a.* striking; shocking; unpleasant.
chocar, *v.* collide, clash, crash; shock.
chocarrear, *v.* joke, jest.

choclo, *m.* clog; overshoe; ear of corn.
chocolate, *m.* chocolate.
chocolatería, *f.* chocolate shop.
chochear, *v.* be in one's dotage.
chochera, *f.* dotage, senility.
chofer, **chófer**, *m.* chauffeur, driver.
chofeta, *f.* chafing dish.
cholo, *m.* half-breed.
chopo, *m.* black poplar.
choque, *m.* collision, clash, crash; shock.
chorizo, *m.* sausage.
chorrear, *v.* spout; drip.
chorro, *m.* spout; spurt, jet. **llover a chorros**, to pour (rain).
choto, *m.* calf, kid.
choza, *f.* hut, cabin.
chozno, *m.* great-grandson.
chubasco, *m.* shower, squall.
chubascoso, *a.* squally.
chuchería, *f.* trinket, knickknack.
chulería, *f.* pleasant manner.
chuleta, *f.* chop, cutlet.
chulo, *m.* rascal, rogue; joker.
chupa, *f.* jacket.
chupada, *f.* suction.
chupado, *a.* very thin.
chupaflor, *m.* hummingbird.
chupar, *v.* suck.
churrasco, *m.* roasted meat.
chuscada, *f.* joke, jest.
chusco, *a.* funny, humorous.
chusma, *f.* mob, rabble.
chuzo, *m.* pike.

D

dable, *a.* possible.
dactilógrafo, *m.* typewriter.
dádiva, *f.* gift.
dadivosamente, *adv.* generously.
dadivoso, *a.* generous, bountiful.
dador, *m.* giver.
dados, *m.pl.* dice.
daga, *f.* dagger.
dalia, *f.* dahlia.
daltonismo, *m.* color blindness.
dallador, *m.* lawn mower.
dallar, *v.* mow.
dama, *f.* lady.
damasco, *m.* apricot.
damisela, *f.* young lady, girl.
danés -esa, *a.* & *n.* Danish, Dane.
danza, *f.* (the) dance. —**danzar**, *v.*
danzante, *m.* dancer.
dañable, *a.* condemnable.
dañar, *v.* hurt, harm; damage.
dañino, **dañoso**, *a.* harmful.
daño, *m.* damage; harm.
dañoso, *a.* harmful.
dar, *v.* give; strike (clock). **d. a**, face, open on. **d. con**, find, locate.
dardo, *m.* dart.
dársena, *f.* dock.
datar, *v.* date.

dátil, *m.* date (fruit).
dativo, *m.* & *a.* dative.
datos, *m.pl.* data.
de, *prep.* of; from; than.
debajo, *adv.* underneath. **d. de**, under.
debate, *m.* debate.
debatir, *v.* debate, argue.
debe, *m.* debit.
debelación, *f.* conquest.
debelar, *v.* conquer.
deber, 1. *v.* owe; must; be to, be supposed to. 2. *m.* obligation.
debido, *a.* due.
débil, *a.* weak, faint.
debilidad, *f.* weakness.
debilitación, *f.* weakness.
debilitar, *v.* weaken.
débito, *m.* debit.
debutante, *f.* debutante.
debutar, *v.* make a debut.
década, *f.* decade.
decadencia, *f.* decadence, decline, decay.
decadente, *a.* decadent, declining, decaying.
decaer, *v.* decay, decline.
decalitro, *m.* decaliter.
decálogo, *m.* decalogue.
decámetro, *m.* decameter.
decano, *m.* dean.
decantado, *a.* much discussed; overexalted.
decapitación, *f.* beheading.
decapitar, *v.* behead.
decencia, *f.* decency.
decenio, *m.* decade.
decente, *a.* decent.
decentemente, *adv.* decently.
decepción, *f.* disappointment; delusion.
decepcionar, *v.* disappoint, disillusion.
decibelio, *m.* decibel.
decididamente, *adv.* decidedly.
decidir, *v.* decide.
decigramo, *m.* decigram.
decilitro, *m.* deciliter.
décima, *f.* ten-line stanza.
decimal, *a.* decimal.
décimo, *a.* tenth.
decir, *v.* tell, say. **es d.**, that is (to say).
decisión, *f.* decision.
decisivamente, *adv.* decisively.
decisivo, *a.* decisive.
declamación, *f.* declamation, speech.
declamar, *v.* declaim.
declaración, *f.* declaration; statement; plea.
declarar, *v.* declare, state.
declarativo, *a.* declarative.
declinación, *f.* descent; decay; decline; declension.
declinar, *v.* decline.
declive, *m.* declivity, slope.
decocción, *f.* decoction.
decomiso, *m.* seizure, confiscation.
decoración, *f.* decoration, trimming.
decorado, *m.* (theat.) scenery, set.

decorar, v. decorate, trim.

decorativo, a. decorative, ornamental.

decoro, m. decorum; decency.

decoroso, a. decorous.

decrecer, v. decrease.

decrépito, a. decrepit.

decreto, m. decree. —decretar, v.

dechado, m. model; sample; pattern; example.

dedal, m. thimble.

dédalo, m. labyrinth.

dedicación, f. dedication.

dedicar, v. devote; dedicate.

dedicatoria, f. dedication, inscription.

dedo, m. finger, toe.

deducción, f. deduction.

deducir, v. deduce; subtract.

defectivo, a. defective.

defecto, m. defect, flaw.

defectuoso, a. defective, faulty.

defender, v. defend.

defensa, f. defense.

defensivo, a. defensive.

defensor, m. defender.

deferencia, f. deference.

deferir, v. defer.

deficiente, a. deficient.

déficit, m. deficit.

definición, f. definition.

definido, a. definite.

definir, v. define; establish.

definitivamente, adv. definitely.

definitivo, a. definite; definitive.

deformación, f. deformation.

deformar, v. deform.

deforme, a. deformed; ugly.

deformidad, f. deformity.

defraudar, v. defraud.

defunción, f. death.

degeneración, f. degeneration.

degenerado, a. degenerate. —degenerar, v.

deglutir, v. swallow.

degollar, v. behead.

degradación, f. degradation.

degradar, v. degrade, debase.

deidad, f. deity.

deificación, f. deification.

deificar, v. deify.

deífico, a. divine, deific.

deísmo, m. deism.

dejadez, f. neglect, untidiness; laziness.

dejado, a. untidy; lazy.

dejar, v. let, allow; leave. d. de, stop, leave off. no d. de, not fail to.

dejo, m. abandonment; negligence; aftertaste; accent.

del, contr. of de + el.

delantal, m. apron.

delante, adv. ahead, forward; in front.

delantero, a. forward, front, first.

delator, m. informer; accuser.

delegación, f. delegation.

delegado -da, n. delegate. —delegar, v.

deleite, m. delight. —deleitar, v.

deleitoso, a. delightful.

deletrear, v. spell; decipher.

delfín, m. dolphin; dauphin.

delgadez, f. thinness, slenderness.

delgado, a. thin, slender, slim, slight.

deliberación, f. deliberation.

deliberadamente, adv. deliberately.

deliberar, v. deliberate.

deliberativo, a. deliberative.

delicadamente, adv. delicately.

delicadeza, f. delicacy.

delicado, a. delicate, dainty.

delicia, f. delight; deliciousness.

delicioso, a. delicious.

delincuencia, f. delinquency.

delincuente, a. & m. delinquent; culprit, offender.

delineación, f. delineation, sketch.

delinear, v. delineate, sketch.

delirante, a. delirious.

delirar, v. rave, be delirious.

delirio, m. delirium; rapture, bliss.

delito, m. crime, offense.

delta, m. delta (of river).

demagogia, f. demagogy.

demagogo, n. demagogue.

demanda, f. demand, claim.

demandador -ra, n. plaintiff.

demandar, v. sue; demand.

demarcación, f. demarcation.

demarcar, v. demarcate, limit.

demás, a. & n. other; (the) rest (of). por d., too much.

demasía, f. excess; audacity; iniquity.

demasiado, a. & adv. too; too much; too many.

demencia, f. dementia; insanity.

demente, a. demented.

democracia, f. democracy.

demócrata, m. & f. democrat.

democrático, a. democratic.

demoler, v. demolish, tear down.

demolición, f. demolition.

demonio, m. demon, devil.

demontre, m. devil.

demora, f. delay. —demorar, v.

demostración, f. demonstration.

demostrador, m. demonstrator.

demostrar, v. demonstrate, show.

demostrativo, a. demonstrative.

demudar, v. change; disguise, conceal.

denegación, f. denial, refusal.

denegar, v. deny, refuse.

dengue, m. prudishness; dengue.

denigración, f. defamation, disgrace.

denigrar, v. defame, disgrace.

denodado, a. brave, dauntless.

denominación, f. denomination.

denominar, v. name, call.

denotación, f. denotation.

denotar, v. denote, betoken, express.

densidad, f. density.

denso, a. dense.

dentado, a. toothed; serrated; cogged.

dentadura, f. set of teeth.

dental, a. dental.

dentífrico, m. dentifrice.

dentista, m. dentist.

dentistería, f. dentistry.

dentro, adv. within, inside. d. de poco, in a short while.

denuedo, m. bravery, courage.

denuesto, m. insult, offense.

denuncia, f. denunciation; declaration.

denunciación, f. denunciation.

denunciar, v. denounce.

deparar, v. offer; grant.

departamento, m. department, section.

departir, v. talk, chat.

dependencia, f. dependence; branch office.

depender, v. depend.

dependiente, a. & m. dependent; clerk.

depilatorio, a. depilatory.

deplorable, a. deplorable, wretched.

deplorablemente, adv. deplorably.

deplorar, v. deplore.

deponer, v. depose.

deportación, f. deportation; exile.

deportar, v. deport.

deporte, m. sport. —deportivo, a.

deposición, f. assertion, deposition; removal; movement.

depositante, m. & f. depositor.

depósito, m. deposit. —depositar, v.

depravación, f. depravation; depravity.

depravado, a. depraved, wicked.

depravar, v. deprave, corrupt, pervert.

depreciación, f. depreciation.

depreciar, v. depreciate.

depredación, f. depredation.

depredar, v. pillage, depredate.

depresión, f. depression.

depresivo, a. depressive.

deprimir, v. depress.

depurar, v. purify.

derecha, f. right (hand, side).

derechera, f. shortcut.

derecho, 1. a. right; straight. 2. m. right; (the) law. derechos, (com.) duty.

derechura, f. straightness.

derelicto, a. abandoned, derelict.

deriva, f. (naut.) drift.

derivación, f. derivation.

derivar, v. derive.

derogar, v. derogate; repeal, abrogate.

derramamiento, m. overflow.

derramar, v. spill, pour, scatter.

derrame, m. overflow; discharge.

derretir, v. melt, dissolve.

derribar, v. demolish, knock down; bowl over, floor, fell.

derrocamiento, m. overthrow.

derrocar, v. overthrow; oust; demolish.

derrochar, v. waste.

derroche, m. waste.

derrota, f. rout, defeat. —derrotar, v.

derrumbamiento, derrumbe, m. collapse; landslide.

derrumbarse, v. collapse, tumble.

derviche, m. dervish.

desabotonar, v. unbutton.

desabrido, a. insipid, tasteless.

desabrigar, v. uncover.

desabrochar, v. unbutton, unclasp.

desacierto, m. error.

desacobardar, v. remove fear; embolden.

desacomodadamente, adv. inconveniently.

desacomodado, a. unemployed.

desacomodar, v. molest; inconvenience; dismiss.

desacomodo, m. loss of employment.

desconsejado, a. imprudent, ill advised, rash.

desaconsejar, v. dissuade.

desacordadamente, adv. unadvisedly.

desacordar, v. differ, disagree; be forgetful.

desacorde, a. discordant.

desacostumbradamente, adv. unusually.

desacostumbrado, a. unusual, unaccustomed.

desacostumbrar, v. give up a habit or custom.

desacreditar, v. discredit.

desacuerdo, m. disagreement.

desadeudar, v. pay one's debts.

desadormecer, v. waken, rouse.

desadornar, v. divest of ornament.

desadvertidamente, adv. inadvertently.

desadvertido, a. imprudent.

desadvertimiento, m. imprudence, rashness.

desadvertir, v. act imprudently.

desafección, f. disaffection.

desafecto, a. disaffected.

desafiar, v. defy; challenge.

desafinar, v. be out of tune.

desafío, m. defiance; challenge.

desaforar, v. infringe one's rights; be outrageous.

desafortunado, a. unfortunate.

desafuero, m. violation of the law; outrage.

desagraciada, a. graceless.

desagradable, a. disagreeable, unpleasant.

desagradablemente, adv. disagreeably.

desagradecido, a. ungrateful.

desagradecimiento, m. ingratitude.

desagrado, m. displeasure.

desagraviar, v. make amends.

desagregar, v. separate, disintegrate.

desagriar, v. mollify, appease.

desaguadero, m. drain, outlet; cesspool; sink.

desaguador, m. water pipe.

desaguar, v. drain.

desaguisado, m. offense; injury.

desahogadamente, adv. impudently; brazenly.

desahogado, a. impudent, brazen; cheeky.

desahogar, v. relieve.

desahogo, m. relief; nerve, cheek.

desahuciar, v. give up hope for; despair of.

desairado, a. graceless.

desaire, m. slight; scorn. —desairar, v.

desajustar, v. mismatch, misfit; make unfit.

desalar, v. hurry, hasten.

desalentar, v. make out of breath; discourage.

desaliento, m. discouragement.

desaliñar, v. disarrange; make untidy.

desaliño, m. slovenliness, untidiness.

desalivar, v. salivate.

desalmadamente, adv. mercilessly.

desalmado, a. merciless.

desalojamiento, m. displacement; dislodging.

desalojar, v. dislodge.

desalquilado, a. vacant, unrented.

desamar, v. cease loving.

desamasado, a. dissolve, undo.

desamistarse, v. quarrel, disagree.

desamor, m. disaffection, dislike; hatred.

desamorado, a. cruel; harsh; rude.

desamparador, m. deserter.

desamparar, v. desert, abandon.

desamparo, m. desertion, abandonment.

desamueblar, v. dismantle.

desandrajado, a. shabby, ragged.

desanimadamente, adv. in a discouraged manner; spiritlessly.

desanimar, v. dishearten, discourage.

desánimo, m. discouragement.

desanudar, v. untie; loosen; disentangle.

desapacible, a. rough, harsh; unpleasant.

desaparecer, v. disappear.

desaparición, f. disappearance.

desapasionadamente, adv. dispassionately.

desapasionado, a. dispassionate.

desapego, m. impartiality.

desapercibido, adj. unprepared.

desapiadado, a. merciless, cruel.

desaplicación, f. indolence, laziness; negligence.

desaplicado, a. indolent, lazy; negligent.

desaposesionar, v. dispossess.

desapreciar, v. depreciate.

desapretador, m. screwdriver.

desapretar, v. loosen; relieve, ease.

desaprisionar, v. set free, release.

desaprobación, f. disapproval.

desaprobar, v. disapprove.

desaprovechado, a. useless, profitless; backward.

desaprovechar, v. waste; be backward.

desarbolar, v. unmast.

desarmado, a. disarmed, defenseless.

desarmar, v. disarm.

desarme, m. disarmament.

desarraigar, v. uproot; eradicate; expel.

desarreglar, v. disarrange, mess up.

desarrollar, v. develop.

desarrollo, m. development.

desarropar, v. undress; uncover.

desarrugar, v. remove wrinkles from.

desaseado, a. dirty; disorderly.

desasear, v. make dirty or disorderly.

desaseo, m. dirtiness; disorder.

desasir, v. loosen; disengage.

desasociable, a. unsociable.

desasosegar, v. disturb.

desasosiego, m. uneasiness.

desastrado, a. ragged, wretched.

desastre, m. disaster.

desastroso, a. disastrous.

desatar, v. untie, undo.

desatención, f. inattention; disrespect; rudeness.

desatender, v. ignore; disregard.

desatentado, a. inconsiderate; imprudent.

desatinado, a. foolish; insane; wild.

desatino, m. blunder. —desatinar, v.

desautorizado, a. unauthorized.

desautorizar, v. deprive of authority.

desavenencia, *f.* disagreement, discord.

desaventajado, *a.* disadvantageous.

desayuno, *m.* breakfast. —**desayunarse**, *v.*

desazón, *f.* insipidity; uneasiness.

desazonado, *a.* insipid; uneasy.

desbandada, *f.* disbanding.

desbandarse, *v.* disband.

desbarajuste, *m.* disorder, confusion.

desbaratar, *v.* destroy.

desbastar, *v.* plane, smoothen.

desbocado, *a.* foul-spoken, indecent.

desbocarse, *v.* use obscene language.

desbordamiento, *m.* overflow, flood.

desbordar, *v.* overflow.

desbrozar, *v.* clear away rubbish.

descabal, *a.* incomplete.

descabalar, *v.* render incomplete; impair.

descabellado, *a.* absurd, preposterous.

descabezar, *v.* behead.

descaecimiento, *m.* weakness; dejection.

descafeinado, *a.* decaffeinated.

descalabrar, *v.* injure, wound (esp. the head).

descalabro, *m.* accident, misfortune.

descalzarse, *v.* take off one's shoes.

descalzo, *a.* shoeless; barefoot.

descaminado, *a.* wrong, misguided.

descaminar, *v.* mislead; lead into error.

descamisado, *a.* shirtless; shabby.

descanso, *m.* rest. —**descansar**, *v.*

descarado, *a.* saucy, fresh.

descarga, *f.* discharge.

descargar, *v.* discharge, unload, dump.

descargo, *m.* acquittal.

descarnar, *v.* skin.

descaro, *m.* gall, effrontery.

descarriar, *v.* lead or go astray.

descarrilamiento, *m.* derailment.

descarrilar, *v.* derail.

descartar, *v.* discard.

descascarar, *v.* peel; boast, brag.

descendencia, *f.* descent, origin; progeny.

descender, *v.* descend.

descendiente, *m.& f.* descendant.

descendimiento, *m.* descent.

descenso, *m.* descent.

descentralización, *f.* decentralizing.

descifrar, *v.* decipher, puzzle out.

descoco, *m.* boldness, brazenness.

descolgar, *v.* take down.

descolorar, *v.* discolor.

descolorido, *a.* pale, faded.

descollar, *v.* stand out; excel.

descomedido, *a.* disproportionate; rude.

descomedirse, *v.* be rude.

descomponer, *v.* decompose; break down, get out of order.

descomposición, *f.* discomposure; disorder, confusion.

descompuesto, *a.* impudent, rude.

descomulgar, *v.* excommunicate.

descomunal, *a.* extraordinary, huge.

desconcertar, *v.* disconcert, baffle.

desconcierto, *m.* confusion, disarray.

desconectar, *v.* disconnect.

desconfiado, *a.* distrustful.

desconfianza, *f.* distrust.

desconfiar, *v.* distrust, mistrust; suspect.

descongestionante, *m.* decongestant.

desconocer, *v.* ignore, fail to recognize.

desconocido -da, *n.* stranger.

desconocimiento, *m.* ingratitude; ignorance.

desconsolado, *a.* disconsolate, wretched.

desconsuelo, *m.* grief.

descontar, *v.* discount, subtract.

descontentar, *v.* dissatisfy.

descontento, *m.* discontent.

descontinuar, *v.* discontinue.

desconvenir, *v.* disagree.

descorazonar, *v.* dishearten.

descorchar, *v.* uncork.

descortés, *a.* discourteous, impolite, rude.

descortesía, *f.* discourtesy, rudeness.

descortezar, *v.* peel.

descoyuntar, *v.* dislocate.

descrédito, *m.* discredit.

describir, *v.* describe.

descripción, *f.* description.

descriptivo, *a.* descriptive.

descuartizar, *v.* dismember, disjoint.

descubridor, *m.* discoverer.

descubrimiento, *m.* discovery.

descubrir, *v.* discover; uncover; disclose.

descubrirse, *v.* take off one's hat.

descuento, *m.* discount.

descuidado, *a.* reckless, careless; slack.

descuido, *m.* neglect. —**descuidar**, *v.*

desde, *prep.* since; from. d. luego, of course.

desdén, *m.* disdain. —**desdeñar**, *v.*

desdeñoso, *a.* contemptuous, disdainful, scornful.

desdicha, *f.* misfortune.

deseable, *a.* desirable.

desear, *v.* desire, wish.

desecar, *v.* dry, desiccate.

desechar, *v.* scrap, reject.

desecho, *m.* remainder, residue; (*pl.*) waste.

desembalar, *v.* unpack.

desembarazado, *a.* free; unrestrained.

desembarazar, *v.* free; extricate; unburden.

desembarcar, *v.* disembark, go ashore.

desembocar, *v.* flow into.

desembolsar, *v.* disburse; expend.

desembolso, *m.* disbursement.

desemejante, *a.* unlike, dissimilar.

desempacar, *v.* unpack.

desempeñar, *v.* carry out; redeem.

desempeño, *m.* fulfillment.

desencajar, *v.* disjoint; disturb.

desencantar, *v.* disillusion.

desencanto, *m.* disillusion.

desencarcelar, *v.* set free; release.

desenfadado, *a.* free; unembarrassed; spacious.

desenfado, *m.* freedom; ease; calmness.

desengaño, *m.* disillusion. —**desengañar**, *v.*

desenlace, *m.* outcome, conclusion.

desenredar, *v.* disentangle.

desensartar, *v.* unthread.

desentenderse, *v.* overlook; avoid noticing.

desenterrar, *v.* disinter, exhume.

desenvainar, *v.* unsheath.

desenvoltura, *f.* impudence, boldness.

desenvolver, *v.* evolve, unfold.

deseo, *m.* wish, desire, urge.

deseoso, *a.* desirous.

deserción, *f.* desertion.

desertar, *v.* desert.

desertor, *m.* deserter.

desesperación, *f.* despair, desperation.

desesperado, *a.* desperate; hopeless.

desesperar, *v.* despair.

desfalcar, *v.* embezzle.

desfavorable, *a.* unfavorable.

desfigurar, *v.* disfigure, mar.

desfiladero, *m.* defile.

desfile, *m.* parade. —**desfilar**, *v.*

desgaire, *m.* slovenly appearance.

desgana, *f.* lack of appetite; repugnance.

desgarrar, *v.* tear, lacerate.

desgastar, *v.* wear away, waste, erode.

desgaste, *m.* wear; erosion.

desgracia, *f.* misfortune.

desgraciado, *a.* unfortunate.

desgranar, *v.* shell.

desgreñar, *v.* dishevel.

deshacer, *v.* undo, take apart, destroy.

deshacerse de, v. get rid of, dispose of.

deshecho, a. undone; wasted.

deshelar, v. thaw; melt.

desheredamiento, m. disinheriting.

desheredar, v. disinherit.

deshielo, m. thaw, melting.

deshinchar, v. reduce a swelling.

deshojarse, v. shed (leaves).

deshonestidad, f. dishonesty.

deshonesto, a. dishonest.

deshonra, f. dishonor.

deshonrar, v. disgrace; dishonor.

deshonroso, a. dishonorable.

desierto, m. desert, wilderness.

designar, v. appoint, name.

designio, m. purpose, intent.

desigual, a. uneven, unequal.

desigualdad, f. inequality.

desilusión, f. disappointment.

desinfección, f. disinfection.

desinfectar, v. disinfect.

desintegrar, v. disintegrate, zap.

desinterés, m. indifference.

desinteresado, a. disinterested, unselfish.

desistir, v. desist, stop.

desleal, a. disloyal.

deslealtad, f. disloyalty.

desleír, v. dilute, dissolve.

desligar, v. untie, loosen; free, release.

deslindar, v. make the boundaries of.

deslinde, m. demarcation.

desliz, m. slip; false step; weakness.

deslizarse, v. slide; slip; glide; coast.

deslumbramiento, m. dazzling glare; confusion.

deslumbrar, v. dazzle; glare.

deslustre, m. tarnish. —deslustrar, v.

desmán, m. mishap; misbehavior; excess.

desmantelar, v. dismantle.

desmañado, a. awkward, clumsy.

desmayar, v. dismay, appall.

desmayo, m. faint. —desmayarse, v.

desmejorar, v. make worse; decline.

desmembrar, v. dismember.

desmemoria, f. forgetfulness.

desmemoriado, a. forgetful.

desmentir, v. contradict, disprove.

desmenuzable, a. crisp, crumbly.

desmenuzar, v. crumble, break into bits.

desmesurado, a. excessive.

desmonetización, f. demonetization.

desmonetizar, v. demonetize.

desmontado, a. dismounted.

desmoralización, f. demoralization.

desmoralizar, v. demoralize.

desmoronar, v. crumble, decay.

desmovilizar, v. demobilize.

desnatar, v. skim.

desnaturalización, f. denaturalization.

desnaturalizar, v. denaturalize.

desnegamiento, m. denial, contradiction.

desnervar, v. enervate.

desnivel, m. unevenness or difference in elevation.

desnudamente, adv. nakedly.

desnudar, v. undress.

desnudez, f. bareness, nudity.

desnudo, a. bare, naked.

desnutrición, f. malnutrition.

desobedecer, v. disobey.

desobediencia, f. disobedience.

desobediente, a. disobedient.

desobedientemente, adv. disobediently.

desobligar, v. release from obligation; offend.

desocupado, a. idle, not busy; vacant.

desocupar, v. vacate.

desolación, f. desolation; ruin.

desolado, a. desolate. —desolar, v.

desollar, v. skin.

desorden, m. disorder.

desordenar, v. disarrange.

desorganización, f. disorganization.

desorganizar, v. disorganize.

despabilado, a. vigilant, watchful; lively.

despacio, adv. slowly.

despachar, v. dispatch, ship, send.

despacho, m. shipment; dispatch, promptness; office.

desparpajo, m. glibness; fluency of speech.

desparramar, v. scatter.

despavorido, a. terrified.

despecho, m. spite.

despedazar, v. tear up.

despedida, f. farewell; leave-taking; discharge.

despedir, v. dismiss, discharge; see off.

despedirse de, v. say good-bye to, take leave of.

despegar, v. unglue; separate.

despego, m. indifference; disinterest.

despejar, v. clear, clear up.

despejo, m. sprightly; clear; unobstructed.

despensa, f. pantry.

despensero, m. butler.

despeñar, v. throw down.

desperdicio, m. waste. —desperdiciar, v.

despertador, m. alarm clock.

despertar, v. wake, wake up.

despesar, m. dislike.

despicar, v. satisfy.

despidida, f. gutter.

despierto, a. awake; alert, wide-awake.

despilfarrado, a. wasteful, extravagant.

despilfarrar, v. waste, squander.

despilfarro, m. waste, extravagance.

despique, m. revenge.

desplazamiento, m. displacement.

desplegar, v. display; unfold.

desplome, m. collapse. —desplomarse, v.

desplumar, v. defeather, pluck.

despoblar, v. depopulate.

despojar, v. strip; despoil, plunder.

despojo, m. plunder, spoils; (pl.) remains, debris.

desposado, a. newly married.

desposar, v. marry.

desposeer, v. dispossess.

déspota, m. & f. despot.

despótico, a. despotic.

despotismo, m. despotism, tyranny.

despreciable, a. contemptible.

despreciar, v. spurn, despise, scorn.

desprecio, m. scorn, contempt.

desprender, v. detach, unfasten.

desprenderse, v. loosen, come apart. d. de, part with.

desprendido, a. disinterested.

despreocupado, a. unprejudiced.

desprevenido, a. unprepared, unready.

desproporción, f. disproportion.

despropósito, m. nonsense.

desprovisto, a. devoid.

después, adv. afterwards, later; then, next. d. de, d. que, after.

despuntar, v. blunt; remove the point of.

desquiciar, v. unhinge; disturb, unsettle.

desquitar, v. get revenge, retaliate.

desquite, m. revenge, retaliation.

destacamento, m. (mil.) detachment.

destacarse, v. stand out, be prominent.

destapar, v. uncover.

destello, m. sparkle, gleam.

destemplar, v. change; soften.

desteñir, v. fade, discolor.

desterrado -da, n. exile.

desterrar, v. banish, exile.

destierro, m. banishment, exile.

destilación, f. distillation.

destilar, v. distill.

destilería, f. distillery.

destinación, f. destination.

destinar, v. destine, intend.

destinatorio -ria, n. addressee.

destino, m. destiny, fate; destination.

destitución, f. dismissal; abandonment.

destituido, a. destitute.

destorcer, v. undo, straighten out.

destornillado, a. reckless, careless.

destornillador, m. screwdriver.

destrallar, v. unleash; set loose.

destral, m. hatchet.

destreza, f. cleverness, dexterity, skill.

destripar, v. eviscerate, disembowel.

destrisimo, a. extremely dexterous.

destronamiento, m. dethronement.

destronar, v. dethrone.

destrozador, m. destroyer, wrecker.

destrozar, v. destroy, wreck.

destrozo, m. destruction, ruin.

destrucción, f. destruction.

destructibilidad, f. destructibility.

destructible, a. destructible.

destructivamente, adv. destructively.

destructivo, a. destructive.

destruir, v. destroy; wipe out.

desuello, m. impudence.

desunión, f. disunion; discord; separation.

desunir, v. disconnect, sever.

desusadamente, adv. unusually.

desusado, a. archaic; obsolete.

desuso, m. disuse.

desvalido, a. helpless, destitute.

desvalijador, m. highwayman.

desván, m. attic.

desvanecerse, v. vanish; faint.

desvariado, a. delirious; disorderly.

desvarío, m. raving. —**desvariar**, v.

desvedado, a. free; unrestrained.

desveladamente, adv. watchfully, alertly.

desvelado, a. watchful; alert.

desvelar, v. be watchful; keep awake.

desvelo, m. vigilance; uneasiness.

desventaja, f. disadvantage.

desventar, v. let air out of.

desventura, f. misfortune.

desventurado, a. unhappy; unlucky.

desvergonzado, a. shameless, brazen.

desvergüenza, f. shamelessness.

desvestir, v. undress.

desviación, f. deviation.

desviado, a. devious.

desviar, v. divert; deviate.

desvío, m. detour; side track; indifference.

desvirtuar, v. decrease the value of.

deszumar, v. remove the juice from.

detalle, m. detail. —**detallar**, v.

detective, m. detective.

detención, f. detention, arrest.

detenedor, m. stopper; catch.

detener, v. detain, stop; arrest.

detenidamente, adv. carefully, slowly.

deteñido, adv. stingy; thorough.

détente, f. detente.

detergente, a. detergent.

deterioración, f. deterioration.

deteriorar, v. deteriorate.

determinable, a. determinable.

determinación, f. determination.

determinar, v. determine.

determinismo, m. determinism.

determinista, n. & a. determinist.

detestable, a. detestable, hateful.

detestablemente, adv. detestably, hatefully, abhorrently.

detestación, f. detestation, hatefulness.

detestar, v. detest.

detonación, f. detonation.

detonar, v. detonate, explode.

detracción, f. detraction, defamation.

detractar, v. detract, defame, vilify.

detraer, v. detract.

detrás, adv. behind; in back.

detrimento, m. detriment, damage.

deuda, f. debt.

deudo -da, n. relative, kin.

deudor -ra, n. debtor.

Deuteronomio, m. Deuteronomy.

devalar, v. drift.

devanar, v. to wind, as on a spool.

devanear, v. talk deliriously, rave.

devaneo, m. frivolity; idle pursuit; delirium.

devantal, m. apron.

devastación, f. devastation, ruin, havoc.

devastador, m. devastator.

devastar, v. devastate.

devenir, v. happen, occur; become.

devoción, f. devotion.

devocionario, m. prayer book.

devocionero, a. devotional.

devolver, v. return, give back.

devorar, v. devour.

devotamente, adv. devotedly, devoutly, piously.

devoto, a. devout; devoted.

deyección, f. depression, dejection.

día, m. day. **buenos días**, good morning.

diabetes, f. diabetes.

diabético, a. diabetic.

diablear, v. play pranks.

diablo, m. devil.

diablura, f. mischief.

diabólicamente, adv. diabolically.

diabólico, a. diabolic, devilish.

diaconado, m. deaconship.

diaconía, f. deaconry.

diácono, m. deacon.

diacrítico, a. diacritic.

diadema, f. diadem, crown.

diáfano, a. transparent.

diafragma, m. diaphragm.

diagnosticar, v. diagnose.

diagonal, f. diagonal.

diagonalmente, adv. diagonally.

diagrama, m. diagram.

dialectal, a. dialectal.

dialéctico, a. dialectic.

dialecto, m. dialect.

diálogo, m. dialogue.

diamante, m. diamond.

diamantista, m. diamond cutter; jeweler.

diametral, a. diametric.

diametralmente, adv. diametrically.

diámetro, m. diameter.

diana, f. reveille.

diapasón, m. pitch; tuning fork.

diaplejía, f. paralysis.

diariamente, adv. daily.

diario, a. & m. daily; daily paper; diary; journal.

diarrea, f. diarrhea.

diatriba, f. diatribe, harangue.

dibujo, m. drawing, sketch. — **dibujar**, v.

dicción, f. diction.

diccionario, m. dictionary.

diccionarista, n. lexicographer.

diciembre, m. December.

dicotomía, f. dichotomy.

dictado, m. dictation.

dictador, m. dictator.

dictadura, f. dictatorship.

dictamen, m. dictate.

dictar, v. dictate; direct.

dictatoría, a. dictatorial; tyrannic.

dicha, f. happiness.

dicho, m. saying.

dichoso, a. happy; fortunate.

didáctico, a. didactic.

diecinueve, a. & pron. nineteen.

dieciocho, a. & pron. eighteen.

dieciseis, a. & pron. sixteen.

diecisiete, a. & pron. seventeen.

diente, m. tooth.

diestramente, adv. skillfully, ably; ingeniously.

diestro, a. dexterous, skillful; clever.

dieta, f. diet; allowance.

dietética, f. dietetic.

diez, a. & pron. ten.

diezmal, a. decimal.

diezmar, v. decimate.

difamación, f. defamation, smear.

difamar, v. defame, smear, libel.

difamatorio, a. defamatory.

diferencia, f. difference.

diferencial, a. & f. differential.

diferenciar, v. differentiate, distinguish.

diferente, a. different.

diferentemente, adv. differently.

diferir, v. differ; defer, put off.

difícil, a. difficult, hard.

difícilmente, adv. with difficulty or hardship.

dificultad, f. difficulty.

dificultar, v. make difficult.

dificultoso, a. difficult, hard.

dificencia, f. diffidence.

dificente, a. diffident.

difteria, f. diphtheria.

difundir, v. diffuse, spread.

difunto, a. deceased, dead, late.

difusamente, adv. diffusely.

difusión, f. diffusion, spread.

digerible, a. digestible.

digerir, v. digest.

digestible, a. digestible.

digestión, f. digestion.

digestivo, a. digestive.

digesto, m. digest or code of laws.

digitado, a. digitate.

digital, 1. a. digital. **2.** f. foxglove.

dignación, f. condescension; deigning.

dignamente, adv. with dignity.

dignarse, v. condescend, deign.

dignidad, f. dignity.

dignificar, v. dignify.

dignatario, m. dignitary.

digno, a. worthy; dignified.

digresión, f. digression.

digresivo, a. digressive.

dij, dije, m. trinket, piece of jewelry.

dilación, f. delay.

dilapidación, f. dilapidation.

dilatación, f. dilatation, enlargement.

dilatar, v. dilate; delay; expand.

dilatoria, f. delay.

dilecto, a. loved.

diluvial, a. diluvial.

diluvio, m. flood, deluge.

dimensión, f. dimension; measurement.

diminución, f. diminution.

diminuto, diminutivo, a. diminutive, little.

dimisión, f. resignation.

dimitir, v. resign.

Dinamarca, f. Denmark.

dinamarqués -esa, a. & n. Danish, Dane.

dinámico, a. dynamic.

dinamita, f. dynamite.

dinamitero, m. dynamiter.

dinamo, m. dynamo.

dinasta, m. dynast, king, monarch.

dinastía, f. dynasty.

dinástico, a. dynastic.

dinero, m. money, currency.

dinosauro, m. dinosaur.

diócesi, f. diocese.

Dios, m. God.

dios -sa, n. god, goddess.

diploma, m. diploma.

diplomacia, f. diplomacy.

diplomado -da, n. graduate.

diplomarse, v. graduate (from a school).

diplomática, f. diplomacy.

diplomático, a. & m. diplomat; diplomatic.

dipsomanía, f. dipsomania.

diptongo, m. diphthong.

diputación, f. deputation, delegation.

diputado, m. deputy.

diputar, v. depute, delegate; empower.

dique, m. dike; dam.

dirección, f. direction; address; guidance; (com.) management.

directamente, adv. directly.

directo, a. direct.

director, m. director; manager.

dirigente, a. directing, controlling, managing.

dirigible, m. dirigible.

dirigir, v. direct; lead; manage.

dirigirse a, v. address; approach, turn to; head for.

dirruir, v. destroy, devastate.

disanto, m. holy day.

discantar, v. sing (esp. in counterpoint); discuss.

disceptación, f. argument, quarrel.

disceptar, v. argue, quarrel.

discernimiento, m. discernment.

discernir, v. discern.

disciplina, f. discipline.

disciplinable, a. disciplinable.

disciplinar, v. discipline, train, teach.

discípulo -la, n. disciple, follower; pupil.

disco, m. disk; (phonograph) record.

discontinuación, f. discontinuation.

discontinuar, v. discontinue, break off, cease.

discordancia, f. discordance.

discordar, v. disagree, conflict.

discordia, f. discord.

discoteca, f. disco, discotheque.

discreción, f. discretion.

discrecional, a. optional.

discrecionalmente, adv. optionally.

discrepancia, f. discrepancy.

discretamente, adv. discreetly.

discreto, a. discreet.

discrimen, m. risk, hazard.

discriminación, f. discrimination.

discriminar, v. discriminate.

disculpa, f. excuse; apology.

disculpar, v. excuse; exonerate.

disculparse, v. apologize.

discurrir, v. roam; flow; think; plan.

discursante, n. lecturer, speaker.

discursivo, a. discursive.

discurso, m. speech, talk.

discusión, f. discussion.

discutible, a. debatable.

discutir, v. discuss; debate; contest.

disecación, f. dissection.

disecar, v. dissect.

disección, f. dissection.

diseminación, f. dissemination.

diseminar, v. disseminate, spread.

disensión, f. dissension; dissent.

disenso, m. dissent.

disentería, f. dysentery.

disentir, v. disagree, dissent.

diseñador -ra, n. designer.

diseño, m. design. —**diseñar,** v.

disertación, f. dissertation.

disfamación, f. defamation.

disforme, a. deformed, monstrous, ugly.

disformidad, f. deformity.

disfraz, m. disguise. —**disfrazar,** v.

disfrutar, v. enjoy.

disfrute, m. enjoyment.

disgustar, v. displease; disappoint.

disgusto, m. displeasure; disappointment.

disidencia, f. dissidence.

disidente, a. & n. dissident.

disímil, a. unlike.

disimilitud, f. dissimilarity.

disimulación, f. dissimulation.

disimulado, a. dissembling, feigning; sly.

disimular, v. hide, dissemble.

disimulo, m. pretense.

disipación, f. dissipation.

disipado, a. dissipated; wasted; scattered.

disipar, v. waste; scatter.

dislexia, f. dyslexia.

dislocación, f. dislocation.

dislocar, v. dislocate; displace.

disminuir, v. diminish, lessen, reduce.

disociación, f. dissociation.

disociar, v. dissociate.

disolubilidad, f. dissolubility.

disoluble, a. dissoluble.

disolución, f. dissolution.

disolutemente, adv. dissolutely.

disoluto, a. dissolute.

disolver, v. dissolve.

disonancia, f. dissonance; discord.

disonante, a. dissonant; discordant.

disonar, v. be discordant; clash in sound.

disono, a. dissonant.

dispar, a. unlike.

disparadamente, *adv.* hastily, hurriedly.

disparar, *v.* shoot, fire (a weapon).

disparatado, *a.* nonsensical.

disparatar, *v.* talk nonsense.

disparate, *m.* nonsense, tall tale.

disparejo, *a.* uneven, unequal.

disparidad, *f.* disparity.

disparo, *m.* shot.

dispendio, *m.* extravagance.

dispendioso, *a.* expensive; extravagant.

dispensa, dispensación, *f.* dispensation.

dispensable, *a.* dispensable; excusable.

dispensar, *v.* dispense, excuse; grant.

dispensario, *m.* dispensary.

dispepsia, *f.* dyspepsia.

dispéptico, *a.* dyspeptic.

dispersar, *v.* scatter; dispel; disband.

dispersión, *f.* dispersion, dispersal.

disperso, *a.* dispersed.

displicente, *a.* unpleasant.

disponer, *v.* dispose. **d. de,** have at one's disposal.

disponible, *a.* available.

disposición, *f.* disposition; disposal.

dispuesto, *a.* disposed, inclined; attractive.

disputa, *f.* dispute, argument.

disputable, *a.* disputable.

disputador, *m.* disputant.

disputar, *v.* argue; dispute.

disquisición, *f.* disquisition.

distancia, *f.* distance.

distante, *a.* distant.

distantemente, *adv.* distantly.

distar, *v.* be distant, be far.

distención, *f.* distension, swelling.

distender, *v.* distend, swell, enlarge.

dístico, *m.* couplet.

distinción, *f.* distinction, difference.

distingo, *m.* restriction.

distinguible, *a.* distinguishable.

distinguido, *a.* distinguished, prominent.

distinguir, *v.* distinguish; make out, spot.

distintamente, *adv.* distinctly, clearly; differently.

distintivo, *a.* distinctive.

distinto, *a.* distinct, different.

distracción, *f.* distraction, pastime; absent-mindedness.

distraer, *v.* distract.

distraídamente, *adv.* absent-mindedly, distractedly.

distraído, *a.* absent-minded; distracted.

distribución, *f.* distribution.

distribuidor -ra, *n.* distributor.

distribuir, *v.* distribute.

distributivo, *a.* distributive.

distribuidor, *m.* distributor.

distrito, *m.* district.

disturbar, *v.* disturb, trouble.

disturbio, *m.* disturbance, outbreak; turmoil.

disuadir, *v.* dissuade.

disuasión, *f.* dissuasion; deterrence.

disuasivo, *a.* dissuasive.

disyunción, *f.* disjunction.

ditirambo, *m.* dithyramb.

diurno, *a.* diurnal.

diva, *f.* singer.

divagación, *f.* digression.

divagar, *v.* digress, ramble.

diván, *m.* couch.

divergencia, *f.* divergence.

divergente, *a.* divergent, differing.

divergir, *v.* diverge.

diversamente, *adv.* diversely.

diversidad, *f.* diversity.

diversificar, *v.* diversify, vary.

diversión, *f.* diversion, pastime.

diverso, *a.* diverse, different; (*pl.*) various, several.

divertido, *a.* humorous, amusing.

divertimiento, *m.* diversion; amusement.

divertir, *v.* entertain, amuse.

divertirse, *v.* enjoy oneself, have a good time.

dividendo, *m.* dividend.

dividero, *a.* divisible.

dividir, *v.* divide, separate.

divieso, *m.* (med.) boil.

divinamente, *adv.* divinely.

divinidad, *f.* divinity.

divinizar, *v.* deify.

divino, *a.* divine; heavenly.

divisa, *f.* badge, emblem.

divisar, *v.* sight, make out.

divisibilidad, *f.* divisibility.

divisible, *a.* divisible.

división, *f.* division.

divisivo, *a.* divisive.

diviso, *a.* divided.

divo, *m.* god.

divorcio, *m.* divorce. —**divorciar,** *v.*

divulgable, *a.* divulgable.

divulgación, *f.* divulgation.

divulgar, *v.* divulge, reveal.

dobladamente, *adv.* doubly.

dobladillo, *m.* hem of a skirt or dress.

dobladura, *f.* fold, bend.

doblar, *v.* fold; bend.

doble, *a.* double.

doblegable, *a.* a flexible, foldable.

doblegar, *v.* fold, bend; yield.

doblez, *m.* fold; duplicity.

doblón, *m.* doubloon.

doce, *a. & pron.* twelve.

docena, *f.* dozen.

docente, *a.* educational.

dócil, *a.* docile.

docilidad, *f.* docility, tractableness.

dócilmente, *adv.* docilely, meekly.

doctamente, *adv.* learnedly, profoundly.

docto, *a.* learned, expert.

doctor, *m.* doctor.

doctorado, *m.* doctorate.

doctoral, *a.* doctoral.

doctrina, *f.* doctrine.

doctrinador, *m.* teacher.

doctrinal, *m.* catechism.

doctrinar, *v.* teach.

documentación, *f.* documentation.

documental, *a.* documentary.

documento, *m.* document.

dogal, *m.* noose.

dogma, *m.* dogma.

dogmáticamente, *adv.* dogmatically.

dogmático, *m.* dogmatic.

dogmatismo, *m.* dogmatism.

dogmatista, *m.* dogmatist.

dogo, *m.* bulldog.

dólar, *v.* cut, chop, hew.

dólar, *m.* dollar.

dolencia, *f.* pain; disease.

doler, *v.* ache, hurt, be sore.

doliente, *a.* ill; aching.

dolor, *m.* pain; grief, sorrow, woe.

dolorido, *a.* painful, sorrowful.

dolorosamente, *adv.* painfully, sorrowfully.

doloroso, *a.* painful, sorrowful.

dolosamente, *adv.* deceitfully.

doloso, *a.* deceitful.

domable, *a.* that can be tamed or managed.

domar, *v.* tame; subdue.

dombo, *m.* dome.

domesticable, *a.* that can be domesticated.

domesticación, *f.* domestication.

domésticamente, *adv.* domestically.

domesticar, *v.* tame.

domesticidad, *f.* domesticity.

doméstico, *a.* domestic.

domicilio, *m.* dwelling, home, residence.

dominación, *f.* domination.

dominador, *a.* dominating.

dominante, *a.* dominant.

dominar, *v.* rule, dominate; master.

dómine, *m.* teacher.

domingo, *m.* Sunday.

dominio, *m.* domain; rule; power.

dominó, *m.* domino.

domo, *m.* dome.

Don, *title used before a man's first name.*

don, *m.* gift.

dona, *f.* woman.

donación, *f.* donation.

donador -ra, *n.* giver, donor.

donaire, *m.* grace.

donairosamente, *adv.* gracefully.

donairoso, *a.* graceful.

donante, *n.* giver, donor.

donar, *v.* donate.

donativo, *m.* donation, contribution; gift.

doncella, *f.* lass; maid.

donde, dónde, *conj. & adv.* where.

dondequiera, *adv.* wherever, anywhere.

donosamente, *adv.* gracefully; wittily.

donoso, *a.* graceful; witty.

donosura, *f.* gracefulness; wittiness.

Doña, *title used before a lady's first name.*

dorado, *a.* gilded.

dorador, *m.* gilder.

dorar, *v.* gild.

dórico, *a.* Doric.

dormidero, *a.* sleep-inducing; soporific.

dormido, *a.* asleep.

dormir, *v.* sleep.

dormirse, *v.* fall asleep, go to sleep.

dormitar, *v.* doze.

dormitorio, m. dormitory; bedroom.

dorsal, *a.* dorsal.

dorso, *m.* spine.

dos, *a. & pron.* two. **los d.,** both.

dosañal, *a.* biennial.

doscientos, *a. & pron.* two hundred.

dosel, *m.* canopy; platform, dais.

dosificación, *f.* dosage.

dosis, *f.* dose.

dotación, *f.* endowment; (naut.) crew.

dotador, *m.* donor.

dotar, *v.* endow; give a dowry to.

dote, *m.* dowry; (*pl.*) talents.

dragaminas, *m.* mine sweeper.

dragar, *v.* dredge; sweep.

dragón, *m.* dragon; dragoon.

dragonear, *v.* pretend to be.

drama, *m.* drama; play.

dramática, *f.* dramatics.

dramáticamente, *adv.* dramatically.

dramático, *a.* dramatic.

dramatizar, *v.* dramatize.

dramaturgo, *m.* playwright, dramatist.

drástico, *a.* drastic.

drenaje, *m.* drainage.

dríada, *f.* dryad.

driza, *f.* halyard.

droga, *f.* drug.

droguería, *f.* drugstore.

droguero, *m.* druggist.

dromedario, *m.* dromedary.

druida, *m.* Druid.

dualidad, *f.* duality.

dubitable, *a.* doubtful.

dubitación, *f.* doubt.

ducado, *m.* duchy.

ducal, *a.* ducal.

dúctil, *a.* ductile.

ductilidad, *f.* ductility.

ducha, *f.* shower (bath).

duda, *f.* doubt.

dudable, *a.* doubtful.

dudar, *v.* doubt; hesitate; question.

dudosamente, *adv.* doubtfully.

dudoso, *a.* dubious; doubtful.

duela, *f.* stave.

duelista, *m.* duelist.

duelo, *m.* duel; grief; mourning.

duende, *m.* elf, hobgoblin.

dueño -ña, *n.* owner; landlord, -lady; master, mistress.

dulce, 1. *a.* sweet. **agua d.,** fresh water. **2.** *m.* piece of candy; (*pl.*) candy.

dulcedumbre, *f.* sweetness.

dulcemente, *adv.* sweetly.

dulcería, *f.* confectionery; candy shop.

dulcificar, *v.* sweeten.

dulzura, *f.* sweetness; mildness.

duna, *f.* dune.

dúo, *m.* duet.

duodenal, *a.* duodenal.

duplicación, *f.* duplication; doubling.

duplicadamente, *adv.* doubly.

duplicado, *a. & m.* duplicate.

duplicar, *v.* double, duplicate, repeat.

duplicidad, *f.* duplicity.

duplo, *a.* double.

duque, *m.* duke.

duquesa, *f.* duchess.

durabilidad, *f.* durability.

durable, *a.* durable.

duración, *f.* duration.

duradero, *a.* lasting, durable.

duramente, *adv.* harshly, roughly.

durante, *prep.* during.

durar, *v.* last.

durazno, *m.* peach.

dureza, *f.* hardness.

durmiente, *a.* dormant.

duro, *a.* hard; stiff; stern; stale.

dux, *m.* doge.

E

e, *conj.* and.

ebanista, *m.* cabinetmaker.

ebanizar, *v.* give an ebony finish to.

ébano, *m.* ebony.

ebonita, *f.* ebonite.

ebrio, *a.* drunken, inebriated.

ebullición, *f.* boiling.

eclecticismo, *m.* eclecticism.

ecléctico, *n. & a.* eclectic.

eclesiástico, *a. & m.* ecclesiastic.

eclipse, *m.* eclipse. —**eclipsar,** *v.*

eclipsis, *f.* ellipsis.

écloga, *f.* eclogue.

eco, *m.* echo.

ecología, *f.* ecology.

ecológico, *f.* ecological.

ecologista, *m. & f.* ecologist.

economía, *f.* economy; thrift. **e. política,** economics.

económicamente, *adv.* economically.

económico, *a.* economic; economical, thrifty.

economista, *f.* economist.

economizar, *v.* save, economize.

ecuación, *f.* equation.

ecuador, *m.* equator.

ecuanimidad, *f.* equanimity.

ecuatorial, *a.* equatorial.

ecuatoriano -na, *a. & n.* Ecuadorian.

ecuestre, *a.* equestrian.

ecuménico, *a.* ecumenical.

echada, *f.* throw.

echadillo, *m.* foundling; orphan.

echar, *v.* throw, toss; pour. **e. a,** start to. **e. a perder,** spoil, ruin. **e. de menos,** miss.

echarse, *v.* lie down.

edad, *f.* age.

edecán, *m.* aide-de-camp.

Edén, *m.* Eden.

edición, *f.* edition; issue.

edicto, *m.* edict, decree.

edificación, *f.* construction.

edificador, *n.* constructor; builder.

edificar, *v.* build.

edificio, *m.* edifice, building.

editar, *v.* publish, issue.

editor, *m.* publisher.

editorial, *m.* editorial.

edredón, *m.* quilt.

educación, *f.* upbringing, breeding; education.

educador, *m.* educator.

educar, *v.* educate, bring up; train.

educativo, *a.* educational.

educción, *f.* deduction.

educir, *v.* educe.

educto, *m.* output.

efectivamente, *adv.* actually, really.

efectivo, *a.* effective; actual, real. **en e.,** (com.) in cash.

efecto, *m.* effect.

efectuar, *v.* effect; cash.

eferente, *a.* efferent.

efervescencia, *f.* effervescence; zeal.

eficacia, *f.* efficacy.

eficaz, *a.* efficient, effective.

eficazmente, *adv.* efficaciously.

eficiencia, *f.* efficiency.

eficiente, *a.* efficient.

efigie, *f.* effigy.

efímera, *f.* May fly.

efímero, *a.* ephemeral, passing.

efluvio, *m.* effluvium.

efundir, *v.* effuse; pour out.

efusión, *f.* effusion.

egipcio -cia, *a. & n.* Egyptian.

Egipto, *m.* Egypt.

égira, *f.* hegira.

egoísmo, *m.* egoism, egotism, selfishness.

egoísta, *a. & n.* selfish, egoistic; egoist.

egotismo, *m.* egotism.

egotista, *m.* egotist.

egreso, *m.* expense, outlay.

eje, *m.* axis; axle.

ejecución, *f.* execution; performance; enforcement.

ejecutar, *v.* execute; enforce; carry out.

ejecutivo, *a. & m.* executive.

ejecutor, *m.* executor.

ejemplar, 1. *a.* exemplary. 2. *m.* copy.

ejemplificación, *f.* exemplification.

ejemplificar, *v.* illustrate.

ejemplo, *m.* example.

ejercer, *v.* exert; practice.

ejercicio, *m.* exercise, drill. —ejercitar, *v.*

ejercitación, *f.* exercise, training, drill.

ejercitar, *v.* exercise, train, drill.

ejército, *m.* army.

ejotes, *m.pl.* string beans.

el, *art. & pron.* the; the one.

él, *pron.* he, him; it.

elaboración, *f.* elaboration; working up.

elaborado, *a.* elaborate.

elaborador, *m.* manufacturer, maker.

elaborar, *v.* elaborate; manufacture; brew.

elación, *f.* elation; magnanimity; turgid style.

elasticidad, *f.* elasticity.

elástico, *m.* elastic.

elección, *f.* election; option, choice.

electivo, *a.* elective.

electo, *a.* elected, chosen, appointed.

electorado, *m.* electorate.

electoral, *a.* electoral.

electricidad, *f.* electricity.

electricista, *m.* electrician.

eléctrico, *a.* electric.

electrización, *f.* electrification.

electrocardiograma, *m.* electrocardiogram.

electrocución, *f.* electrocution.

electrocutar, *v.* electrocute.

electrodo, *m.* electrode.

electroimán, *m.* electromagnet.

electrólisis, *f.* electrolysis.

electrólito, *m.* electrolyte.

electrón, *m.* electron.

elefante, *m.* elephant.

elegancia, *f.* elegance.

elegante, *a.* elegant, smart, stylish, fine.

elegantemente, *adv.* elegantly.

elegía, *f.* elegy.

elegibilidad, *f.* eligibility.

elegible, *a.* eligible.

elegir, *v.* select, choose; elect.

elemental, *a.* elementary.

elementalmente, *adv.* elementally; fundamentally.

elementar, *a.* elementary.

elemento, *m.* element.

elevación, *f.* elevation; height.

elevador, *m.* elevator.

elevamiento, *m.* elevation.

elevar, *v.* elevate; erect, raise.

elidir, *v.* elide.

eliminación, *f.* elimination.

eliminar, *v.* eliminate.

elipse, *f.* ellipse.

elipsis, *f.* ellipsis.

elíptico, *a.* elliptic.

elocuencia, *f.* eloquence.

elocuente, *a.* eloquent.

elocuentemente, *adv.* eloquently.

elogio, *m.* praise, compliment. —elogiar, *v.*

elucidación, *f.* elucidation.

elucidar, *v.* elucidate.

eludir, *v.* elude.

ella, *pron.* she, her; it.

ello, *pron.* it.

ellos -as, *pron. pl.* they, them.

emaciación, *f.* emaciation.

emanar, *v.* emanate, stem.

emancipación, *f.* emancipation, freeing.

emancipador, *n.* emancipator.

emancipar, *v.* emancipate, free.

embajada, *f.* embassy; legation; (coll.) errand.

embajador, *m.* ambassador.

embalar, *v.* pack, bale.

embaldosado, *m.* tile floor.

embalsamador, *m.* embalmer.

embalsamar, *v.* embalm.

embarazada, *a.* pregnant.

embarazadamente, *adv.* embarrassedly.

embarazar, *v.* embarrass.

embarazo, *m.* embarrassment; pregnancy.

embarazado, *a.* difficult; complicated.

embarcación, *f.* boat, ship; embarkation.

embarcadero, *m.* wharf, pier, dock.

embarcador, *m.* shipper, loader, stevedore.

embarcar, *v.* ship.

embarcarse, *v.* embark; sail.

embargador, *m.* one who impedes; one who orders an embargo.

embargante, *a.* impeding, hindering.

embargar, *v.* impede, restrain; (leg.) seize, embargo.

embargo, *m.* seizure, embargo. sin e., however, nevertheless.

embarnizar, *v.* varnish.

embarque, *m.* shipment.

embarrador, *m.* plasterer.

embarrancar, *v.* get stuck in mud.

embarrar, *v.* plaster; besmear with mud.

embasamiento, *m.* foundation of a building.

embastecer, *v.* get fat.

embaucador, *m.* imposter.

embaucar, *v.* deceive, trick, hoax.

embaular, *v.* pack in a trunk.

embausamiento, *m.* amazement.

embebecer, *v.* amaze, astonish; entertain.

embeber, *v.* absorb; incorporate; saturate.

embelecador, *m.* imposter.

embeleco, *m.* fraud, perpetration.

embelesar, *v.* fascinate, charm.

embelesamiento, *m.* rapture.

embeleso, *v.* fascinate, charm.

embeleso, *m.* rapture, bliss.

embellecer, *v.* beautify, embellish.

embestida, *f.* violent assault; attack.

emblandecer, *v.* soften; moisten; move to pity.

emblema, *m.* emblem.

emblemático, *a.* emblematic.

embocadura, *f.* narrow entrance; mouth of a river.

embocar, *v.* eat hastily; gorge.

embolia, *f.* embolism.

embolsar, *v.* pocket.

embonar, *v.* improve, fix, repair.

emborrachador, *a.* intoxicating.

emborrachar, *v.* get drunk.

emboscada, *f.* ambush.

emboscar, *v.* put or lie in ambush.

embotado, *a.* blunt, dull (edged). —embotar, *v.*

embotadura, *f.* bluntness; dullness.

embotellar, *v.* put in bottles.

embozado, *v.* muzzled; muffled.

embozar, *v.* muzzle; muffle.

embozo, *m.* muffler.

embrague, *m.* (auto.) clutch.

embravecer, *v.* be or make angry.

embriagado, *a.* drunken, intoxicated.

embriagar, *v.* intoxicate.

embriaguez, *f.* drunkenness.

embrión, *m.* embryo.

embrionario, *a.* embryonic.

embrochado, *a.* embroidered.

embrollo, *m.* muddle. —embrollar, *v.*

embromar, *v.* tease; joke.

embuchado, *m.* pork sausage.

embudo, *m.* funnel.

embuste, *m.* lie, fib.

embustear, *v.* lie, fib.

embustero -ra, *n.* liar.

embutir, *v.* stuff, cram.

emendación, *f.* emendation, change, correction.

emergencia, *f.* emergency.

emérito, *a.* emeritus.

emético, *m. & a.* emetic.

emigración, *f.* emigration.

emigrante, *a. & n.* emigrant.

emigrar, *v.* emigrate.

eminencia, *f.* eminence, height.

eminente, *a.* eminent.

emisario, *m.* emissary, spy; outlet.

emisión, *f.* issue; emission.

emisor, *m.* radio transmitter.

emitir, *v.* emit.

emoción, *f.* feeling, emotion, thrill.

emocional, *a.* emotional.

emocionante, *a.* exciting.

emocionar, *v.* touch, move, excite.

emolumento, *m.* emolument; perquisite.

empacar, *v.* pack.

empacho, *m.* shyness, timidity; embarrassment.

empadronamiento, *m.* census; list of taxpayers.

empalizada, *f.* palisade, stockade.

empanada, *f.* meat pie.

empañar, *v.* blur; soil, sully.

empapar, *v.* soak.

empapelado, *m.* wallpaper.

empaque, *m.* packing; appearance, mien.

empaquetar, *v.* pack, package.

emparejarse, *v.* match, pair off; level, even off.

emparentado, *a.* related by marriage.

emparrado, *m.* arbor.

empastadura, *f.* (dental) filling.

empastar, *v.* fill (a tooth).

empate, *m.* tie, draw. —**empatarse**, *v.*

empecer, *v.* hurt, harm, injure; prevent.

empedernir, *v.* harden.

empeine, *m.* groin; instep; hoof.

empellar, *v.* shove, jostle.

empellón, *m.* hard push, shove.

empeñar, *v.* pledge; pawn.

empeñarse en, *v.* persist in, be bent on.

empeño, *m.* persistence; pledge; pawning.

empeoramiento, *m.* deterioration.

empeorar, *v.* get worse.

emperador, *m.* emperor.

emperatriz, *f.* empress.

empernar, *v.* nail.

empero, *conj.* however.

emperramiento, *m.* stubbornness.

empezar, *v.* begin, start.

empinado, *a.* steep.

empinar, *v.* raise; exalt.

empíreo, *a.* celestial, heavenly; divine.

empíricamente, *adv.* empirically.

empírico, *a.* empirical.

empirismo, *m.* empiricism.

emplastarse, *v.* get smeared.

emplasto, *m.* salve.

emplazamiento, *m.* court summons.

emplazar, *v.* summon to court.

empleado -da, *n.* employee.

emplear, *v.* employ; use.

empleo, *m.* employment, job; use.

empobrecer, *v.* make or become impoverished.

empobrecimiento, *m.* impoverishment.

empolvado, *a.* dusty.

empolvar, *v.* powder.

empolladior, *m.* incubator.

empollar, *v.* hatch.

emporcar, *v.* soil, make dirty.

emporio, *m.* emporium.

emprendedor, *a.* enterprising.

emprender, *v.* undertake.

empreñar, *v.* make pregnant; beget.

empresa, *f.* enterprise, undertaking.

empresario, *m.* impresario.

empréstito, *m.* loan.

empujón, *m.* push; shove. — **empujar**, *v.*

empuñar, *v.* grasp, seize; wield.

emulación, *f.* emulation; envy; rivalry.

emulador, *m.* emulator; rival.

émulo, *a.* rival. —**emular**, *v.*

emulsión, *f.* emulsion

emulsionar, *v.* emulsify.

en, *prep.* in, on, at.

enaguas, *f.pl.* petticoat; skirt.

enajenable, *a.* alienable.

enajenación, *f.* alienation; derangement, insanity.

enajenar, *v.* alienate.

enamoradamente, *adv.* lovingly.

enamorado, *a.* in love.

enamorador, *m.* wooer; suitor; lover.

enamorarse, *v.* fall in love.

enano -na, *a.* midget; dwarf.

enardecer, *v.* inflame.

enastado, *a.* horned.

encabestrar, *v.* halter.

encabezado, *m.* headline.

encabezador, *m.* reaping machine.

encabezamiento, *m.* title; census; tax roll.

encabezar, *v.* head.

encachar, *v.* hide.

encadenamiento, *m.* connection, linkage.

encadenar, *v.* chain; link, connect.

encajar, *v.* fit in, insert.

encaje, *m.* lace.

encalar, *v.* whitewash.

encalvecer, *v.* lose one's hair.

encallarse, *v.* be stranded.

encallecido, *a.* hardened; calloused.

encaminar, *v.* guide; direct; be on the way to.

encandilar, *v.* dazzle; daze.

encantación, *f.* incantation.

encantado, *a.* charmed, fascinated, enchanted.

encantador, *a.* charming, delightful.

encante, *m.* public auction.

encanto, *m.* charm, delight. — **encantar**, *v.*

encapillado, *m.* clothes one is wearing.

encapotar, *v.* cover, cloak; muffle.

encaramarse, *v.* perch; climb.

encararse con, *v.* face.

encarcelación, *f.* imprisonment.

encarcelar, *v.* jail, imprison.

encarecer, *v.* recommend; extol.

encarecidamente, *adv.* extremely; ardently.

encargado, *m.* agent; attorney; representative.

encargar, *v.* entrust.

encargarse, *v.* take charge, be in charge.

encargo, *m.* errand; assignment; (com.) order.

encarnación, *f.* incarnation.

encarnado, *a.* red.

encarnar, *v.* embody.

encarnecer, *v.* grow fat or heavy.

encarnizado, *a.* bloody, fierce.

encarrilar, *v.* set right; put on the track.

encartar, *v.* ban, outlaw; summon.

encastar, *v.* improve by crossbreeding.

encastillar, *v.* be obstinate or unyielding.

encatarrado, *a.* suffering from a cold.

encausar, *v.* prosecute; take legal action against.

encauzar, *v.* channel; direct.

encefalitis, *f.* encephalitis.

encelamiento, *m.* envy, jealousy.

encenagar, *v.* wallow in mud.

encendedor, *m.* lighter.

encender, *v.* light; set fire to, kindle; turn on.

encendido, *m.* ignition.

encerado, *m.* oilcloth; tarpaulin.

encerar, *v.* wax.

encerrar, *v.* enclose; confine, shut in.

encía, *f.* gum.

encíclico, **1.** *a.* encyclic. **2.** *f.* encyclical.

enciclopedia, *f.* encyclopedia.

enciclopédico, *a.* encyclopedic.

encierro, *m.* confinement; enclosure.

encima, *adv.* on top. e. de, on. por e. de, above.

encina, *f.* oak.

encinta, *a.* pregnant.

enclavar, *v.* nail.

enclenque, *a.* frail, weak, sickly.

encogerse, *v.* shrink. e. de hombros, shrug the shoulders.

encogido, *a.* shy, bashful, timid.

encojar, *v.* make or become lame; cripple.

encolar, *v.* glue, paste, stick.

encolerizar, *v.* make or become angry.

encomendar, *v.* commend; recommend.

encomiar, *v.* praise, laud, extol.

encomienda, *f.* commission, charge; (postal) package.

encomio, *m.* encomium, eulogy.

enconar, *v.* irritate, annoy, anger.

encono, *m.* rancor, resentment.

enconoso, *a.* rancorous, resentful.

encontrado, *a.* opposite.

encontrar, *v.* find; meet.

encorajar, v. encourage; incite.

encorralar, v. corral.

encorvadura, f. bend, curvature.

encorvar, v. arch, bend.

encorvarse, v. stoop.

encrucijada, f. crossroads.

encuadrar, v. frame.

encubierta, a. secret, fraudulent.

encubrir, v. hide, conceal.

encuentro, m. encounter; match, bout.

encurtido, m. pickle.

enchapado, m. veneer.

enchufe, m. (elec.) plug, socket.

endeble, a. rail, weak, sickly.

enderezar, v. straighten; redress.

endiablado, a. devilish.

endibia, f. endive.

endiosar, v. deify.

endorso, endoso, m. endorsement.

endosador, m. endorser.

endosar, v. endorse.

endosatario, m. endorsee.

endulzar, v. sweeten; soothe.

endurar, v. harden; endure.

endurecer, v. harden.

enemigo -ga, f. foe, enemy.

enemistad, f. enmity.

éneo, a. brass.

energía, f. energy.

enérgicamente, adv. energetically.

enérgico, a. forceful; energetic.

enero, m. January.

enervación, f. enervation.

enfadado, a. angry.

enfadar, v. anger, vex.

enfado, m. anger, vexation.

énfasis, m. or f. emphasis, stress.

enfáticamente, adv. emphatically.

enfático, a. emphatic.

enfermar, v. make ill; fall ill.

enfermedad, f. illness, sickness, disease.

enfermera, f. nurse.

enfermería, f. sanitorium.

enfermo -ms, a. & n. ill, sick; sickly; patient.

enfilar, v. line up; put in a row.

enflaquecer, v. make thin; grow thin.

enfoque, m. focus. —**enfocar,** v.

enfrascamiento, m. entanglement.

enfrascarse, v. entangle oneself.

enfrenar, v. bridle, curb; restrain.

enfrente, adv. across, opposite; in front.

enfriadera, f. icebox; cooler.

enfriar, v. chill, cool.

enfurecer, v. infuriate, enrage.

engalanar, v. adorn, trim.

enganchar, v. hook, hitch, attach.

engañar, v. deceive, cheat.

engaño, m. deceit; delusion.

engañoso, a. deceitful.

engarce, m. connection, link.

engastar, v. to put (gems) in a setting.

engaste, m. setting.

engatusar, v. deceive, trick.

engendrar, v. engender, beget, produce.

engendro, m. fetus, embryo.

engolfar, v. be deeply absorbed.

engolosinar, v. allure, charm, entice.

engomar, v. gum.

engordador, a. fattening.

engordar, v. fatten; grow fat.

engranaje, m. (mech.) gear.

engranar, v. gear; mesh together.

engrandecer, v. increase, enlarge; exalt; exaggerate.

engrasación, f. lubrication.

engrasar, v. grease, lubricate.

engreído, a. conceited.

engreimiento, m. conceit.

engullidor, m. devourer.

engullir, v. devour.

enhebrar, v. thread.

enhestadura, f. raising.

enhestar, v. raise, erect, set up.

enhiesto, a. erect, upright.

enhorabuena, f. congratulations.

enigma, m. enigma, puzzle.

enigmáticamente, adv. enigmatically.

enigmático, a. enigmatic.

enjabonar, v. soap, lather.

enjalbegar, v. whitewash.

enjambradera, f. queen bee.

enjambre, m. swarm. —**enjambrar,** v.

enjaular, v. cage, coop up.

enjebe, m. lye.

enjuagar, v. rinse.

enjugar, v. wipe, dry off.

enjutez, f. dryness.

enjuto, a. dried; lean, thin.

enlace, m. attachment; involvement; connection.

enladrillador, m. bricklayer.

enlardar, v. baste.

enlazar, v. lace; join, connect; wed.

enlodar, v. cover with mud.

enloquecer, v. go insane; drive crazy.

enloquecimiento, m. insanity.

enlustrecer, v. polish, brighten.

enmarañar, v. entangle.

enmendación, f. emendation.

enmendador, m. emender, reviser.

enmendar, v. amend, correct.

enmienda, f. amendment; correction.

enmohecer, v. rust; mold.

enmohecido, a. rusty; moldy.

enmudecer, v. silence; become silent.

ennegrecer, v. blacken.

ennoblecer, v. ennoble.

enodio, m. young deer.

enojado, a. angry, cross.

enojarse, v. get angry.

enojo, m. anger. —**enojar,** v.

enojosamente, adv. angrily.

enorme, a. enormous, huge.

enormemente, adv. enormously; hugely.

enormidad, f. enormity; hugeness.

enraizar, v. take root, sprout.

enramada, f. bower.

enredado, a. entangled, snarled.

enredar, v. entangle, snarl; mess up.

enredo, m. tangle, entanglement.

enriquecer, v. enrich.

enrojecerse, v. color; blush.

enrollar, v. wind, coil, roll up.

enromar, v. make dull, blunt.

enronquecimiento, m. hoarseness.

enroscar, v. twist, curl, wind.

ensacar, v. put in a bag.

ensalada, f. salad.

ensaladera, f. salad bowl.

ensalmo, m. charm, enchantment.

ensalzamiento, m. praise.

ensalzar, v. praise, laud, extol.

ensamblar, v. join; unite; connect.

ensanchamiento, m. widening, expansion, extension.

ensanchar, v. widen, expand, extend.

ensangrentado, a. bloody; bloodshot.

ensañar, v. enrage, infuriate, rage.

ensayar, v. try out; rehearse.

ensayista, n. essayist.

ensayo, m. attempt; trial; rehearsal.

ensenada, f. cove.

enseña, f. ensign, standard.

enseñador, m. teacher.

enseñanza, f. education; teaching.

enseñar, v. teach, train; show.

enseres, m. pl. household goods.

ensilaje, m. ensilage.

ensillar, v. saddle.

ensordecer, v. deafen.

ensordecimiento, m. deafness.

ensuciar, v. dirty, muddy, soil.

ensueño, m. illusion, dream.

entablar, v. board up; initiate, begin.

entallador, m. sculptor, carver.

entapizar, v. upholster.

ente, m. being.

entenada, f. stepdaughter.

entenado, m. stepson.

entender, v. understand.

entendimiento, m. understanding.

entenebrecer, v. darken.

enterado, a. aware, informed.

enteramente, adv. entirely, completely.

enterar, v. inform.

enterarse, v. find out.

entereza, f. entirety; integrity; firmness.

entero, a. entire, whole, total.

enterramiento, m. burial, interment.

enterrar, v. bury.

entestado, a. stubborn, willful.

entibiar, v. to cool; moderate.

entidad, f. entity.

entierro, m. interment, burial.

entonación, f. intonation.

entonamiento, m. intonation.

entonar, v. chant; harmonize.

entonces, adv. then.

entono, m. arrogance; affectation.

entortadura, f. crookedness.

entortar, v. make crooked; bend.

entrada, f. entrance; admission, admittance.

entrambos, a. & pron. both.

entrante, a. coming, next.

entrañable, a. affectionate.

entrañas, f.pl. entrails, bowels; womb.

entrar, v. enter, go in, come in.

entre, prep. among; between.

entreabierto, a. ajar, half-open.

entreabrir, v. set ajar.

entreacto, m. intermission.

entrecejo, a. frowning.

entrecuesto, m. spine, backbone.

entredicho, m. prohibition.

entrega, f. delivery.

entregar, v. deliver, hand; hand over.

entrelazar, v. intertwine, entwine.

entremedias, adv. meanwhile; halfway.

entremés, m. side dish.

entremeterse, v. meddle, intrude.

entremetido, m. meddler; intermediary.

entrenador, m. coach. —entrenar, v.

entrenarse, v. train.

entrepalado, a. variegated; spotted.

entrerrenglonar, v. interline.

entresacar, v. select, choose; sift.

entretanto, adv. meanwhile.

entretenedor, m. entertainer.

entretener, v. entertain, amuse; delay.

entretenimiento, m. entertainment, amusement.

entrevista, f. interview. —entrevistar, v.

entristecedor, a. sad.

entristecer, v. sadden.

entronar, v. enthrone.

entroncar, v. be related or connected.

entronización, f. enthronement.

entronque, m. relationship; connection.

entumecer, v. become or be numb; swell.

entusiasmado, a. enthusiastic.

entusiasmo, m. enthusiasm.

entusiasta, m. & f. enthusiast.

entusiástico, a. enthusiastic.

enumeración, f. enumeration.

enumerar, v. enumerate.

enunciación, f. enunciation; statement.

enunciar, v. enunciate.

envainar, v. sheathe.

envalentonar, v. encourage, embolden.

envanecimiento, m. conceit, vanity.

envasar, v. put in a container; bottle.

envase, m. container.

envejecer, v. age, grow old.

envejecimiento, m. oldness, age.

envenenar, v. poison.

envés, m. wrong side; back.

envestir, v. put in office; invest.

enviada, f. shipment.

enviado, m. envoy.

enviar, v. send; ship.

envidia, f. envy. —envidiar, v.

envidiable, a. enviable.

envidioso, a. envious.

envilecer, v. vilify, debase, disgrace.

envío, m. shipment.

envión, m. shove.

envoltura, f. wrapping.

envolver, v. wrap, wrap up.

enyesar, v. plaster.

enyugar, v. yoke.

eperlano, m. smelt (fish).

épica, f. epic writing.

épico, a. epic.

epicureísmo, m. Epicureanism.

epicúreo, n. & a. epicurean.

epidemia, f. epidemic.

epidémico, a. epidemic.

epidermis, f. epidermis.

epigrama, m. epigram.

epigramático, a. epigrammatic.

epilepsia, f. epilepsy.

epiléptico, n. & a. epileptic.

epílogo, m. epilogue.

episcopado, m. bishopric; episcopate.

episcopal, a. episcopal.

episódico, a. episodic.

episodio, m. episode.

epístola, f. epistle, letter.

epitafio, m. epitaph.

epitomadamente, adv. concisely.

epitomar, v. epitomize, summarize.

época, f. epoch, age.

epopeya, f. epic.

epsomita, f. Epsom salts.

equidad, f. equity.

equilibrado, a. stable.

equilibrio, m. equilibrium, balance.

equinoccio, m. equinox.

equipaje, m. luggage, baggage.

equipar, v. equip.

equiparar, v. compare.

equipo, m. equipment; team.

equitación, f. horsemanship.

equitativo, a. fair, equitable.

equivalencia, f. equivalence.

equivalente, a. equivalent.

equivaler, v. equal, be equivalent.

equivocación, f. mistake.

equivocado, a. wrong, mistaken.

equivocarse, v. make a mistake, be wrong.

equívoco, a. equivocal, ambiguous.

era, f. era, age.

erario, m. exchequer.

erección, f. erection; elevation.

eremita, m. hermit.

erguir, v. erect; straighten up.

erigir, v. erect, build.

erisipela, f. erysipelas.

erizado, a. bristly.

erizarse, v. bristle.

erizo, m. hedgehog; sea urchin.

ermita, f. hermitage.

ermitaño, m. hermit.

erogación, f. expenditure. —erogar, v.

erosión, f. erosion.

erótico, a. erotic.

erradicación, f. eradication.

erradicar, v. eradicate.

errado, a. mistaken, erroneous.

errante, a. wandering, roving.

errar, v. be mistaken.

errata, f. erratum.

errático, a. erratic.

erróneamente, adv. erroneously.

erróneo, a. erroneous.

error, m. error, mistake.

eructo, m. belch. —eructar, v.

erudición, f. scholarship, learning.

eruditamente, adv. learnedly.

erudito, m. scholar.

erupción, f. eruption; rash.

eruptivo, a. eruptive.

esbozo, m. outline, sketch. —esbozar, v.

escabechar, v. pickle; preserve.

escabel, m. small stool or bench.

escabroso, a. rough, irregular; craggy; rude.

escabullirse, v. steal away, sneak away.

escala, f. scale; ladder. hacer e., to make a stop.

escalada, f. escalation.

escalador, m. climber.

escalar, v. climb; scale.

escaldar, v. scald.

escalera, f. stairs, staircase; ladder.

escalfado, a. poached.

escalofriado, a. chilled.

escalofrío, m. chill.

escalón, m. step.

escaloña, f. scallion.

escalpar, v. scalp.

escalpelo, m. scalpel.

escama, f. (fish) scale. —escamar, v.

escamondar, v. trim, cut; prune.

escampada, f. stampede.

escandalizar, v. shock, scandalize.

escandalizativo, a. scandalous.

escándalo, m. scandal.

escandaloso, a. scandalous; disgraceful.

escandinavo, n. & a. Scandinavian.

escandir, v. scan.

escanilla, f. cradle.

escañuelo, m. small footstool.

escapada, f. escapade.

escapar, v. escape.

escape, m. escape; (auto.) exhaust.

escápula, f. scapula.

escarabajo, m. black beetle; scarab.

escaramucear, v. skirmish; dispute.

escarbadientes, m. toothpick.

escarbar, v. scratch; poke.

escarcha, f. frost.

escardar, v. weed.

escarlata, f. scarlet.

escarmentar, v. correct severely.

escarnecedor, m. scoffer; mocker.

escarnecer, v. mock, make fun of.

escarola, f. endive.

escarpado, 1. a. steep. 2. m. bluff.

escarpe, m. escarpment.

escasamente, adv. scarcely; sparingly; barely.

escasear, v. be scarce.

escasez, f. shortage, scarcity.

escaso, a. scant; scarce.

escatimoso, a. malicious; sly, cunning.

escena, f. scene; stage.

escenario, m. stage (of theater); scenario.

escénico, a. scenic.

escépticamente, adv. skeptically.

escepticismo, m. skepticism.

escéptico -ca, a. & n. skeptic; skeptical.

esclarecer, v. clear up.

esclavitud, f. slavery; bondage.

esclavizar, v. enslave.

esclavo -va, m. slave.

escoba, f. broom.

escocés, a. & n. Scotch, Scottish; Scot.

Escocia, f. Scotland.

escofinar, v. rasp.

escoger, v. choose, select.

escogido, a. choice, select.

escogimiento, m. choice.

escolar, 1. a. scholastic, (of) school. 2. m. student.

escolasticismo, m. scholasticism.

escolta, f. escort. —**escoltar**, v.

escollo, m. reef.

escombro, m. mackerel.

escombros, m.pl. debris, rubbish.

esconce, m. corner.

escondedero, m. hiding place.

esconder, v. hide, conceal.

escondidamente, adv. secretly.

escondimiento, m. concealment.

escopeta, f. shotgun.

escopetazo, m. gunshot.

escoplo, m. chisel.

escorbuto, m. scurvy.

escorpena, f. grouper.

escorpión, m. scorpion.

escorzón, m. toad.

escribiente, m. & f. clerk.

escribir, v. write.

escritor -ra, n. writer, author.

escritorio, m. desk.

escritura, f. writing, handwriting.

escrófula, f. scrofula.

escroto, m. scrotum.

escrúpulo, m. scruple.

escrupuloso, a. scrupulous.

escrutinio, m. scrutiny; examination.

escuadra, f. squad; fleet.

escuadrón, m. squadron.

escualidez, f. squalor; poverty.

escuálido, a. squalid.

escualo, m. shark.

escuchar, v. listen; listen to.

escudero, m. squire.

escudo, m. shield; protection; coin of certain countries.

escuela, f. school.

escuerzo, m. toad.

esculpir, v. carve, sculpture.

escultor, m. sculptor.

escultura, f. sculpture.

escupidera, f. cuspidor.

escupir, v. spit.

escurridor, m. colander, strainer.

escurrir, v. drain off; wring out.

escurrirse, v. slip; sneak away.

ese, esa, dem. a. that.

ése, ésa, dem. pron. that (one).

esencia, f. essence; perfume.

esencial, a. essential.

esencialmente, adv. essentially.

esfera, f. sphere.

esfinge, f. sphinx.

esforzar, v. strengthen.

esforzarse, v. strive, exert oneself.

esfuerzo, m. effort, attempt; vigor.

esgrima, f. fencing.

eslabón, m. link (of a chain).

eslabonar, v. link, join, connect.

eslavo, a. & n. Slavic; Slav.

esmalte, m. enamel. —**esmaltar**, v.

esmerado, a. careful, thorough.

esmeralda, f. emerald.

esmerarse, v. take pains, do one's best.

esmeril, m. emery.

eso, dem. pron. that.

esófago, m. esophagus.

esotérico, a. esoteric.

espacial, a. spatial.

espacio, m. space. —**espaciar**, v.

espaciosidad, f. spaciousness.

espacioso, a. spacious.

espada, f. sword; spade (in cards).

espadarte, m. swordfish.

espalda, f. back.

espaldera, f. espalier.

espantar, v. frighten, scare; scare away.

espanto, m. fright.

espantoso, a. frightening, frightful.

España, f. Spain.

español -ola, a. & n. Spanish; Spaniard.

esparcir, v. scatter, disperse.

espárrago, m. asparagus.

espartano, n. & a. Spartan.

espasmo, m. spasm.

espasmódico, a. spasmodic.

espata, f. spathe.

espato, m. spar (mineral).

espátula, f. spatula.

especia, f. spice. —**especiar**, v.

especial, a. special, especial.

especialidad, f. specialty.

especialista, m. & f. specialist.

especialización, f. specialization.

especialmente, adv. especially.

especie, f. species; sort.

especiería, f. grocery store.

especiero, m. grocer.

especificar, v. specify.

específico, a. specific.

espécimen, m. specimen.

especioso, a. neat; polished; specious.

espectáculo, m. spectacle, show.

espectador -ra, n. spectator.

espectro, m. specter, ghost.

especulación, f. speculation.

especulador, m. speculator.

especular, v. speculate.

especulativo, a. speculative.

espejo, m. mirror.

espelunca, f. dark cave, cavern.

espera, f. wait.

esperanza, f. hope, expectation.

esperar, v. hope; expect; wait, wait for, watch for.

espesar, v. thicken.

espeso, a. thick, dense, bushy.

espesor, m. thickness, density.

espía, m. & f. spy. —**espiar**, v.

espigón, m. bee sting.

espina, f. thorn.

espinaca, f. spinach.

espinal, a. spinal.

espinazo, m. spine.

espineta, f. spinet.

espino, m. briar.

espinoso, a. spiny, thorny.

espión, m. spy.

espionaje, m. espionage.

espiración, f. expiration.

espiral, a. & m. spiral.

espirar, v. expire; breathe, exhale.

espíritu, m. spirit.

espiritual, a. spiritual.

espiritualidad, f. spirituality.

espiritualmente, adv. spiritually.

espita, f. faucet, spigot.
espléndido, a. splendid.
esplendor, m. splendor.
espolear, v. incite, urge on.
espoleta, f. wishbone.
esponja, f. sponge.
esponjoso, a. spongy.
esponsales, m.pl. engagement, betrothal.
esponsalicio, a. nuptial.
espontáneamente, adv. spontaneously.
espontaneidad, f. spontaneity.
espontáneo, a. spontaneous.
espora, f. spore.
esporádico, a. sporadic.
esposa, f. wife.
esposar, v. shackle.
esposo, m. husband.
espuela, f. spur. —espolear, v.
espuma, f. foam. —espumar, v.
espumadera, f. colander.
espumajear, v. foam at the mouth.
espumajo, m. foam.
espumar, v. foam, froth; skim.
espumoso, a. foamy; sparkling (wine).
espurio, a. spurious.
esputar, v. spit, expectorate.
esputo, m. spit, saliva.
esquela, f. note.
esqueleto, m. skeleton.
esquema, m. scheme; diagram.
esquero, m. leather sack or pouch.
esquiciar, v. outline, sketch roughly.
esquicio, m. rough sketch or outline.
esquife, m. skiff.
esquilar, v. fleece, shear.
esquilmo, m. harvest.
esquimal, n. & a. Eskimo.
esquina, f. corner.
esquivar, v. evade, shun.
estabilidad, f. stability.
estable, a. stable.
establecedor, m. founder, originator.
establecer, v. establish, set up.
establecimiento, m. establishment.
establero, m. groom.
establo, m. stable.
estaca, f. stake.
estación, f. station; season.
estacionar, v. station; park (a vehicle).
estacionario, a. stationary.
estadista, m. statesman.
estadística, f. statistics.
estadístico, a. statistical.
estado, m. state; condition; status.
estafa, f. swindle, fake. —estafar, v.
estafeta, f. post office.
estagnación, f. stagnation.
estallar, v. explode; burst; break out.
estallido, m. crash; crack; explosion.
estampa, f. stamp. —estampar, v.

estampado, m. printed cotton cloth.
estampida, f. stampede.
estampilla, f. (postage) stamp.
estancado, a. stagnant.
estancar, v. stanch, stop, check.
estancia, f. stay; (S.A.) small farm.
estanciero -ra, n. small farmer.
estandarte, m. banner.
estanque, m. pool; pond.
estante, m. shelf.
estaño, m. tin. —estañar, v.
estar, v. be; stand; look.
estática, f. static.
estático, a. static.
estatua, f. statue.
estatura, f. stature.
estatuto, m. statute, law.
este, m. east.
este, esta, dem. a. this.
éste, ésta, dem. pron. this (one); the latter.
estelar, a. stellar.
estenografía, f. stenography.
estenógrafo -fa, n. stenographer.
estera, f. mat, matting.
estereofónico, a. stereophonic.
estéril, a. barren; sterile.
esterilidad, f. sterility, fruitlessness.
esterilizar, v. sterilize.
estética, f. esthetics.
estético, a. esthetic.
estetoscopio, m. stethoscope.
estibador, m. stevedore.
estiércol, m. dung, manure.
estigma, m. stigma; disgrace.
estilo, m. style; sort.
estilográfica, f. (fountain) pen.
estima, f. esteem.
estimable, a. estimable, worthy.
estimación, f. estimation.
estimar, v. esteem; value; estimate; gauge.
estimular, v. stimulate.
estímulo, m. stimulus.
estío, m. summer.
estipulación, f. stipulation.
estipular, v. stipulate.
estirar, v. stretch.
estirpe, m. stock, lineage.
esto, dem. pron. this.
estocada, f. stab, thrust.
estofado, m. stew. —estofar, v.
estoicismo, m. stoicism.
estoico, n. & a. stoic.
estómago, m. stomach.
estorbar, v. bother, hinder, interfere with.
estorbo, m. hindrance.
estornudo, m. sneeze. —estornudar, v.
estrabismo, m. strabismus.
estrago, m. devastation, havoc.
estrangulación, f. strangulation.
estrangular, v. strangle.
estratagema, f. stratagem.
estrategia, f. strategy.
estratégico, a. strategic.
estrato, m. stratum.

estrechar, v. tighten; narrow.
estrechez, f. narrowness; tightness.
estrecho, 1. a. narrow, tight. 2. m. strait.
estregar, v. scour, scrub.
estrella, f. star.
estrellamar, f. starfish.
estrellar, v. shatter, smash.
estremecimiento, m. shudder. —estremecerse, v.
estrenar, v. wear for the first time; open (a play).
estreno, m. debut, first performance.
estrenuo, a. strenuous.
estreptococo, m. streptococcus.
estría, f. groove.
estribillo, m. refrain.
estribo, m. stirrup.
estribor, m. starboard.
estrictamente, adv. strictly.
estrictez, f. strictness.
estricto, a. strict.
estrofa, f. stanza.
estropajo, m. mop.
estropear, v. cripple, damage, spoil.
estructura, f. structure.
estructural, a. structural.
estruendo, m. din, clatter.
estuario, m. estuary.
estuco, m. stucco.
estudiante -ta, n. student.
estudiar, v. study.
estudio, m. study; studio.
estudioso, a. studious.
estufa, f. stove.
estulto, a. foolish.
estupendo, a. wonderful, grand, fine.
estupidez, f. stupidity.
estúpido, a. stupid.
estupor, m. stupor.
estuque, m. stucco.
esturión, m. sturgeon.
etapa, f. stage.
éter, m. ether.
etéreo, a. ethereal.
eternal, a. eternal.
eternidad, f. eternity.
eterno, a. eternal.
ética, f. ethics.
ético, a. ethical.
etimología, f. etymology.
etiqueta, f. etiquette; tag, label.
étnico, a. ethnic.
etrusco, n. & a. Etruscan.
eucaristía, f. Eucharist.
eufemismo, m. euphemism.
eufonía, f. euphony.
Europa, f. Europe.
europeo -pea, a. & n. European.
eutanasia, f. euthanasia.
evacuación, f. evacuation.
evacuar, v. evacuate.
evadir, v. evade.
evangélico, a. evangelical.
evangelio, m. gospel.
evangelista, m. evangelist.
evaporación, f. evaporation.
evaporarse, v. evaporate.

evasión, f. evasion.
evasivamente, adv. evasively.
evasivo, a. evasive.
evento, m. event, occurrence.
eventual, a. eventual.
eventualidad, f. eventuality.
evicción, f. eviction.
evidencia, f. evidence.
evidenciar, v. prove, show.
evidente, a. evident.
evitación, f. avoidance.
evitar, v. avoid, shun.
evocación, f. evocation.
evocar, v. evoke.
evolución, f. evolution.
exacerbar, v. irritate deeply.
exactamente, adv. exactly.
exactitud, f. precision, accuracy.
exacto, a. exact, accurate.
exageración, f. exaggeration.
exagerar, v. exaggerate.
exagonal, a. hexagonal.
exaltación, f. exaltation.
exaltamiento, m. exaltation.
exaltar, v. exalt.
examen, m. test, examination.
examinar, v. test, examine.
exánime, a. spiritless, weak.
exasperación, f. exasperation.
exasperar, v. exasperate.
excavación, f. excavation.
excavar, v. excavate.
exceder, v. exceed, surpass; outrun.
excelencia, f. excellence.
excelente, a. excellent.
excéntrico, a. eccentric.
excepción, f. exception.
excepcional, a. exceptional.
excepto, prep. except, except for.
exceptuar, v. except.
excesivamente, adv. excessively.
excesivo, a. excessive.
exceso, m. excess.
excitabilidad, f. excitability.
excitación, f. excitement.
excitar, v. excite.
exclamación, f. exclamation.
exclamar, v. exclaim.
excluir, v. exclude, bar, shut out.
exclusión, f. exclusion.
exclusivamente, adv. exclusively.
exclusivo, a. exclusive.
excomulgar, v. excommunicate.
excomunión, f. excommunication.
excreción, f. excretion.
excremento, m. excrement.
excretar, v. excrete.
exculpar, v. exonerate.
excursión, f. excursion.
excursionista, n. excursionist.
excusa, f. excuse. —excusar, v.
excusado, m. toilet.
excusarse, v. apologize.
exención, f. exemption.
exento, a. exempt. —exentar, v.
exhalación, f. exhalation.

exhalar, v. exhale, breathe out.
exhausto, a. exhausted.
exhibición, f. exhibit, exhibition.
exhibir, v. exhibit, display.
exhortación, f. exhortation.
exhortar, v. exhort, admonish.
exhumación, f. exhumation.
exhumar, v. exhume.
exigencia, f. requirement, demand.
exigente, a. exacting, demanding.
exigir, v. require, exact, demand.
eximir, v. exempt.
existencia, f. existence; (econ.) supply.
existente, a. existent.
existir, v. exist.
éxito, m. success.
éxodo, m. exodus.
exoneración, f. exoneration.
exonerar, v. exonerate, acquit.
exorar, v. beg, implore.
exorbitancia, f. exorbitance.
exorbitante, a. exorbitant.
exorcismo, m. exorcism.
exornar, v. adorn, decorate.
exótico, a. exotic.
expansibilidad, f. expansibility.
expansión, f. expansion.
expansivo, a. expansive; effusive.
expatriación, f. expatriation.
expatriar, v. expatriate.
expectación, f. expectation.
expectorar, v. expectorate.
expedición, f. expedition.
expediente, m. expedient, means.
expedir, v. send off, ship; expedite.
expeditivo, a. speedy, prompt.
expedito, a. speedy, prompt.
expeler, v. expel, eject.
expendedor, m. dealer.
expender, v. expend.
expensas, f.pl. expenses, costs.
experiencia, f. experience.
experimentado, a. experienced.
experimental, a. experimental.
experimentar, v. experience.
experimento, m. experiment.
expertamente, adv. expertly.
experto, a. & m. expert.
expiación, f. atonement.
expiar, v. atone for.
expiración, f. expiration.
expirar, v. expire.
explanación, f. explanation.
explanar, v. make level.
expletivo, n. & a. expletive.
explicable, a. explicable.
explicación, f. explanation.
explicar, v. explain.
explicativo, a. explanatory.
explícitamente, adv. explicitly.
explícito, adj. explicit.
exploración, f. exploration.
explorador, m. explorer; scout.
explorar, v. explore; scout.
exploratorio, a. exploratory.

explosión, f. explosion; outburst.
explosivo, a. explosive.
explotación, f. exploitation.
explotar, v. exploit.
exponer, v. expose; set forth.
exportación, f. exportation; export.
exportador, m. exporter.
exportar, v. export.
exposición, f. exhibit; exposition; exposure.
expósito, n. foundling; orphan.
expresado, a. aforesaid.
expresamente, adv. clearly, explicitly.
expresar, v. express.
expresión, f. expression.
expresivo, a. expressive; affectionate.
expreso, a. & m. express.
exprimir, v. squeeze.
expropiación, f. expropriation.
expropiar, v. expropriate.
expulsar, v. expel, eject; evict.
expulsión, f. expulsion.
expurgación, f. expurgation.
expurgar, v. expurgate.
exquisitamente, adv. exquisitely.
exquisito, a. exquisite.
éxtasi, m. ecstasy.
extemporáneo, a. extemporaneous, impromptu.
extender, v. extend; spread; widen; stretch.
extensamente, adv. extensively.
extensión, f. extension, spread, expanse.
extenso, a. extensive, widespread.
extenuación, f. weakening; emaciation.
extenuar, v. extenuate.
exterior, a. & m. exterior; foreign.
exterminar, v. exterminate.
exterminio, m. extermination, ruin.
extinción, f. extinction.
extinguir, v. extinguish.
extinto, a. extinct.
extintor, m. fire extinguisher.
extirpar, v. eradicate.
extorsión, f. extortion.
extra, n. extra.
extracción, f. extraction.
extractar, v. summarize.
extracto, m. extract; summary.
extradición, f. extradition.
extraer, v. extract.
extranjero -ra, 1. a. foreign. 2. n. foreigner; stranger.
extrañar, v. surprise; miss.
extraño, a. strange, queer.
extraordinariamente, adv. extraordinarily.
extraordinario, a. extraordinary.
extravagancia, f. extravagance.
extravagante, a. extravagant.
extraviado, a. lost, misplaced.
extraviarse, v. stray, get lost.

extravío, *m.* aberration, deviation.

extremadamente, *adv.* extremely.

extremado, *a.* extreme.

extremaunción, *f.* extreme unction.

extremidad, *f.* extremity.

extremista, *n. & a.* extremist.

extremo, *a. & m.* extreme, end.

extrínseco, *a.* extrinsic.

exuberancia, *f.* exuberance.

exuberante, *a.* exuberant.

exudación, *f.* exudation.

exudar, *v.* exude, ooze.

exultación, *f.* exultation.

F

fábrica, *f.* factory.

fabricación, *f.* manufacture, manufacturing.

fabricante, *m.* manufacturer, maker.

fabricar, *v.* manufacture, make.

fabril, *a.* making, building.

fábula, *f.* fable, myth.

fabuloso, *a.* fabulous.

facción, *f.* faction, party; (*pl.*) features.

faccioso, *a.* factious.

fácil, *a.* easy.

facilidad, *f.* facility, ease.

facilitar, *v.* facilitate, make easy.

fácilmente, *adv.* easily.

facsímil, *m.* facsimile.

factible, *a.* feasible.

factor, *m.* factor.

factótum, *m.* factotum; jack of all trades.

factura, *f.* invoice, bill.

facturar, *v.* check (baggage).

facultad, *f.* faculty; ability.

facultativo, *a.* optional.

fachada, *f.* façade, front.

faena, *f.* task; work.

faja, *f.* band; sash; zone.

falacia, *f.* fallacy; deceitfulness.

falda, *f.* skirt; lap.

falibilidad, *f.* fallibility.

falsear, *v.* falsify, counterfeit; forge.

falsedad, *f.* falsehood; lie; falseness.

falsificación, *f.* falsification; forgery.

falsificar, *v.* falsify, counterfeit, forge.

falso, *a.* false; wrong.

falta, *f.* error, mistake; fault; lack. hacer f., to be lacking, to be necessary. sin f., without fail.

faltar, *v.* be lacking, be missing; be absent.

faltriquera, *f.* pocket.

falla, *f.* failure, fault.

fallar, *v.* fail.

fallecer, *v.* pass away, die.

fallo, *m.* verdict.

fama, *f.* fame; reputation; glory.

familia, *f.* family; household.

familiar, *a.* familiar; domestic; (of) family.

familiaridad, *f.* familiarity, intimacy.

familiarizar, *v.* familiarize, acquaint.

famoso, *a.* famous.

fanal, *m.* lighthouse; lantern, lamp.

fanático -ca, *a. & n.* fanatic.

fanatismo, *m.* fanaticism.

fanfarria, *f.* bluster. —fanfarrear, *v.*

fango, *m.* mud.

fantasía, *f.* fantasy; fancy, whim.

fantasma, *m.* phantom; ghost.

fantástico, *a.* fantastic.

faquín, *m.* porter.

faquir, *m.* fakir.

farallón, *m.* cliff.

Faraón, *m.* Pharaoh.

fardel, *m.* bag; package.

fardo, *m.* bundle.

farináceo, *a.* farinaceous.

faringe, *f.* pharynx.

fariseo, *m.* pharisee, hypocrite.

farmacéutico, *m.* pharmacist.

farmacia, *f.* pharmacy.

faro, *m.* beacon; lighthouse; headlight.

farol, *m.* lantern; (street) light.

farra, *f.* spree.

fárrago, *m.* medley; hodge-podge.

farsa, *f.* farce.

fascinación, *f.* fascination.

fascinar, *v.* fascinate, bewitch.

fase, *f.* phase.

fastidiar, *v.* disgust; irk, annoy.

fastidio, *m.* disgust; annoyance.

fastidioso, *a.* annoying; tedious.

fatal, *a.* fatal.

fatalidad, *f.* fate; calamity, bad luck.

fatalismo, *m.* fatalism.

fatalista, *n. & a.* fatalist.

fatiga, *f.* fatigue. —fatigar, *v.*

fauno, *m.* faun.

favor, *m.* favor; behalf. por f., please.

favorable, *a.* favorable.

favorablemente, *adv.* favorably.

favorecer, *v.* favor; flatter.

favoritismo, *m.* favoritism.

favorito -ta, *a. & n.* favorite.

faz, *f.* face.

fe, *f.* faith.

fealdad, *f.* ugliness, homeliness.

febrero, *m.* February.

febril, *a.* feverish.

fécula, *f.* starch.

fecundar, *v.* fertilize.

fecundidad, *f.* fecundity, fertility.

fecundo, *a.* fecund, fertile.

fecha, *f.* date. —fechar, *v.*

federación, *f.* confederacy.

federal, *a.* federal.

felicidad, *f.* happiness; bliss.

felicitación, *f.* congratulation.

felicitar, *v.* congratulate; compliment.

feligrés -esa, *n.* parishioner.

feliz, *a.* happy; fortunate.

felonía, *f.* felony.

felón, *m.* felon.

felpa, *f.* plush.

felpudo, *m.* doormat.

femenino, *a.* feminine.

feminismo, *m.* feminism.

feminista, *n.* feminist.

fenecer, *v.* conclude; die.

fénix, *m.* phoenix; model.

fenomenal, *a.* phenomenal.

fenómeno, *m.* phenomenon.

feo, *a.* ugly, homely.

feracidad, *f.* feracity, fertility.

feraz, *a.* fertile, fruitful; copious.

feria, *f.* fair; market.

feriado, *a.* día f., holiday.

fermentación, *f.* fermentation.

fermento, *m.* ferment. —fermentar, *v.*

ferocidad, *f.* ferocity, fierceness.

feroz, *a.* ferocious, fierce.

férreo, *a.* of iron.

ferrería, *f.* ironworks.

ferretería, *f.* hardware; hardware store.

ferrocarril, *m.* railroad.

fértil, *a.* fertile.

fertilidad, *f.* fertility.

fertilizar, *v.* fertilize.

férvido, *a.* fervid, ardent.

ferviente, *a.* fervent.

fervor, *m.* fervor, zeal.

fervoroso, *a.* zealous, eager.

festejar, *v.* entertain, fete.

festejo, *m.* feast.

festín, *m.* feast.

festividad, *f.* festivity.

festivo, *a.* festive.

fétido, *adj.* fetid.

feudal, *a.* feudal.

feudo, *m.* feud.

fiado, *adj.* on trust, on credit.

fianza, *f.* bail.

fiar, *v.* trust, sell on credit; give credit.

fiarse de, *v.* trust (in), rely on.

fiasco, *m.* fiasco.

fibra, *f.* fiber; vigor.

fibroso, *a.* fibrous.

ficción, *f.* fiction.

ficticio, *a.* fictitious.

ficha, *f.* slip, card; chip.

fidedigno, *a.* trustworthy.

fideicomisario, *m.* trustee.

fideicomiso, *m.* trust.

fidelidad, *f.* fidelity.

fideo, *m.* noodle.

fiebre, *f.* fever.

fiel, *a.* faithful.

fieltro, *m.* felt.

fiera, *f.* wild animal.

fiereza, *f.* fierceness, wildness.

fiero, *a.* fierce; wild.

fiesta, *f.* festival, feast; party.

figura, *f.* figure. —figurar, *v.*

figurarse, *v.* imagine.

figurón, *m.* dummy.

fijar, *v.* fix; set, establish; post.

fijarse en, *v.* notice.

fijeza, *f.* firmness.

fijo, *a.* fixed, stationary, permanent, set.

fila, *f.* row, rank, file, line.

filantropía, *f.* philanthropy.

filete, *m.* fillet.

film, *m.* film. —**filmar,** *v.*

filo, *m.* (cutting) edge.

filón, *m.* vein (of ore).

filosofía, *f.* philosophy.

filosófico, *a.* philosophical.

filósofo, *m.* philosopher.

filtro, *m.* filter. —**filtrar,** *v.*

fin, *m.* end, purpose, goal. **a f. de que,** in order that. **en f.,** in short. **por f.,** finally, at last.

final, 1. *a.* final. 2. *m.* end.

finalidad, *f.* finality.

finalmente, *adv.* at last.

financiero, 1. *a.* financial. 2. *m.* financier.

finca, *f.* real estate; estate; farm.

finés, *a.* Finnish.

fineza, *f.* courtesy, politeness; fineness.

fingimiento, *m.* pretense.

fingir, *v.* feign, pretend.

fino, *a.* fine; polite, courteous.

firma, *f.* signature; (com.) firm.

firmamento, *m.* firmament, heavens.

firmar, *v.* sign.

firme, *a.* firm, fast, steady, sound.

firmemente, *adv.* firmly.

firmeza, *f.* firmness.

fisco, *m.* exchequer, treasury.

física, *f.* physics.

físico, *a. & n.* physical; physicist.

fisiología, *f.* physiology.

fláccido, *a.* flaccid, soft.

flaco, *a.* thin, gaunt.

flagelación, *f.* flagellation.

flagelar, *v.* flagellate, whip.

flagrancia, *f.* flagrancy.

flagrante, *a.* flagrant.

flama, *f.* flame; ardor, zeal.

flamante, *a.* flaming.

flamenco, *m.* flamingo.

flan, *m.* custard.

flanco, *m.* side; (mil.) flank.

flanquear, *v.* flank.

flaqueza, *f.* thinness; weakness.

fisura, *f.* flute.

flautín, *m.* piccolo.

flautista, *m. & f.* flutist, piper.

fleco, *m.* fringe; flounce.

flecha, *f.* arrow.

flechero, *m.* archer.

flema, *f.* phlegm.

flete, *m.* freight. —**fletar,** *v.*

flexibilidad, *f.* flexibility.

flexible, *a.* flexible, pliable.

flirtear, *v.* flirt.

flojo, *a.* limp; loose, flabby, slack.

flor, *f.* flower; compliment.

flora, *f.* flora.

floral, *a.* floral.

florecer, *v.* flower, bloom; flourish.

floreo, *m.* flourish.

florero, *m.* flower pot; vase.

floresta, *f.* forest.

florido, *a.* flowery; flowering.

florista, *m. & f.* florist.

flota, *f.* fleet.

flotante, *a.* floating.

flotar, *v.* float.

flotilla, *f.* flotilla, fleet.

fluctuación, *f.* fluctuation.

fluctuar, *v.* fluctuate.

fluente, *a.* fluent.

fluidez, *f.* fluency.

flúido, *a. & m.* fluid, liquid.

fluir, *v.* flow.

flujo, *m.* flow, flux.

flúor, *m.* fluorine.

fluorescencia, *f.* fluorescence.

fluorescente, *a.* fluorescent.

fobia, *f.* phobia.

foca, *f.* seal.

foco, *m.* focus, center.

fogata, *f.* bonfire.

fogón, *m.* hearth, fireplace.

fogosidad, *f.* vehemence, ardor.

fogoso, *a.* vehement, ardent.

folklore, *m.* folklore.

follaje, *m.* foliage.

folleto, *m.* pamphlet, booklet.

fomentar, *v.* develop, promote, further, foster.

fomento, *m.* fomentation.

fonda, *f.* eating house, inn.

fondo, *m.* bottom; back (part); background; (pl.) funds; finances. **a f.,** thoroughly.

fonética, *f.* phonetics.

fonético, *a.* phonetic.

fonógrafo, *m.* phonograph.

forastero -ra, 1. *a.* foreign, exotic. 2. *n.* stranger.

forjar, *v.* forge.

forma, *f.* form, shape. —**formar,** *v.*

formación, *f.* formation.

formal, *a.* formal.

formaldehído, *m.* formaldehyde.

formalidad, *f.* formality.

formalizar, *v.* finalize; formulate.

formidable, *a.* formidable.

formidablemente, *adv.* formidably.

formón, *m.* chisel.

fórmula, *f.* formula.

formular, *v.* formulate, draw up.

formulario, *m.* form.

foro, *m.* forum.

forraje, *m.* forage, fodder.

forrar, *v.* line.

forro, *m.* lining.

fortalecer, *v.* fortify.

fortaleza, *f.* fort, fortress; fortitude.

fortificación, *f.* fortification.

fortitud, *f.* fortitude.

fortuitamente, *adv.* fortuitously.

fortuito, *a.* fortuitous.

fortuna, *f.* fortune; luck.

forúnculo, *m.* boil.

forzar, *v.* force, compel, coerce.

forzosamente, *adv.* compulsorily; forcibly.

forzoso, *a.* compulsory; necessary. **paro f.,** unemployment.

forzudo, *a.* powerful, vigorous.

fosa, *f.* grave.

fósforo, *m.* match; phosphorus.

fósil, *m.* fossil.

foso, *m.* ditch, trench; moat.

fotocopiadora, *f.* photocopier.

fotografía, *f.* photograph. —**fotografiar,** *v.*

frac, *m.* dress coat.

fracasar, *v.* fail.

fracaso, *m.* failure.

fracción, *f.* fraction.

fractura, *f.* fracture, break.

fragancia, *f.* fragrance; perfume; aroma.

fragante, *a.* fragrant.

frágil, *a.* fragile, breakable.

fragilidad, *f.* fragility.

fragmentario, *a.* fragmentary.

fragmento, *m.* fragment, bit.

fragor, *m.* noise, clamor.

fragoso, *a.* noisy.

fragua, *f.* forge. —**fraguar,** *v.*

fraile, *m.* monk.

frambuesa, *f.* raspberry.

francamente, *adv.* frankly, candidly.

francés, -esa, *a. & n.* French; Frenchman.

Francia, *f.* France.

franco, *a.* frank.

franela, *f.* flannel.

frangible, *a.* breakable.

franqueo, *m.* postage.

franqueza, *f.* frankness.

franquicia, *f.* franchise.

frasco, *m.* flask, bottle.

frase, *f.* phrase; sentence.

fraseología, *f.* phraseology; style.

fraternal, *a.* fraternal, brotherly.

fraternidad, *f.* fraternity, brotherhood.

fraude, *m.* fraud.

fraudulento, *a.* fraudulent.

frazada, *f.* blanket.

frecuencia, *f.* frequency.

frecuente, *a.* frequent.

frecuentemente, *adv.* frequently, often.

fregadero, *m.* sink.

fregadura, *f.* scouring, scrubbing.

fregar, *v.* scour, scrub, mop.

freír, *v.* fry.

fréjol, *m.* kidney bean.

frenesí, *m.* frenzy.

frenéticamente, *adv.* frantically.

frenético, *a.* frantic, frenzied.

freno, *m.* brake. —**frenar,** *v.*

frente, 1. *f.* forehead. 2. *m.* front. **en f., al f.,** opposite, across. **f. a,** in front of.

fresa, *f.* strawberry.

fresca, *f.* fresh, cool air.

fresco, a. fresh; cool; crisp.

frescura, f. coolness, freshness.

fresno, m. ash tree.

fresquería, f. soda fountain.

friabilidad, f. brittleness.

friable, a. brittle.

frialdad, f. coldness.

friamente, adv. coldly; coolly.

fricandó, m. fricandeau.

fricar, v. rub together.

fricción, f. friction.

friccionar, v. rub.

friega, f. friction.

frigidez, f. frigidity.

frígido, a. frigid.

frijol, m. bean.

frío, a. & n. cold. tener f., to be cold, feel cold. hacer f., to be cold (weather).

friolento, friolero, a. chilly; sensitive to cold.

friolera, f. trifle, trinket.

friso, m. frieze.

fritillas, f.pl. fritters.

frito, a. fried.

fritura, f. fritter.

frívolamente, adv. frivolously.

frivolidad, f. frivolity.

frívolo, a. frivolous.

frondoso, a. leafy.

frontera, f. frontier; border.

frotar, v. rub.

fructífero, a. fruitful.

fructificar, v. bear fruit.

fructuosamente, adv. fruitfully.

fructuoso, a. fruitful.

frugal, a. frugal, thrifty.

frugalidad, f. frugality; thrift.

frugalmente, adv. frugally, thriftily.

fruncir, v. gather, contract. f. el entrecejo, frown.

fruslería, f. trinket.

frustrar, v. frustrate, thwart.

fruta, f. fruit.

fruto, m. fruit; product; profit.

fucsia, f. fuchsia.

fuego, m. fire.

fuelle, m. bellows.

fuente, f. fountain; source; platter.

fuera, adv. without, outside.

fuero, m. statute.

fuerte, 1. a. strong; loud. 2. m. fort.

fuertemente, adv. strongly; loudly.

fuerza, f. force, strength.

fuga, f. flight, escape.

fugarse, v. flee, escape.

fugaz, a. fugitive, passing.

fugitivo -va, a. & n. fugitive.

fulcro, m. fulcrum.

fulgor, m. gleam, glow. —fulgurar, v.

fulminante, a. explosive.

fumador, m. smoker.

fumar, v. smoke.

fumigación, f. fumigation.

fumigador, m. fumigator.

fumigar, v. fumigate.

fumoso, a. smoky.

función, f. function; performance, show.

funcionar, v. function, work, run.

funcionario, m. official, functionary.

funda, f. case, sheath, slip-cover.

fundación, f. foundation.

fundador -ra, n. founder.

fundamental, a. fundamental, basic.

fundamentalmente, adv. fundamentally.

fundamento, m. base, basis, foundation.

fundar, v. found, establish.

fundición, f. foundry; melting, meltdown.

fundir, v. fuse; smelt.

fúnebre, a. dismal.

funeral, m. funeral.

funestamente, adv. sadly.

fungo, m. fungus.

furente, a. furious, enraged.

furia, f. fury.

furiosamente, adv. furiously.

furioso, a. furious.

furor, m. furor; fury.

furtivamente, adv. furtively.

furtivo, a. furtive, sly.

furúnculo, m. boil.

fusibilidad, f. fusibility.

fusible, m. fuse.

fusil, m. rifle, gun.

fusilar, v. shoot.

fusión, f. fusion; merger.

fusionar, v. unite, fuse, merge.

fútbol, m. football, soccer.

fútil, a. trivial.

futilidad, f. triviality.

futuro, a. & m. future.

futurología, f. futurology.

G

gabán, m. overcoat.

gabinete, m. closet; cabinet; study.

gacela, f. gazelle.

gaceta, f. gazette, newspaper.

gacetilla, f. personal news section of a newspaper.

gaélico, a. Gaelic.

gafas, f.pl. eyeglasses.

gaguear, v. stutter, stammer.

gaita, f. bagpipe.

gaje, m. salary; fee.

gala, f. gala, ceremony; (pl.) regalia. tener a g., be proud of.

galán, m. gallant.

galano, a. stylishly dressed; elegant.

galante, a. gallant.

galantería, f. gallantry, compliment.

galápago, m. fresh-water turtle.

galardón, m. prize; reward.

gáleo, m. swordfish.

galera, f. wagon; shed.

galería, f. gallery, (theat.) balcony.

galés, n. & a. Welsh.

galgo, m. greyhound.

galillo, m. uvula.

galocha, f. galosh.

galón, m. gallon; (mil.) stripe.

galope, m. gallop. —galopar, v.

gallardete, m. pennant.

galleta, f. cracker.

gallina, f. hen.

gallinero, m. chicken coop.

gallo, m. rooster.

gambito, m. gambit.

gamuza, f. chamois.

gana, f. desire, wish, mind (to). de buena g., willingly. tener ganas de, to feel like.

ganado, m. cattle.

ganador -ra, n. winner.

ganancia, f. gain, profit; (pl.) earnings.

ganapán, m. drudge.

ganar, v. earn; win; beat.

gancho, m. hook, hanger, clip, hairpin.

gandul -la, n. idler, tramp, hobo.

ganga, f. bargain.

gangrena, f. gangrene.

gansarón, m. gosling.

ganso, m. goose.

garabato, m. hook; scrawl, scribble.

garaje, m. garage.

garantía, f. guarantee; collateral, security.

garantizar, v. guarantee, secure, pledge.

garbanzo, m. chickpea.

garbo, m. grace.

garboso, a. graceful, sprightly.

gardenia, f. gardenia.

garfa, f. claw, talon.

garganta, f. throat.

gárgara, f. gargle. —gargarizar, v.

garita, f. sentry box.

garito, m. gambling house.

garlopa, f. carpenter's plane.

garra, f. claw.

garrafa, f. decanter, carafe.

garrideza, f. elegance, handsomeness.

garrido, a. elegant, handsome.

garrote, m. club, cudgel.

garrotillo, m. croup.

garrudo, a. powerful, brawny.

garza, f. heron.

gas, m. gas.

gasa, f. gauze.

gaseosa, f. carbonated water.

gaseoso, a. gaseous.

gasolina, f. gasoline.

gastar, v. spend; use up, wear out; waste.

gastritis, f. gastritis.

gastrómano, m. glutton.

gastrónomo -ma, n. gourmet, epicure.

gatear, v. creep.

gatillo, m. trigger.

gato -ta, n. cat.

gaucho, m. Argentine cowboy.

gaveta, f. drawer.

gavilla, f. sheaf.

gaviota, f. sea gull.

gayo, a. merry, gay.

gazapera, f. rabbit warren.

gazapo, *m.* rabbit.
gazmonado, *f.* prudishness.
gazmoño, *m.* prude.
gaznate, *m.* windpipe.
gelatina, *f.* gelatine.
gemelo -la, *n.* twin.
gemelos, *m.pl.* cuff links; opera glasses.
gemido, *m.* moan, groan, wail. —gemir, *v.*
genciana, *f.* gentian.
genealogía, *f.* genealogy, pedigree.
generación, *f.* generation.
generador, *m.* generator.
general, *a. & m.* general.
generalidad, *f.* generality.
generalización, *f.* generalization.
generalizar, *v.* generalize.
generalmente, *adv.* generally.
género, *m.* gender; kind; *(pl.)* goods, material.
generosidad, *f.* generosity.
generoso, *a.* generous.
génesis, *m.* genesis.
genial, *a.* genial; brilliant.
genio, *m.* genius; temper; disposition.
genitivo, *m.* genitive.
gente, *f.* people, folk.
gentil, *a.* gracious; graceful.
gentileza, *f.* grace, graciousness.
gentío, *m.* mob, crowd.
genuino, *a.* genuine.
geografía, *f.* geography.
geográfico, *a.* geographical.
geométrico, *a.* geometric.
geranio, *m.* geranium.
gerencia, *f.* management.
gerente, *m.* manager, director.
germen, *m.* germ.
germinar, *v.* germinate.
gerundio, *m.* gerund.
gesticulación, *f.* gesticulation.
gesticular, *v.* gesticulate, gesture.
gestión, *f.* conduct; effort.
gesto, *m.* gesture, facial expression.
gigante, *a. & m.* gigantic, giant.
gigantesco, *a.* gigantic, huge.
gimnasio, *m.* gymnasium.
gimnástica, *f.* gymnastics.
gimotear, *v.* whine.
ginebra, *f.* gin.
girado, *m.* (com.) drawee.
girador, *m.* (com.) drawer.
girar, *v.* revolve, turn, spin, whirl.
giratorio, *a.* rotary, revolving.
giro, *m.* whirl, turn, spin; (com.) draft. **g. postal,** money order.
gitano -na, *a. & n.* Gypsy.
glacial, *a.* glacial, icy.
gladiador, *m.* gladiator.
glándula, *f.* gland.
glasé, *m.* glacé.
glicerina, *f.* glycerine.
globo, *m.* globe; balloon.
gloria, *f.* glory.
glorieta, *f.* bower.

glorificación, *f.* glorification.
glorificar, *v.* glorify.
glorioso, *a.* glorious.
glosa, *f.* gloss. —glosar, *v.*
glosario, *m.* glossary.
glotón -ona, *a. & n.* gluttonous; glutton.
glutin, *m.* gluten; glue.
gobernación, *f.* government.
gobernador, *m.* governor.
gobernalle, *m.* rudder, tiller, helm.
gobernante, *m.* ruler.
gobernar, *v.* govern.
gobierno, *m.* government.
goce, *m.* enjoyment.
gola, *f.* throat.
golfo, *m.* gulf.
golondrina, *f.* swallow.
golosina, *f.* delicacy.
golpe, *m.* blow, stroke. **de g.,** suddenly.
golpear, *v.* strike, beat, pound.
gollete, *m.* upper portion of one's throat.
goma, *f.* rubber; gum; glue; eraser.
gonce, *m.* hinge.
góndola, *f.* gondola.
gordo, *a.* fat.
gordura, *f.* fatness.
gorila, *m.* gorilla.
gorja, *f.* gorge.
gorjeo, *m.* warble, chirp. —gorjear, *v.*
gorrión, *m.* sparrow.
gorro, *m.* cap.
gota, *f.* drop (of liquid).
gotear, *v.* drip, leak.
goteo, *m.* leak.
gotera, *f.* leak; gutter.
gótico, *a.* Gothic.
gozar, *v.* enjoy.
gozne, *m.* hinge.
gozo, *m.* enjoyment, delight, joy.
gozoso, *a.* joyful, joyous.
grabado, *m.* engraving, cut, print.
grabador, *m.* engraver.
grabar, *v.* engrave; record.
gracia, *f.* grace; wit, charm. **hacer g.,** to amuse, strike as funny. **tener g.,** to be funny, to be witty.
gracias, *f.pl.* thanks, thank you.
gracioso, *a.* witty, funny.
grada, *f.* step.
gradación, *f.* gradation.
grado, *m.* grade; rank; degree.
graduado -da, *m.* graduate.
gradual, *a.* gradual.
graduar, *v.* grade, graduate.
gráfico, *a.* graphic, vivid.
grafito, *m.* graphite.
grajo, *m.* jackdaw.
gramática, *f.* grammar.
gramo, *m.* gram.
gran, grande, *a.* big, large; great.
granada, *f.* grenade; pomegranate.
granar, *v.* seed.
grandeza, *f.* greatness.

grandiosidad, *f.* grandeur.
grandioso, *a.* grand, magnificent.
grandor, *m.* size.
granero, *m.* barn; granary.
granito, *m.* granite.
granizada, *f.* hailstorm.
granizo, *m.* hail. —granizar, *v.*
granja, *f.* grange; farm; farmhouse.
granjear, *v.* earn, gain; get.
granjero, *m.* farmer.
grano, *m.* grain; kernel.
granuja, *m.* waif, urchin.
grapa, *f.* clamp, clip.
grasa, *f.* grease, fat.
grasiento, *a.* greasy.
gratificación, *f.* gratification; reward; tip.
gratificar, *v.* gratify; reward; tip.
gratis, *adv.* gratis, free.
gratitud, *f.* gratitude.
grato, *a.* grateful; pleasant.
gratuito, *a.* gratuitous.
gravamen, *m.* tax; burden; obligation.
grave, *a.* grave, serious, severe.
gravedad, *f.* gravity, seriousness.
gravitación, *f.* gravitation.
gravitar, *v.* gravitate.
gravoso, *a.* burdensome.
graznido, *m.* croak. —graznar, *v.*
Grecia, *f.* Greece.
greco, *a. & n.* Greek.
greda, *f.* clay.
gresca, *f.* revelry; quarrel.
griego -ga, *a. & n.* Greek.
grieta, *f.* opening; crevice, crack.
grifo, *m.* faucet.
grillo, *m.* cricket.
grima, *f.* fright.
gringo -ga, *n.* foreigner (usually North American).
gripa, gripe, *f.* grippe.
gris, *a.* gray.
grito, *m.* shout, scream, cry. —gritar, *v.*
grosella, *f.* currant.
grosería, *f.* grossness; coarseness.
grosero, *a.* coarse, vulgar, discourteous.
grotesco, *a.* grotesque.
grúa, *f.* crane.
gruesa, *f.* gross.
grueso, 1. *a.* bulky; stout; coarse, thick. **2.** *m.* bulk.
grulla, *f.* crane.
gruñido, *m.* growl, snarl, mutter. —gruñir, *v.*
grupo, *m.* group, party.
gruta, *f.* cavern.
guadaña, *f.* scythe. —guadañar, *v.*
guagua, *f.* (S.A.) baby; (Carib.) bus.
gualdo, *m.* yellow, golden.
guano, *m.* guano (fertilizer).
guante, *m.* glove.
guapo, *a.* handsome.
guarda, *m. or f.* guard.

guardabarros, *m.* fender.

guardacostas, *m.* revenue ship.

guardar, *v.* keep, store, put away; guard.

guardarropa, *f.* coat room.

guardarse de, *v.* beware of, avoid.

guardia, l. *f.* guard; watch. 2. *m.* policeman.

guardián, *m.* guardian, keeper, watchman.

guardilla, *f.* attic.

guarida, *f.* den.

guarismo, *m.* number, figure.

guarnecer, *v.* adorn.

guarnición, *f.* garrison; trimming.

guasa, *f.* joke, jest.

guayaba, *f.* guava.

gubernativo, *a.* governmental.

guerra, *f.* war.

guerrero, *m.* warrior.

guía, l. *m. & f.* guide. 2. *f.* guidebook, directory.

guiar, *v.* guide; steer, drive.

guija, *f.* pebble.

guillotina, *f.* guillotine.

guindar, *v.* hang.

guinga, *f.* gingham.

guiñada, *f.*, guiño, *m.* wink. — guiñar, *v.*

guión, *m.* dash, hyphen.

guirnalda, *f.* garland, wreath.

guisa, *f.* guise, manner.

guisado, *m.* stew.

guisante, *m.* pea.

guisar, *v.* cook.

guita, *f.* twine.

guitarra, *f.* guitar.

guitarrista, *n.* guitarist.

gula, *f.* gluttony.

gurú, *m.* guru.

gusano, *m.* worm, caterpillar.

gustar, *v.* please; taste.

gusto, *m.* pleasure; taste; liking.

gustoso, *a.* pleasant, tasteful.

gutural, *a.* guttural.

H

haba, *f.* bean.

habanera, *f.* Cuban dance melody.

haber, *v.* have. **h. de,** be to, be supposed to.

haberes, *m.pl.* property; worldly goods.

habichuela, *f.* bean.

hábil, *a.* skillful; capable; clever.

habilidad, *f.* ability; skill; talent.

habilidoso, *a.* able, skillful, talented.

habilitado, *m.* paymaster.

habilitar, *v.* qualify; supply, equip.

hábilmente, *adv.* ably.

habitación, *f.* dwelling; room.

habitante, *m. & f.* inhabitant.

habitar, *v.* inhabit; dwell.

hábito, *m.* habit; custom.

habitual, *a.* habitual.

habituar, *v.* accustom, habituate.

habla, *f.* speech.

hablador, *a.* talkative.

hablar, *v.* talk, speak.

haca, *f.* pony.

hacedor, *m.* maker.

hacendado, *m.* hacienda owner; farmer.

hacendoso, *a.* industrious.

hacer, *v.* do; make. **hace dos años,** etc., two years ago, etc.

hacerse, *v.* become, get to be.

hacia, *prep.* toward.

hacienda, *f.* property; estate; ranch; farm; (govt.) treasury.

hacha, *f.* ax, hatchet.

hada, *f.* fairy.

hado, *m.* fate.

halagar, *v.* flatter.

halar, *v.* haul, pull.

halcón, *m.* hawk, falcon.

haleche, *m.* anchovy.

hallado, *a.* found. **bien h.,** welcome. **mal h.,** uneasy.

hallar, *v.* find, locate.

hallarse, *v.* be located; happen to be.

hallazgo, *m.* find, thing found.

hamaca, *f.* hammock.

hambre, *f.* hunger. **tener h.,** estar con **h.,** to be hungry.

hambrear, *v.* hunger; starve.

hambriento, *a.* starving, hungry.

haragán, *m.* idler, lazy person.

haraganear, *v.* loiter.

harapo, *m.* rag, tatter.

haraposo, *a.* ragged, shabby.

harem, *m.* harem.

harina, *f.* flour, meal.

harnero, *m.* sieve.

hartar, *v.* satiate.

harto, *a.* stuffed; fed up.

hartura, *f.* superabundance, glut.

hasta, l. *prep.* until, till; as far as, up to. **h. luego,** good-bye, so long. 2. *adv.* even.

hastío, *m.* distaste, loathing.

hato, *m.* herd.

hay, *v.* there is, there are. **h. que,** it is necessary to. **no h. de qué,** you're welcome, don't mention it.

haya, *f.* beech tree.

haz, *f.* bundle, sheaf; face.

hazaña, *f.* deed; exploit, feat.

hebdomadario, *a.* weekly.

hebilla, *f.* buckle.

hebra, *f.* thread, string.

hebreo -rea, *a. & n.* Hebrew.

hechicero -ra, *n.* wizard, witch.

hechizar, *v.* bewitch.

hechizo, *m.* spell.

hecho, *m.* fact; act; deed.

hechura, *f.* workmanship, make.

hediondez, *f.* stench.

helada, *f.* frost.

helado, *m.* ice cream.

helar, *v.* freeze.

helecho, *m.* fern.

hélice, *f.* propeller.

helicóptero, *m.* helicopter.

helio, *m.* helium.

hembra, *f.* female.

hemisferio, *m.* hemisphere.

hemoglobina, *f.* hemoglobin.

henchir, *v.* stuff.

hendedura, *f.* crevice, crack.

heno, *m.* hay.

hepática, *f.* liverwort.

heraldo, *m.* herald.

herbáceo, *a.* herbaceous.

herbívoro, *a.* herbivorous.

heredar, *v.* inherit.

heredero -ra, *n.* heir; successor.

hereditario, *a.* hereditary.

hereje, *m. & f.* heretic.

herejía, *f.* heresy.

herencia, *f.* inheritance; heritage.

herético, *a.* heretical.

herida, *f.* wound, injury.

herir, *v.* wound, injure.

hermafrodita, *a. & m.* hermaphrodite.

hermana, *f.* sister.

hermano, *m.* brother.

hermético, *a.* airtight.

hermoso, *a.* beautiful, handsome.

hermosura, *f.* beauty.

hernia, *f.* hernia, rupture.

héroe, *m.* hero.

heroico, *a.* heroic.

heroína, *f.* heroine.

heroísmo, *m.* heroism.

herradura, *f.* horseshoe.

herramienta, *f.* tool; implement.

herrería, *f.* blacksmith's shop.

herrero, *m.* blacksmith.

herrumbre, *f.* rust.

hertzio, *m.* hertz.

hervir, *v.* boil.

hesitación, *f.* hesitation.

heterogéneo, *a.* heterogeneous.

heterosexual, *a.* heterosexual.

hexágono, *m.* hexagon.

hez, *f.* dregs, sediment.

híbrido, *n. & a.* hybrid.

hidalgo -ga, *n.* noble.

hidalguía, *f.* nobility; generosity.

hidráulico, *a.* hydraulic.

hidrofobia, *f.* rabies.

hidrógeno, *m.* hydrogen.

hidropesía, *f.* dropsy.

hiedra, *f.* ivy.

hiel, *f.* gall.

hielo, *m.* ice.

hiena, *f.* hyena.

hierba, *f.* grass; herb; marijuana.

hierbabuena, *f.* mint.

hierro, *m.* iron.

hígado, *m.* liver.

higiene, *f.* hygiene.

higiénico, *a.* sanitary, hygienic.

higo, *m.* fig.

higuera, *f.* fig tree.

hija, *f.* daughter.

hijastro, *m.* stepchild.

hijo, *m.* son.

hila, *f.* line.

hilandero, *m.* spinner.

hilar, *v.* spin.

hilera, f. row, line, tier.

hilo, m. thread; string; wire; linen.

himno, m. hymn.

hincar, v. drive, thrust, sink.

hincarse, v. kneel down.

hinchar, v. swell.

hindú, n. & a. Hindu.

hinojo, m. knee.

hipnótico, a. hypnotic.

hipnotismo, m. hypnotism.

hipnotizar, v. hypnotize.

hipo, m. hiccough.

hipocresía, f. hypocrisy.

hipócrita, a. & n. hypocritical; hypocrite.

hipódromo, m. race track.

hipoteca, f. mortgage. —**hipotecar,** v.

hipótesis, f. hypothesis.

hirsuto, a. hairy, hirsute.

hispano, a. Hispanic, Spanish American.

Hispanoamérica, f. Spanish America.

hispanoamericano -na, a. & n. Spanish American.

histerectomía, f. hysterectomy.

histeria, f. hysteria.

histérico, a. hysterical.

historia, f. history; story.

historiador, m. historian.

histórico, a. historic, historical.

histrión, m. actor.

hocico, m. snout, muzzle.

hogar, m. hearth; home.

hoguera, f. bonfire, blaze.

hoja, f. leaf; sheet (of paper); pane; blade.

hojalata, f. tin.

hojalatero, m. tinsmith.

hojear, v. scan, skim through.

hola, interj. hello.

Holanda, f. Holland, Netherlands.

holandés -esa, a. & n. Dutch; Hollander.

holganza, f. leisure; diversion.

holgazán, 1. a. idle, lazy. **2.** m. idler, loiterer, tramp.

holgazanear, v. idle, loiter.

holografía, f. holography.

holograma, m. hologram.

hollín, m. soot.

hombre, m. man.

hombría, f. manliness.

hombro, m. shoulder.

homenaje, m. homage.

homeópata, m. homeopath.

homicidio, m. homicide.

homilía, f. homily.

homosexual, a. homosexual, gay.

honda, f. sling.

hondo, a. deep.

hondonada, f. ravine.

hondura, f. depth.

honestidad, f. modesty, unpretentiousness.

honesto, a. honest; pure; just.

hongo, m. fungus; mushroom.

honor, m. honor.

honorable, a. honorable.

honorario, 1. a. honorary. **2.** m. honorarium, fee.

honorífico, a. honorary.

honra, f. honor. —**honrar,** v.

honradez, f. honesty.

honrado, a. honest, honorable.

hora, f. hour, time (of day).

horadar, v. perforate.

horario, m. timetable, schedule.

horca, f. gallows; pitchfork.

horda, f. horde.

horizontal, a. horizontal.

horizonte, m. horizon.

hormiga, f. ant.

hormiguear, v. itch.

hormiguero, m. ant hill.

hornero -ra, n. baker.

hornillo, m. stove.

horno, m. oven; kiln.

horóscopo, m. horoscope.

horrendo, a. dreadful, horrendous.

horrible, a. horrible, hideous, awful.

horrido, a. horrid.

horror, m. horror.

horrorizar, v. horrify.

horroroso, a. horrible, frightful.

hortelano, m. horticulturist.

hospedaje, m. lodging.

hospedar, v. give or take lodgings.

hospital, m. hospital.

hospitalario, a. hospitable.

hospitalidad, f. hospitality.

hospitalmente, adv. hospitably.

hostia, f. host.

hostil, a. hostile.

hostilidad, f. hostility.

hotel, m. hotel.

hoy, adv. today. **h. día, h. en día,** nowadays.

hoya, f. dale, valley.

hoyo, m. pit, hole.

hoyuelo, m. dimple.

hoz, f. sickle.

hucha, f. chest, money box; savings.

hueco, 1. a. hollow, empty. **2.** m. hole, hollow.

huelga, f. strike.

huella, f. track, trace; footprint.

huérfano -na, a. & n. orphan.

huero, a. empty.

huerta, f. (vegetable) garden.

huerto, m. orchard.

hueso, m. bone; fruit pit.

huésped, m. & f. guest.

huesudo, a. bony.

huevo, m. egg.

huida, f. flight, escape.

huir, v. flee.

hule, m. oilcloth.

humanidad, f. humanity, mankind; humaneness.

humanista, m. humanist.

humanitario, a. humane.

humano, a. human; humane.

humareda, f. dense cloud of smoke.

humedad, f. humidity, moisture, dampness.

humedecer, v. moisten, dampen.

húmedo, a. humid, moist, damp.

humildad, f. humility, meekness.

humilde, a. humble, meek.

humillación, f. humiliation.

humillar, v. humiliate.

humo, m. smoke; (pl.) airs, affectation.

humor, m. humor, mood.

humorista, m. humorist.

hundimiento, m. collapse.

hundir, v. sink; collapse.

húngaro -ra, a. & n. Hungarian.

Hungría, f. Hungary.

huracán, m. hurricane.

huraño, a. shy, bashful.

hurgar, v. stir.

hurón, m. ferret.

hurraca, f. magpie.

hurtadillas, f.pl. **a h.,** on the sly.

hurtador, m. thief.

hurtar, v. steal, rob of; hide.

hurtarse, v. hide; withdraw.

husmear, v. scent, smell.

huso, m. spindle; bobbin.

I

ibérico, a. Iberian.

iberoamericano -na, a. & n. Latin American.

ida, f. departure; trip out. **i. y vuelta,** round trip.

idea, f. idea.

ideal, a. & m. ideal.

idealismo, m. idealism.

idealista, m. & f. idealist.

idear, v. plan, conceive.

idéntico, a. identical.

identidad, f. identity; identification.

identificar, v. identify.

idilio, m. idyll.

idioma, m. language.

idiota, a. & n. idiotic; idiot.

idiotismo, m. idiom; idiocy.

idolatrar, v. idolize, adore.

ídolo, m. idol.

idóneo, a. suitable, fit, apt.

iglesia, f. church.

ignición, f. ignition.

ignominia, f. ignominy, shame.

ignominioso, a. ignominious, shameful.

ignorancia, f. ignorance.

ignorante, a. ignorant.

ignorar, v. be ignorant of, not know.

ignoto, a. unknown.

igual, 1. a. equal; the same; (pl.) alike. **2.** m. equal.

igualar, v. equal; equalize; match.

igualdad, f. equality.

ijada, f. flank (of an animal).

ilegal, a. illegal.

ilegítimo, a. illegitimate.

ileso, a. unharmed.

ilícito, a. illicit, unlawful.

iluminación, f. illumination.

iluminar, v. illuminate.

ilusión, f. illusion.

ilusorio, a. illusive.

ilustración, f. illustration; learning.

ilustrador, m. illustrator.

ilustrar, v. illustrate.

ilustre, a. illustrious, honorable, distinguished.

imagen, f. image.

imaginación, f. imagination.

imaginar, v. imagine.

imaginario, a. imaginary.

imaginativo, a. imaginative.

imán, m. magnet; imam.

imbécil, a. & n. imbecile; stupid, foolish; fool.

imbuir, v. imbue, instil.

imitación, f. imitation.

imitador, m. imitator.

imitar, v. imitate.

impaciencia, f. impatience.

impaciente, a. impatient.

impar, a. unequal, uneven, odd.

imparcial, a. impartial.

impasible, a. impassive, unmoved.

impávido, adj. fearless, intrepid.

impedimento, m. impediment, obstacle.

impedir, v. impede, hinder, stop, obstruct.

impeler, v. impel; incite.

impensado, a. unexpected.

imperar, v. reign; prevail.

imperativo, a. imperative.

imperceptible, a. imperceptible.

imperdible, n. safety pin.

imperecedero, a. imperishable.

imperfecto, a. imperfect, faulty.

imperial, a. imperial.

imperialismo, m. imperialism.

impericia, f. inexperience.

imperio, m. empire.

imperioso, a. imperious, domineering.

impermeable, 1. a. waterproof. 2. m. raincoat.

impersonal, a. impersonal.

impertinencia, f. impertinence.

ímpetu, m. impulse; impetus.

impetuoso, a. impetuous.

impiedad, f. impiety.

impío, a. impious.

implacable, a. implacable, unrelenting.

implicar, v. implicate, involve.

implorar, v. implore.

imponente, a. impressive.

imponer, v. impose.

importación, f. import, importing.

importancia, f. importance.

importador, m. importer.

importante, a. important.

importar, v. be important, matter; import.

importe, m. value, amount.

importunar, v. beg, importune.

imposibilidad, f. impossibility.

imposibilitado, a. helpless.

imposible, a. impossible.

imposición, f. imposition.

impostor, m. imposter, faker.

impotencia, f. impotence.

impotente, a. impotent.

imprecar, v. curse.

impreciso, adj. inexact.

impregnar, v. impregnate.

imprenta, f. press; printing house.

imprescindible, a. essential.

impresión, f. impression.

impresionable, a. emotional.

impresionar, v. impress.

impresor, m. printer.

imprevisión, f. oversight, thoughtlessness.

imprevisto, a. unexpected, unforeseen.

imprimir, v. print; imprint.

improbable, a. improbable.

improbo, a. dishonest.

improductivo, a. unproductive.

improperio, m. insult.

impropio, a. improper.

improvisación, f. improvisation.

improvisar, v. improvise.

improviso, a. unforeseen.

imprudencia, f. imprudence.

imprudente, a. imprudent, reckless.

impuesto, m. tax.

impulsar, v. prompt, impel.

impulsivo, a. impulsive.

impulso, m. impulse.

impureza, f. impurity.

impuro, a. impure.

imputación, f. imputation.

imputar, v. impute, attribute.

inaccesible, a. inaccessible.

inacción, f. inaction; inactivity.

inaceptable, a. unacceptable.

inactivo, a. inactive; sluggish.

inadecuado, a. inadequate.

inadvertencia, f. oversight.

inadvertido, a. inadvertent, careless; unnoticed.

inagotable, a. inexhaustible.

inalterado, a. unchanged.

inanición, f. starvation.

inanimado, adj. inanimate.

inapetencia, f. lack of appetite.

inaplicable, a. inapplicable; unfit.

inaudito, a. unheard of.

inauguración, f. inauguration.

inaugurar, v. inaugurate, open.

incandescente, a. incandescent.

incansable, a. tireless.

incapacidad, f. incapacity.

incapacitar, v. incapacitate.

incapaz, a. incapable.

incauto, a. unwary.

incendiar, v. set on fire.

incendio, m. fire, conflagration.

incertidumbre, f. uncertainty, suspense.

incesante, a. continual, incessant.

incidente, m. incident, event.

incienso, m. incense.

incierto, a. uncertain, doubtful.

incisión, f. incision, cut.

incitamiento, m. incitement, motivation.

incitar, v. incite, instigate.

incivil, a. impolite, rude.

inclemencia, f. inclemency.

inclemente, a. inclement, merciless.

inclinación, f. inclination, bent; slope.

inclinar, v. incline; influence.

inclinarse, v. slope; lean, bend over; bow.

incluir, v. include; enclose.

inclusivo, a. inclusive.

incluso, prep. including.

incógnito, a. unknown.

incoherente, a. incoherent.

incombustible, a. fireproof.

incomodar, v. disturb, bother, inconvenience.

incomodidad, f. inconvenience.

incómodo, m. uncomfortable; cumbersome; inconvenient.

incomparable, a. incomparable.

incompatible, a. incompatible.

incompetencia, f. incompetence.

incompetente, a. incompetent.

incompleto, a. incomplete.

incondicional, a. unconditional.

inconexo, a. incoherent; unconnected.

incongruente, a. not suitable.

inconsciencia, f. unconsciousness.

inconsciente, a. unconscious.

inconsecuencia, f. inconsistency.

inconsecuente, a. inconsistent.

inconsiderado, a. inconsiderate.

inconstancia, f. changeableness.

inconstante, a. changeable.

inconveniencia, f. unsuitability.

inconveniente, 1. a. unsuitable. 2. m. disadvantage; objection.

incorporar, v. incorporate, embody.

incorporarse, v. sit up.

incorrecto, a. incorrect, wrong.

incredulidad, f. incredulity.

incrédulo, a. incredulous.

increíble, a. incredible.

incremento, m. increase.

incubar, v. hatch.

inculto, a. uncultivated.

incurable, a. incurable.

incurrir, v. incur.

indagación, f. investigation, inquiry.

indagador, m. investigator.

indagar, v. investigate, inquire into.

indebido, a. undue.

indecencia, f. indecency.

indecente, a. indecent.

indeciso, a. undecided.

indefenso, a. defenseless.
indefinido, a. indefinite.
indeleble, a. indelible.
indemnizar, v. indemnify.
independencia, f. independence.
independiente, a. independent.
India, f. India.
indicación, f. indication.
indicar, v. indicate, point out.
indicativo, a. & m. indicative.
índice, m. index; forefinger.
indicio, m. hint, clue.
indiferencia, f. indifference.
indiferente, a. indifferent.
indígena, a. & n. native.
indigente, a. indigent, poor.
indignación, f. indignation.
indignado, a. indignant, incensed.
indignar, v. incense.
indigno, a. unworthy.
indio -dia, a. & n. Indian.
indirecto, a. indirect.
indiscreción, f. indiscretion.
indiscreto, a. indiscreet.
indiscutible, a. unquestionable.
indispensable, a. indispensable.
indisposición, f. indisposition, ailment; reluctance.
indistinto, a. indistinct, unclear.
individual, a. individual.
individualidad, f. individuality.
individuo, a. & m. individual.
indócil, a. headstrong, unruly.
índole, f. nature, character, disposition.
indolencia, f. indolence.
indolente, a. indolent.
indómito, a. untamed, wild; unruly.
inducir, v. induce, persuade.
indudable, a. certain, indubitable.
indulgencia, f. indulgence.
indulgente, a. indulgent.
indultar, v. free; pardon.
industria, f. industry.
industrial, a. industrial.
industrioso, a. industrious.
inédito, a. unpublished.
ineficaz, a. inefficient.
inepto, a. incompetent.
inequívoco, a. unmistakable.
inercia, f. inertia.
inerte, a. inert.
inesperado, a. unexpected.
inestable, a. unstable.
inevitable, a. inevitable.
inexacto, a. inexact.
inexperto, a. unskilled.
inexplicable, a. inexplicable, unexplainable.
infalible, a. infallible.
infame, a. infamous, bad.
infamia, f. infamy.
infancia, f. infancy; childhood.
infante, m. infant.
infantería, f. infantry.
infantil, a. infantile, childish.
infatigable, a. untiring.
infausto, a. unlucky.

infección, f. infection.
infeccioso, a. infectious.
infectar, v. infect.
infeliz, a. unhappy, miserable.
inferior, a. inferior; lower.
inferir, v. infer; inflict.
infernal, a. infernal.
infestar, v. infest.
infiel, a. unfaithful.
infierno, m. hell.
infiltrar, v. infiltrate.
infinidad, f. infinity.
infinito, a. infinite.
inflación, f. inflation.
inflamación, f. inflammation.
inflamar, v. inflame, set on fire.
inflar, v. inflate, pump up, puff up.
inflexible, a. inflexible, rigid.
inflexión, f. inflection.
infligir, v. inflict.
influencia, f. influence.
influenza, f. influenza, flu.
influir, v. influence, sway.
influyente, a. influential.
información, f. information.
informal, a. informal.
informar, v. inform; report.
informe, m. report; (pl.) information, data.
infortunio, m. misfortune.
infracción, f. violation.
infrascrito, m. signer, undersigned.
infringir, v. infringe, violate.
infructuoso, a. fruitless.
infundir, v. instil, inspire with.
ingeniería, f. engineering.
ingeniero, m. engineer.
ingenio, m. wit; talent.
ingeniosidad, f. ingenuity.
ingenioso, a. witty, ingenious.
ingenuidad, f. candor; naïveté.
ingenuo, a. ingenuous, naïve, candid.
Inglaterra, f. England.
ingle, f. groin.
inglés -esa, a. & n. English; Englishman.
ingratitud, f. ingratitude.
ingrato, a. ungrateful.
ingrediente, m. ingredient.
ingresar en, v. enter; join.
ingreso, m. entrance; (pl.) earnings, income.
inhábil, a. unskilled, incapable.
inhabilitar, v. disqualify.
inherente, a. inherent.
inhibir, v. inhibit.
inhumano, a. cruel, inhuman.
iniciador, m. initiator.
inicial, a. initial.
iniciar, v. initiate, begin.
iniciativa, f. initiative.
inicuo, a. wicked.
iniquidad, f. iniquity; sin.
injuria, f. insult. —injuriar, v.
injusticia, f. injustice.
injusto, a. unjust, unfair.
inmaculado, a. immaculate; pure.
inmediato, a. immediate.
inmensidad, f. immensity.

inmenso, a. immense.
inmersión, f. immersion.
inmigración, f. immigration.
inmigrante, a. & n. immigrant.
inmigrar, v. immigrate.
inminente, a. imminent.
inmoderado, a. immoderate.
inmodesto, a. immodest.
inmoral, a. immoral.
inmoralidad, f. immorality.
inmortal, a. immortal.
inmortalidad, f. immortality.
inmóvil, a. immobile, motionless.
inmundicia, f. dirt, filth.
inmune, a. immune.
inmunidad, f. immunity.
innato, a. innate, inborn.
innecesario, a. unnecessary, needless.
innoble, a. ignoble.
innocuo, a. innocuous.
innovación, f. innovation.
innumerable, a. innumerable, countless.
inocencia, f. innocence.
inocente, a. innocent.
inocular, v. inoculate.
inodoro, m. toilet.
inofensivo, a. inoffensive, harmless.
inolvidable, a. unforgettable.
inoportuno, a. inopportune.
inquietar, v. disturb, worry, trouble.
inquieto, a. anxious, uneasy, worried; restless.
inquietud, f. concern, anxiety, worry; restlessness.
inquilino -na, n. occupant, tenant.
inquirir, v. inquire into, investigate.
inquisición, f. inquisition, investigation.
insaciable, a. insatiable.
insalubre, a. unhealthy.
insano, a. insane.
inscribir, v. inscribe; record.
inscribirse, v. register, enroll.
inscripción, f. inscription; registration.
insecto, m. insect.
inseguro, a. unsure, uncertain; insecure, unsafe.
insensato, a. stupid, senseless.
insensible, a. unfeeling, heartless.
inseparable, a. inseparable.
inserción, f. insertion.
insertar, v. insert.
insidioso, a. insidious, crafty.
insigne, a. famous, noted.
insignia, f. insignia, badge.
insignificante, a. insignificant, negligible.
insincero, a. insincere.
insinuación, f. insinuation; hint.
insinuar, v. insinuate, suggest, hint.
insipidez, f. insipidity.
insípido, a. insipid.
insistencia, f. insistence.
insistente, a. insistent.

insistir, v. insist.
insolación, f. sunstroke.
insolencia, f. insolence.
insolente, a. insolent.
insólito, a. unusual.
insolvente, a. insolvent.
insomnio, m. insomnia.
insoportable, a. unbearable.
inspección, f. inspection.
inspeccionar, v. inspect, examine.
inspector, m. inspector.
inspiración, f. inspiration.
inspirar, v. inspire.
instalación, f. installation, fixture.
instalar, v. install, set up.
instantánea, f. snapshot.
instantáneo, a. instantaneous.
instante, a. & m. instant. al l., at once.
instar, v. coax, urge.
instigar, v. instigate, urge.
instintivo, a. instinctive.
instinto, m. instinct.
institución, f. institution.
instituto, m. institute. —instituir, v.
institutriz, f. governess.
instrucción, f. instruction; education.
instructivo, a. instructive.
instructor, a. instructor.
instruir, v. instruct, teach.
instrumento, m. instrument.
insuficiente, a. insufficient.
insufrible, a. intolerable.
insular, a. island, insular.
insulto, m. insult. —insultar, v.
insuperable, a. insuperable.
insurgente, n. & a. insurgent, rebel.
insurrección, f. insurrection, revolt.
insurrecto, a. & m. insurgent.
intacto, a. intact.
integral, a. integral.
integridad, f. integrity; entirety.
íntegro, a. entire; upright.
intelecto, m. intellect.
intelectual, a. & n. intellectual.
inteligencia, f. intelligence.
inteligente, a. intelligent.
inteligible, a. intelligible.
intemperie, f. bad weather.
intención, f. intention.
intendente, m. manager.
intensidad, f. intensity.
intensificar, v. intensify.
intensivo, a. intensive.
intenso, a. intense.
intentar, v. attempt, try.
intento, m. intent.
interceptar, v. intercept.
intercesión, f. intercession.
interés, m. interest; concern; appeal.
interesante, a. interesting.
interesar, v. interest, appeal to.
interferencia, f. interference.
interino, a. temporary.
interior, 1. a. interior, inner; 2. m. interior.
interjección, f. interjection.

intermedio, 1. a. intermediate. 2. m. intermediary; intermission.
interminable, a. interminable, endless.
intermisión, f. intermission.
intermitente, a. intermittent.
internacional, a. international.
internarse en, v. enter into, go into.
interno, a. internal.
interpelar, v. ask questions; quiz.
interponer, v. interpose.
interpretación, f. interpretation.
interpretar, v. interpret; construe.
intérprete, m. & f. interpreter.
interrogación, f. interrogation.
interrogar, v. question, interrogate.
interrogativo, a. interrogative.
interrumpir, v. interrupt.
interrupción, f. interruption.
intersección, f. intersection.
intervalo, m. interval.
intervención, f. intervention.
intervenir, v. intervene, interfere.
intestino, m. intestine.
intimación, f. intimation, hint.
intimar, v. suggest, hint.
intimidad, f. intimacy.
intimidar, v. intimidate.
íntimo -ma, a. & n. intimate.
intolerable, a. intolerable.
intolerancia, f. intolerance, bigotry.
intolerante, a. intolerant.
intranquilo, a. uneasy.
intravenoso, a. intravenous.
intrepidez, f. daring.
intrépido, a. intrepid.
intriga, f. intrigue, plot, scheme. —intrigar, v.
intrincado, a. intricate, involved.
introducción, f. introduction.
introducir, v. introduce.
intruso -sa, m. intruder.
intuición, f. intuition.
inundación, f. flood. —inundar, v.
inútil, a. useless.
invadir, v. invade.
inválido -da, a. & n. invalid.
invariable, a. constant.
invasión, f. invasion.
invasor, m. invader.
invencible, a. invincible.
invención, f. invention.
inventar, v. invent; devise.
inventario, m. inventory.
inventivo, a. inventive.
invento, m. invention.
inventor, m. inventor.
invernáculo, m. greenhouse.
invernal, a. wintry.
inverosímil, a. improbable, unlikely.
inversión, f. inversion; (com.) investment.
inverso, a. inverse, reverse.

invertir, v. invert; reverse; (com.) invest.
investigación, f. investigation.
investigador, m. investigator.
investigar, v. investigate.
invierno, m. winter.
invisible, a. invisible.
invitación, f. invitation.
invitar, v. invite.
invocar, v. invoke.
involuntario, a. involuntary.
inyección, f. injection.
inyectar, v. inject.
ir, v. go. irse, go away, leave.
ira, f. anger, ire.
iracundo, a. wrathful, irate.
iris, m. iris. arco i., rainbow.
Irlanda, f. Ireland.
irlandés -esa, a. & n. Irish; Irishman.
ironía, f. irony.
irónico, a. ironical.
irracional, a. irrational; insane.
irradiación, f. radiation.
irradiar, v. radiate.
irrazonable, a. unreasonable.
irregular, a. irregular.
irreligioso, a. irreligious.
irremediable, a. irremediable, hopeless.
irresistible, a. irresistible.
irresoluto, a. irresolute, wavering.
irrespetuoso, a. disrespectful.
irreverencia, f. irreverence.
irreverente, adj. irreverent.
irrigación, f. irrigation.
irrigar, v. irrigate.
irritación, f. irritation.
irritar, v. irritate.
irrupción, f. raid, attack.
isla, f. island.
isleño -ña, n. islander.
israelita, n. & a. Israelite.
Italia, f. Italy.
italiano -na, a. & n. Italian.
itinerario, m. itinerary; timetable.
izar, v. hoist.
izquierda, f. left (hand, side).
izquierdista, n. & a. leftist.
izquierdo, a. left.

J

jabalí, m. wild boar.
jabón, m. soap.
jabonar, v. soap.
jaca, f. nag.
jacinto, m. hyacinth.
jactancia, f. boast. —jactarse, v.
jactancioso, a. boastful.
jadear, v. pant, puff.
jaez, m. harness; kind.
jalar, v. haul, pull.
jalea, f. jelly.
jaletina, f. gelatin.
jamás, adv. never, ever.
jamón, m. ham.
Japón, m. Japan.
japonés -esa, a. & n. Japanese.
jaqueca, f. headache.

jarabe, *m.* syrup.
jaranear, *v.* jest; carouse.
jardín, *m.* garden.
jardinero -ra, *n.* gardener.
jarra, *f.* jar; pitcher.
jarro, *m.* jug, pitcher.
jaspe, *m.* jasper.
jaula, *f.* cage; coop.
jauría, *f.* pack of hounds.
jazmín, *m.* jasmine.
jefatura, *f.* headquarters.
jefe, *m.* chief, boss.
Jehová, *m.* Jehovah.
jengibre, *m.* ginger.
jerez, *m.* sherry.
jerga, *f.* slang.
jergón, *m.* straw bed.
jerigonza, *f.* jargon.
jeringa, *f.* syringe.
jeringar, *v.* inject; annoy.
jeroglífico, *m.* hieroglyph.
jesuita, *m.* Jesuit.
Jesús, *m.* Jesus.
jeta, *f.* snout.
jícara, *f.* cup.
jinete, *m.* horseman.
jingoísmo, *m.* jingoism.
jingoísta, *n. & a.* jingoist.
jira, *f.* tour, picnic, outing.
jirafa, *f.* giraffe.
jocundo, *a.* jovial.
jornada, *f.* journey; day's work.
jornal, *m.* day's wage.
jornalero, *m.* day laborer, workman.
joroba, *f.* hump.
jorobado, *a.* humpbacked.
joven, 1. *a.* young. 2. *m. & f.* young person.
jovial, *a.* jovial, jolly.
jovialidad, *f.* joviality.
joya, *f.* jewel, gem.
joyelero, *m.* jewel box.
joyería, *f.* jewelry; jewelry store.
joyero, *m.* jeweler.
juanete, *m.* bunion.
jubilación, *f.* retirement; pension.
jubilar, *v.* retire, pension.
jubileo, *m.* jubilee, public festivity.
júbilo, *m.* glee, rejoicing.
jubiloso, *a.* joyful, gay.
judaico, *a.* Jewish.
judaísmo, *m.* Judaism.
judía, *f.* bean, string bean.
judicial, *a.* judicial.
judío -ía, *a. & n.* Jewish; Jew.
juego, *m.* game; play; gambling; set. **j. de damas**, checkers.
juerga, *f.* spree.
jueves, *m.* Thursday.
juez, *m.* judge.
jugador -ra, *n.* player.
jugar, *v.* play; gamble.
juglar, *m.* minstrel.
jugo, *m.* juice.
jugoso, *a.* juicy.
juguete, *m.* toy, plaything.
juguetear, *v.* trifle.
juguetón, *a.* playful.

juicio, *m.* sense, wisdom, judgment.
juicioso, *a.* wise, judicious.
julio, *m.* July.
jumento, *m.* donkey.
junco, *m.* reed, rush.
junio, *m.* June.
junípero, *m.* juniper.
junquillo, *m.* jonquil.
junta, *f.* board, council; joint, coupling.
juntamente, *adv.* jointly.
juntar, *v.* join; connect; assemble.
junto, *a.* together. **j. a**, next to.
juntura, *f.* joint, juncture.
jurado, *m.* jury.
juramento, *m.* oath.
jurar, *v.* swear.
jurisconsulto, *m.* jurist.
jurisdicción, *f.* jurisdiction; territory.
jurisprudencia, *f.* jurisprudence.
justa, *f.* joust. —**justar**, *v.*
justicia, *f.* justice, equity.
justiciero, *a.* just.
justificación, *f.* justification.
justificadamente, *adv.* justifiably.
justificar, *v.* justify, warrant.
justo, *a.* right; exact; just; righteous.
juvenil, *a.* youthful.
juventud, *f.* youth.
juzgado, *m.* court.
juzgar, *v.* judge, estimate.

K, L, LL

káiser, *m.* kaiser.
karate, *m.* karate.
kepis, *m.* military cap.
keroseno, *m.* kerosene.
kilo, kilogramo, *m.* kilogram.
kilohertzio, *m.* kilohertz.
kilolitro, *m.* kiloliter.
kilómetro, *m.* kilometer.
kiosco, *m.* newsstand; pavilion.
la, 1. *art. & pron.* the; the one. 2. *pron.* her, it, you; (*pl.*) them, you.
laberinto, *m.* labyrinth, maze.
labia, *f.* eloquence, fluency.
labio, *m.* lip.
labor, *f.* labor, work.
laborar, *v.* work; till.
laboratorio, *m.* laboratory.
laborioso, *a.* industrious.
labrador, *m.* farmer.
labranza, *f.* farming; farmland.
labrar, *v.* work, till.
labriego -ga, *n.* peasant.
laca, *f.* shellac.
lacio, *a.* withered; limp; straight.
lactar, *v.* nurse, suckle.
lácteo, *a.* milky.
ladear, *v.* tilt, tip; sway.
ladera, *f.* slope.
ladino, *a.* cunning, crafty.
lado, *m.* side. **al l. de**, beside. **de l.**, sideways.

ladra, *f.* barking. —**ladrar**, *v.*
ladrillo, *m.* brisk.
ladrón -ona, *n.* thief, robber.
lagarto, *m.* lizard; (Mex.) alligator.
lago, *m.* lake.
lágrima, *f.* tear.
lagrimear, *v.* weep, cry.
laguna, *f.* lagoon; gap.
laico, *a.* lay.
laja, *f.* stone slab.
lamentable, *a.* lamentable.
lamentación, *f.* lamentation.
lamentar, *v.* lament; wail; regret, be sorry.
lamento, *m.* lament, wail.
lamer, *v.* lick; lap.
lámina, *f.* print, illustration.
lámpara, *f.* lamp.
lampiño, *a.* beardless.
lana, *f.* wool.
lanar, *a.* woolen.
lance, *m.* throw; episode; quarrel.
lancha, *f.* launch; small boat.
lanchón, *m.* barge.
langosta, *f.* lobster; locust.
languidecer, *v.* languish, pine.
languidez, *f.* languidness.
lánguido, *a.* languid.
lanza, *f.* lance, spear.
lanzada, *f.* thrust, throw.
lanzar, *v.* throw, hurl; launch.
lañar, *v.* cramp; clamp.
lapicero, *m.* mechanical pencil.
lápida, *f.* stone; tombstone.
lápiz, *m.* pencil; crayon.
lapso, *m.* lapse.
lardo, *m.* lard.
largar, *v.* loosen; free.
largo, 1. *a.* long. **a lo l. de**, along. 2. *m.* length.
largor, *m.* length.
largueza, *f.* generosity; length.
largura, *f.* length.
laringe, *f.* larynx.
larva, *f.* larva.
lascivia, *f.* lasciviousness.
lascivo, *a.* lascivious.
láser, *m.* laser.
laso, *a.* weary.
lástima, *f.* pity. **ser l.**, to be a pity, to be too bad.
lastimar, *v.* hurt, injure.
lastimoso, *a.* pitiful.
lastre, *m.* ballast. —**lastrar**, *v.*
lata, *f.* tin can; tin (plate); (coll.) annoyance, bore.
latente, *a.* latent.
lateral, *a.* lateral, side.
latigazo, *m.* lash, whipping.
látigo, *m.* whip.
latín, *m.* Latin (language).
latino, *a.* Latin.
latir, *v.* bet, pulsate.
latitud, *f.* latitude.
latón, *m.* brass.
laúd, *m.* lute.
laudable, *a.* laudable.
láudano, *m.* laudanum.
laurel, *m.* laurel.
lava, *f.* lava.
lavabo, lavamanos, *m.* washroom, lavatory.

lavandera, f. washerwoman, laundress.

lavandería, f. laundry.

lavar, v. wash.

lavatorio, m. lavatory.

laya, f. spade. —layar, v.

lazar, v. lasso.

lazareto, m. hospital; quarantine.

lazo, m. tie, knot; bow; loop.

le, pron. him, her, you; (pl.) them, you.

leal, a. loyal.

lealtad, f. loyalty, allegiance.

lebrel, m. greyhound.

lección, f. lesson.

lecito, m. yolk.

lector -ra, n. reader.

lectura, f. reading.

leche, f. milk.

lechería, f. dairy.

lechero, m. milkman.

lecho, m. bed, couch.

lechoso, a. milky.

lechuga, f. lettuce.

lechuza, f. owl.

leer, v. read.

legación, f. legation.

legado, m. bequest.

legal, a. legal, lawful.

legalizar, v. legalize.

legar, v. bequeath, leave, will.

legible, a. legible.

legión, f. legion.

legislación, f. legislation.

legislador, m. legislator.

legislar, v. legislate.

legislativo, a. legislative.

legislatura, f. legislature.

legítimo, a. legitimate.

lego, m. layman.

legua, f. league (measure).

legumbres, f.pl. vegetables.

lejano, a. distant, far-off.

lejía, f. lye.

lejos, adv. far. a lo l., in the distance.

lelo, a. stupid, foolish.

lema, m. theme; slogan.

lengua, f. tongue; language.

lenguado, m. sole, flounder.

lenguaje, m. speech, language.

lenguaraz, a. talkative.

lente, m. or f. lens. m.pl. eyeglasses.

lenteja, f. lentil.

lentitud, f. slowness.

lento, a. slow.

leña, f. wood, firewood.

león, m. lion.

leopardo, m. leopard.

lerdo, a. dull-witted.

lesbiana, f. lesbian.

lesión, f. wound; damage.

letanía, f. litany.

letárgico, a. lethargic.

letargo, m. lethargy.

letra, f. letter (of alphabet); print; words (of a song).

letrado, 1. a. learned. 2. m. lawyer.

letrero, m. sign, poster.

leva, f. (mil.) draft.

levadura, f. yeast, leavening, baking powder.

levantador, m. lifter; rebel, mutineer.

levantar, v. raise, lift.

levantarse, v. rise, get up; stand up.

levar, v. weigh (anchor).

leve, a. slight, light.

levita, f. frock coat.

léxico, m. lexicon, dictionary.

ley, f. law, statute.

leyenda, f. legend.

lezna, f. awl.

libación, f. libation.

libelo, m. libel.

libélula, f. dragonfly.

liberación, f. liberation, release.

liberal, a. liberal.

libertad, f. liberty, freedom.

libertador, m. liberator.

libertar, v. free, liberate.

libertinaje, m. licentiousness.

libertino, m. libertine.

libidine, f. licentiousness; lust.

libidinoso, a. libidinous; lustful.

libra, f. pound.

libranza, f. draft, bill of exchange.

librar, v. free, rid.

libre, a. free, unoccupied.

librería, f. bookstore.

librero, m. bookseller.

libreta, f. notebook; booklet.

libreto, m. libretto.

libro, m. book.

licencia, f. permission, license, leave; furlough.

licenciado -da, n. graduate.

licencioso, a. licentious.

lícito, a. lawful.

licor, m. liquor.

lid, f. fight. —lidiar, v.

líder, m. leader.

liebre, f. hare.

lienzo, m. linen.

liga, f. league, confederacy; garter.

ligadura, f. ligature.

ligar, v. tie, bind, join.

ligero, a. light; fast, nimble.

ligustro, m. privet.

lija, f. sandpaper.

lijar, v. sandpaper.

lima, f. file; lime.

limbo, m. limbo.

limitación, f. limitation.

límite, m. limit. —limitar, v.

limo, m. slime.

limón, m. lemon.

limonada, f. lemonade.

limonero, m. lemon tree.

limosna, f. alms.

limosnero -ra, n. beggar.

limpiabotas, m. bootblack.

limpiadientes, m. toothpick.

limpiar, v. clean, wash, wipe.

límpido, a. limpid, clear.

limpieza, f. cleanliness.

limpio, a. clean.

linaje, m. lineage, ancestry.

linaza, f. linseed.

lince, a. sharp-sighted, observing.

linchamiento, m. lynching.

linchar, v. lynch.

lindar, v. border, bound.

linde, m. boundary; landmark.

lindero, m. boundary.

lindo, a. pretty, lovely, nice.

línea, f. line.

lineal, a. lineal.

linfa, f. lymph.

lingüista, m. & f. linguist.

lingüístico, a. linguistic.

linimento, m. liniment.

lino, m. linen; flax.

linóleo, m. linoleum.

linterna, f. lantern; flashlight.

lío, m. pack, bundle; mess, scrape; hassle.

liquidación, f. liquidation.

liquidar, v. liquidate; settle up.

líquido, a. & m. liquid.

lira, f. lyre.

lírico, a. lyric.

lirio, m. lily.

lirismo, m. lyricism.

lis, f. lily.

lisiar, v. cripple, lame.

liso, a. smooth, even.

lisonja, f. flattery.

lisonjear, v. flatter.

lisonjero -ra, n. flatterer.

lista, f. list; stripe; menu.

listar, v. list; put on a list.

listo, a. ready; smart, clever.

listón, m. ribbon.

litera, f. litter, bunk, berth.

literal, a. literal.

literario, a. literary.

literato, m. literary person, writer.

literatura, f. literature.

litigación, f. litigation.

litigio, m. litigation; lawsuit.

litoral, m. coast.

litro, m. liter.

liturgia, f. liturgy.

liviano, a. light (in weight).

lívido, a. livid.

lo, pron. the; him, it, you; (pl.) them, you.

loar, v. praise, laud.

lobina, f. striped bass.

lobo, m. wolf.

lóbrego, a. murky; dismal.

local, 1. a. local. 2. m. site.

localidad, f. locality, location; seat (in theater).

localizar, v. localize.

loción, f. lotion.

loco -ca, 1. a. crazy, insane, mad. 2. n. lunatic.

locomotora, f. locomotive.

locuaz, a. loquacious.

locución, f. locution, expression.

locura, f. folly; madness, insanity.

lodo, m. mud.

lodoso, a. muddy.

lógica, f. logic.

lógico, a. logical.

lograr, v. achieve; succeed in.

logro, m. accomplishment.

lombriz, f. earthworm.

lomo, *m.* loin; back (of an animal).
lona, *f.* canvas.
longevidad, *f.* longevity.
longitud, *f.* longitude; length.
lonja, *f.* shop; market.
lontananza, *f.* distance.
loro, *m.* parrot.
losa, *f.* slab.
lote, *m.* lot, share.
lotería, *f.* lottery.
loza, *f.* china, crockery.
lozanía, *f.* freshness, vigor.
lozano, *a.* fresh, spirited.
lubricación, *f.* lubrication.
lubricar, *v.* lubricate.
lucero, *m.* (bright) star.
lúcido, *a.* lucid, clear.
luciente, *a.* shining, bright.
luciérnaga, *f.* firefly.
lucimiento, *m.* success; splendor.
lucir, *v.* shine, sparkle; show off.
lucrativo, *a.* lucrative, profitable.
lucha, *f.* fight, struggle; wrestling. —**luchar,** *v.*
luchador, *m.* fighter, wrestler.
luego, *adv.* right away; afterwards, next. **l. que,** as soon as. **desde l.,** of course. **hasta l.,** good-bye, so long.
lugar, *m.* place, spot; space, room.
lúgubre, *a.* gloomy; dismal.
lujo, *m.* luxury. **de l.,** de luxe.
lujoso, *a.* luxurious.
lumbre, *f.* fire; light.
luminoso, *a.* luminous.
luna, *f.* moon.
lunar, *m.* beauty mark, mole; polka dot.
lunático, *a. & n.* lunatic.
lunes, *m.* Monday.
luneta, *f.* (theat.) orchestra seat.
lustre, *m.* polish, shine. —**lustrar,** *v.*
lustroso, *a.* shiny.
luto, *m.* mourning.
luz, *f.* light. **dar a l.,** give birth to.
llaga, *f.* sore.
llama, *f.* flame; llama.
llamada, *f.* call; knock. —**llamar,** *v.*
llamarse, *v.* be called, be named. **se llama . . .** etc., his name is . . . etc.
llamativo, *a.* gaudy, showy.
llamear, *v.* blaze.
llaneza, *f.* simplicity.
llano, l. *a.* flat, level; plain. 2. *m.* plain.
llanta, *f.* tire.
llanto, *m.* crying, weeping.
llanura, *f.* prairie, plain.
llave, *f.* key; wrench; faucet; (elec.) switch. **ll. inglesa,** monkey wrench.
llegada, *f.* arrival.
llegar, *v.* arrive; reach. **ll. a ser,** become, come to be.
llenar, *v.* fill.

lleno, *a.* full.
llenura, *f.* abundance.
llevadero, *a.* tolerable.
llevar, *v.* take, carry, bear; wear (clothes); **ll. a cabo,** carry out.
llevarse, *v.* take away, run away with. **ll. bien,** get along well.
llorar, *v.* cry, weep.
lloroso, *a.* sorrowful, tearful.
llover, *v.* rain.
llovide, *m.* stowaway.
llovizna, *f.* drizzle, sprinkle. —**lloviznar,** *v.*
lluvia, *f.* rain.
lluvioso, *a.* rainy.

M

maca, *f.* blemish, flaw.
macaco, *a.* ugly, horrid.
macareno, *a.* boasting.
macarrones, *m.pl.* macaroni.
macear, *v.* molest, push around.
maceta, *f.* vase; mallet.
macizo, l. *a.* solid. 2. *m.* bulk; flower bed.
macular, *v.* stain.
machacar, *v.* pound; crush.
machina, *f.* derrick.
machista, *a.* macho.
macho, *m.* male.
machucho, *a.* mature, wise.
madera, *f.* lumber; wood.
madero, *m.* beam, timber.
madrastra, *f.* stepmother.
madre, *f.* mother. **m. política,** mother-in-law.
madreperla, *f.* mother-of-pearl.
madriguera, *f.* burrow; lair, den.
madrina, *f.* godmother.
madroncillo, *m.* strawberry.
madrugada, *f.* daybreak.
madrugar, *v.* get up early.
madurar, *v.* ripen.
madurez, *f.* maturity.
maduro, *a.* ripe; mature.
maestría, *f.* mastery.
maestro, *m.* master; teacher.
mafia, *f.* mafia.
maganto, *a.* lethargic, dull.
magia, *f.* magic.
mágico, *a. & m.* magic; magician.
magistrado, *m.* magistrate.
magnánimo, *a.* magnanimous.
magnético, *a.* magnetic.
magnetismo, *m.* magnetism.
magnetófono, *m.* tape recorder.
magnificar, *v.* magnify.
magnificencia, *f.* magnificence.
magnífico, *a.* magnificent.
magnitud, *f.* magnitude.
magno, *a.* great, grand.
magnolia, *f.* magnolia.
mago, *m.* magician; wizard.
magosto, *m.* picnic, outing.
magro, *a.* meager; thin.
magullar, *v.* bruise.

mahometano, *n. & a.* Mohammedan.
mahometismo, *m.* Mohammedanism.
maíz, *m.* corn.
majadero, *a. & m.* foolish; fool.
majar, *v.* mash.
majestad, *f.* majesty.
majestuoso, *a.* majestic.
mal, l. *adv.* badly; wrong. 2. *m.* evil, ill; illness.
mala, *f.* mail.
malacate, *m.* hoist.
malandanza, *f.* misfortune.
malaventura, *f.* misfortune.
malcomido, *a.* underfed; malnourished.
malcontento, *a.* dissatisfied.
maldad, *f.* badness; wickedness.
maldecir, *v.* curse, damn.
maldición, *f.* curse.
maldito, *a.* accursed, damned.
malecón, *m.* embankment.
maledicencia, *f.* slander.
maleficio, *m.* spell, charm.
malestar, *m.* indisposition.
maleta, *f.* suitcase, valise.
malévolo, *a.* malevolent.
maleza, *f.* weeds; underbrush.
malgastar, *v.* squander.
malhechor, *m.* malefactor, evildoer.
malhumorado, *a.* morose, illhumored.
malicia, *f.* malice.
maliciar, *v.* suspect.
malicioso, *a.* malicious.
maligno, *a.* malignant, evil.
malo, *a.* bad; evil, wicked; naughty; ill.
malograr, *v.* miss, lose.
malparto, *m.* abortion, miscarriage.
malquerencia, *f.* hatred.
malquerer, *v.* dislike; bear ill will.
malsano, *a.* unhealthy; unwholesome.
malsín, *m.* malicious gossip.
malta, *f.* malt.
maltratar, *v.* mistreat.
malvado, l. *a.* wicked. 2. *n.* villain.
malviz, *m.* redwing.
malla, *f.* mesh, net.
mallete, *m.* mallet.
mamá, *f.* mama, mother.
mamar, *v.* suckle; suck.
mamífero, *m.* mammal.
mampara, *f.* screen.
mampostería, *f.* masonry.
mamut, *m.* mammoth.
manada, *f.* flock, herd, drove.
manantial, *m.* spring (of water).
manar, *v.* gush, flow out.
mancebo, *m.* young man.
mancilla, *f.* stain; blemish.
manco, *a.* armless; one-armed.
mancha, *f.* stain, smear, blemish, spot. —**manchar,** *v.*
mandadero, *m.* messenger.
mandado, *m.* order, command.
mandamiento, *m.* commandment; command.

mandar, v. send; order, command.

mandatario, m. attorney; representative.

mandato, m. mandate, command.

mandíbula, f. jaw; jawbone.

mando, m. command, order; leadership.

mandón, a. domineering.

mandril, m. baboon.

manejar, v. handle, manage; drive (a car).

manejo, m. management; horsemanship.

manera, f. way, manner, means. **de m. que,** so, as a result.

manga, f. sleeve.

mangana, f. lariat, lasso.

manganeso, m. manganese.

mango, m. handle; mango (fruit).

mangosta, f. mongoose.

manguera, f. hose.

manguito, m. muff.

maní, m. peanut.

manía, f. mania, madness; hobby.

maníaco, maniático, a. & m. maniac.

manicomio, m. insane asylum.

manicura, f. manicure.

manifactura, f. manufacture.

manifestación, f. manifestation.

manifestar, v. manifest, show.

manifiesto, a. & m. manifest.

manija, f. handle; crank.

maniobra, f. maneuver. —**maniobrar,** v.

manipulación, f. manipulation.

manipular, v. manipulate.

maniquí, m. mannequin.

manivela, f. (mech.) crank.

manjar, m. food, dish.

manlieve, v. swindle.

mano, f. hand.

manojo, m. handful; bunch.

manómetro, m. gauge.

manopla, f. gauntlet.

manosear, v. handle, feel, touch.

manotada, f. slap, smack. —**manotear,** v.

mansedumbre, f. meekness, tameness.

mansión, f. mansion; abode.

manso, a. tame, gentle.

manta, f. blanket.

manteca, f. fat, lard; butter.

mantecado, m. ice cream.

mantecoso, a. buttery.

mantel, m. tablecloth.

mantener, v. maintain, keep; sustain; support.

mantenimiento, m. maintenance.

mantequera, f. butter dish; churn.

mantequilla, f. butter.

mantilla, f. mantilla; baby clothes.

mantillo, m. humus; manure.

manto, m. mantle, cloak.

manual, a. & m. manual.

manubrio, m. handle; crank.

manufacturar, v. manufacture; make.

manuscrito, m. manuscript.

manzana, f. apple; block (of street).

manzano, m. apple tree.

maña, f. skill; cunning; trick.

mañana, 1. adv. tomorrow. 2. f. morning.

mañanear, v. rise early in the morning.

mañero, a. clever; skillful; lazy.

mapa, m. map, chart.

mapache, m. raccoon.

mapurito, m. skunk.

máquina, f. machine.

maquinación, f. machination; plot.

maquinador, m. plotter, schemer.

maquinal, a. mechanical.

maquinar, v. scheme, plot.

maquinaria, f. machinery.

maquinista, m. machinist; engineer.

mar, m. or f. sea.

marabú, m. marabou.

maraña, f. tangle; maze; snarl; plot.

maravilla, f. marvel, wonder. —**maravillarse,** v.

maravilloso, a. marvelous, wonderful.

marbete, m. tag, label; check.

marca, f. mark, sign; brand, make.

marcar, v. mark; observe, note.

marcial, a. martial.

marco, m. frame.

marcha, f. march, progress. —**marchar,** v.

marchante, m. merchant; customer.

marcharse, v. go away, depart.

marchitable, a. perishable.

marchitar, v. fade, wilt, wither.

marchito, a. faded, withered.

marea, f. tide.

mareado, a. seasick.

marearse, v. get dizzy; be seasick.

mareo, m. dizziness, seasickness.

marfil, m. ivory.

margarita, f. pearl; daisy.

margen, m. or f. margin, edge, rim.

marido, m. husband.

marijuana, f. marijuana, pot, grass.

marimba, f. marimba.

marina, f. navy; seascape.

marinero, m. sailor, seaman.

marino, a. & m. marine, (of) sea; mariner, seaman.

marión, m. sturgeon.

mariposa, f. butterfly.

mariquita, f. ladybird.

mariscal, m. marshal.

marisco, m. shellfish; mollusk.

marital, a. marital.

marítimo, a. maritime.

marmita, f. pot, kettle.

mármol, m. marble.

marmóreo, a. marble.

maroma, f. rope.

marqués, m. marquis.

marquesa, f. marquise.

Marte, m. Mars.

martes, m. Tuesday.

martillo, m. hammer. —**martillar,** v.

mártir, m. & f. martyr.

martirio, m. martyrdom.

martirizar, v. martyrize.

marzo, m. March.

mas, conj. but.

más, a. & adv. more, most; plus. **no m.,** only.

masa, f. mass; dough.

masaje, m. massage.

mascar, v. chew.

máscara, f. mask.

mascarada, f. masquerade.

mascota, f. mascot; good-luck charm.

masculino, a. masculine.

mascullar, v. mumble.

masón, m. Freemason.

masticar, v. chew.

mástil, m. mast; post.

mastín, m. mastiff.

mastuerzo, m. fool, ninny.

mata, f. plant; bush.

matadero, m. slaughterhouse.

matador, m. matador.

matanza, f. killing, bloodshed, slaughter.

matar, v. kill, slay; slaughter.

matasanos, m. quack.

mate, m. checkmate; Paraguayan tea.

matemáticas, f.pl. mathematics.

matemático, a. mathematical.

materia, f. material; subject (matter).

material, a. & m. material.

materialismo, m. materialism.

materializar, v. materialize.

maternal, materno, a. maternal.

maternidad, f. maternity.

matiné, m. matinee.

matiz, m. hue, shade.

matizar, v. blend; tint.

matón, m. bully.

matorral, m. thicket.

matoso, a. weedy.

matraca, f. rattle. —**matraquear,** v.

matrícula, f. registration; tuition.

matricularse, v. enroll, register.

matrimonio, m. matrimony, marriage, married couple.

matriz, f. womb; (mech.) die, mold.

matrona, f. matron.

maullar, v. mew.

máxima, f. maxim.

máxime, a. principally.

máximo, a. & m. maximum.

maya, f. daisy.

mayo, m. May.

mayonesa, f. mayonnaise.

mayor, 1. a. larger, largest;

greater, greatest; elder, eldest, senior. **m. de edad**, major, of age. **al por m.**, at wholesale. **2. m.** major.

mayoral, *m.* head shepherd; boss; foreman.

mayordomo, *m.* manager; butler, steward.

mayoría, *f.* majority, bulk.

mazmorra, *f.* dungeon.

mazorca, *f.* ear of corn.

me, *pron.* me; myself.

mecánico, *a. & m.* mechanical; mechanic.

mecanismo, *m.* mechanism.

mecanizar, *v.* mechanize.

mecanografía, *f.* typewriting.

mecanógrafo -fa, *n.* typist.

mecedor, *m.* swing.

mecedora, *f.* rocking chair.

mecer, *v.* rock; swing, sway.

mecha, *f.* wick; fuse.

mechón, *m.* lock (of hair).

medalla, *f.* medal.

médano, *m.* sand dune.

media, *f.* stocking.

mediación, *f.* mediation.

mediador, *m.* mediator.

mediados, *m.pl.* **a m.** de, about the middle of (a period of time).

medianero, *m.* mediator.

medianía, *f.* mediocrity.

mediano, *a.* medium; moderate; mediocre.

medianoche, *f.* midnight.

mediante, *prep.* by means of.

mediar, *v.* mediate.

medicamento, *m.* medicine, drug.

medicastro, *m.* quack.

medicina, *f.* medicine.

medicinar, *v.* treat (as a doctor).

médico, **1.** *a.* medical. **2.** *m.* doctor, physician.

medida, *f.* measure, step.

medidor, *m.* meter.

medio, **1.** *a.* half; mid, middle of. **2.** *m.* middle; means.

mediocre, *a.* mediocre.

mediocridad, *f.* mediocrity.

mediodía, *m.* midday, noon.

medioeval, *a.* medieval.

medir, *v.* measure, gauge.

meditación, *f.* meditation.

meditar, *v.* meditate.

mediterráneo, *a.* Mediterranean.

medrar, *v.* thrive.

medroso, *a.* fearful, cowardly.

megáfono, *m.* megaphone.

megahertzio, *f.* megahertz.

mejicano, *a. & m.* Mexican.

mejilla, *f.* cheek.

mejor, *a. & adv.* better; best. **a lo m.**, perhaps.

mejora, *f.*, **mejoramiento**, *m.* improvement.

mejorar, *v.* improve, better.

mejoría, *f.* improvement; superiority.

melancolía, *f.* melancholy.

melancólico, *a.* melancholy.

melaza, *f.* molasses.

melena, *f.* mane; long or loose hair.

melindroso, *a.* fussy.

melocotón, *m.* peach.

melodía, *f.* melody.

melodioso, *a.* melodious.

melón, *m.* melon.

meloso, *a.* like honey.

mella, *f.* notch; dent. —**mellar**, *v.*

mellizo -za, *n. & a.* twin.

membrana, *f.* membrane.

membrete, *m.* memorandum, letterhead.

membrillo, *m.* quince.

membrudo, *a.* strong, muscular.

memorable, *a.* memorable.

memorándum, *m.* memorandum; notebook.

memoria, *f.* memory; memoir; memorandum.

mención, *f.* mention. —**mencionar**, *v.*

mendigar, *v.* beg (for alms).

mendigo -a, *n.* beggar.

mendrugo, *m.* crumb, bit.

menear, *v.* shake, wag; stir.

menester, *m.* need, want; duty, task. **ser m.**, to be necessary.

menesteroso, *a.* needy.

mengua, *f.* decrease; lack; poverty.

menguar, *v.* abate, decrease.

menor, *a.* smaller, smallest; lesser, least; younger, youngest, junior. **m. de edad**, minor, under age. **al por m.**, at retail.

menos, *a. & adv.* less, least; minus. **a m. que**, unless. **echar de m.**, to miss.

menospreciar, *v.* cheapen; despise; slight.

mensaje, *m.* message.

mensajero -ra, *n.* messenger.

menstruar, *v.* menstruate.

mensual, *a.* monthly.

mensualidad, *f.* monthly income or allowance; monthly payment.

menta, *f.* mint, peppermint.

mentado, *a.* famous.

mental, *a.* mental.

mentalidad, *f.* mentality.

mente, *f.* mind.

mentecato, *a.* foolish, stupid.

mentir, *v.* lie, tell a lie.

mentira, *f.* lie, falsehood. **parece m.**, it seems impossible.

mentiroso, *a.* lying, untruthful.

mentol, *m.* menthol.

menú, *m.* menu.

menudeo, *m.* retail.

menudo, *a.* small, minute. **a m.**, often.

meñique, *a.* tiny.

meple, *m.* maple.

merca, *f.* purchase.

mercader, *m.* merchant.

mercaderías, *f.pl.* merchandise, commodities.

mercado, *m.* market.

mercancía, *f.* merchandise; (*pl.*) wares.

mercante, *a.* merchant.

mercantil, *a.* mercantile.

merced, *f.* mercy, grace.

mercenario -ria, *a. & m.* mercenary.

mercurio, *m.* mercury.

merecedor, *a.* worthy.

merecer, *v.* merit, deserve.

merecimiento, *m.* merit.

merendar, *v.* eat lunch.

merendero, *m.* lunchroom.

meridional, *a.* southern.

merienda, *f.* midday meal, lunch.

mérito, *m.* merit, worth.

meritorio, *a.* meritorious.

merla, *f.* blackbird.

merluza, *f.* haddock.

mermelada, *f.* marmalade.

mero, *a.* mere.

mes, *m.* month.

mesa, *f.* table.

meseta, *f.* plateau.

mesón, *m.* inn.

mesonero, *m.* innkeeper.

mestizo -za, *a. & n.* half-caste.

meta, *f.* goal, objective.

metabolismo, *m.* metabolism.

metafísica, *f.* metaphysics.

metáfora, *f.* metaphor.

metal, *m.* metal.

metálico, *a.* metallic.

metalurgia, *f.* metallurgy.

meteoro, *m.* meteor.

meteorología, *f.* meteorology.

meter, *v.* put (in).

meterse, *v.* interfere, meddle.

metódico, *a.* methodic.

método, *m.* method, approach.

metralla, *f.* shrapnel.

métrico, *a.* metric.

metro, *m.* meter (measure); subway.

metrópoli, *f.* metropolis.

mexicano -na, *a. & n.* Mexican.

mezcla, *f.* mixture; blend.

mezclar, *v.* mix; blend.

mezcolanza, *f.* mixture; hodgepodge.

mezquino, *a.* stingy; petty.

mi, *a.* my.

mí, *pron.* me; myself.

microbio, *m.* microbe, germ.

microficha, *f.* microfiche.

micrófono, *m.* microphone.

microforma, *f.* microform.

microscópico, *a.* microscopic.

microscopio, *m.* microscope.

miedo, *m.* fear. **tener m.**, fear, be afraid.

miedoso, *a.* fearful.

miel, *f.* honey.

miembro, *m.* member; limb.

mientras, *conj.* while. **m. tanto**, meanwhile. **m. más . . . más**, the more . . . the more.

miércoles, *m.* Wednesday.

miga, **migaja**, *f.* scrap, crumb.

migración, *f.* migration.

migratorio, *a.* migratory.

mil, *a. & pron.* thousand.

milagro, *m.* miracle.

milagroso, *a.* miraculous.

milicia, *f.* militia.

militante, *a.* militant.

militar, 1. *a.* military. **2.** *m.* military man.

militarismo, *m.* militarism.

milla, *f.* mile.

millar, *m.* (a) thousand.

millón, *m.* million.

millonario -ria, *n.* millionaire.

mimar, *v.* pamper; spoil (a child).

mimbre, *m.* willow; wicker.

mímico, *a.* mimic.

mimo, *m.* mime, mimic.

mina, *f.* mine. **—minar,** *v.*

mineral, *a. & m.* mineral.

minero, *m.* miner.

miniatura, *f.* miniature.

miniaturizar, *v.* miniaturize.

mínimo, *a. & m.* minimum.

ministerio, *m.* ministry; cabinet.

ministro, *m.* (govt.) minister, secretary.

minoría, *f.* minority.

minoridad, *f.* minority; nonage.

minucioso, *a.* minute; thorough.

minué, *m.* minuet.

minuta, *f.* minute; draft.

mío, *a.* mine.

miopía, *f.* myopia.

mira, *f.* gunsight.

mirada, *f.* look; gaze, glance.

miramiento, *m.* consideration; respect.

mirar, *v.* look, look at; watch. **m. a,** face.

miríada, *f.* myriad.

mirlo, *m.* blackbird.

mirón, *m.* bystander, observer.

mirra, *f.* myrrh.

mirto, *m.* myrtle.

misa, *f.* mass, church service.

misceláneo, *a.* miscellaneous.

miserable, *a.* miserable, wretched.

miseria, *f.* misery.

misericordia, *f.* mercy.

misericordioso, *a.* merciful.

misión, *f.* assignment; mission.

misionario -ria, misionero -ra, *n.* missionary.

mismo, 1. *a. & pron.* same; -self, -selves. **2.** *adv.* right, exactly.

misterio, *m.* mystery.

misterioso, *a.* mysterious, weird.

místico, *a. & m.* mystical, mystic.

mitad, *f.* half.

mítico, *a.* mythical.

mitigar, *v.* mitigate.

mitin, *m.* meeting.

mito, *m.* myth.

mitón, *m.* mitten.

mitra, *f.* miter (bishop's).

mixto, *a.* mixed.

mixtura, *f.* mixture.

mobiliario, *m.* household goods.

mocasín, *m.* moccasin.

mocedad, *f.* youthfulness.

moción, *f.* motion.

mocoso -sa, *n.* brat.

mochila, *f.* knapsack, backpack.

mocho, *a.* cropped, trimmed, shorn.

moda, *f.* mode, fashion, style.

modales, *m.pl.* manners.

modelo, *m.* model, pattern.

moderación, *f.* moderation.

moderado, *a.* moderate. **— moderar,** *v.*

modernizar, *v.* modernize.

moderno, *a.* modern.

modestia, *f.* modesty.

modesto, *a.* modest.

módico, *a.* reasonable, moderate.

modificación, *f.* modification.

modificar, *v.* modify.

modismo, *m.* (gram.) idiom.

modista, *f.* dressmaker; milliner.

modo, *m.* way, means.

modular, *v.* modulate.

mofarse, *v.* scoff, sneer.

mofletudo, *a.* fat-cheeked.

mohín, *m.* grimace.

moho, *m.* mold, mildew.

mohoso, *a.* moldy.

mojar, *v.* wet.

mojón, *m.* landmark; heap.

molde, *m.* mold, form.

molécula, *f.* molecule.

moler, *v.* grind, mill.

molestar, *v.* molest, bother, disturb, annoy, trouble.

molestia, *f.* bother, annoyance, trouble; hassle.

molesto, *a.* bothersome; annoyed; uncomfortable.

molicie, *f.* softness.

molinero, *m.* miller.

molino, *m.* mill.

molusco, *m.* mollusk.

mollera, *f.* top of the head.

momentáneo, *a.* momentary.

momento, *m.* moment.

mona, *f.* female monkey.

monarca, *m.* monarch.

monarquía, *f.* monarchy.

monarquista, *n. & a.* monarchist.

monasterio, *m.* monastery.

mondadientes, *m.* toothpick.

moneda, *f.* coin; money.

monetario, *a.* monetary.

monición, *f.* warning.

monigote, *m.* puppet.

monja, *f.* nun.

monje, *m.* monk.

mono -na, 1. *a.* (coll.) cute. **2.** *m. & f.* monkey.

monólogo, *m.* monologue.

monopatín, *m.* skateboard.

monopolio, *m.* monopoly.

monopolizar, *v.* monopolize.

monosílabo, *m.* monosyllable.

monotonía, *f.* monotony.

monótono, *a.* monotonous, dreary.

monstruo, *m.* monster.

monstruosidad, *f.* monstrosity.

monstruoso, *a.* monstrous.

monta, *f.* amount; price.

montaña, *f.* mountain.

montañoso, *a.* mountainous.

montar, *v.* mount, climb; amount; (mech.) assemble. **m. a caballo,** ride horseback.

montaraz, *a.* wild, barbaric.

monte, *m.* mountain, forest.

montón, *m.* heap, pile.

montuoso, *a.* mountainous.

montura, *f.* riding horse, mount.

monumental, *a.* monumental.

monumento, *m.* monument.

mora, *f.* blackberry.

morada, *f.* residence, dwelling.

morado, *a.* purple.

moral, 1. *a.* moral. **2.** *f.* morale.

moraleja, *f.* moral.

moralidad, *f.* morality, morals.

moralista, *m. & f.* moralist.

morar, *v.* dwell, live, reside.

mórbido, *a.* morbid.

mordaz, *a.* caustic; sarcastic.

mordedura, *f.* bite.

morder, *v.* bite.

moreno -na, *a. & n.* brown; dark-skinned; dark-haired, brunette.

morfina, *f.* morphine.

moribundo, *a.* dying.

morir, *v.* die.

morisco -ca, moro -ra, *a. & n.* Moorish; Moor.

morriña, *f.* sadness.

morro, *m.* bluff.

mortaja, *f.* shroud.

mortal, *a. & m.* mortal.

mortalidad, *f.* mortality.

mortero, *m.* mortar.

mortífero, *a.* fatal, mortal.

mortificar, *v.* mortify.

mortuorio, *a.* funereal.

mosaico, *a. & m.* mosaic.

mosca, *f.* fly.

mosquito, *m.* mosquito.

mostacho, *m.* mustache.

mostaza, *f.* mustard.

mostrador, *m.* counter; showcase.

mostrar, *v.* show, display.

mote, *m.* nickname; alias.

motín, *m.* mutiny; riot.

motivo, *m.* motive, reason.

motocicleta, *f.* motorcycle.

motor, *m.* motor.

motorista, *n.* motorist.

movedizo, *a.* movable; shaky.

mover, *v.* move; stir.

movible, *a.* movable.

móvil, *a.* mobile.

movilización, *f.* mobilization.

movilizar, *v.* mobilize.

movimiento, *m.* movement, motion.

mozo, *m.* boy; servant, waiter, porter.

muaré, *m.* moiré.

mucoso, *a.* mucous.

muchacha, *f.* girl; maid (servant).

muchachez, *m.* boyhood, girlhood.

muchacho, *m.* boy.

muchedumbre, *f.* crowd, mob.

mucho, 1. *a.* much, many. **2.** *adv.* much.

muda, *f.* change.

N, Ñ

mudanza, f. change; change of residence.
mudar, v. change, shift.
mudarse, v. change residence, move.
mudo -da, a. & n. mute.
mueble, m. piece of furniture; (pl.) furniture.
mueca, f. grimace.
muela, f. (back) tooth.
muelle, m. pier, wharf; (mech.) spring.
muerte, f. death.
muerto -ta, 1. a. dead. 2. n. dead person.
muescas, f. notch; groove.
muestra, f. sample, specimen, sign.
mugido, m. lowing; mooing.
mugir, v. low, moo.
mugre, f. filth, dirt.
mugriento, a. dirty.
mujer, f. woman; wife.
mujeril, a. womanly, feminine.
mula, f. mule.
mulato, a. & m. mulatto.
muleta, f. crutch; prop.
mulo, m. mule.
multa, f. fine, penalty.
multicolor, a. many-colored.
multinacional, a. multinational.
múltiple, a. multiple.
multiplicación, f. multiplication.
multiplicar, v. multiply.
multiplicidad, f. multiplicity.
multitud, f. multitude, crowd.
mundanal, a. worldly.
mundano, a. worldly, mundane.
mundial, a. worldwide; (of the) world.
mundo, m. world.
munición, f. ammunition.
municipal, a. municipal.
muñeca, f. doll; wrist.
muñeco, m. doll; puppet.
mural, a. & m. mural.
muralla, f. wall.
murciélago, m. bat.
murga, f. musical band.
murmullo, m. murmur; rustle.
murmurar, v. murmur; rustle; grumble.
murta, f. myrtle.
musa, f. muse.
muscular, a. muscular.
músculo, m. muscle.
muselina, f. muslin.
museo, m. museum.
música, f. music.
musical, a. musical.
músico, a. & m. musical; musician.
muslo, m. thigh.
mustio, a. sad.
muta, f. pack of hounds.
mutabilidad, f. mutability.
mutación, f. mutation.
mutilación, f. mutilation.
mutilar, v. mutilate; mangle.
mutuo, a. mutual.
muy, adv. very.

nabo, m. turnip.
nacar, m. mother-of-pearl.
nacarado, a. pearly.
nacer, v. be born.
naciente, a. rising.
nacimiento, m. birth.
nación, f. nation.
nacional, a. national.
nacionalidad, f. nationality.
nacionalismo, m. nationalism.
nacionalista, n. & a. nationalist.
nacionalización, f. nationalization.
nacionalizar, v. nationalize.
nada, 1. pron. nothing; any-thing de n., you're welcome. 2. adv. at all.
nadador, m. swimmer.
nadar, v. swim.
nadie, pron. no one, nobody; anyone, anybody.
nafta, f. naphtha.
naipe, m. (playing) card.
naranja, f. orange.
naranjada, f. orangeade.
naranjo, m. orange tree.
narciso, m. daffodil; narcissus.
narcótico, a. & m. narcotic.
nardo, m. spikenard.
nariz, f. nose; (pl.) nostrils.
narración, f. account.
narrador, m. narrator.
narrar, v. narrate.
narrativo, f. narrative.
nata, f. cream.
natal, a. native, natal.
natalicio, m. birthplace.
natalidad, f. birth rate.
natilla, f. custard.
nativo, a. native; innate.
natural, 1. a. natural. 2. m. & f. native. m. nature, disposition.
naturaleza, f. nature.
naturalidad, f. naturalness; naturality.
naturalista, a. & m. naturalistic; naturalist.
naturalización, f. naturalization.
naturalizar, v. naturalize, accustom.
naufragar, v. be shipwrecked; fail.
naufragio, m. shipwreck; disaster.
náufrago -ga, a. & n. shipwrecked (person).
náusea, f. nausea.
nausear, v. feel nauseous.
náutico, a. nautical.
navaja, f. razor; pen knife.
naval, a. naval.
nave, f. ship.
navegable, a. navigable.
navegación, f. navigation.
navegador, m. navigator.
navegante, m. navigator.
navegar, v. sail; navigate.
Navidad, f. Christmas.
navío, m. ship.

neblina, f. mist, fog.
nebuloso, a. misty; nebulous.
necedad, f. stupidity; nonsense.
necesario, a. necessary.
necesidad, f. necessity, need, want.
necesitado, a. needy, poor.
necesitar, v. need.
necio -cia, 1. a. stupid, silly. 2. n. fool.
néctar, m. nectar.
nefando, a. nefarious.
negable, a. deniable.
negación, f. denial, negation.
negar, v. deny.
negarse, v. refuse, decline.
negativa, f. negative, refusal.
negativamente, adv. negatively.
negativo, a. negative.
negligencia, f. negligence, neglect.
negligente, a. negligent.
negociación, f. negotiation, deal.
negociador, m. negotiator.
negociante, m. businessman.
negociar, v. negotiate, trade.
negocio, m. trade; business.
negro -gra, 1. a. black. 2. m. Black.
nene -na, n. baby.
neo, neón, m. neon.
nervio, m. nerve.
nervioso, a. nervous.
nervosamente, adv. nervously.
nesciencia, f. ignorance.
nesciente, a. ignorant.
neto, a. net.
neumático, 1. a. pneumatic. 2. m. (pneumatic) tire.
neumonía, f. pneumonia.
neurótico, a. neurotic.
neutral, a. neutral.
neutralidad, f. neutrality.
neutro, a. neuter; neutral.
neutrón, m. neutron.
nevada, f. snowfall.
nevado, a. snow-white; snow-capped.
nevar, v. snow.
nevera, f. icebox.
nevoso, a. snowy.
ni, 1. conj. nor. ni . . . ni, nei-ther . . . nor. 2. adv. not even.
nicho, m. recess.
nido, m. nest.
niebla, f. fog; mist.
nieto -ta, n. grandchild.
nieve, f. snow.
nilón, m. nylon.
nimio, adj. stingy.
ninfa, f. nymph.
ningún -no -na, a. & pron. no, none, neither (one); any, ei-ther (one).
niñera, f. nursemaid.
niñez, f. childhood.
niño -ña 1. a. young; childish; childlike. 2. n. child.
níquel, m. nickel.
niquelado, a. nickel-plated.
nítido, a. neat, clean, bright.
nitrato, m. nitrate.
nitro, m. niter.

nitrógeno, *m.* nitrogen.

nivel, *m.* level; grade. —**nivelar**, *v.*

no, 1. *adv.* not. **no más**, only. 2. *interj.* no.

noble, *a. & n.* noble; nobleman.

nobleza, *f.* nobility; nobleness.

noción, *f.* notion, idea.

nocivo, *a.* harmful.

noctiluca, *f.* glowworm.

nocturno, *a.* nocturnal.

noche, *f.* night; evening.

Nochebuena, *f.* Christmas Eve.

nodriza, *f.* wet nurse.

nogal, *m.* walnut.

nombradía, *f.* fame.

nombramiento, *m.* appointment, nomination.

nombrar, *v.* name, appoint, nominate; mention.

nombre, *m.* name; noun.

nómina, *f.* list; payroll.

nominación, *f.* nomination.

nominal, *a.* nominal.

nominar, *v.* name.

non, *a.* uneven, odd.

nonada, *f.* trifle.

nordeste, *m.* northeast.

nórdico, *a.* Nordic.

norma, *f.* norm, standard.

normal, *a.* normal, standard.

normalidad, *f.* normality.

normalizar, *v.* normalize; standardize.

noroeste, *m.* northwest.

norte, *m.* north.

norteamericano -na, *a. & n.* North American.

Noruega, *f.* Norway.

noruego -ga, *a. & n.* Norwegian.

nos, *pron.* us; ourselves.

nosotros -as, *pron.* we, us; ourselves.

nostalgia, *f.* nostalgia, homesickness.

nostálgico, *a.* nostalgic.

nota, *f.* note; grade, mark.

notable, *a.* notable, remarkable.

notación, *f.* notation; note.

notar, *v.* note, notice.

notario, *m.* notary.

noticia, *f.* notice; piece of news; (*pl.*) news.

notificación, *f.* notification.

notificar, *v.* notify.

notorio, *a.* well-known.

novato -ta, *n.* novice.

novecientos, *a. & pron.* nine hundred.

novedad, *f.* novelty; piece of news.

novel, *a.* new, inexperienced.

novela, *f.* novel.

novelista, *m. & f.* novelist.

novena, *f.* novena.

noveno, *a.* ninth.

noventa, *a. & pron.* ninety.

novia, *f.* bride; sweetheart, fiancée.

noviazgo, *m.* engagement, match.

novicio -cia, *n.* novice, beginner.

noviembre, *m.* November.

novilla, *f.* heifer.

novio, *m.* bridegroom; sweetheart, fiancé.

nube, *f.* cloud.

nubile, *a.* marriageable.

nublado, *a.* cloudy.

nuclear, *a.* nuclear.

núcleo, *m.* nucleus.

nudo, *m.* knot.

nuera, *f.* daughter-in-law.

nuestro, *a.* our, ours.

nueva, *f.* news.

nueve, *a. & pron.* nine.

nuevo, *a.* new. **de n.**, again, anew.

nuez, *f.* nut; walnut.

nulidad, *f.* nonentity.

nulo, *a.* null, void.

numeración, *f.* numeration.

numerar, *v.* number.

numérico, *a.* numerical.

número, *m.* number; size (of shoe, etc.)

numeroso, *a.* numerous.

numismática, *f.* numismatics.

nunca, *adv.* never; ever.

nupcial, *a.* nuptial.

nupcias, *f.pl.* nuptials, wedding.

nutrición, *f.* nutrition.

nutrimiento, *m.* nourishment.

nutrir, *v.* nourish.

nutritivo, *a.* nutritious.

ñame, *m.* yam.

ñapa, *f.* something extra.

ñoñería, *f.* dotage.

ñoño, *a.* feeble-minded, senile.

O

o, *conj.* or. **o . . . o**, either . . . or.

oasis, *m.* oasis.

obedecer, *v.* obey, mind.

obediencia, *f.* obedience.

obediente, *a.* obedient.

obelisco, *m.* obelisk.

obertura, *f.* overture.

obeso, *a.* obese.

obispo, *m.* bishop.

obituario, *m.* obituary.

objeción, *f.* objection.

objetivo, *a. & m.* objective.

objeto, *m.* object. —**objetar**, *v.*

oblicuo, *a.* oblique.

obligación, *f.* obligation, duty.

obligar, *v.* oblige, require, compel; obligate.

obligatorio, *a.* obligatory, compulsory.

oblongo, *a.* oblong.

oboe, *m.* oboe.

obra, *f.* work. —**obrar**, *v.*

obrero -ra, *n.* worker, laborer.

obscenidad, *f.* obscenity.

obsceno, *a.* obscene.

obscurecer, *v.* obscure; darken.

obscuridad, *f.* obscurity; darkness.

obscuro, *a.* obscure; dark.

obsequiar, *v.* court; make presents to, fete.

obsequio, *m.* obsequiousness; gift; attention.

observación, *f.* observation.

observador, *m.* observer.

observancia, *f.* observance.

observar, *v.* observe, watch.

observatorio, *m.* observatory.

obsesión, *f.* obsession.

obstáculo, *m.* obstacle.

obstante, *adv.* **no o.**, however, yet, nevertheless.

obstar, *v.* hinder, obstruct.

obstetricia, *f.* obstetrics.

obstinación, *f.* obstinacy.

obstinado, *a.* obstinate, stubborn.

obstinarse, *v.* persist, insist.

obstrucción, *f.* obstruction.

obstruir, *v.* obstruct, clog, block.

obtener, *v.* obtain, get, secure.

obtuso, *a.* obtuse.

obvio, *a.* obvious.

ocasión, *f.* occasion; opportunity, chance. **de o.**, secondhand.

ocasional, *a.* occasional.

ocasionalmente, *adv.* occasionally.

ocasionar, *v.* cause, occasion.

occidental, *a.* western.

occidente, *m.* west.

océano, *m.* ocean.

ocelote, *m.* ocelot.

ocio, *m.* idleness, leisure.

ociosidad, *f.* idleness, laziness.

ocioso, *a.* idle, lazy.

ocre, *m.* ochre.

octava, *f.* octave.

octavo, *a.* eighth.

octogonal, *a.* octagonal.

octubre, *m.* October.

oculista, *m.* oculist.

ocultación, *f.* concealment.

ocultar, *v.* hide, conceal.

oculto, *a.* hidden.

ocupación, *f.* occupation.

ocupado, *a.* occupied; busy.

ocupante, *m.* occupant.

ocupar, *v.* occupy.

ocuparse de, *v.* take care of, take charge of.

ocurrencia, *f.* occurrence; witticism.

ocurrir, *v.* occur, happen.

ochenta, *a. & pron.* eighty.

ocho, *a. & pron.* eight.

ochocientos, *a. & pron.* eight hundred.

oda, *f.* ode.

odio, *m.* hate. —**odiar**, *v.*

odiosidad, *f.* odiousness; hatred.

odioso, *a.* obnoxious, odious.

odisea, *f.* odyssey.

oeste, *m.* west.

ofender, *v.* offend, wrong.

ofenderse, *v.* be offended, take offense.

ofensa, *f.* offense.

ofensiva, *f.* offensive.

ofensivo, *a.* offensive.

ofensor -ra, *n.* offender.

oferta, f. offer, proposal.
ofertorio, m. offertory.
oficial, a. & m. official; officer.
oficialmente, adv. officially.
oficiar, v. officiate.
oficina, f. office.
oficio, m. office; trade; church service.
oficioso, a. officious.
ofrecer, v. offer.
ofrecimiento, m. offer, offering.
ofrenda, f. offering.
oftalmía, f. ophthalmia.
ofuscamiento, m. obfuscation; bewilderment.
ofuscar, v. obfuscate; bewilder.
ogro, m. ogre.
oído, m. ear; hearing.
oír, v. hear; listen.
ojal, m. buttonhole.
ojalá, interj. expressing wish or hope. **o. que . . .** would that . . .
ojeada, f. glance; peep; look.
ojear, v. eye, look at, glance at, stare at.
ojeriza, f. spite; grudge.
ojiva, f. pointed arch; ogive.
ojo, m. eye. **¡Ojo!** Look out!
ola, f. wave.
olaje, m. surge of waves.
oleada, f. swell.
oleo, m. oil; holy oil; extreme unction.
oleomargarina, f. oleomargarine.
oleoso, a. oily.
oler, v. smell.
olfatear, v. smell.
olfato, m. scent, smell.
oliva, f. olive.
olivar, m. olive grove.
olivo, m. olive tree.
olmo, m. elm.
olor, m. odor, smell, scent.
oloroso, a. fragrant, scented.
olvidadizo, a. forgetful.
olvidar, v. forget.
olvido, m. omission; forgetfulness.
olla, f. pot, kettle. **o. podrida**, stew.
ombligo, m. navel.
ominar, v. foretell.
ominoso, a. ominous.
omisión, f. omission.
omitir, v. omit, leave out.
ómnibus, m. bus.
omnipotencia, f. omnipotence.
omnipotente, a. almighty.
omnipresencia, f. omnipresence.
omnisciencia, f. omniscience.
omnívoro, a. omnivorous.
once, a. & pron. eleven.
onda, f. wave, ripple.
ondear, v. ripple.
ondulación, f. wave, undulation.
ondular, v. undulate, ripple.
onza, f. ounce.
opaco, a. opaque.
ópalo, m. opal.
opción, f. option.

ópera, f. opera.
operación, f. operation.
operar, v. operate; operate on.
operario -ria, m. operator; (skilled) worker.
operarse, v. have an operation.
operativo, a. operative.
opereta, f. operetta.
opiato, m. opiate.
opinar, v. opine.
opinión, f. opinion, view.
opio, m. opium.
oponer, v. oppose.
oporto, m. port (wine).
oportunidad, f. opportunity.
oportunismo, m. opportunism.
oportunista, n. & a. opportunist.
oportuno, a. opportune, expedient.
oposición, f. opposition.
opresión, f. oppression.
opresivo, a. oppressive.
oprimir, v. oppress.
oprobio, m. infamy.
optar, v. select, choose.
óptica, f. optics.
óptico, a. optic.
optimismo, m. optimism.
optimista, a. & n. optimistic; optimist.
óptimo, a. best.
opuesto, a. opposite; opposed.
opugnar, v. attack.
opulencia, f. opulence, wealth.
opulento, a. opulent, wealthy.
oración, f. sentence; prayer; oration.
oráculo, m. oracle.
orador, m. orator, speaker.
oral, a. oral.
orangután, m. orangutan.
orar, v. pray.
oratoria, f. oratory.
oratorio, a. oratorical.
orbe, m. orb; globe.
órbita, f. orbit.
orden, m. or f. order.
ordenador, m. computer; regulator.
ordenanza, f. ordinance.
ordenar, v. order; put in order; ordain.
ordeñar, v. milk.
ordinal, n. & a. ordinal.
ordinario, a. ordinary; common, usual.
oreja, f. ear.
orejera, f. earmuff.
orfanato, m. orphanage.
organdí, m. organdy.
orgánico, a. organic.
organismo, m. organism.
organista, m. & f. organist.
organización, f. organization.
organizar, v. organize.
órgano, m. organ.
orgía, f. orgy, revel.
orgullo, m. pride.
orgulloso, a. proud.
orientación, f. orientation.
oriental, a. Oriental; eastern.
orientar, v. orient.
oriente, m. orient, east.

orificación, f. gold filling (for tooth).
origen, m. origin; parentage, descent.
original, a. original.
originalidad, f. originality.
originalmente, adv. originally.
originar, v. originate.
orilla, f. shore; bank; edge.
orín, m. rust.
orina, f. urine.
orinar, v. urinate.
orines, n.pl. urine.
oriol, m. oriole.
orla, f. border; edging.
ornado, a. ornate.
ornamentación, f. ornamentation.
ornamento, m. ornament. — **ornamentar**, v.
ornar, v. ornament, adorn.
oro, m. gold.
oropel, m. tinsel.
orquesta, f. orchestra.
ortiga, f. nettle.
ortodoxo, a. orthodox.
ortografía, f. orthography, spelling.
ortóptero, a. orthopterous.
oruga, f. caterpillar.
orzuelo, m. sty.
os, pron. you (pl.); yourselves.
osadía, f. daring.
osar, v. dare.
oscilación, f. oscillation.
oscilar, v. oscillate, rock.
ósculo, m. kiss.
oscurecer, oscuridad, oscuro = **obscur--**.
oso, osa, n. bear.
ostentación, f. ostentation, showiness.
ostentar, v. show off.
ostentoso, a. ostentatious, flashy.
ostra, f. oyster.
ostracismo, m. ostracism.
otalgia, f. earache.
otero, m. hill, knoll.
otoño, m. autumn, fall.
otorgar, v. grant, award.
otro, a. & pron. other, another. **o. vez**, again. **el uno al o.**, one another, each other.
ovación, f. ovation.
oval, ovalado, a. oval.
óvalo, m. oval.
ovario, m. ovary.
oveja, f. sheep.
ovejero, m. shepherd.
ovillo, m. ball of yarn.
oxidación, f. oxidation.
oxidar, v. oxidize; rust.
óxido, m. oxide.
oxígeno, m. oxygen.
oyente, m. hearer; (pl.) audience.
ozono, m. ozone.

P

pabellón, m. pavilion.
pabilo, m. wick.
paciencia, f. patience.

paciente, *a.* & *n.* patient.

pacificar, *v.* pacify.

pacífico, *a.* pacific.

pacifismo, *m.* pacifism.

pacifista, *n.* & *a.* pacifist.

pacto, *m.* pact, treaty.

padecer, *v.* suffer.

padrasto, *m.* stepfather.

padre, *m.* father; priest; (*pl.*) parents.

padrenuestro, *m.* paternoster.

padrino, *m.* godfather; sponsor.

paella, *f.* dish of rice with meat or chicken.

paga, *f.* pay, wages.

pagadero, *a.* payable.

pagador, *m.* payer.

paganismo, *m.* paganism.

pagano -na, *a.* & *n.* heathen, pagan.

pagar, *v.* pay, pay for.

página, *f.* page.

pago, *m.* pay, payment.

país, *m.* country, nation.

paisaje, *m.* landscape, scenery, countryside.

paisano -na, *n.* countryman; compatriot; civilian.

paja, *f.* straw.

pajar, *m.* barn.

pájaro, *m.* bird.

paje, *m.* page (person).

pala, *f.* shovel, spade.

palabra, *f.* word.

palabrero, *a.* talkative.

palabrista, *m.* talkative person.

palacio, *m.* palace.

paladar, *m.* palate.

paladear, *v.* taste; relish.

palanca, *f.* lever.

palangana, *f.* washbasin.

palco, *m.* theater box.

palenque, *m.* palisade.

palidecer, *v.* turn pale.

palidez, *f.* paleness.

pálido, *a.* pale.

paliza, *f.* beating.

palizada, *m.* palisade.

palma, palmera, *f.* palm (tree).

palmada, *f.* slap, clap.

palmear, *v.* applaud.

palo, *m.* pole, stick; suit (in cards); (naut.) mast.

paloma, *f.* dove, pigeon.

palpar, *v.* touch, feel.

palpitación, *f.* palpitation.

palpitar, *v.* palpitate.

paludismo, *m.* malaria.

palleta, *f.* mat, pallet.

pampa, *f.* (South America) prairie, plain.

pan, *m.* bread; loaf.

pana, *f.* corduroy.

pánacea, *f.* panacea.

panadería, *f.* bakery.

panadero -ra, *n.* baker.

panameño -ña, *a.* & *n.* Panamanian, of Panama.

panamericano, *a.* Pan-American.

páncreas, *m.* pancreas.

pandeo, *m.* bulge.

pandilla, *f.* band, gang.

panecillo, *m.* roll, muffin.

panegírico, *m.* panegyric.

pánico, *m.* panic.

panocha, *f.* ear of corn.

panorámico, *a.* panoramic.

pantalones, *m.pl.* trousers, pants.

pantalla, *f.* (movie) screen; lamp shade.

pantano, *m.* bog, marsh, swamp.

pantanoso, *a.* swampy, marshy.

pantera, *f.* panther.

pantomima, *f.* pantomime.

panza, *f.* belly, paunch.

pañal, *m.* diaper.

paño, *m.* piece of cloth.

pañuelo, *m.* handkerchief.

Papa, *m.* Pope.

papa, *f.* potato.

papá, *m.* papa, father.

papado, *m.* papacy.

papagayo, *m.* parrot.

papal, *a.* papal.

papel, *m.* paper; role, part.

papelera, *f.* file or folder for papers.

papelería, *f.* stationery store.

papera, *f.* mumps.

paquete, *m.* package.

par, 1. *a.* even, equal. 2. *m.* pair; equal, peer. **abierto de p. en p.**, wide open.

para, *prep.* for; in order to. **p. que**, in order that. **estar p.**, to be about to.

parabién, *m.* greeting; congratulation.

parabrisa, *m.* windshield.

paracaídas, *m.* parachute.

parachoques, *m.* (auto.) bumper.

parada, *f.* stop, halt; parade.

paradero, *m.* whereabouts; stopping place.

paradigma, *m.* paradigm.

paradoja, *f.* paradox.

parafina, *f.* paraffin.

parafrasear, *v.* paraphrase.

paraguas, *m.* umbrella.

paraguayano -na, *n.* & *a.* Paraguayan.

paraíso, *m.* paradise.

paralelo, *a.* & *m.* parallel.

parálisis, *f.* paralysis.

paralizar, *v.* paralyze.

paramédico, *m.* paramedic.

parámetro, *m.* parameter.

parapeto, *m.* parapet.

parar, *v.* stop, stem, ward off; stay.

pararse, *v.* stop; stand up.

parasismo, *m.* paroxysm.

parasítico, *a.* parasitic.

parásito, *m.* parasite.

parcela, *f.* plot of ground.

parcial, *a.* partial.

parcialidad, *f.* partiality; bias.

parcialmente, *adv.* partially.

pardo, *a.* brown.

parear, *v.* pair, match, mate.

parecer, 1. *m.* opinion. 2. *v.* seem, appear, look.

parecerse, *v.* look alike. **p. a**, look like.

parecido, *a.* similar.

pared, *f.* wall.

pareja, *f.* pair, couple; (dancing) partner.

parentela, *f.* kinfolk.

parentesco, *m.* parentage, lineage; kin.

paréntesis, *m.* parenthesis.

paria, *m.* outcast.

paridad, *f.* parity.

pariente, *m.* & *f.* relative.

parir, *v.* give birth to young.

parisiense, *n.* & *a.* Parisian.

parlamentario, *a.* parliamentary.

parlamento, *m.* parliament.

paro, *m.* stoppage; strike. **p. forzoso**, unemployment.

parodia, *f.* parody.

parodista, *m.* parodist.

paroxismo, *m.* paroxysm.

párpado, *m.* eyelid.

parque, *m.* park.

parra, *f.* grapevine.

párrafo, *m.* paragraph.

parranda, *f.* spree.

parrandear, *v.* carouse.

parrilla, *f.* grill.

párroco, *m.* parish priest.

parroquia, *f.* parish.

parroquial, *a.* parochial.

parsimonia, *f.* economy, thrift.

parsimonioso, *a.* economical, thrifty.

parte, *f.* part. **de p. de**, on behalf of. **alguna p.**, somewhere. **por otra p.**, on the other hand. **dar p. a**, to notify.

partera, *f.* midwife.

partición, *f.* distribution.

participación, *f.* participation.

participante, *m.* & *f.* participant.

participar, *v.* participate; announce.

participio, *m.* participle.

partícula, *f.* particle.

particular, 1. *a.* particular; private. 2. *m.* particular; detail; individual.

particularmente, *adv.* particularly.

partida, *f.* departure; (mil.) party; (sport) game.

partidario -ria, *n.* partisan.

partido, *m.* side, party, faction; game, match.

partir, *v.* leave, depart; part, cleave, split.

parto, *m.* delivery, childbirth.

pasa, *f.* raisin.

pasado, 1. *a.* past; last. 2. *m.* past.

pasaje, *m.* passage, fare.

pasajero -ra, 1. *a.* passing, transient. 2. *n.* passenger.

pasamano, *m.* banister.

pasaporte, *m.* passport.

pasar, *v.* pass; happen; spend (time). **p. por alto**, overlook. **p. lista**, call the roll. **p. sin**, do without.

pasatiempo, *m.* pastime, hobby.

pascua, *f.* religious holiday;

(pl.) Christmas (season). **P. Florida,** Easter.

paseo, m. walk, stroll; drive. —**pasear,** v.

pasillo, m. aisle; hallway.

pasión, f. passion.

pasivo, a. passive.

pasmar, v. astonish, astound, stun.

pasmo, m. spasm; wonder.

paso, 1. a. dried (fruit). **2.** m. pace, step; (mountain) pass.

pasta, f. paste; batter; plastic.

pastar, v. graze.

pastel, m. pastry; pie.

pastelería, f. pastry; pastry shop.

pasteurización, f. pasteurization.

pasteurizar, v. pasteurize.

pastilla, f. tablet, lozenge, drop.

pasto, m. pasture; grass.

pastor, m. pastor, shepherd.

pastorear, v. pasture, tend (a flock).

pastura, f. pasture.

pata, f. foot (of animal).

patada, f. kick.

patán, m. boor.

patanada, f. rudeness.

patata, f. potato.

patear, v. stamp, tramp, kick.

patente, a. & m. patent. —**patentar,** v.

paternal, paterno, a. paternal.

paternidad, f. paternity, fatherhood.

patético, a. pathetic.

patíbulo, m. scaffold, gallows.

patín, m. skate. —**patinar,** v.

patio, m. yard, court, patio.

pato, m. duck.

patria, f. native land.

patriarca, m. patriarch.

patrimonio, m. inheritance.

patriota, m. & f. patriot.

patriótico, a. patriotic.

patriotismo, m. patriotism.

patrocinar, v. patronize, sponsor.

patrón, m. patron; boss; (dress) pattern.

patrulla, f. patrol. —**patrullar,** v.

pausa, f. pause. —**pausar,** v.

pavesa, f. embers.

pavimentar, v. pave.

pavimento, m. pavement.

pavo, m. turkey. **p. real,** peacock.

payaso, m. clown.

paz, f. peace.

peatón -na, n. pedestrian.

peca, f. freckle.

pecado, m. sin. —**pecar,** v.

pecador -ra, a. & n. sinful; sinner.

pecera, f. aquarium, fishbowl.

peculiar, a. peculiar.

peculiaridad, f. peculiarity.

pechera, f. shirt front.

pecho, m. chest; breast; bosom.

pedagogía, f. pedagogy.

pedagogo, m. pedagogue, teacher.

pedal, m. pedal.

pedantesco, a. pedantic.

pedazo, m. piece.

pedernal, m. flint.

pedestal, m. pedestal.

pediatría, f. pediatrics.

pedicuro, m. chiropodist.

pedir, v. ask, ask for, request; apply for; order.

pedregoso, a. rocky.

pegajoso, a. sticky.

pegar, v. beat, strike; adhere, fasten, stick.

peinado, m. coiffure, hairdo.

peine, m. comb. —**peinar,** v.

peineta, f. (ornamental) comb.

pelagra, f. pellagra.

pelar, v. skin, pare, peel.

pelea, f. fight, row. —**pelearse,** v.

pelícano, m. pelican.

película, f. movie, motion picture, film.

peligrar, v. be in danger.

peligro, m. peril, danger.

peligroso, a. perilous, dangerous.

pelo, m. hair.

pelota, f. ball.

peltre, m. pewter.

peluca, f. wig.

peludo, a. hairy.

peluquería, f. hairdresser's shop, beauty parlor.

peluquero, m. hairdresser.

pellejo, m. skin, peel (of fruit).

pellizco, m. pinch. —**pellizcar,** v.

pena, f. pain, grief, trouble, woe; penalty. **valer la p.,** to be worthwhile.

penacho, m. plume.

penalidad, f. trouble; penalty.

pender, v. hang, dangle; be pending.

pendiente, 1. a. hanging; pending. **2.** m. incline, slope; earring, pendant.

pendón, m. pennant, flag.

penetración, f. penetration.

penetrar, v. penetrate, pierce.

penicilina, f. penicillin.

península, f. peninsula.

penitencia, f. penitence, penance.

penitenciaría, f. penitentiary.

penoso, a. painful, troublesome, grievous.

pensador -ra, n. thinker.

pensamiento, m. thought.

pensar, v. think; intend, plan.

pensativo, a. pensive, thoughtful.

pensión, f. pension; boardinghouse.

pensionista, m. & f. boarder.

pentagonal, a. pentagonal.

penuria, f. penury, poverty.

peña, f. rock.

peñascoso, a. rocky.

peón, m. unskilled laborer; infantryman.

peonada, f. group of laborers.

peonía, f. peony.

peor, a. worse, worst.

pepino, m. cucumber.

pepita, f. seed (in fruit).

pequeñez, f. smallness; trifle.

pequeño -ña, 1. a. small, little, short, slight. **2.** n. child.

pera, f. pear.

peral, m. pear tree.

perca, f. perch (fish).

percal, m. calico, percale.

percentaje, m. percentage.

percepción, f. perception.

perceptivo, a. perceptive.

percibir, v. perceive, sense; collect.

percha, f. perch; clothes hanger, rack.

perder, v. lose; miss; waste. **echar a p.,** spoil.

perdición, f. perdition, downfall.

pérdida, f. loss.

perdiz, f. partridge.

perdón, m. pardon, forgiveness.

perdonar, v. forgive, pardon; spare.

perdurable, a. enduring, everlasting.

perdurar, v. endure, last.

perecedero, a. perishable.

perecer, v. perish.

peregrinación, f. peregrination; pilgrimage.

peregrino -na, n. pilgrim.

perejil, m. parsley.

perenne, a. perennial.

pereza, f. laziness.

perezoso, a. lazy, sluggish.

perfección, f. perfection.

perfeccionar, v. perfect.

perfectamente, adv. perfectly.

perfecto, a. perfect.

perfidia, f. falseness, perfidy.

pérfido, a. perfidious.

perfil, m. profile.

perforación, f. perforation.

perforar, v. pierce, perforate.

perfume, m. perfume, scent. —**perfumar,** v.

pergamino, m. parchment.

pericia, f. skill, expertness.

perico, m. parakeet.

perímetro, m. perimeter.

periódico, 1. a. periodic. **2.** m. newspaper.

periodista, m. journalist.

período, m. period.

periscopio, m. periscope.

perito -ta, a. & n. experienced; expert, connoisseur.

perjudicar, v. damage, hurt; impair.

perjudicial, a. harmful, injurious.

perjuicio, m. injury, damage.

perjurar, v. commit perjury.

perjurio, m. perjury.

perla, f. pearl.

permanecer, v. remain, stay.

permanencia, f. permanence; stay.

permanente, a. permanent.

permiso, m. permission; permit; furlough.

permitir, v. permit, enable, let, allow.

permuta, f. exchange; barter.

pernicioso, a. pernicious.

perno, m. bolt.

pero, conj. but.

peróxido, m. peroxide.

perpendicular, m. & a. perpendicular.

perpetración, f. perpetration.

perpetrar, v. perpetrate.

perpetuar, v. perpetuate.

perpetuidad, f. perpetuity.

perpetuo, a. perpetual.

perplejo, a. perplexed, puzzled.

perro -rra, n. dog.

persecución, f. persecution.

perseguir, v. pursue; persecute.

perseverancia, f. perseverance.

perseverar, v. persevere.

persiana, f. shutter, Venetian blind.

persistente, a. persistent.

persistir, v. persist.

persona, f. person.

personaje, m. personage; (theat.) character.

personal, 1. a. personal. 2. m. personnel, staff.

personalidad, f. personality.

personalmente, adv. personally.

perspectiva, f. perspective; prospect.

perspicaz, a. perspicacious, acute.

persuadir, v. persuade.

persuasión, f. persuasion.

persuasivo, a. persuasive.

pertenecer, v. pertain, belong.

pertinencia, f. pertinence.

pertinente, a. pertinent; relevant.

perturbar, v. perturb, disturb.

peruano -na, a. & n. Peruvian.

perversidad, f. perversity.

perverso, a. perverse.

pesadez, f. dullness, importunity.

pesadilla, f. nightmare.

pesado, a. heavy; dull, dreary, boring.

pésame, m. condolence.

pesar, 1. m. sorrow; regret. a pesar de, in spite of. 2. v. weigh.

pesca, f. fishing; catch (of fish).

pescado, m. fish. —pescar, v.

pescador, m. fisherman.

pesebre, m. stall, manger, crib.

peseta, f. monetary unit of Spain.

pesimismo, m. pessimism.

pesimista, a. & n. pessimistic; pessimist.

peso, m. weight; load; peso (monetary unit).

pesquera, f. fishery.

pesquisa, f. investigation.

pestaña, f. eyelash.

pestañeo, m. wink, blink. —pestañear, v.

peste, f. plague.

pestilencia, f. pestilence.

pétalo, m. petal.

petición, f. petition.

petirrojo, m. robin.

petrel, m. petrel.

pétreo, a. rocky.

petrificar, v. petrify.

petróleo, m. petroleum.

petunia, f. petunia.

pez, m. fish (in the water). f. pitch, tar.

pezuña, f. hoof.

piadoso, a. pious.

pianista, m. & f. pianist.

piano, m. piano.

picadura, f. sting, bite, prick.

picamaderos, m. woodpecker.

picante, a. hot, spicy.

picaporte, m. latch.

picar, v. sting, bite, prick; itch; chop up, grind up.

pícaro -ra, 1. a. knavish, mischievous. 2. n. rogue, rascal.

picarse, v. be offended, piqued.

picazón, f. itch.

picea, f. spruce.

pico, m. peak; pick; beak; spout; small amount.

picotazo, m. peck. —picotear, v.

pictórico, a. pictorial.

pichón, m. pigeon, squab.

pie, m. foot. al p. de la letra, literally; thoroughly.

piedad, f. piety; pity, mercy.

piedra, f. stone.

piel, f. skin, hide; fur.

pierna, f. leg.

pieza, f. piece; room; (theat.) play.

pijamas, m. or f.pl. pajamas.

pila, f. pile, stack; battery; sink.

pilar, m. pillar, column.

píldora, f. pill.

piloto, m. pilot.

pillo, m. thief; rascal.

pimienta, f. pepper (spice).

pimiento, m. pepper (vegetable).

pináculo, m. pinnacle.

pincel, m. (artist's) brush.

pinchazo, m. puncture. —pinchar, v.

pingajo, m. rag, tatter.

pino, m. pine.

pinta, f. pint.

pintar, v. paint; portray, depict.

pintor -ra, n. painter.

pintoresco, a. picturesque.

pintura, f. paint; painting.

pinzas, f.pl. pincers, tweezers; claws.

piña, f. pineapple.

pío, a. pious; merciful.

piojo, m. louse.

pionero -ra, n. pioneer.

pipa, f. tobacco pipe.

pique, m. resentment, pique. echar a p., sink (ship).

pira, f. pyre.

pirámide, f. pyramid.

pirata, m. pirate. p. de aviones, hijacker.

pisada, f. tread, step. —pisar, v.

piscina, f. fishpond; swimming pool.

piso, m. floor.

pista, f. trace, clue, track; racetrack.

pistola, f. pistol.

pistón, m. piston.

pitillo, m. cigarette.

pito, m. whistle. —pitar, v.

pizarra, f. slate; blackboard.

pizca, f. bit, speck; pinch.

pizza, f. pizza.

placentero, a. pleasant.

placer, 1. m. pleasure. 2. v. please.

plácido, a. placid.

plaga, f. plague, scourge.

plagio, m. plagiarism; (S.A.) kidnapping.

plan, m. plan. —planear, v.

plancha, f. plate, slab, flatiron.

planchar, v. iron, press.

planeta, m. planet.

plano, 1. a. level, flat. 2. m. plan; plane.

planta, f. plant; sole (of foot).

plantación, f. plantation.

plantar, v. plant.

plantear, v. pose, present.

plantel, m. educational institution; (agr.) nursery.

plasma, m. plasma.

plástico, a. & m. plastic.

plata, f. silver; (coll.) money.

plataforma, f. platform.

plátano, m. plantain, cooking banana.

platel, m. platter.

plática, f. chat, talk. —platicar, v.

platillo, m. saucer.

plato, m. plate, dish.

playa, f. beach, shore.

plaza, f. square. p. de toros, bullring.

plazo, m. term, deadline; installment.

plebe, f. common people; masses.

plebiscito, m. plebiscite.

plegadura, f. fold, pleat. —plegar, v.

pleito, m. lawsuit; dispute.

plenitud, f. fullness; abundance.

pleno, a. full. en pleno . . . in the middle of . . .

pliego, m. sheet of paper.

pliegue, m. fold, pleat, crease.

plomería, f. plumbing.

plomero, m. plumber.

plomizo, a. leaden.

plomo, m. lead; fuse.

pluma, f. feather; (writing) pen.

plumafuente, f. fountain pen.

plumaje, m. plumage.

plumero, m. feather duster; plume.

plumoso, a. feathery.

plural, a. & m. plural.

población, f. population; town.

poblador -ra, n. settler.

poblar, v. populate; settle.

pobre, a. & n. poor; poor person.

pobreza, f. poverty, need.

pocilga, f. pigpen.

poción, f. drink; potion.

poco, 1. a. & adv. little, not much, (pl.) few. **por p.,** almost, nearly. **2.** m. **un p. (de),** a little, a bit (of).

poder, 1. m. power. **2.** v. be able to, can; be possible, may, might. **no p. menos de,** not be able to help.

poderío, m. power, might.

poderoso, a. powerful, mighty, potent.

podrido, a. rotten.

poema, m. poem.

poesía, f. poetry; poem.

poeta, m. poet.

poético, a. poetic.

polaco -ca, a. & n. Polish; Pole.

polar, a. polar.

polaridad, f. polarity.

polea, f. pulley.

polen, m. pollen.

policía, f. police. m. policeman.

poligamia, f. polygamy.

polígloto -ta, n. polyglot.

polilla, f. moth.

política, f. politics; policy.

político, a. & m. politic; political; politician.

póliza, f. (insurance) policy; permit, ticket.

polizonte, m. policeman.

polo, m. pole; polo.

polonés, a. Polish.

Polonia, f. Poland.

polvera, f. powder box; powder puff.

polvo, m. powder; dust.

pólvora, f. powder, gunpowder.

pollada, f. brood.

pollería, f. poultry shop.

pollino, m. donkey.

pollo, m. chicken.

pompa, f. pomp.

pomposo, a. pompous.

ponche, m. punch (beverage).

ponchera, f. punch bowl.

ponderar, v. ponder.

ponderoso, a. ponderous.

poner, v. put, set, lay, place.

ponerse, v. put on; become, get; set (sun). **p. a,** start to.

poniente, m. west.

pontífice, m. pontiff.

popa, f. stern.

popular, a. popular.

popularidad, f. popularity.

populazo, m. populace; masses.

por, prep. by, through, because of; via; for. **p. qué,** why?

porcelana, f. porcelain, chinaware.

porcentaje, m. percentage.

porción, f. portion, lot.

porche, m. porch; portico.

porfiar, v. persist; argue.

pormenor, m. detail.

pornografía, f. pornography.

poro, m. pore.

poroso, a. porous.

porque, conj. because.

porqué, m. reason, motive.

porra, f. stick, club.

porrazo, m. blow.

portaaviones, m. aircraft carrier.

portador -ra, n. bearer.

portal, m. portal.

portar, v. carry.

portarse, v. behave, act.

portátil, a. portable.

portavoz, m. megaphone.

porte, m. bearing; behavior; postage.

portero, m. porter; janitor.

pórtico, m. porch.

portorriqueño -ña, n. & a. Puerto Rican.

portugués -esa, a. & n. Portuguese.

posada, f. lodge, inn.

posar, v. pose.

posdata, f. postscript.

poseer, v. possess, own.

posesión, f. possession.

posibilidad, f. possibility.

posible, a. possible.

posiblemente, adv. possibly.

posición, f. position, stand.

positivo, a. positive.

posponer, v. postpone.

postal, a. postal.

poste, m. post, pillar.

posteridad, f. posterity.

posterior, a. posterior, rear.

postizo, a. false, artificial.

postrado, a. prostrate. —**postrar,** v.

postre, m. dessert.

póstumo, a. posthumous.

postura, f. posture, pose; bet.

potable, a. drinkable.

potaje, m. porridge; pot stew.

potasa, f. potash.

potasio, m. potassium.

pote, m. pot, jar.

potencia, f. potency, power.

potencial, a. & f. potential.

potentado, m. potentate.

potente, a. potent, powerful.

potestad, f. power.

potro, m. colt.

pozo, m. well.

práctica, f. practice. —**practicar,** v.

práctico, a. practical.

pradera, f. prairie, meadow.

prado, m. meadow; lawn.

pragmatismo, m. pragmatism.

preámbulo, m. preamble.

precario, a. precarious.

precaución, f. precaution.

precaverse, v. beware.

precavido, a. cautious, guarded, wary.

precedencia, f. precedence, priority.

precedente, a. & m. preceding; precedent.

preceder, v. precede.

precepto, m. precept.

preciar, v. value, prize.

preciarse de, v. take pride in.

precio, m. price.

precioso, a. precious; beautiful, gorgeous.

precipicio, m. precipice, cliff.

precipitación, f. precipitation.

precipitar, v. precipitate, rush; throw headlong.

precipitoso, a. precipitous; rash.

precisar, v. fix, specify; be necessary.

precisión, f. precision; necessity.

preciso, a. precise; necessary.

precocidad, f. precocity.

precoz, a. precocious.

precursor -ra 1. a. preceding. **2.** m. precursor, forerunner.

predecesor -ra, a. & n. predecessor.

predecir, v. predict, foretell.

predicación, f. sermon.

predicador, m. preacher.

predicar, v. preach; publish.

predicción, f. prediction.

predilecto, a. favorite, preferred.

predisponer, v. predispose.

predisposición, f. predisposition; bias.

predominante, a. prevailing, prevalent, predominant.

predominar, v. prevail, predominate.

predominio, m. predominance, sway.

prefacio, m. preface.

preferencia, f. preference.

preferentemente, adv. preferably.

preferible, a. preferable.

preferir, v. prefer.

prefijo, m. prefix; area code. —**prefijar,** v.

pregón, m. proclamation, cry.

pregonar, v. proclaim, cry out.

pregunta, f. question, inquiry. **hacer una p.,** to ask a question.

preguntar, v. ask, inquire.

preguntarse, v. wonder.

prehistórico, a. prehistoric.

prejuicio, m. prejudice.

prelacía, f. prelacy.

preliminar, a. & m. preliminary.

preludio, m. prelude.

prematuro, a. premature.

premeditación, f. premeditation.

premeditar, v. premeditate.

premiar, v. reward; award a prize to.

premio, m. prize, award; reward.

premisa, f. premise.

premura, f. pressure; urgency.

prenda, f. jewel; (personal) quality. **p. de vestir,** garment.

prender, v. seize, arrest, catch; attack, pin, clip. **p. fuego a,** set fire to.

prensa, f. printing press; (the) press.

prensar, v. press, compress.

preñado, a. pregnant.

preocupación, f. worry, preoccupation.

preocupar, v. worry, preoccupy.

preparación, f. preparation.

preparar, v. prepare.

preparativo, m. preparation.

preparatorio, m. preparatory.

preponderante, a. preponderant.

preposición, f. preposition.

prerrogativa, f. prerogative, privilege.

presa, f. capture; prey; (water) dam.

presagiar, v. presage, forebode.

presbiteriano -na, n. & a. Presbyterian.

presbítero, m. priest.

prescindir de, v. dispense with; omit.

prescribir, v. prescribe.

prescripción, f. prescription.

presencia, f. presence.

presenciar, v. witness, be present at.

presentable, a. presentable.

presentación, f. presentation; introduction.

presentar, v. present; introduce.

presente, a. & m. present.

preservación, f. preservation.

preservar, v. preserve, keep.

preservativo, a. & m. preservative.

presidencia, f. presidency.

presidencial, a. presidential.

presidente -ta, n. president.

presidio, m. prison; garrison.

presidir, v. preside.

presión, f. pressure.

preso, m. prisoner.

presta, f. mint (plant).

prestador, m. lender.

prestamista, m. & f. money lender.

préstamo, m. loan.

prestar, v. lend.

presteza, f. haste, promptness.

prestidigitación, f. sleight of hand.

prestigio, m. prestige.

presto, 1. a. quick, prompt; ready. 2. adv. quickly; at once.

presumido, a. conceited, presumptuous.

presumir, v. presume; boast; claim; be conceited.

presunción, f. presumption; conceit.

presunto, a. presumed; prospective.

presuntuoso, a. presumptuous.

presupuesto, m. motive, pretext; budget.

pretender, v. pretend; intend; aspire.

pretendiente, m. suitor; pretender (to throne).

pretensión, f. pretension; claim.

pretérito, a. & m. preterit, past (tense).

pretexto, m. pretext.

prevalecer, v. prevail.

prevención, f. prevention.

prevenir, v. prevent; forewarn; prearrange.

preventivo, a. preventive.

prever, v. foresee.

previamente, adv. previously.

previo, a. previous.

previsión, f. foresight. **p. social,** social security.

prieto, a. blackish, very dark.

primacía, f. primacy.

primario, a. primary.

primavera, f. spring (season).

primero, a. & adv. first.

primitivo, a. primitive.

primo -ma, n. cousin.

primor, m. beauty; excellence; lovely thing.

primoroso, a. exquisite, elegant; graceful.

princesa, f. princess.

principal, 1. a. principal, main. 2. m. chief, head, principal.

principalmente, adv. principally.

príncipe, m. prince.

principiar, v. begin, initiate.

principio, m. beginning, start; principle.

prioridad, f. priority.

prisa, f. hurry, haste. **darse p.,** hurry, hasten. **tener p.,** be in a hurry.

prisión, f. prison; imprisonment.

prisionero -ra, n. captive, prisoner.

prisma, m. prism.

prismático, a. prismatic.

privación, f. privation, want.

privado, a. private, secret; deprived.

privar, v. deprive.

privilegio, m. privilege.

pro, m. or f. benefit, advantage. **en p. de,** in behalf of. **en p. y en contra,** pro and con.

proa, f. prow, bow.

probabilidad, f. probability.

probable, a. probable, likely.

probablemente, adv. probably.

probar, v. try, sample; taste; test; prove.

probarse, v. try on.

probidad, f. honesty, integrity.

problema, m. problem.

probo, a. honest.

procaz, a. impudent, saucy.

proceder, v. proceed.

procedimiento, m. procedure.

procesar, v. prosecute; sue; process.

procesión, f. procession.

proceso, m. process; (court) trial.

proclama, proclamación, f. proclamation.

proclamar, v. proclaim.

procreación, f. procreation.

procrear, v. procreate.

procurar, v. try; see to it; get; procure.

prodigalidad, f. prodigality.

prodigar, v. lavish, squander, waste.

prodigio, m. prodigy.

pródigo, a. prodigal, profuse, lavish.

producción, f. production.

producir, v. produce.

productivo, a. productive.

producto, m. product.

proeza, f. prowess.

profanación, f. profanation.

profanar, v. defile, desecrate.

profanidad, f. profanity.

profano, a. profane.

profecía, f. prophecy.

proferir, v. utter, express.

profesar, v. profess.

profesión, f. profession.

profesional, a. professional.

profesor -ra, n. professor; teacher.

profeta, m. prophet.

profético, a. prophetic.

profetizar, v. prophesy.

proficiente, a. proficient.

profundamente, adv. profoundly, deeply.

profundidad, f. profundity, depth.

profundizar, v. deepen.

profundo, a. profound, deep.

profuso, a. profuse.

progenie, f. progeny, offspring.

programa, m. program; schedule.

progresar, v. progress, advance.

progresión, f. progression.

progresista, progresivo, a. progressive.

progreso, m. progress.

prohibición, f. prohibition.

prohibir, v. prohibit, forbid.

prohibitivo, a. prohibitive.

prole, f. progeny.

proletariado, m. proletariat.

proliferación, f. proliferation.

prolijo, a. prolix, tedious; long-winded.

prólogo, m. prologue; preface.

prolongar, v. prolong.

promedio, m. average.

promesa, f. promise.

prometer, v. promise.

prometido, a. promised; engaged (to marry).

prominencia, f. prominence.

promiscuamente, adv. promiscuously.

promiscuo, a. promiscuous.

promisorio, a. promissory.

promoción, f. promotion.

promover, v. promote, further.

promulgación, f. promulgation.

promulgar, v. promulgate.

pronombre, m. pronoun.

pronosticación, f. prediction, forecast.

pronosticar, v. predict, forecast.

pronóstico, m. prediction.

prontamente, *adv.* promptly.

prontitud, *f.* promptness.

pronto, 1. *a.* prompt; ready. **2.** *adv.* soon; quickly. **de p.,** abruptly.

pronunciación, *f.* pronunciation.

pronunciar, *v.* pronounce.

propagación, *f.* propagation.

propaganda, *f.* propaganda.

propagandista, *n.* propagandist.

propagar, *v.* propagate.

propicio, *a.* propitious, auspicious, favorable.

propiedad, *f.* property.

propietario -ria, *n.* proprietor; owner; landlord, landlady.

propina, *f.* gratuity, tip.

propio, *a.* proper, suitable; typical; (one's) own; -self.

proponer, *v.* propose.

proporción, *f.* proportion.

proporcionado, *a.* proportionate.

proporcionar, *v.* provide with, supply, afford.

proposición, *f.* proposition, offer; proposal.

propósito, *m.* purpose; plan; **a p.,** by the way, apropos; on purpose.

propuesta, *f.* proposal, motion.

prorrata, *f.* quota.

prórroga, *f.* renewal, extension.

prorrogar, *v.* renew, extend.

prosa, *f.* prose.

prosaico, *a.* prosaic.

proscribir, *v.* prohibit, proscribe, ban.

prosecución, *f.* prosecution.

proseguir, *v.* pursue; proceed, go on.

prosélito, *m.* proselyte.

prospecto, *m.* prospectus.

prosperar, *v.* prosper, thrive, flourish.

prosperidad, *f.* prosperity.

próspero, *a.* prosperous, successful.

prosternado, *a.* prostrate.

prostitución, *f.* prostitution.

prostituir, *v.* prostitute; debase.

prostituta, *f.* prostitute.

protagonista, *m. & f.* protagonist, hero, heroine.

protección, *f.* protection.

protector -ra, *a. & n.* protective; protector.

proteger, *v.* protect, safeguard.

protegido -da, *n.* protégé.

proteína, *f.* protein.

protesta, *f.* protest. **—protestar,** *v.*

protestante, *a. & n.* Protestant.

protocolo, *m.* protocol.

protuberancia, *f.* protuberance, lump.

provecho, *m.* profit, gain, benefit. **¡Buen provecho!** May you enjoy your meal!

provechoso, *a.* beneficial, advantageous, profitable.

proveer, *v.* provide, furnish.

provenir de, *v.* originate in, be due to, come from.

proverbial, *a.* proverbial.

proverbio, *m.* proverb.

providencia, *f.* providence.

providente, *a.* provident.

provincia, *f.* province.

provincial, *a.* provincial.

provinciano -na, *a. & n.* provincial.

provisión, *f.* provision, supply, stock.

provisional, *a.* provisional.

provocación, *f.* provocation.

provocador, *m.* provoker.

provocar, *v.* provoke, excite.

provocativo, *a.* provocative.

proximidad, *f.* proximity, vicinity.

próximo, *a.* next; near.

proyección, *f.* projection.

proyectar, *v.* plan, project.

proyectil, *m.* projectile, missile, shell.

proyecto, *m.* plan, project, scheme.

proyector, *m.* projector.

prudencia, *f.* prudence.

prudente, *a.* prudent.

prueba, *f.* proof; trial; test.

psicoanálisis, *m. or f.* psychoanalysis.

psicología, *f.* psychology.

psicológico, *a.* psychological.

psicólogo, *m.* psychologist.

psiquedélico, *a.* psychedelic.

psiquiatra, *m.* psychiatrist.

psiquiatría, *f.* psychiatry.

publicación, *f.* publication.

publicar, *v.* publish.

publicidad, *f.* publicity.

público, *a. & m.* public.

puchero, *m.* pot.

pudiente, *a.* powerful; wealthy.

pudín, *m.* pudding.

pudor, *m.* modesty.

pudoroso, *a.* modest.

pudrirse, *v.* rot.

pueblo, *m.* town, village; (the) people.

puente, *m.* bridge.

puerco -ca, *n.* pig.

pueril, *a.* childish.

puerilidad, *f.* puerility.

puerta, *f.* door; gate.

puerto, *m.* port, harbor.

puertorriqueño -ña, *a. & n.* Puerto Rican.

pues, 1. *adv.* well . . . **2.** *conj.* as, since, for.

puesto, *m.* appointment, post, job; place; stand. **p. que,** since.

pugilato, *m.* boxing.

pugna, *f.* conflict.

pugnacidad, *f.* pugnacity.

pugnar, *v.* fight; oppose.

pulcritud, *f.* beauty.

pulga, *f.* flea.

pulgada, *f.* inch.

pulgar, *m.* thumb.

pulir, *v.* polish; beautify.

pulmón, *m.* lung.

pulmonía, *f.* pneumonia.

pulpa, *f.* pulp.

púlpito, *m.* pulpit.

pulque, *m.* pulque (fermented maguey juice).

pulsación, *f.* pulsation, beat.

pulsar, *v.* pulsate, beat.

pulsera, *f.* wristband; bracelet; wristwatch.

pulso, *m.* pulse.

pulverizar, *v.* pulverize.

puma, *f.* puma.

pundonor, *m.* point of honor.

punta, *f.* point, tip, end.

puntada, *f.* stitch.

puntapié, *m.* kick.

puntería, *f.* (marksman's) aim.

puntiagudo, *a.* sharp-pointed.

puntillas, *f.pl.* **de p., en p.,** on tiptoe.

punto, *m.* point; period; spot, dot. **dos puntos,** (punct.) colon. **a p. de,** about to. **al p.,** instantly.

puntuación, *f.* punctuation.

puntual, *a.* punctual, prompt.

puntuar, *v.* punctuate.

puñada, *f.* fist, blow.

puñado, *m.* handful.

puñal, *m.* dagger.

puñalada, *f.* stab.

puñetazo, *m.* punch, fist blow.

puño, *m.* fist; cuff; handle.

pupila, *f.* pupil (of eye).

pupitre, *m.* writing desk, school desk.

pureza, *f.* purity; chastity.

purgante, *m.* laxative.

purgar, *v.* purge, cleanse.

purgatorio, *m.* purgatory.

puridad, *f.* purity.

purificación, *f.* purification.

purificar, *v.* purify.

purismo, *m.* purism.

purista, *n.* purist.

puritanismo, *m.* puritanism.

puro, 1. *a.* pure. **2.** *m.* cigar.

púrpura, *f.* purple.

purpúreo, *a.* purple.

purulencia, *f.* purulence.

purulento, *a.* purulent.

pus, *m.* pus.

pusilánime, *a.* pusillanimous.

puta, *f.* prostitute.

putrefacción, *f.* putrefaction, rot.

putrefacto, *a.* putrid, rotten.

pútrido, *a.* putrid.

puya, *f.* goad.

Q

que, 1. *rel. pron.* who, whom; that, which. **2.** *conj.* than.

qué, 1. *a. & pron.* what. **por q., para q.,** why? **2.** *adv.* how.

quebrada, *f.* ravine, gully, gulch; stream.

quebradizo, *a.* fragile, brittle.

quebrar, *v.* break.

queda, *f.* curfew.

quedar, *v.* remain, be located; be left. **q. bien a,** be becoming to.

quedarse, *v.* stay, remain. **q. con,** keep, hold on to.

quedo, *a.* quiet; gentle.
quehacer, *m.* task; chore.
queja, *f.* complaint.
quejarse, *v.* complain, grumble.
quejido, *m.* moan.
quejoso, *a.* complaining.
quema, *f.* burning.
quemadura, *f.* burn.
quemar, *v.* burn.
querella, *f.* quarrel; complaint.
querencia, *f.* affection, love.
querer, *v.* want, wish; will; love (a person). **q. decir**, mean. **sin q.**, without meaning to; unwillingly.
querido, *a.* dear, loved, beloved.
quesería, *f.* dairy.
queso, *m.* cheese.
quiebra, *f.* break, fracture; damage; bankruptcy.
quien, *rel. pron.* who, whom.
quién, *interrog. pron.* who, whom.
quienquiera, *pron.* whoever, whomever.
quietamente, *adv.* quietly.
quieto, *a.* quiet, still.
quietud, *f.* quiet, quietude.
quijada, *f.* jaw.
quijotesco, *a.* quixotic.
quilate, *m.* carat.
quilla, *f.* keel.
quimera, *f.* chimera, vision; quarrel.
química, *f.* chemistry.
químico, *a. & m.* chemical; chemist.
quimoterapia, *f.* chemotherapy.
quincalleri, *f.* hardware store.
quince, *a. & pron.* fifteen.
quinientos, *a. & pron.* five hundred.
quinina, *f.* quinine.
quintana, *f.* country home.
quinto, *a.* fifth.
quirúrgico, *m.* surgeon.
quiste, *m.* cyst.
quitamanchas, *m.* stain remover.
quitanieve, *m.* snowplow.
quitar, *v.* take away, remove.
quitarse, *v.* take off; get rid of.
quitasol, *m.* parasol, umbrella.
quizá, **quizás**, *adv.* perhaps, maybe.
quórum, *m.* quorum.

R

rábano, *m.* radish.
rabí, **rabino**, *m.* rabbi.
rabia, *f.* rage; grudge; rabies.
rabiar, *v.* rage, be furious.
rabieta, *f.* tantrum.
rabioso, *a.* furious; rabid.
rabo, *m.* tail.
racimo, *m.* bunch, cluster.
ración, *f.* ration. —**racionar**, *v.*
racionabilidad, *f.* rationality.
racional, *a.* rational.
racionalismo, *m.* rationalism.

racionalmente, *adv.* rationally.
racha, *f.* streak.
radar, *m.* radar.
radiación, *f.* radiation.
radiador, *m.* radiator.
radiante, *a.* radiant.
radical, *a. & m.* radical.
radicalismo, *m.* radicalism.
radicoso, *a.* radical.
radio, *m. or f.* radio.
radioactividad, *f.* radioactivity.
radioactivo, *a.* radioactive.
radiodifundir, *v.* broadcast.
radiodifusión, *f.* (radio) broadcasting.
ráfaga, *f.* gust (of wind).
raíz, *f.* root.
raja, *f.* rip; split, crack. —**rajar**, *v.*
ralea, *f.* stock, breed.
ralo, *a.* thin, scattered.
rama, *f.* branch, bough.
ramillete, *m.* bouquet.
ramo, *m.* branch, bough.
ramonear, *v.* browse.
rampa, *f.* ramp.
rana, *f.* frog.
rancidez, *f.* rancidity.
rancio, *a.* rancid, rank, stale, sour.
ranchero -ra, *n.* small farmer.
rancho, *m.* ranch.
rango, *m.* rank.
ranúnculo, *m.* ranunculus; buttercup.
ranura, *f.* slot.
rapacidad, *f.* rapacity.
rapaz, **1.** *a.* rapacious. **2.** *m.* young boy.
rapé, *m.* snuff.
rápidamente, *adv.* rapidly.
rapidez, *f.* rapidity, speed.
rápido, **1.** *a.* rapid, fast, speedy. **2.** *m.* express (train).
rapiña, *f.* robbery, plundering.
rapsodia, *f.* rhapsody.
raqueta, *f.* (tennis) racket.
rareza, *f.* rarity, freak.
raridad, *f.* rarity.
raro, *a.* rare, strange, unusual, odd, queer.
rasar, *v.* skim.
rascar, *v.* scrape; scratch.
rasgadura, *f.* tear, rip. —**rasgar**, *v.*
rasgo, *m.* trait.
rasgón, *m.* tear.
rasguño, *m.* scratch. —**rasguñar**, *v.*
raso, **1.** *a.* plain. **soldado r.**, (mil.) private. **2.** *m.* satin.
raspar, *v.* scrape; erase.
rastra, *f.* trail, track. —**rastrear**, *v.*
rastrillar, *v.* rake.
rastro, *m.* track, trail, trace; rake.
rata, *f.* rat.
ratificación, *f.* ratification.
ratificar, *v.* ratify.
rato, *m.* while, spell, short time.
ratón, *m.* mouse.
ratonera, *f.* mousetrap.

raya, *f.* dash, line, streak, stripe.
rayar, *v.* rule, stripe; scratch; cross out.
rayo, *m.* lightning bolt; ray; flash.
rayón, *m.* rayon.
raza, *f.* race; breed, stock.
razón, *f.* reason; ratio. **a r. de**, at the rate of. **tener r.**, to be right.
razonable, *a.* reasonable, sensible.
razonamiento, *m.* argument.
razonar, *v.* reason.
reacción, *f.* reaction.
reaccionar, *v.* react.
reaccionario, *m.* reactionary.
reacondicionar, *v.* recondition.
reactivo, *a. & m.* reactive; (chem.) reagent.
reactor, *m.* reactor.
real, *a.* royal, regal; real, actual.
realdad, *f.* royal authority.
realeza, *f.* royalty.
realidad, *f.* reality.
realista, *a. & n.* realistic; realist.
realización, *f.* achievement, accomplishment.
realizar, *v.* accomplish; fulfill; effect; (com.) realize.
realmente, *adv.* in reality.
realzar, *v.* enhance.
reata, *f.* rope; lasso, lariat.
rebaja, *f.* reduction.
rebajar, *v.* cheapen; reduce (in price); lower.
rebanada, *f.* slice. —**rebanar**, *v.*
rebaño, *m.* flock, herd.
rebato, *m.* alarm; sudden attack.
rebelarse, *v.* rebel, revolt.
rebelde, *a. & n.* rebellious; rebel.
rebelión, *f.* rebellion, revolt.
reborde, *m.* border.
rebotar, *v.* rebound.
rebozo, *m.* shawl.
rebuscar, *v.* search thoroughly.
rebuznar, *v.* bray.
recado, *m.* message; errand.
recaída, *f.* relapse. —**recaer**, *v.*
recalcar, *v.* stress, emphasize.
recámara, *f.* (Mex.) bedroom.
recapitulación, *f.* recapitulation.
recapitular, *v.* recapitulate.
recatado, *m.* coy; prudent.
recelar, *v.* fear, distrust.
receloso, *a.* distrustful.
recepción, *f.* reception.
receptáculo, *m.* receptacle.
receptividad, *f.* receptivity.
receptivo, *a.* receptive.
receptor, *m.* receiver.
receta, *f.* recipe; prescription.
recetar, *v.* prescribe.
recibimiento, *m.* reception; cordiality.
recibir, *v.* receive.
recibo, *m.* receipt.
reciclar, *v.* recycle.
recidiva, *f.* relapse.

recién, *adv.* recently, newly, just.

reciente, *a.* recent.

recinto, *m.* enclosure.

recipiente, *m.* recipient.

reciprocación, *f.* reciprocation.

recíprocamente, *adv.* reciprocally.

reciprocar, *v.* reciprocate.

reciprocidad, *f.* reciprocity.

recitación, *f.* recitation.

recitar, *v.* recite.

reclamación, *f.* claim; complaint.

reclamar, *v.* claim; complain.

reclamo, *m.* claim; advertisement, advertising; decoy.

reclinar, *v.* recline, repose, lean.

recluta, *m.* recruit.

reclutar, *v.* recruit, draft.

recobrar, *v.* recover, salvage, regain.

recobro, *m.* recovery.

recoger, *v.* gather; collect; pick up.

recogerse, *v.* retire (for night).

recolectar, *v.* gather, assemble; harvest.

recomendación, *f.* recommendation; commendation.

recomendar, *v.* recommend; commend.

recompensa, *f.* recompense, compensation.

recompensar, *v.* reward; compensate.

reconciliación, *f.* reconciliation.

reconciliar, *v.* reconcile.

reconocer, *v.* recognize; acknowledge; inspect, examine; (mil.) reconnoiter.

reconocimiento, *m.* recognition; appreciation, gratitude.

reconstituir, *v.* reconstitute.

reconstruir, *v.* reconstruct, rebuild.

record, *m.* (sports) record.

recordar, *v.* recall, recollect; remind.

recorrer, *v.* go over; read over; cover (distance).

recorte, *m.* clipping, cutting.

recostarse, *v.* recline, lean back, rest.

recreación, *f.* recreation.

recreo, *m.* recreation.

recriminación, *f.* recrimination.

rectangular, *a.* rectangular.

rectángulo, *m.* rectangle.

rectificación, *f.* rectification.

rectificar, *v.* rectify.

recto, *a.* straight; just, fair. ángulo r., right angle.

recuento, *m.* recount.

recuerdo, *m.* memory, souvenir, remembrance; (*pl.*) regards.

reculada, *f.* recoil. —**recular,** *v.*

recuperación, *f.* recuperation.

recuperar, *v.* recuperate.

recurrir, *v.* revert; resort, have recourse.

recurso, *m.* resource; recourse.

rechazar, *v.* reject, spurn, discard.

rechinar, *v.* chatter.

red, *f.* net; trap.

redacción, *f.* (editorial) staff; composition (of written material).

redactar, *v.* draft, draw up; edit.

redactor, *m.* editor.

redada, *f.* netful, catch, haul.

redargución, *f.* retort. —**redargüir,** *v.*

redención, *f.* redemption, salvation.

redentor, *m.* redeemer.

redimir, *v.* redeem.

redoblante, *m.* drummer.

redonda, *f.* neighborhood, vicinity.

redondo, *a.* round, circular.

reducción, *f.* reduction.

reducir, *v.* reduce.

reembolso, *m.* refund. —**reembolsar,** *v.*

reemplazar, *v.* replace, supersede.

reencarnación, *f.* reincarnation.

reexaminar, *v.* reexamine.

reexpedir, *v.* forward (mail).

referencia, *f.* reference.

referéndum, *m.* referendum.

referir, *v.* relate, report on.

referirse, *v.* refer.

refinamiento, *m.* refinement.

refinar, *v.* refine.

refinería, *f.* refinery.

reflejar, *v.* reflect; think, ponder.

reflejo, *m.* reflection; glare.

reflexión, *f.* reflection, thought.

reflexionar, *v.* reflect, think.

reflujo, *m.* ebb; ebb tide.

reforma, *f.* reform. —**reformar,** *v.*

reformación, *f.* reformation.

reformador, *m.* reformer.

reforzar, *v.* reinforce, strengthen; encourage.

refractario, *a.* refractory.

refrán, *m.* proverb, saying.

refrenar, *v.* curb, rein; restrain.

refrescar, *v.* refresh, freshen, cool.

refresco, *m.* refreshment; cold drink.

refrigeración, *f.* refrigeration.

refrigerador, *m.* refrigerator.

refrigerar, *v.* refrigerate.

refuerzo, *m.* reinforcement.

refugiado -da, refugee.

refugiarse, *v.* take refuge.

refugio, *m.* refuge, asylum, shelter.

refulgencia, *f.* refulgence.

refulgente, *a.* refulgent.

refulgir, *v.* shine.

refunfuñar, *v.* mutter, grumble, growl.

refutación, *f.* refutation; rebuttal.

refutar, *v.* refute.

regadizo, *a.* irrigable.

regadura, *f.* irrigation.

regalar, *v.* give (a gift), give away.

regalo, *m.* gift, present, con r., in luxury.

regañar, *v.* reprove; scold.

regaño, *m.* reprimand, scolding.

regar, *v.* water, irrigate.

regatear, *v.* haggle.

regateo, *m.* bargaining, haggling.

regazo, *m.* lap.

regencia, *f.* regency.

regeneración, *f.* regeneration.

regenerar, *v.* regenerate.

regente, *m.* regent.

régimen, *m.* regime; diet.

regimentar, *v.* regiment.

regimiento, *m.* regiment.

región, *f.* region.

regional, *a.* regional, sectional.

regir, *v.* rule; be in effect.

registrar, *v.* register; record; search.

registro, *m.* register; record; search.

regla, *f.* rule, regulation. en r., in order.

reglamento, *m.* code of regulations.

regocijarse, *v.* rejoice, exult.

regocijo, *f.* rejoicing; merriment, joy.

regordete, *a.* chubby, plump.

regresar, *v.* go back, return.

regresión, *f.* regression.

regresivo, *a.* regressive.

regreso, *m.* return.

regulación, *f.* regulation.

regular, 1. *a.* regular; fair, middling. 2. *v.* regulate.

regularidad, *f.* regularity.

regularmente, *adv.* regularly.

rehabilitación, *f.* rehabilitation.

rehabilitar, *v.* rehabilitate.

rehén, *m.* hostage.

rehusar, *v.* refuse; decline.

reina, *f.* queen.

reinado, *m.* reign. —**reinar,** *v.*

reino, *m.* kingdom; realm; reign.

reír, *v.* laugh.

reiteración, *f.* reiteration.

reiterar, *v.* reiterate.

reja, *f.* grating, grillwork.

relación, *f.* relation; account, report.

relacionar, *v.* relate, connect.

relajamiento, *m.* laxity, laxness.

relajar, *v.* relax, slacken.

relámpago, *m.* lightning; flash (of lightning).

relatador, *m.* teller.

relatar, *v.* relate, recount.

relativamente, *adv.* relatively.

relatividad, *f.* relativity.

relativo, *a.* relative.

relato, *m.* account, story.

relegación, *f.* relegation.

relegar, *v.* relegate.

relevar, *v.* relieve.

relicario, *m.* reliquary; locket.

relieve, *m.* (sculpture) relief.

religión, *f.* religion.

religiosidad, *f.* religiosity.

religioso -sa, 1. *a.* religious. 2. *m.* member of a religious order.

reliquia, *f.* relic.

reloj, *m.* clock; watch.

relojería, *f.* watchmaker's shop.

relojero, *m.* watchmaker.

relucir, *v.* glow, shine; excel.

relumbrar, *v.* glitter, sparkle.

rellenar, *v.* refill; fill up, stuff.

relleno, *m.* filling; stuffing.

remache, *m.* rivet. —remachar, *v.*

remar, *v.* row (a boat).

rematado, *a.* finished; sold.

remate, *m.* end, finish; auction. de r., utterly.

remedador, *m.* imitator.

remedar, *v.* imitate.

remedio, *m.* remedy. —remediar, *v.*

remendar, *v.* mend, patch.

remesa, *f.* shipment; remittance.

remiendo, *m.* patch.

remilgado, *a.* prudish; affected.

reminiscencia, *f.* reminiscence.

remitir, *v.* remit.

remo, *m.* oar.

remolacha, *f.* beet.

remolcador, *m.* tug (boat).

remolino, *m.* whirl; whirlpool; whirlwind.

remolque, *m.* tow. —remolcar, *v.*

remontar, *v.* ascend, go up.

remontarse, *v.* get excited; soar. r. a, date from; go back to (in time).

remordimiento, *m.* remorse.

remotamente, *adv.* remotely.

remoto, *a.* remote.

remover, *v.* remove; stir; shake; loosen.

rempujar, *v.* jostle.

remuneración, *f.* remuneration.

remunerar, *v.* remunerate.

renacido, *a.* reborn, born-again.

renacimiento, *m.* rebirth; renaissance.

rencor, *m.* rancor, bitterness, animosity; grudge.

rencoroso, *a.* rancorous, bitter.

rendición, *f.* surrender.

rendido, *a.* weary, worn out.

rendir, *v.* yield; surrender, give up; win over.

renegado, *m.* renegade.

renglón, *m.* line; (com.) item.

reno, *m.* reindeer.

renombre, *m.* renown.

renovación, *f.* renovation, renewal.

renovar, *v.* renew; renovate.

renta, *f.* income; rent.

rentar, *v.* yield; rent for.

renuencia, *f.* reluctance.

renuente, *a.* reluctant.

renuncia, *f.* resignation; renunciation.

renunciar, *v.* resign; renounce; give up.

reñir, *v.* scold, berate; quarrel, wrangle.

reo, *a.* & *n.* criminal; convict.

reorganizar, *v.* reorganize.

reparación, *f.* reparation, atonement; repair.

reparar, *v.* repair; mend; stop, stay over. r. en, notice; consider.

reparo, *m.* repair; remark; difficulty; objection.

repartición, *f.*, repartimiento, reparto, *m.* division, distribution.

repartir, *v.* divide, apportion, distribute; (theat.) cast.

repaso, *m.* review. —repasar, *v.*

repatriación, *f.* repatriation.

repatriar, *v.* repatriate.

repeler, *v.* repel.

repente, *m.* de r., suddenly; unexpectedly.

repentinamente, *adv.* suddenly.

repentino, *a.* sudden.

repercusión, *f.* repercussion.

repertorio, *m.* repertoire.

repetición, *f.* repetition.

repetidamente, *adv.* repeatedly.

repetir, *v.* repeat.

repisa, *f.* shelf.

réplica, *f.* reply; objection.

replicar, *v.* reply; answer back.

repollo, *m.* cabbage.

reponer, *v.* replace; repair.

reponerse, *v.* recover, get well.

reporte, *m.* report; news.

repórter, reportero, *m.* reporter.

reposado, *a.* tranquil, peaceful, quiet.

reposo, *m.* repose, rest. —reposar, *v.*

reposte, *f.* pantry.

represalia, *f.* reprisal.

representación, *f.* representation; (theat.) performance.

representante, *m.* representative, agent.

representar, *v.* represent, depict; (theat.) perform.

representativo, *a.* representative.

represión, *f.* repression.

represivo, *a.* repressive.

reprimenda, *f.* reprimand.

reprimir, *v.* repress, quell.

reproche, *m.* reproach. —reprochar, *v.*

reproducción, *f.* reproduction.

reproducir, *v.* reproduce.

reptil, *m.* reptile.

república, *f.* republic.

republicano -na, *a.* & *n.* republican.

repudiación, *f.* repudiation.

repudiar, *v.* repudiate; disown.

repuesto, *m.* spare part. de r., spare.

repugnancia, *f.* repugnance.

repugnante, *a.* repugnant, repulsive.

repugnar, *v.* disgust.

repulsa, *f.* refusal; repulse.

repulsivo, *a.* repulsive.

reputación, *f.* reputation.

reputar, *v.* repute; appreciate.

requerir, *v.* require.

requesón, *m.* cottage cheese.

requisición, *f.* requisition.

requisito, *m.* requisite, requirement.

res, *f.* head of cattle.

resbalar, *v.* slide; slip.

resbaloso, *a.* slippery.

rescate, *m.* rescue, ransom. — rescatar, *v.*

rescindir, *v.* rescind.

resentimiento, *m.* resentment.

resentirse, *v.* resent.

reserva, *f.* reserve. —reservar, *v.*

reservación, *f.* reservation.

resfriado, *m.* (med.) cold.

resfriarse, *v.* catch cold.

resguardar, *v.* guard, protect.

residencia, *f.* residence, seat.

residente, *a.* & *n.* resident.

residir, *v.* reside.

residuo, *m.* remainder.

resignación, *f.* resignation.

resignar, *v.* resign.

resina, *f.* resin; rosin.

resistencia, *f.* resistance.

resistir, *v.* resist; endure.

resolución, *f.* resolution.

resolutivamente, *adv.* resolutely.

resolver, *v.* resolve; solve.

resonante, *a.* resonant.

resonar, *v.* resound.

resorte, *m.* (mech.) spring.

respaldar, *v.* endorse; back.

respaldo, *m.* back (of a seat).

respectivo, *a.* respective.

respecto, *m.* relation, proportion; r. a, concerning, regarding.

respetabilidad, *f.* respectability.

respetable, *a.* respectable.

respeto, *m.* respect. —respetar, *v.*

respetuosamente, *adv.* respectfully.

respetuoso, *a.* respectful.

respiración, *f.* respiration, breath.

respirar, *v.* breathe.

resplandeciente, *a.* resplendent.

resplandor, *m.* brightness, glitter.

responder, *v.* respond, answer.

responsabilidad, *f.* responsibility.

responsable, *a.* responsible.

respuesta, *f.* answer, response, reply.

resquicio, *m.* crack, slit.

resta, *f.* subtraction, remainder.

restablecer, *v.* restore, reestablish.

restablecerse, v. recover, get well.

restar, v. remain; subtract.

restauración, f. restoration.

restaurante, m. restaurant.

restaurar, v. restore.

restitución, f. restitution.

restituir, v. restore, give back.

resto, m. remainder, rest; (pl.) remains.

restorán, m. restaurant.

restregar, v. scrape.

restricción, f. restriction.

restrictivo, a. restrictive.

restringir, v. restrict, curtail.

resucitar, v. resuscitate; resurrect.

resuelto, a. resolute.

resultado, m. result.

resultar, v. result; turn out; ensue.

resumen, m. résumé, summary, en r., in brief.

resumir, v. sum up.

resurgir, v. resurge, reappear.

resurrección, f. resurrection.

retaguardia, f. rear guard.

retal, m. remnant.

retardar, v. retard, show.

retardo, m. delay.

retención, f. retention.

retener, v. retain, keep, withhold.

reticencia, f. reticence.

reticente, a. reticent.

retirada, f. retreat, retirement.

retirar, v. retire, retreat, withdraw.

retiro, m. retirement.

retorcer, v. wring.

retórica, f. rhetoric.

retórico, a. rhetorical.

retorno, m. return.

retozo, m. frolic, romp. —**retozar**, v.

retozón, a. frisky.

retracción, f. retraction.

retractor, v. retract.

retrasar, v. delay, set back; be slow.

retraso, m. delay, lag, slowness.

retratar, v. portray; photograph.

retrato, m. portrait, picture; photograph.

retreta, f. (mil.) retreat.

retrete, m. alcove; toilet.

retribución, f. retribution.

retroactivo, a. retroactive.

retroalimentación, f. feedback.

retroceder, v. recede, go back, draw back, back up.

retumbar, v. resound, rumble.

reumático, a. rheumatic.

reumatismo, m. rheumatism.

reunión, f. gathering, meeting, party; reunion.

reunir, v. gather, collect, bring together.

reunirse, v. meet, assemble, get together.

revelación, f. revelation.

revelar, v. reveal, betray; (phot.) develop.

reventa, f. resale.

reventar, v. burst; split apart.

reventón, m. blowout (of tire).

reverencia, f. reverence.

reverendo, a. reverend.

reverente, a. reverent.

revertir, v. revert.

revés, m. reverse; back, wrong side. al r., just the opposite; inside out.

revisar, v. revise; review.

revisión, f. revision.

revista, f. magazine, periodical; review.

revivir, v. revive.

revocación, f. revocation.

revocar, v. revoke, reverse.

revolotear, v. hover.

revolución, f. revolution.

revolucionario -ria, a. & n. revolutionary.

revólver, v. revolve; stir, agitate.

revólver, m. revolver, pistol.

revuelta, f. revolt; turn.

rey, m. king.

reyerta, f. quarrel, wrangle.

rezar, v. pray.

rezongar, v. grumble; mutter.

ría, f. estuary.

riachuelo, m. creek.

riba, f. embankment.

rico, a. rich, wealthy; delicious.

ridículamente, adv. ridiculously.

ridiculizar, v. ridicule.

ridículo, a. & m. ridiculous; ridicule.

riego, m. irrigation.

rienda, f. rein.

riesgo, m. risk, gamble.

rifa, f. raffle; lottery; scuffle.

rifle, m. rifle.

rígidamente, adv. rigidly.

rigidez, f. rigidity.

rígido, a. rigid, stiff.

rigor, m. rigor.

riguroso, a. rigorous, strict.

rima, f. rhyme. —**rimar**, v.

rincón, m. corner, nook.

rinoceronte, m. rhinoceros.

riña, f. quarrel, feud.

riñón, m. kidney.

río, m. river.

ripio, m. debris.

riqueza, f. wealth.

risa, f. laugh; laughter.

risco, m. cliff.

risibilidad, f. risibility.

risotada, f. peal of laughter.

risueño, a. cheerful, smiling.

rítmico, a. rhythmical.

ritmo, m. rhythm.

rito, m. rite.

ritual, a. & m. ritual.

rivalidad, f. rivalry.

rivera, f. brook.

rizado, a. curly.

rizo, m. curl. —**rizar**, v.

robar, v. rob, steal.

roble, m. oak.

roblón, m. rivet. —**roblar**, v.

robo, m. robbery, theft.

robustamente, adv. robustly.

robusto, a. robust.

roca, f. rock; cliff.

rociada, f. spray, sprinkle. —**rociar**, v.

rocío, m. dew.

rodar, v. roll; roam.

rodear, v. surround, encircle.

rodeo, m. turn, winding; roundup.

rodilla, f. knee.

rodillo, m. roller.

rodio, m. rhodium.

rododendro, m. rhododendron.

roedor, m. rodent.

roer, v. gnaw.

rogación, f. request, entreaty.

rogar, v. beg, plead with, supplicate.

rojizo, a. reddish.

rojo, a. red.

rollo, m. roll; coil.

romadizo, m. head cold.

romance, m. romance, ballad.

románico, a. Romance.

romano -na, a. & n. Roman.

romántico, a. romantic.

romería, f. pilgrimage; picnic.

romero -ra, n. pilgrim.

rompecabezas, m. puzzle (pastime).

romper, v. break, smash, shatter; sever; tear.

rompible, a. breakable.

ron, m. rum.

roncar, v. snore.

ronco, a. hoarse.

ronda, f. round.

rondar, v. prowl.

ronquido, m. snore.

ronzal, m. halter.

roña, f. scab; filth.

ropa, f. clothes, clothing. r. blanca, linen. r. interior, underwear.

ropero, m. closet.

rosa, f. rose. r. náutica, compass.

rosado, a. pink, rosy.

rosal, m. rose bush.

rosario, m. rosary.

rosbif, m. roast beef.

rosca, f. thread (of screw).

róseo, a. rosy.

rostro, m. face, countenance.

rota, f. defeat; (naut.) course.

rotación, f. rotation.

rotatorio, a. rotary.

rótulo, m. label. —**rotular**, v.

rotundo, a. round; sonorous.

rotura, f. break, fracture, rupture.

rozar, v. rub against, chafe; graze.

rubí, m. ruby.

rubio -bia, a. & n. blond.

rubor, m. blush; bashfulness.

rúbrica, f. caption; scroll.

rucho, m. donkey.

rudeza, f. rudeness; roughness.

rudimento, m. rudiment.

rudo, a. rude, rough.

rueda, f. wheel.

ruego, m. plea; entreaty.

rufián, m. ruffian.

rufo, a. sandy (colored).

rugir, v. bellow, roar.

rugoso, a. wrinkled.

ruibarbo, m. rhubarb.

ruido, m. noise.

ruidoso, a. noisy.

ruina, f. ruin, wreck.

ruinar, v. ruin, destroy.

ruinoso, a. ruinous.

ruiseñor, m. nightingale.

ruleta, f. roulette.

rumba, f. rumba (dance or music).

rumbo, m. course, direction.

rumor, m. rumor; murmur.

runrún, m. rumor.

ruptura, f. rupture, break.

rural, a. rural.

Rusia, f. Russia.

ruso -sa, a. & n. Russian.

rústico -ca, a. & n. rustic. en r., paperback f.

ruta, f. route.

rutina, f. routine.

rutinario, a. routine.

S

sábado, m. Saturday.

sábalo, m. shad.

sábana, f. sheet.

sabañón, m. chilblain.

saber, 1. n. knowledge. 2. v. know; learn, find out; know how to; taste. a s., namely, to wit.

sabiduría, f. wisdom; learning.

sabio, 1. a. wise; scholarly. 2. m. sage; scholar.

sable, m. saber.

sabor, m. flavor, taste, savor.

saborear, v. savor, relish.

sabotaje, m. sabotage.

sabroso, a. savory, tasty.

sabueso, m. hound.

sacacorchos, m. corkscrew.

sacar, v. draw out; take out; take.

sacerdocio, m. priesthood.

sacerdote, m. priest.

saciar, v. satiate.

saco, m. sack, bag, pouch; suit coat, jacket.

sacramento, m. sacrament.

sacrificio, m. sacrifice. —sacrificar, v.

sacrilegio, m. sacrilege.

sacristán, m. sexton.

sacro, a. sacred, holy.

sacrosanto, a. sacrosanct.

sacudir, v. shake, jerk, jolt.

sádico, a. sadistic.

sadismo, m. sadism.

sagacidad, f. sagacity.

sagaz, a. sagacious, sage.

sagrado, a. sacred, holy.

sal, f. salt; (coll.) wit.

sala, f. room; living room, parlor; hall, auditorium.

salado, a. salted, salty; (coll.) witty.

salar, v. salt; steep in brine.

salario, m. salary, wages.

salchicha, f. sausage.

saldo, m. remainder, balance; (bargain) sale.

salero, m. salt shaker.

salida, f. exit, outlet; departure.

salir, v. go out, come out; set out, leave, start; turn out; result.

salirse de, v. get out of. s. con la suya, have one's own way.

salitre, m. saltpeter.

saliva, f. saliva.

salmo, m. psalm.

salmón, m. salmon.

salmuera, f. pickle; brine.

salobre, a. salty.

salón, m. parlor, living room; hall.

salpicar, v. spatter, splash.

salpullido, m. rash.

salsa, f. sauce; gravy.

saltamontes, m. grasshopper.

salteador, m. highwayman.

salto, m. jump, leap, spring. —saltar, v.

saltón, m. grasshopper.

salubre, a. salubrious, healthful.

salubridad, f. health.

salud, f. health.

saludable, a. healthful, wholesome.

saludar, v. greet; salute.

saludo, m. greeting; salutation; salute.

salutación, f. salutation.

salva, f. salvo.

salvación, f. salvation; deliverance.

salvador -ra, n. savior; rescuer.

salvaguardia, m. safeguard.

salvaje, a. & m. savage, wild (man).

salvamento, m. salvation; rescue.

salvar, v. save; salvage; rescue; jump over.

salvavidas, m. life preserver.

salvia, f. sage (plant).

salvo, 1. a. safe. 2. prep. except, save (for). s. que, unless.

San, title. Saint.

sanar, v. heal, cure.

sanatorio, m. sanatorium.

sanción, f. sanction. —sancionar, v.

sandalia, f. sandal.

sandez, f. stupidity.

sandía, f. watermelon.

saneamiento, m. sanitation.

sangrar, v. bleed.

sangre, f. blood.

sangriento, a. bloody.

sanguinario, a. bloodthirsty.

sanidad, f. health.

sanitario, a. sanitary.

sano, a. healthy, sound, sane; healthful, wholesome.

santidad, f. sanctity, holiness.

santificar, v. sanctify.

santo -ta, 1. a. holy, saintly. 2. m. saint.

Santo -ta, title. Saint.

santuario, m. sanctuary, shrine.

saña, f. rage, anger.

sapiente, a. wise.

sapo, m. toad.

saquera, v. sack, ransack, plunder.

sarampión, m. measles.

sarape, m. (Mex.) woven blanket; shawl.

sarcasmo, m. sarcasm.

sarcástico, a. sarcastic.

sardina, f. sardine.

sargento, m. sergeant.

sarna, f. itch.

sartén, m. frying pan.

sastre, m. tailor.

satánico, a. satanic.

satélite, m. satellite.

sátira, f. satire.

satírico, a. & m. satirical; satirist.

satirizar, v. satirize.

sátiro, m. satyr.

satisfacción, f. satisfaction.

satisfacer, v. satisfy.

satisfactorio, a. satisfactory.

saturación, f. saturation.

saturar, v. saturate.

sauce, m. willow.

savia, f. sap.

saxófono, m. saxophone.

saya, f. skirt.

sazón, f. season; seasoning. a la s., at that time.

sazonar, v. flavor, season.

se, pron. -self, -selves.

seca, f. drought.

secante, a. papel s., blotting paper.

secar, v. dry.

sección, f. section.

seco, a. dry; curt.

secreción, f. secretion.

secretar, v. secrete.

secretaría, f. secretary's office; secretariat.

secretario -ra, n. secretary.

secreto, a. & m. secret.

secta, f. denomination, sect.

secuela, f. result; sequel.

secuestrar, v. abduct, kidnap; hijack.

secuestro, m. abduction, kidnapping.

secular, a. secular.

secundario, a. secondary.

sed, f. thirst. tener s., estar con s., to be thirsty.

seda, f. silk.

sedar, v. quiet, allay.

sedativo, a. & m. sedative.

sede, f. seat, headquarters.

sedentario, a. sedentary.

sedición, f. sedition.

sedicioso, a. seditious.

sediento, a. thirsty.

sedimento, m. sediment.

sedoso, a. silky.

seducir, v. seduce.

seductivo, a. seductive, alluring.

segar, v. reap, harvest; mow.

seglar, m. layman.

segmento, m. segment.

segregar, v. segregate.

seguida, *f.* succession. **en s.,** right away, at once.

seguido, *a.* consecutive.

seguir, *v.* follow; continue, keep on, go on.

según, **1.** *prep.* according to, **2.** *conj.* as.

segundo, *a. & m.* second. **—segundar**, *v.*

seguridad, *f.* safety, security; assurance.

seguro, **1.** *a.* safe, secure; sure, certain. **2.** *m.* insurance.

seis, *a. & pron.* six.

seiscientos, *a. & pron.* six hundred.

selección, *f.* selection, choice.

seleccionar, *v.* select, choose.

selecto, *a.* select, choice, elite.

selva, *f.* forest; jungle.

selvoso, *a.* sylvan.

sello, *m.* seal; stamp. **—sellar**, *v.*

semáforo, *m.* semaphore.

semana, *f.* week.

semanal, *a.* weekly.

semántica, *f.* semantics.

semblante, *m.* look, expression.

sembrado, *m.* sown field.

sembrar, *v.* sow, seed.

semejante, **1.** *a.* like, similar; such (a). **2.** *m.* fellowman.

semejanza, *f.* similarity, likeness.

semejar, *v.* resemble.

semilla, *f.* seed.

seminario, *m.* seminary.

senado, *m.* senate.

senador -ra, *n.* senator.

sencillez, *f.* simplicity; naturalness.

sencillo, *a.* simple, natural; single.

senda, *f.* **sendero**, *m.* path.

senectud, *f.* old age.

senil, *a.* senile.

seno, *m.* breast, bosom.

sensación, *f.* sensation.

sensacional, *a.* sensational.

sensato, *a.* sensible, wise.

sensibilidad, *f.* sensibility; sensitiveness.

sensible, *a.* sensitive; emotional.

sensitivo, *a.* sensitive.

sensual, *a.* sensual.

sensualidad, *f.* sensuality.

sentar, *v.* seat. **s. bien**, fit well, be becoming.

sentarse, *v.* sit, sit down.

sentencia, *f.* (court) sentence.

sentidamente, *adv.* feelingly.

sentido, *m.* meaning, sense; consciousness.

sentimental, *a.* sentimental.

sentimiento, *m.* sentiment, feeling.

sentir, *v.* feel, sense; hear; regret, be sorry.

seña, *f.* sign, indication; (*pl.*) address.

señal, *f.* sign, signal; mark.

señalar, *v.* designate, point out; mark.

señor, *m.* gentleman; lord; (title) Mr., Sir.

señora, *f.* lady; wife; (title) Mrs., Madam.

señorita, *f.* young lady; (title) Miss.

sépalo, *m.* sepal.

separación, *f.* separation, parting.

separadamente, *adv.* separately.

separado, *a.* separate. **—separar**, *v.*

septentrional, *a.* northern.

septiembre, *m.* September.

séptimo, *a.* seventh.

sepulcro, *m.* sepulcher.

sepultar, *v.* bury, entomb.

sepultura, *f.* grave.

sequedad, *f.* dryness.

sequía, *f.* drought.

ser, *v.* be.

serenata, *f.* serenade.

serenidad, *f.* serenity.

sereno, **1.** *a.* serene, calm. **2.** *m.* dew; watchman.

serie, *f.* series, sequence.

seriedad, *f.* seriousness.

serio, *a.* serious. **en s.**, seriously.

sermón, *m.* sermon.

seroso, *a.* watery.

serpiente, *f.* serpent, snake.

serrano, *m.* mountaineer.

serrar, *v.* saw.

serrín, *m.* sawdust.

servicial, *a.* helpful, of service.

servicio, *m.* service; toilet.

servidor -ra, *n.* servant.

servidumbre, *f.* bondage; staff of servants.

servil, *a.* servile, menial.

servilleta, *f.* napkin.

servir, *v.* serve. **s. para**, be good for.

servirse, *v.* help oneself.

sesenta, *a. & pron.* sixty.

sesgo, *a.* slant. **—sesgar**, *v.*

sesión, *f.* session; sitting.

seso, *m.* brain.

seta, *f.* mushroom.

setecientos, *a. & pron.* seven hundred.

setenta, *a. & pron.* seventy.

seto, *m.* hedge.

severamente, *adv.* severely.

severidad, *f.* severity.

severo, *a.* severe, strict, stern.

sexismo, *m.* sexism.

sexista, *m. & a.* sexist.

sexo, *m.* sex.

sexto, *a.* sixth.

sexual, *a.* sexual.

si, *conj.* if; whether.

sí, **1.** *pron.* -self, -selves. **2.** *interj.* yes.

sicómoro, *m.* sycamore.

sidra, *f.* cider.

siempre, *adv.* always. **para s.**, forever. **s. que**, whenever; provided that.

sierra, *f.* saw; mountain range.

siervo, *m.* slave; serf.

siesta, *f.* (afternoon) nap.

siete, *a. & pron.* seven.

sifón, *m.* siphon; siphon bottle.

siglo, *m.* century.

signatura, *f.* signature.

significación, *f.* significance.

significado, *m.* meaning.

significante, *a.* significant.

significar, *v.* signify, mean.

significativo, *a.* significant.

signo, *m.* sign, symbol; mark.

siguiente, *a.* following, next.

sílaba, *f.* syllable.

silbar, *v.* whistle; hiss, boo.

silbato, **silbido**, *m.* whistle.

silencio, *m.* silence, stillness.

silenciosamente, *a.* silently.

silencioso, *a.* silent, still.

silicato, *m.* silicate.

silicio, *m.* silicon.

silueta, *f.* silhouette.

silvestre, *a.* wild, uncultivated. **fauna s.**, wildlife.

silla, *f.* chair; saddle.

sillón, *m.* armchair.

sima, *f.* chasm; cavern.

simbólico, *a.* symbolic.

símbolo, *m.* symbol.

simetría, *f.* symmetry.

simétrico, *a.* symmetrical.

símil, **similar**, *a.* similar, alike.

similitud, *f.* similarity.

simpatía, *f.* congeniality; friendly feeling.

simpático, *a.* likeable, nice, congenial.

simple, *a.* simple.

simpleza, *f.* silliness; trifle.

simplicidad, *f.* simplicity.

simplificación, *f.* simplification.

simplificar, *v.* simplify.

simular, *v.* simulate.

simultáneo, *a.* simultaneous.

sin, *prep.* without.

sinagoga, *f.* synagogue.

sinceridad, *f.* sincerity.

sincero, *a.* sincere.

sincronizar, *v.* synchronize.

sindicato, *m.* syndicate; labor union.

síndrome, *m.* syndrome.

sinfonía, *f.* symphony.

sinfónico, *a.* symphonic.

singular, *a. & m.* singular.

siniestro, *a.* sinister, ominous.

sino, *conj.* but.

sinónimo, *m.* synonym.

sinrazón, *f.* wrong, injustice.

sinsabor, *m.* displeasure, distaste.

sintaxis, *f.* syntax.

síntesis, *f.* synthesis.

sintético, *a.* synthetic.

síntoma, *m.* symptom.

siquiera, *adv.* **ni s.**, not even.

sirena, *f.* siren.

sirviente -ta, *n.* servant.

sistema, *m.* system.

sistemático, *a.* systematic.

sistematizar, *v.* systematize.

sitiar, *v.* besiege.

sitio, *m.* site, location, place, spot.

situación, *f.* situation; location.

situar, v. situate; locate.

smoking, m. tuxedo, dinner jacket.

so, prep. under.

soba, f. massage. —sobar, v.

sobaco, m. armpit.

sobaquero, f. armhole.

soberano -na, a. & m. sovereign.

soberbia, f. arrogance.

soberbio, a. superb; arrogant.

soborno, m. bribe. —sobornar, v.

sobra, f. excess, surplus. de sobra, to spare.

sobrado, m. attic.

sobrante, a. & m. surplus.

sobre, 1. prep. about; above, over. 2. m. envelope.

sobrecama, f. bedspread.

sobrecargo, m. supercargo.

sobredicho, a. aforesaid.

sobrehumano, a. superhuman.

sobrenatural, a. supernatural, weird.

sobrepasar, v. surpass.

sobresalir, v. excel.

sobretodo, m. overcoat.

sobrevivir, v. survive, outlive.

sobriedad, f. sobriety; moderation.

sobrina, f. niece.

sobrino, m. nephew.

sobrio, a. sober, temperate.

socarrén, m. eaves.

sociable, a. sociable.

social, a. social.

socialismo, m. socialism.

socialista, a. & m. socialistic; socialist.

sociedad, f. society; association.

socio -cia, n. associate, partner; member.

sociología, f. sociology.

socorro, m. help, aid. —socorrer, v.

soda, f. soda.

sodio, m. sodium.

sofá, m. sofa, couch.

sofisma, m. sophism.

sofista, m. sophist.

sofocación, f. suffocation.

sofocar, v. smother, suffocate, stifle, choke.

soga, f. rope.

soja, f. soybean.

sol, m. sun.

solada, f. dregs.

solanera, f. sunbath.

solapa, f. lapel.

solar, 1. a. solar. 2. m. building lot.

solaz, m. solace, comfort. —solazar, v.

soldado, m. soldier.

soldar, v. solder, weld.

soledad, f. solitude, privacy.

solemne, a. solemn.

solemnemente, adv. solemnly.

solemnidad, f. solemnity.

soler, v. be in the habit of.

solicitador, m. solicitor.

solicitar, v. solicit; apply for.

solícito, a. solicitous.

solicitud, f. solicitude; application.

sólidamente, adv. solidly.

solidaridad, f. solidarity.

solidez, f. solidity.

solidificar, v. solidify.

sólido, a. & m. solid.

soliloquio, m. soliloquy.

solitario, a. solitary, lone.

solo, 1. a. only; single; alone; lonely. a solas, alone. 2. m. solo.

sólo, adv. only, just.

soltar, v. release; loosen.

soltero -ra, a. & n. single, unmarried (person).

soltura, f. poise, ease, facility.

solubilidad, f. solubility.

solución, f. solution.

solucionar, v. solve, settle.

solvente, a. solvent.

sollozo, m. sob. —sollozar, v.

sombra, f. shade; shadow. —sombrear, v.

sombrero, m. hat.

sombrilla, f. parasol.

sombrío, a. somber, bleak, gloomy.

sombroso, a. shady.

someter, v. subject; submit.

somnolencia, f. drowsiness.

son, m. sound. —sonar, v.

sonata, f. sonata.

sondar, v. sound, fathom.

sonido, m. sound.

sonoridad, f. sonority.

sonoro, a. sonorous.

sonrisa, f. smile. —sonreír, v.

sonrojo, m. flush, blush. —sonrojarse, v.

soñador -ra, a. & n. dreamy; dreamer.

soñar, v. dream.

soñoliento, a. sleepy.

sopa, f. soup.

soplar, v. blow.

soplete, m. blowtorch.

soplo, m. breath; puff, gust.

soportar, v. abide, bear, stand.

soprano, m. & f. soprano.

sorbete, m. sherbet.

sorbo, m. sip. —sorber, v.

sordera, f. deafness.

sórdidamente, adv. sordidly.

sordidez, f. sordidness.

sórdido, a. sordid.

sordo, a. deaf; muffled, dull.

sordomudo -da, a. & n. deafmute.

sorpresa, f. surprise. —sorprender, v.

sorteo, m. drawing lots; raffle.

sortija, f. ring.

sosa, f. (chem.) soda.

soso, a. dull, insipid, tasteless.

sospecha, f. suspicion.

sospechar, v. suspect.

sospechoso, a. suspicious.

sostén, m. support; brassiere.

sostener, v. hold; support; maintain.

sostenimiento, m. sustenance.

sota, f. jack (in cards).

sótano, m. basement, cellar.

soto, m. grove.

soviet, m. soviet.

soya, f. soybean.

su, a. his, her, its, their, your.

suave, a. smooth; gentle, soft, mild.

suavidad, f. smoothness; gentleness, softness, mildness.

suavizar, v. soften.

subalterno, a. & m. subordinate.

subasta, f. auction.

subconsciencia, f. subconscious.

súbdito -ta, n. subject.

subida, f. ascent, rise.

subilla, f. awl.

subir, v. rise, climb, ascend, mount. s. a, amount to.

súbito, a. sudden.

subjetivo, a. subjective.

subjuntivo, a. & m. subjunctive.

sublimación, f. sublimation.

sublimar, v. elevate; sublimate.

sublime, a. sublime.

submarino, a. & m. submarine.

subordinación, f. subordination.

subordinado, a. & m. subordinate. —subordinar, v.

subrayar, v. underline.

subscribirse, v. subscribe; sign one's name.

subscripción, f. subscription.

subsecuente, a. subsequent.

subsidiaria, a. subsidiary.

subsiguiente, a. subsequent.

substancia, f. substance.

substancial, a. substantial.

substantivo, m. substantive, noun.

substitución, f. substitution.

substituir, v. replace; substitute.

substitutivo, a. substitute.

substituto -ta, n. substitute.

substraer, v. subtract.

subterfugio, m. subterfuge.

subterráneo, 1. a. subterranean, underground. 2. m. place underground; subway.

suburbio, m. suburb.

subvención, f. subsidy, grant.

subversión, f. subversion.

subversivo, a. subversive.

subvertir, v. subvert.

subyugación, f. subjugation.

subyugar, v. subjugate, quell.

succión, f. suction.

suceder, v. happen, occur, befall. s. a, succeed, follow.

sucesión, f. succession.

sucesivo, a. successive. en lo s., in the future.

suceso, m. event.

sucesor -ra, n. successor.

suciedad, f. filth, dirt.

sucio, a. filthy, dirty.

suculento, a. succulent.

sucumbir, v. succumb.

sud, m. south.

sudamericano -na, a. & n. South American.

sudar, v. perspire, sweat.

sudeste, m. southeast.

sudoeste, *m.* southwest.

sudor, *m.* perspiration, sweat.

Suecia, *f.* Sweden.

sueco -ca, *a. & n.* Swedish; Swede.

suegra, *f.* mother-in-law.

suegro, *m.* father-in-law.

suela, *f.* sole.

sueldo, *m.* salary, wages.

suelo, *m.* soil; floor; ground.

suelto, *a.* loose; free; odd, separate.

sueño, *m.* sleep; sleepiness; dream. tener s., to be sleepy.

suero, *m.* serum.

suerte, *f.* luck; chance; lot.

suéter, *m.* sweater.

suficiente, *a.* sufficient.

sufragio, *m.* suffrage.

sufrimiento, *m.* suffering, agony.

sufrir, *v.* suffer; undergo; endure.

sugerencia, *f.* suggestion.

sugerir, *v.* suggest.

sugestión, *f.* suggestion.

sugestionar, *v.* influence; hypnotize.

suicida, *m. & f.* suicide (person).

suicidarse, *v.* commit suicide.

suicidio, *m.* (act of) suicide.

Suiza, *f.* Switzerland.

suizo -za, *a. & n.* Swiss.

sujeción, *f.* subjection.

sujetar, *v.* hold, fasten, clip.

sujeto, 1. *a.* subject, liable. 2. *m.* (gram.) subject.

sulfato, *m.* sulfate.

sulfuro, *m.* sulfide.

sultán, *m.* sultan.

suma, *f.* sum, amount. en s., in short.

sumar, *v.* add up.

sumaria, *f.* indictment.

sumario, *m. & a.* summary.

sumergir, *v.* submerge.

sumersión, *f.* submersion.

sumisión, *f.* submission.

sumiso, *a.* submissive.

sumo, *a.* great, high, utmost.

suntuoso, *a.* sumptuous.

superar, *v.* overcome, surpass.

superficial, *a.* superficial, shallow.

superficie, *f.* surface.

superfluo, *a.* superfluous.

superhombre, *m.* superman.

superintendente, *m.* superintendent.

superior, 1. *a.* superior; upper, higher. 2. *m.* superior.

superioridad, *f.* superiority.

superlativo, *m. & a.* superlative.

superstición, *f.* superstition.

supersticioso, *a.* superstitious.

supervisar, *v.* supervise.

supervivencia, *f.* survival.

suplantar, *v.* supplant.

suplementario, *a.* supplementary.

suplemento, *m.* supplement. — suplementar, *v.*

suplente, *a. & m.* substitute.

súplica, *f.* request, entreaty, plea.

suplicación, *f.* supplication; request, entreaty.

suplicar, *v.* request, entreat; implore.

suplicio, *m.* torture, ordeal.

suplir, *v.* supply.

suponer, *v.* suppose, pressume, assume.

suposición, *f.* supposition, assumption.

supremacía, *f.* supremacy.

supremo, *a.* supreme.

supresión, *f.* suppression.

suprimir, *v.* suppress; abolish.

supuesto, *a.* supposed. por s., of course.

sur, *m.* south.

surco, *m.* furrow. —surcar, *v.*

surgir, *v.* arise; appear suddenly.

surtido, *m.* assortment; supply, stock.

surtir, *v.* furnish, supply.

susceptibilidad, *f.* susceptibility.

susceptible, *a.* susceptible.

suscitar, *v.* stir up.

suscri- = subscri-

suspender, *v.* withhold; suspend; fail (in a course).

suspensión, *f.* suspension.

suspenso, *m.* failing grade. en s., in suspense.

suspicacia, *f.* suspicion, distrust.

suspicaz, *a.* suspicious.

suspicazmente, *adv.* suspiciously.

suspiro, *m.* sigh. —suspirar, *v.*

sustan- = substan-

sustentar, *v.* sustain, support.

sustento, *m.* sustenance, support, living.

susti- = substi-

susto, *m.* fright, scare.

sustraer = substraer.

susurro, *m.* rustle; whisper. — susurrar, *v.*

sutil, *a.* subtle.

sutileza, sutilidad, *f.* subtlety.

sutura, *f.* suture.

suyo, *a.* his, hers, theirs, yours.

T

tabaco, *m.* tobacco.

tábano, *m.* horsefly.

taberna, *f.* tavern, bar.

tabernáculo, *m.* tabernacle.

tabique, *m.* dividing wall, partition.

tabla, *f.* board, plank; table, list.

tablado, *m.* stage, platform.

tablero, *m.* panel.

tableta, *f.* tablet.

tablilla, *f.* bulletin board.

tabú, *m.* taboo.

tabular, *a.* tabular.

tacaño, *a.* stingy.

tácitamente, *adv.* tacitly.

tácito, *a.* tacit.

taciturno, *a.* taciturn.

taco, *m.* heel (of shoe); billiard cue.

tacón, *m.* heel (of shoe).

táctico, *a.* tactical.

tacto, *m.* (sense of) touch; tact.

tacha, *f.* fault, defect.

tachar, *v.* find fault with; cross out.

tachuela, *f.* tack.

tafetán, *m.* taffeta.

taimado, *a.* sly.

tajada, *n.* cut, slice, chop. — tajar, *v.*

tajea, *f.* channel.

tal, *a.* such. con t. que., provided that. t. vez, perhaps.

taladrar, *v.* drill.

taladro, *m.* (mech.) drill.

talante, *m.* humor, disposition.

talco, *m.* talc.

talega, *f.* bag, sack.

talento, *m.* talent.

talón, *m.* heel (of foot); (baggage) check, stub.

talla, *f.* engraving; stature; size (of suit).

tallador -ra, *n.* engraver; dealer (at cards).

talle, *m.* figure; waist; fit.

taller, *m.* workshop, factory.

tallo, *m.* stem, stalk.

tamal, *m.* tamale.

tamaño, *m.* size.

tambalear, *v.* stagger, totter.

también, *adv.* also, too.

tambor, *m.* drum.

tamiz, *m.* sieve, sifter.

tampoco, *adv.* neither, either.

tan, *adv.* so.

tanda, *f.* turn, relay.

tándem, *m.* tandem bicycle.

tangencia, *f.* tangency.

tangible, *a.* tangible.

tango, *m.* tango (dance or music).

tanque, *m.* tank.

tanteo, *m.* estimate. —tantear, *v.*

tanto, 1. *a. & pron.* so much, so many; as much, as many. entre t., mientras t., meanwhile. por lo t., therefore. un t., somewhat, a bit. 2. *m.* point (in games); (pl.) score. estar al t., to be up to date.

tañer, *v.* play (an instrument); ring (bells).

tapa, *f.* cap, cover. —tapar, *v.*

tapadero, *m.* stopper, lid.

tápara, *f.* caper.

tapete, *m.* small rug, mat, cover.

tapia, *f.* wall.

tapicería, *f.* tapestry.

tapioca, *f.* tapioca.

tapiz, *m.* tapestry; carpet.

tapizado (de pared), *m.* (wall) covering.

tapón, *m.* plug; cork.

taquigrafía, *f.* shorthand.

taquilla, *f.* ticket office; ticket window.

tara, *f.* hang-up.

tarántula, *f.* tarantula.

tararear, v. hum.

tardanza, f. delay; lateness.

tardar, v. delay; be late; take (of time). a más t., at the latest.

tarde, 1. adv. late. 2. f. afternoon; early evening.

tardío, a. late, belated.

tarea, f. task, assignment.

tarifa, f. rate; tariff; price list.

tarjeta, f. card.

tarta, f. tart.

tartamudear, v. stammer, falter.

tasa, f. rate.

tasación, f. valuation.

tasar, v. assess, appraise.

tasugo, m. badger.

tautología, f. tautology.

taxi, taxímetro, m. taxi.

taxonomía, f. taxonomy.

taza, f. cup.

te, pron. you; yourself.

té, m. tea.

teátrico, a. theatrical.

teatro, m. theater.

tecla, f. key (of a piano, etc.).

técnica, f. technique.

técnicamente, adv. technically.

técnico, a. technical.

tecnología, f. technology.

techo, m. roof. —techar, v.

tedio, m. tedium, boredom.

tedioso, a. tedious.

teísmo, m. theism.

teja, f. tile.

tejado, m. roof.

tejer, v. weave; knit.

tejido, m. fabric; weaving.

tejón, m. badger.

tela, f. cloth, fabric, web. t. metálica, screen; screening.

telar, m. loom.

telaraña, f. cobweb.

telefonista, m. & f. (telephone) operator.

teléfono, m. telephone. —telefonear, v.

telégrafo, m. telegraph. —telegrafiar, v.

telegrama, m. telegram.

telescopio, m. telescope.

televisión, f. television.

telón, m. (theat.) curtain.

telurio, m. tellurium.

tema, m. theme, subject.

temblar, v. tremble, quake; shake, shiver.

temblor, m. tremor; shiver.

temer, v. fear, be afraid of, dread.

temerario, a. rash.

temeridad, f. temerity.

temerosamente, adv. timorously.

temeroso, a. fearful.

temor, m. fear.

témpano, m. kettledrum; iceberg.

temperamento, m. temperament.

temperancia, f. temperance.

temperatura, f. temperature.

tempestad, f. tempest, storm.

tempestuoso, a. tempestuous, stormy.

templado, a. temperate, mild, moderate.

templanza, f. temperance; mildness.

templar, v. temper; tune (an instrument).

templo, m. temple.

temporada, f. season, time, spell.

temporal, temporáneo, a. temporary.

temprano, a. & adv. early.

tenacidad, f. tenacity.

tenaz, a. tenacious, stubborn.

tenazmente, adv. tenaciously.

tendencia, f. tendency, trend.

tender, v. stretch, stretch out.

tendero -ra, n. shopkeeper, storekeeper.

tendón, m. tendon, sinew.

tenebrosidad, f. gloom.

tenebroso, a. dark, gloomy.

tenedor, m. keeper; holder; fork.

tener, v. have; own; hold. t. que, have to, must.

teniente, m. lieutenant.

tenis, m. tennis.

tenor, m. tenor.

tensión, f. tension, stress, strain.

tenso, a. tense.

tentación, f. temptation.

tentáculo, m. tentacle.

tentador, a. alluring, tempting.

tentar, v. tempt, lure; grope, probe.

tentativa, f. attempt.

tentativo, a. tentative.

teñir, v. tint, dye.

teología, f. theology.

teológico, a. theological.

teoría, f. theory.

teórico, a. theoretical.

terapéutico, a. therapeutic.

tercero, a. third.

tercio, m. third.

terciopelo, m. velvet.

terco, a. obstinate, stubborn.

termal, a. thermal.

terminación, f. termination, completion.

terminar, v. terminate, finish.

término, m. term; end.

terminología, f. terminology.

termómetro, m. thermometer.

termos, m. thermos.

ternero -ra, n. calf.

ternura, f. tenderness.

terquedad, f. stubbornness.

terraza, f. terrace.

terremoto, m. earthquake.

terreno, 1. a. earthly, terrestrial. 2. m. ground; terrain; lot, plot.

terrible, a. terrible, awful.

terrífico, a. terrific.

territorio, m. territory.

terrón, m. clod, lump; mound.

terror, m. terror.

terso, a. smooth, glossy; terse.

tertulia, f. social gathering, party.

tesis, f. thesis.

tesorería, f. treasury.

tesorero -ra, n. treasurer.

tesoro, m. treasure.

testamento, m. will, testament.

testarudo, a. stubborn.

testificar, v. testify.

testigo, m. witness; testimony.

testimonial, a. testimonial.

testimonio, m. testimony.

teta, f. teat.

tetera, f. teapot.

tétrico, a. sad; gloomy.

texto, m. text.

textura, f. texture.

tez, f. complexion.

ti, pron. you; yourself.

tía, f. aunt.

tibio, a. lukewarm.

tiburón, m. shark.

tiemblo, m. aspen.

tiempo, m. time; weather; (gram.) tense.

tienda, f. shop, store; tent.

tientas, f.pl. andar a t., to grope (in the dark).

tierno, a. tender.

tierra, f. land; ground; earth, dirt, soil.

tieso, a. taut, stiff, hard, strong.

tiesto, m. flower pot.

tiesura, f. stiffness; harshness.

tifo, m. typhus.

tifoideo, a. typhoid fever.

tigre, m. tiger.

tijeras, f.pl. scissors.

tila, f. linden.

timbre, m. seal, stamp; tone; (electric) bell.

tímidamente, adv. timidly.

timidez, f. timidity.

tímido, a. timid, shy.

timón, m. rudder, helm.

tímpano, m. kettledrum; eardrum.

tina, f. tub, vat.

tinaja, f. jar.

tinta, f. ink.

tinte, m. tint, shade.

tintero, m. inkwell.

tinto, a. wine-colored; red (of wine).

tintorería, f. dry cleaning shop.

tintorero -ra, n. dyer; dry cleaner.

tintura, f. tincture; dye.

tiñoso, a. scabby; stingy.

tío, m. uncle.

tiovivo, m. merry-go-round.

típico, a. typical.

tipo, m. type, sort; (interest) rate; (coll.) guy, fellow.

tira, f. strip.

tirabuzón, m. corkscrew.

tirada, f. edition.

tiranía, f. tyranny.

tiránico, m. tyrannical; domineering.

tirano, m. tyrant.

tirante, 1. a. tight, taut; tense. 2. m. (pl.) suspenders.

tirar, v. throw; draw; pull; fire (a weapon).

tiritar, v. shiver.

tiro, *m.* throw; shot.

tirón, *m.* pull. **de un t.,** at a stretch, at one stroke.

tísico, *n. & a.* consumptive.

tisis, *f.* consumption, tuberculosis.

titanio, *m.* titanium.

títere, *m.* puppet.

titilación, *f.* twinkle.

titilbear, *v.* stagger; totter; waver.

titulado, *a.* entitled; so-called.

titular, 1. *a.* titular. **2.** *v.* entitle.

título, *m.* title, headline.

tiza, *f.* chalk.

tiznar, *v.* smudge; stain.

toalla, *f.* towel.

toalleta, *f.* small towel.

tobillo, *m.* ankle.

tocadiscos, *m.* record player.

tocado, *m.* hairdo.

tocador, *m.* boudoir; dressing table.

tocante, *a.* touching. **t. a,** concerning, relative to.

tocar, *v.* touch; play (an instrument). **t. a uno,** be one's turn; be up to one.

tocayo, *m.* namesake.

tocino, *m.* bacon.

todavía, *adv.* yet, still.

todo, 1. *a.* all, whole. **todos los,** every. **2.** *pron.* all, everything. **con t.,** still, however. **del t.,** wholly; at all.

todopoderoso, *a.* almighty.

toldo, *m.* awning.

tolerancia, *f.* tolerance.

tolerante, *a.* tolerant.

tolerar, *v.* tolerate.

toma, *f.* taking, capture, seizure.

tomaína, *f.* ptomaine.

tomar, *v.* take; drink.

tomate, *m.* tomato.

tomillo, *m.* thyme.

tomo, *m.* volume.

tonada, *f.* tune.

tonel, *m.* barrel, cask.

tonelada, *f.* ton.

tonelaje, *m.* tonnage.

tónico, *a. & m.* tonic.

tono, *m.* tone, pitch, shade. **darse t.,** to put on airs.

tonsila, *f.* tonsil.

tonsilitis, *f.* tonsilitis.

tontería, *f.* nonsense, foolishness.

tonto -ta, *a. & n.* foolish, silly; fool.

topacio, *m.* topaz.

topar, *v.* run into. **t. con,** come upon.

tópico, 1. *a.* topical. **2.** *m.* topic.

topo, *m.* mole (animal).

toque, *m.* touch.

tórax, *m.* thorax.

torbellino, *m.* whirlwind.

torcer, *v.* twist; wind; distort.

toreador, *m.* toreador.

torero, *m.* bullfighter.

torio, *m.* thorium.

tormenta, *f.* storm.

tormento, *m.* torment.

tornado, *m.* tornado.

tornar, *v.* return; turn.

tornarse en, *v.* turn into, become.

torneo, *m.* tournament.

tornillo, *m.* screw.

toro, *m.* bull.

toronja, *f.* grapefruit.

torpe, *a.* awkward, clumsy; sluggish.

torpedero, *m.* torpedo boat.

torpedo, *m.* torpedo.

torre, *f.* tower.

torrente, *m.* torrent.

tórrido, *a.* torrid.

torta, *f.* cake; loaf.

tortilla, *f.* omelet; (Mex.) tortilla, pancake.

tórtola, *f.* dove.

tortuga, *f.* turtle.

tortuoso, *a.* tortuous.

tortura, *f.* torture. **—torturar,** *v.*

tos, *m.* cough. **—toser,** *v.*

tosco, *a.* coarse, rough, uncouth.

tosquedad, *f.* coarseness, roughness.

tostar, *v.* toast; tan.

total, *a. & m.* total.

totalidad, *f.* totality, entirety, whole.

totalitario, *a.* totalitarian.

totalmente, *adv.* totally; entirely.

tótem, *m.* totem.

tóxico, *a.* toxic.

trabajador -ra, 1. *a.* hardworking. **2.** *n.* worker.

trabajo, *m.* work; labor. **—trabajar,** *v.*

trabar, *v.* fasten, shackle; grasp; strike up.

tracción, *f.* traction.

tracto, *m.* tract.

tractor, *m.* tractor.

tradición, *f.* tradition.

tradicional, *a.* traditional.

traducción, *f.* translation.

traducir, *v.* translate.

traductor, *m.* translator.

traer, *v.* bring; carry; wear.

tráfico, *m.* traffic. **—traficar,** *v.*

tragar, *v.* swallow.

tragedia, *f.* tragedy.

trágicamente, *adv.* tragically.

trágico -ca, 1. *a.* tragic. **2.** *n.* tragedian.

trago, *m.* swallow; drink.

traición, *f.* treason, betrayal.

traicionar, *v.* betray.

traidor -ra, *a. & n.* traitorous; traitor.

traje, *m.* suit; dress; garb, apparel.

trama, *v.* plot (of a story).

tramador, *m.* weaver; plotter.

tramar, *v.* weave; plot, scheme.

trámite, *m.* (business) deal, transaction.

tramo, *m.* span, stretch, section.

trampa, *f.* trap, snare.

trampista, *m.* cheater; swindler.

trance, *m.* critical moment or stage. **a todo t.,** at any cost.

tranco, *m.* stride.

tranquilidad, *f.* tranquility, calm, quiet.

tranquilizar, *v.* quiet, calm down.

tranquilo, *a.* tranquil, calm, quiet.

transacción, *f.* transaction.

transbordador, *m.* ferry.

transcribir, *v.* transcribe.

transcripción, *f.* transcription.

transcurrir, *v.* elapse.

transeúnte, *a. & n.* transient; passerby.

transexual, *a.* transsexual.

transferencia, *f.* transference.

transferir, *v.* transfer.

transformación, *f.* transformation.

transformar, *v.* transform.

transfusión, *f.* transfusion.

transgresión, *f.* transgression.

transgresor, *m.* transgressor.

transición, *f.* transition.

transigir, *v.* compromise, settle; agree.

transitivo, *a.* transitive.

tránsito, *m.* transit, passage.

transitorio, *a.* transitory.

transmisión, *f.* transmission; broadcast.

transmisora, *f.* broadcasting station.

transmitir, *v.* transmit; broadcast.

transparencia, *f.* transparency.

transparente, 1. *a.* transparent. **2.** *m.* (window) shade.

transportación, *f.* transportation.

transportar, *v.* transport, convey.

transporte, *m.* transportation; transport.

tranvía, *m.* streetcar, trolley.

trapacero, *n.* cheat; swindler.

trapo, *m.* rag.

tráquea, *f.* trachea.

tras, *prep.* after; behind.

trasegar, *v.* upset, overturn.

trasero, *a.* rear, back.

traslado, *m.* transfer. **—trasladar,** *v.*

traslapo, *m.* overlap. **—traslapar,** *v.*

trasnochar, *v.* sit up all night.

traspalar, *v.* shovel.

traspasar, *v.* go beyond; cross; violate; pierce.

trasquilar, *v.* shear; clip.

trastornar, *v.* overturn, overthrow, upset.

trastorno, *m.* overthrow; upheaval.

tratado, *m.* treaty; treatise.

tratamiento, *m.* treatment.

tratar, *v.* treat, handle. **t. de,** deal with; try to; call (a name).

tratarse de, *v.* be a question of.

trato, *m.* treatment; manners; (com.) deal.

través, adv. a t. de, through, across. de t., sideways.

travesía, f. crossing; voyage.

travestí, m. transvestite.

travestido, a. disguised.

travesura, f. prank; mischief.

travieso, a. naughty, mischievous.

trayectoria, f. trajectory.

trazar, v. plan, devise; trace; draw.

trazo, n. plan, outline; line, stroke.

trébol, m. clover.

trece, a. & pron. thirteen.

trecho, m. space, distance, stretch.

tregua, f. truce, respite, lull.

treinta, a. & pron. thirty.

tremendo, a. tremendous.

tremer, v. tremble.

tren, m. train.

trenza, f. braid. —trenzar, v.

trepar, v. climb, mount.

trepidación, f. trepidation.

tres, a. & pron. three.

trescientos, a. & pron. three hundred.

triángulo, m. triangle.

tribu, f. tribe.

tribulación, f. tribulation.

tribuna, f. rostrum, stand; (pl.) grandstand.

tribunal, m. court, tribunal.

tributario, a. & m. tributary.

tributo, m. tribute.

triciclo, m. tricycle.

trigo, m. wheat.

trigonometría, f. trigonometry.

trigueño, a. swarthy, dark.

trilogía, f. trilogy.

trimestral, a. quarterly.

trinchar, v. carve (meat).

trinchera, f. trench, ditch.

trineo, m. sled; sleigh.

trinidad, f. trinity.

tripa, f. tripe, entrails.

triple, a. triple. —triplicar, v.

tripulación, f. (ship's) crew.

triste, a. sad, sorrowful; dreary.

tristemente, adv. sadly.

tristeza, f. sadness; gloom.

triunfal, a. triumphal.

triunfante, a. triumphant.

triunfo, m. triumph, trump. —triunfar, v.

trivial, a. trivial, commonplace.

trivialidad, f. triviality.

trocar, v. exchange, switch; barter.

trofeo, m. trophy.

trombón, m. trombone.

trompa, trompeta, f. trumpet, horn.

tronada, f. thunderstorm.

tronar, v. thunder.

tronco, m. trunk, stump.

trono, m. throne.

tropa, f. troop.

tropel, m. crowd, throng.

tropezar, v. trip, stumble, t. con, come upon, run into.

trópico, a. & m. tropical; tropics.

tropiezo, m. stumble; obstacle; slip, error.

trote, m. trot. —trotar, v.

trovador, m. troubadour.

trozo, m. piece, portion, fragment, selection, passage.

trucha, f. trout.

trueco, trueque, m. exchange, barter.

trueno, m. thunder.

tu, a. your.

tú, pron. you.

tuberculosis, f. tuberculosis.

tubo, m. tube, pipe.

tuerca, f. (mech.) nut.

tulipán, m. tulip.

tumba, f. tomb, grave.

tumbar, v. knock down.

tumbarse, v. tumble.

tumbo, m. tumble; somersault.

tumor, m. tumor; growth.

tumulto, m. tumult, commotion.

tumultuoso, a. tumultuous, boisterous.

tunante, m. rascal, rogue.

tunda, f. spanking, whipping.

túnel, m. tunnel.

tungsteno, m. tungsten.

túnica, f. tunic, robe.

tupir, v. pack tight, stuff; stop up.

turbación, f. confusion, turmoil.

turbamulta, f. mob; crowd.

turbar, v. disturb, upset; embarrass.

turbina, f. turbine.

turbio, a. turbid; muddy.

turco -ca, a. & n. Turkish; Turk.

turismo, m. touring, (foreign) travel.

turista, m. & f. tourist.

turno, m. turn; (work) shift.

turquesa, f. turquoise.

Turquía, f. Turkey.

turrón, m. nougat.

tusa, f. corncob; corn.

tutear, v. use the pronoun tú, etc., in addressing a person.

tutela, f. guardianship; aegis.

tutor, m. tutor; guardian.

tuyo, a. your, yours.

U

u, conj. or.

ubre, f. udder.

ufano, a. proud, haughty.

úlcera, f. ulcer.

ulterior, a. ulterior.

último, a. last, final; ultimate; latest. por ú., finally.

ultraje, m. outrage. —ultrajar, v.

umbral, m. threshold.

umbroso, a. shady.

un, una, art. & a. a, an; one; (pl.) some.

unánime, a. unanimous.

unanimidad, f. unanimity.

unción, f. unction.

ungüento, m. ointment, salve.

único, a. only, sole; unique.

unicornio, m. unicorn.

unidad, f. unit; unity.

unificar, v. unify.

uniforme, a. & m. uniform.

uniformidad, f. uniformity.

unión, f. union; joining.

unir, v. unite, join.

universal, a. universal.

universalidad, f. universality.

universidad, f. university; college.

universo, m. universe.

uno, una, pron. one; (pl.) some.

untar, v. spread; grease; anoint.

uña, f. fingernail.

urbanidad, f. urbanity; good breeding.

urbano, a. urban; urbane; well-bred.

urbe, f. large city.

urgencia, f. urgency.

urgente, a. urgent, pressing. entrega u., special delivery.

urgir, v. be urgent.

urna, f. urn; ballot box; (pl.) polls.

usanza, f. usage, custom.

usar, v. use; wear.

uso, m. use; usage; wear.

usted, pron. you.

usual, a. usual.

usualmente, adv. usually.

usura, f. usury.

usurero, m. usurer.

usurpación, f. usurpation.

usurpar, v. usurp.

utensilio, m. utensil.

útero, m. uterus.

útil, a. useful, handy.

utilidad, f. utility, usefulness.

utilizar, v. use, utilize.

útilmente, adv. usefully.

utópico, a. utopian.

uva, f. grape.

V

vaca, f. cow; beef.

vacaciones, f.pl. vacation, holidays.

vacancia, f. vacancy.

vacante, 1. a. vacant. 2. f. vacancy.

vaciar, v. empty; pour out.

vacilación, f. vacillation, hesitation.

vacilante, a. vacillating.

vacilar, v. falter, hesitate; waver; stagger.

vacío, 1. a. empty. 2. m. void, empty space.

vacuna, f. vaccine.

vacunación, f. vaccination.

vacunar, v. vaccinate.

vacuo, 1. a. empty, vacant. 2. m. vacuum.

vadear, v. wade through, ford.

vado, m. ford.

vagabundo, a. & m. vagabond.

vagar, v. wander, rove, roam; loiter.

vago -ga, 1. a. vague, hazy; wandering, vagrant. 2. n. vagrant, tramp.

vagón, m. railroad car.

vahído, m. dizziness.

vaina, f. sheath; pod.

vainilla, f. vanilla.

vaivén, m. vibration, sway.

vajilla, f. (dinner) dishes.

valentía, f. valor, courage.

valer, 1. m. worth. 2. v. be worth.

valerse de, v. make use of, avail oneself of.

valía, f. value.

validez, f. validity.

válido, a. valid.

valiente, a. valiant, brave, courageous.

valija, f. valise.

valioso, a. valuable.

valor, m. value, worth; bravery, valor; (pl., com.) securities.

valoración, f. appraisal.

valorar, v. value, appraise.

vals, m. waltz.

valsar, v. waltz.

valuación, f. valuation.

valuar, v. value; rate.

válvula, f. valve.

valla, f. fence, barrier.

valle, m. valley.

vándalo, m. vandal.

vanidad, f. vanity.

vanidoso, a. vain, conceited.

vano, a. vain; inane.

vapor, m. vapor; steam; steamer, steamship.

vaquero, m. cowboy.

vara, f. wand, stick, switch.

varadero, m. shipyard.

varar, v. launch; be stranded; run aground.

variable, a. variable.

variación, f. variation.

variar, v. vary.

variedad, f. variety.

varios, a. & pron. pl. various; several.

varón, m. man; male.

varonil, a. manly, virile.

vasallo, m. vassal.

vasectomía, f. vasectomy.

vasija, f. bowl, container (for liquids).

vaso, m. water glass; vase.

vástago, m. bud, shoot; twig; offspring.

vasto, a. vast.

vecindad, f. **vecindario**, m. neighborhood, vicinity.

vecino -na, a. & n. neighboring; neighbor.

vedar, v. forbid; impede.

vega, f. meadow.

vegetación, f. vegetation.

vegetal, m. vegetable.

vehemente, a. vehement.

vehículo, m. vehicle; conveyance.

veinte, a. & pron. twenty.

vejez, f. old age.

vejiga, f. bladder.

vela, f. vigil, watch; candle; sail.

velar, v. stay up, sit up; watch over.

velo, m. veil.

velocidad, f. velocity; speed; rate.

velomotor, m. motorbike, moped.

veloz, a. speedy, fast, swift.

vellón, m. fleece.

velloso, a. hairy; fuzzy.

velludo, a. downy.

vena, f. vein.

venado, m. deer.

vencedor -ra, n. victor.

vencer, v. defeat, overcome, conquer; (com.) become due, expire.

vencimiento, m. defeat.

venda, f. **vendaje**, m. bandage.
   —**vendar**, v.

vendedor -ra, n. seller, trader; sales clerk.

vender, v. sell.

vendimia, f. vintage.

veneno, m. poison.

venenoso, a. poisonous.

veneración, f. veneration.

venerar, v. venerate, revere.

venero, m. spring, origin.

véneto, a. Venetian.

venezolano, a. & n. Venezuelan.

vengador, m. avenger.

venganza, f. vengeance, revenge.

vengar, v. avenge.

venida, f. arrival, advent, coming.

venidero, a. future; coming.

venir, v. come.

venta, f. sale; sales.

ventaja, f. advantage; profit.

ventajoso, a. advantageous; profitable.

ventana, f. window.

ventero, m. innkeeper.

ventilación, m. ventilation.

ventilador, m. ventilator, fan.

ventilar, v. ventilate, air.

ventoso, a. windy.

ventura, f. venture; happiness; luck.

ver, v. see. **tener que v. con**, have to do with.

vera, f. edge.

veracidad, f. truthfulness, veracity.

verano, m. summer. —**veranear**, v.

veras, f.pl. **de v.**, really, truly.

veraz, a. truthful.

verbigracia, adv. for example.

verbo, m. verb.

verboso, a. verbose.

verdad, f. truth. **ser v.**, to be true.

verdadero, a. true, real.

verde, a. green; risqué, off-color.

verdor, m. greenness, verdure.

verdugo, m. hangman.

verdura, f. verdure, vegetation; (pl.) vegetables.

vereda, f. path.

veredicto, m. verdict.

vergonzoso, a. shameful, embarrassing; shy, bashful.

vergüenza, f. shame; disgrace; embarrassment.

verificar, v. verify, check.

verja, f. grating, railing.

verosímil, a. likely, plausible.

verraco, m. boar.

verruga, f. wart.

versátil, a. versatile.

verse, v. look, appear.

versión, f. version.

verso, m. verse, stanza; line (of poetry).

verter, v. pour, spill; shed; empty.

vertical, a. vertical.

vertiente, f. slope; watershed.

vertiginoso, a. dizzy.

vértigo, m. vertigo, dizziness.

vestíbulo, m. vestibule, lobby.

vestido, m. dress; clothing.

vestigio, m. vestige, trace.

vestir, v. dress, clothe.

veterano -na, a. & n. veteran.

veterinario, m. veterinary.

veto, m. veto.

vetusto, a. ancient, very old.

vez, f. time; turn. **tal v.**, perhaps. **a la v.**, at the same time. **en v. de**, instead of. **una v.**, once. **otra v.**, again.

vía, f. track; route, way.

viaducto, m. viaduct.

viajante, a. & n. traveling; traveler.

viajar, v. travel; journey, tour.

viaje, m. trip, journey, voyage; (pl.) travels.

viajero -ra, n. traveler; passenger.

viandas, f.pl. victuals, food.

víbora, f. viper.

vibración, f. vibration.

vibrar, v. vibrate.

vicepresidente, m. vice president.

vicio, m. vice.

vicioso, a. vicious; licentious.

víctima, f. victim.

victoria, f. victory.

victorioso, a. victorious.

vid, f. grapevine.

vida, f. life; living.

vídeo, m. videotape.

videodisco, m. videodisc.

vidrio, m. glass.

viejo -ja, a. & n. old; old person.

viento, m. wind. **hacer v.**, to be windy.

vientre, m. belly.

viernes, m. Friday.

viga, f. beam, rafter.

vigente, a. in effect (prices, etc.).

vigilante, a. & m. vigilant, watchful; watchman.

vigilar, v. guard, watch over.

vigilia, f. vigil, watchfulness; (rel.) fast.

vigor, *m.* vigor. **en v.,** in effect, in force.

vil, *a.* vile, low, contemptible.

vileza, *f.* baseness; vileness.

villa, *f.* town; country house.

villancico, *m.* Christmas carol.

villanía, *f.* villainy.

villano, *m.* boor.

vinagre, *m.* vinegar.

vínculo, *m.* link. **—vincular,** *v.*

vindicar, *v.* vindicate.

vino, *m.* wine.

viña, *f.* vineyard.

violación, *f.* violation.

violar, *v.* violate.

violencia, *f.* violence.

violento, *a.* violent; impulsive.

violeta, *f.* violet.

violín, *m.* violin.

violón, *m.* bass viol.

virar, *v.* veer, change course.

virgen, *f.* virgin.

viril, *a.* virile, manly.

virilidad, *f.* virility; manhood.

virtual, *a.* virtual.

virtud, *f.* virtue; efficacy, power.

virtuoso, *a.* virtuous.

viruela, *f.* smallpox.

visa, *f.* visa.

visaje, *m.* grimace.

visera, *f.* visor.

visible, *a.* visible.

visión, *f.* vision.

visionario -ria, *a. & n.* visionary.

visita, *f.* visit; visitor, caller.

visitación, *f.* visitation.

visitante, *a. & n.* visiting; visitor.

visitar, *v.* visit; inspect, examine.

vislumbre, *m.* glimpse.

viso, *m.* looks; outlook.

víspera, *f.* eve, day before.

vista, *f.* view; scene; sight.

vistazo, *m.* glance, glimpse.

vistoso, *a.* beautiful; showy.

visual, *a.* visual.

vital, *a.* vital.

vitalidad, *f.* vitality.

vitamina, *f.* vitamin.

vitando, *a.* hateful.

vituperar, *v.* vituperate; revile.

viuda, *f.* widow.

viudo, *m.* widower.

vivaz, *a.* vivacious, buoyant; clever.

víveres, *m.pl.* provisions.

viveza, *f.* animation, liveliness.

vívido, *a.* vivid, bright.

vivienda, *f.* (living) quarters, dwelling.

vivificar, *v.* vivify, enliven.

vivir, *v.* live.

vivo, *a.* live, alive, living; vivid; animated, brisk.

vocablo, *m.* word.

vocabulario, *m.* vocabulary.

vocación, *f.* vocation, calling.

vocal, 1. *a.* vocal. **2.** *f.* vowel.

vocear, *v.* vociferate.

vodevil, *m.* vaudeville.

volante, 1. *a.* flying. **2.** *m.* memorandum; (steering) wheel.

volar, *v.* fly; explode.

volcán, *m.* volcano.

volcar, *v.* upset, capsize.

voltear, *v.* turn, whirl; overturn.

voltio, *m.* volt.

volumen, *m.* volume.

voluminoso, *a.* voluminous.

voluntad, *f.* will.

voluntario -ria, *a. & n.* voluntary; volunteer.

voluntarioso, *a.* willful.

volver, *v.* turn; return, go back, come back. **v. a hacer** (etc.), do (etc.) again.

volverse, *v.* turn around; turn, become.

vómito, *m.* vomit. **—vomitar,** *v.*

voracidad, *f.* voracity; greed.

voraz, *a.* greedy, ravenous.

vórtice, *m.* whirlpool.

vosotros -as, *pron.pl.* you; yourselves.

votación, *f.* voting, vote.

voto, *m.* vote; vow. **—votar,** *v.*

voz, *f.* voice; word. **a voces,** by shouting. **en v. alta,** aloud.

vuelco, *m.* upset.

vuelo, *m.* flight. **v. libre,** hang gliding.

vuelta, *f.* turn, bend; return. **a la v. de,** around. **dar una v.,** to take a walk.

vuestro, *a.* your, yours.

vulgar, *a.* vulgar, common.

vulgaridad, *f.* vulgarity.

vulgo, *m.* (the) masses, (the) common people.

vulnerable, *a.* vulnerable.

Y, Z

y, *conj.* and.

ya, *adv.* already; now; at once. **y. no,** no longer, any more. **y. que,** since.

yacer, *v.* lie.

yanqui, *a. & n.* North American.

yate, *m.* yacht.

yegua, *f.* mare.

yelmo, *m.* helmet.

yema, *f.* yolk (of an egg).

yerba, *f.* grass; herb.

yerno, *m.* son-in-law.

yerro, *m.* error, mistake.

yeso, *m.* plaster.

yo, *pron.* I.

yodo, *m.* iodine.

yoduro, *m.* iodide.

yugo, *m.* yoke.

yunque, *m.* anvil.

yunta, *f.* team (of animals).

zafarse, *v.* run away, escape. **z. de,** get rid of.

zafio, *a.* coarse, uncivil.

zafiro, *m.* sapphire.

zaguán, *m.* vestibule, hall.

zalamero -ra, *n.* flatterer, wheedler.

zambullir, *v.* plunge, dive.

zanahoria, *f.* carrot.

zanja, *f.* ditch, trench.

zapatería, *f.* shoe store; shoemaker's shop.

zapatero, *m.* shoemaker.

zapato, *m.* shoe.

zar, *m.* czar.

zaraza, *f.* calico; chintz.

zarza, *f.* bramble.

zarzuela, *f.* musical comedy.

zona, *f.* zone.

zoología, *f.* zoology.

zoológico, *a.* zoological.

zorro -rra, *n.* fox.

zozobra, *f.* worry, anxiety; capsizing.

zozobrar, *v.* capsize.

zumba, *f.* spanking.

zumbido, *m.* buzz, hum. **—zumbar,** *v.*

zumo, *m.* juice, sap.

zurcir, *v.* darn, mend.

zurdo, *a.* left-handed.

zurrar, *v.* flog, drub.

English-Spanish

A

a, *art.* un, una.

abacus, *n.* ábaco *m.*

abandon, 1. *n.* desenfreno, abandono *m.* 2. *v.* abandonar, desamparar.

abandoned, *a.* abandonado.

abandonment, *n.* abandono, desamparo *m.*

abase, *v.* degradar, humillar.

abasement, *n.* degradación, humillación *f.*

abash, *v.* avergonzar.

abate, *v.* menguar, moderarse.

abatement, *n.* disminución *f.*

abbess, *n.* abadesa *f.*

abbey, *n.* abadía *f.*

abbot, *n.* abad *m.*

abbreviate, *v.* abreviar.

abbreviation, *n.* abreviatura *f.*

abdicate, *v.* abdicar.

abdication, *n.* abdicación *f.*

abdomen, *n.* abdomen *m.*

abdominal, *a.* abdominal.

abduct, *v.* secuestrar.

abduction, *n.* secuestración *f.*

abductor, *n.* secuestrador *m.*

aberrant, *a.* extraviado.

aberration, *n.* error, extravío *m.*

abet, *v.* apoyar, favorecer.

abetment, *n.* apoyo *m.*

abettor, *n.* cómplice *m.* & *f.*

abeyance, *n.* suspensión *f.*

abhor, *v.* abominar, odiar.

abhorrence, *n.* detestación *f.*; aborrecimiento *m.*

abhorrent, *a.* detestable, aborrecible.

abide, *v.* soportar. **to a. by,** cumplir con.

abiding, *a.* perdurable.

ability, *n.* habilidad *f.*

abject, *a.* abyecto; desanimado.

abjuration, *n.* renuncia *f.*

abjure, *v.* renunciar.

ablative, *a.* & *n.* (gram.) ablativo *m.*

ablaze, *a.* en llamas.

able, *a.* capaz; competente. **to be a.,** poder.

able-bodied, *a.* robusto.

ablution, *n.* ablución *f.*

ably, *adv.* hábilmente.

abnegate, *v.* repudiar; negar.

abnegation, *n.* abnegación; repudiación *f.*

abnormal, *a.* anormal.

abnormality, *n.* anormalidad, deformidad *f.*

abnormally, *adv.* anormalmente.

aboard, *adv.* a bordo.

abode, *n.* residencia *f.*

abolish, *v.* suprimir.

abolishment, *n.* abolición *f.*

abolition, *n.* abolición *f.*

abominable, *a.* abominable.

abominate, *v.* abominar, detestar.

abomination, *n.* abominación; enormidad *f.*

aboriginal, *a.* primitivo.

abortion, *n.* aborto *m.*

abortive, *a.* abortivo.

abound, *v.* abundar.

about, 1. *adv.* como. **about to,** para; a punto de. 2. *prep.* de, sobre, acerca de.

about-face, *n.* (mil.) media vuelta.

above, 1. *adv.* arriba. 2. *prep.* sobre; por encima de.

aboveboard, *a.* & *adv.* sincero, franco.

abrasion, *n.* raspadura *f.* (med.) abrasión *f.*

abrasive, 1. *a.* raspante. 2. *n.* abrasivo *m.*

abreast, *adv.* de frente.

abridge, *v.* abreviar.

abridgment, *n.* abreviación *f.*; compendio *m.*

abroad, *adv.* en el extranjero, al extranjero.

abrogate, *v.* abrogar, revocar.

abrogation, *n.* abrogación, revocación *f.*

abrupt, *a.* repentino; brusco.

abruptly, *adv.* bruscamente, precipitadamente.

abruptness, *n.* precipitación; brusquedad *f.*

abscess, *n.* absceso *m.*

abscond, *v.* fugarse.

absence, *n.* ausencia, falta *f.*

absent, *a.* ausente.

absentee, *a.* & *n.* ausente *m.*

absent-minded, *a.* distraído.

absinthe, *n.* absenta *f.*

absolute, *a.* absoluto.

absolutely, *adv.* absolutamente.

absoluteness, *n.* absolutismo *m.*

absolution, *n.* absolución *f.*

absolutism, *n.* absolutismo, despotismo *m.*

absolve, *v.* absolver.

absorb, *v.* absorber; preocupar.

absorbed, *a.* absorbido; absorto.

absorbent, *a.* absorbente.

absorbing, *a.* interesante.

absorption, *n.* absorción; preocupación *f.*

abstain, *v.* abstenerse.

abstemious, *a.* abstemio, sobrio.

abstinence, *n.* abstinencia *f.*

abstract, 1. *n.* resumen *m.* 2. *v.* abstraer.

abstracted, *a.* distraído.

abstraction, *n.* abstracción *f.*

abstruse, *a.* abstruso.

absurd, *a.* absurdo, ridículo.

absurdity, *n.* absurdo *m.*

absurdly, *adv.* absurdamente.

abundance, *n.* abundancia *f.*

abundant, *a.* abundante.

abundantly, *adv.* abundantemente.

abuse, 1. *n.* abuso *m.* 2. *v.* abusar de; maltratar.

abusive, *a.* abusivo.

abusively, *adv.* abusivamente, ofensivamente.

abut (en), *v.* terminar (en); lindar (con).

abutment, *n.* (building) estribo, contrafuerte *m.*

abyss, *n.* abismo *m.*

Abyssinian, *a.* & *n.* abisinio - nia.

academic, *a.* académico.

academy, *n.* academia *f.*

acanthus, *n.* (bot.) acanto *m.*

accede, *v.* acceder; consentir.

accelerate, *v.* acelerar.

acceleration, *n.* aceleración *f.*

accelerator, *n.* (auto.) acelerador *m.*

accent, 1. *n.* acento *m.* 2. *v.* acentuar.

accentuate, *v.* acentuar.

accept, *v.* aceptar.

acceptability, *n.* aceptabilidad *f.*

acceptable, *a.* aceptable.

acceptably, *adv.* aceptablemente.

acceptance, *n.* aceptación *f.*

access, *n.* acceso *m.*, entrada *f.*

accessible, *a.* accesible.

accessory, 1. *a.* accesorio. 2. *n.* cómplice *m.* & *f.*

accident, *n.* accidente *m.* **by a.,** por casualidad.

accidental, *a.* accidental.

accidentally, *adv.* accidentalmente, casualmente.

acclaim, *v.* aclamar.

acclamation, *n.* aclamación *f.*

acclimate, *v.* aclimatar.

acclivity, *n.* subida *f.*

accolade, *n.* acolada *f.*

accommodate, *v.* acomodar.

accommodating, *a.* bondadoso, complaciente.

accommodation, *n.* servicio *m.*; (pl.) alojamiento *m.*

accompaniment, *n.* acompañamiento *m.*

accompanist, *n.* acompañador *m.*

accompany, *v.* acompañar.

accomplice, *n.* cómplice *m.* & *f.*

accomplish, *v.* llevar a cabo; realizar.

accomplished, *a.* acabado, cumplido; culto.

accomplishment, *n.* realización *f.*; logro *m.*

accord, 1. *n.* acuerdo *m.* 2. *v.* otorgar.

accordance, *n.*: **in a. with,** de acuerdo con.

accordingly, *adv.* en conformidad.

according to, *prep.* según.

accordion, *n.* (mus.) acordeón *m.*

accost, *v.* dirigirse a.

account, 1. *n.* relato *m.*; (com.) cuenta *f.* **on a. of,** a causa de.

on no a., de ninguna manera.
2. v. a. for, explicar.

accountable, a. responsable.

accountant, n. contador -ra.

accounting, n. contabilidad f.

accouter, v. equipar, ataviar.

accoutrements, n. equipo, atavío m.

accredit, v. acreditar.

accretion, n. aumento m.

accrual, n. aumento, incremento m.

accrue, v. provenir; acumularse.

accumulate, v. acumular.

accumulation, n. acumulación f.

accumulative, a. acumulativo.

accumulator, n. acumulador m.

accuracy, n. exactitud, precisión f.

accurate, a. exacto.

accursed, a. maldito.

accusation, n. acusación f., cargo m.

accusative, a. & n. acusativo m.

accuse, v. acusar.

accused, a. & n. acusado, procesado m.

accuser, n. acusador -ra.

accustom, v. acostumbrar.

accustomed, a. acostumbrado.

ace, 1. a. sobresaliente. 2. n. as m.

acerbity, n. acerbidad, amargura f.

acetate, n. (chem.) acetato m.

acetic, a. acético.

acetylene, 1. a. acetilénico. 2. n. (chem.) acetileno m.

ache, 1. n. dolor m. 2. v. doler.

achieve, v. lograr, llevar a cabo.

achievement, n. realización f.; hecho notable.

acid, a. & n. ácido m.

acidify, v. acidificar.

acidity, n. acidez f.

acidosis, n. (med.) acidismo m.

acid test, prueba decisiva.

acidulous, a. agrio, acídulo.

acknowledge, v. admitir (receipt) acusar.

acme, n. apogeo, colmo m.

acne, n. (med.) acne m. & f.; barros m.pl.

acolyte, n. acólito m.

acorn, n. bellota f.

acoustics, n. acústica f.

acquaint, v. familiarizar. to be acquainted with, conocer.

acquaintance, n. conocimiento m. (person known) conocido -da. to make the a. of, conocer.

acquainted, be acquainted with, v. conocer.

acquiesce, v. consentir.

acquiescence, n. consentimiento m.

acquire, v. adquirir.

acquirement, n. adquisición f.; (pl.) conocimientos m.pl.

acquisition, n. adquisición f.

acquisitive, a. adquisitivo.

acquit, v. exonerar, absolver.

acquittal, n. absolución f.

acre, n. acre m.

acreage, número de acres.

acrid, a. acre, picante.

acrimonious, a. acrimonioso, mordaz.

acrimony, n. acrimonia, aspereza f.

acrobat, n. acróbata m.

across, 1. adv. a través, al otro lado. 2. prep. al otro lado de, a través de.

acrostic, n. acróstico m.

act, 1. n. acción f.; acto m. 2. v. actuar, portarse. act as, hacer de. act on, decidir sobre.

acting, 1. a. interino. 2. n. acción f.; (theat.) representación f.

actinism, n. actinismo m.

actinium, n. (chem.) actinio m.

action, n. acción f. take a., tomar medidas.

activate, v. activar.

activation, n. activación f.

activator, n. (chem.) activador m.

active, a. activo.

activity, n. actividad f.

actor, n. actor m.

actress, n. actriz f.

actual, a. real, efectivo.

actuality, n. realidad, actualidad f.

actually, adv. en realidad.

actuary, n. actuario m.

actuate, v. impulsar, mover.

acumen, n. cacumen m., perspicacia f.

acupuncture, n. acupuntura f.

acute, a. agudo; perspicaz.

acutely, adv. agudamente.

acuteness, n. agudeza f.

adage, n. refrán, proverbio m.

adamant, a. firme.

Adam's apple, nuez de la garganta.

adapt, v. adaptar.

adaptable, a. adaptable.

adaptability, n. adaptabilidad f.

adaptation, n. adaptación f.

adapter, n. (tech.) adaptador m.; (mech.) ajustador m.

adaptive, a. adaptable, acomodable.

add, v. agregar, añadir. a. up, sumar.

adder, n. víbora f.; serpiente m.

addict, n. adicto; ('fan') aficionado m.

addition, n. adición f. in a. to, además de.

additional, a. adicional.

addle, v. confundir.

address, 1. n. dirección f.; señas f.pl. (speech) discurso m. 2. v. dirigirse a.

addressee, n. destinatario -ia.

adduce, v. aducir.

adenoid, a. adenoideo.

adept, a. adepto.

adeptly, adv. diestramente.

adeptness, n. destreza f.

adequacy, n. suficiencia f.

adequate, a. adecuado.

adequately, adv. adecuadamente.

adhere, v. adherirse, pegarse.

adherence, n. adhesión f.; apego m.

adherent, n. adherente, partidario m.

adhesion, n. adhesión f.

adhesive, a. adhesivo. a. tape, esparadrapo m.

adhesiveness, n. adhesividad f.

adieu, 1. interj. adiós. 2. n. despedida f.

adjacent, a. adyacente.

adjective, n. adjectivo m.

adjoin, v. lindar (con).

adjoining, a. contiguo.

adjourn, v. suspender, levantar.

adjournment, n. suspensión f.; (leg.) espera f.

adjunct, n. adjunto m.; (gram.) atributo m.

adjust, v. ajustar, acomodar; arreglar.

adjuster, n. ajustador m.

adjustment, n. ajuste; arreglo m.

adjutant, n. (mil.) ayudante m.

administer, v. administrar.

administration, n. administración f.; gobierno m.

administrative, a. administrativo.

administrator, n. administrador m.

admirable, a. admirable.

admirably, adv. admirablemente.

admiral, n. almirante m.

admiralty, n. ministerio de marina.

admiration, n. admiración f.

admire, v. admirar.

admirer, n. admirador -ra; enamorado -da.

admiringly, adv. admirativamente.

admissible, a. admisible, aceptable.

admission, n. admisión; entrada f.

admit, v. admitir.

admittance, n. entrada f.

admittedly, adv. reconocidamente.

admixture, n. mezcla f.

admonish, v. amonestar.

admonition, n. admonición f.

adolescence, n. adolescencia f.

adolescent, n. & a. adolescente.

adopt, v. adoptar.

adoption, n. adopción f.

adorable, a. adorable.

adoration, n. adoración f.

adore, v. adorar.

adorn, v. adornar.

adornment, n. adorno m.

adrenalin, n. adrenalina f.

adrift, adv. a la ventura.

adroit, a. diestro.

adulate, *v.* adular.

adulation, *n.* adulación *f.*

adult, *a. & n.* adulto *m.*

adulterant, *a. & n.* adulterante *m.*

adulterate, *v.* adulterar.

adulterer, *n.* adúltero *m.*

adulteress, *n.* adúltera *f.*

adultery, *n.* adulterio *m.*

advance, 1. *n.* avance; adelanto *m.* **in a.,** de antemano, antes. **2.** *v.* avanzar, adelantar.

advanced, *a.* avanzado, adelantado.

advancement, *n.* adelantamiento *m.;* promoción *f.*

advantage, *n.* ventaja *f.* **take a. of,** aprovecharse de.

advantageous, *a.* provechoso, ventajoso.

advantageously, *adv.* ventajosamente.

advent, *n.* venida, llegada *f.*

adventitious, *a.* adventicio, espontáneo.

adventure, *n.* aventura *f.*

adventurer, *n.* aventurero *m.*

adventurous, *a.* aventurero, intrépido.

adventurously, *adv.* arriesgadamente.

adverb, *n.* adverbio *m.*

adverbial, *a.* adverbial.

adversary, *n.* adversario *m.*

adverse, *a.* adverso.

adversely, *adv.* adversamente.

adversity, *n.* adversidad *f.*

advert, *v.* hacer referencia a.

advertise, *v.* avisar, anunciar.

advertisement, *n.* aviso, anuncio *m.*

advertiser, *n.* anunciante, avisador *m.*

advertising, *n.* publicidad *f.*

advice, *n.* consejos *m.pl.*

advisability, *n.* prudencia, propiedad *f.*

advisable, *a.* aconsejable, prudente.

advisably, *adv.* prudentemente.

advise, *v.* aconsejar.

advisedly, *adv.* avisadamente, prudentemente.

advisement, *n.* consideración *f.;* **take under a.,** someter a estudio.

adviser, *n.* consejero *m.*

advocacy, *n.* abogacía; defensa *f.*

advocate, 1. *n.* abogado *m.* **2.** *v.* apoyar.

aegis, *n.* amparo *m.*

aerate, *v.* airear, ventilar.

aeration, *n.* aeración, ventilación *f.*

aerial, *a.* aéreo.

aerie, *n.* nido de águila.

aeronautics, *n.* aeronáutica *f.*

aerosol bomb, *n.* bomba insecticida.

afar, *adv.* lejos. **from a.,** de lejos, desde lejos.

affability, *n.* afabilidad, amabilidad *f.*

affable, *a.* afable.

affably, *adv.* afablemente.

affair, *n.* asunto *m.* **love a.,** aventura amorosa.

affect, *v.* afectar; (emotionally) conmover.

affectation, *n.* afectación *f.*

affected, *a.* artificioso.

affecting, *a.* conmovedor.

affection, *n.* cariño *m.*

affectionate, *a.* afectuoso, cariñoso.

affectionately, *adv.* afectuosamente, con cariño.

affiance, *v.* dar palabra de casamiento; **become affianced,** comprometerse.

affidavit, *n.* (leg.) declaración, deposición *f.*

affiliate, 1. *n.* afiliado *m.* **2.** *v.* afiliar.

affiliation, *n.* afiliación *f.*

affinity, *n.* afinidad *f.*

affirm, *v.* afirmar.

affirmation, *n.* afirmación, aserción *f.*

affirmative, 1. *n.* afirmativa *f.* **2.** *a.* afirmativo.

affirmatively, *adv.* afirmativamente, aseveradamente.

affix, 1. *n.* (gram.) afijo *m.* **2.** *v.* fijar, pegar, poner.

afflict, *v.* afligir.

affliction, *n.* aflicción *f.;* mal *m.*

affluence, *n.* abundancia, opulencia *f.*

affluent, *a.* opulento, afluente.

afford, *v.* proporcionar. **be able to a.,** tener con que comprar.

affront, 1. *n.* afrenta *f.* **2.** *v.* afrentar, insultar.

afield, *adv.* lejos de casa; lejos del camino; lejos del asunto.

afire, *adv.* ardiendo.

afloat, *adv.* (naut.) a flote.

aforementioned, aforesaid, *a.* dicho, susodicho.

afraid, *a.* **to be a.,** tener miedo, temer.

African, *n. & a.* africano -na.

aft, *adv.* (naut.) a popa, en popa.

after, 1. *prep.* después de. **2.** *conj.* después que.

aftermath, *n.* resultados *m.pl.,* consecuencias *f.pl.*

afternoon, *n.* tarde *f.* **good a.,** buenas tardes.

afterthought, *n.* idea tardía.

afterward(s), *adv.* después.

again, *adv.* otra vez, de nuevo. **to do a.,** volver a hacer.

against, *prep.* contra; en contra de.

agape, *adv.* con la boca abierta.

agate, *n.* ágata *f.*

age, 1. *n.* edad *f.* **of a.,** mayor de edad. **old a.,** vejez *f.* **2.** *v.* envejecer.

aged, *a.* viejo, anciano, añejo.

ageism, *n.* discriminación contra las personas de edad.

ageless, *a.* sempiterno.

agency, *n.* agencia *f.*

agenda, *n.* agenda *f.,* orden *m.*

agent, *n.* agente; representante *m.*

agglutinate, *v.* aglutinar.

agglutination, *n.* aglutinación *f.*

aggrandize, *v.* agrandar; elevar.

aggrandizement, *n.* engrandecimiento *m.*

aggravate, *v.* agravar; irritar.

aggravation, *n.* agravamiento; empeoramiento *m.*

aggregate, *a. & n.* agregado *m.*

aggregation, *n.* agregación *f.*

aggression, *n.* agresión *f.*

aggressive, *n.* agresivo.

aggressively, *adv.* agresivamente.

aggressiveness, *n.* agresividad *f.*

aggressor, *n.* agresor *m.*

aghast, *a.* horrorizado.

agile, *a.* ágil.

agility, *n.* agilidad, ligereza, prontitud *f.*

agitate, *v.* agitar.

agitation, *n.* agitación *f.*

agitator, *n.* agitador *m.*

agnostic, *a. & n.* agnóstico *m.*

ago, *adv.* hace. **two days a.,** hace dos días.

agonized, *a.* angustioso.

agony, *n.* sufrimiento *m.;* angustia *f.*

agrarian, *a.* agrario.

agree, *v.* estar de acuerdo; convenir. **a. with one,** sentar bien.

agreeable, *a.* agradable.

agreeably, *adv.* agradablemente.

agreement, *n.* acuerdo *m.*

agriculture, *n.* agricultura *f.*

ahead, *adv.* adelante.

aid, 1. *n.* ayuda *f.* **2.** *v.* ayudar.

aide, *n.* ayudante *m.*

ailing, *adj.* enfermo.

ailment, *n.* enfermedad *f.*

aim, 1. *n.* puntería *f.;* (purpose) propósito *m.* **2.** *v.* apuntar.

aimless, *a.* sin objeto.

air, 1. *n.* aire *m.* **by a.,** por avión. **2.** *v.* ventilar, airear.

airbag, *n.* (in automobiles) saco de aire *m.*

air-conditioned, *a.* enfriado por aire.

air-conditioning, acondicionamiento del aire.

aircraft, *n.* máquina de volar.

aircraft carrier, *n.* portaaviones *m.*

airing, *n.* ventilación *f.*

airline, *n.* línea aérea.

airliner, *n.* avión de transporte.

airmail, *n.* correo aéreo.

airplane, *n.* avión, aeroplano *m.*

air pollution, contaminación atmosférica.

airport, *n.* aeropuerto *m.*

air pressure, presión atmosférica.

air raid, ataque aéreo.

airsick, a. mareado.

airtight, a. hermético.

aisle, n. pasillo m.

ajar, a. entreabierto.

akin, a. emparentado, semejante.

alacrity, n. alacridad, presteza f.

alarm, 1. n. alarma f. 2. v. alarmar.

alarmist, n. alarmista m. & f.

albino, n. albino -na.

album, n. album m.

alcohol, n. alcohol m.

alcoholic, a. alcohólico.

alcove, n. alcoba f.

ale, n. cerveza inglesa

alert, 1. n. alarma f. on the a., alerta, sobre aviso. 2. a. listo, vivo. 3. v. poner sobre aviso.

alfalfa, n. alfalfa f.

algebra, n. álgebra f.

alias, n. alias m.

alibi, n. excusa f.; (leg.) coartada f.

alien, 1. a. ajeno, extranjero. 2. n. extranjero -ra.

alienate, v. enajenar.

alight, v. bajar, apearse.

align, v. alinear.

alike, 1. a. semejante, igual. 2. adv. del mismo modo, igualmente.

alimentary canal, tubo digestivo.

alive, a. vivo; animado.

alkali, n. (chem.) álcali, cali m.

alkaline, a. alcalino.

all, a. & pron. todo. not at a., de ninguna manera, nada.

allay, v. aquietar.

allegation, n. alegación f.

allege, v. alegar; pretender.

allegiance, n. lealtad f.; (to country) homenaje m.

allegory, n. alegoría f.

allergy, n. alergia f.

alleviate, v. aliviar.

alley, n. callejón m. bowling a., bolera f., boliche m.

alliance, n. alianza f.

allied, a. aliado.

alligator, n. caimán m.; (Mex.) lagarto m. a. pear, aguacate m.

allocate, v. colocar, asignar.

allot, v. asignar.

allotment, n. lote, porción f.

allow, v. permitir, dejar.

allowance, n. abono m.; dieta f. make a. for, tener en cuenta.

alloy, n. mezcla f. (metal) aleación f.

all right, está bien.

allude, v. aludir.

allure, 1. n. atracción f. 2. v. atraer, tentar.

alluring, a. tentador, seductivo.

allusion, n. alusión f.

ally, 1. n. aliado m. 2. v. aliar.

almanac, n. almanaque m.

almighty, a. todopoderoso.

almond, n. almendra f.

almost, adv. casi.

alms, n. limosna f.

aloft, adv. arriba, en alto.

alone, adv. solo, a solas. to leave a., dejar en paz.

along, prep. por; a lo largo de. a. with, junto con.

alongside, 1. adv. al lado. 2. prep. junto a.

aloof, a. apartado.

aloud, adv. en voz alta.

alpaca, n. alpaca f.

alphabet, n. alfabeto m.

alphabetical, a. alfabético.

alphabetize, v. alfabetizar.

already, adv. ya.

also, adv. también.

altar, n. altar m.

alter, v. alterar.

alteration, n. alteración f.

alternate, 1. a. alterno. 2. n. substituto -ta. 3. v. alternar.

alternative, 1. a. alternativo. 2. n. alternativa f.

although, conj. aunque.

altitude, n. altura f.

alto, n. contralto m.

altogether, adv. en junto; enteramente.

altruism, n. altruismo m.

alum, n. alumbre m.

aluminum, n. aluminio m.

always, adv. siempre.

amalgam, n. amalgama f.

amalgamate, v. amalgamar.

amass, v. amontonar.

amateur, n. aficionado -da.

amaze, v. asombrar; sorprender.

amazement, n. asombro m.

amazing, a. asombroso, pasmoso.

ambassador, n. embajador m.

amber, 1. a. ambarino. 2. n. ámbar m.

ambidextrous, a. ambidextro.

ambiguity, n. ambigüedad f.

ambiguous, a. ambiguo.

ambition, n. ambición f.

ambitious, a. ambicioso.

ambulance, n. ambulancia f.

ambush, 1. n. emboscada f. 2. v. acechar.

ameliorate, v. mejorar.

amenable, a. tratable, dócil.

amend, v. enmendar.

amendment, n. enmienda f.

amenity, n. amenidad f.

American, a. & n. americano -na, norteamericano -na.

amethyst, n. amatista f.

amiable, a. amable.

amicable, a. amigable.

amid, prep. entre, en medio de.

amidships, adv. (naut.) en medio del navío.

amiss, adv. mal. to take a., llevar a mal.

amity, n. amistad, armonía f.

ammonia, n. amoníaco m.

ammunition, n. munición f.

amnesia, n. (med.) amnesia f.

amnesty, n. amnistía f., indulto m.

amniocentesis, n. amniocéntesis m.

amoeba, n. amiba f.

among, prep. entre.

amoral, a. amoral.

amorous, a. amoroso.

amorphous, a. amorfo.

amortize, v. (com.) amortizar.

amount, 1. n. cantidad, suma f. 2. v. a. to, subir a.

ampere, n. (elec.) amperio m.

amphibian, a. & n. anfibio m.

amphitheater, n. anfiteatro, circo m.

ample, a. amplio; suficiente.

amplify, v. amplificar.

amputate, v. amputar.

amuse, v. entretener, divertir.

amusement, n. diversión f.

an, art. un, una.

anachronism, n. anacronismo, m.

analogous, a. análogo, parecido.

analogy, n. analogía f.

analysis, n. análisis m. & f.

analyst, n. analizador m.

analytic, a. analítico.

analyze, v. analizar.

anarchy, n. anarquía f.

anatomy, n. anatomía f.

ancestor, n. antepasado m.

ancestral, a. de los antepasados, hereditario.

ancestry, n. linaje, abolengo m.

anchor, 1. n. ancla f. to weigh a., levar el ancla. 2. v. anclar.

anchorage, n. (naut.) ancladero, anclaje m.

anchovy, n. anchoa f.

ancient, a. & n. antiguo.

and, conj. y, (before i-, hi-) e.

anecdote, n. anécdota f.

anemia, n. (med.) anemia f.

anesthetic, n. anestesia f.

anew, adv. de nuevo.

angel, n. ángel m.

anger, n. ira f., enojo m. 2. v. enfadar, enojar.

angle, n. ángulo m.

angry, a. enojado, enfadado.

anguish, n. angustia f.

angular, a. angular.

aniline, n. (chem.) anilina f.

animal, a.& n. animal m.

animate, 1. adj. animado. 2. v. animar.

animated, a. vivo, animado.

animation, n. animación, viveza f.

animosity, n. rencor m.

anise, n. anís m.

ankle, n. tobillo m.

annals, n.pl. anales m.pl.

annex, 1. n. anexo m., adición f. 2. v. anexar.

annexation, n. anexión, adición f.

annihilate, v. aniquilar, destruir.

anniversary, n. aniversario m.

annotate, v. anotar.

annotation, n. anotación f., apunte m.

announce, v. anunciar.

announcement, n. anuncio, aviso m.

announcer, n. anunciador m.; (radio) anunciador, noticiador m.

annoy, v. molestar.

annoyance, n. molestia, incomodidad f.

annual, a. anual.

annuity, n. anualidad, pensión f.

annul, v. anular, invalidar.

anode, n. (elec.) ánodo m.

anoint, v. untar; (rel.) ungir.

anomalous, a. anómalo, irregular.

anonymous, a. anónimo.

another, a. & pron. otro.

answer, 1. n. contestación, respuesta f. 2. v. contestar, responder. a. for, ser responsable de.

answerable, a. discutible, refutable.

ant, n. hormiga f.

antacid, a. & n. antiácido m.

antagonism, n. antagonismo m.

antagonist, n. antagonista m.

antagonistic, a. antagónico, hostil.

antagonize, v. contrariar.

antarctic, a. & n. antártico m.

antecedent, a. & n. antecedente m.

antedate, v. antedatar.

antelope, n. antílope m., gacela f.

antenna, n. antena f.

anterior, a. anterior.

anteroom, n. antecámara f.

anthem, n. himno m.; (religious) antífona f.

anthology, n. antología f.

anthracite, n. antracita f.

anthrax, n. (med.) ántrax m.

anthropology, n. antropología f.

antiaircraft, a. antiaéreo.

antibody, n. anticuerpo m.

anticipate, v. esperar, anticipar.

anticipation, n. anticipación f.

anticlerical, a. anticlerical.

anticlimax, n. anticlímax m.

antidote, n. antídoto m.

antimony, n. antimonio m.

antinuclear, a. antinuclear.

antipathy, n. antipatía f.

antiquated, a. anticuado.

antique, 1. a. antiguo. 2. n. antigüedad f.

antiquity, n. antigüedad f.

antiseptic, a. & n. antiséptico m.

antisocial, a. antisocial.

antitoxin, n. (med.) antitoxina f.

antler, n. asta f.

anvil, n. yunque m.

anxiety, n. ansia, ansiedad f.

anxious, a. inquieto, ansioso.

any, a. alguno; (at all) cualquiera; (after not) ninguno.

anybody, pron. alguien; (at all) cualquiera; (after not) nadie.

anyhow, adv. de todos modos; en todo caso.

anyone, pron. = anybody.

anything, pron. algo; (at all) cualquier cosa; (after not) nada.

anyway, adv. = anyhow.

anywhere, adv. en alguna parte; (at all) dondequiera; (after not) en ninguna parte.

apart, adv. aparte. to take a., deshacer.

apartheid, n. apartheid m.

apartment, n. apartamento, piso m.

apathetic, a. apático.

apathy, n. apatía f.

ape, 1. n. mono m. 2. v. imitar.

aperture, n. abertura f.

apex, n. ápice m.

aphorism, n. aforismo m.

apiary, n. apiario, abejar m.

apiece, adv. por persona; cada uno.

apologetic, a. apologético.

apologist, n. apologista m. & f.

apologize, v. excusarse, disculparse.

apology, n. excusa; apología f.

apoplectic, a. apopléptico.

apoplexy, n. apoplejía f.

apostate, n. apóstata m. & f.

apostle, n. apóstol m.

apostolic, a. apostólico.

appall, v. espantar; desmayar.

apparatus, n. aparato m.

apparel, n. ropa f.

apparent, a. aparente; claro.

apparition, n. fantasma f.

appeal, 1. n. súplica f.; interés m.; (leg.) apelación f. 2. v. apelar, suplicar; interesar.

appear, v. aparecer, asomar; (seem) parecer; (leg.) comparecer.

appearance, n. apariencia f., aspecto m.

appease, v. aplacar, apaciguar.

appeasement, n. apaciguamiento m.

appeaser, n. apaciguador, pacificador m.

appellant, n. apelante, demandante m.

appellate, a. (leg.) de apelación.

appendage, n. pertenencia f.

appendectomy, n. (med.) apendectomía f.

appendicitis, n. (med.) apendicitis m.

appendix, n. apéndice m.

appetite, n. apetito m.

appetizer, n. apertivo m.

appetizing, a. apetitivo.

applaud, v. aplaudir.

applause, n. aplauso m.

apple, n. manzana f. a. tree, manzano m.

applesauce, n. compota de manzana.

appliance, n. utensilio, aparato m.

applicable, a. aplicable.

applicant, n. suplicante m. & f.; candidato -ta.

application, n. solicitud f.

applied, a. aplicado. a. for, pedido.

appliqué, n. (sewing) aplicación f.

apply, v. aplicar. a. for, solicitar, pedir.

appoint, v. nombrar.

appointment, n. nombramiento, puesto m.

apportion, v. repartir.

apposition, n. (gram.) aposición f.

appraisal, n. valoración f.; apremio m.

appraise, v. avaluar, tasar; estimar.

appreciable, a. apreciable; notable.

appreciate, v. apreciar, estimar.

appreciation, n. aprecio; reconocimiento m.

apprehend, v. prender, capturar.

apprehension, n. aprensión f.

apprehensive, a. aprensivo.

apprentice, n. aprendiz m.

apprise, v. informar.

approach, 1. n. acceso; método m. 2. v. acercarse.

approachable, a. accesible.

approbation, n. aprobación f.

appropriate, 1. a. apropiado. 2. v. apropiar.

appropriation, n. apropiación f.

approval, n. aprobación f.

approve, v. aprobar.

approximate, 1. a. aproximado. 2. v. aproximar.

approximately, adv. aproximadamente.

approximation, n. aproximación f.

appurtenance, n. pertenencia f.

apricot, n. albaricoque, damasco m.

April, n. abril m.

apron, n. delantal m.

apropos, adv. a propósito.

apt, a. apto; capaz.

aptitude, n. aptitud; facilidad f.

aquarium, n. acuario m., pecera f.

aquatic, a. acuático.

aqueduct, n. acueducto m.

aqueous, a. ácueo, acuoso, aguoso.

aquiline, a. aquilino, aguileño.

Arab, a. & n. árabe m. & f.

arable, a. cultivable.

arbitrary, a. arbitrario.

arbitrate, v. arbitrar.

arbitration, n. arbitraje m., arbitración f.

arbitrator, n. arbitrador -ra.

arbor, n. emparrado m.

arboreal, a. arbóreo.

arc, n. arco m.

arch, 1. n. arco m. 2. v. arquear, encorvar.

archaeology, n. arqueología f.

archaic, a. arcaico.

archbishop, n. arzobispo m.

archdiocese, n. archidiócesis m.

archduke, n. archiduque m.

archer, n. arquero m.

archery, n. ballestería f.

archipelago, n. archipiélago m.

architect, n. arquitecto m.

architectural, a. arquitectural.

architecture, n. arquitectura f.

archive, n. archivo m.

archway, n. arcada f.

arctic, a. ártico.

ardent, a. ardiente.

ardor, n. ardor m., pasión f.

arduous, a. arduo, difícil.

area, n. área; extensión f.

area code, prefijo m.

arena, n. arena f.

Argentine, a. & n. argentino-na.

argue, v. disputar; sostener.

argument, n. disputa f.; razonamiento m.

argumentative, a. argumentoso.

aria, n. (mus.) aria f.

arid, a. árido, seco.

arise, v. surgir.

aristocracy, n. aristocracia f.

aristocrat, n. aristócrata m.

aristocratic, a. aristocrático.

arithmetic, n. aritmética f.

ark, n. arca f.

arm, 1. n. brazo m.; (weapon) arma f. 2. v. armar.

armament, n. armamento m.

armchair, n. sillón m., butaca f.

armed forces, fuerzas militares.

armful, n. brazada f.

armhole, n. (sew.) sobaquera f.

armistice, n. armisticio m.

armor, n. armadura f., blindaje m.

armored, a. blindado.

armory, n. armería f., arsenal m.

armpit, n. sobaco m.

army, n. ejército m.

arnica, n. árnica f.

aroma, n. fragancia f.

aromatic, a. aromático.

around, prep. alrededor de, a la vuelta de; cerca de a. here, por aquí.

arouse, v. despertar; excitar.

arraign, v. (leg.) procesar criminalmente.

arrange, v. arreglar; concertar; (mus.) adaptar.

arrangement, n. arreglo; orden m.

array, 1. n. orden; adorno m. 2. v. adornar.

arrears, n. atrasos m.pl.

arrest, 1. n. detención f. 2. v. detener, arrestar.

arrival, n. llegada f.

arrive, v. llegar.

arrogance, n. arrogancia f.

arrogant, a. arrogante.

arrogate, v. arrogarse, usurpar.

arrow, n. flecha f.

arrowhead, n. punta de flecha.

arsenal, n. arsenal m.

arsenic, n. arsénico m.

arson, n. incendio premeditado.

art, arte m. (f. in pl.); (skill) maña f.

arterial, a. arterial.

arteriosclerosis, n. arteriosclerosis m.

artery, n. arteria f.

artesian well, pozo artesiano.

artful, a. astuto.

arthritis, n. artritis m.

artichoke, n. alcachofa f.

article, n. artículo m.

articulate, v. articular.

articulation, n. articulación f.

artifice, n. artificio m.

artificial, a. artificial.

artificially, adv. artificialmente.

artillery, n. artillería f.

artisan, n. artesano m.

artist, n. artista m. & f.

artistic, a. artístico.

artistry, n. arte m. & f.

artless, a. natural, cándido.

as, adv. & conj. como; as ... as ... tan ... como.

asbestos, n. asbesto m.

ascend, v. ascender.

ascendancy, n. ascendiente m.

ascendant, a. ascendente.

ascent, n. subida f., ascenso m.

ascertain, v. averiguar.

ascetic, 1. a. ascético. 2. n. asceta m. & f.

ascribe, v. atribuir.

ash, n. ceniza f.

ashamed, a. avergonzado.

ashen, a. pálido.

ashore, adv. a tierra. go a., desembarcar.

ashtray, n. cenicero m.

Asiatic, a. & n. asiático -ca.

aside, adv. al lado. a. from, aparte de.

ask, v. preguntar; invitar; (request) pedir. a. for, pedir. a. a question, hacer una pregunta.

askance, adv. de soslayo; con recelo.

asleep, a. dormido. to fall a., dormirse.

asparagus, n. espárrago m.

aspect, n. aspecto m., apariencia f.

asperity, n. aspereza f.

aspersion, n. calumnia f.

asphalt, n. asfalto m.

asphyxia, n. asfixia f.

asphyxiate, v. asfixiar, sofocar.

aspirant, a. & n. aspirante.

aspirate, v. aspirar.

aspiration, n. aspiración f.

aspirator, n. aspirador m.

aspire, v. aspirar. a. to, ambicionar.

aspirin, n. aspirina f.

ass, n. asno, burro m.

assail, v. asaltar, acometer.

assailant, n. asaltador m.

assassin, n. asesino m.

assassinate, v. asesinar.

assassination, n. asesinato m.

assault, 1. n. asalto m. 2. v. asaltar, atacar.

assay, v. examinar; ensayar.

assemblage, n. asamblea f.

assemble, v. juntar, convocar; (mechanism) montar.

assembly, n. asamblea, concurrencia f.

assent, 1. n. asentimiento m. 2. v. asentir, convenir.

assert, v. afirmar, aseverar. a. oneself, hacerse sentir.

assertion, n. aserción, aseveración f.

assertive, a. asertivo.

assess, v. tasar, avaluar.

assessor, n. asesor m.

asset, n. ventaja f. assets (com.) capital m.

asseverate, v. aseverar, afirmar.

asseveration, n. aseveración f.

assiduous, a. asiduo.

assiduously, adv. asiduamente.

assign, v. asignar; destinar.

assignable, a. asignable, transferible.

assignation, n. asignación f.

assignment, n. misión; tarea f.

assimilate, v. asimilar.

assimilation, n. asimilación f.

assimilative, a. asimilativo.

assist, v. ayudar, auxiliar.

assistance, n. ayuda f., auxilio m.

assistant, n. ayudante, asistente m.

associate, 1. n. socio m. 2. v. asociar.

association, n. asociación; sociedad f.

assonance, n. asonancia f.

assort, v. surtir con variedad.

assorted, a. variado, surtido.

assortment, n. surtido m.

assuage, v. mitigar, aliviar.

assume, v. suponer; asumir.

assuming, a. presuntuoso. a. that, dado que.

assumption, n. suposición; (rel.) asunción f.

assurance, n. seguridad; confianza f.

assure, v. asegurar; dar confianza.

assured, 1. a. seguro. 2. a. & n. (com.) asegurado m.

assuredly, adv. ciertamente.

aster, n. (bot.) aster m.

asterisk, n. asterisco m.

astern, adv. (naut.) a popa.

asteroid, n. asteroide m.

asthma, n. (med.) asma f.

astigmatism, n. astigmatismo m.

astir, adv. en movimiento.

astonish, v. asombrar, pasmar.

astonishment, n. asombro m., sorpresa f.

astound, v. pasmar, sorprender.

astral, a. astral, estelar.

astray, a. desviado.

astride. adv. a horcajadas.

astringent, a. & n. astringente m.

astrology, n. astrología f.

astronaut, n. astronauta m.

astronomy, n. astronomía f.

astute, a. astuto; agudo.

asunder, adv. en dos.

asylum, n. asilo, refugio m.

asymmetry, n. asimetría f.

at, prep. a, en; cerca de.

ataxia, n. (med.) ataxia f.

atheist, n. ateo m.

athlete, n. atleta m.

athletic, a. atlético.

athletics, n. atletismo m., deportes m.pl.

athwart, prep. á través de.

Atlantic, 1. a. atlántico. 2. n. Atlántico m.

Atlantic Ocean, el mar atlántico.

atlas, n. atlas m.

atmosphere, n. atmósfera f.; (fig.) ambiente m.

atmospheric, a. atmosférico.

atoll, n. atolón m.

atom, n. átomo m.

atomic, a. atómico.

atomic bomb, bomba atómica.

atomic energy, energía atómica.

atomic theory, teoría atómica.

atomic weight, peso atómico.

atonal, a. (mus.) atonal.

atone, v. expiar, compensar.

atonement, n. expiación; reparación f.

atrocious, a. atroz.

atrocity, n. atrocidad f.

atrophy, 1. n. (med.) atrofia f. 2. v. atrofiar.

atropine, n. (chem.) atropina f.

attach, v. juntar; prender; (hook) enganchar; (fig.) atribuir.

attaché, n. agregado m.

attachment, 1. enlace m.; accesorio m.; (emotional) afecto, cariño m.

attack, 1. n. ataque m. 2. v. atacar.

attacker, n. asaltador m.

attain, v. lograr, alcanzar.

attainable, a. accesible, realizable.

attainment, n. logro; (pl.) dotes f.pl.

attempt, 1. n. ensayo; esfuerzo m.; tentativa f. 2. v. ensayar, intentar.

attend, v. atender; (a meeting) asistir a.

attendance, n. asistencia; presencia f.

attendant, 1. a. concomitante. 2. n. servidor -ra.

attention, n. atención f.; obsequio m. to pay a. to, hacer caso a.

attentive, a. atento.

attentively, adv. atentamento.

attenuate, v. atenuar, adelgazar.

attest, v. confirmar, atestiguar.

attic, n. desván m, guardilla f.

attire, 1. n. traje m. 2. v. vestir.

attitude, n. actitud f.; ademán m.

attorney, n. abogado, apoderado m.

attract, v. atraer. a. attention, llamar la atención.

attraction, n. atracción f., atractivo m.

attractive, a. atractivo; simpático.

attributable, a. atribuible, imputable.

attribute, 1. n. atributo m. 2. v. atribuir.

attrition, n. roce, desgaste m.; atrición f.

attune, v. armonizar.

auction, n. subasta f., (S.A.) venduta f.

auctioneer, n. subastador m., (S.A.) martillero m.

audacious, a. audaz.

audacity, n. audacia f.

audible, a. audible.

audience, n. auditorio, público m.; entrevista f.

audiovisual, a. audiovisual.

audit, v. revisar cuentas.

audition, n. audición f.

auditor, n. interventor, revisor m.

auditorium, n. sala f.; teatro m.

auditory, a. & n. auditorio m.

augment, v. aumentar.

augur, v. augurar, pronosticar.

August, n. agosto m.

aunt, n. tía f.

auspice, n. auspicio m.

auspicious, a. favorable; propicio.

austere, a. austero.

austerity, n. austeridad, severidad f.

Austrian, a. & n. austríaco -ca.

authentic, a. auténtico.

authenticate, v. autenticar.

authenticity, n. autenticidad f.

author, n. autor, escritor m.

authoritarian, a. & n. autoritario m.

authoritative, a. autoritario; autorizado.

authoritatively, adv. autorizadamente.

authority, n. autoridad f.

authorization, n. autorización f.

authorize, v. autorizar.

auto, n. auto, automóvil m.

autobiography, n. autobiografía f.

autocracy, n. autocracia f.

autocrat, n. autócrata m. & f.

autograph, n. autógrafo m.

automatic, a. automático.

automatically, adv. automáticamente.

automobile, n. automóvil, coche m.

automotive, a. automotriz.

autonomy, n. autonomía f.

autopsy, n. autopsia f.

autumn, n. otoño m.

auxiliary, a. auxiliar.

avail, 1. n. of no a., en vano. 2. v. a. oneself of, aprovechar.

available, a. disponible.

avalanche, n. alud m.

avarice, n. avaricia, codicia f.

avariciously, adv. avaramente.

avenge, v. vengar.

avenger, n. vengador -ra.

avenue, n. avenida f.

average, 1. a. medio; común. 2. n. promedio, término medio m. 3. v. calcular el promedio.

averse, a. adverso.

aversion, n. aversión f.

avert, v. desviar; impedir.

aviary, n. pajarera, avería f.

aviation, n. aviación f.

aviator, n. aviador -ra.

aviatrix, n. aviatriz f.

avid, a. ávido.

avocation, n. pasatiempo f.

avoid, v. evitar.

avoidable, a. evitable.

avoidance, n. evitación f.; (leg.) anulación f.

avow, v. declarar; admitir.

avowal, n. admisión f.

avowed, a. reconocido; admitido.

avowedly, adv. reconocidamente; confesadamente.

await, v. esperar, aguardar.

awake, a. despierto.

awake, v. despertar.

awaken, v. despertar.

award, 1. n. premio m. 2. v. otorgar.

aware, a. enterado, consciente.

awash, a. & adv. (naut.) a flor de agua.

away, adv. (see under verb: go away, put away, take away, etc.)

awe, n. pavor m.

awesome, a. pavoroso; aterrador.

awful, a. horrible, terrible, muy malo.

awhile, adv. por un rato.

awkward, a. torpe, desmañado; (fig.) delicado, embarazoso.

awning, n. toldo m.

awry, a. oblicuo, torcido.

ax, axe, n. hacha f.

axiom, n. axioma m.

axis, n. eje m.

axle, n. eje m.

ayatollah, n. ayatola m.

azure, a. azulado.

B

babble, 1. n. balbuceo, murmullo m. 2 v. balbucear.

babbler, n. hablador -ra, charlador -ra.

baboon, n. mandril m.

baby, n. nene, bebé m.

babyish, a. infantil.

bachelor, n. soltero m.

bacillus, n. bacilo, microbio m.

back, 1. adv. atrás. to be b., estar de vuelta. b. of, detrás de. 2. n. espalda f.; (of animal) lomo m.

backbone, n. espinazo m.; (fig.) firmeza f.

backer, n. sostenedor -ra.

background, n. fondo m. antecedentes m.pl.

backing, n. apoyo m., garantía f.

backlash, n. repercusión negativa.

backlog, n. rezago m.

backpack, n. mochila f.

backstage, n. entre bastidores m.

backward, 1. a. atrasado. 2. adv. hacia atrás.

backwardness, n. atraso m.

backwater, n. remolino m.; contracorriente f.

backwoods, n. monte m.; región apartada.

bacon, n. tocino m.

bacteria, n. bacterias f.pl.

bacteriologist, n. bacteriólogo m.

bacteriology, n. bacteriología f.

bad, a. malo.

badge, n. insignia, divisa f.

badger, 1. n. tejón m. 2. v. atormentar.

badly, adv. mal.

badness, n. maldad f.

bad-tempered, a. de mal humor.

baffle, v. desconcertar.

bafflement, n. contrariedad; confusión f.

bag, 1. n. saco m.; bolsa f. 2. v. ensacar, cazar.

baggage, n. equipaje m. b. check, talón m.

baggage cart (airport), carrillo para llevar equipaje.

baggy, a. abotagado; bolsudo; hinchado.

bagpipe, n. gaita f.

bail, 1. n. fianza f. 2. v. desaguar.

bailiff, n. alguacil m.

bait, 1. n. cebo m. 2. v. cebar.

bake, v. cocer en horno.

baker, n. panadero, hornero m.

bakery, n. panadería f.

baking, n. hornada f. b. powder, levadura f.

balance, n. balanza f.; equilibrio m.; (com.) saldo m.

balcony, n. balcón m.; (theat.) galería f.

bald, a. calvo.

baldness, n. calvicie f.

bale, 1. n. bala f. 2. v. embalar.

balk, v. frustrar; rebelarse.

balky, a. rebelón.

ball, n. bola, pelota f.; (dance) baile m.

ballad, n. romance m.; balada f.

ballast, 1. n. lastre m. 2. v. lastrar.

ball bearing, n. cojinete de bolas m.

ballerina, n. bailarina f.

ballet, n. danza f.; ballet m.

ballistics, n. balística f.

balloon, n. globo m. b. tire, neumático de balón.

ballot, 1. n. balota f., voto m. 2. v. balotar, votar.

ballroom, n. salón de baile m.

balm, n. bálsamo; ungüento m.

balmy, a. fragante; reparador; calmante.

balsa, n. bálsamo m.

balsam, n. bálsamo m.

balustrade, n. barandilla f.

bamboo, n. bambú m., caña f.

ban, 1. n. prohibición f. 2. v. prohibir; proscribir.

banal, a. trivial; vulgar.

banana, n. banana f., cambur m. b. tree, banano, plátano m.

band, 1. n. venda f.; (of men) banda, cuadrilla, partida f. 2. v. asociarse.

bandage, 1. n. vendaje m. 2. v. vendar.

bandanna, n. pañuelo (grande) m.; bandana f.

bandbox, n. caja de cartón.

bandit, n. bandido -da.

bandmaster, n. músico mayor m.

bandstand, n. kiosco de música m.

bang, 1. interj. ¡pum! 2. n. ruido de un golpe. 3. v. golpear ruidosamente.

banish, v. desterrar.

banishment, n. destierro m.

banister, n. pasamano m.

bank, 1. n. banco m.; (of a river) margen m. or f. 2. v. depositar.

bankbook, n. libreta de depositos f.

banker, n. banquero m.

banking, 1. a. bancaria. 2. n. banca f.

bank note, n. billete de banco m.

bankrupt, n. insolvente.

bankruptcy, n. bancarrota f.

banner, n. bandera f.; estandarte m.

banquet, n. banquete m.

banter, 1. n. choteo m.; zumba; burla f. 2. v. chotear; zumbar; burlarse.

baptism, n. bautismo, bautizo m.

baptismal, a. bautismal.

Baptist, n. bautista m.

baptize, v. bautizar.

bar, 1. n. barra f.; obstáculo m.; (tavern) taberna f., bar m. 2. v. barrear; prohibir, excluir.

barbarian, 1. a. bárbaro. 2. n. bárbaro -ra.

barbarism, n. barbarismo m., barbarie f.

barbarous, n. bárbaro, cruel.

barbecue, n. animal asado entero; (Mex.) barbacoa f.

barber, n. barbero m. b. shop, barbería f.

barbiturate, n. barbiturado m.

bare, 1. a. desnudo; descubierto. 2. v. desnudar; descubrir.

bareback, adv. sin silla.

barefoot(ed), a. descalzo.

barely, adv. escasamente, apenas.

bareness, n. desnudez f.; pobreza f.

bargain, 1. n. ganga f., compra ventajosa f.; contrato m. 2. v. regatear; negociar.

barge, n. lanchón m., barcaza f.

baritone, n. barítono m.

barium, n. bario m.

bark, 1. n. corteza f.; (of dog) ladra f. 2. v. ladrar.

barley, n. cebada f.

barn, n. granero m.

barnacle, n. lapa f.

barnyard, n. corral m.

barometer, n. barómetro m.

barometric, a. barométrico.

baron, n. barón m.

baroness, n. baronesa f.

baronial, a. baronial.

baroque, a. barroco.

barracks, n. cuartel m.

barrage, n. cortina de fuego f.

barred, a. excluido; prohibido.

barrel, n. barril m.; (of gun) cañón m.

barren, a. estéril.

barrenness, n. esterilidad f.

barricade, n. barricada, barrera f.

barrier, n. barrera f.; obstáculo m.

barroom, n. cantina f.

bartender, n. tabernero; cantinero m.

barter, 1. n. cambio, trueque m. 2. v. cambiar, trocar.

base, 1. a. bajo, vil. 2. n. base f. 3. v. basar.

baseball, n. beisbol m.

baseboard, n. tabla de resguardo.

basement, n. sótano m.

baseness, n. bajeza, vileza f.

bashful, a. vergonzoso, tímido.

bashfully, adv. timidamente; vergonzosamente.

bashfulness, n. vergüenza; timidez f.

basic, a. fundamental, básico.

basin, n. bacia f.; (of river) cuenca f.

basis, n. base f.

bask, v. tomar el sol.

basket, n. cesta, canasta f.

bass, n. (fish) lobina f.; (mus.) bajo profundo m. b. viol, violón m.

bassinet, n. bacinete m.

bassoon, n. bajón m.

bastard, a. & n. bastardo; hijo natural m.

baste, v. (sew) bastear; (cooking) pringar.

bat, 1. n. (animal) murciélago m.; (baseball) bate m. **2.** v. batear.

batch, n. cantidad de cosas.

bath, n. baño m.

bathe, v. bañar.

bather, n. bañista.

bathing resort, n. balneario m.

bathrobe, n. bata de baña f., peinador m.

bathroom, n. cuarto de baño.

bathtub, n. bañera f.

baton, n. bastón m.; (mus.) batuta f.

battalion, n. batallón m.

batter, 1. n. (cooking) batido m.; (baseball) voleador m. **2.** v. batir; derribar.

battery, n. batería f.; (elec.) pila f.

batting, n. agramaje, moldeaje m.

battle, 1. n. batalla f.; combate m. **2.** v. batallar.

battlefield, n. campo de batalla.

battleship, n. acorazado m.

bauxite, n. bauxita f.

bawl, v. gritar; vocear.

bay, 1. n. bahía f. **2.** v. aullar.

bayonet, n. bayoneta f.

bazaar, n. bazar m., feria f.

be, v. ser; estar. (See **hacer;** **hay;** tener in Sp.-Eng. section).

beach, n. playa f.

beacon, n. faro m.

bead, n. cuenta f.; pl. (rel.) rosario m.

beading, n. abalorio m.

beady, a. globuloso; burbujoso.

beak, n. pico m.

beaker, n. vaso con pico m.

beam, n. viga f.; (of wood) madero m.; (of light) rayo m.

beaming, a. radiante.

bean, n. haba, habichuela f., frijol m.

bear, 1. n. oso -sa. **2.** v. llevar; (endure) aguantar.

bearable, a. sufrible; suportable.

beard, n. barba f.

bearded, a. barbado; barbudo.

beardless, a. lampiño; imberbe.

bearer, n. portador -ra.

bearing, n. porte, aguante m.

bearskin, n. piel de oso f.

beast, n. bestia f.; bruto m.

beat, v. golpear; batir; pulsar; (in games) ganar, vencer.

beaten, a. vencido; batido.

beatify, v. beatificar.

beating, n. paliza f.

beau, n. novio m.

beautiful, a. hermoso, bello.

beautifully, adv. bellamente.

beautify, v. embellecer.

beauty, n. hermosura, belleza f.

beaver, n. castor m.

becalm, v. calmar; sosegar; encalmarse.

becuse, conj. porque. **b. of,** a causa de.

beckon, v. hacer señas.

become, v. hacerse; ponerse.

becoming, a. propio, correcto; **be b.,** quedar bien, sentar bien.

bed, n. cama f.; lecho m.; (of river) cauce m.

bedbug, n. chinche m.

bedclothes, n. ropa de cama.

bedding, n. colchones m.pl.

bedfellow, n. compañero de cama m.

bedizen, v. adornar; aderezar.

bedridden, a. postrado (en cama).

bedrock, n. (mining) lecho de roca m.; (fig.) fundamento m.

bedroom, n. alcoba f.; (Mex.) recámara f.

bedside, n. lado de cama m.

bedspread, n. cubrecama, sobrecama f.

bedstead, n. armadura de cama f.

bedtime, n. hora de acostarse.

bee, n. abeja f.

beef, n. carne de vaca.

beefsteak, n. bistec, bisté m.

beehive, n. colmena f.

beer, n. cerveza f.

beeswax, n. cera de abejas.

beet, n. remolacha f.; (Mex.) betabel m.

beetle, n. escarabajo m.

befall, v. suceder, sobrevenir.

befitting, a. conveniente; propio; digno.

before, 1. adv. antes. **2.** prep. antes de; (in front of) delante de. **3.** conj. antes que.

beforehand, adv. de antemano.

befriend, v. amparar.

befuddle, v. confundir; aturdir.

beg, v. rogar, suplicar; (for alms) mendigar.

beget, v. engendrar; producir.

beggar, n. mendigo -ga; (Sp. Am.) limosnero -ra.

beggarly, a. pobre, miserable.

begin, v. empezar, comenzar, principiar.

beginner, n. principiante m.

beginning, n. principio, comienzo m.

begrudge, v. envidiar.

behalf: in, on b. of, a favor de, en pro de.

behave, v. portarse comportarse.

behavior, n. conducta f.; comportamiento m.

behead, v. decapitar.

behind, 1. adv. atrás, detrás. **2.** prep. detrás de.

behold, v. contemplar.

beige, a. crema.

being, n. existencia f.; (person) ser m.

bejewel, v. adornar con joyas.

belated, a. atrasado, tardío.

belch, 1. n. eructo m. **2.** v. vomitar; eructar.

belfry, n. campanario m.

Belgian, 1. a. belga. **2.** n. belga m. & f.

Belgium, n. Bélgica f.

belie, v. desmentir.

belief, n. creencia f.; parecer m.

believable, a. creíble.

believe, v. creer.

believer, n. creyente m.

belittle, v. dar poca importancia a.

bell, n. campana f.; (of house) campanilla f.; (electric) timbre m.

bellboy, n. mozo, botones m.

bellicose, a. guerrero.

belligerence, n. beligerancia f.

belligerent, a. & n. beligerante.

belligerently, adv. belicosamente.

bellow, v. bramar, rugir.

bellows, n. fuelle m.

belly, n. vientre m.; panza, barriga f.

belong, v. pertenecer.

belongings, n. propiedad f.

beloved, a. querido, amado.

below, 1. adv. debajo, abajo. **2.** prep. debajo de.

belt, n. cinturón m.

bench, n. banco m.

bend, 1. n. vuelta; curva f. **2.** v. encorvar, doblar.

beneath, 1. adv. debajo, abajo. **2.** prep. debajo de.

benediction, n. bendición f.

benefactor, n. bienhechor -ra.

benefactress, n. bienhechora f.

beneficial, a. provechoso, beneficioso.

beneficiary, n. beneficiario, beneficiado m.

benefit, 1. n. provecho, beneficio m. **2.** v. beneficiar.

benevolence, n. benevolencia f.

benevolent, a. benévolo.

benevolently, adv. benignamente.

benign, a. benigno.

benignity, n. benignidad; bondad f.

bent, 1. a. encorvado. **b. on,** resuelto a. **2.** n. inclinación f.

benzene, n. bencina f.

bequeath, v. legar.

bequest, n. legado m.

berate, v. reñir, regañar.

bereave, v. despojar; desolar.

bereavement, n. privación f.; despojo m.

berry, n. baya f.

berth, n. camarote m.; (naut.) litera f.; (for vessel) amarradero m.

beseech, v. suplicar; implorar.

beseechingly, adv. suplicantemente.

beset, v. acosar; rodear.

beside, prep. al lado de.

besides, adv. además, por otra parte.

besiege, v. sitiar; asediar.

besieged, a. sitiado.

besieger, n. sitiador m.

besmirch, v. manchar; deshonrar.

best, a. & adv. mejor. **at b.,** a lo más.

bestial, a. bestial; brutal.

bestir, v. incitar; intrigar.

best man, n. padrino de boda.

bestow, v. conferir.

bestowal, n. dádiva; presentación f.

bet, 1. n. apuesta f. **2.** v. apostar.

betoken, v. denotar, significar.

betray, v. traicionar; revelar.

betrayal, n. traición f.

betroth, v. contraer esponsales; prometer.

betrothal, n. esponsales m.pl.

better, 1. a. & adv. mejor. **2.** v. mejorar.

between, prep. entre, en medio de.

bevel, 1. n. cartabón m. **2.** v. cortar al sesgo.

beverage, n. bebida f.; (cold) refresco m.

bewail, v. llorar; lamentar.

beware, v. guardarse, precaverse.

bewilder, v. aturdir.

bewildered, a. descarriado.

bewildering, a. aturdente.

bewilderment, n. aturdimiento m.; perplejidad f.

bewitch, v. hechizar; embrujar.

beyond, prep. más allá de.

biannual, a. semianual; semestral.

bias, 1. n. parcialidad f.; prejuicio m. **on the b.,** al sesgo **2.** v. predisponer, influir.

bib, n. babador m.

Bible, n. Biblia f.

Biblical, a. bíblico.

bibliography, n. bibliografía f.

bicarbonate, n. bicarbonato m.

bicentennial, a. & n. bicentenario m.

biceps, n. biceps m.

bicker, v. altercar.

bicycle, n. bicicleta f.

bicyclist, n. biciclista m.

bid, 1. n. proposición, oferta f. **2.** v. mandar; ofrecer.

bidder, n. postor m.

bide, v. aguardar; esperar.

bier, n. ataúd m.

bifocal, a. bifocal.

big, a. grande.

bigamist, n. bígamo -ma.

bigamy, n. bigamia f.

bigot, n. persona intolerante.

bigotry, n. intolerancia f.

bilateral, a. bilateral.

bile, n. bilis f.

bilingual, a. bilingüe.

bilious, a. bilioso.

bill, 1. n. cuenta, factura f.; (money) billete m.; (of bird) pico m. **2.** v. facturar.

billet, 1. n. billete m.; (mil.) boleta f. **2.** v. aposentar.

billfold, n. cartera f.

billiard balls, n. bolas de billar.

billiards, n. billar m.

billion, n. billón m.

bill of health, n. certificado de sanidad.

bill of lading, n. conocimiento de embarque.

bill of sale, n. escritura de venta.

billow, n. ola; oleada f.

bimetallic, a. bimetálico.

bimonthly, a. & adv. bimestral.

bin, n. hucha f.; depósito m.

bind, v. atar; obligar; (book) encuadernar.

bindery, n. taller de encuadernación m.

binding, n. encuadernación f.

binocular, 1. a. binocular. **2.** n.pl. gemelos m.pl.

biochemistry, n. bioquímica f.

biodegradable, a. biodegradable.

biofeedback, n. retroalimentación biológica.

biographer, n. biógrafo m.

biographical, a. biográfico.

biography, n. biografía f.

biological, a. biológico.

biologically, adv. biológicamente.

biology, n. biología f.

bipartisan, a. bipartito.

biped, n. bípedo m.

bird, n. pájaro m.; ave f.

bird of prey, n. ave de rapiña m.

birth, n. nacimiento m. **give b. to,** dar a luz.

birth control, n. contracepción f.

birthday, n. cumpleaños m.

birthmark, n. estigma f., marca de nacimiento.

birthplace, n. natalicio m.

birth rate, n. natalidad f.

birthright, n. primogenitura f.

biscuit, n. bizcocho m.

bisect, v. bisecar.

bishop, n. obispo m.; (chess) alfil m.

bishopric, n. obispado m.

bismuth, n. bismuto m.

bison, n. bisonte m.

bit, n. pedacito m.; (mech.) taladro m.; (for horse) bocado m.; (computer) bit m.

bitch, n. perra f.

bite, 1. n. bocado m.; picada f. **2.** v. morder; picar.

biting, a. penetrante; mordaz.

bitter, a. amargo.

bitterly, adv. amargamente; agriamente.

bitterness, n. amargura f.; rencor m.

bivouac, 1. n. vivaque m. **2.** v. vivaquear.

biweekly, a. quincenal.

black, a. negro.

Black, n. (person) negro -gra; persona de color.

blackberry, n. mora f.

blackbird, n. mirlo m.

blackboard, n. pizarra f.

blacken, v. ennegrecer.

black eye, n. ojo amoratado.

blackguard, n. tunante; pillo m.

blackmail, 1. n. chantaje m. **2.** v. amenazar con chantaje.

black market, n. mercado negro.

blackout, n. oscurecimiento, apagamiento m.

blacksmith, n. herrero m.

bladder, n. vejiga f.

blade, n. (sword) hoja f.; (oar) pala f.; (grass) brizna f.

blame, v. culpar, echar la culpa a.

blameless, a. inculpable.

blanch, v. blanquear; escaldar.

bland, a. blando.

blank, a. & n. blanco.

blanket, n. manta f.; cobertor m.

blare, 1. n. sonido de trompeta. **2.** v. sonar como trompeta.

blaspheme, v. blasfemar.

blasphemer, n. blasfemo, blasfemador m.

blasphemous, a. blasfemo, impío.

blasphemy, n. blasfemia f.

blast, 1. n. barreno m.; (wind) ráfaga f. **2.** v. barrenar.

blatant, a. bramante.

blaze, 1. n. llama, hoguera f. **2.** v. encenderse en llama.

blazing, a. flameante.

bleach, v. blanquear.

bleachers, n. asientos al aire libre.

bleak, a. frío y sombrío.

bleakness, n. intemperie f.

bleed, v. sangrar.

blemish, 1. n. mancha f.; lunar m. **2.** v. manchar.

blend, 1. n. mezcla f. **2.** v. mezclar, combinar.

blended, a. mezclado.

bless, v. bendecir.

blessed, a. bendito.

blessing, n. bendición f.

blight, 1. n. plaga f.; tizón m. **2.** v. atizonar.

blind, a. ciego.

blindfold, v. vendar los ojos.

blinding, a. deslumbrante; ofuscante.

blindly, adv. ciegamente.

blindness, n. ceguedad, ceguera f.

blink, 1. n. guiñada f. **2.** v. guiñar.

bliss, n. felicidad f.

blissful, a. dichoso; bienaventurado.

blissfully, adv. felizmente.

blister, n. ampolla f.

blithe, a. alegre; jovial; gozoso.

blizzard, n. chubasco de nieve.

bloat, v. hinchar.

bloc, n. grupo (político); bloc.

block, 1. n. bloque m.; (street) manzana, cuadra f. **2.** v. bloquear.

blockade, 1. *n.* bloqueo *m.* **2.** *v.* bloquear.

blond, *a.* & *n.* rubio -ia.

blood, *n.* sangre *f.;* parentesco, linaje *m.*

bloodhound, *n.* sabueso *m.*

bloodless, *a.* exangüe; desangrado.

blood poisoning, *n.* envenenamiento de sangre.

blood pressure, *n.* presión arterial.

bloodshed, *n.* matanza *f.*

bloodthirsty, *a.* cruel, sanguinario.

bloody, *a.* ensangrentado, sangriento.

bloom, 1. *n.* flor *f.* **2.** *v.* florecer.

blooming, *a.* lozano; fresco.

blossom, 1. *n.* flor *f.* **2.** *v.* florecer.

blot, 1. *n.* mancha *f.* **2.** *v.* manchar.

blotch, 1. *n.* mancha, roncha *f.* **2.** *v.* manchar.

blotter, *n.* papel secante.

blouse, *n.* blusa *f.*

blow, 1. *n.* golpe *m.;* (fig.) chasco *m.* **2.** *v.* soplar.

blowout, *n.* reventón de neumático.

blubber, *n.* grasa de ballena.

bludgeon, *n.* porra *f.*

blue, *a.* azul; triste, melancólico.

bluebird, *n.* azulejo *m.*

blue jeans, *n.* jeans *m.pl.*

blueprint, *n.* heliografía *f.*

bluff, 1. *n.* risco *m.* **2.** *v.* alardear; baladronar.

bluing, *n.* añil *m.*

blunder, 1. *n.* desatino *m.* **2.** *v.* desatinar.

blunderer, *n.* desatinado *m.*

blunt, 1. *a.* embotado; descortés. **2.** *v.* embotar.

bluntly, *a.* bruscamente.

bluntness, *n.* grosería *f.*

blur, 1. *n.* trazo confuso. **2.** *v.* hacer indistinto.

blush, 1. *n.* rubor, sonrojo *m.* **2.** *v.* sonrojarse.

bluster, 1. *n.* fanfarria *f.* **2.** *v.* fanfarrear.

boar, *n.* verraco *m.* **wild b.,** jabalí *m.*

board, 1. *n.* tabla; (govt.) consejo *m.;* junta *f.* **b. and room,** cuarto y comida, casa y comida. **2.** *v.* (ship) abordar.

boarder, *n.* pensionista *m.* & *f.*

boardinghouse, pensión *f.,* casa de huéspedes.

boast, 1. *n.* jactancia *f.* **2.** *v.* jactarse.

boaster, *n.* fanfarrón *m.*

boastful, *a.* jactancioso.

boastfulness, *n.* jactancia *f.*

boat, *n.* barco, buque, bote *m.*

boathouse, *n.* casilla de botes *f.*

boatswain, *n.* contramaestre *m.*

bob, *v.* menear.

bobbin, *n.* bobina *f.*

bobby pin, *n.* invisible *f.;* gancho *m.*

bodice, *n.* corpiño *m.*

bodily, *a.* corporal.

body, *n.* cuerpo *m.*

bodyguard, *n.* guardia de corps.

bog, *n.* pantano *m.*

Bohemian, *a.* & *n.* bohemio -mia.

boil, 1. *n.* (med.) divieso *m.* **2.** *v.* hervir.

boiler, *n.* marmita; caldera *f.*

boisterous, *a.* tumultuoso.

boisterously, *adv.* tumultuosamente.

bold, *a.* atrevido, audaz.

boldface, *n.* (type) letra negra.

boldly, *adv.* audazmente; descaradamente.

boldness, *n.* atrevimiento *m.;* osadía *f.*

Bolivian, *a.* & *n.* boliviano -na.

bologna, *n.* salchicha *f.*

bolster, 1. *n.* travesero, cojín *m.* **2.** *v.* apoyar, sostener.

bolt, 1. *n.* perno *m.;* (of door) cerrojo *m.;* (lightning) rayo *m.* **2.** *v.* acerrojar.

bomb, 1. *n.* bomba *f.* **2.** *v.* bombardear.

bombard, *v.* bombardear.

bombardier, *n.* bombardero *m.*

bombardment, *n.* bombardeo *m.*

bomber, *n.* avión de bombardeo.

bombproof, *a.* a prueba de granadas.

bombshell, *n.* bomba *f.*

bonbon, *n.* dulce, bombón *m.*

bond, *n.* lazo *m.;* (com.) bono *m.*

bondage, *n.* esclavitud, servidumbre *f.*

bonded, *a.* garantizado.

bone, *n.* hueso *m.*

boneless, *a.* sin huesos.

bonfire, *n.* hoguera, fogata *f.*

bonnet, *n.* gorra *f.*

bonus, *n.* bono *m.*

bony, *a.* huesudo.

book, *n.* libro *m.*

bookbinder, *n.* encuadernador *m.*

bookcase, *n.* armario para libros.

bookkeeper, *n.* tenedor de libros.

bookkeeping, *n.* contabilidad *f.*

booklet, *n.* folleto *m.,* libreta *f.*

bookseller, *n.* librero *m.*

bookstore, *n.* librería *f.*

boom, *n.* (naut.) botalón *m.;* prosperidad repentina.

boon, *n.* dádiva *f.*

boor, *n.* patán, rústico *m.*

boorish, *a.* villano.

boost, 1. *n.* alza; ayuda *f.* **2.** *v.* levantar, alzar; fomentar.

booster, *n.* fomentador *m.*

boot, *n.* bota *f.*

bootblack, *n.* limpiabotas *m.*

booth, *n.* cabaña; casilla *f.*

booty, *n.* botín *m.*

border, 1. *n.* borde *m.;* frontera *f.* **2.** *v.* **b. on,** lindar con.

borderline, 1. *a.* marginal. **2.** *n.* margen *m.*

bore, 1. *n.* lata *f.;* persona pesada. **2.** *v.* aburrir, fastidiar; (mech.) taladrar.

boredom, *n.* aburrimiento *m.*

boric acid, *n.* ácido bórico *m.*

boring, *a.* aburrido, pesado.

born, *a.* nacido. **be born,** nacer.

born-again, *a.* renacido.

borrow, *v.* pedir prestado.

bosom, *v.* seno, pecho *m.*

boss, *n.* jefe, patrón *m.*

botany, *n.* botánica *f.*

both, *pron.* & *a.* ambos, los dos.

bother, 1. *n.* molestia *f.* **2.** *v.* molestar, incomodar.

bothersome, *a.* molesto.

bottle, 1. *n.* botella *f.* **2.** *v.* embotellar.

bottom, *n.* fondo *m.*

boudoir, *n.* tocador *m.*

bough, *n.* rama *f.*

boulder, *n.* canto rodado.

boulevard, *n.* bulevar *m.*

bounce, 1. *n.* brinco *m.* **2.** *v.* brincar; hacer saltar.

bound, 1. *n.* salto *m.* **2.** *v.* limitar.

boundary, *n.* límite, lindero *m.*

bouquet, *n.* ramillete de flores.

bourgeois, *a.* & *n.* burgués.

bout, *n.* encuentro; combate *m.*

bow, 1. *n.* saludo *m.;* (of ship) proa *f.;* (archery) arco *m.;* (ribbon) lazo *m.* **2.** *v.* saludar, inclinar.

bowels, *n.* intestinos *m.pl.;* entrañas *f.pl.*

bowl, 1. *n.* vasija *f.;* platón *m.* **2.** *v.* jugar a los bolos. **b. over,** derribar.

bowlegged, *a.* perniabierto.

bowling, *n.* bolos *m.pl.*

box, 1. *n.* caja *f.;* (theat.) palco *m.* **2.** *v.* (sports) boxear.

boxcar, *n.* vagón *m.*

boxer, *n.* boxeador, pugilista *m.*

boxing, *n.* boxeo *m.*

box office, *n.* taquilla *f.*

boy, *n.* muchacho, chico *m.*

boycott, 1. *n.* boicoteo *m.* **2.** *v.* boicotear.

boyhood, *n.* muchachez *f.*

boyish, *a.* pueril.

boyishly, *adv.* puerilmente.

brace, 1. *n.* grapón *m.;* *pl.* tirantes *m.pl.* **2.** *v.* reforzar.

bracelet, *n.* brazalete *m.,* pulsera *f.*

bracket, *n.* ménsula *f.*

brag, *v.* jactarse.

braggart, 1. *a.* jactancioso. **2.** *n.* jaque *m.*

braid, 1. *n.* trenza *f.* **2.** *v.* trenzar.

brain, *n.* cerebro, seso *m.*

brainy, *a.* sesudo, inteligente.

brake, 1. *n.* freno *m.* **2.** *v.* frenar.

bran, *n.* salvado *m.*

branch, *n.* ramo *m.;* (of tree) rama *f.*

brand, *n.* marca *f.*

brandish, *v.* blandir.

brand-new, *a.* enteramente nuevo.

brandy, *n.* aguardiente, coñac *m.*

brash, *a.* impetuoso.

brass, *n.* bronce, latón *m.*

brassiere, *n.* corpiño, sostén *m.*

brat, *n.* mocoso *m.*

bravado, *n.* bravata *f.*

brave, *a.* valiente.

bravery, *n.* valor *m.*

brawl, 1. *n.* alboroto *m.* **2.** *v.* alborotar.

brawn, *n.* músculo *m.*

bray, *v.* rebuznar.

brazen, *a.* desvergonzado.

Brazil, *n.* Brasil *m.*

Brazilian, *a.* & *n.* brasileño -ña.

breach, *n.* rotura, infracción *f.*

bread, *n.* pan *m.*

breadth, *n.* anchura *f.*

break, 1. *n.* rotura; pausa *f.* **2.** *v.* quebrar, romper.

breakable, *a.* rompible, frágil.

breakage, *n.* rotura *f.,* destrozo *m.*

breakfast, 1. *n.* desayuno, almuerzo *m.* **2.** *v.* desayunarse, almorzar.

breakneck, *a.* rápido, precipitado, atropellado.

breast, *n.* pecho, seno *m.*

breath, *n.* aliento; soplo *m.*

breathe, *v.* respirar.

breathless, *a.* desalentado.

breathlessly, *adv.* jadeantemente, intensamente.

bred, *a.* criado; educado.

breeches, *n.pl.* calzones; pantalones, *m.pl.*

breed, 1. *n.* raza *f.* **2.** *v.* engendrar; criar.

breeder, *n.* criador *m.*

breeding, *n.* cría *f.*

breeze, *n.* brisa *f.*

breezy, *a.:* **it is b.,** hace brisa.

brevity, *n.* brevedad *f.*

brew, *v.* fraguar, elaborar.

brewer, *n.* cervecero *m.*

brewery, *n.* cervecería *f.*

bribe, 1. *n.* soborno, cohecho *m.* **2.** *v.* sobornar, cohechar.

briber, *n.* sobornador *m.*

bribery, *n.* soborno, cohecho *m.*

brick, *n.* ladrillo *m.*

bricklayer, *n.* albañil *m.*

bridal, *a.* nupcial.

bride, *n.* novia *f.*

bridegroom, *n.* novio *m.*

bridesmaid, *n.* madrina de boda.

bridge, *n.* puente *m.*

bridged, *a.* conectado.

bridgehead, *n.* (mil.) cabeza de puente.

bridle, *n.* brida *f.*

brief, *a.* breve.

briefcase, *n.* maletín *m.*

briefly, *adv.* brevemente.

briefness, *n.* brevedad *f.*

brier, *n.* zarza *f.*

brig, *n.* bergantín *m.*

brigade, *n.* brigada *f.*

bright, *a.* claro, brillante.

brighten, *v.* abrillantar; alegrar.

brightness, *n.* resplandor *m.*

brilliance, *n.* brillantez *f.*

brilliant, *a.* brillante.

brim, *n.* borde *m.;* (of hat) ala *f.*

brine, *n.* salmuera *f.*

bring, *v.* traer. **b. about,** efectuar, llevar a cabo.

brink, *n.* borde *m.*

briny, *a.* salado.

brisk, *a.* vivo; enérgico.

briskly, *adv.* vivamente.

briskness, *n.* viveza *f.*

bristle, *n.* cerda *f.*

bristly, *a.* hirsuto.

Britain, *n.* **Great B.,** Gran Bretaña *f.*

British, *a.* británico.

British Empire, imperio británico.

British Isles, islas británicas.

Briton, *n.* inglés *m.*

brittle, *a.* quebradizo, frágil.

broad, *a.* ancho.

broadcast, 1. *n.* radiodifusión *m.* **2.** *v.* radiodifundir.

broadcaster, *n.* locutor *m.*

broadcloth, *n.* paño fino.

broaden, *v.* ensanchar.

broadly, *adv.* ampliamente.

broadminded, *a.* tolerante, liberal.

brocade, *n.* brocado *m.*

brocaded, *a.* espolinado.

broil, *v.* asar.

broiler, *n.* parilla *f.*

broken, *a.* roto, quebrado.

broken-hearted, *a.* angustiado.

broker, *n.* corredor, cambista *m.*

brokerage, *n.* corretaje *m.*

bronchial, *a.* bronquial.

bronchitis, *n.* bronquitis *f.*

bronze, *n.* bronce *m.*

brooch, *n.* broche *m.*

brood, 1. *n.* cría, progenie *f.* **2.** *v.* empollar; cobijar.

brook, *n.* arroyo *m.,* quebrada *f.*

broom, *n.* escoba *f.*

broomstick, *n.* palo de escoba.

broth, *n.* caldo *m.*

brothel, *n.* burdel *m.*

brother, *n.* hermano *m.*

brotherhood, *n.* fraternidad *f.*

brother-in-law, *n.* cuñado *m.*

brotherly, *a.* fraternal.

brow, *n.* ceja; frente *f.*

brown, *a.* pardo, moreno.

browse, *v.* ramonear.

bruise, 1. *n.* contusión *f.* **2.** *v.* magullar.

brunette, *a.* & *n.* moreno -na, trigueño -ña.

brush, 1. *n.* cepillo *m.;* brocha *f.* **2.** *v.* cepillar.

brushwood, *n.* matorral *m.*

brusque, *a.* brusco.

brusquely, *adv.* bruscamente.

brutal, *a.* brutal.

brutality, *n.* brutalidad *f.*

brutalize, *v.* embrutecer.

brute, *n.* bruto *m.,* bestia *f.*

bubble, *n.* ampolla *f.*

bucket, *n.* cubo *m.*

buckle, *n.* hebilla *f.*

buckram, *n.* bucarán *m.*

bucksaw, *n.* sierra de bastidor.

buckshot, *n.* posta *f.*

buckwheat, *n.* trigo sarraceno.

bud, 1. *n.* brote *m.* **2.** *v.* brotar.

budding, *a.* en capullo.

budge, *v.* moverse.

budget, *n.* presupuesto *m.*

buffalo, *n.* búfalo *m.*

buffer, *n.* parachoques *m.*

buffet, *n.* bufet *m.;* (furniture) aparador *m.*

buffoon, *n.* bufón *m.*

bug, *n.* insecto *m.*

bugle, *n.* clarín *m.;* corneta *f.*

build, *v.* construir.

builder, *n.* constructor *m.*

building, *n.* edificio *m.*

bulb, *n.* bulbo *m.;* (of lamp) bombilla, ampolla *f.*

bulge, 1. *n.* abultamiento *m.* **2.** *v.* abultar.

bulk, *n.* masa *f.;* grueso *m.;* mayoría *f.*

bulkhead, *n.* frontón *m.*

bulky, *a.* grueso, abultado.

bull, *n.* toro *m.*

bulldog, *n.* perro de presa.

bullet, *n.* bala *f.*

bulletin, *n.* boletín *m.*

bulletproof, *a.* a prueba de bala.

bullfight, *n.* corrida de toros.

bullfighter, *n.* torero *m.*

bullfinch, *n.* pinzón real *m.*

bully, 1. *n.* rufián *m.* **2.** *v.* bravear.

bulwark, *n.* baluarte *m.*

bum, *n.* holgazán *m.*

bump, 1. *n.* golpe, choque *m.* **2.** *v.* **b. into,** chocar contra.

bumper, *n.* parachoques *m.*

bun, *n.* bollo *m.*

bunch, *n.* racimo; montón *m.*

bundle, 1. *n.* bulto *m.* **2.** *v.* **b. up,** abrigar.

bungalow, *n.* casa de un solo piso.

bungle, *v.* estropear.

bunion, *n.* juanete *m.*

bunk, *n.* litera *f.*

bunny, *n.* conejito *m.*

bunting, *n.* lanilla, banderas *f.*

buoy, *n.* boya *f.*

buoyant, *a.* boyante; vivaz.

burden, 1. *n.* carga *f.* **2.** *v.* cargar.

burdensome, *a.* gravoso.

bureau, *n.* (furniture) cómoda *f.;* departamento *m.*

burglar, *n.* ladrón *m.*

burglarize, *v.* robar.

burglary, *n.* robo *m.*

burial, *n.* entierro *m.*

burlap, *n.* arpillera *f.*

burly, *a.* corpulento.

burn, v. quemar; arder.
burner, n. mechero m.
burning, a. ardiente.
burnish, v. pulir; acicalar.
burrow, v. minar; horadar.
burst, v. reventar.
bury, v. enterrar.
bus, n. autobús m.
bush, n. arbusto m.
bushy, a. matoso; peludo.
business, n. negocios m.pl.; comercio m.
businesslike, a. directo.
businessman, n. comerciante m.
businesswoman, n. mujer de negocios.
bust, n. busto; pecho m.
bustle, n. bullicio m.; animación f.
busy, a. ocupado, atareado.
busybody, n. entremetido m.
but, conj. pero; sino.
butcher, n. carnicero m.
butchery, n. carnicería; matanza f.
butler, n. mayordomo m.
butt, n. punta f.; cabo extremo m.
butter, n. manteca, mantequilla f.
buttercup, n. ranúnculo m.
butterfat, n. mantequilla f.
butterfly, n. mariposa f.
buttermilk, n. suero (de leche) m.
button, n. botón m.
buttonhole, n. ojal m.
buttress, n. sostén; refuerzo m.
buxom, a. regordete.
buy, v. comprar.
buyer, n. comprador -ra.
buzz, 1. n. zumbido m. 2. v. zumbar.
buzzard, n. gallinazo m.
buzzer, n. zumbador m.
buzz saw, n. sierra circular f.
by, prep. por; (near) cerca de, al lado de; (time) para.
by-and-by, adv. pronto; luego.
bygone, a. pasado.
bylaw, n. estatuto, reglamento m.
bypass, n. desvío m.
byproduct, n. producto accesorio m.
bystander, n. espectador; mirón m.
byte, n. en teoría de la información: ocho bits.
byway, n. camino desviado m.

C

cab, n. coche de alquiler.
cabaret, n. cabaret m.
cabbage, n. repollo m.
cabin, n. cabaña f.
cabinet, n. gabinete; ministerio m.
cabinetmaker, n. ebanista m.
cable, n. cable m.
cablegram, n. cablegrama m.
cache, n. escondite m.

cackle, 1. n. charla f., cacareo m. 2. v. cacarear.
cacophony, n. cacofonía f.
cactus, n. cacto m.
cad, n. persona vil.
cadaver, n. cadáver m.
cadaverous, a. cadavérico.
cadence, n. cadencia f.
cadet, n. cadete m.
cadmium, n. cadmio m.
cadre, n. núcleo; (mil.) cuadro m.
café, n. café, cantina f.
cafeteria, n. cafetería f.
caffeine, n. cafeína f.
cage, 1. n. jaula f. 2. v. enjaular.
caged, a. enjaulado.
caisson, n. arcón m.; (mil.) furgón m.
cajole, v. lisonjear; adular.
cake, n. torta f.; bizcocho m.
calamitous, a. calamitoso.
calamity, n. calamidad f.
calcify, v. calcificar.
calcium, n. calcio m.
calculable, a. calculable.
calculate, v. calcular.
calculating, a. interesado.
calculation, n. calculación f.; cálculo m.
calculus, n. cálculo m.
caldron, n. caldera f.
calendar, n. calendario m.
calf, n. ternero m.
calfskin, n. piel de becerro.
caliber, n. calibre m.
calico, n. percal m.
caliper, n. calibrador f.
calisthenics, n. calistenia, gimnasia f.
calk, v. calafatear; rellenar.
calker, n. calafate m.
call, 1. n. llamada f. 2. v. llamar.
calligraphy, n. caligrafía f.
calling, n. vocación f.
calling card, n. tarjeta (de visita) f.
callously, adv. insensiblemente.
callow, a. sin experiencia.
callus, n. callo m.
calm, 1. a. tranquilo, calmado. 2. n. calma f. 3. v. calmar.
calmly, adv. serenamente.
calmness, n. calma f.
caloric, a. calórico.
calorie, n. caloría f.
calorimeter, n. calorímetro m.
calumniate, v. calumniar.
calumny, n. calumnia f.
Calvary, n. Calvario m.
calve, v. parir (la vaca).
calyx, n. cáliz m.
camaraderie, n. compañerismo m., compadrería f.
cambric, n. batista f.
camel, n. camello m.
camellia, n. camelia f.
camel's hair, n. piel de camello.
cameo, n. camafeo m.
camera, n. cámara f.
camouflage, n. camuflaje m.

camouflaging, n. simulacro, disfraz m.
camp, 1. n. campamento m. 2. v. acampar.
campaign, n. campaña f.
camper, n. acampado m.
campfire, n. fogata de campamento.
camphor, n. alcanfor m.
camphor ball, n. bola de alcanfor.
campus, n. campo de colegio (o universidad)
can, v. (be able) poder.
can, 1. n. lata f. 2. v. conservar en latas.
Canada, n. Canadá m.
Canadian, a. & n. canadiense.
canal, n. canal m.
canalize, v. canalizar.
canard, n. embuste m.
canary, n. canario m.
cancel, v. cancelar.
cancellation, n. cancelación f.
cancer, n. cáncer m.
candelabrum, n. candelabro m.
candid, a. cándido, sincero.
candidacy, n. candidatura f.
candidate, n. candidato -ta.
candidly, adv. candidamente.
candidness, n. candidez; sinceridad f.
candied, a. garapiñado.
candle, n. vela f.
candlestick, n. candelero m.
candor, n. candor m.; sinceridad f.
candy, n. dulces m.pl.
cane, n. caña f.; (for walking) bastón m.
canine, a. canino.
canister, n. frasco m.; lata f.
canker, n. llaga; úlcera f.
cankerworm, n. oruga f.
canned, a. envasado.
canner, n. envasador m.
cannery, n. fábrica de conservas alimenticias f.
cannibal, n. caníbal m.
cannon, n. cañón m.
cannonade, n. cañoneo m.
cannoneer, n. cañonero m.
canny, a. sagaz; prudente.
canoe, n. canoa f.
canon, n. canon m.; (rel.) canónigo m.
canonical, a. canónico.
canonize, v. canonizar.
canopy, n. dosel m.
cant, n. hipocresía f.
cantaloupe, n. melón m.
canteen, n. cantina f.
canter, 1. n. medio galope m. 2. v. galopar.
cantonment, n. (mil.) acuartelamiento m.
canvas, n. lona f.
canyon, n. cañón, desfiladero m.
cap, 1. n. tapa f.; (headwear) gorro m. 2. v. tapar.
capability, n. capacidad f.
capable, a. capaz.
capably, adv. hábilmente.
capacious, a. espacioso.

capacity, n. capacidad f.

cape, n. capa f., (geog.) cabo m.

caper, n. zapateta f.; (bot.) alcaparra f.

capillary, a. capilar.

capital, n. capital m.; (govt.) capital f.

capitalism, n. capitalismo m.

capitalist, n. capitalista m.

capitalistic, a. capitalista.

capitalization, n. capitalización f.

capitalize, v. capitalizar.

capitulate, v. capitular.

capon, n. capón m.

caprice, n. capricho m.

capricious, a. caprichoso.

capriciously, adv. caprichosamente.

capriciousness, n. capricho m.

capsize, v. zozobrar, volcar.

capsule, n. cápsula f.

captain, n. capitán m.

caption, n. título m.; (motion pictures) subtítulo m.

captious, a. capcioso.

captivate, v. cautivar.

captivating, a. encantador.

captive, n. cautivo -va, prisionero -ra.

captivity, n. cautividad f.

captor, n. apresador m.

capture, 1. n. captura f. 2. v. capturar.

car, n. coche, carro m.; (of train) vagón, coche m. baggage c., vagón de equipajes. parlor c., coche salón.

carafe, n. garrafa f.

caramel, n. caramelo m.

carat, n. quilate m.

caravan, n. caravana f.

caraway, n. alcaravea f.

carbide, n. carburo m.

carbine, n. carabina f.

carbohydrate, n. hidrato de carbono.

carbon, n. carbón m.

carbon dioxide, anhídrido carbónico.

carbon monoxide, monóxido de carbono.

carbon paper, n. papel carbón m.

carbuncle, n. carbunclo m.

carburetor, n. carburador m.

carcinogenic, a. carcinogénico.

card, n. tarjeta f. playing c., naipe m.

cardboard, n. cartón m.

cardiac, a. cardíaco.

cardigan, n. chaqueta de punto.

cardinal, 1. a. cardinal. 2. n. cardenal m.

care, 1. n. cuidado. 2. v. c. for, cuidar.

careen, v. carenar; encharse de costado.

career, n. carrera f.

carefree, a. descuidado.

careful, a. cuidadoso. be c., tener cuidado.

carefully, adv. cuidadosamente.

carefulness, n. esmero; cuidado m.; cautela f.

careless, a. descuidado.

carelessly, adv. descuidadamente; negligentemente.

carelessness, n. descuido m.

caress, 1. n. caricia f. 2. v. acariciar.

caretaker, n. guardián m.

cargo, n. carga f.

caricature, n. caricatura f.

caries, n. carias f.

carload, a. furgonada, vagonada.

carnal, a. carnal.

carnation, n. clavel m.

carnival, n. carnaval m.

carnivorous, a. carnívoro.

carol, n. villancico m.

carouse, v. parrandear.

carpenter, n. carpintero m.

carpet, n. alfombra f.

carpeting, n. alfombrado m.

car pool, n. uso habitual, por varias personas, de un automóvil perteneciente a una de ellas.

carriage, n. carruaje; (bearing) porte m.

carrier, n. portador -ra.

carrier pigeon, n. paloma mensajera.

carrot, n. zanahoria f.

carrousel, n. volantín m.

carry, v. llevar, cargar. c. out, cumplir; llevar a cabo.

cart, n. carreta f.

cartage, n. acarreo, carretaje m.

cartel, n. cartel m.

cartilage, n. cartílago m.

carton, n. caja de cartón.

cartoon, n. caricatura f.

cartoonist, n. caricaturista m.

cartridge, n. cartucho m.

carve, v. esculpir; (meat) trinchar.

carver, n. tallador; grabador m.

carving, n. entalladura f.; arte de trinchar. c. knife, trinchante m.

cascade, n. cascada f.

case, n. caso m.; (box) caja f. in any c., sea como sea.

cash, 1. n. dinero contante. 2. v. efectuar, cambiar.

cashier, n. cajero -ra.

cashmere, n. casimir m.

casino, n. casino m.

cask, n. barril m.

casket, n. ataúd m.

casserole, n. cacerola f.

cassette, n. cassette m., cartucho m.

cast, 1. n. (theat.) reparto de papeles. 2. v. echar; (theat.) repartir.

castanet, n. castañuela f.

castaway, n. náufrago m.

caste, n. casta f.

caster, n. tirador m.

castigate, v. castigar.

Castilian, a. castellano.

cast iron, n. hierro colado m.

castle, n. castillo m.

castoff, a. descartado.

casual, a. casual.

casually, adv. casualmente.

casualness, n. casualidad f.

casualty, n. víctima f.; (mil.) baja f.

cat, n. gato -ta.

cataclysm, n. cataclismo m.

catacomb, n. catacumba f.

catalogue, n. catálogo m.

catapult, n. catapulta f.

cataract, n. catarata f.

catarrh, n. catarro m.

catastrophe, n. catástrofe m.

catch, v. alcanzar, atrapar, coger.

catchy, a. contagioso.

catechism, n. catequismo m.

catechize, v. catequizar.

categorical, a. categórico.

category, n. categoría f.

cater, v. abastecer; proveer. c. to, complacer.

caterpillar, n. gusano m.

catgut, n. cuerda (de tripa).

catharsis, n. purga f.

cathartic, 1. a. catártico; purgante. 2. n. purgante m.

cathedral, n. catedral f.

cathode, n. cátodo m.

Catholic, 1. a. católico. 2. n. católico -ca.

Catholicism, n. catolicismo m.

catnap, n. siesta corta.

catsup, n. salsa de tomate.

cattle, n. ganado m.

cattleman, n. ganadero m.

cauliflower, n. coliflor m.

causation, n. causalidad f.

cause, n. causa f.

causeway, n. calzada f.; terraplén m.

caustic, a. cáustico.

cauterize, v. cauterizar.

cautery, n. cauterio m.

caution, n. cautela f.

cautious, a. cauteloso.

cavalcade, n. cabalgata f.

cavalier, n. caballero m.

cavalry, n. caballería f.

cave, n. cueva, caverna f.

cave-in, n. hundimiento m.

caviar, n. caviar m.

cavity, n. hueco m.

cayman, n. caimán m.

cease, v. cesar.

ceaseless, a. incesante.

cedar, n. cedro m.

cede, v. ceder.

ceiling, n. cielo m.

celebrant, n. celebrante m.

celebrate, v. celebrar.

celebration, n. celebración f.

celebrity, n. persona célebre.

celerity, n. celeridad; prontitud f.

celery, n. apio m.

celestial, a. celeste.

celibacy, n. celibato m.

celibate, a. & n. célibe m.

cell, n. celda f.; (biol.) célula f.

cellar, n. sótano m.

cellist, a. celista m.

cello, n. violoncelo m.

cellophane, n. celofán m.

cellular, a. celular.

celluloid, n. celuloide m.

cellulose, 1. a. celuloso. 2. n. celulosa f.

Celtic, a. céltico.

cement, n. cemento m.

cemetery, n. cementerio m.; campo santo m.

censor, n. censor m.

censorious, a. severo; crítico.

censorship, n. censura f.

censure, 1. n. censura f. 2. v. censurar.

census, n. censo m.

cent, n. centavo m., céntimo m.

centenary, a. & n. centenario m.

centennial, a. & n. centenario m.

center, n. centro m.

centerfold, n. página central desplegable en una revista.

centerpiece, n. centro de mesa.

centigrade, a. centígrado.

centigrade thermometer, termómetro centígrado.

central, a. central.

Central American, a. & n. centroamericano -na.

centralize, v. centralizar.

century, n. siglo m.

century plant, n. maguey f.

ceramic, a. cerámico.

ceramics, n. cerámica f.

cereal, n. cereal m.

cerebral, a. cerebral.

ceremonial, a. ceremonial.

ceremonious, a. ceremonioso.

ceremony, n. ceremonia f.

certain, a. cierto, seguro.

certainly, adv. sin duda, seguramente.

certainty, n. certeza f.

certificate, n. certificado m.

certification, n. certificación f.

certified, a. certificado.

certify, v. certificar.

certitude, n. certeza f.

cessation, n. cesación f., discontinuación f.

cession, n. cesión f.

chafe, v. irritar.

chafing dish, n. escalfador m.

chagrin, n. disgusto m.

chain, 1. n. cadena f. 2. v. encadenar.

chair, n. silla f.

chairman, n. presidente m.

chairperson, n. presidente -ta; persona que preside.

chalk, n. tiza f.

challenge, 1. n. desafío m. 2. v. desafiar.

challenger, n. desafiador m.

chamber, n. cámara f.

chamberlain, n. camarero m.

chambermaid, n. camarera f.

chameleon, n. camaleón m.

chamois, n. gamuza f.

champagne, n. champán m., champaña f.

champion, 1. n. campeón m. 2. v. defender.

championship, n. campeonato m.

chance, n. oportunidad, ocasión f. by c., por casualidad, por acaso. take a c., aventurarse.

chancel, n. antealtar m.

chancellery, n. cancillería f.

chancellor, n. canciller m.

chandelier, n. araña de luces.

change, 1. n. cambio; (from a bill) moneda f. 2. v. cambiar f.

changeability, n. mutabilidad f.

changeable, a. variable, inconstante.

changer, n. cambiador m.

channel, 1. n. canal m. 2. v. encauzar.

chant, 1. n. canto llano m. 2. v. cantar.

chaos, n. caos m.

chaotic, a. caótico.

chap, 1. n. (coll.) tipo m. 2. v. rajar.

chapel, n. capilla f.

chaperon, n. dueña m.

chaplain, n. capellán m.

chapter, n. capítulo m.

char, v. carbonizar.

character, n. carácter m.

characteristic, 1. a. característico. 2. n. característica f.

characterization, n. caracterización f.

characterize, v. caracterizar.

charcoal, n. carbón leña.

charge, 1. n. acusación f.; ataque m. 2. v. cargar; acusar; atacar.

chariot, n. carroza f.

charisma, n. carisma m.

charitable, a. caritativo.

charitableness, n. caridad f.

charitably, adv. caritativamente.

charity, n. caridad f.; (alms) limosna f.

charlatan, n. charlatán -na.

charlatanism, n. charlatanería f.

charm, 1. n. encanto m.; (witchcraft) hechizo m. 2. v. encantar; hechizar.

charming, a. encantador.

charred, a. carbonizado.

chart, n. mapa m.

charter, 1. n. carta f. 2. v. alquilar.

charter flight, vuelo charter m.

chase, 1. n. caza f. 2. v. cazar; perseguir.

chaser, n. perseguidor m.

chasm, n. abismo m.

chassis, n. chasis m.

chaste, a. casto.

chasten, v. corregir, castigar.

chastise, v. castigar.

chastisement, n. castigo m.

chastity, n. castidad, pureza f.

chat, 1. n. plática, charla f. 2. v. platicar, charlar.

chateau, n. castillo m.

chattels, n.pl. bienes m.

chatter, 1. v. cotorrear; (teeth) rechinar. 2. n. cotorreo m.

chatterbox, n. charlador m.

chauffeur, n. chofer m.

cheap, a. barato.

cheapen, v. rebajar, menospreciar.

cheaply, adv. barato.

cheapness, n. baratura f.

cheat, v. engañar.

cheater, n. engañador m.

check, 1. v. verificación f.; (bank) cheque m.; (restaurant) cuenta f.; (chess) jaque m. 2. v. verificar.

checkers, n. juego de damas.

checkmate, v. dar mate.

cheek, n. mejilla f.

cheer, 1. n. alegría f.; aplauso m. 2. v. alegrar; aplaudir.

cheerful, a. alegre.

cheerfully, adv. alegremente.

cheerfulness, n. alegría f.

cheerless, a. triste.

cheery, a. alegre.

cheese, n. queso m. cottage c., requesón m.

chef, n. cocinero en jefe.

chemical, 1. a. químico. 2. n. reactivo m.

chemically, adv. químicamente.

chemist, n. químico m.

chemistry, n. química f.

chemotherapy, n. quimoterapia f.

chenille, n. felpilla f.

cherish, v. apreciar.

cherry, n. cereza f.

cherub, n. querubín m.

chess, n. ajedrez m.

chest, n. arca f.; (physiology) pecho m.

chestnut, n. castaña f.

chevron, n. sardineta f.

chew, v. mascar, masticar.

chewer, n. mascador m.

chic, a. elegante, paquete.

chicanery, n. trampería f.

chick, n. pollito.

chicken, n. pollo m., gallina f.

chicken-hearted, a. cobarde.

chicken pox, n. viruelas locas f.

chicle, n. chicle m.

chicory, n. achicoria f.

chide, v. regañar, reprender.

chief, 1. a. principal. 2. n. jefe m.

chiefly, adv. principalmente, mayormente.

chieftain, n. caudillo m.; (Indian c.) cacique m.

chiffon, n. chifón m.

chilblain, n. sabañón m.

child, n. niño -ña; hijo -ja.

childbirth, n. parto m.

childhood, n. niñez f.

childish, a. pueril.

childishness, n. puerilidad f.

childless, a. sin hijos.

childlike, a. infantil.

Chilean, a. & n. chileno -na m.

chili, n. chile ají m.

chill, 1. *n.* frío; escalofrío *m.* 2. *v.* enfriar.

chilliness, *n.* frialdad *f.*

chilly, *a.* frío; friolento.

chimes, *n.* juego de campanas.

chimney, *n.* chimenea *f.*

chimpanzee, *n.* chimpancé *m.*

chin, *n.* barba *f.*

china, *n.* loza *f.*

chinchilla, *n.* chinchilla *f.*

Chinese, *a.* & *n.* chino -na.

chink, *n.* grieta *f.*

chintz, *n.* zaraza *f.*

chip, 1. *n.* astilla *f.* 2. *v.* astillar.

chiropodist, *n.* pedicuro *m.*

chiropractor, *n.* quiroprático *m.*

chirp, 1. *n.* chirrido *m.* 2. *v.* chirriar, piar.

chisel, 1. *n.* cincel *m.* 2. *v.* cincelar, talar.

chivalrous, *a.* caballeroso.

chivalry, *n.* caballería *f.*

chive, *n.* cebollino *m.*

chloride, *n.* cloruro *m.*

chlorine, *n.* cloro *m.*

chloroform, *n.* cloroformo *m.*

chlorophyll, *n.* clorófila *f.*

chock-full, *a.* repleto, colmado.

chocolate, *n.* chocolate *m.*

choice, 1. *a.* selecto, escogido. 2. *n.* selección *f.;* escogimiento *m.*

choir, *n.* coro *m.*

choke, *v.* sofocar, ahogar.

cholera, *n.* cólera *f.*

choleric, *a.* colérico, irascible.

choose, *v.* elegir, escoger.

chop, 1. *n.* chuleta, costilla *f.* 2. *v.* tajar; cortar.

chopper, *n.* tajador *m.*

choppy, *a.* agitado.

choral, *a.* coral.

chord, *n.* cuerda *f.*

chore, *n.* tarea *f.,* quehacer *m.*

choreography, *n.* coreografía *f.*

chorister, *n.* corista *m.*

chorus, *n.* coro *m.*

christen, *v.* bautizar.

Christendom, *n.* cristiandad *f.*

Christian, *a.* & *n.* cristiano -na.

Christianity, *n.* cristianismo *m.*

Christmas, *n.* navidad, pascua *f.* Merry C., felices pascuas. C. Eve, nochebuena *f.*

chromatic, *a.* cromático.

chromium, *n.* cromo *m.*

chromosome, *n.* cromosoma *m.*

chronic, *a.* crónico.

chronicle, *n.* crónica *f.*

chronological, *a.* cronológico.

chronology, *n.* cronología *f.*

chrysalis, *n.* crisálida *f.*

chrysanthemum, *n.* crisantemo *m.*

chubby, *a.* regordete.

chuck, *v.* (cluck) cloquear; (throw) echar, tirar.

chuckle, *v.* reír entre dientes.

chum, *n.* amigo *m.;* compinche *m.*

chummy, *a.* íntimo.

chunk, *n.* trozo *m.*

chunky, *a.* fornido, trabado.

church, *n.* iglesia *f.*

churchman, *n.* eclesiástico *m.*

churchyard, *n.* cementerio *m.*

churn, 1. *n.* mantequera *f.* 2. *v.* agitar, revolver.

chute, *n.* conducto *m.;* canal *f.*

cicada, *n.* cigarra, chicharra *f.*

cider, *n.* sidra *f.*

cigar, *n.* cigarro, puro *m.*

cigarette, *n.* cigarrillo, pitillo *m.* c. case, cigarrillera *f.*

cinchona, *n.* cinchona *f.*

cinder, *n.* ceniza *f.*

cinema, *n.* cine *m.*

cinnamon, *n.* canela *f.*

cipher, *n.* cifra *f.*

circle, *n.* círculo *m.*

circuit, *n.* circuito *m.*

circuitous, *a.* tortuoso.

circuitously, *adv.* tortuosamente.

circular, *a.* circular, redondo.

circularize, *v.* hacer circular.

circulate, *v.* circular.

circulation, *n.* circulación *f.*

circulator, *n.* diseminador *m.*

circulatory, *a.* circulatorio.

circumcise, *v.* circuncidar.

circumcision, *n.* circuncisión *f.*

circumference, *n.* circunferencia *f.*

circumlocution, *n.* circunlocución *f.*

circumscribe, *v.* circunscribir; limitar.

circumspect, *a.* discreto.

circumstance, *n.* circunstancia *f.*

circumstantial, *a.* circunstancial, indirecto.

circumstantially, *adv.* minuciosamente.

circumvent, *v.* evadir, evitar.

circumvention, *n.* trampa *f.;* estratagema *f.*

circus, *n.* circo *m.*

cirrhosis, *n.* cirrosis *f.*

cistern, *n.* cisterna *f.*

citadel, *n.* ciudadela *f.*

citation, *n.* citación *f.*

cite, *v.* citar.

citizen, *n.* ciudadano -na.

citizenship, *n.* ciudadanía *f.*

citric, *a.* cítrico.

city, *n.* ciudad *f.*

civic, *a.* cívico.

civics, *n.* ciencia del gobierno civil.

civil, *a.* civil; cortés.

civilian, *a.* & *n.* civil *m.*

civility, *n.* cortesía *f.*

civilization, *n.* civilización *f.*

civilize, *v.* civilizar.

civil service, *n.* servicio civil oficial *m.*

civil war, *n.* guerra civil *f.*

clabber, 1. *n.* cuajo *m.* 2. *v.* cuajarse.

clad, *a.* vestido.

claim, 1. *n.* demanda; pretensión *f.* 2. *v.* demandar, reclamar.

claimant, *n.* reclamante *m.*

clairvoyance, *n.* clarividencia *f.*

clairvoyant, *a.* clarividente.

clam, *n.* almeja *f.*

clamber, *v.* trepar.

clamor, 1. *n.* clamor *m.* 2. *v.* clamar.

clamorous, *a.* clamoroso.

clamp, 1. *n.* prensa de sujeción *f.* 2. *v.* asegurar, sujetar.

clan, *n.* tribu *f.*

clandestine, *a.* clandestino.

clandestinely, *adv.* clandestinamente.

clangor, *n.* estruendo *m.,* estrépito *m.*

clannish, *a.* unido; exclusivista.

clap, *v.* aplaudir.

clapboard, *n.* chilla *f.*

claque, *n.* claque *f.*

claret, *n.* clarete *m.*

clarification, *n.* clarificación *f.*

clarify, *v.* clarificar.

clarinet, *n.* clarinete *m.*

clarinetist, *n.* clarinero *m.*

clarity, *n.* claridad *f.*

clash, 1. *n.* choque *m.* 2. *v.* chocar.

clasp, 1. *n.* broche *m.* 2. *v.* abrochar.

class, *n.* clase *f.*

classic, classical, *a.* clásico.

classicism, *n.* clasicismo *m.*

classifiable, *a.* clasificable, calificable.

classification, *n.* clasificación *f.*

classify, *v.* clasificar.

classmate, *n.* compañero de clase.

classroom, *n.* sala de clase.

clatter, 1. *n.* alboroto *m.* 2. *v.* alborotar.

clause, *n.* cláusula *f.*

claustrophobia, *n.* claustrofobia *f.*

claw, *n.* garra *f.*

clay, *n.* arcilla *f.;* barro *m.*

clean, 1. *a.* limpio. 2. *v.* limpiar.

cleaner, *n.* limpiador -ra.

cleanliness, *n.* limpieza *f.*

cleanse, *v.* limpiar, purificar.

cleanser, *n.* limpiador *m.,* purificador *m.*

clear, *a.* claro.

clearance, *n.* espacio libre. c. sale, venta de liquidación.

clearing, *n.* despejo *m.;* desmonte *m.*

clearly, *adv.* claramente, evidentemente.

clearness, *n.* claridad *f.*

cleavage, *n.* resquebradura *f.*

cleaver, *n.* partidor *m.,* hacha *f.*

clef, *n.* clave, llave *f.*

clemency, *n.* clemencia *f.*

clench, *v.* agarrar.

clergy, *n.* clero *m.*

clergyman, *n.* clérigo *m.*

clerical, *a.* clerical. c. work, trabajo de dependientes.

clericalism, *n.* clericalismo *m.*

clerk, *n.* dependiente, escribiente *m.*

clerkship, *n.* escribanía *f.,* secretaría *f.*

clever, a. diestro, hábil.

cleverly, adv. diestramente, hábilmente.

cleverness, n. destreza f.

cliché, n. cliché m.

client, n. cliente m.

clientele, n. clientela f.

cliff, n. precipicio, risco m.

climate, n. clima m.

climatic, a. climático.

climax, n. colmo m., culminación f.

climb, v. escalar; subir.

climber, n. trepador m., escalador m; (bot.) enredadera f.

clinch, v. afirmar.

cling, v. pegarse.

clinic, n. clínica f.

clinical, a. clínico.

clinically, adv. clinicalmente.

clip, 1. n. grapa f. paper c., gancho m. 2. v. prender; (shear) trasquilar.

clipper, n. recortador m.; (aero.) clíper m.

clipping, n. recorte m.

clique, n. camarilla f., compadraje m.

cloak, n. capa f., manto m.

clock, n. reloj m. alarm c., despertador m.

clod, n. terrón m.; césped m.

clog, v. obstruir.

cloister, n. claustro m.

clone, m. ser viviente reproducido a base de las células de otro.

close, 1. a. cercano. 2. adv. cerca. c. to, cerca de. 3. v. cerrar; tapar.

closely, adv. (near) de cerca; (tight) estrechamente; (care) cuidadosamente.

closeness, n. contigüidad f., apretamiento m.; (airless) falta de ventilación f.

closet, n. gabinete m. clothes c., ropero m.

clot, 1. n. coagulación f. 2. v. coagularse.

cloth, n. paño m.; tela f.

clothe, v. vestir.

clothes, clothing, n. ropa f.

clothing, n. vestidos m., ropa f.

cloud, n. nube f.

cloudburst, n. chaparrón m.

cloudiness, n. nebulosidad f.; obscuridad f.

cloudless, a. despejado, sin nubes.

cloudy, a. nublado.

clove, n. clavo m.

clover, n. trébol m.

clown, n. bufón m.

clownish, a. grosero; bufonesco.

cloy, v. saciar.

club, 1. n. porra f.; (social) círculo, club m.; (cards) basto m. 2. v. golpear con una porra.

clubfoot, n. pateta m., pie zambo m.

clue, n. seña, pista f.

clump, n. grupo m., masa f.

clumsiness, n. tosquedad f., desmaña f.

clumsy, a. torpe, desmañado.

cluster, 1. n. grupo m.; (fruit) racimo m. 2. v. agrupar.

clutch, 1. n. (auto.) embrague m. 2. v. agarrar.

clutter, 1. n. confusión f. 2. v. poner en desorden.

coach, 1. n. coche, vagón m.; coche ordinario; (sports) entrenador m. 2. v. entrenar.

coachman, n. cochero m.

coagulate, v. coagular.

coagulation, n. coagulación f.

coal, n. carbón m.

coalesce, v. unirse, soldarse.

coalition, n. coalición f.

coal oil, n. petróleo m.

coal tar, n. alquitrán m.

coarse, a. grosero, burdo; (material) tosco, grueso.

coarsen, v. vulgarizar.

coarseness, n. grosería; tosquedad f.

coast, 1. n. costa f., litoral m. 2. v. deslizarse.

coastal, a. costanero.

coast guard, n. costanero m.

coat, 1. n. saco m., chaqueta f.; (paint) capa f. 2. v. cubrir.

coat of arms, n. escudo m.

coax, v. instar.

cobalt, n. cobalto m.

cobbler, n. zapatero m.

cobblestone, n. guijarro m.

cobra, n. cobra f.

cobweb, n. telaraña f.

cocaine, n. cocaína f.

cock, n. (rooster) gallo m.; (water, etc.) llave f.; (gun) martillo m.

cockfight, n. riña de gallos f.

cockpit, n. gallera f.; reñidero de gallos m.

cockroach, n. cucaracha f.

cocktail, n. coctel m.

cocky, a. confiado, atrevido.

cocoa, n. cacao m.

coconut, n. coco m.

cocoon, n. capullo m.

cod, n. bacalao m.

code, n. código m.; clave f.

codeine, n. codeína f.

codfish, n. bacalao m.

codify, v. compilar.

coeducation, n. coeducación f.

coequal, a. mutuamente igual.

coerce, v. forzar.

coercion, n. coerción f.

coercive, a. coercitivo.

coexist, v. coexistir.

coffee, n. café m. c. plantation, cafetal m.

coffer, n. cofre m.

coffin, n. ataúd m.

cog, n. diente de rueda m.

cogent, a. convincente.

cogitate, v. pensar, reflexionar.

cognizance, n. conocimiento m., comprensión f.

cognizant, a. conocedor, informado.

cogwheel, n. rueda dentada f.

cohere, v. pegarse.

coherent, a. coherente.

cohesion, n. cohesión f.

cohesive, a. cohesivo.

cohort, n. cohorte f.

coiffure, n. peinado, tocado m.

coil, 1. n. rollo m.; (naut.) adujada f. 2. v. enrollar.

coin, n. moneda f.

coinage, n. sistema monetario f.

coincide, v. coincidir.

coincidence, n. coincidencia; casualidad f.

coincident, a. coincidente.

coincidental, a. coincidental.

coincidentally, adv. coincidentalmente, al mismo tiempo.

colander, n. colador m.

cold, a. & n. frío m.; (med.) resfriado m. to be c., tener frío; (weather) hacer frío.

coldly, adv. friamente.

coldness, n. frialdad f.

collaborate, v. colaborar.

collaboration, n. colaboración f.

collaborator, n. colaborador m.

collapse, 1. n. desplome m.; (med.) colapso m. 2. v. desplomarse.

collar, n. cuello m.

collarbone, n. clavícula f.

collate, v. comparar.

collateral, 1. a. colateral. 2. n. garantía f.

collation, n. comparación f.; (food) colación f., merienda f.

colleague, n. colega m. & f.

collect, v. cobrar; recoger; coleccionar.

collection, n. colección f.

collective, a. colectivo.

collectively, adv. colectivamente, en masa.

collector, n. colector -ra; coleccionista m. & f.

college, n. colegio m.; universidad f.

collegiate, a. colegiado m.

collide, v. chocar.

collision, n. choque m.

colloquial, a. familiar.

colloquially, adv. familiarmente.

colloquy, n. conversación f., coloquio m.

collusion, n. colusión f., connivencia f.

Colombian, a. & n. colombiano -na.

colon, n. colon m.; (punct.) dos puntos.

colonel, n. coronel m.

colonial, a. colonial.

colonist, n. colono m.

colonization, n. colonización f.

colonize, v. colonizar.

colony, n. colonia f.

color, 1. n. color; colorido m. 2. v. colorar; colorir.

coloration, n. colorido m.

colored, a. de color.

colorful, a. vívido.

colorless, a. descolorido, sin color.

colossal, *a.* colosal.

colt, *n.* porto *m.*

column, *n.* columna *f.*

coma, *n.* coma *m.*

comb, 1. *n.* peine *m.* 2. *v.* peinar.

combat, 1. *n.* combate *m.* 2. *v.* combatir.

combatant, *n.* combatiente *m.*

combative, *a.* combativo.

combination, *n.* combinación *f.*

combine, *v.* combinar.

combustible, *a. & n.* combustible *m.*

combustion, *n.* combustión *f.*

come, *v.* venir. c. **back**, volver. c. **in**, entrar. c. **out**, salir. c. **up**, subir. c. **upon**, encontrarse con.

comedian, *n.* cómico -ca.

comedienne, *n.* cómica *f.*, actriz *f.*

comedy, *n.* comedia *f.*

comet, *n.* cometa *m.*

comfort, 1. *n.* confort *m.*; solaz *m.* 2. *v.* confortar; solazar.

comfortable, *a.* cómodo.

comfortably, *adv.* cómodamente.

comforter, *n.* colcha *f.*

comfortingly, *adv.* confortantemente.

comfortless, *a.* sin consuelo; sin comodidades.

comic, comical, *a.* cómico.

coming, 1. *n.* venida *f.*, llegada *f.* 2. *a.* próximo, que viene, entrante.

comma, *n.* coma *f.*

command, 1. *n.* mando *m.* 2. *v.* mandar.

commandeer, *v.* reclutar forzosamente, expropiar.

commander, *n.* comandante *m.*

commander in chief, *n.* generalísimo, jefe supremo.

commandment, *n.* mandato; mandamiento *m.*

commemorate, *v.* conmemorar.

commemoration, *n.* conmemoración *f.*

commemorative, *a.* conmemorativo.

commence, *v.* comenzar, principiar.

commencement, *n.* comienzo *m.*; graduación *f.*

commend, *v.* encomendar.

commendable, *a.* recomendable.

commendably, *adv.* loablemente.

commendation, *n.* recomendación *f.*

commensurate, *a.* proporcionado.

comment, 1. *n.* comento *m.* 2. *v.* comentar.

commentary, *n.* comentario *m.*

commentator, *n.* comentador -ra.

commerce, *n.* comercio *m.*

commercial, *a.* comercial.

commercialism, *n.* comercialismo *m.*

commercialize, *v.* mercantilizar, explotar.

commercially, *a. & adv.* comercial.

commiserate, *v.* compadecerse.

commissary, *n.* comisario *m.*

commission, 1. *n.* comisión *f.* 2. *v.* comisionar.

commissioner, *n.* comisionista *m. & f.*

commit, *v.* cometer.

commitment, *n.* compromiso *m.*

committee, *n.* comité *m.*

commodious, *a.* cómodo.

commodity, *n.* mercadería *f.*

common, *a.* común; ordinario.

commonly, *adv.* comúnmente, vulgarmente.

commonplace, *a.* trivial, banal.

commonwealth, *n.* estado *m.*; nación *f.*

commotion, *n.* tumulto *m.*

communal, *a.* comunal, público.

commune, 1. *n.* distrito municipal *m.*; comuna *f.* 2. *v.* conversar.

communicable, *a.* comunicativo.

communicate, *v.* comunicar.

communication, *n.* comunicación *f.*

communicative, *a.* comunicativo.

communion, *n.* comunión *f.* **take c.**, comulgar.

communiqué, *n.* comunicación *f.*

communism, *n.* comunismo *m.*

communist, *n.* comunista *m. & f.*

communistic, *a.* comunístico.

community, *n.* comunidad *f.*

commutation, *n.* conmutación *f.*

commuter, *n.* empleado que viaja diariamente desde su domicilio hasta la ciudad donde trabaja.

compact, 1. *a.* compacto. 2. *n.* pacto *m.*; (lady's) polvera *f.*

companion, *n.* compañero -ra.

companionable, *a.* sociable.

companionship, *n.* compañerismo *m.*

company, *n.* compañía *f.*

comparable, *a.* comparable.

comparative, *a.* comparativo.

comparatively, *a.* relativamente.

compare, *v.* comparar.

comparison, *n.* comparación *f.*

compartment, *n.* compartimiento *m.*

compass, *n.* compás *m.*; (naut.) brújula *f.*

compassion, *n.* compasión *f.*

compassionate, *a.* compasivo.

compassionately, *adv.* compasivamente.

compatible, *a.* compatible.

compatriot, *n.* compatriota *m. & f.*

compel, *v.* obligar.

compensate, *v.* compensar.

compensation, *n.* compensación *f.*

compensatory, *a.* compensatorio.

compete, *v.* competir.

competence, *n.* competencia *f.*

competent, *a.* competente, capaz.

competently, *adv.* competentemente.

competition, *n.* concurrencia *f.*; concurso *m.*

competitive, *a.* competidor.

competitor, *n.* competidor -ra.

compile, *v.* compilar.

complacency, *n.* complacencia *f.*

complacent, *a.* complaciente.

complacently, *adv.* complacientemente.

complain, *v.* quejarse.

complaint, *n.* queja *f.*

complement, *n.* complemento *m.*

complete, 1. *a.* completo 2. *v.* completar.

completely, *adv.* completamente, enteramente.

completeness, *n.* integridad *f.*

completion, *n.* terminación *f.*

complex, *a.* complejo.

complexion, *n.* tez *f.*

complexity, *n.* complejidad *f.*

compliance, *n.* consentimiento *m.* **in c. with**, de acuerdo con.

compliant, *a.* dócil; complaciente.

complicate, *v.* complicar.

complicated, *a.* complicado.

complication, *n.* complicación *f.*

complicity, *n.* complicidad *f.*

compliment, 1. *n.* flor *f.* 2. *v.* felicitar; echar flores.

complimentary, *a.* galante, obsequioso, regaloso.

comply, *v.* cumplir.

component, *a. & n.* componente *m.*

comport, *v.* portarse.

compose, *v.* componer.

composed, *a.* tranquilo; (made up) compuesto.

composer, *n.* compositor -ra.

composite, *a.* compuesto.

composition, *n.* composición *f.*

composure, *n.* serenidad *f.*; calma *f.*

compote, *n.* compota *f.*

compound, *a. & n.* compuesto *m.*

comprehend, *v.* comprender.

comprehensible, *a.* comprensible.

comprehension, *n.* comprensión *f.*

comprehensive, *a.* comprensivo.

compress, 1. *n.* cabezal *m.* 2. *v.* comprimir.

compressed, *a.* comprimido.

compression, *n.* compresión *f.*

compressor, *n.* compresor *m.*

comprise, v. comprender; abarcar.

compromise, 1. n. compromiso m. 2. v. comprometer.

compromiser, n. compromisario m.

compulsion, n. compulsión f.

compulsive, a. compulsivo.

compulsory, a. obligatorio.

compunction, n. compunción f.; escrúpulo m.

computation, n. computación f.

compute, v. computar, calcular.

computer, n. computadora f., ordenador m.

computerize, v. procesar en computadora.

comrade, n. camarada m. & f.; compañero -ra.

comradeship, n. camaradería f.

concave, a. cóncavo.

conceal, v. ocultar, esconder.

concealment, n. ocultación f.

concede, v. conceder.

conceit, n. amor propio; engreimiento m.

conceited, a. engreído.

conceivable, a. concebible.

conceive, v. concebir.

concentrate, v. concentrar.

concentration, n. concentración f.

concept, n. concepto m.

conception, n. concepción f.; concepto m.

concern, 1. n. interés m.; inquietud f.; (com.) negocio m. 2. v. concernir.

concerning, prep. respecto a.

concert, n. concierto m.

concerted, a. convenido.

concession, n. concesión f.

conciliate, v. conciliar.

conciliation, n. conciliación f.

conciliator, n. conciliador m.

conciliatory, a. conciliatorio.

concise, a. conciso.

concisely, adv. concisamente.

conciseness, n. concisión f.

conclave, n. conclave m.

conclude, v. concluir.

conclusion, n. conclusión f.

conclusive, a. conclusivo, decisivo.

conclusively, adv. concluyentemente.

concoct, v. confeccionar.

concomitant, n. & a. concomitante.

concord, n. concordia f.

concordat, n. concordato m.

concourse, n. concurso m.; confluencia f.

concrete, a. concreto.

concretely, adv. concretamente.

concubine, n. concubina, amiga f.

concur, v. concurrir.

concurrence, n. concurrencia f.; casualidad f.

concurrent, a. concurrente.

concussion, n. concusión f.; (c.

of the brain) conmoción cerebral f.

condemn, v. condenar.

condemnable, a. culpable, condenable.

condemnation, n. condenación f.

condensation, n. condensación f.

condense, v. condensar.

condenser, n. condensador m.

condescend, v. condescender.

condescension, n. condescendencia f.

condiment, n. condimento m.

condition, 1. n. condición f.; estado m. 2. v. acondicionar.

conditional, a. condicional.

conditionally, adv. condicionalmente.

condole, v. condolerse.

condolence, n. pésame m.

condominium, n. apartamento en propiedad m.

condone, v. condonar.

conducive, a. conducente.

conduct, 1. n. conducta f. 2. v. conducir.

conductivity, n. conductividad f.

conductor, n. conductor m.

conduit, n. caño m., canal f.; conducto m.

cone, n. cono m. ice-cream c., barquillo de helado.

confection, n. confitura f.

confectioner, n. confitero m.

confectionery, n. dulcería f.

confederacy, n. federación f.

confederate, a. & n. confederado m.

confederation, n. confederación f.

confer, v. conferenciar; conferir.

conference, n. conferencia f.; congreso m.

confess, v. confesar.

confession, n. confesión f.

confessional, 1. n. confesionario m. 2. a. confesional.

confessor, n. confesor m.

confetti, n. confetti m.

confidant, confidante, n. confidente m. & f.

confide, v. confiar.

confidence, n. confianza f.

confident, a. confiado; cierto.

confidential, a. confidencial.

confidentially, adv. confidencialmente, en secreto.

confidently, adv. confiadamente.

confine, 1. n. confín m. 2. v. confinar; encerrar.

confirm, v. confirmar.

confirmation, n. confirmación f.

confiscate, v. confiscar.

confiscation, n. confiscación f.

conflagration, n. incendio m.

conflict, 1. n. conflicto m.; oponerse; estar en conflicto.

conform, v. conformar.

conformation, n. conformación f.

conformer, n. conformista m. & f.

conformist, n. conformista m. & f.

conformity, n. conformidad f.

confound, v. confundir.

confront, v. confrontar.

confuse, v. confundir.

confusion, n. confusión f.

congeal, v. congelar, helar.

congealment, n. congelación f.

congenial, a. congenial.

congeniality, a. congénito.

congenitally, adv. congenitalmente.

congestion, n. congestión f.

conglomerate, 1. v. conglomerar. 2. a. conglomerado.

conglomeration, n. conglomeración f.

congratulate, v. felicitar.

congratulation, n. felicitación f.

congratulatory, a. congratulatorio.

congregate, v. congregar.

congregation, n. congregación f.

congress, n. congreso m.

conic, 1. n. cónica f. 2. a. cónico.

conjecture, 1. n. conjetura f. 2. v. conjeturar.

conjugal, a. conyugal, matrimonial.

conjugate, v. conjugar.

conjugation, n. conjugación f.

conjunction, n. conjunción f.

conjunctive, 1. n. (gram.) conjunción f. 2. a. conjuntivo.

conjunctivitis, n. conjuntivitis f.

conjure, v. conjurar.

connect, v. juntar; relacionar.

connection, n. conexión f.

connivance, n. consentimiento m.

connive, v. disimular.

connoisseur, n. perito -ta.

connotation, n. connotación f.

connote, v. connotar.

connubial, a. conyugal.

conquer, v. conquistar.

conquerable, a. conquistable, vencible.

conqueror, n. conquistador m.

conquest, n. conquista f.

conscience, n. conciencia f.

conscientious, a. concienzudo.

conscientiously, adv. escrupulosamente.

conscious, a. consciente.

consciously, adv. con conocimiento.

consciousness, n. consciencia f.

conscript, 1. n. conscripto m., recluta m. 2. v. reclutar, alistar.

conscription, n. conscripción f., alistamiento m.

consecrate, v. consagrar.

consecration, n. consagración f.

consecutive, a. consecutivo, seguido.

consecutively, adv. consecutivamente, de seguida.

consensus, n. consenso m., acuerdo general m.

consent, 1. n. consentimiento m. 2. v. consentir.

consequence, n. consecuencia f.

consequent, a. consiguiente.

consequential, a. importante.

consequently, adv. por lo tanto, por consiguiente.

conservation, n. conservación f.

conservatism, n. conservatismo m.

conservative, a. conservador, conservativo.

conservatory, n. (plants) invernáculo m.; (school) conservatorio m.

conserve, v. conservar.

consider, v. considerar.

considerable, a. considerable.

considerably, adv. considerablemente.

considerate, a. considerado.

considerately, adv. consideradamente.

consideration, n. consideración f.

considering, prep. visto que, en vista de.

consign, v. consignar.

consignment, n. consignación f., envío m.

consist, v. consistir.

consistency, n. consistencia f.

consistent, a. consistente.

consolation, n. consolación f.

console, v. consolar.

consolidate, v. consolidar.

consommé, n. caldo m.

consonant, n. consonante f.

consort, 1. n. conyuge m. & f.; socio. 2. v. asociarse.

conspicuous, a. conspicuo.

conspicuously, adv. visiblemente, llamativamente.

conspicuousness, n. visibilidad f.; evidencia f.; fama f.

conspiracy, n. conspiración f.; complot m.

conspirator, n. conspirador -ra.

conspire, v. conspirar.

conspirer, n. conspirante m. & f.

constancy, n. constancia f., lealtad f.

constant, a. constante.

constantly, adv. constantemente, de continuo.

constellation, n. constelación f.

consternation, n. consternación f.

constipation, n. constipación f.

constituency, n. distrito electoral m.

constituent, 1. a. constituyente. 2. n. elector m.

constitute, v. constituir.

constitution, n. constitución f.

constitutional, a. constitucional.

constrain, v. constreñir.

constraint, n. constreñimiento m., compulsión f.

constrict, v. apretar, estrechar.

construct, v. construir.

construction, n. construcción f.

constructive, a. constructivo.

constructively, adv. constructivamente; por deducción.

constructor, n. constructor m.

construe, v. interpretar.

consul, n. cónsul m.

consular, a. consular.

consulate, n. consulado m.

consult, v. consultar.

consultant, n. consultante m. & f.

consultation, n. consulta f.

consume, v. consumir.

consumer, n. consumidor -ra.

consummation, n. consumación f.

consumption, n. consumo m.

consumptive, 1. n. tísico m. 2. a. consuntivo.

contact, 1. n. contacto m. 2. v. ponerse en contacto con.

contagion, n. contagio m.

contagious, a. contagioso.

contain, v. contener.

container, n. envase m.

contaminate, v. contaminar.

contemplate, v. contemplar.

contemplation, n. contemplación f.

contemplative, a. contemplativo.

contemporary, n. & a. contemporáneo -nea.

contempt, n. desprecio m.

contemptible, v. vil, despreciable.

contemptuous, a. desdeñoso.

contemptuously, adv. desdeñosamente.

contend, v. contender; competir.

contender, n. competidor m.

content, 1. a. contento. 2. n. contenido m. 3. v. contentar.

contented, a. contento.

contention, n. contención f.

contentment, n. contentamiento m.

contest, 1. n. concurso m. 2. v. disputar.

contestable, a. contestable.

context, n. contexto m.

contiguous, a. contiguo.

continence, n. continencia f., castidad f.

continent, n. continente m.

continental, a. continental.

contingency, n. eventualidad f., casualidad f.

contingent, a. contingente.

continual, a. continuo.

continuation, n. continuación f.

continue, v. continuar.

continuity, n. continuidad f.

continuous, a. continuo.

continuously, adv. continualmente.

contour, n. contorno m.

contraband, n. contrabando m.

contraception, n. contracepción f.

contract, 1. n. contrato m. 2. v. contraer.

contraction, n. contracción f.

contractor, n. contratista m.

contradict, v. contradecir.

contradiction, n. contradicción f.

contradictory, a. contradictorio, opuesto.

contralto, n. contralto m.

contrary, a. & n. contrario m.

contrast, 1. n. contraste m. 2. v. contrastar.

contribute, v. contribuir.

contribution, n. contribución f.

contributive, contributory, a. contribuyente.

contributor, n. contribuidor m.

contrite, a. contrito.

contrition, n. contrición f.

contrivance, n. aparato m.; estratagema f.

contrive, v. inventar, tramar; darse maña.

control, 1. n. control m. 2. v. controlar.

controllable, a. controlable, dominable.

controller, n. interventor m., contralor m.

controversial, a. contencioso.

controversy, n. controversia f.

contusion, n. contusión f.

convalesce, v. convalecer.

convalescence, n. convalecencio f.

convalescent, n. convaleciente m. & f.

convene, v. juntarse; convocar.

convenience, n. comodidad f.

convenient, a. cómodo. to be c., convenir.

conveniently, adv. cómodamente.

convent, n. convento m.

convention, n. convención f.

conventional, a. convencional.

conventionally, adv. convencionalmente.

converge, v. convergir.

convergence, n. convergencia f.

convergent, a. convergente.

conversant, a. versado; entendido (de).

conversation, n. conversación, plática f.

conversational, a. de conversación.

conversationalist, n. conversador m.

converse, v. conversar.

conversely, adv. a la inversa.

convert, 1. n. convertido m. 2. v. convertir.

converter, n. convertidor m.

convertible, a. convertible.

convex, a. convexo.

convey, v. transportar; comunicar.

conveyance, n. transporte; vehículo m.

conveyor, n. conductor m.; (mech.) transportador m.

convict, 1. n. reo m. 2. v. probar de culpa.

conviction, n. convicción f.

convince, v. convencer.

convincing, a. convincente.

convivial, a. cónvival.

convocation, n. convocación; asamblea f.

convoke, v. convocar, citar.

convoy, n. convoy m.; escolta f.

convulse, v. convulsionar; agitar violentamente.

convulsion, n. convulsión f.

convulsive, a. convulsivo.

cook, 1. n. cocinero -ra. 2 v. cocinar, cocer.

cookbook, n. libro de cocina m.

cooky, n. galleta dulce f.

cool, 1. a. fresco. 2. v. refrescar.

cooler, n. enfriadera f.

coolness, n. frescura f.

coop, 1. n. jaula f. chicken c., gallinero m. 2. v. enjaular.

cooperate, v. cooperar.

cooperation, n. cooperación f.

cooperative, a. cooperativo.

cooperatively, adv. cooperativamente.

coordinate, v. coordinar.

coordination, n. coordinación f.

coordinator, n. coordinador m.

cope, v. contender. c. with, superar, hacer frente a.

copier, n. copiadora f.

copious, a. copioso, abundante.

copiously, adv. copiosamente.

copiousness, n. copia f., abundancia f.

copper, n. cobre m.

copy, 1. n. copia f.; ejemplar m. 2. v. copiar.

copyist, n. copista m. & f.

copyright, n. derechos de propiedad literaria m.pl.

coquetry, n. coquetería f.

coquette, n. coqueta f.

coral, n. coral m.

cord, n. cuerda f.

cordial, a. cordial.

cordiality, n. cordialidad f.

cordially, adv. cordialmente.

cordovan, n. cordobán m.

corduroy, n. pana f.

core, n. corazón; centro m.

cork, n. corcho m.

corkscrew, n. tirabuzón m.

corn, n. maíz m.

cornea, n. córnea f.

corner, n. rincón m.; (of street) esquina f.

cornet, n. corneta f.

cornetist, n. cornetín m.

cornice, n. cornisa f.

cornstarch, n. maicena f.

corollary, n. corolario m.

coronary, a. coronario.

coronation, n. coronación f.

corporal, 1. a. corpóreo. 2. n. cabo m.

corporate, a. corporativo.

corporation, n. corporación f.

corps, n. cuerpo m.

corpse, n. cadáver m.

corpulent, a. corpulento.

corpuscle, n. corpúsculo m.

corral, 1. n. corral m. 2. v. acorralar.

correct, 1. a. correcto. 2. v. corregir.

correction, n. corrección; enmienda f.

corrective, & a. correctivo.

correctly, adv. correctamente.

correctness, n. exactitud f.

correlate, v. correlacionar.

correlation, n. correlación f.

correspond, v. corresponder.

correspondence, n. correspondencia f.

correspondent, a. correspondiente.

corresponding, a. correspondiente.

corridor, n. corredor, pasillo m.

corroborate, v. corroborar.

corroboration, n. corroboración f.

corroborative, a. corroborante.

corrode, v. corroer.

corrosion, n. corrosión f.

corrugate, v. arrugar; ondular.

corrupt, 1. a. corrompido. 2. v. corromper.

corruptible, a. corruptible.

corruption, n. corrupción f.

corruptive, a. corruptivo.

corset, n. corsé m., (girdle) faja f.

cortege, n. comitiva f., séquito m.

corvette, n. corbeta f.

cosmetic, a. & n. cosmético.

cosmic, a. cósmico.

cosmopolitan, a. & n. cosmopolita m. & f.

cosmos, n. cosmos m.

cost, 1. n. coste m.; costa f. 2. v. costar.

Costa Rican, a. & n. costarricense m. & f.

costly, a. costoso, caro.

costume, n. traje; disfraz m.

cot, n. catre m.

coterie, n. camarilla f.

cotillion, n. cotillón f.

cottage, n. casita f.

cottage cheese, n. requesón m.

cotton, n. algodón m.

cottonseed, n. semilla del algodón f.

couch, n. sofá m.

cougar, n. cuguar m.

cough, 1. n. tos f. 2. v. toser.

council, n. consejo, concilio m.

counsel, 1. n. consejo; (law) abogado m. 2. v. aconsejar. to keep one's c., no decir nada.

counselor, n. consejero; (law) abogado m.

count, 1. n. cuenta f.; (title) conde m. 2. v. contar.

countenance, 1. n. aspecto m.; cara f. 2. v. aprobar.

counter, 1. adv. c. to, contra, en contra de. 2. n. mostrador m.

counteract, v. contrariar.

counteraction, n. oposición f.

counterbalance, 1. n. contrapeso m. 2. v. contrapesar.

counterfeit, 1. a. falsificado. 2. v. falsear.

countermand, v. contramandar.

counteroffensive, n. contraofensiva f.

counterpart, n. contraparte f.

countess, n. condesa f.

countless, a. innumerable.

country, n. campo m.; (pol.) país m.; (homeland) patria f.

countryman, n. paisano m. fellow c., compatriota m.

countryside, n. campo, paisaje m.

county, n. condado m.

coupé, n. cupé m.

couple, 1. n. par m. 2. v. unir.

coupon, n. cupón, talón m.

courage, n. valor m.

courageous, a. valiente.

course, n. curso m. of c., por supuesto, desde luego.

court, 1. n. corte f.; cortejo m.; (of law) tribunal m. 2. v. cortejar.

courteous, a. cortés.

courtesy, n. cortesía f.

courthouse, n. palacio de justicia m., tribunal m.

courtier, n. cortesano m.

courtly, a. cortés, galante.

courtroom, n. sala de justicia f.

courtship, n. corte f.

courtyard, n. patio m.

cousin, n. primo -ma.

covenant, n. contrato, convenio m.

cover, 1. n. cubierta, tapa f. 2. v. cubrir, tapar.

covet, v. ambicionar, suspirar por.

covetous, a. codicioso.

cow, n. vaca f.

coward, n. cobarde m. & f.

cowardice, n. cobardía f.

cowardly, a. cobarde.

cowboy, n. vaquero, gaucho m.

cower, v. agacharse.

cowhide, n. cuero m.

coy, a. recatado, modesto.

coyote, n. coyote m.

cozy, a. cómodo y agradable.

crab, n. cangrejo m.

crab apple, n. manzana silvestre f.

crack, 1. n. hendedura f.; (noise) crujido m. 2. v. hender; crujir.

cracker, n. galleta f.

cradle, n. cuna f.

craft, n. arte m.

craftsman, *n.* artesano *m.*

craftsmanship, *n.* mano de obra *f.*

crafty, *a.* ladino.

crag, *n.* despeñadero *m.*

cram, *v.* rellenar, hartar.

cramp, *n.* calambre *m.*

cranberry, *n.* arándano *m.*

crane, 1. *n.* (bird) grulla *f.;* (mech.) grúa *f.*

cranium, *n.* cráneo *m.*

crank, *n.* (mech.) manivela *f.*

cranky, *a.* chiflado, caprichoso.

crash, 1. *n.* choque; estallido *m.* 2. *v.* estallar.

crate, *n.* canasto *f.*

crater, *n.* cráter *m.*

crave, *v.* desear; anhelar.

craven, *a.* cobarde.

craving, *n.* sed *m.*, anhelo *m.*

crawl, *v.* andar a gatas, arrastrarse.

crayon, *n.* creyón; lápiz *m.*

crazy, *a.* loco.

creak, *v.* crujir.

creaky, *a.* crujidero.

cream, *n.* crema *f.*

creamery, *n.* lechería *f.*

crease, 1. *n.* pliegue *m.* 2. *v.* plegar.

create, *v.* crear.

creation, *n.* creación *f.*

creative, *a.* creativo, creador.

creator, *n.* criador -ra.

creature, *n.* criatura *f.*

credence, *n.* creencia *f.*

credentials, *n.* credenciales *f.pl.*

credibility, *n.* credibilidad *f.*

credible, *a.* creíble.

credit, 1. *n.* crédito *m.* on c., al fiado. 2. *v.* (com.) abonar.

creditable, *a.* fidedigno.

credit card, *n.* tarjeta de crédito *f.*

creditor, *n.* acreedor -ra.

credo, *n.* credo *m.*

credulity, *n.* credulidad *f.*

credulous, *a.* crédulo.

creed, *n.* credo *m.*

creek, *n.* riachuelo *m.*

creep, *v.* gatear.

cremate, *v.* cremar.

crematory, *n.* crematorio *m.*

creosote, *n.* creosota *f.*

crepe, *n.* crespón *m.*

crescent, *a. & n.* creciente *f.*

crest, *n.* cresta; cima *f.;* (heraldry) timbre *m.*

cretonne, *n.* cretona *f.*

crevice, *n.* grieta *f.*

crew, *n.* tripulación *f.*

crib, *n.* pesebre *m.;* camita de niño.

cricket, *n.* grillo *m.*

crime, *n.* crimen *m.*

criminal, *a. & n.* criminal.

criminologist, *n.* criminologo *m.*

criminology, *n.* criminología *f.*

crimson, *a. & n.* carmesí *m.*

cringe, *v.* encogerse, temblar.

cripple, 1. *n.* lisiado -da. 2. *v.* estropear, lisiar.

crisis, *n.* crisis *f.*

crisp, *a.* crespo, fresco.

crispness, *n.* encrespadura *f.*

crisscross, *a.* entrelazado.

criterion, *n.* criterio *m.*

critic, *n.* crítico *m.*

critical, *a.* crítico.

criticism, *n.* crítica; censura *f.*

criticize, *v.* criticar; censurar.

critique, *n.* crítica *f.*

croak, 1. *n.* graznido *m.* 2. *v.* graznar.

crochet, 1. *n.* crochet *m.* 2. *v.* hacer crochet.

crock, *n.* cazuela *f.;* olla de barro.

crockery, *n.* loza *f.*

crocodile, *n.* cocodrilo *m.*

crony, *n.* compinche *m.*

crooked, *a.* encorvado; deshonesto.

croon, *v.* canturrear.

crop, *n.* cosecha *f.*

croquet, *n.* juego de croquet *m.*

croquette, *n.* croqueta *f.*

cross, 1. *a.* enojado, mal humorado. 2. *n.* cruz *f.* 3. *v.* cruzar, atravesar.

crossbreed, 1. *n.* mestizo *m.* 2. *v.* cruzar.

cross-examine, *v.* interrogar.

cross-eyed, *a.* bisco.

cross-fertilization, *n.* alogamia *f.*

crossing, crossroads, *n.* cruce *m.*

cross section, *n.* corte transversal *m.*

crotch, *n.* bifurcación *f.;* (anat.) bragadura *f.*

crouch, *v.* agacharse.

croup, *n.* (med.) crup *m.*

croupier, *n.* crupié *m.*

crow, *n.* cuervo *m.*

crowd, 1. *n.* muchedumbre *f.;* tropel *m.* 2. *v.* apretar.

crowded, *a.* lleno de gente.

crown, 1. *n.* corona *f.* 2. *v.* coronar.

crown prince, *n.* príncipe heredero *m.*

crucial, *a.* crucial.

crucible, *n.* crisol *m.*

crucifix, *n.* crucifijo *m.*

crucifixion, *n.* crucifixión *f.*

crucify, *v.* crucificar.

crude, *a.* crudo; (oil) bruto.

crudeness, *n.* crudeza *f.*

cruel, *a.* cruel.

cruelty, *n.* crueldad *f.*

cruet, *n.* vinagrera *f.*

cruise, 1. *n.* viaje por mar. 2. *v.* navegar.

cruiser, *n.* crucero *m.*

crumb, *n.* miga; migaja *f.*

crumble, *v.* desmigajar; moronar.

crumple, *v.* arrugar; encogerse.

crusade, *n.* cruzada *f.*

crusader, *n.* cruzado *m.*

crush, *v.* aplastar.

crust, *n.* costra *f.*

crustacean, *n.* crustáceo *m.*

crutch, *n.* muleta *f.*

cry, 1. *n.* grito *m.* 2. *v.* gritar; (weep) llorar.

cryosurgery, *n.* criocirugía *f.*

crypt, *n.* gruta *f.,* cripta *f.*

cryptic, *a.* secreto.

cryptography, *n.* criptografía *f.*

crystal, *n.* cristal *m.*

crystalline, *a.* cristalino, transparente.

crystallize, *v.* cristalizar.

cub, *n.* cachorro *m.*

Cuban, *n. & a.* cubano -na.

cube, *n.* cubo *m.*

cubic, *a.* cúbico.

cubicle, *n.* cubículo *m.*

cubic measure, *n.* medida de capacidad *f.*

cubism, *n.* cubismo *m.*

cuckoo, *n.* cuco *m.*

cucumber, *n.* pepino *m.*

cuddle, *v.* abrazar.

cudgel, *n.* palo *m.*

cue, *n.* apunte *m.;* (billiards) taco *m.*

cuff, *n.* puño de camisa. c. links, gemelos.

cuisine, *n.* arte culinario *f.*

culinary, *a.* culinario.

culminate, *v.* culminar.

culmination, *n.* culminación *f.*

culpable, *a.* culpable.

culprit, *n.* criminal; delincuente *m.*

cult, *n.* culto *m.*

cultivate, *v.* cultivar.

cultivated, *a.* cultivado.

cultivation, *n.* cultivo *m.;* cultivación *f.*

cultivator, *n.* cultivador *m.*

cultural, *a.* cultural.

culture, *n.* cultura *f.*

cultured, *a.* culto.

cumbersome, *a.* pesado, incómodo.

cumulative, *a.* acumulativo.

cunning, 1. *a.* astuto. 2. *n.* astucia *f.*

cup, *n.* taza, jícara *f.*

cupboard, *n.* armario, aparador *m.*

cupidity, *n.* avaricia *f.*

curable, *a.* curable.

curator, *n.* guardián *m.*

curb, 1. *n.* freno *m.* 2. *v.* refrenar.

curd, *n.* cuajada *f.*

curdle, *v.* cuajarse, coagularse.

cure, 1. *n.* remedio *m.* 2. *v.* curar, sanar.

curfew, *n.* toque de queda *m.*

curio, *n.* objeto curioso.

curiosity, *n.* curiosidad *f.*

curious, *a.* curioso.

curl, 1. *n.* rizo *m.* 2. *v.* rizar.

curly, *a.* rizado.

currant, *n.* grosella *f.*

currency, *n.* circulación *f.;* dinero *m.*

current, *a. & n.* corriente *f.*

currently, *adv.* corrientemente.

curriculum, *n.* plan de estudio *m.*

curse, 1. *n.* maldición *f.* 2. *v.* maldecir.

cursory, *a.* sumario.

curt, *a.* brusco.

curtail, *v.* reducir; restringir.

curtain, *n.* cortina *f.;* (theat.) telón *m.*

curtsy, 1. *n.* reverencia *f.* **2.** *v.* hacer una reverencia.

curvature, *n.* curvatura *f.*

curve, 1. *n.* curva *f.* **2.** *v.* encorvar.

cushion, *n.* cojín *m.;* almohada *f.*

cuspidor, *n.* escupidera *f.*

custard, *n.* flan *m.;* natillas *f.pl.*

custodian, *n.* custodio *m.*

custody, *n.* custodia *f.*

custom, *n.* custumbre *f.*

customary, *a.* acostumbrado, usual.

customer, *n.* cliente *m. & f.*

customhouse, customs, *n.* aduana *f.*

cut, 1. *n.* corte *m.;* cortada *f.;* tajada *f.;* (printing) grabado *m.* **2.** *v.* cortar; tajar.

cute, *a.* mono, lindo.

cut glass, *n.* cristal tallado *m.*

cuticle, *n.* cutícula *f.*

cutlery, *n.* cuchillería *f.*

cutlet, *n.* coteleta, chuleta *f.*

cutter, *n.* cortador -ra; (naut.) cúter *m.*

cutthroat, *n.* asesino *m.*

cyclamate, *n.* ciclamato *m.*

cycle, *n.* ciclo *m.*

cyclist, *n.* ciclista *m. & f.*

cyclone, *n.* ciclón, huracán *m.*

cyclotron, *n.* ciclotrón *m.*

cylinder, *n.* cilindro *m.*

cylindrical, *a.* cilíndrico.

cymbal, *n.* címbalo *m.*

cynic, *n.* cínico *m.*

cynical, *a.* cínico.

cynicism, *n.* cinismo *m.*

cypress, *n.* ciprés *m.* **c. nut,** piñuela *f.*

cyst, *n.* quiste *m.*

D

dad, *n.* papa *m.,* papito *m.*

daffodil, *n.* narciso *m.*

dagger, *n.* puñal *m.*

dahlia, *n.* dalia *f.*

daily, *a.* diario, cotidiano.

daintiness, *n.* delicadeza *f.*

dainty, *a.* delicado.

dairy, *n.* lechería, quesería *f.*

dais, *n.* tablado *m.*

daisy, *n.* margarita *f.*

dale, *n.* valle *m.*

dally, *v.* holgar; perder el tiempo.

dam, *n.* presa *f.;* dique *m.*

damage, 1. *n.* daño *m.* **2.** *v.* dañar.

damask, *n.* damasco *m.*

damn, *v.* condenar.

damnation, *n.* condenación *f.*

damp, *a.* húmedo.

dampen, *v.* humedecer.

dampness, *n.* humedad *f.*

damsel, *n.* doncella *f.*

dance, 1. *n.* baile *m.;* danza *f.* **2.** *v.* bailar.

dancer, *n.* bailador -ra; (professional) bailarín -na.

dancing, *n.* baile *m.*

dandelion, *n.* amargón *m.*

dandruff, *n.* caspa *f.*

dandy, *n.* petimetre *m.*

danger, *n.* peligro *m.*

dangerous, *a.* peligroso.

dangle, *v.* colgar.

Danish, *a. & n.* danés -sa; dinamarqués -sa.

dapper, *a.* gallardo.

dare, *v.* atreverse, osar.

daredevil, *n.* atrevido *m,* -da *f.*

daring, 1. *a.* atrevido. **2.** *n.* osadía *f.*

dark, 1. *a.* obscuro; moreno. **2.** *n.* obscuridad *f.*

darken, *v.* obscurecer.

darkness, *n.* obscuridad *f.*

darkroom, *n.* cámara obscura *f.*

darling, *a. & n.* querido, amado.

darn, *v.* zurcir.

darning needle, *n.* agujar de zurcir *m.*

dart, *n.* dardo *m.*

dash, *n.* arranque *m.;* (punct.) guión *m.*

data, *n.* datos *m.*

data processing, proceso de datos *m.*

date, *n.* fecha *f.;* (engagement) cita *f.;* (fruit) dátil *m.*

daughter, *n.* hija *f.*

daughter-in-law, *n.* nuera *f.*

daunt, *v.* intimidar.

dauntless, *a.* intrépido.

davenport, *n.* sofá *m.*

dawn, 1. *n.* alba, madrugada *f.* **2.** *v.* amanecer.

day, *n.* día *m.* **good d.,** buenos días.

daybreak, *n.* alba, madrugada *f.*

daydream, *n.* fantasía *f.*

daylight, *n.* luz del día.

daze, *v.* aturdir.

dazzle, *v.* deslumbrar.

deacon, *n.* diácono *m.*

dead, *a.* muerto.

deaden, *v.* amortecer.

deadline, *n.* límite absoluto *m.*

deadlock, *n.* paro *m.*

deadly, *a.* mortal.

deaf, *a.* sordo.

deafen, *v.* ensordecer.

deaf-mute, *n.* sordomudo *m.*

deafness, *n.* sordera *f.*

deal, 1. *n.* trato *m.;* negociación *f.* **a great d., a good d.,** mucho. **2.** *v.* tratar; negociar.

dealer, *n.* comerciante *m.,* (at cards) tallador -ra.

dean, *n.* decano *m.*

dear, *a.* querido; caro.

dearth, *n.* escasez *f.*

death, *n.* muerte *f.*

deathless, *a.* inmortal.

debacle, *n.* desastre *m.*

debase, *v.* degradar.

debatable, *a.* discutible.

debate, 1. *n.* debate *m.* **2.** *v.* disputar, deliberar.

debauch, *v.* corromper.

debilitate, *v.* debilitar.

debit, *n.* débito *m.*

debonair, *a.* cortés; alegre, vivo.

debris, *n.* escombros *m.pl.*

debt, *n.* deuda *f.*

debtor, *n.* deudor -ra.

debunk, *v.* traer a la realidad.

debut, *n.* debut, estreno *m.*

debutante, *n.* debutante *f.*

decade, *n.* década *f.*

decadence, *n.* decadencia *f.*

decadent, *a.* decadente.

decaffeinated, *a.* descafeinado.

decalcomania, *n.* calcomanía *f.*

decanter, *n.* garrafa *f.*

decapitate, *v.* descabezar.

decay, 1. *n.* descaecimiento *m.;* (dental) caries *f.* **2.** *v.* decaer; (dental) cariarse.

deceased, *a.* muerto, difunto.

deceit, *n.* engaño *m.*

deceitful, *a.* engañoso.

deceive, *v.* engañar.

December, *n.* diciembre *m.*

decency, *n.* decencia *f.;* decoro *m.*

decent, *a.* decente.

decentralize, *v.* descentralizar.

deception, *n.* decepción *f.*

deceptive, *a.* deceptivo.

decibel, *n.* decibelio *m.*

decide, *v.* decidir.

decimal, *a.* decimal.

decipher, *v.* descifrar.

decision, *n.* decisión *f.*

decisive, *a.* decisivo.

deck, *n.* cubierta *f.*

declamation, *n.* declamación *f.*

declaration, *n.* declaración *f.*

declarative, *a.* declarativo.

declare, *v.* declarar.

declension, *n.* declinación *f.*

decline, 1. *n.* decadencia *f.* **2.** *v.* decaer; negarse; (gram.) declinar.

decompose, *v.* descomponer.

decongestant, *n.* descongestionante *m.*

decorate, *v.* decorar, adornar.

decoration, *n.* decoración *f.*

decorative, *a.* decorativo.

decorator, *n.* decorador *m.*

decorous, *a.* correcto.

decorum, *n.* decoro *m.*

decrease, *v.* disminuir.

decree, *n.* decreto *m.*

decrepit, *a.* decrépito.

decry, *v.* descreditar.

dedicate, *v.* dedicar; consagrar.

dedication, *n.* dedicación; dedicatoria *f.*

deduce, deduct, *v.* deducir.

deduction, *n.* rebaja *f.*

deductive, *a.* deductivo.

deed, *n.* acción; hazaña *f.*

deem, *v.* estimar.

deep, *a.* hondo, profundo.

deepen, *v.* profundizar, ahondar.

deep freeze, *n.* congelación *f.*

deeply, *adv.* profundamente.

deer, *n.* venado, ciervo *m.*

deface, *v.* mutilar.

defamation, n. calumnia f.
defame, v. difamar.
default, 1. n. defecto m. 2. v. faltar.
defeat, 1. n. derrota f. 2. v. derrotar.
defect, n. defecto m.
defective, a. defectivo.
defend, v. defender.
defendant, n. acusado -da.
defender, n. defensor -ra.
defense, n. defensa f.
defensive, a. defensivo.
defer, v. aplazar; deferir.
deference, n. deferencia f.
defiance, n. desafío m.
defiant, a. desafiador.
deficiency, n. defecto m.
deficient, a. deficiente.
deficit, n. déficit, descubierto m.
defile, 1. n. desfiladero m. 2. v. profanar.
define, v. definir.
definite, a. exacto; definitivo.
definitely, adv. definidamente.
definition, n. definición f.
definitive, a. definitivo.
deflation, n. desinflación f.
deflect, v. desviar.
deform, v. deformar.
deformity, n. deformidad f.
defraud, v. defraudar.
defray, v. costear.
deft, a. diestro.
defy, v. desafiar.
degenerate, 1. a. degenerado. 2. v. degenerar.
degeneration, n. degeneración f.
degradation, n. degradación f.
degrade, v. degradar.
degree, n. grado m.
deign, v. condescender.
deity, n. deidad f.
dejected, a. abatido.
dejection, n. tristeza f.
delay, 1. n. retardo m., demora f. 2. v. tardar, demorar.
delegate, 1. n. delegado -da. 2. v. delegar.
delegation, n. delegación f.
delete, v. suprimir.
deliberate, 1. a. premeditado. 2. v. deliberar.
deliberately, adv. deliberadamente.
deliberation, n. deliberación f.
deliberative, a. deliberativo.
delicacy, n. delicadeza f.
delicate, a. delicado.
delicious, a. delicioso.
delight, n. deleite m.
delightful, a. deleitoso.
delinquency, n. delincuencia f.
delinquent, a. & n. delincuente.
delirious, a. delirante.
deliver, v. entregar.
deliverance, n. liberación; salvación f.
delivery, n. entrega f.; (med.) parto m.
delude, v. engañar.
deluge, n. inundación f.

delusion, n. decepción f.; engaño m.
delve, v. cavar, sondear.
demagogue, n. demagogo m.
demand, 1. n. demanda f. 2. v. demandar; exigir.
demarcation, n. demarcación f.
demeanor, n. conducta f.
demented, a. demente, loco.
demilitarize, v. desmilitarizar.
demobilize, v. desmovilizar.
democracy, n. democracia f.
democrat, n. demócrata m. & f.
democratic, a. democrático.
demolish, v. demoler.
demon, n. demonio m.
demonstrate, v. demostrar.
demonstration, n. demostración f.
demonstrative, a. demostrativo.
demoralize, v. desmoralizar.
demure, a. modesto, serio.
den, n. caverna f.; retrete m.
denature, v. alterar.
denial, n. negación f.
denim, n. tela para jeans, azul de Vergara.
Denmark, n. Dinamarca f.
denomination, n. denominación; secta f.
denote, v. denotar.
denounce, v. denunciar.
dense, a. denso, espeso; estúpido.
density, n. densidad f.
dent, 1. n. abolladura f. 2. v. abollar.
dental, a. dental.
dentist, n. dentista m.
dentistry, n. odontología f.
denture, n. dentadura f.
denunciation, n. denunciación f.
deny, v. negar, rehusar.
deodorant, n. desodorante m.
depart, v. partir; irse, marcharse.
department, n. departamento m.
departmental, a. departamental.
departure, n. salida; desviación f.
depend, v. depender.
dependability, n. confiabilidad f.
dependable, a. confiable.
dependence, n. dependencia f.
dependent, a. & n. dependiente m.
depict, v. pintar; representar.
deplete, v. agotar.
deplorable, a. deplorable.
deplore, v. deplorar.
deport, v. deportar.
deportation, n. deportación f.
deportment, n. conducta f.
depose, v. deponer.
deposit, 1. n. depósito m. 2. v. depositar.
depositor, n. depositante m. & f.
depot, n. depósito m.; (railway) estación f.

depravity, n. depravación f.
deprecate, v. deprecar.
depreciate, v. depreciar.
depreciation, n. depreciación f.
depredation, n. depredación f.
depress, v. deprimir; desanimar.
depression, n. depresión f.
deprive, v. privar.
depth, n. profundidad, hondura f.
depth charge, n. carga de profundidad f.
deputy, n. diputado m.
deride, v. burlar.
derision, n. burla f.
derivation, n. derivación f.
derivative, a. derivativo.
derive, v. derivar.
derogatory, a. derogatorio.
derrick, n. grúa f.
descend, v. descender, bajar.
descendant, n. descendiente m. & f.
descent, n. descenso m.; origen m.
describe, v. describir.
description, n. descripción f.
descriptive, a. descriptivo.
desecrate, v. profanar.
desert, 1. n. desierto m. 2. v. abandonar.
deserter, n. desertor m.
desertion, n. deserción f.
deserve, v. merecer.
design, 1. n. diseño m. 2. v. diseñar.
designate, v. señalar, apuntar.
designation, n. designación f.
designer, n. diseñador -ra; (technical) proyectista m. & f.
desirability, n. conveniencia f.
desirable, a. deseable.
desire, 1. n. deseo m. 2. v. desear.
desirous, a. deseoso.
desist, v. desistir.
desk, n. escritorio m.
desolate, 1. a. desolado. 2. v. desolar.
desolation, n. desolación, ruina f.
despair, 1. n. desesperación f. 2. v. desesperar.
despatch, dispatch, 1. n. despacho m.; prontitud f. 2. v. despachar.
desperado, n. bandido m.
desperate, a. desesperado.
desperation, n. desesperación f.
despicable, a. vil.
despise, v. despreciar.
despite, prep. a pesar de.
despondent, a. abatido; desanimado.
despot, n. déspota m.
despotic, a. despótico.
dessert, n. postre m.
destination, n. destinación f.
destine, v. destinar.
destiny, n. destino m.
destitute, a. destituido.
destitution, n. destitución f.
destroy, v. destrozar, destruir.

destroyer, *n.* destruidor *m.*; (naval) destróyer *m.*
destruction, *n.* destrucción *f.*
destructive, *a.* destructivo.
desultory, *a.* inconexo; casual.
detach, *v.* separar, desprender.
detachment, *n.* (mil.) destacamento *m.*
detail, 1. *n.* detalle *m.* 2. *v.* detallar.
detain, *v.* detener.
detect, *v.* descubrir.
detection, *n.* detección *f.*
detective, *n.* detective *m.*
detente, *n.* détente *f.*
detention, *n.* detención; cautividad *f.*
deter, *v.* disuadir.
detergent, *n. & a.* detergente *m.*
deteriorate, *v.* deteriorar.
deterioration, *n.* deterioración *f.*
determination, *n.* determinación *f.*
determine, *v.* determinar.
deterrence, *n.* disuasión *f.*
detest, *v.* detestar.
detonate, *v.* detonar.
detour, *n.* desvío *m.*
detract, *v.* disminuir.
detriment, *n.* detrimento *m.*, daño *m.*
detrimental, *a.* dañoso.
devaluate, *v.* depreciar.
devastate, *v.* devastar.
develop, *v.* desarrollar; (phot.) revelar.
developing nation, nación en desarrollo.
development, *n.* desarrollo *m.*
deviate, *v.* desviar.
deviation, *n.* desviación *f.*
device, *n.* aparato; artificio *m.*
devil, *n.* diablo, demonio *m.*
devious, *a.* desviado.
devise, *v.* inventar.
devoid, *a.* desprovisto.
devote, *v.* dedicar, consagrar.
devoted, *a.* devoto.
devotee, *n.* aficionado *m.*
devotion, *n.* devoción *f.*
devour, *v.* devorar.
devout, *a.* devoto.
dew, *n.* rocío, sereno *m.*
dexterity, *n.* destreza *f.*
dexterous, *a.* diestro.
diabetes, *n.* diabetes *f.*
diabolic, *a.* diabólico.
diadem, *n.* diadema *f.*
diagnose, *v.* diagnosticar.
diagnosis, *n.* diagnóstico *m.*
diagonal, *n.* diagonal *f.*
diagram, *n.* diagrama *m.*
dial, *n.* cuadrante *m.*, carátula *f.*
dialect, *n.* dialecto *m.*
dialogue, *n.* diálogo *m.*
diameter, *n.* diámetro *m.*
diamond, *n.* diamante, brillante *m.*
diaper, *n.* pañal *m.*
diarrhea, *n.* diarrea *f.*
diary, *n.* diario *m.*
diathermy, *n.* diatermia *f.*

dice, *n.* dados *m.pl.*
dictate, 1. *n.* dictamen *m.* 2. *v.* dictar.
dictation, *n.* dictado *m.*
dictator, *n.* dictador *m.*
dictatorship, *n.* dictadura *f.*
diction, *n.* dicción *f.*
dictionary, *n.* diccionario *m.*
die, 1. *n.* matriz *f.*; (game) dado *m.* 2. *v.* morir.
diet, *n.* dieta *f.*
dietary, *a.* dietético.
dietitian, *n.* dietista *m. & f.*
differ, *v.* diferir.
difference, *n.* diferencia *f.* **to make no d.**, no importar.
different, *a.* diferente, distinto.
differential, *n.* diferencial *f.*
differentiate, *v.* diferenciar.
difficult, *a.* difícil.
difficulty, *n.* dificultad *f.*
diffident, *a.* tímido.
diffuse, *v.* difundir.
diffusion, *n.* difusión *f.*
dig, *v.* cavar.
digest, 1. *n.* extracto *m.* 2. *v.* digerir.
digestible, *a.* digerible.
digestion, *n.* digestión *f.*
digestive, *a.* digestivo.
digital, *a.* digital.
digitalis, *n.* digital *f.*
dignified, *a.* digno.
dignify, *v.* dignificar.
dignitary, *n.* dignatario *m.*
dignity, *n.* dignidad *f.*
digress, *v.* divagar.
digression, *n.* digresión *f.*
dike, *n.* dique *m.*
dilapidated, *a.* dilapidado.
dilapidation, *n.* dilapidación *f.*
dilate, *v.* dilatar.
dilatory, *a.* dilatorio.
dilemma, *n.* dilema *m.*
dilettante, *n.* diletante *m. & f.*
diligence, *n.* diligencia *f.*
diligent, *a.* diligente, aplicado.
dilute, *v.* diluir.
dim, 1. *a.* oscuro. 2. *v.* oscurecer.
dimension, *n.* dimensión *f.*
diminish, *v.* disminuir.
diminution, *n.* disminución *f.*
diminutive, *a.* diminutivo.
dimness, *n.* oscuridad *f.*
dimple, *n.* hoyuelo *m.*
din, *n.* alboroto *m.*
dine, *v.* comer, cenar.
diner, *n.* coche comedor *m.*
dingy, *a.* deslucido, deslustrado.
dinner, *n.* comida, cena *f.*
dinosaur, *n.* dinosauro *m.*
diocese, *n.* diócesis *m.*
dip, *v.* sumergir, hundir.
diphtheria, *n.* difteria *f.*
diploma, *n.* diploma *m.*
diplomacy, *n.* diplomacia *f.*
diplomat, *n.* diplomático *m.*
diplomatic, *a.* diplomático.
dipper, *n.* cucharón *m.*
dire, *a.* horrendo.
direct, 1. *a.* directo. 2. *v.* dirigir.
direction, *n.* dirección *f.*

directive, *n.* directivo *m.*
directly, *adv.* directamente.
director, *n.* director -ra.
directory, *n.* directorio *m.*, guía *f.*
dirigible, *n.* dirigible *m.*
dirt, *n.* basura *f.*; (earth) tierra *f.*
dirty, *a.* sucio.
disability, *n.* inhabilidad *f.*; invalidez *m.*
disable, *v.* incapacitar.
disabuse, *v.* desengañar.
disadvantage, *n.* desventaja *f.*
disagree, *v.* desconvenir; disentir.
disagreeable, *a.* desagradable.
disagreement, *n.* desacuerdo *m.*
disappear, *v.* desaparecer.
disappearance, *n.* desaparición *f.*
disappoint, *v.* disgustar, desilusionar.
disappointment, *n.* disgusto *m.*, desilusión *f.*
disapproval, *n.* desaprobación *f.*
disapprove, *v.* desaprobar.
disarm, *v.* desarmar.
disarmament, *n.* desarme *m.*
disarrange, *v.* desordenar; desarreglar.
disaster, *n.* desastre *m.*
disastrous, *a.* desastroso.
disavow, *v.* repudiar.
disavowal, *n.* repudiación *f.*
disband, *v.* dispersarse.
disbelieve, *v.* descreer.
disburse, *v.* desembolsar, pagar.
discard, *v.* descartar.
discern, *v.* discernir.
discerning, *a.* discernidor, perspicaz.
discernment, *n.* discernimiento *m.*
discharge, *v.* descargar; despedir.
disciple, *n.* discípulo *m.*
disciplinary, *a.* disciplinario.
discipline, *n.* disciplina *f.*
disclaim, *v.* repudiar.
disclaimer, *n.* negador *m.*
disclose, *v.* revelar.
disclosure, *n.* descubrimiento *m.*
disco, *n.* discoteca *f.*
discolor, *v.* descolorar.
discomfort, *n.* incomodidad *f.*
disconcert, *v.* desconcertar.
disconnect, *v.* desunir; desconectar.
disconnected, *a.* desunido.
disconsolate, *a.* desconsolado.
discontent, *n.* descontento *m.*
discontented, *a.* descontento.
discontinue, *v.* descontinuar.
discord, *n.* discordia *f.*
discordant, *a.* disonante.
discotheque, *n.* discoteca *f.*
discount, *n.* descuento *m.*
discourage, *v.* desalentar, desanimar.

discouragement, *n.* desaliento, desánimo *m.*

discourse, *n.* discurso *m.*

discourteous, *a.* descortés.

discourtesy, *n.* descortesía *f.*

discover, *v.* descubrir.

discoverer, *n.* descubridor -ra.

discovery, *n.* descubrimiento *m.*

discreet, *a.* discreto.

discrepancy, *n.* discrepancia *f.*

discretion, *n.* discreción *f.*

discriminate, *v.* distinguir; diferenciar parcialmente.

discrimination, *n.* discernimiento *m.;* discriminación *f.*

discuss, *v.* discutir.

discussion, *n.* discusión *f.*

disdain, 1. *n.* desdén *m.* 2. *v.* desdeñar.

disdainful, *a.* desdeñoso.

disease, *n.* enfermedad *f.,* mal *m.*

disembark, *v.* desembarcar.

disentangle, *v.* desenredar.

disfigure, *v.* desfigurar.

disgrace, 1. *n.* vergüenza; deshonra *f.* 2. *v.* deshonrar.

disgraceful, *a.* vergonzoso.

disguise, 1. *n.* disfraz *m.* 2. *v.* disfrazar.

disgust, 1. *n.* fastidio *m.* 2. *v.* fastidiar.

dish, *n.* plato *m.*

dishearten, *v.* desanimar; descorazonar.

dishonest, *a.* deshonesto.

dishonesty, *n.* deshonestidad *f.*

dishonor, 1. *n.* deshonra *f.* 2. *v.* deshonrar.

dishonorable, *a.* deshonroso.

disillusion, 1. *n.* desengaño *m.* 2. *v.* desengañar.

disinfect, *v.* desinfectar.

disinfectant, *n.* desinfectante *m.*

disinherit, *v.* desheredar.

disintegrate, *v.* desintegrar.

disinterested, *a.* desinteresado.

disk, *n.* disco *m.*

dislike, 1. *n.* antipatía *f.* 2. *v.* no gustar de.

dislocate, *v.* dislocar.

dislodge, *v.* desalojar.

disloyal, *a.* desleal; infiel.

disloyalty, *n.* deslealtad *f.*

dismal, *a.* lúgubre.

dismantle, *v.* desmantelar.

dismay, 1. *n.* consternación *f.* 2. *v.* consternar.

dismiss, *v.* despedir.

dismissal, *n.* despedida *f.*

dismount, *v.* apearse.

disobedience, *n.* desobediencia *f.*

disobedient, *a.* desobediente.

disobey, *v.* desobedecer.

disorder, *n.* desorden *m.*

disorderly, *a.* desarreglado, desordenado.

disown, *v.* repudiar.

dispassionate, *a.* desapasionado; templado.

dispatch, 1. *n.* despacho *m.* 2. *v.* despachar.

dispel, *v.* despersar.

dispensary, *n.* dispensario *m.*

dispensation, *n.* dispensación *f.*

dispense, *v.* dispensar.

dispersal, *n.* dispersión *f.*

disperse, *v.* dispersar.

displace, *v.* dislocar.

display, 1. *n.* despliegue *m.,* exhibición *f.* 2. desplegar, exhibir.

displease, *v.* disgustar; ofender.

displeasure, *n.* disgusto, sinsabor *m.*

disposable, *a.* disponible.

disposal, *n.* disposición *f.*

dispose, *v.* disponer.

disposition, *n.* disposición *f.;* índole *f.,* genio *m.*

dispossess, *v.* desposeer.

disproportionate, *a.* desproporcionado.

disprove, *v.* confutar.

dispute, 1. *n.* disputa *f.* 2. *v.* disputar.

disqualify, *v.* inhabilitar.

disregard, 1. *n.* desatención *f.* 2. *v.* desatender.

disrepair, *n.* descompostura *f.*

disreputable, *a.* desacreditado.

disrespect, *n.* falta de respecto.

disrespectful, *a.* irrespetuoso.

disrobe, *v.* desvestir.

disrupt, *v.* romper; desbaratar.

dissatisfaction, *n.* descontento *m.*

dissatisfy, *v.* descontentar.

dissect, *v.* disecar.

dissemble, *v.* disimular.

disseminate, *v.* diseminar.

dissension, *n.* disensión *f.*

dissent, 1. *n.* disensión *f.* 2. *v.* disentir.

dissertation, *n.* disertación *f.*

dissimilar, *a.* desemejante.

dissipate, *v.* disipar.

dissipation, *n.* disipación *f.;* libertinaje *m.*

dissolute, *a.* disoluto.

dissolution, *n.* disolución *f.*

dissolve, *v.* disolver; derretirse.

dissonant, *a.* disonante.

dissuade, *v.* disuadir.

distance, *n.* distancia *f.* **at a d., in the d.,** a lo lejos.

distant, *a.* distante, lejano.

distaste, *n.* disgusto, sinsabor *m.*

distasteful, *a.* desagradable.

distill, *v.* destilar.

distillation, *n.* destilación *f.*

distillery, *n.* destilería *f.*

distinct, *a.* distinto.

distinctive, *a.* distintivo; característico.

distinctly, *adv.* distintamente.

distinction, *n.* distinción *f.*

distinguish, *v.* distinguir.

distinguished, *a.* distinguido.

distort, *v.* falsear; torcer.

distract, *v.* distraer.

distraction, *n.* distracción *f.*

distraught, *a.* aturrullado; demente.

distress, 1. *n.* dolor *m.* 2. *v.* afligir.

distribute, *v.* distribuir.

distribution, *n.* distribución *f.,* reparto *m.*

distributor, *n.* distribuidor -ra.

district, *n.* distrito *m.*

distrust, 1. *n.* desconfianza *f.* 2. *v.* desconfiar.

distrustful, *a.* desconfiado; sospechoso.

disturb, *v.* incomodar; inquietar.

disturbance, *n.* disturbio *m.*

ditch, *n.* zanja *f.;* foso *m.*

divan, *n.* diván *m.*

dive, 1. *n.* clavado *m.;* (coll.) leonera *f.* 2. *v.* echar un clavado; bucear.

diver, *n.* buzo *m.*

diverge, *v.* divergir.

divergence, *n.* divergencia *f.*

divergent, *a.* divergente.

diverse, *a.* diverso.

diversion, *n.* diversión *f.;* pasatiempo *m.*

diversity, *n.* diversidad *f.*

divert, *v.* desviar; divertir.

divest, *v.* desnudar, despojar.

divide, *v.* dividir.

dividend, *n.* dividendo *m.*

divine, *a.* divino.

divinity, *n.* divinidad *f.*

division, *n.* división *f.*

divorce, 1. *n.* divorcio *m.* 2. *v.* divorciar.

divorcee, *n.* divorciada *f.*

divulge, *v.* divulgar, revelar.

dizziness, *n.* vértigo, mareo *m.*

dizzy, *a.* mareado.

do, *v.* hacer.

docile, *a.* dócil.

dock, 1. *n.* muelle *m.* **dry d.,** astillero *m.* 2. *v.* entrar en muelle.

doctor, *n.* médico *m.;* doctor -ra.

doctrine, *n.* doctrina *f.*

document, *n.* documento *m.*

documentary, *a.* documental.

documentation, *n.* documentación *f.*

dodge, 1. *n.* evasión *f.* 2. *v.* evadir.

doe, *n.* gama *f.*

dog, *n.* perro *m.*

dogma, *n.* dogma *m.*

dogmatic, *a.* dogmático.

dogmatism, *n.* dogmatismo *m.*

doily, *n.* servilletita *f.*

doleful, *a.* triste.

doll, *n.* muñeca *f.*

dollar, *n.* dólar *m.*

dolorous, *a.* lastimoso.

dolphin, *n.* delfín *m.*

domain, *n.* dominio *m.*

dome, *n.* domo *m.*

domestic, *a.* doméstico.

domesticate, *v.* domesticar.

domicile, *n.* domicilio *m.*

dominance, *n.* dominación *f.*

dominant, *a.* dominante.

dominate, *v.* dominar.

domination, *n.* dominación *f.*

domineer, *v.* dominar.

domineering, *a.* tiránico, mandón.

dominion, n. dominio; territorio m.

domine, n. dominó m.

donate, v. donar; contribuir.

donation, n. donación f.

donkey, n. asno, burro m.

doom, 1. n. perdición, ruina f. 2. v. perder, ruinar.

door, n. puerta f.

doorman, n. portero m.

doorway, n. entrada f.

dope, n. narcótico m.

dormant, a. durmiente.

dormitory, n. dormitorio m.

dosage, n. dosificación f.

dose, n. dosis f.

dot, n. punto m.

double, 1. a. doble. 2. v. duplicar.

double-breasted, a. cruzado.

double-cross, v. traicionar.

doubly, adv. doblemente.

doubt, 1. n. duda f. 2. v. dudar.

doubtful, a. dudoso, incierto.

doubtless, 1. a. indudable. 2. adv. sin duda.

dough, n. pasta, masa f.

doughnut, n. buñuelo m.

dove, n. paloma f.

dowager, n. viuda f.

down, 1. adv. abajo. 2. prep. d. the street, etc. calle abajo, etc.

downcast, a. cabizbajo.

downfall, n. ruina, perdición f.

downhearted, a. descorazonado.

downpour, n. chaparrón m.

downright, a. absoluto, completo.

downstairs, 1. adv. abajo. 2. n. primer piso.

downtown, adv. al centro, en el centro.

downward, 1. a. descendente. 2. adv. hacia abajo.

dowry, n. dote m.

doze, v. dormitar.

dozen, n. docena f.

draft, 1. n. dibujo m.; (com.) giro m.; (mil.) conscripción f. 2. v. dibujar; (mil.) reclutar.

draftee, n. conscripto m.

drag, v. arrastrar.

dragon, n. dragón m.

drain, 1. n. desaguadero m. 2. v. desaguar.

drainage, n. drenaje m.

drama, n. drama m.

dramatic, a. dramático.

dramatics, n. dramática f.

dramatist, n. dramaturgo m.

dramatize, v. dramatizar.

drape, n. cortina f.

drapery, n. colgaduras f.pl.; ropaje m.

drastic, a. drástico.

draw, v. dibujar; atraer. d. up, formular.

drawback, n. desventaja f.

drawer, n. cajón m.

drawing, n. dibujo m.; rifa f.

dread, 1. n. terror m. 2. v. temer.

dreadful, a. terrible.

dreadfully, adv. horrendamente.

dream, 1. n. sueño, ensueño m. 2. v. soñar.

dreamer, n. soñador -ra; visionario -ia.

dreamy, a. soñador, contemplativo.

dreary, a. monótono y pesado.

dredge, 1. n. rastra f. 2. v. rastrear.

dregs, n. sedimento m.

drench, v. mojar.

dress, 1. n. vestido; traje m. 2. v. vestir.

dresser, n. (furniture) tocador.

dressing, n. (med.) curación f.; (cookery) condimento, relleno m.

dressing gown, n. batá f.

dressmaker, n. modista m. & f.

drift, 1. n. tendencia f.; (naut.) deriva f. 2. v. (naut.) derivar; (snow) amontonarse.

drill, 1. n. ejercicio m.; (mech.) taladro m. 2. v. (mech.) taladrar.

drink, 1. n. bebida f. 2. v. beber, tomar.

drinkable, a. potable, bebible.

drip, v. gotear.

drive, 1. n. paseo m. 2. v. impeler; (auto.) guiar, conducir.

driver, n. chofer m.

driveway, n. entrada para coches.

drizzle, 1. n. llovizna f. 2. v. lloviznar.

dromedary, n. dromedario m.

droop, v. inclinarse.

drop, 1. n. gota f. 2. v. soltar; dejar, caer.

dropout, n. joven que abandona sus estudios.

dropper, n. cuentagotas f.

dropsy, n. hidropesía f.

drought, n. seca, sequía f.

drove, n. manada f.

drown, v. ahogar.

drowse, v. adormecer.

drowsiness, n. somnolencia f.

drowsy, a. soñoliento.

drudge, n. ganapán m.

drudgery, n. trabajo penoso.

drug, 1. n. droga f. 2. v. narcotizar.

druggist, n. farmacéutico, boticario m.

drugstore, n. farmacia, botica, droguería f.

drum, n. tambor m.

drummer, n. tambor m.

drumstick, n. palillo m.; (leg) pierna f.

drunk, a. & n. borracho.

drunkard, n. borrachón m.

drunken, a. borracho; ebrio.

drunkenness, n. embriaguez f.

dry, 1. a. seco, árido. 2. v. secar.

dry cell, n. pila seca f.

dry-cleaner, n. tintorero m.

dryness, n. sequedad f.

dual, a. doble.

dubious, a. dudoso.

duchess, n. duquesa f.

duck, 1. n. pato m. 2. v. zabullir; (avoid) esquivar.

duct, n. canal m.

due, 1. a. debido; (com.) vencido. 2. dues, n. cuota f.

duel, n. duelo m.

duelist, n. duelista m.

duet, n. dúo m.

duke, n. duque m.

dull, a. apagado, desteñido; sin punta; (fig.) pesado, soso.

dullness, n. estupidez; pesadez f.; deslustre m.

duly, adv. debidamente.

dumb, a. mudo; (coll.) estúpido.

dumbwaiter, n. montaplatos m.

dumfound, v. confundir.

dummy, n. figurón m.

dump, 1. n. depósito m. 2. v. descargar.

dune, n. duna f.

dungeon, n. calabozo m.

dunk, v. mojar.

dupe, v. engañar.

duplicate, 1. a. & n. duplicado m. 2. v. duplicar.

duplication, n. duplicación f.

duplicity, n. duplicidad f.

durability, n. durabilidad f.

durable, a. durable, duradero.

duration, n. duración f.

duress, n. compulsión m.; encierro m.

during, prep. durante.

dusk, n. crepúsculo m.

dusky, a. oscuro; moreno.

dust, 1. n. polvo m. 2. v. polvorear; despolvorear.

dusty, a. empolvado.

Dutch, a. holandés -sa.

dutiful, a. respetuoso.

dutifully, adv. respetuosamente, obedientemente.

duty, n. deber m.; (com.) derechos m.pl.

duty-free, a. libre de derechos.

dwarf, 1. n. enano -na. 2. v. achicar.

dwell, v. habitar, residir. d. on, espaciarse en.

dwelling, n. morada, casa f.

dwindle, v. disminuirse.

dye, 1. n. tintura f. 2. v. teñir.

dyer, n. tintorero -ra.

dynamic, a. dinámico.

dynamite, n. dinamita f.

dynamo, n. dínamo m.

dynasty, n. dinastía f.

dysentery, n. disentería f.

dyslexia, n. dislexia f.

dyspepsia, n. dispepsia f.

E

each, 1. a. cada. 2. pron. cada uno -na. e. other, el uno al otro.

eager, a. ansioso.

eagerly, adv. ansiosamente.

eagerness, n. ansia f.

eagle, n. águila f.

ear, n. oído m.; (outer) oreja f.; (of corn) mazorca f.
earache, n. dolor de oído m.
earl, n. conde m.
early, a. & adv. temprano.
earn, v. ganar.
earnest, a. serio.
earnestly, adv. seriamente.
earnings, n. ganancias f.pl.; (com.) ingresos m.pl.
earphone, n. auricular m.
earring, n. pendiente, arete m.
earth, n. tierra f.
earthquake, n. terremoto m.
ease, 1. n. reposo m.; facilidad f. 2. v. aliviar.
easel, n. caballete m.
easily, adv. fácilmente.
east, n. oriente, este m.
Easter, n. Pascua Florida.
eastern, a. oriental.
eastward, adv. hacia el este.
easy, a. fácil.
eat, v. comer.
eaves, n. socarrén m.
ebb, 1. n. menguante f. 2. v. menguar.
ebony, n. ébano m.
eccentric, a. excéntrico.
eccentricity, n. excentricidad f.
ecclesiastic, a. & n. eclesiástico. m.
ecclesiastical, a. eclasiástico.
echelon, n. escalón m.
echo, n. eco m.
eclipse, 1. n. eclipse m. 2. v. eclipsar.
ecological, a. ecológico.
ecology, n. ecología f.
economic, a. económico.
economical, a. económico.
economics, n. economía política.
economist, n. economista m.
economize, v. economizar.
economy, n. economía f.
ecstasy, n. éxtasis m.
Ecuadorian, a. & n. ecuatoriano -na.
ecumenical, a. ecuménico.
eczema, n. eczema f.
eddy, 1. n. remolino m. 2. v. remolinar.
edge, 1. n. filo; borde m. 2. v. e. one's way, abrirse paso.
edible, a. comestible.
edict, n. edicto m.
edifice, n. edificio m.
edify, v. edificar.
edition, n. edición f.
editor, n. redactor m.
editorial, a. editorial m. e. staff, redacción f.
educate, v. educar.
education, n. instrucción; enseñanza f.
educational, a. educativo.
educator, n. educador, pedagogo m.
eel, n. anguila f.
efface, v. tachar.
effect, 1. n. efecto m. in e., en vigor. 2. v. efectuar, realizar.
effective, a. eficaz; efectivo; en vigor.

effectively, adv. eficazmente.
effectiveness, n. efectividad f.
effectual, a. eficaz.
effeminate, a. afeminado.
efficacy, n. eficacia f.
efficiency, n. eficiencia f.
efficient, a. eficaz.
efficiently, adv. eficazmente.
effigy, n. efigie m.
effort, n. esfuerzo m.
effrontery, n. impudencia f.
effusive, a. expansivo.
egg, n. huevo m. fried e., huevo frito. soft-boiled e., h. pasado por agua. scrambled eggs, huevos revueltos.
eggplant, n. berenjena f.
egoism, egotism, n. egoísmo m.
egoist, egotist, n. egoísta m. & f.
egotism, n. egotismo m.
egotist, n. egotista m.
Egypt, n. Egipto m.
Egyptian, a. & n. egipcio -ia.
eight, a. & pron. ocho.
eighteen, a. & pron. dieciocho.
eighth, a. octavo.
eightieth, n. octogésimo m.
eighty, a. & pron. ochenta.
either, 1. a. & pron. cualquiera de los dos. 2. adv. tampoco. 3. conj. either . . . or, o . . . o.
ejaculate, v. exclamar.
eject, v. expeler.
ejection, n. expulsión f.
elaborate, 1. a. elaborado. 2. v. elaborar; ampliar.
elapse, v. transcurrir; pasar.
elastic, a. & n. elástico m.
elasticity, n. elasticidad f.
elate, v. exaltar.
elation, n. exaltación f.
elbow, n. codo m.
elder, 1. a. mayor. 2. n. anciano m.
elderly, a. de edad.
eldest, a. mayor.
elect, v. elegir.
election, n. elección f.
elective, a. electivo.
electorate, n. electorado m.
electric, electrical, a. eléctrico.
electrician, n. electricista m.
electricity, n. electricidad f.
electrocardiogram, n. electrocardiograma m.
electrocute, v. electrocutar.
electrode, n. electrodo m.
electrolysis, n. electrólisis f.
electron, n. electrón m.
electronics, n. electrónica f.
elegance, n. elegancia f.
elegant, a. elegante.
elegy, n. elegía f.
element, n. elemento m.
elemental, a. elemental.
elementary, a. elemental.
elephant, n. elefante m.
elevate, v. elevar.
elevation, n. elevación f.
elevator, n. ascensor m.
eleven, a. & pron. once.
eleventh, a. undécimo.
elf, n. duende m.
elicit, v. sacar; despertar.

eligibility, n. elegibilidad f.
eligible, a. elegible.
eliminate, v. eliminar.
elimination, n. eliminación f.
elixir, n. elixir m.
elk, n. alce m., anta f.
elm, n. olmo m.
elocution, n. elocución f.
elongate, v. alargar.
elope, v. fugarse.
eloquence, n. elocuencia f.
eloquent, a. elocuente.
eloquently, adv. elocuentemente.
else, adv. más. someone e., otra persona. something e., otra cosa. or e., de otro modo.
elsewhere, adv. en otra parte.
elucidate, v. elucidar.
elude, v. eludir.
elusive, a. evasivo.
emaciated, a. enflaquecido.
emanate, v. emanar.
emancipate, v. emancipar.
emancipation, n. emancipación f.
emancipator, n. libertador m.
embalm, v. embalsamar.
embankment, n. malecón, dique m.
embargo, n. embargo m.
embark, v. embarcar.
embarrass, v. avergonzar; turbar.
embarrassing, a. penoso, vergonzoso.
embarrassment, n. turbación; vergüenza f.
embassy, n. embajada f.
embellish, v. hermosear, embellecer.
embellishment, n. embellecimiento m.
embezzle, v. apropiarse dinero ilícitamente.
emblem, n. emblema m.
embody, v. incorporar.
embrace, 1. n. abrazo m. 2. v. abrazar.
embroider, v. bordar.
embroidery, n. bordado m.
embryo, n. embrión m.
embryonic, a. embrionario.
emerald, n. esmeralda f.
emerge, v. salir.
emergency, n. emergencia f.
emergent, a. emergente.
emery, n. esmeril m.
emetic, n. emético m.
emigrant, a. & n. emigrante m. & f.
emigrate, v. emigrar.
emigration, n. emigración f.
eminence, n. altura; eminencia f.
eminent, a. eminente.
emissary, n. emisario m.
emission, n. emisión f.
emit, v. emitir.
emolument, n. emolumento m.
emotion, n. emoción f.
emotional, a. sensible.
emperor, n. emperador m.
emphasis, n. énfasis m. or f.

emphasize, v. acentuar, recalcar.

emphatic, a. enfático.

empire, n. imperio m.

empirical, a. empírico.

employ, v. emplear.

employee, n. empleado -da.

employer, n. patrón -ona.

employment, n. empleo m.

empower, v. autorizar.

emptiness, n. vaciedad; futilidad f.

empty, 1. a. vacío. 2. v. vaciar.

emulate, v. emular.

emulsion, n. emulsión f.

enable, v. capacitar; permitir.

enact, v. promulgar, decretar.

enactment, n. ley f., estatuto m.

enamel, 1. n. esmalte m. 2. v. esmaltar.

enamored, a. enamorado.

enchant, v. encantar.

enchantment, n. encanto m.

encircle, v. circundar.

enclose, v. encerrar. **enclosed,** (in letter) adjunto.

enclosure, n. recinto m.; (in letter) incluso m.

encompass, v. circundar.

encounter, 1. n. encuentro m. 2. v. encontrar.

encourage, v. animar.

encouragement, n. estímulo m.

encroach, v. usurpar; meterse.

encyclical, n. encíclica f.

encyclopedia, n. enciclopedia f.

end, 1. n. fin, término, cabo; extremo; (aim) propósito m. 2. v. acabar; terminar.

endanger, v. poner en peligro.

endear, v. hacer querer.

endeavor, 1. n. esfuerzo m. 2. v. esforzarse.

ending, n. conclusión f.

endless, a. sin fin.

endorse, v. endosar; apoyar.

endorsement, n. endoso m.

endow, v. dotar, fundar.

endowment, n. dotación f., fundación f.

endurance, n. resistencia f.

endure, v. soportar, resistir, aguantar.

enema, n. enema; lavativa f.

enemy, n. enemigo -ga.

energetic, a. enérgico.

energy, n. energía f.

enervate, v. enervar.

enervation, n. enervación f.

enfold, v. envolver.

enforce, v. ejecutar.

enforcement, n. ejecución f.

engage, v. emplear; ocupar.

engaged, (to marry) comprometido.

engagement, n. combate; compromiso; contrato m.; cita f.

engine, n. máquina f. (railroad) locomotora f.

engineer, n. ingeniero; maquinista m.

engineering, n. ingeniería f.

England, n. Inglaterra f.

English, a. & n. inglés m.

Englishman, n. inglés m.

Englishwoman, n. inglesa f.

engrave, v. grabar.

engraver, n. grabador m.

engraving, n. grabado m.

engross, v. absorber.

enhance, v. aumentar en valor; realzar.

enigma, n. enigma f.

enigmatic, a. enigmático.

enjoy, v. gozar de; disfrutar de. **e. oneself,** divertirse.

enjoyable, a. agradable.

enjoyment, n. goce m.

enlarge, v. agrandar; ampliar.

enlargement, n. ensanchamiento m., ampliación f.

enlarger, n. amplificador m.

enlighten, v. informar.

enlightenment, n. esclarecimiento m.; cultura f.

enlist, v. reclutar; alistarse.

enlistment, n. alistamiento m.

enliven, v. avivar.

enmesh, v. entrampar.

enmity, n. enemistad f.

enormity, v. enormidad f.

enormous, a. enorme.

enough, a. & adv. bastante. **to be e.,** bastar.

enrage, v. enfurecer.

enrich, v. enriquecer.

enroll, v. registrar; matricularse.

enrollment, n. matriculación f.

ensign, n. bandera f.; (naval) sub-teniente m.

enslave, v. esclavizar.

ensue, v. seguir, resultar.

entail, v. envolver.

entangle, v. enredar.

enter, v. entrar.

enterprise, n. empresa f.

enterprising, a. emprendedor.

entertain, v. entretener; divertir.

entertainment, n. entretenimiento m.; diversión f.

enthrall, v. esclavizar.

enthusiasm, n. entusiasmo m.

enthusiast, n. entusiasta m. & f.

enthusiastic, a. entusiasmado.

entice, v. inducir.

entire, a. entero.

entirely, adv. enteramente.

entirety, n. totalidad f.

entitle, v. autorizar; (book) titular.

entity, n. entidad f.

entrails, n. entrañas f.pl.

entrance, n. entrada f.

entrant, n. competidor m.

entreat, v. rogar, suplicar.

entreaty, n. ruego m., súplica f.

entrench, v. atrincherar.

entrust, v. confiar.

entry, n. entrada f.; (com.) partida f.

enumerate, v. enumerar.

enumeration, n. enumeración f.

enunciate, v. enunciar.

enunciation, n. enunciación f.

envelop, v. envolver.

envelope, n. sobre m., cubierta f.

enviable, a. envidiable.

envious, a. envidioso.

environment, n. ambiente m.

environmentalist, n. activista ecológico, ecologista m.

environmental protection, protección del ambiente.

environs, n. alrededores m.

envoy, n. enviado m.

envy, 1. n. envidia f. 2. v. envidiar.

eon, n. eón m.

ephemeral, a. efímero.

epic, 1. a. épico. 2. n. epopeya f.

epicure, n. epicúreo m.

epidemic, 1. a. epidémico. 2. n. epidemia f.

epidermis, n. epidermis f.

epigram, n. epigrama m.

epilepsy, n. epilepsia f.

epilogue, n. epílogo m.

episode, n. episodio m.

epistle, n. epístola f.

epitaph, n. epitafio m.

epithet, n. epíteto m.

epitome, n. epítome m.

epoch, n. época, era f.

equal, 1. a. & n. igual m. 2. v. igualar; equivaler.

equality, n. igualdad f.

equalize, v. igualar.

equanimity, n. ecuanimidad f.

equate, v. igualar.

equation, n. ecuación f.

equator, n. ecuador m.

equatorial, n. & a. ecuatorial f.

equestrian, 1. n. jinete m. 2. a. ecuestre.

equilibrium, n. equilibrio m.

equinox, n. equinoccio m.

equip, v. equipar.

equipment, n. equipo m.

equitable, a. equitativo.

equity, n. equidad, justicia f.

equivalent, a. & n. equivalente m.

equivocal, a. equívoco, ambiguo.

era, n. era, época, edad f.

eradicate, v. extirpar.

erase, v. borrar.

eraser, n. borrador m.

erasure, n. borradura f.

erect, 1. a. derecho, erguido. 2. v. erigir.

erection, erectness, n. erección f.

ermine, n. armiño m.

erode, v. corroer.

erosion, n. erosión f.

erotic, a. erótico.

err, v. equivocarse.

errand, n. encargo, recado m.

errant, a. errante.

erratic, a. errático.

erroneous, a. erróneo.

error, n. error m.

erudite, a. erudito.

erudition, n. erudición f.

eruption, n. erupción, irrupción f.

escalate, v. realizar una escalada.

escalator, n. escalera mecánica f.

escapade, n. escapada; correría f.

escape, 1. n. fuga, huida f. fire e., escalera de salvamento. 2. v. escapar; fugarse.

eschew, v. evadir.

escort, 1. n. escolta f. 2. v. escoltar.

escrow, n. plica f.

escutcheon, n. escudo de armas m.

esophagus, n. esófago m.

esoteric, a. esotérico.

especially, adv. especialmente.

espionage, n. espionaje m.

essay, n. ensayo m.

essayist, n. ensayista.

essence, n. esencia f.; perfume m.

essential, a. esencial.

essentially, adv. esencialmente.

establish, v. establecer.

establishment, n. establecimiento m.

estate, n. estado m.; hacienda f.; bienes m.pl.

esteem, 1. n. estima f. 2. v. estimar.

estimable, a. estimable.

estimate, 1. n. cálculo; presupuesto m. 2. v. estimar.

estimation, n. estimación f.; cálculo m.

estrange, v. extrañar; enajenar.

estuary, n. estuario m.

etching, n. grabado al agua fuerte.

eternal, a. eterno.

eternity, n. eternidad f.

ether, n. éter m.

ethereal, a. etéreo.

ethical, a. ético.

ethics, n. ética f.

ethnic, a. étnico.

etiquette, n. etiqueta f.

etymology, n. etimología f.

eucalyptus, n. eucalipto m.

eugenic, a. eugenésico.

eugenics, n. eugenesia f.

eulogize, v. elogiar.

eulogy, n. elogio m.

eunuch, n. eunuco m.

euphonious, a. eufónico.

Europe, n. Europa f.

European, a. & n. europeo pea.

euthanasia, n. eutanasia f.

evacuate, v. evacuar.

evade, v. evadir.

evaluate, v. avaluar.

evaluation, n. valoración f.

evangelist, n. evangelista m.

evaporate, v. evaporarse.

evaporation, n. evaporación f.

evasion, n. evasión f.

evasive, a. evasivo.

eve, n. víspera f.

even, 1. a. llano; igual. 2. adv. aun; hasta. not e., ni siquiera.

evening, n. noche, tarde f. good e., buenas noches.

evenness, n. uniformidad f.

event, n. acontecimiento, suceso m.

eventful, a. memorable.

eventual, a. eventual.

ever, adv. alguna vez; (after not) nunca. e. since, desde que.

everlasting, a. eterno.

every, a. cada, todos los.

everybody, pron. todo el mundo; cada uno.

everyday, a. ordinario, de cada día.

everyone, pron. cada uno; cada cual; todos.

everything, pron. todo m.

everywhere, adv. por todas partes, en todas partes.

evict, v. expulsar.

eviction, n. evicción f.

evidence, n. evidencia f.

evident, a. evidente.

evidently, adv. evidentemente.

evil, 1. a. malo; maligno. 2. n. mal m.

evince, v. revelar.

evoke, v. evocar.

evolution, n. evolución f.

evolve, v. desenvolver; desarrollar.

ewe, n. oveja f.

exact, 1. a. exacto. 2. v. exigir.

exacting, a. exigente.

exactly, adv. exactamente.

exaggerate, v. exagerar.

exaggeration, n. exageración f.

exalt, v. exaltar.

exaltation, n. exaltación f.

examination, n. examen m.; (legal) interrogatorio m.

examine, v. examinar.

example, n. ejemplo m.

exasperate, v. exasperar.

exasperation, n. exasperación f.

excavate, v. excavar, cavar.

exceed, v. exceder.

exceedingly, adv. sumamente, extremadamente.

excel, v. sobresalir.

excellence, n. excelencia f.

Excellency, n. (title) Excelencia f.

excellent, a. excelente.

except, 1. prep. salvo, excepto. 2. v. exceptuar.

exception, n. excepción f.

exceptional, a. excepcional.

excerpt, n. extracto.

excess, n. exceso m.

excessive, a. excesivo.

exchange, 1. n. cambio; canje m. stock e., bolsa f. telephone e., central telefónica. 2. v. cambiar, canjear.

exchangeable, a. cambiable.

excise, 1. n. sisa f. 2. v. extirpar.

excite, v. agitar; provocar; emocionar.

excitement, n. agitación, conmoción f.

exciting, a. emocionante.

exclaim, v. exclamar.

exclamation, n. exclamación f.

exclamation point or mark, n. punto de admiración m.

exclude, v. excluir.

exclusion, n. exclusión f.

exclusive, a. exclusivo.

excommunicate, v. excomulgar, descomulgar.

excommunication, n. excomunión f.

excrement, n. excremento m.

excruciating, a. penosísimo.

exculpate, v. justificar.

excursion, n. excursión; jira f.

excuse, 1. n. excusa f. 2. v. excusar, perdonar; dispensar; disculpar.

execrable, a. execrable.

execute, v. ejecutar.

execution, n. ejecución f.

executioner, n. verdugo m.

executive, a. & n. ejecutivo m.

executor, n. testamentario m.

exemplary, a. ejemplar.

exemplify, v. ejemplificar.

exempt, 1. a. exento. 2. v. exentar.

exercise, 1. n. ejercicio m. 2. v. ejercitar.

exert, v. esforzar.

exertion, n. esfuerzo m.

exhale, v. exhalar.

exhaust, 1. n. (auto.) escape m. 2. v. agotar.

exhaustion, n. agotamiento m.

exhaustive, a. agotador.

exhibit, 1. n. exhibición, exposición f. 2. v. exhibir.

exhibition, n. exhibición f.

exhilarate, v. alegrar; estimular.

exhort, v. exhortar.

exhortation, n. exhortación f.

exhume, v. exhumar.

exigency, n. exigencia f., urgencia f.

exile, 1. n. destierro m., (person) desterrado m. 2. v. desterrar.

exist, v. existir.

existence, n. existencia f.

existent, a. existente.

exit, n. salida f.

exodus, n. éxodo m.

exonerate, v. exonerar.

exorbitant, a. exorbitante.

exorcise, v. exorcizar.

exotic, a. exótico.

expand, v. dilatar; ensanchar.

expanse, n. espacio m.; extensión f.

expansion, n. expansión f.

expansive, a. expansivo.

expatiate, v. espaciarse.

expatriate, 1. n. & a. expatriato m. 2. v. expatriar.

expect, v. esperar; contar con.

expectancy, n. esperanza f.

expectation, n. esperanza f.

expectorate, v. expectorar.

expediency, n. conveniencia f.

expedient, 1. a. oportuno. 2. n. expediente m.

expedite, v. acelerar, despachar.

expedition, n. expedición f.

expel, v. expeler, expulsar.

expend, v. desembolsar, expender.

expenditure, n. desembolso; gasto m.

expense, n. gasto m.; costa f.

expensive, a. caro, costoso.

expensively, adv. costosamente.

experience, 1. n. experiencia f. **2.** v. experimentar.

experienced, a. experimentado, perito.

experiment, 1. n. experimento m. **2.** v. experimentar.

experimental, a. experimental.

expert, a. & n. experto m.

expiate, v. expiar.

expiration, n. expiración f.

expire, v. expirar; (com.) vencerse.

explain, v. explicar.

explanation, n. explicación f.

explanatory, a. explicativo.

expletive, 1. n. interjección f. **2.** a. expletivo.

explicit, a. explícito, claro.

explode, v. estallar, volar; refutar.

exploit, 1. n. hazaña f. **2.** v. explotar.

exploitation, n. explotación f.

exploration, n. exploración f.

exploratory, a. exploratorio.

explore, v. explorar.

explorer, n. explorador m.

explosion, n. explosión f.

explosive, a. explosivo.

export, 1. n. exportación f. **2.** v. exportar.

exportation, n. exportación f.

expose, v. exponer; descubrir.

exposition, n. exposición f.

expository, a. expositivo.

expostulate, v. altercar.

exposure, n. exposición f.

expound, v. exponer, explicar.

express, 1. a. & n. expreso m. **e. company,** compañía de porteo. **2.** v. expresar.

expression, n. expresión f.

expressive, a. expresivo.

expressly, adv. expresamente.

expressman, n. empresario de expresos m.

expropriate, v. expropriar.

expulsion, n. expulsión f.

expunge, v. borrar, expurgar.

expurgate, v. expurgar.

exquisite, a. exquisito.

extant, a. existente.

extemporaneous, a. improvisado.

extend, v. extender.

extension, n. extensión f.

extensive, a. extenso.

extensively, adv. por extenso.

extent, n. extensión f.; grado m. **to a certain e.,** hasta cierto punto.

extenuate, v. extenuar.

exterior, a. & n. exterior m.

exterminate, v. exterminar.

extermination, n. exterminio m.

external, a. externo, exterior.

extinct, a. extinto.

extinction, n. extinción f.

extinguish, v. extinguir, apagar.

extol, v. alabar.

extort, v. exigir dinero sin derecho.

extortion, n. extorsión f.

extra, 1. a. extraordinario; adicional. **2.** n. (newspaper) extra m.

extract, 1. n. extracto m. **2.** v. extraer.

extraction, n. extracción f.

extraneous, a. extraño; ajeno.

extraordinary, a. extraordinario.

extravagance, n. extravagancia f.

extravagant, a. extravagante.

extreme, a. & n. extremo m.

extremity, n. extremidad f.

extricate, v. desenredar.

exuberant, a. exuberante.

exude, v. exudar.

exult, v. regocijarse.

exultant, a. triunfante.

eye, 1. n. ojo m. **2.** v. ojear.

eyeball, n. globo del ojo.

eyebrow, n. ceja f.

eyeglasses, n. lentes m.

eyelash, n. pestaña f.

eyelid, n. párpado m.

eyesight, n. vista f.

F

fable, n. fábula; ficción f.

fabric, n. tejido m., tela f.

fabricate, v. fabricar.

fabulous, a. fabuloso.

façade, n. fachada f.

face, 1. n. cara f. **to make faces,** hacer muecas. **2.** encararse con. **f. the street,** dar a la calle.

facet, n. faceta f.

facetious, a. chistoso.

facial, 1. n. masaje facial m. **2.** a. facial.

facile, a. fácil.

facilitate, v. facilitar.

facility, n. facilidad f.

facsimile, n. facsímile m.

fact, n. hecho m. **in f.,** en realidad.

faction, n. facción f.

factor, n. factor m.

factory, n. fábrica f.

factual, a. verdadero.

faculty, n. facultad f.

fad, n. boga; novedad f.

fade, v. desteñirse; (flowers) marchitarse.

fail, 1. n. **without f.,** sin falta. **2.** v. fallar; fracasar. **not to f. to,** no dejar de.

failure, n. fracaso m.

faint, 1. a. débil; vago; pálido. **2.** n. desmayo m. **3.** v. desmayarse.

faintly, adv. débilmente; indistintamente.

fair, 1. a. razonable, justo; (hair) rubio; (weather) bueno. **2.** n. feria f.

fairly, adv. imparcialmente; regularmente; claramente; bellamente.

fairness, n. justicia f.

fairy, n. hada f., duende m.

faith, n. fe; confianza f.

faithful, a. fiel.

fake, 1. a. falso; postizo. **2.** n. imitación; estafa f. **3.** v. imitar; fingir.

faker, n. imitador m.; farsante m.

falcon, n. halcón m.

fall, 1. n. caída; catarata f.; (season) otoño m.; (in price) baja f. **2.** v. caer; bajar. **f. asleep,** dormirse; **f. in love,** enamorarse.

fallacious, a. falaz.

fallacy, n. falacia f.

fallible, a. falible.

fallout, n. precipitación resultante de una explosión nuclear.

fallow, a. sin cultivar.

false, a. falso; postizo.

falsehood, n. falsedad; mentira f.

falseness, n. falsedad, perfidia f.

falsetto, n. falsete m.

falsification, n. falsificación f.

falsify, v. falsificar.

falter, v. vacilar; (in speech) tartamudear.

fame, n. fama f.

familiar, 1. a. familiar; conocido. **to be f. with,** estar familiarizado con.

familiarity, n. familiaridad f.

familiarize, v. familiarizar.

family, n. familia; especie naje m.

famine, n. hambre; carestía f.

famished, a. muerto de hambre.

famous, a. famoso, célebre.

fan, n. abanico; ventilador m. (sports) aficionado -da.

fanatic, a. & n. fanático -ca.

fanatical, a. fanático.

fanaticism, n. fanatismo m.

fanciful, a. caprichoso; fantástico.

fancy, 1. a. fino, elegante. **f. foods,** novedades f.pl. **2.** n. fantasía f.; capricho m. **3.** v. imaginar.

fanfare, n. fanfarria f.

fang, n. colmillo m.

fantastic, a. fantástico.

fantasy, n. fantasía f.

far, 1. a. lejano, distante. **2.** adv. lejos. **how f.,** a qué distancia. **as f. as,** hasta. **so f.,** thus f., hasta aquí.

farce, n. farsa f.

fare, n. pasaje m.

farewell, 1. n. despedida f. **to**

say f. despedirse. 2. *interj.* ¡adiós!

farfetched, *a.* forzado.

farm, 1. *n.* granja; hacienda *f.* 2. *v.* cultivar, labrar la tierra.

farmer, *n.* labrador, agricultor *m.*

farmhouse, *n.* hacienda, alquería *f.*

farming, *n.* agricultura *f.;* cultivo *m.*

fascinate, *v.* fascinar, embelesar.

fascination, *n.* fascinación *f.*

fascism, *n.* fascismo *m.*

fashion, 1. *n.* moda; costumbre; guisa *f.* 2. *v.* formar.

fashionable, *a.* de moda, en boga.

fast, 1. *a.* rápido, veloz; (watch) adelantado; (color) firme. 2. *adv.* ligero, de prisa. 3. *n.* ayuno *m.* 4. *v.* ayunar.

fasten, *v.* afirmar, atar; fijar.

fastener, *n.* asegurador *m.*

fastidious, *a.* melindroso.

fat, 1. *a.* gordo. 2. *n.* grasa, manteca *f.*

fatal, *a.* fatal.

fatality, *n.* fatalidad *f.*

fatally, *adv.* fatalmente.

fate, *n.* destino *m.;* suerte *f.*

fateful, *a.* fatal; ominoso.

father, *n.* padre *m.*

fatherhood, *n.* paternidad *f.*

father-in-law, *n.* suegro *m.*

fatherland, *n.* patria *f.*

fatherly, 1. *a.* paternal. 2. *adv.* paternalmente.

fathom, 1. *n.* braza *f.* 2. *v.* sondar; (fig.) penetrar en.

fatigue, 1. *n.* fatiga *f.,* cansancio *m.* 2. *v.* fatigar, cansar.

fatten, *v.* engordar, cebar.

faucet, *n.* grifo *m.,* llave *f.*

fault, *n.* culpa *f.;* defecto *m.* at f., culpable.

faultless, *a.* sin tacha, perfecto.

faultlessly, *adv.* perfectamente.

faulty, *a.* defectuoso, imperfecto.

favor, 1. *n.* favor *m.* 2. *v.* favorecer.

favorable, *a.* favorable.

favorite, *a.* & *n.* favorito -ta.

favoritism, *n.* favoritismo *m.*

fawn, 1. *n.* cervato *m.* 2. *v.* halagar, adular.

faze, *v.* desconcertar.

fear, 1. *n.* miedo, temor *m.* 2. *v.* temer.

fearful, *a.* temeroso, medroso.

fearless, *a.* intrépido; sin temor.

fearlessness, *n.* intrepidez *f.*

feasible, *a.* factible.

feast, *n.* banquete *m.;* fiesta *f.*

feat, *n.* hazaña *f.;* hecho *m.*

feather, *n.* pluma *f.*

feature, 1. *n.* facción *f.;* rasgo *m.;* (movies) película principal. 2. *v.* presentar como atracción especial.

February, *n.* febrero *m.*

federal, *a.* federal.

federation, *n.* confederación, federación *f.*

fee, *n.* honorarios *m.pl.*

feeble, *a.* débil.

feebleminded, *a.* imbécil.

feebleness, *a.* debilidad *f.*

feed, 1. *n.* pasto *m.* 2. *v.* alimentar; dar de comer. fed up with, harto de.

feedback, *n.* feedback *m.,* retroalimentación *f.*

feel, 1. *n.* sensación *f.* 2. *v.* sentir; palpar. f. like, tener ganas de.

feeling, *n.* sensación; sensibilidad *f.*

feign, *v.* fingir.

felicitate, *v.* felicitar.

felicitous, *a.* feliz.

felicity, *n.* felicidad *f.,* dicha *f.*

feline, *a.* felino.

fellow, *n.* compañero; socio *m.;* (coll.) tipo *m.*

fellowship, *n.* compañía, (for study) beca *f.*

felon, *n.* reo *m.,* felón *f.*

felony, *n.* felonía *f.*

felt, *n.* fieltro *m.*

female, *a.* & *n.* hembra *f.*

feminine, *a.* femenino.

fence, 1. *n.* cerca *f.* 2. *v.* cercar.

fender, *n.* guardabarros *m.*

ferment, 1. *n.* fermento *m.;* (fig.) agitación *f.* 2. *v.* fermentar.

fermentation, *n.* fermentación *f.*

fern, *n.* helecho *m.*

ferocious, *a.* feroz; fiero.

ferociously, *adv.* ferozmente.

ferocity, *n.* ferocidad, fiereza *f.*

ferry, *n.* transbordador *m.,* barca de transporte.

fertile, *a.* fecundo; (land) fértil.

fertility, *n.* fertilidad *f.*

fertilization, *n.* fertilización *f.*

fertilize, *v.* fertilizar, abonar.

fertilizer, *n.* abono *m.*

fervency, *n.* ardor *m.*

fervent, *a.* ferviente.

fervently, *adv.* fervorosamente.

fervid, *a.* férvido.

fervor, *n.* fervor *m.*

fester, *v.* ulcerarse.

festival, *n.* fiesta *f.*

festive, *a.* festivo.

festivity, *n.* festividad *f.*

festoon, 1. *n.* festón *m.* 2. *v.* festonear.

fetch, *v.* ir por; traer.

fete, 1. *n.* fiesta *f.* 2. *v.* festejar.

fetid, *a.* fétido.

fetish, *n.* fetiche *m.*

fetter, 1. *n.* grillete *m.* 2. *v.* engrillar.

fetus, *n.* feto *m.*

feud, *n.* riña *f.;* feudo *m.*

feudal, *a.* feudal.

feudalism, *n.* feudalismo *m.*

fever, *n.* fiebre *f.*

feverish, *a.* febril.

feverishly, *adv.* febrilmente.

few, *a.* pocos. a. f., algunos, unos cuantos.

fiancé, fiancée, *n.* novio -via.

fiasco, *n.* fiasco *m.*

fiat, *n.* fiat *m.,* orden *f.*

fib, 1. *n.* mentira *f.* 2. *v.* mentir.

fiber, *n.* fibra *f.*

fibrous, *a.* fibroso.

fickle, *a.* caprichoso.

fickleness, *n.* inconstancia *f.*

fiction, *n.* ficción *f.;* (literature) novelas *f.pl.*

fictitious, *a.* ficticio.

fidelity, *n.* fidelidad *f.*

fidget, *v.* inquietar.

field, *n.* campo *m.*

fiend, *n.* demonio *m.*

fiendish, *a.* diabólico, malvado.

fierce, *a.* fiero, feroz.

fiery, *a.* ardiente.

fiesta, *n.* fiesta *f.*

fife, *n.* pífano *m.*

fifteen, *a.* & *pron.* quince.

fifteenth, *n.* & *a.* décimoquinto.

fifth, *a.* quinto.

fifty, *a.* & *pron.* cincuenta.

fig, *n.* higo *m.* f. tree, higuera *f.*

fight, 1. *n.* lucha, pelea *f.* 2. *v.* luchar, pelear.

fighter, *n.* peleador -ra, luchador -ra.

figment, *n.* invención *f.*

figurative, *a.* metafórico.

figuratively, *adv.* figuradamente.

figure, 1. *n.* figura; cifra *f.* 2. *v.* figurar; calcular.

filament, *n.* filamento *m.*

file, 1. *n.* archivo *m.;* (instrument) lima *f.;* (row) fila *f.* 2. *v.* archivar; limar.

filial, *a.* filial.

filigree, *n.* filigrana *f.*

fill, *v.* llenar.

fillet, *n.* filete *m.*

filling, *n.* relleno *m.;* (dental) empastadura *f.* f. station, bomba *f.*

film, 1. *n.* película *f.,* film *m.* 2. *v.* filmar.

filter, 1. *n.* filtro *m.* 2. *v.* filtrar.

filth, *n.* suciedad, mugre *f.*

filthy, *a.* sucio.

fin, *n.* aleta *f.*

final, 1. *a.* final, último. 2. *n.* examen final. finals, (sports) final *f.*

finalist, *n.* finalista.

finally, *adv.* finalmente.

finances, *n.* recursos, fondos *m.pl.*

financial, *a.* financiero.

financier, *n.* financiero *m.*

find, 1. *n.* hallazgo *m.* 2. *v.* hallar; encontrar. f. out, averiguar, enterarse, saber.

fine, 1. *a.* fino; bueno. 2. *adv.* muy bien. 3. *n.* multa *f.* 4. *v.* multar.

finery, *n.* gala *f.,* adorno *m.*

finesse, 1. *n.* artificio *m.* 2. *v.* valerse de artificio.

finger, *n.* dedo *m.*

finger bowl, *n.* enjuagatorio *m.*

fingernail, *n.* uña *f.*

fingerprint, 1. *n.* impresión digital *f.* **2.** *v.* tomar las impresiones digitales.

finicky, *a.* melindroso.

finish, 1. *n.* conclusión *f.* **2.** *v.* acabar, terminar.

finished, *a.* acabado.

finite, *a.* finito.

fir, *n.* abeto *m.*

fire, 1. *n.* fuego; incendio *m.* **2.** *v.* disparar, tirar; (coll.) despedir.

fire alarm, *n.* alarma de incendio *f.*

firearm, *n.* arma de fuego.

firecracker, *n.* triquitraque *m.*, buscapiés *m.*, petardo *m.*

fire engine, *n.* bomba de incendios *f.*

fire escape, *n.* escalera de incendios *f.*

fire extinguisher, *n.* matafuego *m.*

firefly, *n.* luciérnaga *f.*

fireman, *n.* bombero *m.;* (railway) fogonero *m.*

fireplace, *n.* hogar, fogón *m.*

fireproof, *a.* incombustible.

fireside, *n.* hogar *m.* fogón *m.*

fireworks, *n.* fuegos artificiales.

firm, 1. *a.* firme. **2.** *n.* casa de comercio.

firmness, *n.* firmeza *f.*

first, *a.* & *adv.* primero. **at f.,** al principio.

first aid, *n.* primeros auxilios *m.*

first-class, *a.* de primera clase.

fiscal, *a.* fiscal.

fish, 1. *n.* (food) pescado *m.;* (alive) pez *m.* **2.** *v.* pescar.

fisherman, *n.* pescador *m.*

fishhook, *n.* anzuelo *m.*

fishing, *n.* pesca *f.* **to go f.,** ir de pesca.

fishmonger, *n.* pescadero *m.*

fission, *n.* fisura *f.*

fissure, *n.* grieta *f.*, quebradura *f.*

fist, *n.* puño *m.*

fit, 1. *a.* capaz; justo. **2.** *n.* corte, talle *m.;* (med.) convulsión *f.* **3.** *v.* caber; quedar bien, sentar bien.

fitful, *a.* espasmódico; caprichoso.

fitness, *n.* aptitud; conveniencia *f.*

fitting, 1. *a.* conveniente. **to be f.,** convenir. **2.** *n.* ajuste *m.*

five, *a.* & *pron.* cinco.

fix, 1. *n.* apuro *m.* **2.** *v.* fijar; arreglar; componer, reparar.

fixation, *n.* fijación *f.;* fijeza *f.*

fixed, *a.* fijo.

fixture, *n.* instalación; guarnición *f.*

flabby, *a.* flojo.

flaccid, *a.* flojo; flácido.

flag, *n.* bandera *f.*

flagellant, *n.* & *a.* flagelante *m.*

flagon, *n.* frasco *m.*

flagrant, *a.* flagrante.

flagrantly, *adv.* notoriamente.

flair, *n.* afición *f.*

flake, 1. *n.* lámina *f.;* copo de nieve. **2.** *v.* romperse en láminas.

flamboyant, *a.* flamante, llamativo.

flame, 1. *n.* llama *f.* **2.** *v.* llamear.

flaming, *a.* llameante, flamante.

flamingo, *n.* flamenco *m.*

flank, 1. *n.* ijada *f.;* (mil.) flanco *m.* **2.** *v.* flanquear.

flannel, *n.* franela *f.*

flap, 1. *n.* cartera *f.* **2.** *v.* aletear; sacudirse.

flare, 1. *n.* llamarada *f.* **2.** *v.* brillar; (fig.) enojarse.

flash, 1. *n.* resplandor *m.;* (lightning) rayo, relámpago *m.;* (fig.) instante *m.* **2.** *v.* brillar.

flashcube, *n.* cubo de flash *m.*

flashlight, *n.* linterna eléctrica.

flashy, *a.* resplandeciente; ostentoso.

flask, *n.* frasco *m.*

flat, 1. *a.* llano; (tire) desinflado. **2.** *n.* llanura *f.;* apartamiento *m.*

flatness, *n.* llanura *f.*

flatten, *v.* aplastar, allanar; abatir.

flatter, *v.* adular, lisonjear.

flatterer, *n.* lisonjero -ra. zalamero -ra.

flattery, *n.* adulación, lisonja *f.*

flaunt, *v.* ostentar.

flavor, 1. *n.* sabor *m.* **2.** *v.* sazonar.

flavoring, *n.* condimento *m.*

flaw, *n.* defecto *m.*

flax, *n.* lino *m.*

flay, *v.* despellejar; excoriar.

flea, *n.* pulga *f.*

fleck, 1. *n.* mancha *f.* **2.** *v.* varetear.

flee, *v.* huir.

fleece, 1. *n.* vellón *m.* **2.** *v.* esquilar.

fleet, 1. *a.* veloz. **2.** *n.* flota *f.*

fleeting, *a.* fugaz, pasajero.

flesh, *n.* carne *f.*

fleshy, *a.* gordo; carnoso.

flex, 1. *n.* doblez *m.* **2.** *v.* doblar.

flexibility, *n.* flexibilidad *f.*

flexible, *a.* flexible -ra.

flier, *n.* aviador -ra.

flight, *n.* vuelo *m.;* fuga *f.*

flight attendant, *n.* azafata *f.;* ayudante de vuelo *m.*

flimsy, *a.* débil.

flinch, *v.* acobardarse.

fling, *v.* lanzar.

flint, *n.* pedernal *m.*

flip, *v.* lanzar.

flippant, *a.* impertinente.

flippantly, *adv.* impertinentemente.

flirt, 1. *n.* coqueta *f.* **2.** *v.* coquetear, flirtear.

flirtation, *n.* coqueteo *m.*

float, *v.* flotar.

flock, 1. *n.* rebaño *m.* **2.** *v.* congregarse.

flog, *v.* azotar.

flood, 1. *n.* inundación *f.* **2.** *v.* inundar.

floor, 1. *n.* suelo, piso *m.* **2.** *v.* derribar.

floral, *a.* floral.

florid, *a.* florido.

florist, *n.* florista *m.* & *f.*

flounce, 1. *n.* (sewing) volante *m.* **2.** *v.* pernear.

flounder, *n.* rodaballo *m.*

flour, *n.* harina *f.*

flourish, 1. *n.* floreo *m.* **2.** *v.* florecer; prosperar; blandir.

flow, 1. *n.* flujo *m.* **2.** *v.* fluir.

flower, 1. *n.* flor *f.* **2.** *v.* florecer.

flowerpot, *n.* maceta de flores *f.*

flowery, *a.* florido.

fluctuate, *v.* fluctuar.

fluctuation, *n.* fluctuación *f.*

flue, *n.* humero *m.*

fluency, *n.* fluidez *f.*

fluent, *a.* fluente.

fluffy, *a.* velloso.

fluid, *a.* & *n.* flúido *m.*

fluidity, *n.* fluidez *f.*

fluoroscope, *n.* fluoroscopio *m.*

flurry, *n.* agitación *f.*

flush, 1. *a.* bien provisto. **2.** *n.* sonrojo *m.* **3.** *v.* limpiar con un chorro de agua; sonrojarse.

flute, *n.* flauta *f.*

flutter, 1. *n.* agitación *f.* **2.** *v.* agitarse.

flux, *n.* flujo *m.*

fly, 1. *n.* mosca *f.* **2.** *v.* volar.

foam, 1. *n.* espuma *f.* **2.** *v.* espumar.

focal, *a.* focal.

focus, 1. *n.* enfoque *m.* **2.** *v.* enfocar.

fodder, *n.* forraje *m.*

foe, *n.* adversario -ria, enemigo -ga.

fog, *n.* niebla *f.*

foggy, *a.* brumoso.

foil, *v.* frustrar.

foist, *v.* emponer.

fold, 1. *n.* pliegue *m.* **2.** *v.* doblar, plegar.

folder, *n.* circular *m.;* (for filing) carpeta *f.*

foliage, *n.* follaje *m.*

folio, *n.* infolio; folio *m.*

folklore, *n.* folklore *m.*

folks, *n.* gente, familia *f.*

follicle, *n.* folículo *m.*

follow, *v.* seguir.

follower, *n.* partidario -ria.

folly, *n.* locura *f.*

foment, *v.* fomentar.

fond, *a.* cariñoso, tierno. **be f. of,** ser aficionado a.

fondle, *v.* acariciar.

fondly, *adv.* tiernamente.

fondness, *n.* afición *f.;* cariño *m.*

food, *n.* alimento *m.;* comida *f.*

foodstuffs, *n.pl.* comestibles, víveres *m.pl.*

fool, 1. *a.* tonto -ta; bobo -ba; bufón -ona. 2. *v.* engañar.

foolhardy, *a.* temerario.

foolish, *a.* bobo, tonto, majadero.

foolproof, *a.* seguro.

foot, *n.* pie *m.*

footage, *n.* longitud en pies.

football, *n.* fúbol, balompié *m.*

foothold, *n.* posición establecida.

footing, *n.* base *f.*, fundamento *m.*

footlights, *n.pl.* luces del proscenio.

footnote, *n.* nota al pie de una página.

footprint, *n.* huella *f.*

footstep, *n.* paso *m.*

footstool, *n.* escañuelo *m.*, banqueta *f.*

fop, *n.* petimetre *m.*

for, 1. *prep.* para; por. as f., en cuanto a. what f., ¿para qué? 2. *conj.* porque, pues.

forage, 1. *n.* forraje *m.* 2. *v.* forrajear.

foray, *n.* correría *f.*

forbear, *v.* cesar; abstenerse.

forbearance, *n.* paciencia *f.*

forbid, *v.* prohibir.

forbidding, *a.* repugnante.

force, 1. *n.* fuerza *f.* 2. *v.* forzar.

forceful, *a.* fuerte; enérgico.

forcible, *a.* fuerte; enérgico.

ford, 1. *n.* vado *m.* 2. *v.* vadear.

fore, 1. *a.* delantero. 2. *n.* delantera *f.*

fore and aft, de popa a proa.

forearm, *n.* antebrazo *m.*

forebears, *n.pl.* antepasados *m.pl.*

forebode, *v.* presagiar.

foreboding, *n.* presentimiento *m.*

forecast, 1. *n.* pronóstico *m.*; profecía *f.* 2. *v.* pronosticar.

forecastle, *n.* (naut.) castillo de proa.

forefather, *n.* antepasado *m.*

forefinger, *n.* índice *m.*

forego, *v.* renunciar.

foregone, *a.* predeterminado.

foreground, *n.* primer plano.

forehead, *n.* frente *f.*

foreign, *a.* extranjero.

foreign aid, ayuda exterior.

foreigner, *n.* extranjero -ra; forastero -ra.

foreleg, *n.* pierna delantera.

foreman, *n.* capataz *m.*

foremost, 1. *a.* primero. 2. *adv.* en primer lugar.

forenoon, *n.* mañana *f.*

forensic, *a.* forense.

forerunner, *n.* precursor -ra.

foresee, *v.* prever.

foreshadow, *v.* prefigurar, anunciar.

foresight, *n.* previsión *f.*

forest, *n.* bosque *m.*; selva *f.*

forestall, *v.* anticipar; prevenir.

forester, *n.* silvicultor; guardamonte *m.*

forestry, *n.* silvicultura *f.*

foretell, *v.* predecir.

forever, *adv.* por siempre, para siempre.

forevermore, *adv.* siempre.

forewarn, *v.* advertir, avisar.

foreword, *n.* prefacio *m.*

forfeit, 1. *n.* prenda, multa *f.* 2. *v.* perder.

forfeiture, *n.* decomiso *m.*, multa *f.*

forgather, *v.* reunirse.

forge, 1. *n.* fragua *f.* 2. *v.* forjar; falsear.

forger, *n.* forjador; falsificador *m.*

forgery, *n.* falsificación *f.*

forget, *v.* olvidar.

forgetful, *a.* olvidadizo.

forgive, *v.* perdonar.

forgiveness, *n.* perdón *m.*

fork, 1. *n.* tenedor *m.*; bifurcación *f.* 2. *v.* bifurcarse.

forlorn, *a.* triste.

form, 1. *n.* forma *f.*; (document) formulario *m.* 2. *v.* formar.

formal, *a.* formal; ceremonioso. f. dance, baile de etiqueta. f. dress, traje de etiqueta.

formality, *n.* formalidad *f.*

formally, *adv.* formalmente.

format, *n.* formato *m.*

formation, *n.* formación *f.*

formative, *a.* formativo.

former, *a.* anterior; antiguo. the f., aquél.

formerly, *adv.* antiguamente.

formidable, *a.* formidable.

formless, *a.* sin forma.

formula, *n.* fórmula *f.*

formulate, *v.* formular.

formulation, *n.* formulación *f.*; expresión *f.*

forsake, *v.* abandonar.

fort, *n.* fortaleza *f.*; fuerte *m.*

forte, *a. & adv.* (mus.) forte, fuerte.

forth, *adv.* adelante. back and f., de aquí allá. and so f., etcétera.

forthcoming, *a.* futuro, próximo.

forthright, *a.* franco.

forthwith, *adv.* inmediatamente.

fortification, *n.* fortificación *f.*

fortify, *v.* fortificar.

fortissimo, *a. & adv.* (mus.) fortísimo.

fortitude, *n.* fortaleza; fortitud *f.*

fortnight, *n.* quincena *f.*

fortress, *n.* fuerte *m.*, fortaleza *f.*

fortuitous, *a.* fortuito.

fortunate, *a.* afortunado.

fortune, *n.* fortuna; suerte *f.*

fortune-teller, *n.* sortílego, adivino *m.*

forty, *a. & pron.* cuarenta.

forum, *n.* foro *m.*

forward, 1. *a.* delantero; atrevido. 2. *adv.* adelante. 3. *v.* trasmitir, reexpedir.

foster, 1. *a.* f. child, hijo adoptivo. 2. *v.* fomentar, criar.

foul, *a.* sucio; impuro.

found, *v.* fundar.

foundation, *n.* fundación *f.*; (of building) cimientos *m.pl.*

founder, 1. *n.* fundador -ra. 2. *v.* irse a pique.

foundry, *n.* fundición *f.*

fountain, *n.* fuente *f.*

four, *a. & pron.* cuatro.

fourteen, *a. & pron.* catorce.

fourth, *a. & n.* cuarto *m.*

fowl, *n.* ave *f.*

fox, *n.* zorro -rra.

fox trot, *n.* foxtrot *m.*

foxy, *a.* astuto.

foyer, *n.* salón de entrada.

fracas, *n.* riña *f.*

fraction, *n.* fracción *f.*

fracture, 1. *n.* fractura, rotura *f.* 2. *v.* fracturar, romper.

fragile, *a.* frágil.

fragment, *n.* fragmento, trozo *m.*

fragmentary, *a.* fragmentario.

fragrance, *n.* fragancia *f.*

fragrant, *a.* fragante.

frail, *a.* débil, frágil.

frailty, *n.* debilidad, fragilidad *f.*

frame, 1. *n.* marco; armazón; cuadro, cuerpo *m.* 2. *v.* fabricar; formar; encuadrar.

frame-up, *n.* (coll.) conspiración *f.*

framework, *n.* armazón *m.*

France, *n.* Francia *f.*

franchise, *n.* franquicia *f.*

frank, 1. *a.* franco. 2. *n.* carta franca. 3. *v.* franquear.

frankfurter, *n.* salchicha *f.*

frankly, *adv.* francamente.

frankness, *n.* franqueza *f.*

frantic, *a.* frenético.

fraternal, *a.* fraternal.

fraternity, *n.* fraternidad *f.*

fraternization, *n.* fraternización *f.*

fraternize, *v.* confraternizar.

fratricide, *n.* fratricida *m. & f.*

fraud, *n.* fraude *m.*

fraudulent, *a.* fraudulento.

fraudulently, *adv.* fraudulentamente.

fraught, *a.* cargado.

freak, *n.* rareza *f.*

freckle, *n.* peca *f.*

free, 1. *a.* libre; gratis. 2. *v.* libertar, librar.

freedom, *n.* libertad *f.*

freeze, *v.* helar, congelar.

freezer, *n.* heladora *f.*

freight, 1. *n.* carga *f.*; flete *m.* 2. *v.* cargar; fletar.

freighter, *n.* (naut.) fletador *m.*

French, *a. & n.* francés *m.*

Frenchman, *n.* francés *m.*

frenzied, *a.* frenético.

frenzy, *n.* frenesí *m.*

frequency, *n.* frecuencia *f.*

frequency modulation, modulación de frequencia.

frequent, *a.* frecuente.

frequently, adv. frecuentemente.

fresco, n. pintura al fresco.

fresh, a. fresco. f. water, agua dulce.

freshen, v. refrescar.

freshness, n. frescura f.

fret, v. quejarse, irritarse.

fretful, a. irritable.

fretfully, adv. de mala gana.

fretfulness, n. mal humor.

friar, n. fraile m.

fricassee, n. fricasé m.

friction, n. fricción f.

Friday, n. viernes m. Good F., Viernes Santo.

fried, a. frito.

friend, n. amigo -ga.

friendless, a. sin amigos.

friendliness, n. amistad f.

friendly, a. amistoso.

friendship, n. amistad f.

fright, n. susto m.

frighten, v. asustar, espantar.

frightful, a. espantoso.

frigid, a. frígido, frío.

frill, n. (sewing) lechuga f.

fringe, n. fleco; borde m.

frisky, a. retozón.

fritter, n. fritura f.

frivolity, n. frivolidad f.

frivolous, a. frívolo.

frivolousness, n. frivolidad f.

frock, n. vestido de mujer. f. coat, levita f.

frog, n. rana f.

frolic, 1. n. retozo m. 2. v. retozar.

from, prep. de; desde.

front, n. frente; (of building) fachada f. in f. of, delante de.

frontal, a. frental.

frontier, n. frontera f.

frost, n. helada, escharcha f.

frosty, a. helado.

froth, n. espuma f.

frown, 1. n. ceño m. 2. v. fruncir el entrecejo.

frowzy, a. desaliñado.

frozen, a. helado; congelado.

fructify, v. fructificar.

frugal, a. frugal.

frugality, n. frugalidad f.

fruit, n. fruta f.; (benefits) frutos m.pl. f. tree, árbol frutal.

fruitful, a. productivo.

fruition, n. fruición f.

fruitless, a. inútil, vano.

frustrate, v. frustrar.

frustration, n. frustración f.

fry, v. freír.

fuel, n. combustible m.

fugitive, a. & n. fugitivo -va.

fugue, n. (mus.) fuga f.

fulcrum, n. fulcro m.

fulfill, v. cumplir.

fulfillment, n. cumplimiento m.; realización f.

full, a. lleno; completo; pleno.

fullness, n. plenitud f.

fulminate, v. volar; fulminar.

fulmination, n. fulminación, detonación f.

fumble, v. chapucear.

fume, 1. n. humo m. 2. v. humear.

fumigate, v. fumigar.

fumigator, n. fumigador m.

fun, n. diversión f. to make f. of, burlarse de. to have f., divertirse.

function, 1. n. función f. 2. v. funcionar.

functional, a. funcional.

fund, n. fondo m.

fundamental, a. fundamental.

funeral, n. funeral m.

fungus, n. hongo m.

funnel, n. embudo m.; (of ship) chimenea f.

funny, a. divertido, gracioso. to be f., tener gracia.

fur, n. piel f.

furious, a. furioso.

furlough, n. permiso m.

furnace, n. horno m.

furnish, v. surtir, proveer; (a house) amueblar.

furniture, n. muebles m.pl.

furrow, 1. n. surco m. 2. v. surcar.

further, 1. a. & adv. más. 2. v. adelantar, fomentar.

furthermore, adv. además.

fury, n. furor m.; furia f.

fuse, 1. n. fusible m. 2. v. fundir.

fuss, 1. n. alboroto m. 2. v. preocuparse por pequeñeces.

fussy, a. melindroso.

futile, a. fútil.

future, 1. a. futuro. 2. n. porvenir m.

futurology, n. futurología f.

G

gag, n. chiste m.

gaiety, n. alegría f.

gain, 1. n. ganancia f. 2. v. ganar.

gait, n. paso m.

gale, n. ventarrón m.

gall, n. hiel f.; (fig.) amargura f.; descaro m.

gallant, 1. a. galante. 2. n. galán m.

gallery, n. galería f.; (theat.) paraíso m.

gallon, n. galón m.

gallop, 1. n. galope m. 2. v. galopar.

gallows, n. horca f.

gamble, 1. n. riesgo m. 2. v. jugar; aventurar.

game, n. juego m.; (match) partida f.; (hunting) caza f.

gang, n. cuadrilla; pandilla f.

gangster, n. rufián m.

gap, n. raja f.

gape, v. boquear.

garage, n. garaje m.

garbage, n. basura f.

garden, n. jardín m.; (vegetable) huerta f.

gardener, n. jardinero -ra.

gargle, 1. n. gárgara f. 2. v. gargarizar.

garland, n. guirnalda f.

garlic, n. ajo m.

garment, n. prenda de vestir.

garrison, n. guarnición f.

garter, n. liga f.; ataderas f.pl.

gas, n. gas m.

gasohol, n. gasohol m.

gasoline, n. gasolina f.

gasp, 1. n. boqueada f. 2. v. boquear.

gate, n. puerta; entrada f.

gather, v. recoger; inferir; reunir.

gaudy, a. brillante; llamativo.

gauge, 1. n. manómetro, indicador m. 2. v. medir; estimar.

gaunt, a. flaco.

gauze, n. gasa f.

gay, 1. a. alegre; homosexual. 2. n. homosexual.

gaze, 1. n. mirada f. 2. v. mirar con fijeza.

gear, n. engranaje m. in g., en juego.

gem, n. joya f.

gender, n. género m.

general, a. & n. general m.

generality, n. generalidad f.

generalize, v. generalizar.

generation, n. generación f.

generator, n. generador m.

generosity, n. generosidad f.

generous, a. generoso.

genial, a. genial.

genius, n. genio m.

gentle, a. suave; manso; benigno.

gentleman, n. señor, caballero m.

gentleness, n. suavidad f.

genuine, a. genuino.

genuineness, n. pureza f.

geographical, a. geográfico.

geography, n. geografía f.

geometric, a. geométrico.

geranium, n. geranio m.

germ, n. germen; microbio m.

German, a. & n. alemán mana.

Germany, n. Alemania f.

gesticulate, v. gesticular.

gesture, 1. n. gesto m. 2. v. gesticular, hacer gestos.

get, v. obtener; conseguir; (become) ponerse. go and g., ir a buscar; g. away, irse; escaparse; g. together, reunirse; g. on, subir; g. off, bajar; g. up, levantarse; g. there, llegar.

ghastly, a. pálido; espantoso.

ghost, n. espectro, fantasma m.

giant, n. gigante m.

gift, n. regalo, don; talento m.

gild, v. dorar.

gin, n. ginebra f.

ginger, n. jengibre m.

gingerbread, n. pan de jengibre.

gingham, n. guinga f.

gird, v. ceñir.

girdle, n. faja f.

girl, n. muchacha, niña, chica f.

give, v. dar; regalar. g. back,

devolver. g. up, rendirse; renunciar.

giver, n. dador -ra; donador -ra.

glacier, n. ventisquero m.

glad, a. alegre, contento. to be g., alegrarse.

gladly, adj. con mucho gusto.

gladness, n. alegría f.; placer m.

glamor, n. encanto m.; elegancia f.

glamorous, a. encantador, elegante.

glance, 1. n. vistazo m., ojeada f. 2. v. ojear.

gland, n. glándula f.

glare, 1. n. reflejo; brillo m. 2. v. deslumbrar; echar miradas indignadas.

glass, n. vidrio; vaso m.; (eyeglasses), lentes anteojos m.pl.

gleam, 1. n. fulgor m. 2. v. fulgurar.

glee, n. alegría f.; júbilo m.

glide, v. deslizarse.

glimpse, 1. n. vistazo m. 2. v. ojear.

glisten, 1. n. brillo m. 2. v. brillar.

glitter, 1. n. resplandor m. 2. v. brillar.

globe, n. globo; orbe m.

gloom, n. oscuridad; tristeza f.

gloomy, a. oscuro; sombrío, triste.

glorify, v. glorificar.

glorious, a. glorioso.

glory, n. gloria, fama f.

glossary, n. glosario m.

glove, n. guante m.

glow, 1. n. fulgor m. 2. v. relucir; arder.

glue, 1. n. cola f. 2. v. encolar, pegar.

glum, a. de mal humor.

glutton, n. glotón -ona.

gnaw, v. roer.

go, v. ir, irse. g. away, irse, marcharse. g. back, volver, regresar. g. down, bajar. g. in, entrar. g. on, seguir. g. out, salir. g. up, subir.

goal, n. meta f.; objeto m.

goat, n. cabra f.

goblet, n. copa f.

God, n. Dios m.

gold, n. oro m.

golden, a. áureo.

good, 1. a. bueno. 2. n. bienes m.pl.; (com.) géneros m.pl.

good-bye, 1. n. adiós m. 2. interj. ¡adiós!, ¡hasta la vista!, ¡hasta luego! to say g. to, despedirse de.

goodness, n. bondad f.

goose, n. ganso m.

gooseberry, n. uva crespa f.

gooseneck, 1. n. cuello de cisne m. 2. a. curvo.

goose step, n. paso de ganso m.

gore, 1. n. sangre f. 2. v. acornear.

gorge, 1. n. gorja f. 2. v. engullir.

gorgeous, a. magnífico; precioso.

gorilla, n. gorila f.

gory, a. sangriento.

gosling, n. gansarón m.

gospel, n. evangelio m.

gossamer, 1. n. telaraña f. 2. a. delgado.

gossip, 1. n. chisme m. 2. v. chismear.

Gothic, a. gótico.

gouge, 1. n. gubia f. 2. v. escoplear.

gourd, n. calabaza f.

gourmand, n. glotón m.

gourmet, a. gastrónomo -ma.

govern, v. gobernar.

governess, n. aya, institutriz f.

government, n. gobierno m.

governmental, a. gubernamental.

governor, n. gobernador m.

governorship, n. gobernatura f.

gown, n. vestido m. dressing g., bata f.

grab, v. agarrar, arrebatar.

grace, n. gracia; gentileza; merced f.

graceful, a. agraciado.

graceless, a. réprobo.

gracious, a. gentil, cortés.

grackle, n. grajo m.

grade, 1. n. grado; nivel m.; pendiente; nota; calidad f. 2. v. graduar.

grade crossing, n. paso a nivel m.

gradual, a. gradual.

gradually, adv. gradualmente.

graduate, 1. n. graduado -da, diplomado-da. 2. v. graduar; diplomarse.

graft, 1. n. injerto m.; soborno público. 2. v. injertar.

graham, a. centeno; acemita.

grail, n. grial m.

grain, n. grano; cereal m.

grain alcohol, n. alcohol de madera m.

grama, n. gramo m.

grammar, n. gramática f.

grammarian, n. gramático m.

grammar school, n. escuela elemental f.

grammatical, a. gramatical.

gramophone, n. gramófono m.

granary, n. granero m.

grand, a. grande, ilustre; estupendo.

grandchild, n. nieto -ta.

granddaughter, n. nieta f.

grandee, n. noble m.

grandeur, n. grandeza f.

grandfather, n. abuelo m.

grandiloquent, a. grandílocuo.

grandiose, a. grandioso.

grand jury, n. gran jurado m.

grandly, adv. grandiosamente.

grandmother, n. abuela f.

grand opera, n. ópera grande f.

grandparents, n. abuelos m.pl.

grandson, n. nieto m.

grandstand, n. andanada f., tribuna f.

grange, n. granja f.

granger, n. labriego m.

granite, n. granito m.

granny, n. abuelita f.

grant, 1. n. concesión; subvención f. 2. v. otorgar; conceder; conferir. take for granted, tomar por cierto.

granular, a. granular.

granulate, v. granular.

granulation, n. granulación f.

granule, n. gránulo m.

grape, n. uva f.

grapefruit, n. toronja f.

grapeshot, n. metralla f.

grapevine, n. vid; parra f.

graph, n. gráfia f.

graphic, a. gráfico.

graphite, n. grafito m.

graphology, n. grafología f.

grapple, v. agarrar.

grasp, 1. n. puño; poder; conocimiento m. 2. v. empuñar agarrar; comprender.

grasping, a. codicioso.

grass, n. hierba f.; (marijuana) marijuana f.

grasshopper, n. saltamontes m.

grassy, a. herboso.

grate, n. reja f.

grateful, a. agradecido.

gratify, v. satisfacer.

grating, 1. n. enrejado m. 2. a. discordante.

gratis, adv. & a. gratis.

gratitude, n. agradecimiento m.

gratuitous, adv. gratismente.

gratuity, n. propina f.

grave, 1. a. grave. 2. n. sepultura; tumba f.

gravel, n. cascajo m.

gravely, adv. gravemente.

gravestone, n. lápida sepulcral f.

graveyard, n. cementerio m.

gravitate, v. gravitar.

gravitation, n. gravitación f.

gravity, n. gravedad; seriedad f.

gravure, n. grabado m.

gravy, n. salsa f.

gray, a. gris; (hair) cano.

grayish, a. pardusco.

gray matter, n. substancia gris f.

graze, v. rozar; (cattle) pastar.

grazing, a. pastando.

grease, 1. n. grasa f. 2. v. engrasar.

greasy, a. grasiento.

great, a. grande, ilustre; estupendo.

Great Dane, n. mastín danés m.

greatness, n. grandeza f.

Greece, n. Grecia f.

greed, greediness, n. codicia, voracidad f.

greedy, a. voraz.

Greek, a. & n. griego -ga.

green, a. & n. verde m. greens, n. verduras f.pl.

greenery, n. verdor m.

greenhouse, n. invernáculo m.

greet, v. saludar.

greeting, n. saludo m.

gregarious, a. gregario.

grenade, n. granada; bomba f.

greyhound, n. galgo m.

grid, n. parrilla f.

griddle, n. tortera f.

griddlecake, n. tortita de harina f.

gridiron, n. parrilla f., campo de fútbol m.

grief, n. dolor m.; pena f.

grievance, n. pesar; agravio m.

grieve, v. afligir.

grievous, a. penoso.

grill, 1. n. parrilla f. 2. v. asar a la parrilla.

grillroom, n. restaurante de servicio rápido m.

grim, a. ceñudo.

grimace, 1. n. mueca f. 2. v. hacer muecas.

grime, n. mugre f.

grimy, a. sucio; mugroso.

grin, 1. n. sonrisa f. 2. v. sonreír.

grind, v. moler; afilar.

grindstone, n. esmeriladora f.

gringo, n. gringo; yanqui m.

grip, 1. n. maleta f. 2. v. agarrar.

gripe, 1. v. agarrar. 2. n. asimiento m., opresión f.

grippe, n. gripe f.

grisly, a. espantoso.

grist, n. molienda f.

gristle, n. cartílago m.

grit, n. arena f., entereza f.

grizzled, a. tordillo.

groan, 1. n. gemido m. 2. v. gemir.

grocer, n. abacero m.

grocery, n. tienda de comestibles, bodega f.

grog, n. brebaje m.

groggy, a. medio borracho; vacilante.

groin, n. ingle f.

groom, n. (of horses) establero; (at wedding) novio m.

groove, 1. n. estría f. 2. v. acanalar.

grope, v. tentar; andar a tientas.

gross, 1. a. grueso; grosero. 2. n. gruesa f.

grossly, adv. groseramente.

grossness, n. grosería f.

grotesque, a. grotesco.

grotto, n. gruta f.

grouch, n. gruñón; descontento m.

ground, n. tierra f.; terreno; suelo; campo; fundamento m.

groundhog, n. marmota f.

groundless, a. infundado.

groundwork, n. base f., fundamento m.

group, 1. n. grupo m. 2. v. agrupar.

groupie, n. muchacha que acompaña a un grupo de música moderna.

grouse, n. chachalaca f.

grove, n. arboleda f.

grovel, v. rebajarse; envilecerse.

grow, v. crecer; cultivar.

growl, 1. n. gruñido m. 2. v. gruñir.

grown, a. crecido; desarrollado.

grownup, n. adulto m.

growth, n. crecimiento; vegetación f.; (med.) tumor m.

grub, n. gorgojo m., larva f.

grubby, a. guasarapiento.

grudge, n. rencor m. bear a g., guardar rencor.

gruel, 1. n. atole m. 2. v. estropear.

gruesome, a. horripilante.

gruff, a. ceñudo.

grumble, v. quejarse.

grumpy, a. gruñón; quejoso.

grunt, v. gruñir.

guarantee, 1. n. garantía f. 2. v. garantizar.

guarantor, n. fiador m.

guaranty, n. garantía f.

guard, 1. n. guardia m. or f. 2. v. vigilar.

guarded, a. cauteloso.

guardhouse, n. prisión militar f.

guardian, n. guardián m.

guardianship, n. tutela f.

guardsman, n. centinela m.

guava, n. guayaba f.

gubernatorial, a. gubernativo.

guerrilla, n. guerrillero m.

guess, 1. n. conjetura f. 2. v. adivinar; (coll.) creer.

guesswork, n. conjetura f.

guest, n. huésped m. & f.

guffaw, n. risotada f.

guidance, n. dirección f.

guide, 1. n. guía m. & f. 2. v. guiar.

guidebook, n. guía f.

guidepost, n. poste indicador m.

guild, n. gremio m.

guile, n. engaño m.

guillotine, 1. n. guillotina f. 2. v. guillotinar.

guilt, n. culpa f.

guiltily, adv. culpablemente.

guiltless, a. inocente.

guilty, a. culpable.

guinea fowl, n. gallina de Guinea f.

guinea pig, n. cobayo m.

guise, n. modo m.

guitar, n. guitarra f.

gulch, n. quebrada f.

gulf, n. golfo m.

gull, n. gaviota f.

gullet, n. esófago m., zanja f.

gullible, a. crédulo.

gully, n. barranca f.

gulp, 1. n. trago m. 2. v. tragar.

gum, 1. n. goma f.; (anat.) encía f.; chewing g., chicle m. 2. v. engomar.

gumbo, n. quimbombó m.

gummy, a. gomoso.

gun, n. fusil; cañón m.

gunboat, n. cañonero m.

gunman, n. bandido m.

gunner, n. artillero m.

gunpowder, n. pólvora f.

gunshot, n. escopetazo m.

gunwale, n. borda f.

gurgle, 1. n. gorgoteo m. 2. v. gorgotear.

guru, n. gurú m.

gush, 1. n. chorro m. 2. v. brotar, chorrear.

gusher, n. pozo de chorro de petróleo m.

gust, n. soplo m.; ráfaga f.

gustatory, a. del sentido del gusto.

gusto, n. gusto; placer m.

gusty, a. borrascoso.

gut, n. intestino m., tripa f.

gutter, n. canal; zanja f.

guttural, a. gutural.

guy, n. tipo m.

guzzle, v. engullir; tragar.

gym, n. gimnasio m.

gymnasium, n. gimnasio m.

gymnast, n. gimnasta m.

gymnastic, a. gimnástico.

gymnastics, n. gimnasia f.

gynecology, n. ginecología f.

gypsum, n. yeso m.

Gypsy, a. & n. gitano -na.

gyrate, v. girar.

gyroscope, n. giroscopio m.

H

habeas corpus, n. habeas corpus m.

haberdasher, n. camisero m.

haberdashery, n. camisería f.

habiliment, n. vestuario m.

habit, n. costumbre f., hábito m. be in the h. of, estar acostumbrado a; soler.

habitable, a. habitable.

habitat, n. habitación f., ambiente m.

habitation, n. habitación f.

habitual, a. habitual.

habituate, v. habituar.

habitué, n. parroquiano m.

hack, 1. n. coche de alquiler. 2. v. tajar.

hackneyed, a. trillado.

hacksaw, n. sierra para cortar metal f.

haddock, n. merluza f.

haft, n. mango m.

hag, n. bruja f.

haggard, a. trasnochado.

haggle, v. regatear.

hail, 1. n. granizo; (greeting) saludo m. 2. v. granizar; saludar.

Hail Mary, n. Ave María m.

hailstone, n. piedra de granizo f.

hailstorm, n. granizada f.

hair, n. pelo; cabello m.

haircut, n. corte de pelo.

hairdo, n. peinado m.

hairdresser, n. peluquero m.

hairpin, *n.* horquilla *f.;* gancho *m.*

hair's-breadth, *n.* ancho de un pelo *m.*

hairspray, *n.* aerosol para cabello.

hairy, *a.* peludo.

halcyon, 1. *n.* alcedón *m.* 2. *a.* tranquilo.

hale, *a.* sano.

half, 1. *a.* medio. 2. *n.* mitad *f.*

half-and-half, *a.* mitad y mitad.

half-baked, *a.* medio crudo.

half-breed, *n.* mestizo *m.*

half brother, *n.* medio hermano *m.*

half-hearted, *a.* sin entusiasmo.

half-mast, *a.* & *n.* media asta *m.*

halfpenny, *n.* media penique *m.*

halfway, *adv.* a medio camino.

half-wit, *n.* bobo *m.*

halibut, *n.* hipogloso *m.*

hall, *n.* corredor *m.;* (for assembling) sala *f.* **city h.,** ayuntamiento *m.*

hallmark, *n.* marca del contraste *f.*

hallow, *v.* consagrar.

Halloween, *n.* víspera de Todos los Santos *f.*

hallucination, *n.* alucinación *f.*

hallway, *n.* pasadizo *m.*

halo, *n.* halo *m.;* corona *f.*

halt, 1. *a.* cojo. 2. *n.* parada *f.* 3. *v.* parar. 4. *interj.* ¡alto!

halter, *n.* cabestro *m.*

halve, *v.* dividir en dos partes.

halyard, *n.* driza *f.*

ham, *n.* jamón *m.*

hamburger, *n.* albóndiga *f.*

hamlet, *n.* aldea *f.*

hammer, 1. *n.* martillo *m.* 2. *v.* martillar.

hammock, *n.* hamaca *f.*

hamper, *n.* canasta *f.,* cesto *m.*

hamstring, 1. *n.* tendón de la corva *m.* 2. *v.* desjarretar.

hand, 1. mano *f.* **on the other h.,** en cambio. 2. *v.* pasar. **h. over,** entregar.

handbag, *n.* cartera *f.*

handball, *n.* pelota *f.*

handbook, *n.* manual *m.*

handcuff, *n.* esposas *f.*

handful, *n.* puñado *m.*

handicap, *n.* desventaja *f.*

handicraft, *n.* artífice *m.*

handiwork, *n.* artefacto *m.*

handkerchief, *n.* pañuelo *m.*

handle, 1. *n.* mango *m.* 2. *v.* manejar.

handmade, *a.* hecho a mano *m.*

handmaid, *n.* criada de mano *f.*

hand organ, *n.* organillo *m.*

handsome, *a.* guapo; hermoso.

hand-to-hand, *adv.* de mano a mano.

handwriting, *n.* escritura *f.*

handy, *a.* diestro; útil; a la mano.

hang, *v.* colgar; ahorcar.

hangar, *n.* hangar *m.*

hangdog, *a.* & *n.* camastrón *m.*

hanger, *n.* colgador, gancho *m.*

hanger-on, *n.* dependiente; mogollón *m.*

hang glider, *n.* aparato para vuelo libre.

hanging, 1. *n.* ahorcadura *f.* 2. *a.* colgante.

hangman, *n.* verdugo *m.*

hangnail, *n.* padrastro *m.*

hang out, *v.* enarbolar.

hangup, *n.* tara (psicológica) *f.*

hank, *n.* madeja *f.*

hanker, *v.* ansiar; apetecer.

haphazard, *a.* casual.

happen, *v.* acontecer, suceder, pasar.

happening, *n.* acontecimiento *m.*

happiness, *n.* felicidad; dicha *f.*

happy, *a.* feliz; contento; dichoso.

happy-go-lucky, *a.* & *n.* descuidado *m.*

harakiri, *n.* harakiri (suicidio japonés) *m.*

harangue, 1. *n.* arenga *f.* 2. *v.* arengar.

harass, *v.* acosar; atormentar.

harbinger, *n.* presagio *m.*

harbor, 1. *n.* puerto; albergue *m.* 2. *v.* abrigar.

hard, 1. *a.* duro; difícil. 2. *adv.* mucho.

hard coal, antracita *f.*

harden, *v.* endurecer.

hard-headed, *a.* terco.

hard-hearted, *a.* empedernido.

hardiness, *n.* vigor *m.*

hardly, *adv.* apenas.

hardness, *n.* dureza; dificultad *f.*

hardship, *n.* penalidad *f.;* trabajo *m.*

hardware, *n.* ferretería *f.*

hardwood, *n.* madera dura *f.*

hardy, *a.* fuerte, robusto.

hare, *n.* liebre *f.*

harebrained, *a.* tolondro.

harelip, 1. *n.* labio leporino *m.* 2. *a.* labihendido.

harem, *n.* harén *m.*

hark, *v.* escuchar; atender.

Harlequin, *n.* arlequín *m.*

harlot, *n.* ramera *f.*

harm, 1. *n.* mal, daño; perjuicio *m.* 2. *v.* dañar.

harmful, *a.* dañoso.

harmless, *a.* inocente.

harmonic, *n.* armónico *m.*

harmonica, *n.* armónica *f.*

harmonious, *a.* armonioso.

harmonize, *v.* armonizar.

harmony, *n.* armonía *f.*

harness, *n.* arnés *m.*

harp, *n.* arpa *f.*

harpoon, *n.* arpón *m.*

harridan, *n.* vieja regañona *f.*

harrow, 1. *n.* rastro *m.;* grada *f.* 2. *v.* gradar.

harry, *v.* acosar.

harsh, *a.* áspero.

harshness, *n.* aspereza *f.*

harvest, 1. *n.* cosecha *f.* 2. *v.* cosechar.

hash, *n.* picadillo *m.*

hashish, *n.* haxis *m.*

hasn't, *v.* no tiene (neg. + tener).

hassle, *n.* lío *m.,* molestia *f.;* controversia *f.*

hassock, *n.* cojín *m.*

haste, *n.* prisa *f.*

hasten, *v.* apresurarse, darse prisa.

hasty, *a.* apresurado.

hat, *n.* sombrero *m.*

hatch, 1. *n.* (naut.) cuartel *m.* 2. *v.* incubar; (fig.) tramar.

hatchery, *n.* criadero *m.*

hatchet, *n.* hacha pequeña.

hate, 1. *n.* odio *m.* 2. *v.* odiar, detestar.

hateful, *a.* detestable.

hatred, *n.* odio *m.*

haughtiness, *n.* arrogancia *f.*

haughty, *a.* altivo.

haul, 1. *n.* (fishery) redada *f.* 2. *v.* tirar, halar.

haunch, *n.* anca *f.*

haunt, 1. *n.* lugar frecuentado. 2. *v.* frecuentar, andar por.

have, *v.* tener; haber.

haven, *n.* puerto; asilo *m.*

haven't, *v.* no tiene (neg. + tener).

havoc, *n.* ruina *f.*

hawk, *n.* halcón *m.*

hawker, *n.* buhonero *m.*

hawser, *n.* cable *m.*

hawthorn, *n.* espino *m.*

hay, *n.* heno *m.*

hay fever, *n.* catarro anual de la nariz *m.;* alergia nasal.

hayfield, *n.* henar *m.*

hayloft, *n.* henil *m.*

haystack, *n.* hacina de heno *f.*

hazard, 1. *n.* azar *m.* 2. *v.* aventurar.

hazardous, *a.* peligroso.

haze, *n.* niebla *f.*

hazel, *n.* avellano *m.*

hazy, *a.* brumoso.

he, *pron.* él *m.*

head, 1. *n.* cabeza *f.;* jefe *m.* 2. *v.* dirigir; encabezar.

headache, *n.* dolor de cabeza.

headband, *n.* venda para cabeza *f.*

headfirst, *adv.* de cabeza.

headgear, *n.* tocado *m.*

headlight, *n.* linterna delantera *f.,* farol de tope *m.*

headline, *n.* encabezado *m.*

headlong, *a.* precipitoso.

head-on, *adv.* de frente.

headquarters, *n.* jefatura *f.;* (mil.) cuartel general.

headstone, *n.* lápida mortuoria *f.*

headstrong, *a.* terco.

headwaters, *n.* cabeceras *f.*

headway, *n.* avance *m.,* progreso *m.*

headwork, *n.* trabajo mental *m.*

heady, *a.* impetuoso.

heal, *v.* curar, sanar.

health, *n.* salud *f.*

healthful, *a.* saludable.

healthy, *a.* sano; salubre.

heap, *n.* montón *m.*

hear, *v.* oír. **h. from,** tener noticias de. **h. about, h. of,** oír hablar de.

bearing, *n.* oído *m.*

hearsay, *n.* rumor *m.*

bearse, *n.* ataúd *m.*

heart, *n.* corazón; ánimo *m.* **by h.,** de memoria.

heartache, *n.* angustia *f.*

heartbreak, *n.* angustia *f.;* pesar *m.*

heartbroken, *a.* acongojado.

heartburn, *n.* acedía *f.*

heartfelt, *a.* sentido.

hearth, *n.* hogar *m.,* chimenea *f.*

heartless, *a.* empedernido.

heartsick, *a.* desconsolado.

heart-stricken, *a.* afligido.

heart-to-heart, *adv.* franco; sincero.

hearty, *a.* cordial; vigoroso.

heat, 1. *n.* calor; ardor *m.;* calefacción *f.* 2. *v.* calentar.

beated, *a.* acalorado.

beater, *n.* calentador *m.*

heath, *n.* matorral *m.*

heathen, *a.* & *n.* pagano -na.

heather, *n.* brezo *m.*

heatstroke, *n.* insolación *f.*

heat wave, *n.* onda de calor *f.*

heave, *v.* tirar.

heaven, *n.* cielo *m.*

heavenly, *a.* divino.

heavy, *a.* pesado; oneroso.

Hebrew, *a.* & *n.* hebreo -ea.

hectic, *a.* turbulento.

hedge, *n.* seto *m.*

hedgehog, *n.* erizo *m.*

hedonism, *n.* hedonismo *m.*

heed, 1. *n.* cuidado *m.* 2. *v.* atender.

heedless, *a.* desatento; incauto.

heel, *n.* talón *m.;* (of shoe) tacón *m.*

heifer, *n.* novilla *f.*

height, *n.* altura *f.*

heighten, *n.* elevar; exaltar.

heinous, *a.* nefando.

heir, heiress, *n.* heredero -ra.

helicopter, *n.* helicóptero *m.*

heliotrope, *n.* heliotropo *m.*

helium, *n.* helio *m.*

hell, *n.* infierno *m.*

Hellenism, *n.* helenismo *m.*

hellish, *a.* infernal.

hello, *interj.* ¡hola!; (on telephone) aló; bueno.

helm, *n.* timón *m.*

helmet, *n.* yelmo, casco *m.*

helmsman, *n.* limonero *m.*

help, 1. *n.* ayuda *f.* **help!** ¡socorro! 2. *v.* ayudar. **h. oneself,** servirse. **can't help (but),** no poder menos de.

helper, *n.* ayudante *m.*

helpful, *a.* útil; servicial.

helpfulness, *n.* utilidad *f.*

helpless, *a.* imposibilitado.

hem, 1. *n.* ribete *m.* 2. *v.* ribetear.

hemisphere, *n.* hemisferio *m.*

hemlock, *n.* abeto *m.*

hemoglobin, *n.* hemoglobina *f.*

hemophilia, *n.* hemofilia *f.*

hemorrhage, *n.* hemorragia *f.*

hemorrhoid, *n.* hemorriodes *f.pl.*

hemp, *n.* cáñamo *m.*

hemstitch, 1. *n.* vainica *f.* 2. *v.* hacer una vainica.

hen, *n.* gallina *f.*

hence, *adv.* por lo tanto.

henceforth, *adv.* de aquí en adelante.

benchman, *n.* paniaguado *m.*

henna, *n.* alheña *f.*

her, 1. *a.* su. 2. *pron.* ella; la; le.

herald, *n.* heraldo *m.*

heraldic, *a.* heráldico.

heraldry, *n.* heráldica *f.*

herb, *n.* yerba, hierba *f.*

herbaceous, *a.* herbáceo.

herbarium, *n.* herbario *m.*

herd, 1. *n.* hato, rebaño *m.* 2. *v.* reunir en hatos.

here, *adv.* aquí; acá.

hereafter, *adv.* en lo futuro.

hereby, *adv.* por éstas, por la presente.

hereditary, *a.* hereditario.

heredity, *n.* herencia *f.*

herein, *adv.* aquí dentro; incluso.

heresy, *n.* herejía *f.*

heretic, 1. *a.* herético. 2. *n.* hereje *m.* & *f.*

heretical, *a.* herético.

heretofore, *adv.* hasta ahora.

herewith, *adv.* con esto, adjunto.

heritage, *n.* herencia *f.*

hermetic, *a.* hermético.

hermit, *n.* ermitaño *m.*

hernia, *n.* hernia *f.*

hero, *n.* héroe *m.*

heroic, *a.* heroico.

heroically, *adv.* heroicamente.

heroin, *n.* heroína *f.*

heroine, *n.* heroína *f.*

heroism, *n.* heroísmo *m.*

heron, *n.* garza *f.*

herring, *n.* arenque *m.*

hers, *pron.* suyo, de ella.

herself, *pron.* sí, sí misma, se. **she h.,** ella misma. **with h.,** consigo.

hertz, *n.* hertzio *m.*

hesitancy, *n.* hesitación *f.*

hesitant, *a.* indeciso.

hesitate, *v.* vacilar.

hesitation, *n.* duda; vacilación *f.*

heterogeneous, *a.* heterogéneo.

heterosexual, *a.* heterosexual.

hexagon, *n.* hexágono *m.*

hibernate, *v.* invernar.

hibernation, *n.* invernada *f.*

hibiscus, *n.* hibisco *m.*

hiccup, 1. *n.* hipo *m.* 2. *v.* tener hipo.

hickory, *n.* nogal americano *m.*

hidden, *a.* oculto; escondido.

hide, 1. *n.* cuero *m.;* piel *f.* 2. *v.* esconder; ocultar.

hideous, *a.* horrible.

hide-out, *n.* escondite *m.*

hierarchy, *n.* jerarquía *f.*

high, *a.* alto, elevado; (in price) caro.

highbrow, *n.* erudito *m.*

high fidelity, de alta fidelidad.

highly, *adv.* altamente; sumamente.

high school, *n.* escuela secundaria *f.*

highway, *n.* carretera *f.;* camino real *m.*

hijacker, *n.* secuestrador, pirata de aviones *m.*

hike, *n.* caminata *f.*

hilarious, *a.* alegre, bullicioso.

hilariousness, hilarity, *n.* hilaridad *f.*

hill, *n.* colina *f.;* cerro *m.;* **down h.,** cuesta abajo. **up h.,** cuesta arriba.

hilt, *n.* puño *m.* **up to the h.,** a fondo.

him, *pron.* él; lo; le.

himself, *pron.* sí, sí mismo; se. **he h.,** él mismo. **with h.,** consigo.

hinder, *v.* impedir.

hindmost, *a.* último.

hindquarter, *n.* cuarto trasero *m.*

hindrance, *n.* obstáculo *m.*

hinge, 1. *n.* gozne *m.* 2. *v.* engoznar. **h. on,** depender de.

hint, 1. *n.* insinuación *f.;* indicio *m.* 2. *v.* insinuar.

hip, *n.* cadera *f.*

hippopotamus, *n.* hipopótamo *m.*

hire, *v.* alquilar.

his, 1. *a.* su. 2. *pron.* suyo, de él.

Hispanic, *a.* hispano.

hiss, *v.* silbar, sisear.

historian, *n.* historiador *m.*

historic, historical, *a.* histórico.

history, *n.* historia *f.*

histrionic, *a.* histriónico.

hit, 1. *n.* golpe *m.;* (coll.) éxito *m.* 2. *v.* golpear, dar.

hitch, *v.* amarrar; enganchar.

hither, *adv.* acá, hacia acá.

hitherto, *adv.* hasta ahora.

hive, *n.* colmena *f.*

hives, *n.* urticaria *f.*

hoard, 1. *n.* acumulación *f.* 2. *v.* acaparar; atesorar.

hoarse, *a.* ronco.

hoax, 1. *n.* engaño *m.* 2. *v.* engañar.

hobby, *n.* afición *f.,* pasatiempo *m.*

hobgoblin, *n.* trasgo *m.*

hobnob, *v.* tener intimidad.

hobo, *n.* vagabundo *m.*

hockey, *n.* hockey *m.* **ice-h.,** hockey sobre hielo.

hod, *n.* esparavel *m.*

hodgepodge, *n.* baturillo *m.;* mezcolanza *f.*

hoe, 1. *n.* azada *f.* 2. *v.* cultivar con azada.

hog, *n.* cerdo, puerco *m.*

hoist, 1. *n.* grúa *f.,* elevador *m.* 2. *v.* elevar, enarbolar.

hold, 1. *n.* presa *f.;* agarro *m.;*

(naut.) bodega f. **to get h. of,** conseguir, apoderarse de. **2.** v. tener; detener; sujetar; celebrar.

holder, n. tenedor m. **cigarette h.,** boquilla f.

boldup, n. salteamiento m.

hole, n. agujero; hoyo; hueco m.

holiday, n. día de fiesta.

holiness, n. santidad f.

Holland, n. Holanda f.

hollow, 1. a. hueco. **2.** n. cavidad f. **3.** v. ahuecar; excavar.

holly, n. acebo m.

hollyhock, n. malva real f.

holocaust, n. holocausto m.

hologram, n. holograma m.

holography, n. holografía f.

holster, n. pistolera f.

holy, a. santo.

holy day. n. disanto m.

Holy See, n. Santa Sede f.

Holy Spirit, n. Espíritu Santo m.

Holy Week, n. Semana Santa f.

homage, n. homenaje m.

home, n. casa, morada f; hogar m. **at h.,** en casa. **to go h.,** ir a casa.

homeland, n. patria f.

homely, a. feo; casero.

home rule, n. autonomía f.

homesick, a. nostálgico.

homespun, a. casero; tosco.

homeward, adv. hacia casa.

homicide, n. homicida m. & f.

homily, n. homilía f.

homogeneous, a. homogéneo.

homogenize, v. homogenizar.

homosexual, n. & a. homosexual m.

Honduras, n. Honduras f.

hone, 1. n. piedra de afilar f. **2.** v. afilar.

honest, a. honrado, honesto; sincero.

honestly, adv. honradamente; de veras.

honesty, n. honradez, honestidad f.

honey, n. miel f.

honeybee, n. abeja obrera f.

honeymoon, n. luna de miel.

honeysuckle, n. madreselva f.

honor, 1. n. honra f.; honor m. **2.** v. honrar.

honorable, a. honorable; ilustre.

honorary, a. honorario.

hood, n. capota; capucha f.; (auto.) cubierta del motor.

hoodlum, n. pillo m., rufián m.

hoof, n. pezuña f.

hook, 1. n. gancho m. **2.** v. enganchar.

hoop, n. cerco m.

hop, 1. n. salto m. **2.** v. saltar.

hope, 1. n. esperanza f. **2.** v. esperar.

hopeful, a. lleno de esperanzas.

hopeless, a. desesperado; sin remedio.

horde, n. horda f.

horehound, n. marrubio m.

horizon, n. horizonte m.

horizontal, a. horizontal.

hormone, n. hormón m.

horn, n. cuerno m.; (music) trompa f.; (auto.) bocina f.

hornet, n. avispón m.

horny, a. córneo; calloso.

horoscope, n. horóscopo m.

horrendous, a. horrendo.

horrible, a. horrible.

horrid, a. horrible.

horrify, v. horrorizar.

horror, n. horror m.

horse, n. caballo m. **to ride a h.,** cabalgar.

horseback, n. **on h.,** a caballo. **to ride h.,** montar a caballo.

horsefly, n. tábano m.

horsehair, n. pelo de caballo m.; tela de crin f.

horseman, n. jinete m.

horsemanship, n. manejo m., equitación f.

horsepower, n. caballo de fuerza m.

horseradish, n. rábano picante m.

horseshoe, n. herradura f.

hortatory, a. exhortatorio.

horticulture, n. horticultura f.

hose, n. medias f.pl; (garden) manguera f.

hosiery, n. calcetería f.

hospitable, a. hospitalario.

hospital, n. hospital m.

hospitality, n. hospitalidad f.

hospitalization, n. hospitalización f.

hospitalize, v. hispitalizar.

host, n. anfitrión m., dueño de la casa; (rel.) hostia f.

hostage, n. rehén m.

hostel, n. hostería f.

hostelry, n. fonda f., parador m.

hostess, n. anfitriona f., dueña de la casa.

hostile, a. hostil.

hostility, n. hostilidad f.

hot, a. caliente; (sauce) picante. **to be h.,** tener calor; (weather) hacer calor.

hotbed, n. estercolero m. (fig.) foco m.

hotel, n. hotel m.

hot-headed, a. turbulente, alborotadizo.

hothouse, n. invernáculo m.

hound, 1. n. sabueso m. **2.** v. perseguir; seguir la pista.

hour, n. hora f.

hourglass, n. reloj de arena m.

hourly, 1. a. por horas. **2.** adv. a cada hora.

house, 1. casa f.; (theat.) público m. **2.** v. alojar, albergar.

housefly, n. mosca ordinaria f.

household, n. familia; casa f.

housekeeper, n. ama de llaves.

housemaid, n. criada f., sirvienta f.

housewife, n. ama de casa.

housework, n. tareas domésticas f.

hovel, n. choza f.

hover, v. revolotear.

hovercraft, n. hovercraft m.

how, adv. cómo. **h. much,** cuánto. **h. many,** cuántos. **h. far,** a qué distancia.

however, adv. como quiera; sin embargo.

howl, 1. n. aullido m. **2.** v. aullar.

hub, n. centro m.; eje m. **h. of a wheel,** cubo de la rueda m.

hubbub, n. alborota f., bulla f.

hue, n. matiz; color m.

hug, 1. n. abrazo m. **2.** v. abrazar.

huge, a. enorme.

hulk, n. casco de buque m.

hull, 1. n. cáscara f.; (naval) casco m. **2.** v. decascarar.

hum, 1. n. zumbido m. **2.** v. tararear; zumbar.

human, a. & n. humano -na.

humane, a. humano, humanitario.

humanism, n. humanidad f.; benevolencia f.

humanitarian, a. humanitario.

humanity, n. humanidad f.

humanly, a. humanamente.

humble, a. humilde.

humbug, n. farsa f., embaucador m.

humdrum, a. monótono.

humid, a. húmedo.

humidity, n. humedad f.

humiliate, v. humillar.

humiliation, n. mortificación f.; bochorno m.

humility, n. humildad f.

humor, 1. n. humor; capricho m. **2.** v. complacer.

humorist, n. humorista m.

humorous, a. divertido.

hump, n. joroba f.

humpback, n. jorobado m.

humus, n. humus m.

hunch, n. giba f.; (idea) corazonada f.

hunchback, n. jorobado m.

hundred, 1. a. & pron. cien, ciento. **200,** doscientos. **300,** trescientos. **400,** cuatrocientos. **500,** quinientos. **600,** seiscientos. **700,** setecientos. **800,** ochocientos. **900,** novecientos. **2.** n. centenar m.

hundredth, n. & a. centésimo m.

Hungarian, a. & n. húngaro -ra.

Hungary, n. Hungría f.

hunger, n. hambre f.

hungry, a. hambriento. **to be h.,** tener hambre.

hunt, 1. n. caza f. **2.** v. cazar. **h. up,** buscar.

hunter, n. cazador m.

hunting, n. caza f. **to go h.,** ir de caza.

hurdle, n. zarzo m., valla f.; dificultad f.

hurl, v. arrojar.

hurricane, n. huracán m.

hurry, 1. n. prisa f. **to be in a h.,** tener prisa. **2.** v. apresurar; darse prisa.

hurt, 1. n. daño, perjuicio m. **2.** v. dañar; lastimar; doler; ofender.

hurtful, a. perjudicial, dañino.

hurtle, v. lanzar.

husband, n. marido, esposo m.

husk, 1. n. cáscara f. **2.** v. descascarar.

husky, a. fornido.

hustle, v. empujar.

hut, n. choza f.

hyacinth, n. jacinto m.

hybrid, a. híbrido.

hydrangea, n. hortensia f.

hydraulic, a. hidráulico.

hydroelectric, a. hidroeléctrico.

hydrogen, n. hidrógeno m.

hydrophobia, n. hidrofobia. f.

hydroplane, n. hidroavión m.

hydrotherapy, n. hidroterapia f.

hyena, n. hiena f.

hygiene, n. higiene f.

hygienic, a. higiénico.

hymn, n. himno m.

hymnal, n. himnario m.

hypercritical, a. hipercrítico.

hyphen, n. guión m.

hyphenate, v. separar con guión.

hypnosis, n. hipnosis f.

hypnotic, a. hipnótico.

hypnotism, n. hipnotismo m.

hypnotize, v. hipnotizar.

hypochondria, n. hipocondría f.

hypochondriac, n. & a. hipocondríaco m.

hypocrisy, n. hipocresía f.

hypocrite, n. hipócrita m. & f.

hypocritical, a. hipócrita.

hypodermic, a. hipodérmico.

hypotenuse, n. hipotenusa f.

hypothesis, n. hipótesis f.

hypothetical, a. hipotético.

hysterectomy, n. histerectomía f.

hysteria, hysterics, n. histeria f.

hysterical, a. histérico.

I

I, pron. yo.

iambic, a. yámbico.

ice, n. hielo m.

iceberg, n. iceberg m.

icebox, n. refrigerador m.

ice cream, n. helado, mantecado m.; **i.-c. cone,** barquillo de helado.

ice skate, n. patín de cuchilla m.

icon, n. icón m.

icy, a. helado; indiferente.

idea, n. idea f.

ideal, a. ideal.

idealism, n. idealismo m.

idealist, n. idealista m. & f.

idealistic, a. idealista.

idealize, v. idealizar.

ideally, adv. idealmente.

identical, a. idéntico.

identifiable, a. identificable.

identification, n. identificación f. **i. papers,** cédula de identidad f.

identify, v. identificar.

identity, n. identidad f.

ideology, n. ideología f.

idiocy, n. idiotez f.

idiom, n. modismo m.; idioma m.

idiot, n. idiota m. & f.

idiotic, a. idiota, tonto.

idle, a. desocupado; perezoso.

idleness, n. ociosidad, pereza f.

idol, n. ídolo m.

idolatry, n. idolatría f.

idolize, v. idolatrar.

idyl, n. idilio m.

idyllic, a. idílico.

if, conj. si. **even if,** aunque.

ignite, v. encender.

ignition, n. ignición f.

ignoble, a. innoble, indigno.

ignominious, a. ignominioso.

ignoramus, n. ignorante m.

ignorance, n. ignorancia f.

ignorant, a. ignorante. **to be i. of,** ignorar.

ignore, v. desconocer, pasar por alto.

ill, a. enfermo, malo.

illegal, a. ilegal.

illegible, a. ilegible.

illegibly, a. ilegiblemente.

illegitimacy, n. ilegitimidad f.

illegitimate, a. ilegítimo; desautorizado.

illicit, a. ilícito.

illiteracy, n. analfabetismo m.

illiterate, a. & n. analfabeto - ta.

illness, n. enfermedad, maldad f.

illogical, a. ilógico.

illuminate, v. iluminar.

illumination, n. iluminación f.

illusion, n. ilusión f.; ensueño m.

illusive, a. ilusivo.

illustrate, v. ilustrar; ejemplificar.

illustration, n. ilustración f.; ejemplo; grabado m.

illustrative, a. ilustrativo.

illustrious, a. ilustre.

ill will, n. malevolencia f.

image, n. imagen, estatua f.

imagery, n. imaginación f.

imaginable, a. imaginable.

imaginary, a. imaginario.

imagination, n. imaginación f.

imaginative, a. imaginativo.

imagine, v. imaginarse, figurarse.

imam, n. imán m.

imbecile, a. & n. imbécil m.

imitate, v. imitar.

imitation, n. imitación f.

imitative, a. imitativo.

immaculate, a. inmaculado.

immanent, a. inmanente.

immaterial, a. inmaterial; sin importancia.

immature, a. inmaturo.

immediate, a. inmediato.

immediately, adv. inmediatamente.

immense, a. inmenso.

immerse, v. sumergir.

immigrant, n. & a. inmigrante m.

immigrate, v. inmigrar.

imminent, a. inminente.

immobile, a. inmóvil.

immoderate, a. inmoderado.

immodest, a. inmodesto; atrevido.

immoral, a. inmoral.

immorality, n. inmoralidad f.

immorally, adv. licenciosamente.

immortal, a. inmortal.

immortality, n. inmortalidad f.

immortalize, v. inmortalizar.

immune, a. inmune.

immunity, n. inmunidad f.

immunize, v. inmunizar.

impact, n. impacto m.

impair, v. empeorar, perjudicar.

impale, v. empalar.

impart, v. impartir, comunicar.

impartial, a. imparcial.

impatience, n. impaciencia f.

impatient, a. impaciente.

impede, v. impedir, estorbar.

impediment, n. impedimento m.

impel, v. impeler.

impenetrable, a. impenetrable.

impenitent, a. & a. impenitente m.

imperative, a. imperativo.

imperceptible, a. imperceptible.

imperfect, a. imperfecto.

imperfection, n. imperfección f.

imperial, a. imperial.

imperialism, n. imperialismo m.

imperious, a. imperioso.

impersonal, a. impersonal.

impersonate, v. personificar; imitar.

impersonation, n. personificación f.; imitación f.

impertinence, n. impertinencia f.

impervious, a. impermeable.

impetuous, a. impetuoso.

impetus, n. ímpetu m., impulso m.

impinge, v. tropezar; infringir.

implacable, a. implacable.

implant, v. implantar; inculcar.

implement, n. herramienta f.

implicate, v. implicar; embrollar.

implication, n. inferencia f.; complicidad f.

implicit, a. implícito.

implied, a. implícito.

implore, v. implorar.

imply, v. significar; dar a entender.

impolite, *a.* descortés.

import, **1.** *n.* importación *f.* **2.** *v.* importar.

importance, *n.* importancia *f.*

important, *a.* importante.

importation, *n.* importación *f.*

importune, *v.* importunar.

impose, *v.* imponer.

imposition, *n.* imposición *f.*

impossibility, *n.* imposibilidad *f.*

impossible, *a.* imposible.

impotence, *n.* impotencia *f.*

impotent, *a.* impotente.

impregnable, *a.* impregnable.

impregnate, *v.* impregnar; fecundizar.

impresario, *n.* empresario *m.*

impress, *v.* impresionar.

impression, *n.* impresión *f.*

impressive, *a.* imponente.

imprison, *v.* encarcelar.

imprisonment, *n.* prisión, encarcelación *f.*

improbable, *a.* improbable.

impromptu, *a.* extemporáneo.

improper, *a.* impropio.

improve, *v.* mejorar; progresar.

improvement, *n.* mejoramiento; progreso *m.*

improvise, *v.* improvisar.

impudent, *a.* descarada.

impugn, *v.* impugnar.

impulse, *n.* impulso *m.*

impulsive, *a.* impulsivo.

impunity, *n.* impunidad *f.*

impure, *a.* impuro.

impurity, *n.* impureza *f.*; deshonestidad *f.*

impute, *v.* imputar.

in, **1.** *prep.* en; dentro de. **2.** *adv.* adentro.

inadvertent, *a.* inadvertido.

inalienable, *a.* inalienable.

inane, *a.* mentecato.

inaugural, *a.* inaugural.

inaugurate, *v.* inaugurar.

inauguration, *n.* inauguración *f.*

Inca, *n.* inca *m.*

incandescent, *a.* incandescente.

incantation, *n.* encantación *f.*, conjuro *m.*

incapacitate, *v.* incapacitar.

incarcerate, *v.* encarcelar.

incarnate, *a.* encarnado; personificado.

incarnation, *n.* encarnación *f.*

incendiary, *a.* incendiario.

incense, **1.** *n.* incienso *m.* **2.** *v.* indignar.

incentive, *n.* incentivo *m.*

inception, *n.* cimiento *m.*

incessant, *a.* incesante.

incest, *n.* incesto *m.*

inch, *n.* pulgada *f.*

incidence, *n.* incidencia *f.*

incident, *n.* incidente *m.*

incidental, *a.* incidental.

incidentally, *adv.* incidentalmente; entre paréntesis.

incinerator, *n.* incinerador *m.*

incipient, *a.* incipiente.

incision, *n.* incisión *f.*; cortadura *f.*

incisive, *a.* incisivo; mordaz.

incisor, *n.* incisivo *m.*

incite, *v.* incitar, instigar.

inclination, *n.* inclinación *f.*; declive *m.*

incline, **1.** *n.* pendiente *m.* **2.** *v.* inclinar.

inclose, *v.* incluir.

include, *v.* incluir.

including, *prep.* incluso.

inclusive, *a.* inclusivo.

incognito, *n. & adv.* incógnito *m.*

income, *n.* renta *f.*; ingresos *m.pl.*

incomparable, *a.* incomparable.

inconvenience, **1.** *n.* incomodidad *f.* **2.** *v.* incomodar.

inconvenient, *a.* incómodo.

incorporate, *v.* incoporar; dar cuerpo.

incorrigible, *a.* incorregible.

increase, *v.* crecer; aumentar.

incredible, *a.* increíble.

incredulity, *n.* incredulidad *f.*

incredulous, *a.* incrédulo.

increment, *n.* incremento *m.*, aumento *m.*

incriminate, *v.* incriminar.

incrimination, *n.* incriminación *f.*

incrust, *v.* incrustar.

incubator, *n.* incubadora *f.*

inculcate, *v.* inculcar.

incumbency, *n.* incumbencia *f.*

incumbent, *a.* obligatorio; colocado sobre.

incur, *v.* incurrir.

incurable, *a.* incurable.

indebted, *a.* obligado; adeudado.

indeed, *adv.* verdaderamente, de veras. **no i.**, de ninguna manera.

indefatigable, *a.* incansable.

indefinite, *a.* indefinido.

indefinitely, *adv.* indefinidamente.

indelible, *a.* indeleble.

indemnify, *v.* indemnizar.

indemnity, *n.* indemnificación *f.*

indent, **1.** *n.* diente *f.*, mella *f.* **2.** *v.* indentar, mellar.

indentation, *n.* indentación *f.*

independence, *n.* independencia *f.*

independent, *a.* independiente.

in-depth, *adj.* en profundidad.

index, *n.* índice *m.*; (of book) tabla *f.*

India, *n.* India *f.*

Indian, *a. & n.* indio -dia.

indicate, *v.* indicar.

indication, *n.* indicación *f.*

indicative, *a. & n.* indicativo *m.*

indict, *v.* encausar.

indictment, *n.* (law) sumaria *m.*; denuncia *f.*

indifference, *n.* indiferencia *f.*

indifferent, *a.* indiferente.

indigenous, *a.* indígena.

indigent, *a.* indigente, pobre.

indigestion, *n.* indigestión *f.*

indignant, *a.* indignado.

indignation, *n.* indignación *f.*

indignity, *n.* indignidad *f.*

indirect, *a.* indirecto.

indiscreet, *a.* indiscreto.

indiscretion, *n.* indiscreción *f.*

indiscriminate, *a.* promiscuo.

indispensable, *a.* indispensable.

indisposed, *a.* indispuesto.

individual, *a. & n.* individuo *m.*

individuality, *n.* individualidad *f.*

individually, *adv.* individualmente.

indivisible, *a.* indivisible.

indoctrinate, *v.* doctrinar, enseñar.

indolent, *a.* indolente.

indoor, *a.* interior. **indoors**, *adv.* en casa; bajo techo.

indorse, *v.* endosar.

induce, *v.* inducir, persuadir.

induct, *v.* instalar, iniciar.

induction, *n.* introducción *f.*; instalación *f.*

inductive, *a.* inductivo; introductor.

indulge, *v.* favorecer. **i. in**, entregarse a.

indulgence, *n.* indulgencia *f.*

indulgent, *a.* indulgente.

industrial, *a.* industrial.

industrialist, *n.* industrial *m.*

industrious, *a.* industrioso, trabajador.

industry, *n.* industria *f.*

ineligible, *a.* inelegible.

inept, *a.* inepto.

inert, *a.* inerte.

inertia, *n.* inercia *f.*

inevitable, *a.* inevitable.

inexplicable, *a.* inexplicable.

infallible, *a.* infalible.

infamous, *a.* infame.

infamy, *n.* infamia *f.*

infancy, *n.* infancia *f.*

infant, *n.* nene *m.*; criatura *f.*

infantile, *a.* infantil.

infantry, *n.* infantería *f.*

infatuated, *a.* infatuado.

infect, *v.* infectar.

infection, *n.* infección *f.*

infectious, *a.* infeccioso.

infer, *v.* inferir.

inference, *n.* inferencia *f.*

inferior, *a.* inferior.

infernal, *a.* infernal.

inferno, *n.* infierno *m.*

infest, *v.* infestar.

infidel, **1.** *n.* infiel *m.*; pagano *m.* **2.** *a.* infiel.

infidelity, *n.* infidelidad *f.*

infiltrate, *v.* infiltrar.

infinite, *a.* infinito.

infinitesimal, *a.* infinitesimal.

infinitive, *n. & a.* infinitivo *m.*

infinity, *n.* infinidad *f.*

infirm, *a.* enfermizo.

infirmary, *n.* hospital *m.*, enfermería *f.*

infirmity, *n.* enfermedad *f.*

inflame, *v.* inflamar.

inflammable, a. inflamable.

inflammation, n. inflamación f.

inflammatory, a. inflamante; (med.) inflamatorio.

inflate, v. inflar.

inflation, n. inflación f.

inflection, n. inflexión f.; (of the voice) modulación de la voz f.

inflict, v. infligir.

infliction, n. imposición f.

influence, 1. n. influencia f. 2. v. influir en.

influential, a. influyente.

influenza, n. gripe f.

inform, v. informar. i. oneself, enterarse.

informal, a. informal.

information, n. informaciones f.pl.

infringe, v. infringir.

infuriate, v. enfurecer.

ingenious, a. ingenioso.

ingenuity, n. ingeniosidad; destreza f.

ingredient, n. ingrediente m.

inhabit, v. habitar.

inhabitant, n. habitante m. & f.

inhale, v. inhalar.

inherent, a. inherente.

inherit, v. heredar.

inheritance, n. herencia f.

inhibit, v. inhibir.

inhibition, n. inhibición f.

inhuman, a. inhumano.

inimical, a. hostil.

inimitable, a. inimitable.

iniquity, n. iniquidad f.

initial, a. & n. inicial f.

initiate, v. iniciar.

initiation, n. iniciación f.

initiative, n. iniciativa f.

inject, v. inyectar.

injection, n. inyección f.

injunction, n. mandato m.; (law) embargo m.

injure, v. herir; lastimar; ofender.

injurious, a. perjudicial.

injury, n. herida; afrenta f. perjuicio m.

injustice, n. injusticia f.

ink, n. tinta f.

inland, 1. a. interior. 2. adv. tierra adentro.

inlet, n. entrada f.; ensenada f.; estuario m.

inmate, n. residente m.; (of a prison) preso m.

inn, n. posada f.; mesón m.

inner, a. interior. i. tube, cámara de aire.

innocence, n. inocencia f.

innocent, a. inocente.

innocuous, a. innocuo.

innovation, n. innovación f.

innuendo, n. insinuación f.

innumerable, a. innumerable.

inoculate, v. inocular.

inoculation, n. inoculación f.

input, n. aducto m.

inquest, n. indagación f.

inquire, v. preguntar; inquirir.

inquiry, n. pregunta; investigación f.

inquisition, n. escudriñamiento m.; (church) Inquisición f.

insane, a. loco. to go i., perder la razón; volverse loco.

insanity, n. locura f.; demencia f.

inscribe, v. inscribir.

inscription, n. inscripción; dedicatoria f.

insect, n. insecto m.

insecticide, n. & a. insecticida f.

inseparable, a. inseparable.

insert, v. insertar, meter.

insertion, n. cosa insertada f.

inside, 1. a. & n. interior m. 2. adv. adentro, por dentro. i. out, al revés. 3. prep. dentro de.

insidious, a. insidioso.

insight, n. perspicacia f.; comprensión f.

insignia, n. insignias f.pl.

insignificance, n. insignificancia f.

insignificant, a. insignificante.

insinuate, v. insinuar.

insinuation, n. insinuación f.

insipid, a. insípido.

insist, v. insistir.

insistence, n. insistencia f.

insistent, a. insistente.

insolence, n. insolencia f.

insolent, a. insolente.

insomnia, n. insomnio m.

inspect, v. inspeccionar, examinar.

inspection, n. inspección f.

inspector, n. inspector m.

inspiration, n. inspiración f.

inspire, v. inspirar.

install, v. instalar.

installation, n. instalación f.

installment, n. plazo m.

instance, n. ocasión f. for i., por ejemplo.

instant, a. & n. instante m.

instantaneous, a. instantáneo.

instantly, adv. al instante.

instead, adv. en lugar de eso. i. of, en vez de, en lugar de.

instigate, v. instigar.

instill, v. instilar.

instinct, n. instinto m.

instinctive, a. instintivo.

institute, 1. n. instituto m. 2. v. instituir.

institution, n. institución f.

instruct, v. instruir.

instruction, n. instrucción f.

instructive, a. instructivo.

instructor, n. instructor m.

instrument, n. instrumento m.

instrumental, a. instrumental.

insufficient, a. insuficiente.

insular, a. insular; estrecho de miras.

insulate, v. aislar.

insulation, n. aislamiento m.

insulator, n. aislador m.

insulin, n. insulina f.

insult, 1. n. insulto m. 2. v. insultar.

insuperable, a. insuperable.

insurance, n. seguro m.

insure, v. asegurar.

insurgent, a. & n. insurgente m.

insurrection, n. insurrección f.

intact, a. intacto.

intangible, a. intangible, impalpable.

integral, a. íntegro.

integrate, v. integrar.

integrity, n. integridad f.

intellect, n. intelecto m.

intellectual, a. & n. intelectual m. & f.

intelligence, n. inteligencia f.

intelligent, a. inteligente.

intelligible, a. inteligible.

intend, v. pensar; intentar; destinar.

intense, a. intenso.

intensify, v. intensificar.

intensity, n. intensidad f.

intensive, a. intensivo.

intent, n. intento m.

intention, n. intención f.

intentional, a. intencional.

intercede, v. interceder.

intercept, v. interceptar; detener.

intercourse, n. tráfico m.; comunicación f.; coito m.

interest, 1. n. interés m. 2. v. interesar.

interesting, a. interesante.

interface, n. aparato o zona de contacto.

interfere, v. meterse; intervenir. i. with, estorbar.

interference, n. intervención f.; obstáculo m.

interior, a. interior.

interject, v. interponer; intervenir.

interjection, n. interjección f.; interposición f.

interlude, n. intervalo m.; (theat.) intermedio m.; (music) interludio m.

intermediary, n. intermediario m.

intermediate, a. intermedio.

interment, n. entierro m.

intermission, n. intermisión f.; (theat.) entreacto m.

intermittent, a. intermitente.

intern, 1. n. interno m. 2. v. internar.

internal, a. interno.

international, a. internacional.

internationalism, n. internacionalismo m.

interne, n. practicante de hospital m.

interpose, v. interponer.

interpret, v. interpretar.

interpretation, n. interpretación f.

interpreter, n. intérprete m. & f.

interrogate, v. interrogar.

interrogation, n. interrogación; pregunta f.

interrogative, a. interrogativo.

interrupt, v. interrumpir.

interruption, n. interrupción f.

intersect, v. cortar.

intersection, n. intersección f.; (street) bocacalle f.
intersperse, v. entremezclar.
interval, n. intervalo m.
intervene, v. intervenir.
intervention, n. intervención f.
interview, 1. n. entrevista f. **2.** v. entrevistar.
intestine, n. intestino m.
intimacy, n. intimidad; familiaridad f.
intimate, 1. a. íntimo, familiar. **2.** n. amigo íntimo. **3.** v. insinuar.
intimidate, v. intimidar.
intimidation, n. intimidación f.
into, prep. en, dentro de.
intonation, n. entonación f.
intone, v. entonar.
intoxicate, v. embriagar.
intoxication, n. embriaguez f.
intravenous, a. intravenoso.
intrepid, a. intrépido.
intricacy, n. intrincación f.; enredo m.
intricate, a. intrincado; complejo.
intrigue, 1. n. intriga f. **2.** v. intrigar.
intrinsic, a. intrínseco.
introduce, v. introducir; (a person) presentar.
introduction, n. presentación; introducción f.
introductory, a. introductivo.
introvert, n. & a. introverso m.
intrude, v. entremeterse.
intruder, n. intruso -sa.
intuition, n. intuición f.
intuitive, a. intuitivo.
inundate, v. inundar.
invade, v. invadir.
invader, n. invasor m.
invalid, a. & n. inválido -da.
invariable, a. invariable.
invasion, n. invasión f.
invective, 1. n. invectiva f. **2.** a. ultrajante.
inveigle, v. seducir.
invent, v. inventar.
invention, n. invención f.
inventive, a. inventivo.
inventor, n. inventor m.
inventory, n. inventario m.
invertebrate, n. & a. invertebrado m.
invest, v. investir; (com.) invertir.
investigate, v. investigar.
investigation, n. investigación f.
investment, n. inversión f.
inveterate, a. inveterado.
invidious, a. difamatorio.
invigorate, v. vigorizar, fortificar.
invincible, a. invencible.
invisible, a. invisible.
invitation, n. invitación f.
invite, v. invitar, convidar.
invocation, n. invocación f.
invoice, n. factura f.
invoke, v. invocar.
involuntary, a. involuntario.

involve, v. envolver; implicar.
involved, a. complicado.
invulnerable, a. invulnerable.
inward, adv. hacia adentro.
inwardly, adv. interiormente.
iodine, n. iodo m.
irate, a. encolerizado.
Ireland, n. Irlanda f.
iris, n. (anat.) iris m.; (botany) flor de lis f.
Irish, a. irlandés.
irk, v. fastidiar.
iron, 1. n. hierro m.; (appliance) plancha f. **2.** v. planchar.
ironical, a. irónico.
irony, n. ironía f.
irrational, a. irracional; ilógico.
irregular, a. irregular.
irregularity, n. irregularidad f.
irrelevant, a. ajeno.
irresistible, a. irresistible.
irresponsible, a. irresponsable.
irreverent, a. irreverente.
irrevocable, a. irrevocable.
irrigate, v. regar; (med.) irrigar.
irrigation, n. riego m.
irritability, n. irritabilidad f.
irritable, a. irritable.
irritant, n. & a. irritante m.
irritate, v. irritar.
irritation, n. irritación f.
island, n. isla f.
isolate, v. aislar.
isolation, n. aislamiento m.
isosceles, a. isósceles.
issuance, n. emisión f.; publicación f.
issue, 1. n. emisión; edición; progenie f.; número m.; punto en disputa. **2.** v. emitir; publicar.
isthmus, n. istmo m.
it, pron. ello; él, ella; lo, la.
Italian, a. & n. italiano -na.
Italy, n. Italia f.
itch, 1. n. picazón f. **2.** v. picar.
item, n. artículo; detalle m.; inserción f.; (com.) renglón m.
itemize, v. detallar.
itinerant, 1. n. viandante m. **2.** a. ambulante.
itinerary, n. itinerario m.
its, a. su.
itself, pron. sí; se.
ivory, n. marfil m.
ivy, n. hiedra f.

J

jab, 1. n. pinchazo m. **2.** v. pinchar.
jack, n. (for lifting) gato m.; (cards) sota f.
jackal, n. chacal m.
jackass, n. asno m.
jacket, n. chaqueta f.; saco m.
jack-of-all-trades, n. estuche m.
jade, n. (horse) rocín m.;

(woman) picarona f.; (mineral) jade m.
jaded, a. rendido.
jagged, a. mellado.
jaguar, n. jaguar m.
jail, n. cárcel f.
jailer, n. carcelero m.
jam, 1. n. conserva f.; apretura f. **2.** v. apiñar, apretar; trabar.
janitor, n. portero m.
January, n. enero m.
Japan, n. Japón m.
Japanese, a. & n. japonés -esa.
jar, 1. n. jarro m. **2.** v. chocar; agitar.
jargon, n. jerga f.
jasmine, n. jazmín m.
jaundice, n. ictericia f.
jaunt, n. paseata f.
javelin, n. jabalina f.
jaw, n. quijada f.
jay, n. grajo m.
jazz, n. jazz m.
jealous, a. celoso. **to be j.,** tener celos.
jealousy, n. celos m.pl.
jeans, n. jeans m.pl.
jeer, 1. n. burla f., mofa f. **2.** v. burlar, mofar.
jelly, n. jalea f.
jellyfish, n. aguamar m.
jeopardize, v. arriesgar.
jeopardy, n. riesgo m.
jerk, 1. n. sacudida f. **2.** v. sacudir.
jerky, a. espasmódico.
Jerusalem, n. Jerusalén m.
jest, 1. n. broma f. **2.** v. bromear.
jester, n. bufón m.; burlón m.
Jesuit, n. jesuíta m. **2.** a. jesuítico.
Jesus Christ, n. Jesucristo m.
jet, n. chorro m.; (gas) mechero m.
jet lag, n. fatiga que sufre un viajero en avión, por causa del cambio de horas.
jetsam, n. echazón f.
jettison, v. echar mercancías al mar.
jetty, n. muelle m.
Jew, n. judío -día.
jewel, n. joya f.
jeweler, n. joyero m.
jewelry, n. joyería f. **j. store,** joyería f.
Jewish, a. judío.
jib, n. (naut.) foque m.
jiffy, n. instante m.
jig, n. jiga f. **j-saw,** sierra de vaivén f.
jilt, v. dar calabazas.
jingle, 1. n. retintín m.; rima pueril f. **2.** v. retiñir.
jinx, 1. n. aojo m. **2.** v. aojar.
jittery, a. nervioso.
job, n. empleo m.
jobber, n. destajista m., remendero m.
jockey, n. jockey m.
jocular, a. jocoso.
jog, 1. n. empujoncito m. **2.** v. empujar; estimular. **to j. along,** ir a un trote corto.

join, v. juntar; unir.
joiner, n. ebanista m.
joint, n. juntura f.
jointly, adv. conjuntamente.
joke, 1. n. broma, chanza f.; chiste m. 2. v. bromear.
joker, n. bromista m. & f.
jolly, a. alegre, jovial.
jolt, 1. n. sacudida m. 2. v. sacudir.
jonquil, n. junquillo m.
jostle, v. rempujar.
journal, n. diario m.; revista f.
journalism, n. periodismo m.
journalist, n. periodista m. & f.
journey, 1. n. viaje m.; jornada f. 2. v. viajar.
journeyman, n. jornalero m., oficial m.
jovial, a. jovial.
jowl, n. carrillo m.
joy, n. alegría f.
joyful, joyous, a. alegre, gozoso.
jubilant, a. jubiloso.
jubilee, n. jubileo m.
Judaism, n. judaísmo m.
judge, 1. n. juez m. 2. v. juzgar.
judgment, n. juicio m.
judicial, a. judicial.
judiciary, a. judiciario.
judicious, a. juicioso.
jug, n. jarro m.
juggle, v. escamotear.
juice, n. jugo, zumo m.
juicy, a. jugoso.
July, n. julio m.
jumble, 1. n. revoltillo m. 2. v. arrebujar, revolver.
jump, 1. n. salto m. 2. v. saltar, brincar.
junction, n. confluencia f.; (railway) empalme m.
juncture, n. junta f.
June, n. junio m.
jungle, n. selva f.
junior, a. menor; más joven. Jr., hijo.
juniper, n. enebro m.
junk, n. basura f.
junket, 1. n. leche cuajada f. 2. v. festejar.
jurisdiction, n. jurisdicción f.
jurisprudence, n. jurisprudencia f.
jurist, n. jurista m.
juror, n. jurado m.
jury, n. jurado m.
just, 1. a. justo; exacto. 2. adv. exactamente; (only) sólo. **j. now,** ahora mismo. **to have j.,** acabar de.
justice, n. justicia f.; (person) juez m.
justifiable, a. justificable.
justification, n. justificación f.
justify, v. justificar.
jut, v. sobresalir.
jute, n. yute m.
juvenile, a. juvenil.

K

kaleidoscope, n. calidoscopio m.

kangaroo, n. canguro m.
karakul, n. caracul m.
karat, n. quilate m.
karate, n. karate m.
keel, 1. n. quilla f. 2. v. **to k. over,** volcarse.
keen, a. agudo; penetrante.
keep, v. mantener, retener; guardar; preservar. **k. on,** seguir, continuar.
keeper, n. guardián m.
keepsake, n. recuerdo m.
keg, n. barrilito m.
kennel, n. perrera f.
kerchief, n. pañuelo m.
kernel, n. pepita f.; grano m.
kerosene, n. kerosén m.
ketchup, n. salsa de tomate f.
kettle, n. caldera, olla f.
kettledrum, n. tímpano m.
key, n. llave f.; (music) clave f.; (piano) tecla f.
keyhole, n. bocallave f.
khaki, a. caqui.
kick, 1. n. patada f. 2. v. patear; (coll.) quejarse.
kid, 1. n. cabrito m.; (coll.) niño -ña, chico, -ca. 2. v. (coll.) bromear.
kidnap, v. secuestrar.
kidnaper, n. secuestrador m.
kidney, n. riñón m.
kidney bean, n. frijol m.
kill, v. matar.
killer, n. matador m.
kiln, n. horno m.
kilogram, n. kilogramo m.
kilohertz, n. kilohertzio m.
kilometer, n. kilómetro m.
kilowatt, n. kilovatio m.
kin, n. parentesco m.; parientes m.pl.
kind, 1. a. bondadoso, amable. 2. n. género m.; clase f. **k. of,** algo, un poco.
kindergarten, n. kindergarten m.
kindle, v. encender.
kindling, n. encendimiento m. **k.-wood,** leña menuda f.
kindly, a. bondadoso.
kindness, n. bondad f.
kindred, n. parentesco m.
kinetic, a. cinético.
king, n. rey m.
kingdom, n. reino m.
kink, n. retorcimiento m.
kiosk, n. kiosco m.
kiss, 1. n. beso m. 2. v. besar.
kitchen, n. cocina f.
kite, n. cometa f.
kitten, n. gatito -ta.
kleptomania, n. cleptomanía f.
kleptomaniac, n. cleptómano m.
knack, n. don m., destreza f.
knapsack, n. alforja f.
knead, v. amasar.
knee, n. rodilla f.
kneecap, n. rodillera f.
kneel, v. arrodillarse.
knickers, n. calzón corto m., pantalones m.

knife, n. cuchillo m.
knight, n. caballero m.; (chess) caballo m.
knit, v. tejer.
knob, n. tirador m.
knock, 1. n. golpe m.; llamada f. 2. v. golpear; tocar, llamar.
knot, 1. n. nudo; lazo m. 2. v. anudar.
knotty, a. nudoso.
know, v. saber; (a person) conocer.
knowledge, n. conocimiento, saber m.
knuckle, n. nudillo m. **k. bone,** jarrete m. **to k. under,** ceder a.
Korea, n. Corea f.

L

label, 1. n. rótulo m. 2. v. rotular; designar.
labor, 1. n. trabajo m.; la clase obrera. 2. v. trabajar.
laboratory, n. laboratorio m.
laborer, n. trabajador, obrero m.
laborious, a. laborioso, difícil.
labor union, n. gremio obrero m.
labyrinth, n. laberinto m.
lace, 1. n. encaje m.; (of shoe) lazo m. 2. v. amarrar.
lacerate, v. lacerar, lastimar.
laceration, n. laceración f., desgarro m.
lack, 1. n. falta f. 2. v. faltar, carecer.
lackadaisical, a. indiferente; soñador.
laconic, a. lacónico.
lacquer, 1. n. laca f., barniz m. 2. v. laquear, barnizar.
lactic, a. láctico.
lactose, n. lactosa f.
ladder, n. escalera f.
ladle, 1. n. cucharón m. 2. v. servir con cucharón.
lady, n. señora, dama f.
ladybug, n. mariquita f.
lag, 1. n. retraso m. 2. v. quedarse atrás.
lagoon, n. laguna f.
laid-back, a. de buen talante.
laity, n. laicidad f.
lake, n. lago m.
lamb, n. cordero m.
lame, 1. a. cojo; estropeado. 2. v. estropear.
lament, 1. n. lamento m. 2. v. lamentar.
lamentable, a. lamentable.
lamentation, n. lamento m.; lamentación f.
laminate, a. laminado.
lamp, n. lámpara f.
lampoon, 1. n. pasquín m. 2. v. pasquinar.
lance, 1. n. lanza f. 2. v. (med.) abrir.
land, 1. n. país m.; tierra f. **native l.,** patria f. 2. v. desembarcar; (plane) aterrizar.

landholder, n. hacendado m.

landing, n. (of stairs) descanso m.; (ship) desembarcadero m.; (airplane) aterrizaje m.

landlady, landlord, n. propietario -ria.

landmark, n. mojón m., señal f.; rasgo sobresaliente m.

landscape, n. paisaje m.

landslide, n. derrumbe m.

lane, n. senda f.

language, n. lengua f., idioma; lenguaje m.

languid, a. lánguido.

languish, v. languidecer.

languor, n. languidez f.

lanolin, n. lanolina f.

lantern, n. linterna f.; farol m.

lap, 1. n. regazo m.; falda f. 2. v. lamer.

lapel, n. solapa f.

lapse, 1. n. lapso m. 2. v. pasar; decaer; caer en error.

larceny, n. ratería f.

lard, n. manteca f.

large, a. grande.

largely, v. ampliamente; mayormente; muy.

largo, n. & a. (mus.) largo m.

lariat, n. lazo m.

lark, n. (bird) alondra f.

larva, n. larva f.

laryngitis, n. laringitis f.

larynx, n. laringe f.

lascivious, a. lascivo.

laser, n. láser m.

lash, 1. n. azote, latigazo m. 2. v. azotar.

lass, n. doncella f.

lassitude, n. lasitud f.

lasso, 1. n. lazo m. 2. v. enlazar.

last, 1. a. pasado; (final) último. **at l.,** por fin. 2. v. durar.

lasting, a. duradero.

latch, n. aldaba f.

late, 1. a. tardío; (deceased) difunto. **to be l.,** llegar tarde. 2. adv. tarde.

lately, adv. recientemente.

latent, a. latente.

lateral, a. lateral.

lather, 1. n. espuma de jabón. 2. v. enjabonar.

Latin, n. latín m.

Latin America, n. Hispanoamérica, América Latina f.

Latin American, a. & n. hispanoamericano -na.

latitude, n. latitud f.

latrine, n. letrina f.

latter, a. posterior. **the l.,** éste.

lattice, n. celosía f.

laud, v. loar.

laudable, a. laudable.

laudanum, n. láudano m.

laudatory, a. laudatorio.

laugh, 1. n. risa, risotada f. 2. v. reír. **l. at,** reírse de.

laughable, a. risible.

laughter, n. risa f.

launch, 1. n. (naut.) lancha f. 2. v. lanzar.

launder, v. lavar y planchar la ropa.

laundry, n. lavandería f.

laundryman, n. lavandero m.

laureate, n. & a. laureado m.

laurel, n. laureado.

lava, n. lava f.

lavatory, n. lavatorio m.

lavender, n. lavándula f.

lavish, 1. a. pródigo. 2. v. prodigar.

law, n. ley f.; derecho m.

lawful, a. legal.

lawless, a. sin ley.

lawn, n. césped; prado m.

lawsuit, n. pleito m.

lawyer, n. abogado m.

lax, a. flojo, laxo.

laxative, n. purgante m.

laxity, n. laxidad f.; flojedad f.

lay, 1. a. secular. 2. v. poner.

layer, n. capa f.

layman, n. lego, seglar m.

lazy, a. perezoso.

lead, 1. n. plomo m.; (theat.) papel principal. **to take the l.,** tomar la delantera. 2. v. conducir; dirigir.

leaden, a. plomizo; pesado; abatido.

leader, n. líder; jefe; director m.

leadership, n. dirección f.

leaf, n. hoja f.

leaflet, n. (bot.) hojilla f.; folleto m.

league, n. liga; (measure) legua f.

leak, 1. n. escape; goteo m. 2. v. gotear; (naut.) hacer agua.

leakage, n. goteo m., escape m., pérdida f.

leaky, a. llovedizo, resquebrajado.

lean, 1. a. flaco, magro. 2. v. apoyarse, arrimarse.

leap, 1. n. salto m. 2. v. saltar.

leap year, n. año bisiesto m.

learn, v. aprender; saber.

learned, a. erudito.

learning, n. erudición f., instrucción f.

lease, 1. n. arriendo m. 2. v. arrendar.

leash, 1. n. correa f. 2. v. atraillar.

least, a. menor; mínimo. **the l.,** lo menos. **at l.,** por lo menos.

leather, n. cuero m.

leathery, a. coriáceo.

leave, 1. n. licencia f. **to take l.,** despedirse. 2. v. dejar; (depart) salir, irse. **l. out,** omitir.

leaven, 1. n. levadura f. 2. v. fermentar, imbuir.

lecherous, a. lujurioso.

lecture, n. conferencia f.

lecturer, n. conferencista m.; catedrático m.

ledge, n. borde m.; capa f.

ledger, n. libro mayor m.

lee, n. sotavento m.

leech, n. sanguijuela f.

leek, n. porro m.

leer, v. mirar de soslayo.

leeward, a. sotavento.

left, a. izquierdo. **the l.,** la iz-

quierda. **to be left,** quedarse.

leftist, n. izquierdista m. & f.

leg, n. pierna f.

legacy, n. legado m., herencia f.

legal, a. legal.

legalize, v. legalizar.

legation, n. legación, embajada f.

legend, n. leyenda f.

legendary, a. legendario.

legible, a. legible.

legion, n. legión f.

legislate, v. legislar.

legislation, n. legislación f.

legislator, n. legislador m.

legislature, n. legislatura f.

legitimate, a. legítimo.

legume, n. legumbre f.

leisure, n. desocupación f.; horas libres.

leisurely, 1. a. deliberado. 2. adv. despacio.

lemon, n. limón m.

lemonade, n. limonada f.

lend, v. prestar.

length, n. largo m.; duración f.

lengthen, v. alargar.

lengthwise, adv. a lo largo.

lengthy, a. largo.

lenient, a. indulgente.

lens, n. lente m. or f.

Lent, n. cuaresma f.

Lenten, a. cuaresmal.

lentil, n. lenteja f.

leopard, n. leopardo m.

leper, n. leproso m.

leprosy, n. lepra.

lesbian, a. lesbiana f.

lesion, n. lesión f.

less, a. & adv. menos.

lessen, v. disminuir.

lesser, a. menor; más pequeño.

lesson, n. lección f.

lest, conj. para que no.

let, v. dejar; permitir; arrendar.

lethal, a. letal.

lethargic, a. letárgico.

lethargy, n. letargo m.

letter, n. carta; (of alphabet) letra f.

letterhead, n. membrete m.

lettuce, n. lechuga f.

leukemia, n. leucemia f.

levee, n. recepción f.

level, 1. a. llano, nivelado. 2. n. nivel m.; llanura f. 3. v. allanar; nivelar.

lever, n. palanca f.

levity, n. levedad f.

levy, 1. n. leva f. 2. v. imponer.

lewd, a. lascivo.

lexicon, n. léxico m.

liability, n. riesgo m.; obligación f.

liable, a. sujeto; responsable.

liaison, n. vinculación f., enlace m.; concubinaje m.

liar, n. embustero -ra.

libel, 1. n. libelo m. 2. v. difamar.

libelous, a. difamatorio.

liberal, a. liberal; generoso.

liberalize, n. liberalismo m.

liberality, n. liberalidad f.

liberate, v. libertar.

liberty, n. libertad f.

libidinous, a. libidinoso.

librarian, n. bibliotecario m.

library, n. biblioteca f.

libretto, n. libreto m.

license, n. licencia f.; permiso m.

licentious, a. licencioso.

lick, v. lamer.

licorice, n. regaliz m.

lid, n. tapa f.

lie, 1. n. mentira f. 2. v. mentir. **l. down,** acostarse, echarse.

lieutenant, n. teniente m.

life, n. vida f.

lifeboat, n. bote salvavidas m.

life buoy, n. buya f.

life insurance, n. seguro de vida m.

lifeless, a. sin vida.

life preserver, n. salvavidas m.

life style, n. modo de vida m.

lift, v. levantar, alzar, elevar.

ligament, n. ligamento m.

ligature, n. ligadura f.

light, 1. a. ligero; liviano; (in color) claro. 2. n. luz; candela f. 3. v. encender; iluminar.

lighten, v. aligerar; aclarar; iluminar.

lighter, n. encendedor m.

lighthouse, n. faro m.

lightness, n. ligereza; agilidad f.

lightning, n. relámpago m.

like, 1. a. semejante. 2. prep. como. 3. v. **I like . . . me gusta, me gustan . . . I should like,** quisiera.

likeable, a. simpático, agradable.

likelihood, n. probabilidad f.

likely, a. probable; verosímil.

liken, v. comparar; asemejar.

likeness, n. semejanza f.

likewise, adv. igualmente.

lilac, n. lila f.

lilt, 1. n. cadencia alegre f. 2. v. cantar alegremente.

lily, n. lirio m.

lily of the valley, n. muguete m.

limb, n. rama f.

limber, a. flexible. **to l. up,** ponerse flexible.

limbo, n. limbo m.

lime, n. cal f.; (fruit) limoncito m., lima f.

limestone, n. piedra caliza f.

limewater, n. agua de cal f.

limit, 1. n. límite m. 2. v. limitar.

limitation, n. limitación f.

limitless, a. ilimitado.

limousine, n. limousine f.

limp, 1. n. cojera f. 2. a. flojo. 3. v. cojear.

limpid, a. límpido.

line, 1. n. línea; fila; raya f. (of print) renglón m. 2. v. forrar; rayar.

lineage, n. linaje m.

lineal, a. lineal.

linear, a. linear, longitudinal.

linen, n. lienzo, lino m.; ropa blanca.

liner, n. vapor m.

linger, v. demorarse.

lingerie, n. ropa blanca f.

linguist, n. lingüista m. & f.

linguistic, a. lingüístico.

liniment, n. linimento m.

lining, n. forro m.

link, 1. n. eslabón; vínculo m. 2. v. vincular.

linoleum, n. linóleo m.

linseed, n. linaza f.; simiente de lino f.

lint, n. hilacha f.

lion, n. león m.

lip, n. labio m.

lipstick, n. lápiz de labios.

liqueur, n. cordial m.

liquid, a. & n. líquido m.

liquidate, v. liquidar.

liquidation, n. liquidación f.

liquor, n. licor m.

lisp, 1. n. ceceo m. 2. v. cecear.

list, 1. n. lista f. 2. v. registrar.

listen (to), v. escuchar.

listless, a. indiferente.

litany, n. letanía f.

liter, n. litro m.

literal, a. literal.

literary, a. literario.

literate, a. literato.

literature, n. literatura f.

litigant, n. & a. litigante m.

litigation, n. litigio, pleito m.

litter, 1. n. litera f.; cama de paja. 2. v. poner en desorden.

little, a. pequeño; (quantity) poco.

liturgical, a. litúrgico.

liturgy, n. liturgia f.

live, 1. a. vivo. 2. v. vivir.

livelihood, n. subsistencia f.

lively, a. vivo; rápido; animado.

liver, n. hígado m.

livery, n. librea f.

livestock, n. ganadería f.

livid, a. lívido.

living, 1. a. vivo. 2. n. sustento m. **to earn (make) a living,** ganarse la vida.

lizard, n. lagarto m., lagartija f.

llama, n. llama f.

load, 1. n. carga f. 2. v. cargar.

loaf, 1. n. pan m. 2. v. holgazanear.

loam, n. marga f.

loan, 1. n. préstamo m. 2. v. prestar.

loathe, v. aborrecer, detestar.

lobby, n. vestíbulo m.

lobe, n. lóbulo m.

lobster, n. langosta f.

local, a. local.

locale, n. localidad f.

locality, n. localidad f., lugar m.

localize, v. localizar.

locate, v. situar; hallar.

location, n. sitio m.; posición f.

lock, 1. n. cerradura f.; (pl.) cabellos m.pl. 2. v. cerrar con llave.

locker, n. cajón m.; ropero m.

locket, n. guardapelo m., medallón m.

lockjaw, n. trismo m.

locksmith, n. cerrajero m.

locomotive, n. locomotora f.

locust, n. cigarra f., saltamontes m.

locution, n. locución f.

lode, n. filón m., vena f.

lodge, 1. n. logia; (inn) posada f. 2. v. fijar; alojar, morar.

lodger, n. inquilino m.

lodging, n. posada f.

loft, n. piso m., sobrado m.

lofty, a. alto; altivo.

log, n. tronco de árbol; (naut.) barquilla f.

loge, n. palco m.

logic, n. lógica f.

logical, a. lógico.

loin, n. lomo m.

loiter, v. haraganear.

lone, a. solitario.

loneliness, n. soledad f.; tristeza f.

lonely, lonesome, a. solo y triste.

lonesome, a. solitario; triste.

long, 1. a. largo. a l. time, mucho tiempo. 2. adv. mucho tiempo. **how l.,** cuánto tiempo. **no longer,** ya no. 3. v. **l. for,** anhelar.

longevity, n. longevidad f.

longing, n. anhelo m.

longitude, n. longitud m.

look, 1. n. mirada f.; aspecto m. 2. v. parecer; mirar. **l. at,** mirar. **l. for,** buscar. **l. like,** parecerse a. **l. out!,** ¡cuidado! **l. up,** buscar; ir a ver, venir a ver.

looking glass, n. espejo m.

loom, 1. n. telar m. 2. v. asomar.

loop, n. vuelta f.

loophole, n. abertura f., mirador m.

loose, a. suelto; flojo.

loosen, v. soltar; aflojar.

loot, 1. n. botín m., saqueo m. 2. v. saquear.

lopsided, a. desequilibrado.

loquacious, a. locuaz.

lord, n. señor m.; (Brit. title) lord m.

lordship, n. señorío m.

lose, v. perder.

loss, n. pérdida f.

lost, a. perdido.

lot, n. suerte f.; building l., solar m. **a lot (of), lots of,** mucho.

lotion, n. loción f.

lottery, n. lotería f.

loud, 1. a. fuerte; ruidoso. 2. adv. alto.

loudspeaker, n. altavoz m.

lounge, n. sofá m.; salón de fumar m.

louse, n. piojo m.

love, 1. n. amor m. **in l.,** enamorado. **to fall in l.,** enamorarse. 2. v. querer; amar; adorar.

lovely, *a.* hermoso.
lover, *n.* amante *m.*
low, *a.* bajo; vil.
lower, *v.* bajar; (in price) rebajar.
lowly, *a.* humilde.
loyal, *a.* leal, fiel.
loyalist, *n.* lealista *m. & f.*
loyalty, *n.* lealtad *f.*
lozenge, *n.* pastilla *f.*
lubricant, *n.* lubricante *m.*
lubricate, *v.* engrasar, lubricar.
lucid, *a.* claro, lúcido.
luck, *n.* suerte; fortuna *f.*
lucky, *a.* afortunado. **to be l.,** tener suerte.
lucrative, *a.* lucrativo.
ludicrous, *a.* ridículo.
luggage, *n.* equipaje *m.*
lukewarm, *a.* tibio.
lull, 1. *n.* momento de calma. 2. *v.* calmar.
lullaby, *n.* arrullo *m.*
lumbago, *n.* lumbago *m.*
lumber, *n.* madera *f.*
luminous, *a.* luminoso.
lump, *n.* protuberancia *f.*; (of sugar) terrón *m.*
lunacy, *n.* locura *f.*
lunar, *a.* lunar.
lunatic, *a. & n.* loco -ca.
lunch, luncheon, 1. *n.* merienda *f.*, almuerzo *m.* 2. *v.* merendar, almorzar.
lung, *n.* pulmón *m.*
lunge, 1. *n.* estocada *f.* 2. *v.* dar un estocada.
lure, *v.* atraer.
lurid, *a.* rojizo; fantástico.
lurk, *v.* esconderse; espiar.
luscious, *a.* sabroso, delicioso.
lust, *n.* sensualidad; codicia *f.*
luster, *n.* lustre *m.*
lustful, *a.* sensual, lascivo.
lusty, *a.* vigoroso.
lute, *n.* laúd *m.*
Lutheran, *n. & a.* luterano *m.*
luxuriant, *a.* exuberante, frondoso.
luxurious, *a.* lujoso.
luxury, *n.* lujo *m.*
lying, *a.* mentiroso.
lymph, *n.* linfa *f.*
lynch, *v.* linchar.
lyre, *n.* lira *f.*
lyric, *a.* lírico.
lyricism, *n.* lirismo *m.*

M

macabre, *a.* macabre.
macaroni, *n.* macarrones *m.*
machine, *n.* máquina *f.*
machine gun, *n.* ametralladora *f.*
machinery, *n.* maquinaria *f.*
machinist, *n.* maquinista, mecánico *m.*
macho, *a.* machista.
mackerel, *n.* escombro *m.*
mad, *a.* loco; furioso.
madam, *n.* señora *f.*
mafia, *n.* mafia *f.*
magazine, *n.* revista *f.*

magic, 1. *a.* mágico. 2. *n.* magia *f.*
magician, *n.* mágico *m.*
magistrate, *n.* magistrado *m.*
magnanimous, *a.* magnánimo.
magnate, *n.* magnate *m.*
magnesium, *n.* magnesio *m.*
magnet, *n.* imán *m.*
magnetic, *a.* magnético.
magnificence, *n.* magnificencia *f.*
magnificent, *a.* magnífico.
magnify, *v.* magnificar.
magnitude, *n.* magnitud *f.*
mahogany, *n.* caoba *f.*
maid, *n.* criada *f.* **old m.,** soltera *f.*
maiden, *a.* soltero.
mail, 1. *n.* correo *m.* **air m.,** correo aéreo. **by return m.,** a vuelta de correo. 2. *v.* echar al correo.
mailbox, *n.* buzón *m.*
mailman, *n.* cartero *m.*
maim, *v.* mutilar.
main, *a.* principal.
mainframe, *n.* componente central de una computadora.
mainland, *n.* continente *m.*
maintain, *v.* mantener; sostener.
maintenance, *n.* mantenimiento; sustento *m.;* conservación *f.*
maize, *n.* maíz *m.*
majestic, *a.* majestuoso.
majesty, *n.* majestad *f.*
major, 1. *a.* mayor. 2. *n.* (mil.) comandante *m.;* (study) especialidad *f.*
majority, *n.* mayoría *f.*
make, 1. *n.* marca *f.* 2. *v.* hacer; fabricar; (earn) ganar.
maker, *n.* fabricante *m.*
makeshift, *a.* provisional.
make-up, *n.* cosméticos *m.pl.*
malady, *n.* mal *m.,* enfermedad *f.*
malaria, *n.* paludismo *m.*
male, *a. & n.* macho *m.*
malevolent, *a.* malévolo.
malice, *n.* malicia *f.*
malicious, *a.* malicioso.
malign, 1. *v.* difamar. 2. *a.* maligno.
malignant, *a.* maligno.
malnutrition, *n.* desnutrición *f.*
malt, *n.* malta *m. & f.*
mammal, *n.* mamífero *m.*
man, *n.* hombre; varón *m.*
manage, *v.* manejar; dirigir; administrar; arreglárselas. **m. to,** lograr.
management, *n.* dirección, administración *f.*
manager, *n.* director *m.*
mandate, *n.* mandato *m.*
mandatory, *a.* obligatorio.
mandolin, *n.* mandolina *f.*
mane, *n.* crines *f.*
maneuver, 1. *n.* maniobra *f.* 2. *v.* maniobrar.
manganese, *n.* manganeso *m.*
manger, *n.* pesebre *m.*

mangle, 1. *n.* planchadora mecánica. 2. *v.* mutilar.
manhood, *n.* virilidad *f.*
mania, *n.* manía *f.*
maniac, *a. & n.* maniático *m.*
manicure, *n.* manicuro *m.*
manifest, 1. *a. & n.* manifiesto *m.* 2. *v.* manifestar.
manifesto, *n.* manifiesto *m.*
manifold, 1. *a.* muchos. 2. *n.* (auto.) tubo múltiple.
manipulate, *v.* manipular.
mankind, *n.* humanidad *f.*
manly, *a.* varonil.
manner, *n.* manera *f.,* modo *m.*
manners, *n.* modales *m.pl.*
mannerism, *n.* manerismo *m.*
mansion, *n.* mansión *f.*
mantel, *n.* manto de chimenea.
mantle, *n.* manto *m.*
manual, *a. & n.* manual *m.*
manufacture, *v.* fabricar.
manufacturer, *n.* fabricante *m.*
manufacturing, *n.* fabricación *f.*
manure, *n.* abono, estiércol *m.*
manuscript, *n.* manuscrito *m.*
many, *a.* muchos. **how m., so m.,** tantos. **too m.,** demasiados, cuántos. **as m. as,** tantos como.
map, *n.* mapa *m.*
maple, *n.* arce *m.*
mar, *v.* estropear; desfigurar.
marble, *n.* mármol *m.*
march, 1. *n.* marcha *f.* 2. *v.* marchar.
mare, *n.* yegua *f.*
margarine, *n.* margarina *f.*
margin, *n.* margen *m. or f.*
marijuana, *n.* marijuana *f.*
marine, 1. *a.* marino. 2. *n.* soldado de marina.
mariner, *n.* marinero *m.*
marionette, *n.* marioneta *f.*
marital, *a.* marital.
maritime, *a.* marítimo.
mark, 1. *n.* marca *f.* 2. *v.* marcar.
market, *n.* mercado *m.* **meat m.,** carnicería *f.* **stock m.,** bolsa *f.*
marmalade, *n.* mermelada *f.*
maroon, *a. & n.* color rojo oscuro.
marquis, *n.* marqués *m.*
marriage, *n.* matrimonio *m.*
married, *a.* casado. **to get m.,** casarse.
marrow, *n.* medula *f.;* substancia *f.*
marry, *v.* casarse con; casar.
marsh, *n.* pantano *m.*
marshal, *n.* mariscal *m.*
marshmallow, *n.* malvarisco *m.;* bombón de altea *m.*
martial, *a.* marcial. **m. law,** gobierno militar.
martyr, *n.* mártir *m. & f.*
martyrdom, *n.* martirio *m.*
marvel, 1. *n.* maravilla *f.* 2. *v.* maravillarse.
marvelous, *a.* maravilloso.
mascot, *n.* mascota *f.*
masculine, *a.* masculino.

mash, v. majar. **mashed potatoes,** puré de papas m.

mask, n. máscara f.

mason, n. albañil m.

masquerade, n. mascarada f.

mass, n. masa f.; (rel.) misa f. **to say m.,** cantar misa. **m. production,** producción en serie.

massacre, 1. n. carnicería, matanza f. 2. v. matar atrozmente, destrozar.

massage, 1. n. masaje m.; soba f. 2. v. sobar.

masseur, n. masajista m. & f.

massive, a. macizo, sólido.

mast, n. palo, árbol m.

master, 1. n. amo; maestro m. 2. v. domar, dominar.

masterpiece, n. obra maestra.

mastery, n. maestría f.

mat, 1. n. estera; palleta f. 2. v. enredar.

match, 1. n. igual m; fósforo m.; (sport) partida, contienda f.; (marriage) noviazgo; casamiento. 2. v. ser igual a; igualar.

mate, 1. n. consorte m. & f.; compañero -ra. 2. v. igualar; casar.

material, a. & n. material m. **raw materials,** materias primas.

materialism, n. materialismo m.

materialize, v. materializar.

maternal, a. materno.

maternity, n. maternidad f.

mathematical, a. matemático.

mathematics, n. matemáticas f.pl.

matinee, n. matiné m.

matrimony, n. matrimonio m.

matron, n. matrona; directora f.

matter, 1. n. materia f.; asunto m. **what's the m.?,** ¿qué pasa? 2. v. importar.

mattress, n. colchón m.

mature, 1. a. maduro. 2. v. madurar.

maturity, n. madurez f.

maudlin, a. sentimental en exceso; peneque.

maul, v. maltratar a golpes.

maxim, n. máxima f.

maximum, a. & n. máximo.

may, v. poder.

May, n. mayo m.

maybe, adv. quizá, quizás, tal vez.

mayonnaise, n. mayonesa f.

mayor, n. alcalde m.

maze, n. laberinto m.

me, pron. mí; me. **with me,** conmigo.

meadow, n. prado m.; vega f.

meager, a. magro; pobre.

meal, n. comida; (flour) harina f.

mean, 1. a. bajo; malo. 2. n. medio (see also **means**). 3. v. significar; querer decir.

meaning, n. sentido, significado m.

means, n.pl. medios, recursos. **by all m.,** sin falta. **by no m.,** de ningún modo. **by m. of,** por medio de.

meanwhile, adv. mientras tanto.

measles, n. sarampión m.

measure, 1. n. medida f.; (music) compás m. 2. v. medir.

measurement, n. medida, dimensión f.

meat, n. carne f.

mechanic, n. mecánico m.

mechanical, a. mecánico.

mechanism, n. mecanismo m.

mechanize, v. mecanizar.

medal, n. medalla f.

meddle, v. meterse, entremeterse.

mediate, v. mediar.

medical, a. médico.

medicine, n. medicina f.

medieval, a. medioeval.

mediocre, a. mediocre.

mediocrity, n. mediocridad f.

meditate, v. meditar.

meditation, n. meditación f.

Mediterranean, n. Mediterráneo m.

medium, 1. a. mediano, medio. 2. n. medio m.

medley, n. mezcla f., ensalada f.

meek, a. manso; humilde.

meekness, n. modestia; humildad f.

meet, 1. a. propio. 2. n. concurso m. 3. v. encontrar; reunirse; conocer.

meeting, n. reunión f.; mitin m.

megahertz, n. megahertzio m.

megaphone, n. megáfono m.

melancholy, 1. a. melancólico. 2. n. melancolía f.

mellow, a. suave; blando; maduro.

melodious, a. melodioso.

melodrama, n. melodrama m.

melody, n. melodía f.

melon, n. melón m.

melt, v. derretir.

meltdown, n. fundición resultante de un accidente en un reactor nuclear.

member, n. socio -ia; miembro m.

membership, n. membrecía f.

membrane, n. membrana f.

memento, n. recuerdo m.

memoir, n. memoria f.

memorable, a. memorable.

memorandum, n. memorándum, volante m.

memorial, 1. a. conmemorativo. 2. n. memorial m.

memorize, v. aprender de memoria.

memory, n. memoria f.; recuerdo m.

menace, 1. n. amenaza f. 2. v. amenazar.

mend, v. reparar, remendar.

menial, 1. a. servil. 2. n. sirviente m.

menopause, n. menopausia f.

menstruation, n. menstruación f.

menswear, n. ropa de caballeros f.

mental, a. mental.

mentality, n. mentalidad f.

menthol, n. mentol m.

mention, 1. n. mención f. 2. v. mencionar.

menu, n. menú m., lista f.

mercantile, a. mercantil.

mercenary, a. & n. mercenario -ria.

merchandise, n. mercancía f.

merchant, 1. a. mercante. 2. n. comerciante m.

merciful, a. misericordioso, compasivo.

merciless, a. cruel, inhumano.

mercury, n. mercurio m.

mercy, n. misericordia; merced f.

mere, a. mero, puro.

merely, adv. solamente; simplemente.

merge, v. unir, combinar.

merger, n. consolidación, fusión.

meringue, n. merengue m.

merit, 1. n. mérito m. 2. v. merecer.

meritorious, a. meritorio.

mermaid, n. sirena f.

merriment, n. regocijo m.

merry, a. alegre, festivo.

merry-go-round, n. caballitos m.

mesh, n. malla f.

mess, 1. n. lío m.; confusión f.; (mil.) salón comedor, rancho m. 2. v. **m. up,** ensuciar; enredar.

message, n. mensaje, recado m.

messenger, n. mensajero -ra.

messy, a. confuso, desarreglado.

metabolism, n. metabolismo m.

metal, n. metal m.

metallic, a. metálico.

metaphysics, n. metafísica f.

meteor, n. meteoro m.

meteorology, n. meteorología f.

meter, n. medidor; (measure) metro m.

method, n. método m.

meticulous, a. meticuloso.

metric, a. métrico.

metropolis, n. metrópoli f.

metropolitan, a. metropolitano.

Mexican, a. & n. mexicano -na.

Mexico, n. México m.

mezzanine, n. entresuelo m.

microbe, n. microbio m.

microfiche, n. microficha f.

microfilm, n. microfilm m.

microform, n. microforma f.

microphone, n. micrófono m.

microscope, n. microscopio m.
microscopic, a. microscópico.
mid, a. medio.
middle, a. & n. medio m. in the m. of, en medio de, a mediados de.
middle-aged, a. de edad madura.
Middle East, n. Medio Oriente m.
midget, n. enano -na.
midnight, n. medianoche f.
midwife, n. partera f.
might, n. poder m., fuerza f.
mighty, a. poderoso.
migraine, n. migraña f.; jaqueca f.
migrate, v. emigrar.
migration, n. emigración f.
migratory, a. migratorio.
mild, a. moderado, suave; templado.
mildew, n. añublo m., moho m.
mile, n. milla f.
militant, a. militante.
militarism, n. militarismo m.
military, a. militar.
militia, n. milicia f.
milk, 1. n. leche f. 2. v. ordeñar.
milkman, n. lechero m.
milky, a. lácteo; lechoso.
mill, 1. n. molino m.; fábrica f. 2. v. moler.
miller, n. molinero m.
millimeter, n. milímetro m.
milliner, n. modista m. & f.
millinery, n. sombrerería f.
million, n. millón m.
millionaire, n. millonario -ria.
mimic, 1. n. mimo m. 2. v. imitar.
mind, 1. n. mente; opinión f. 2. v. obedecer. never m., no se ocupe.
mindful, a. atento.
mine, 1. pron. mío. 2. n. mina f. 3. v. minar.
miner, n. minero m.
mineral, a. & n. mineral m.
mine sweeper, n. dragaminas f.
mingle, v. mezclar.
miniature, n. miniatura f.
miniaturize, v. miniaturizar.
minimize, v. menospreciar.
minimum, a. & n. mínimo m.
mining, n. minería f.
minister, 1. n. ministro; (rel.) pastor m. 2. v. ministrar.
ministry, n. ministerio m.
mink, n. visón m.; (fur) piel de visón m.
minor, 1. a. menor. 2. n. menor de edad.
minority, n. minoría f.
minstrel, n. juglar m.
mint, 1. n. menta f.; casa de moneda. 2. v. acuñar.
minus, prep. menos.
minute, 1. a. minucioso. 2. n. minuto, momento m.
miracle, n. milagro m.
miraculous, a. milagroso.
mirage, n. miraje m.
mire, n. lodo m.

mirror, n. espejo m.
mirth, n. alegría; risa f.
misbehave, v. portarse mal.
miscellaneous, a. misceláneo.
mischief, n. travesura, diablura f.
mischievous, a. travieso, dañino.
miser, n. avaro -ra.
miserable, a. miserable; infeliz.
miserly, a. avariento, tacaño.
misfortune, n. desgracia f., infortunio, revés m.
misgiving, n. recelo m., desconfianza f.
mishap, n. desgracia f., contratiempo m.
mislead, v. extraviar, despistar; pervertir.
misplaced, a. extraviado.
mispronounce, v. pronunciar mal.
miss, 1. n. señorita f. 2. v. perder; echar de menos, extrañar. be missing, faltar.
missile, n. proyectil m.
mission, n. misión; comisión f.
missionary, n. misionero -ra.
mist, n. niebla, bruma f.
mistake, 1. n. equivocación f.; error m. to make a m., equivocarse.
mistaken, a. equivocado.
mister, n. señor m.
mistletoe, n. muérdago m.
mistreat, v. maltratar.
mistress, n. ama; señora; concubina f.
mistrust, v. desconfiar; sospechar.
misty, a. nebuloso, brumoso.
misunderstand, v. entender mal.
misuse, v. maltratar; abusar.
mite, n. pizca f., blanca f.
mitten, n. mitón, confortante m.
mix, v. mezclar. m. up, confundir.
mixture, n. mezcla, mixtura f.
mix-up, n. confusión f.
moan, 1. n. quejido, gemido m. 2. v. gemir.
mob, n. muchedumbre f.; gentío m.
mobilization, n. movilización f.
mobilize, v. movilizar.
mock, v. burlar.
mockery, n. burla f.
mod, a. a la última; en boga.
mode, n. modo m.
model, 1. n. modelo m. 2. v. modelar.
moderate, 1. a. moderado. 2. v. moderar.
moderation, n. moderación; sobriedad f.
modern, a. moderno.
modernize, v. modernizar.
modest, a. modesto.
modesty, n. modestia f.
modify, v. modificar.
modulate, v. modular.
moist, a. húmedo.

moisten, v. humedecer.
moisture, n. humedad f.
molar, n. molar m.
molasses, n. melaza f.
mold, 1. n. molde; moho m. 2. v. moldar, formar; enmohecerse.
moldy, a. mohoso.
mole, n. lunar m.; (animal) topo m.
molecule, n. molécula f.
molest, v. molestar.
mollify, v. molificar.
moment, n. momento m.
momentary, a. momentáneo.
momentous, a. importante.
monarch, n. monarca m.
monarchy, n. monarquía f.
monastery, n. monasterio m.
Monday, n. lunes m.
monetary, a. monetario.
money, n. dinero m. m. order, giro postal.
mongrel, 1. n. mestizo m. 2. a. mestizo, cruzado.
monitor, n. amonestador m.
monk, n. monje m.
monkey, n. mono -na.
monocle, n. monóculo m.
monologue, n. monólogo m.
monopolize, v. monopolizar.
monopoly, n. monopolio m.
monosyllable, n. monosílabo m.
monotone, n. monotonía f.
monotonous, a. monótono.
monotony, n. monotonía f.
monsoon, n. monzón m.
monster, n. monstruo m.
monstrosity, n. monstruosidad f.
monstrous, a. monstruoso.
month, n. mes m.
monthly, a. mensual.
monument, n. momumento m.
monumental, a. monumental.
mood, n. humor m.; (gram.) modo m.
moody, a. caprichoso, taciturno.
moon, n. luna f.
moonlight, n. luz de la luna.
moor, 1. n. páramo m. 2. v. anclar.
mop, 1. n. estropajo m. 2. v. fregar.
moped (vehicle), n. velomotor m.
moral, 1. a. moral. 2. n. moraleja f. morals, moralidad f.
morale, n. espíritu m.
moralist, n. moralista m. & f.
morality, n. moralidad, ética f.
morbid, a. mórbido.
more, a. & adv. más. m. and m., cada vez más.
moreover, adv. además.
morgue, n. necrocomio m.
morning, n. mañana f. good m., buenos días.
morose, a. malhumorado.
morphine, n. morfina f.
morsel, n. bocado m.
mortal, a. & n. mortal m.
mortality, n. mortalidad f.

mortar, n. mortero m.

mortgage, l. n. hipoteca f. 2. v. hipotecar.

mortify, v. mortificar.

mosaic, n. & a. mosaico m.

mosquito, n. mosquito m.

moss, n. musgo m.

most, 1. a. más. 2. adv. más; sumamente. 3. pron. m. of, la mayor parte de.

mostly, adv. principalmente; en su mayor parte.

moth, n. polilla f.

mother, n. madre f.

mother-in-law, n. suegra f.

motif, n. tema m.

motion, 1. n. moción f.; movimiento m. 2. v. hacer señas.

motionless, a. inmóvil.

motion picture, n. película f.

motivate, v. motivar.

motive, n. motivo m.

motor, n. motor m.

motorboat, n. bote de gasolina.

motorcycle, n. motocicleta f.

motorist, n. motorista m. & f.

motto, n. lema m.

mound, n. terrón; montón m.

mount, 1. n. monte m.; (horse) montura f. 2. v. montar; subir.

mountain, n. montaña f.

mountaineer, n. montañés m.

mountainous, a. montañoso.

mourn, v. lamentar, llorar; llevar luto.

mournful, a. triste.

mourning, n. luto; lamento m.

mouse, n. ratón, ratoncito m.

mouth, n. boca f.; (of river) desembocadura f.

movable, a. movible, movedizo.

move, 1. n. movimiento m.; mudanza f. 2. v. mover; mudarse; emocionar conmover. m. away, quitar; alejarse; mudarse.

movement, n. movimiento m.

movie, n. película f. m. theater, movies, cine m.

moving, a. conmovedor; persuasivo.

mow, v. guadañar, segar.

Mr., title. Señor (Sr.).

Mrs., title. Señora (Sra.).

much, a. & adv. mucho. how m., cuánto. so m., tanto. too m., demasiado. as m. as, tanto como.

mucilage, n. mucilago m.

mucous, a. mucoso.

mucous membrane, n. mucosa f.

mud, n. fango, lodo m.

muddy, 1. a. lodoso; turbio. 2. v. ensuciar; enturbiar.

muff, n. manguito m.

muffin, n. panecillo m.

mug, n. cubilete m.

mulatto, n. mulato m.

mule, n. mula f.

mullah, n. mullah m.

multinational, a. multinacional.

multiple, a. múltiple.

multiplication, n. multiplicación f.

multiplicity, n. multiplicidad f.

multiply, v. multiplicar.

multitude, n. multitud f.

mummy, n. momia f.

mumps, n. poperas f.pl.

municipal, a. municipal.

munificent, a. munífico.

mural, a. & n. mural m.

murder, 1. n. asesinato; homicidio m. 2. v. asesinar.

murderer, n. asesino -na.

murmur, 1. n. murmullo m. 2. v. murmurar.

muscle, n. músculo m.

muscular, a. muscular.

muse, 1. n. musa f. 2. v. meditar.

museum, n. museo m.

mushroom, n. seta f., hongo m.

music, n. música f.

musical, a. musical; melodioso.

musician, n. músico m.

muslin, n. muselina f., percal m.

must, v. deber; tener que.

mustache, n. bigotes m.pl.

mustard, n. mostaza f.

muster, 1. n. (mil.) revista f. 2. v. agregar.

mute, a. & n. mudo m.

mutilate, v. mutilar.

mutiny, 1. n. motín m. 2. amotinarse.

mutter, v. refunfuñar, gruñir.

mutton, n. carnero m.

mutual, a. mutuo.

muzzle, 1. n. hocico m.; bozal m. 2. v. embozar.

my, a. mi.

myriad, n. miríada f.

myrtle, n. mirto m.

myself, pron. mí, mí mismo; me. I m., yo mismo.

mysterious, a. misterioso.

mystery, n. misterio m.

mystic, a. místico.

mystify, v. confundir.

myth, n. mito m.

mythical, a. mítico.

mythology, n. mitología f.

N

nag, 1. n. jaca f. 2. v. regañar; sermonear.

nail, 1. n. clavo m.; (finger) uña f. 2. v. clavar.

naïve, a. ingenuo.

naked, a. desnudo.

name, 1. n. nombre m.; reputación f. 2. v. nombrar, mencionar.

namely, adv. a saber; es decir.

namesake, n. tocayo m.

nap, n. siesta f. to take a n., echar una siesta.

naphtha, n. nafta f.

napkin, n. servilleta f.

narcissus, n. narciso m.

narcotic, a. & n. narcótico m.

narrate, v. narrar.

narrative, 1. a. narrativo. 2. n. cuento, relato m.

narrow, a. estrecho, angosto. n.-minded, intolerante.

nasal, a. nasal.

nasty, a. desagradable; antipático.

nation, n. nación f.

national, a. nacional.

nationalism, n. nacionalismo m.

nationality, n. nacionalidad f.

nationalization, n. nacionalización f.

nationalize, v. nacionalizar.

native, 1. a. nativo. 2. n. natural; indígena m. & f.

nativity, n. natividad f.

natural, a. natural.

naturalist, n. naturalista m.

naturalize, v. naturalizar.

naturalness, n. naturalidad f.

nature, n. naturaleza f.; índole f.; humor m.

naughty, a. travieso, desobediente.

nausea, n. náusea f.

nauseous, a. nauseoso.

nautical, a. náutico.

naval, a. naval.

nave, n. nave f.

navel, n. ombligo m.

navigable, a. navegable.

navigate, v. navegar.

navigation, n. navigación f.

navigator, n. navegante m.

navy, n. marina f.

near, 1. a. cercano, próximo. 2. adv. cerca. 3. prep. cerca de.

nearby, 1. a. cercano. 2. adv. cerca.

nearly, adv. casi.

nearsighted, a. corto de vista.

neat, a. aseado; ordenado.

neatness, n. aseo m.

nebulous, a. nebuloso.

necessary, a. necesario.

necessity, n. necesidad f.

neck, n. cuello m.

necklace, n. collar m.

necktie, n. corbata f.

nectar, n. néctar m.

need, 1. n. necesidad; (poverty) pobreza f. 2. v. necesitar.

needle, n. aguja f.

needless, a. innecesario, inútil.

needy, a. indigente, necesitado, pobre.

nefarious, a. nefario.

negative, 1. n. negativo. 2. n. negativa f.

neglect, 1. n. negligencia f.; descuido m. 2. v. descuidar.

negligee, n. negligee m., bata de casa f.

negligent, a. negligente, descuidado.

negligible, a. insignificante.

negotiate, v. negociar.

negotiation, n. negociación f.

Negro, n. negro -ra.

neighbor, n. vecino -na.

neighborhood, *n.* vecindad *f.*

neither, **1.** *a. & pron.* ninguno de los dos. **2.** *adv.* tampoco. **3.** *conj.* **neither ... nor**, ni ... ni.

neon, *n.* neón *m.* **n. light**, tubo neón *m.*

nephew, *n.* sobrino *m.*

nerve, *n.* nervio *m.;* (coll.) audacia *f.*

nervous, *a.* nervioso.

nest, *n.* nido *m.*

net, *n.* a neto. **2.** *n.* red *f.* **hair n.**, albanega *f.* **3.** redar; (com.) ganar.

netting, *n.* red *m.;* obra de malla *f.*

network, *n.* (radio) red radiodifusora.

neuralgia, *n.* neuralgia *f.*

neurology, *n.* neurología *f.*

neurotic, *a.* neurótico.

neutral, *a.* neutral.

neutrality, *n.* neutralidad *f.*

neutron, *n.* neutrón *m.*

neutron bomb, bomba de neutrones *f.*

never, *adv.* nunca, jamás; **n. mind**, no importa.

nevertheless, *adv.* no obstante, sin embargo.

new, *a.* nuevo.

news, *n.* noticias *f.pl.*

newsboy, *n.* vendedor de periódicos.

newspaper, *n.* periódico *m.*

New Testament, *n.* Nuevo Testamento *m.*

new year, *n.* año nuevo *m.*

next, **1.** *a.* próximo; siguiente; contiguo. **2.** *adv.* luego, después. **n. door**, al lado de. **n. to**, al lado de.

nibble, *v.* picar.

nice, *a.* simpático, agradable; amable; hermoso; exacto.

nick, *n.* muesca *f.*, picadura *f.* **in the n. of time**, apunto.

nickel, *n.* níquel *m.*

nickname, **1.** *n.* apodo, mote *m.* **2.** *v.* apodar.

nicotine, *n.* nicotina *f.*

niece, *n.* sobrina *f.*

niggardly, *a.* mezquino.

night, *n.* noche *f.* **good n.**, buenas noches. **last n.**, anoche. **n. club**, cabaret *m.*

nightclub, *n.* cabaret *m.*

nightgown, *n.* camisa de dormir.

nightingale, *n.* ruiseñor *m.*

nightly, *adv.* todas las noches.

nightmare, *n.* pesadilla *f.*

nimble, *a.* ágil.

nine, *a. & pron.* nueve.

nineteen, *a. & pron.* diecinueve.

ninety, *a. & pron.* noventa.

ninth, *a.* noveno.

nipple, *n.* teta *f.;* pezón *m.*

nitrogen, *n.* nitrógeno *m.*

no, **1.** *a.* ninguno. **no one**, nadie. **2.** *adv.* no.

nobility, *n.* nobleza *f.*

noble, *a. & n.* noble *m.*

nobleman, *n.* noble *m.*

nobody, *pron.* nadie.

nocturnal, *a.* nocturno.

nocturne, *n.* nocturno *m.*

nod, **1.** *n.* seña con la cabeza. **2.** *v.* inclinar la cabeza; (doze) dormitar.

no-frills, *a.* sin extras.

noise, *n.* ruido *m.*

noiseless, *a.* silencioso.

noisy, *a.* ruidoso.

nominal, *a.* nominal.

nominate, *v.* nombrar.

nomination, *n.* nombramiento *m.*, nominación *f.*

nominee, *n.* nombrado *m.*

nonaligned (in political sense), *a.* no alineado.

nonchalant, *a.* indiferente.

noncombatant, *n.* no combatiente *m.*

noncommittal, *a.* evasivo; reservado.

nondescript, *a.* difícil de describir.

none, *pron.* ninguno.

nonentity, *n.* nulidad *f.*

nonpartisan, *a.* sin afiliación.

non-proliferation, *n.* no proliferación *m.*

nonsense, *n.* tontería *f.*

noodle, *n.* fideo *m.*

noon, *n.* mediodía *m.*

noose, *n.* lazo corredizo *m.;* dogal *m.*

nor, *conj.* ni.

normal, *a.* normal.

north, *n.* norte *m.*

North America, *n.* Norte América *f.*

North American, *a. & n.* norteamericano -na.

northeast, *n.* nordeste *m.*

northern, *a.* septentrional.

North Pole, *n.* polo norte *m.*

northwest, *n.* noroeste *m.*

Norway, *n.* Noruega *f.*

Norwegian, *a. & n.* noruego -ga.

nose, *n.* nariz *f.*

nostalgia, *n.* nostalgia *f.*

nostril, *n.* ventana de la nariz; (pl.) narices.

not, *adv.* no. **n. at all**, de ninguna manera. **n. even**, ni siquiera.

notable, *a.* notable.

notary, *n.* notario *m.*

notation, *n.* notación *f.*

notch, *n.* muesca *f.;* corte *m.*

note, **1.** *n.* nota *f.;* apunte *m.* **2.** *v.* notar.

notebook, *n.* libreta *f.*, cuaderno *m.*

noted, *a.* célebre.

notepaper, *n.* papel de notas *m.*

noteworthy, *a.* notable.

nothing, *pron.* nada.

notice, **1.** *n.* aviso *m.;* noticia *f.* **2.** *v.* observar, fijarse en.

noticeable, *a.* notable.

notification, *n.* notificación *f.*

notify, *v.* notificar.

notion, *n.* noción; idea *f.;* (pl.) novedades *f.pl.*

notoriety, *n.* notoriedad *f.*

notorious, *a.* notorio.

noun, *n.* nombre, sustantivo *m.*

nourish, *v.* nutrir, alimentar.

nourishment, *n.* nutrimento, alimento *m.*

novel, **1.** *a.* nuevo, original. **2.** *n.* novela *f.*

novelist, *n.* novelista *m. & f.*

novelty, *n.* novedad *f.*

November, *n.* noviembre *m.*

novena, *n.* novena *f.*

novice, *n.* novicio -cia, novato -ta.

Novocaine, *n.* novocaína *f.*

now, *adv.* ahora. **n. and then**, de vez en cuando. **by n.**, ya. **from n. on**, de ahora en adelante. **just n.**, ahorita. **right n.**, ahora mismo.

nowhere, *adv.* en ninguna parte.

nozzle, *n.* boquilla *f.*

nuance, *n.* matiz *m.*

nuclear, *a.* nuclear.

nuclear warhead, cabeza nuclear *f.*

nuclear waste, desechos nucleares *m.pl.*

nucleus, *n.* núcleo *m.*

nude, *a.* desnudo.

nuisance, *n.* molestia *f.*

nuke, *n.* armamento o reactor nuclear.

nullify, *v.* anular.

number, **1.** *n.* número *m.;* cifra *f.* **license n.**, matrícula *f.* **2.** *v.* numerar, contar.

numerical, *a.* numérico.

numerous, *a.* numeroso.

nun, *n.* monja *f.*

nuptial, *a.* nupcial.

nurse, **1.** *n.* enfermera *f.;* (child's) ama, niñera *f.* **2.** *v.* criar, alimentar, amamantar; cuidar.

nursery, *n.* cuarto destinado a los niños; (agr.) plantel, criadero *m.*

nurture, *v.* nutrir.

nut, *n.* nuez *f.;* (mech.) tuerca *f.*

nutrition, *n.* nutrición *f.*

nutritious, *a.* nutritivo.

nylon, *n.* nilón *f.*

nymph, *n.* ninfa *f.*

O

oak, *n.* roble *m.*

oar, *n.* remo *m.*

oasis, *n.* oasis *m.*

oat, *n.* avena *f.*

oath, *n.* juramento *m.*

oatmeal, *n.* harina de avena *f.*

obedience, *n.* obediencia *f.*

obedient, *a.* obediente.

obese, *a.* obeso, gordo.

obey, *v.* obedecer.

obituary, *n.* obituario *m.*

object, **1.** *n.* objeto *m.;* (gram.)

complemento *m.* 2. *v.* oponerse; objectar.
objection, *n.* objección *f.*
objectionable, *a.* censurable.
objective, *a.* & *n.* objetivo *m.*
obligation, *n.* obligación *f.*
obligatory, *a.* obligatorio.
oblige, *v.* obligar; complacer.
oblique, *a.* oblicuo.
obliterate, *v.* borrar; destruir.
oblivion, *n.* olvido *m.*
oblong, *a.* oblongo.
obnoxious, *a.* ofensivo, odioso.
obscene, *a.* obsceno, indecente.
obscure, 1. *a.* obscuro. 2. *v.* obscurecer.
observance, *n.* observancia; ceremonia *f.*
observation, *n.* observación *f.*
observatory, *n.* observatorio *m.*
observe, *v.* observar; celebrar.
observer, *n.* observador -ra.
obsession, *n.* obsesión *f.*
obsolete, *a.* anticuado.
obstacle, *n.* obstáculo *m.*
obstetrician, *n.* obstétrico *m.*
obstinate, *a.* obstinado, terco.
obstruct, *v.* obstruir, impedir.
obstruction, *n.* obstrucción *f.*
obtain, *v.* obtener, conseguir.
obtuse, *a.* obtuso.
obviate, *v.* obviar.
obvious, *a.* evidente, obvio.
occasion, 1. *n.* ocasión *f.* 2. *v.* ocasionar.
occasional, *a.* ocasional.
occult, *a.* oculto.
occupant, *n.* ocupante *m.*; inquilino -na.
occupation, *n.* ocupación *f.*; empleo *m.*
occupy, *v.* ocupar; emplear.
occur, *v.* ocurrir.
occurrence, *n.* ocurrencia *f.*
ocean, *n.* océano *m.*
o'clock: it's one o., es la una. it's two o., son las dos, etc. at ... o., a las ...
octagon, *n.* octágono *m.*
octave, *n.* octava *f.*
October, *n.* octubre *m.*
octopus, *n.* pulpo *m.*
oculist, *n.* oculista *m.*
odd, *a.* impar; suelto; raro.
odious, *a.* odioso.
odor, *n.* olor *m.*; fragancia *f.*
of, *prep.* de.
off, *adv.* (see under verb: stop off, take off, etc.)
offend, *v.* ofender.
offender, *n.* ofensor -ra; delincuente *m.*
offense, *n.* ofensa *f.*; crimen *m.*
offensive, 1. *a.* ofensivo. 2. *n.* ofensiva *f.*
offer, 1. *n.* oferta *f.* 2. *v.* ofrecer.
offering, *n.* oferta *f.*
office, *n.* oficina *f.*; despacho *m.*; oficio, cargo *m.*
officer, *n.* oficial *m.* police o., agente de policía.
official, 1. *a.* oficial. 2. *n.* oficial, funcionario *m.*

officiate, *v.* oficiar.
officious, *a.* oficioso.
offspring, *n.* hijos *m.pl.*; progenie *f.*
often, *adv.* muchas veces, a menudo. how o., con qué frecuencia.
oil, 1. *n.* aceite; óleo; petróleo *m.* 2. *v.* aceitar; engrasar.
oily, *a.* aceitoso.
ointment, *n.* ungüento *m.*
okay, *adv.* bien; de acuerdo.
old, *a.* viejo; antiguo. o. man, o. woman, viejo -ja.
old-fashioned, *a.* fuera de moda.
Old Testament, *n.* Antiguo Testamento *m.*
olive, *n.* aceituna, oliva *f.*
ombudsman, *n.* ombudsman *m.*
omelet, *n.* tortilla de huevos.
omen, *n.* agüero *m.*
ominous, *a.* ominoso, siniestro.
omission, *n.* omisión *f.*; olvido *m.*
omit, *v.* omitir.
omnibus, *n.* ómnibus *m.*
omnipotent, *a.* omnipotente.
on, *prep.* en, sobre, encima de. 2. *adv.* adelante.
once, *adv.* una vez. at o., en seguida. o. in a while, de vez en cuando.
one, *a.* & *pron.* uno.
oneself, *pron.* sí mismo; se. with o., consigo.
onion, *n.* cebolla *f.*
only, 1. *a.* único, solo. 2. *adv.* sólo, solamente.
onward, *adv.* adelante.
opal, *n.* ópalo *m.*
opaque, *a.* opaco.
open, 1. *a.* abierto; franco. o. air, aire libre. 2. *v.* abrir.
opening, *n.* abertura *f.*
opera, *n.* ópera *f.* o. glasses, anteojos de ópera; gemelos *m.pl.*
operate, *v.* operar.
operation, *n.* operación *f.* to have an o., operarse, ser operado.
operative, *a.* eficaz, operativo.
operator, *n.* operario -ria. elevator o., ascensorista *m.* & *f.* telephone o., telefonista *m.* & *f.*
operetta, *n.* opereta *f.*
ophthalmic, *a.* oftálmico.
opinion, *n.* opinión *f.*
opponent, *n.* antagonista *m.* & *f.*
opportunism, *n.* oportunismo *m.*
opportunity, *n.* ocasión, oportunidad *f.*
oppose, *v.* oponer.
opposite, 1. *a.* opuesto, contrario. 2. *prep.* al frente de. 3. *n.* contrario *m.*
opposition, *n.* oposición *f.*
oppress, *v.* oprimir.
oppression, *n.* opresión *f.*
oppressive, *a.* opresivo.

optic, *a.* óptico.
optician, *n.* óptico *m.*
optics, *n.* óptica *f.*
optimism, *n.* optimismo.
optimistic, *a.* optimista.
option, *n.* opción, elección *f.*
optional, *a.* discrecional, facultativo.
optometry, *n.* optometría *f.*
opulent, *a.* opulento.
or, *conj.* o, (before o-, ho-) u.
oracle, *n.* oráculo *m.*
oral, *a.* oral, vocal.
orange, *n.* naranja *f.*
oration, *n.* discurso *m.*; oración *f.*
orator, *n.* orador *m.*
oratory, *n.* elocuencia *f.*; (church) oratorio *m.*
orbit, *n.* órbita *f.*
orchard, *n.* huerto *m.*
orchestra, *n.* orquesta *f.* o. seat, butaca *f.*
orchid, *n.* orquídea *f.*
ordain, *v.* ordenar.
ordeal, *n.* prueba *f.*
order, 1. *n.* orden, *m. or f.*; clase *f.*; (com.) pedido *m.* in o. that, para que. 2. *v.* ordenar; mandar; pedir.
orderly, *a.* ordenado.
ordinance, *n.* ordenanza *f.*
ordinary, *a.* ordinario.
ordination, *n.* ordenación *f.*
ore, *n.* mineral *m.*
organ, *n.* órgano *m.*
organdy, *n.* organdí *m.*
organic, *a.* orgánico.
organism, *n.* organismo *m.*
organist, *n.* organista *m.* & *f.*
organization, *n.* organización *f.*
organize, *v.* organizar.
orgy, *n.* orgía *f.*
orient, 1. *n.* oriente *m.* 2. *v.* orientar.
Oriental, *a.* oriental.
orientation, *n.* orientación *f.*
origin, *n.* origen *m.*
original, *a.* & *n.* original *m.*
originality, *n.* originalidad *f.*
ornament, 1. *n.* ornamento *m.* 2. *v.* ornamentar.
ornamental, *a.* ornamental, decorativo.
ornate, *a.* ornado.
ornithology, *n.* ornitología *f.*
orphan, *a.* & *n.* huérfano -na.
orphanage, *n.* orfanato *m.*
orthodox, *a.* ortodoxo.
ostentation, *n.* ostentación *f.*
ostentatious, *a.* ostentoso.
ostrich, *n.* avestruz *m.*
other, *a.* & *pron.* otro. every o. day, un día sí otro no.
otherwise, *adv.* de otra manera.
ought, *v.* deber.
ounce, *n.* onza *f.*
our, ours, *a.* & *pron.* nuestro.
ourselves, *pron.* nosotros mismos; nos.
oust, *v.* desalojar.
ouster, *n.* desahucio *m.*
out, 1. *adv.* fuera, afuera. out of, fuera de. 2. *prep.* por.

outbreak, n. erupción f.
outcast, n. paria m. & f.
outcome, n. resultado m.
outdoors, adv. fuera de casa; al aire libre.
outer, a. exterior, externo.
outfit, 1. n. equipo; traje m. 2. v. equipar.
outgrowth, n. resultado m.
outing, n. paseo m.
outlaw, 1. n. bandido m. 2. v. proscribir.
outlet, n. salida f.
outline, 1. n. contorno; esbozo m.; silueta f. 2. v. esbozar.
outlive, v. sobrevivir.
out-of-date, a. pasado.
outpost, n. puesto avanzado.
output, n. capacidad f.; educto m.
outrage, 1. n. ultraje m.; atrocidad f. 2. v. ultrajar.
outrageous, a. atroz.
outrun, v. exceder.
outside, 1. a. & n. exterior m. 2. adv. afuera, por fuera. 3. prep. fuera de.
outskirt, n. borde m.
outward, adv. hacia afuera.
outwardly, adv. exteriormente.
oval, 1. a. oval, ovalado. 2. n. óvalo m.
ovary, n. ovario m.
ovation, n. ovación f.
oven, n. horno m.
over, 1. prep. sobre, encima de; por. 2. adv. o. here, aquí. o. there, allí, por allí. to be o., estar terminado.
overcoat, n. abrigo, sobretodo m.
overcome, v. superar, vencer.
overdue, a. restrasado.
overflow, 1. n. inundación f. 2. v. inundar.
overhaul, v. repasar.
overhead, adv. arriba, en lo alto.
overkill, n. efecto mayor que el pretendido.
overlook, v. pasar por alto.
overnight, adv. to stay or stop o., pasar la noche.
overpower, v. vencer.
overrule, v. predominar.
overrun, v. invadir.
oversee, v. superintender.
oversight, n. equivocación f.
overt, a. abierto.
overtake, v. alcanzar.
overthrow, 1. n. trastorno m. 2. v. trastornar.
overture, n. obertura f.
overturn, v. trastornar.
overview, n. visión de conjunto f.
overweight, a. demasiado pesado.
overwhelm, v. abrumar.
overwork, v. trabajar demasiado.
owe, v. deber. owing to, debido a.
owl, n. lechuza f.

own, 1. a. propio. 2. v. poseer.
owner, n. dueño -ña.
ox, n. buey m.
oxygen, n. oxígeno m.
oxygen tent, n. tienda de oxigeno f.
oyster, n. ostra f.

P

pace, 1. n. paso m. 2. v. pasearse. p. off, medir a pasos.
pacific, a. pacífico.
pacifier, n. pacificador m.; (baby p.) chupete m.
pacifism, n. pacifismo m.
pacifist, n. pacifista m. & f.
pacify, v. pacificar.
pack, 1. n. fardo; paquete m.; (animals) muta f. p. of cards, baraja f. 2. v. empaquetear; (baggage) empacar.
package, n. paquete, bulto m.
pact, n. pacto m.
pad, 1. n. colchoncillo m. p. of paper, bloc de papel. 2. v. rellenar.
paddle, 1. n. canalete m. 2. v. remar.
padlock, n. candado m.
pagan, a. & n. pagano -na.
page, n. página f.; (boy) paje m.
pageant, n. espectáculo m.; procesión f.
pail, n. cubo m.
pain, 1. n. dolor m. to take pains, esmerarse.
painful, a. doloroso; penoso.
paint, 1. n. pintura f. 2. v. pintar.
painter, n. pintor -ra.
painting, n. pintura f.; cuadro m.
pair, 1. n. par m.; pareja f. 2. v. parear. p. off, emparejarse.
pajamas, n. pijama m.
palace, n. palacio m.
palatable, a. sabroso, agradable.
palate, n. paladar m.
palatial, a. palaciego, suntuoso.
pale, a. pálido. to turn pale, palidecer.
paleness, n. palidez f.
palette, n. paleta f.
pallbearer, n. andero m.
pallid, a. pálido.
palm, n. palma f. p. tree, palmera f.
palpitate, v. palpitar.
paltry, a. miserable.
pamper, v. mimar.
pamphlet, n. folleto m.
pan, n. cacerola f.
panacea, n. panacea f.
Pan-American, a. panamericano.
pane, n. hoja f., cuadro m.
panel, n. tablero m.
pang, n. dolor; remordimiento m.
panic, n. pánico m.

panorama, n. panorama m.
pant, v. jadear.
panther, n. pantera f.
pantomime, n. pantomima f.; mímica f.
pantry, n. despensa f.
pants, n. pantalones, m.pl.
panty hose, n. pantyhose m. (medias hasta la cintura).
papal, a. papal.
paper, n. papel; periódico; artículo m.
paperback, n. libro en rústica m.
paper hanger, n. empapelador m.
par, n. paridad f.; (com.) par f.
parable, n. parábola f.
parachute, n. paracaídas m.
parade, 1. n. desfile m., procesión f. 2. v. desfilar.
paradise, n. paraíso m.
paradox, n. paradoja f.
paraffin, n. parafina f.
paragraph, n. párrafo m.
parakeet, n. perico m.
parallel, 1. a. paralelo. 2. v. correr parejas con.
paralysis, n. parálisis f.
paralyze, v. paralizar.
paramedic, n. paramédico m.
parameter, n. parámetro m.
paramount, a. supremo.
paraphrase, 1. n. paráfrasis f. 2. v. parafrasear.
parasite, n. parásito m.
parcel, n. paquete m. p. of land, lote de terreno.
parchment, n. pergamino m.
pardon, 1. n. perdón m. 2. v. perdonar.
pare, v. pelar.
parentage, n. origen m.; extracción f.
parenthesis, n. paréntesis m.
parents, n. padres m.pl.
parish, n. parroquia f.
Parisian, a. & n. parisiense m. & f.
park, 1. n. parque m. 2. v. estacionar.
parkway, n. bulevar m.
parley, n. conferencia f.; (mil.) parlamento m.
parliament, n. parlamento m.
parliamentary, a. parlamentario.
parlor, n. sala f., salón m.
parochial, a. parroquial.
parody, 1. n. parodia f. 2. v. parodiar.
parole, 1. n. palabra f.; (mil.) santo y seña. 2. v. poner en libertad bajo palabra.
paroxysm, n. paroxismo m.
parrot, n. loro, papagayo m.
parsimony, n. parsimonia f.
parsley, n. perejil m.
parson, n. párroco m.
part, 1. n. parte f.; (theat.) papel m. 2. v. separarse; partirse. p. with, desprenderse de.
partake, v. tomar parte.
partial, a. parcial.

participant, n. participante m. & f.

participate, v. participar.

participation, n. participación f.

participle, n. participio m.

particle, n. partícula f.

particular, a. & n. particular m.

parting, n. despedida f.

partisan, a. & n. partidario -ria.

partition, n. tabique m.

partly, adv. en parte.

partner, n. socio -cia; compañero -ra.

partridge, n. perdiz f.

party, n. tertulia, fiesta f.; grupo m.; (political) partido m.

pass, 1. n. pase; (mountain) paso m. 2. v. pasar. p. away, fallecer.

passable, a. transitable; regular.

passage, n. pasaje; (corridor) pasillo m.

passé, a. anticuado.

passenger, n. pasajero -ra.

passerby, n. transeúnte m. & f.

passion, n. pasión f.

passionate, a. apasionado.

passive, a. pasivo.

passport, n. pasaporte m.

past, 1. a. & n. pasado m. 2. prep. más allá de; después de.

paste, 1. n. pasta f. 2. v. empastar; pegar.

pasteurize, v. pasteurizar.

pastime, n. pasatiempo m.; diversión f.

pastor, n. pastor m.

pastry, n. pastelería f.

pasture, 1. n. pasto m.; pradera f. 2. v. pastar.

pat, 1. n. golpecito m. to stand p., mantenerse firme. 2. v. dar golpecillos.

patch, 1. n. remiendo m. 2. v. remendar.

patent, 1. a. & n. patente m. 2. v. patentar.

patent leather, n. charol m.

paternal, a. paterno, paternal.

paternity, n. paternidad f.

path, n. senda f.

pathetic, a. patético.

pathology, n. patología f.

pathos, n. rasgo conmovedor m.

patience, n. paciencia f.

patient, 1. a. paciente. 2. n. enfermo, paciente m.

patio, n. patio m.

patriarch, n. patriarca m.

patriot, n. patriota m.

patriotic, a. patriótico.

patriotism, n. patriotismo m.

patrol, 1. n. patrulla f. 2. v. patrullar.

patrolman, n. vigilante m.; patrullador m.

patron, n. patrón m.

patronize, v. condescender; patrocinar; ser cliente de.

pattern, n. modelo m.

pauper, n. indigent m. & f.

pause, 1. n. pausa f. 2. v. pausar.

pave, v. pavimentar. p. the way, preparar el camino.

pavement, n. pavimento m.

pavilion, n. pabellón m.

paw, 1. n. pata f. 2. v. patear.

pawn, 1. n. prenda f.; (chess) peón de ajedrez m. 2. v. empeñar.

pay, 1. n. pago; sueldo, salario m.; 2. v. pagar. p. back, pagar; vengarse de.

payment, n. pago m.; recompensa f.

pea, n. guisante m.

peace, n. paz f.

peaceable, a. pacífico.

peaceful, a. tranquilo.

peach, n. durazno, melocotón m.

peacock, n. pavo real m.

peak, n. pico, cumbre; máximo m.

peal, n. repique; estruendo m. p. of laughter, risotada f.

peanut, n. maní, cacahuete m.

pear, n. pera f.

pearl, n. perla f.

peasant, n. campesino -na.

pebble, n. guija f.

peck, 1. n. picotazo m. 2. v. picotear.

peculiar, a. peculiar.

pecuniary, a. pecuniario.

pedagogue, n. pedagogo m.

pedagogy, n. pedagogía f.

pedal, n. pedal m.

pedant, n. pedante m.

peddler, n. buhonero m.

pedestal, n. pedestal m.

pedestrian, n. peatón -na.

pediatrician, n. pediatra m. & f.

pedigree, n. genealogía f.

peek, 1. n. atisbo m. 2. v. atisbar.

peel, 1. n. corteza f.; (fruit) pellejo m. 2. v. descortezar; pelar.

peep, n. ojeada f.

peer, 1. n. par m. 2. v. mirar fijamente.

peg, n. clavija; estaquilla f.; gancho m.

pelt, 1. n. pellejo m. 2. v. apedrear; (rain) caer con fuerza.

pelvis, n. pelvis f.

pen, n. pluma f.; corral m. fountain p., pluma fuente.

penalty, n. pena; multa f.; castigo m.

penance, n. penitencia f. to do p., penar.

penchant, n. propensión f.

pencil, n. lápiz m.

pending, a. pendiente. to be p., pender.

penetrate, v. penetrar.

penetration, n. penetración f.

penicillin, n. penicilina f.

peninsula, n. península f.

penitent, n. & a. penitente m.

penknife, n. cortaplumas f.

penniless, a. indigente.

penny, n. penique m.

pension, n. pensión f.

pensive, a. pensativo.

penury, n. penuria f.

people, 1. n. gente f.; (of a nation) pueblo m. 2. v. poblar.

pepper, n. pimienta f.; (plant) pimiento m.

per, prep. por.

perambulator, n. cochecillo de niño m.

perceive, v. percibir.

percent, adv. por ciento.

percentage, n. porcentaje m.

perceptible, a. perceptible.

perception, n. percepción f.

perch, n. percha f.; (fish) perca f.

perdition, n. perdición f.

peremptory, a. perentorio, terminante.

perennial, a. perenne.

perfect, 1. a. perfecto. 2. v. perfeccionar.

perfection, n. perfección f.

perforation, n. perforación f.

perform, v. hacer; ejecutar; (theat.) representar.

performance, n. ejecución f.; (theat.) representación f.

perfume, 1. n. perfume m.; fragancia f. 2. v. perfumar.

perfunctory, a. perfunctorio, superficial.

perhaps, adv. quizá, quizás, tal vez.

peril, n. peligro m.

perilous, a. peligroso.

perimeter, n. perímetro m.

period, n. periodo m.; (punct.) punto m.

periodic, a. periódico.

periodical, n. revista f.

periphery, n. periferia f.

perish, v. perecer.

perishable, a. perecedero.

perjury, n. perjurio m.

permanent, a. permanente. p. wave, ondulado permanente.

permeate, v. penetrar.

permissible, a. permisible.

permission, n. permiso m.

permit, 1. n. permiso m. 2. v. permitir.

pernicious, a. pernicioso.

perpendicular, n. & a. perpendicular m.

perpetrate, v. perpetrar.

perpetual, a. perpetuo.

perplex, v. confundir.

perplexity, n. perplejidad f.

persecute, v. perseguir.

persecution, n. persecución f.

perseverance, n. perseverancia f.

persevere, v. perseverar.

persist, v. persistir.

persistent, a. persistente.

person, n. persona f.

personage, n. personaje m.

personal, a. personal.

personality, n. personalidad f.

personnel, n. personal m.

perspective, n. perspectiva f.

perspiration, n. sudor m.

perspire, v. sudar.

persuade, v. persuadir.

persuasive, a. persuasivo.

pertain, v. pertenecer.

pertinent, a. pertinente.

perturb, v. perturbar.

peruse, v. leer con cuidado.

pervade, v. penetrar; llenar.

perverse, a. perverso.

perversion, n. perversión f.

pessimism, n. pesimismo m.

pestilence, n. pestilencia f.

pet, 1. n. favorito -ta. 2. v. mimar.

petal, n. pétalo m.

petition, 1. n. petición, súplica f. 2. v. pedir, suplicar.

petrify, v. petrificar.

petroleum, n. petróleo m.

petticoat, n. enagua f.

petty, a. mezquino, insignificante.

petulant, a. quisquilloso.

pew, n. banco de iglesia m.

pewter, n. peltre m.

phantom, n. espectro, fantasma m.

pharmacist, n. farmacéutico, boticario m.

pharmacy, n. farmacia, botica f.

phase, n. fase f.

pheasant, n. faisan m.

phenomenal, a. fenomenal.

phenomenon, n. fenómeno f.

philanthropy, n. filantropía f.

philately, n. filatelia f.

philosopher, n. filósofo m.

philosophical, a. filosófico.

philosophy, n. filosofía f.

phlegm, n. flema f.; frialdad de ánimo f.

phobia, n. fobia f.

phonetic, a. fonético.

phonograph, n. fonógrafo m.

phosphorus, n. fósforo m.

photocopier, n. fotocopiadora f.

photocopy, 1. n. fotocopia f. 2. v. fotocopiar.

photoelectric, a. fotoeléctrico.

photogenic, a. fotogénico.

photograph, 1. n. fotografía f. 2. v. fotografiar; retratar.

photography, n. fotografía f.

Photostat, n. fotocopia f.

phrase, 1. n. frase f. 2. v. expresar.

physical, a. físico.

physician, n. médico m.

physics, n. física f.

physiology, n. fisiología f.

physiotherapy, n. fisioterapia f.

physique, n. físico m.

pianist, n. pianista m. & f.

piano, n. piano m.

picayune, a. insignificante.

piccolo, n. flutín m.

pick, 1. n. pico m. 2. v. escoger. p. up, recoger.

picket, n. piquete m.

pickle, 1. n. salmuera f.; encurtido m. 2. v. escabechar.

pickpocket, n. cortabolsas m. & f.

picnic, n. picnic m.

picture, 1. n. cuadro; retrato m.; fotografía f.; (movie) película f. 2. v. imaginarse.

picturesque, a. pintoresco.

pie, n. pastel m.

piece, n. pedazo m.; pieza f.

pier, n. muelle m.

pierce, v. perforar; pinchar; traspasar.

piety, n. piedad f.

pig, n. puerco, cerdo, lechón m.

pigeon, n. paloma f.

pigeonhole, n. casilla f.

pigment, n. pigmento m.

pile, 1. n. pila f.; montón m.pl.; (med.) hemorroides m.pl. 2. v. amontonar.

pilfer, v. ratear.

pilgrim, n. peregrino -na, romero -ra.

pilgrimage, n. romería f.

pill, n. píldora f.

pillage, 1. n. pillaje m. 2. v. pillar.

pillar, n. columna f.

pillow, n. almohada f.

pillowcase, n. funda de almohada f.

pilot, 1. n. piloto m. 2. v. pilotear.

pimple, n. grano m.

pin, 1. n. alfiler; broche m.; (mech.) clavija f. 2. v. prender. p. up, fijar.

pinch, 1. n. pellizco m. 2. v. pellizcar.

pine, 1. n. pino m. 2. v. p. away, languidecer. p. for, anhelar.

pineapple, n. piña f., ananá m.

pink, n. rosado.

pinnacle, n. pináculo m.; cumbre f.

pint, n. pinta f.

pioneer, n. pionero -ra.

pious, a. piadoso.

pipe, n. pipa f.; tubo; (of organ) cañón m.

piper, n. flautista m. & f.

piquant, a. picante.

pirate, n. pirata m.

pistol, n. pistola f.

piston, n. pistón m.

pit, n. hoyo m.; (fruit) hueso m.

pitch, 1. n. brea f.; grado de inclinación; (music) tono m.; 2. v. lanzar; (ship) cabecear.

pitchblende, n. pechblenda f.

pitcher, n. cántaro m.; (baseball) lanzador m.

pitchfork, n. horca f.; tridente m.

pitfall, n. trampa f., hoya cubierta f.

pitiful, a. lastimoso.

pitiless, a. cruel.

pity, 1. n. compasión, piedad f. to be a p., ser lástima. 2. v. compadecer.

pivot, 1. n. espiga f., pivote m.; punto de partido m. 2. v. girar sobre un pivote.

pizza, n. pizza f.

placard, 1. n. cartel m. 2. v. fijar carteles.

placate, v. aplacar.

place, 1. n. lugar, sitio, puesto m. 2. v. colocar, poner.

placid, a. plácido.

plagiarism, n. plagio m.

plague, 1. n. plaga, peste f. 2. v. atormentar.

plain, 1. a. sencillo; puro; evidente. 2. n. llano m.

plaintiff, n. demandador -ra.

plan, 1. n. plan, propósito m. 2. v. planear; pensar. p. on, contar con.

plane, 1. n. plano; (tool) cepillo m. 2. v. allanar; acepillar.

planet, n. planeta m.

planetarium, n. planetario m.

plank, n. tablón m.

plant, 1. n. mata, planta f. 2. v. sembrar, plantar.

plantation, n. plantación f. coffee p., cafetal m.

planter, n. plantador; hacendado m.

plasma, n. plasma f.

plaster, 1. n. yeso; emplasto m. 2. v. enyesar; emplastar.

plastic, a. plástico.

plate, 1. n. plato m.; plancha de metal. 2. v. planchear.

plateau, n. meseta f.

platform, n. plataforma f.

platinum, n. platino m.

platitude, n. perogrullada f.

platter, n. fuente f.; platel m.

plaudit, n. aplauso m.

plausible, a. plausible.

play, 1. n. juego m.; (theat.) pieza f. 2. v. jugar; (music) tocar; (theat.) representar. p. a part, hacer un papel.

player, n. jugador -ra; (music) músico m.; (theat.) actor m., actriz f.

playful, a. juguetón.

playground, n. campo de deportes; patio de recreo.

playmate, n. compañero -ra de juego.

playwright, n. dramaturgo m.

plea, n. ruego m.; súplica f.; (legal) declaración f.

plead, v. suplicar; declararse. p. a case, defender un pleito.

pleasant, a. agradable.

please, 1. v. gustar, agradar. Pleased to meet you, Mucho gusto en conocer a Vd. 2. adv. por favor. Please . . . Haga el favor de . . . , Tenga la bondad de . . . , Sírvase . . .

pleasure, n. gusto, placer m.

pleat, 1. n. pliegue m. 2. v. plegar.

plebiscite, n. plebiscito m.

pledge, 1. n. empeño m. 2. v. empeñar.

plentiful, a. abundante.

plenty, n. abundancia f. p. of, bastante. p. more, mucho más.

pleurisy, n. pleuritis f.

pliable, pliant, a. flexible.

pliers, n.pl. alicates m.pl.

plight, n. apuro, aprieto m.

plot, 1. n. conspiración; (of a story) trama; (of land) parcela f. **2.** v. conspirar; tramar.

plow, 1. n. arado m. **2.** v. arar.

pluck, 1. n. valor m. **2.** v. arrancar; desplumar.

plug, 1. n. tapón; (elec.) enchufe m. **spark p.,** bujía f. **2.** v. tapar.

plum, n. ciruela f.

plumage, n. plumaje m.

plumber, n. plomero m.

plume, n. pluma f.

plump, a. regordete.

plunder, 1. n. botín m.; despojos m.pl. **2.** v. saquear.

plunge, v. zambullir; precipitar.

plural, a. & n. plural m.

plus, prep. más.

plutocrat, n. plutócrata m. & f.

pneumatic, a. neumático.

pneumonia n. pulmonía f.

poach, v. (eggs) escalfar; invadir; cazar en vedado.

pocket, 1. n. bolsillo m. **2.** v. embolsar.

pocketbook, n. cartera f.

podiatry, n. podiatría f.

poem, n. poema m.

poet, n. poeta m.

poetic, a. poético.

poetry, n. poesía f.

poignant, a. conmovedor.

point, 1. n. punta f.; punto m. **2.** v. apuntar. **p. out,** señalar.

pointed, a. puntiagudo; directo.

pointless, a. inútil.

poise, 1. n. equilibrio m.; serenidad f. **2.** v. equilibrar; estar suspendido.

poison, 1. n. veneno m. **2.** v. envenenar.

poisonous, a. venenoso.

poke, n. empuje m., hurgonada f. **2.** v. picar; haronear.

Poland, n. Polonia f.

polar, a. polar.

pole, n. palo; (geog.) polo m.

police, n. policía f.

policeman, n. policía m.

policy, n. política f. **insurance p.,** póliza de seguro.

Polish, a. & n. polaco m.

polish, 1. n. lustre m. **2.** v. pulir, lustrar.

polite, a. cortés.

politic, political, a. político.

politician, n. político m.

politics, n. política f.

poll, n. encuesta f.; (pl.) urnas f.pl.

pollen, n. polen m.

pollute, v. contaminar.

polo, n. polo m.

polygamy, n. poligamia f.

polygon, n. polígono m.

pomp, n. pompa f.

pompous, a. pomposo.

poncho, n. poncho m.

pond, n. charca f.

ponder, v. ponderar, meditar.

ponderous, a. ponderoso, pesado.

pontiff, n. pontífice m.

pontoon, n. pontón m.

pony, n. caballito m.

pool, n. charco m. **swimming p.,** piscina f.

poor, a. pobre; (not good) malo.

pop, n. chasquido m.

popcorn, n. maíz tostado m.

pope, n. papa m.

popular, a. popular.

popularity, n. popularidad f.

population, n. población f.

porcelain, n. porcelana f.

porch, n. pórtico m.; galería f.

pore, n. poro m.

pork, n. carne de puerco.

pornography, n. pornografía f.

porous, a. poroso, esponjoso.

port, n. puerto; (naut.) babor m. **p. wine,** oporto m.

portable, a. portátil.

portal, n. portal m.

portend, v. pronosticar.

portent, n. presagio m., portento m.

porter, n. portero m.

portfolio, n. cartera f.

porthole, n. porta f.

portion, n. porción f.

portly, a. corpulento.

portrait, n. retrato m.

portray, v. pintar.

Portugal, n. Portugal m.

Portuguese, a. & n. portugués - sa.

pose, 1. n. postura; actitud f. **2.** v. posar. **p. as,** pretender ser.

position, n. posición f.

positive, a. positivo.

possess, v. poseer.

possession, n. posesión f.

possessive, a. posesorio.

possibility, n. posibilidad f.

possible, a. posible.

post, 1. n. poste; puesto m. **2.** v. fijar; situar; echar al correo.

postage, n. porte de correo. **p. stamp,** sello m.

postal, a. postal.

post card, tarjeta postal.

poster, n. cartel, letrero m.

posterior, a. posterior.

posterity, n. posteridad f.

postgraduate, a. postgraduado.

postmark, n. matasellos m.

post office, casa de correos.

postpone, v. posponer, aplazar.

postscript, n. posdata f.

posture, n. postura f.

pot, n. olla, marmita; (marijuana) marijuana, hierba f. **flower p.,** tiesto m.

potassium, n. potasio m.

potato, n. patata, papa f. **sweet p.,** batata f.

potent, a. potente, poderoso.

potential, a. & n. potencial f.

potion, n. poción f., pócima f.

pottery, n. alfarería f.

pouch, n. saco m.; bolsa f.

poultry, n. aves de corral.

pound, 1. n. libra f. **2.** v. golpear.

pour, v. echar; verter; llover a cántaros.

poverty, n. pobreza f.

powder, 1. n. polvo m.; (gun) pólvora f. **2.** v. empolvar; pulverizar.

power, n. poder m.; potencia f.

powerful, a. poderoso, fuerte.

powerless, a. impotente.

practical, a. prático.

practically, adv. casi; práticamente.

practice, 1. n. prática; costumbre; clientela f. **2.** v. practicar; ejercer.

practiced, a. experto.

practitioner, n. practicante m.

pragmatic, a. pragmática.

prairie, n. llanura; (So. Amer.) pampa f.

praise, 1. n. alabanza f. **2.** v. alabar.

prank, n. travesura f.

pray, v. rezar; (beg) rogar.

prayer, n. oración; súplica f.; ruego m.

preach, v. predicar; sermonear.

preacher, n. predicador m.

preamble, n. preámbulo m.

precarious, a. precario.

precaution, n. precaución f.

precede, v. preceder, anteceder.

precedent, a. & n. precedente m.

precept, n. precepto m.

precinct, n. recinto m.

precious, a. precioso.

precipice, n. precipicio m.

precipitate, v. precipitar.

precise, a. preciso, exacto.

precision, n. precisión f.

preclude, v. evitar.

precocious, a. precoz.

predatory, a. de rapiña, rapaz.

predecessor, n. predecesor, antecesor m.

predicament, n. dificultad f.; apuro m.

predict, v. pronosticar, predecir.

predilection, n. predilección f.

predispose, v. predisponer.

predominant, a. predominante.

prefabricate, v. fabricar de antemano.

preface, n. prefacio m.

prefer, v. preferir.

preferable, a. preferible.

preference, n. preferencia f.

prefix, 1. n. prefijo m. **2.** v. prefijar.

pregnant, a. preñada.

prehistoric, a. prehistórico.

prejudice, n. prejuicio m.

prejudiced, a. prejuiciado.

preliminary, a. preliminar.

prelude, n. preludio m.

premature, a. prematuro.

premeditate, v. premeditar.

premier, n. premer ministro.

première, n. estreno m.

premise, n. premisa f.

premium, n. premio m.

premonition, n. presentimiento m.

prenatal, a. prenatal.

preparation, n. preparativo m.; preparación f.

preparatory, a. preparatorio. p. to, antes de.

prepare, v. preparar.

preponderant, a. preponderante.

preposition, n. preposición f.

preposterous, a. prepóstero, absurdo.

prerequisite, n. requisito previo.

prerogative, n. prerrogativa f.

prescribe, v. prescribir; (med.) recetar.

prescription, n. prescripción; (med.) receta f.

presence, n. presencia f.; porte m.

present, 1. a. presente. to be present at, asistir a. 2. n. presente; (gift) regalo m. at p., ahora. for the p., por ahora. 3. v. presentar.

presentable, a. presentable.

presentation, n. presentación; introducción f.; (theat.) presentación f.

presently, adv. luego; dentro de poco.

preservative, a. & n. preservativo m.

preserve, 1. n. conserva f.; (hunting) vedado m. 2. v. preservar.

preside, v. presidir.

presidency, n. presidencia f.

president, n. presidente -ta.

press, 1. n. prensa f. 2. v. apretar; urgir; (clothes) planchar.

pressing, a. urgente.

pressure, n. presión f.

pressure cooker, n. cocina de presión f.

prestige, n. prestigio m.

presume, v. presumir; suponer.

presumptuous, a. presumtuoso.

presuppose, v. presuponer.

pretend, v. fingir. p. to the throne, aspirar al trono.

pretense, n. pretensión f.; fingimiento m.

pretension, n. pretensión f.

pretentious, a. presumido.

pretext, n. pretexto m.

pretty, 1. a. bonito, lindo. 2. adv. bastante.

prevail, v. prevalecer.

prevailing, prevalent, a. predominante.

prevent, v. impedir; evitar.

prevention, n. prevención f.

preventive, a. preventivo.

preview, n. vista previa f.

previous, a. anterior, previo.

prey, n. presa f.

price, n. precio m.

priceless, a. sin precio.

prick, 1. n. punzada f. 2. v. punzar.

pride, n. orgullo m.

priest, n. sacerdote, cura m.

prim, a. severamente modesto.

primary, a. primario, principal.

prime, 1. a. primero. 2. n. flor f. 3. v. alistar.

prime minister, n. primer ministro m.

primitive, a. primitivo.

prince, n. príncipe m.

princess, n. princesa f.

principal, 1. a. principal. 2. n. principal; director m.

principle, n. principio m.

print, 1. n. letra f.; (art) grabado m. 2. v. imprimir; estampar.

printing, n. imprenta f.

printing press, n. prensa f.

printout, n. impreso producido por una computadora.

priority, n. prioridad, precedencia f.

prism, n. prisma m.

prison, n. prisión, cárcel f.

prisoner, n. prisionero, preso m.

privacy, n. soledad f.

private, 1. a. particular. 2. n. soldado raso. in p., en particular.

privation, n. privación f.

privet, n. ligustro m.

privilege, n. privilegio m.

privy, n. letrina f.

prize, 1. n. premio m. 2. v. apreciar, estimar.

probability, n. probabilidad f.

probable, a. probable.

probate, a. testamentario.

probation, n. prueba f.; probación f.; libertad condicional f.

probe, 1. n. indagación f. 2. v. indagar; tentar.

probity, n. probidad f.

problem, n. problema m.

procedure, n. procedimiento m.

proceed, v. proceder; proseguir.

process, n. proceso m.

procession, n. procesión f.

proclaim, v. proclamar, anunciar.

proclamation, n. proclamación f.; decreto m.

procrastinate, v. dilatar.

procure, v. obtener, procurar.

prodigal, n. & a. pródigo m.

prodigy, n. prodigio m.

produce, v. producir.

product, n. producto m.

production, n. producción f.

productive, a. productivo.

profane, 1. a. profano. 2. v. profanar.

profanity, n. profanidad f.

profess, v. profesar; declarar.

profession, n. profesión f.

professional, a. & n. profesional m.

professor, n. profesor -ra; catedrático m.

proficient, a. experto, proficiente.

profile, n. perfil m.

profit, 1. n. provecho m.; ventaja f.; (com.) ganancia f. 2. v. aprovechar; beneficiar.

profitable, a. provechoso, ventajoso, lucrativo.

profiteer, 1. n. explotador m. 2. v. explotar.

profound, a. profundo, hondo.

profuse, a. pródigo, profuso.

prognosis, n. pronóstico m.

program, n. programa m.

progress, 1. n. progreso m.pl. in p., en marcha. 2. v. progresar; marchar.

progressive, a. progresivo; progresista.

prohibit, v. prohibir.

prohibition, n. prohibición f.

prohibitive, a. prohibitivo.

project, 1. n. proyecto m. 2. v. proyectar.

projectile, n. proyectil m.

projection, n. proyección f.

projector, n. proyector m.

proliferation, n. proliferación f.

prolific, a. prolífico.

prologue, n. prólogo m.

prolong, v. prolongar.

prominent, a. prominente; eminente.

promiscuous, a. promiscuo.

promise, 1. n. promesa f. 2. v. prometer.

promote, v. fomentar; estimular; adelantar.

promotion, n. promoción f.; adelanto m.

prompt, 1. a. pronto; puntual. 2. v. impulsar; (theat.) apuntar.

promulgate, v. promulgar.

pronoun, n. pronombre m.

pronounce, v. pronunciar.

pronunciation, n. pronunciación f.

proof, n. prueba f.

proofread, v. corregir pruebas.

prop, 1. n. apoyo, m. 2. v. sostener.

propaganda, n. propaganda f.

propagate, v. propagar.

propel, v. propulsar.

propeller, n. hélice f.

propensity, n. tendencia f.

proper, a. propio; correcto.

property, n. propiedad f.

prophecy, n. profecía f.

prophesy, v. predecir, profetizar.

prophet, n. profeta m.

prophetic, a. profético.

propitious, a. propicio.

proponent, n. & a. proponente m.

proportion, n. proporción f.

proportionate, a. proporcionado.

proposal, n. propuesta; oferta f.; (marriage) declaración f.

propose, v. proponer; pensar; declararse.

proposition, n. proposición f.

proprietor, *n.* propietario, dueño *m.*

propriety, *n.* corrección *f.,* decoro *m.*

prosaic, *a.* prosaico.

proscribe, *v.* proscribir.

prose, *n.* prosa *f.*

prosecute, *v.* acusar, procesar.

prospect, *n.* perspectiva; esperanza *f.*

prospective, *a.* anticipado, presunto.

prosper, *v.* prosperar.

prosperity, *n.* prosperidad *f.*

prosperous, *a.* próspero.

prostitute, 1. *n.* prostituta *f.* 2. *v.* prostituir. 3. *a.* prostituido.

prostrate, 1. *a.* postrado. 2. *v.* postrar.

protect, *v.* proteger; amparar.

protection, *n.* protección *f.;* amparo *m.*

protective, *a.* protector.

protector, *n.* protector *m.*

protégé, *n.* protegido -da.

protein, *n.* proteína *f.*

protest, 1. *n.* protesta *f.* 2. *v.* protestar.

Protestant, *a. & n.* protestante *m.*

protocol, *n.* protocolo *m.*

proton, *n.* protón *m.*

protract, *v.* alargar, demorar.

protrude, *v.* salir fuera.

protuberance, *n.* protuberancia *f.*

proud, *a.* orgulloso.

prove, *v.* comprobar.

proverb, *n.* proverbio, refrán *m.*

provide, *v.* proporcionar; proveer.

provided, *conj.* con tal que.

providence, *n.* providencia *f.*

province, *n.* provincia *f.*

provincial, 1. *a.* provincial. 2. *n.* provinciano -na.

provision, 1. *n.* provisión *f.;* (pl.) comestibles *m.pl.* 2. *v.* abastecer.

provocation, *n.* provocación *f.*

provoke, *v.* provocar.

prowess, *n.* proeza *f.*

prowl, *v.* rondar.

proximity, *n.* proximidad *f.*

proxy, *n.* delegado *m.* by p., mediante apoderado.

prudence, *n.* prudencia *f.*

prudent, *a.* prudente, cauteloso.

prune, *n.* ciruela pasa.

pry, *v.* atisbar; curiosear; (mech.) alzaprimar.

psalm, *n.* salmo *m.*

pseudonym, *n.* seudónimo *m.*

psychedelic, *a.* psiquedélico.

psychiatrist, *n.* psiquiatra *m.*

psychiatry, *n.* psiquiatría *f.*

psychoanalysis, *n.* psicoanálisis *m.* or *f.*

psychological, *a.* psicológico.

psychology, *n.* psicología *f.*

psychosis, *n.* psicosis.

ptomaine, *n.* tomaína *f.*

public, *a. & n.* público *m.*

publication, *n.* publicación; revista *f.*

publicity, *n.* publicidad *f.*

publish, *v.* publicar.

publisher, *n.* editor *m.*

pudding, *n.* pudín *m.*

puddle, *n.* charco, lodazal *m.*

Puerto Rico, *n.* Puerto Rico *m.*

Puerto Rican, *a. & n.* puertorriqueño -ña.

puff, 1. *n.* soplo *m.;* (of smoke) bocanada *f.* powder p., polvera *f.* 2. *v.* jadear; echar bocanadas. p. up, hinchar; (fig.) engreír.

pugnacious, *a.* pugnaz.

pull, 1. *n.* tirón *m.;* (coll.) influencia *f.* 2. *v.* tirar; halar.

pulley, *n.* polla *f.,* motón *m.*

pulmonary, *a.* pulmonar.

pulp, *n.* pulpa; (of fruit) carne *f.*

pulpit, *n.* púlpito *m.*

pulsar, *n.* pulsar *m.*

pulsate, *v.* pulsar.

pulse, *n.* pulso *m.*

pump, 1. *n.* bomba *f.* 2. *v.* bombear. p. up, inflar.

pumpkin, *n.* calabaza *f.*

pun, *n.* juego de palabras.

punch, 1. *n.* puñetazo *m.;* (mech.) punzón; (beverage) ponche *m.* 2. *v.* dar puñetazos; punzar.

punctual, *a.* puntual.

punctuate, *v.* puntuar.

puncture, 1. *n.* pinchazo *m.,* perforación *f.* 2. *v.* pinchar, perforar.

pungent, *a.* picante, pungente.

punish, *v.* castigar.

punishment, *n.* castigo *m.*

punitive, *a.* punitivo.

puny, *a.* encanijado.

pupil, *n.* alumno -na; (anat.) pupila *f.*

puppet, *n.* muñeco *m.*

puppy, *n.* perrito *m.*

purchase, 1. *n.* compra *f.* 2. *v.* comprar.

pure, *a.* puro.

purée, *n.* puré *m.*

purge, *v.* purgar.

purify, *v.* purificar.

puritanical, *a.* puritano.

purity, *n.* pureza *f.*

purple, 1. *a.* purpúreo. 2. *n.* púrpura *f.*

purport, 1. *n.* significación *f.* 2. *v.* significar.

purpose, *n.* propósito *m.* on p., de propósito.

purse, *n.* bolsa *f.*

pursue, *v.* perseguir.

pursuit, *n.* caza; busca; ocupación *f.* p. plane, caza *m.*

push, 1. *n.* empuje; impulso *m.* 2. *v.* empujar.

put, *v.* poner, colocar. p. away, guardar. p. in, meter. p. off, dejar. p. on, ponerse. p. out, apagar. p. up with, aguantar.

putrid, *a.* podrido.

puzzle, 1. *n.* enigma; rompecabe-

zas *m.* 2. *v.* dejar perplejo. p. out, descifrar.

pyramid, *n.* pirámide *f.*

pyromania, *n.* piromanía *f.*

Q

quadrangle, *n.* cuandrángulo *m.*

quadraphonic, *a.* cuadrafónico.

quadruped, *n. & a.* cuadrúpedo *m.*

quail, 1. *n.* codorniz *f.* 2. *v.* descorazonarse.

quaint, *a.* arcaico y curioso.

quake, 1. *n.* temblor *m.* 2. *v.* temblar.

qualification, *n.* requisito *m.;* (pl.) preparaciones.

qualified, *a.* calificado, competente; preparado.

qualify, *v.* calificar, modificar; llenar los requisitos.

quality, *n.* calidad *f.*

quandary, *n.* incertidumbre *f.*

quantity, *n.* cantidad *f.*

quarantine, *n.* cuarentena *f.*

quarrel, 1. *n.* riña, disputa *f.* 2. *v.* reñir, disputar.

quarry, *n.* cantera; (hunting) presa *f.*

quarter, *n.* cuarto *m.;* (pl.) vivienda *f.*

quarterly, 1. *a.* trimestral. 2. *adv.* por cuartos.

quartet, *n.* cuarteto *m.*

quartz, *n.* cuarzo *m.*

quasar, *n.* quasar *m.*

quaver, *v.* temblar.

queen, *n.* reina *f.;* (chess) dama *f.*

queer, *a.* extraño, raro.

quell, *v.* reprimir.

quench, *v.* apagar.

query, 1. *n.* pregunta *f.* 2. *v.* preguntar.

quest, *n.* busca *f.*

question, 1. *n.* pregunta; cuestión *f.* q. mark, signo de interrogación. 2. *v.* preguntar; interrogar; dudar.

questionable, *a.* dudoso.

questionnaire, *n.* cuestionario *m.*

quick, *a.* rápido.

quicken, *v.* acelerar.

quicksand, *n.* arena movediza *f.*

quiet, 1. *a.* quieto, tranquilo; callado. to be q., keep q., callarse. 2. *n.* calma; quietud *f.* 3. *v.* tranquilizar. q. down, callarse; calmarse.

quilt, *n.* colcha *f.*

quinine, *n.* quinina *f.*

quintet, *n.* (mus.) quinteto *m.*

quip, 1. *n.* pulla *f.* 2. *v.* echar pullas.

quit, *v.* dejar; renunciar a. q. doing (etc.) dejar de hacer (etc.).

quite, *adv.* bastante; completamente. not q., no precisamente; no completamente.

quiver, 1. n. aljabe f.; temblor m. **2.** v. temblar.
quixotic, a. quijotesco.
quorum, n. quórum m.
quota, n. cuota f.
quotation, n. citación; (com.) cotización f. **q. marks,** comillas f.pl.
quote, v. citar; (com.) cotizar.

R

rabbi, n. rabí, rabino m.
rabbit, n. conejo m.
rabble, n. canalla f.
rabid, a. rabioso.
rabies, n. hidrofobia f.
race, 1. n. raza; carrera f. **2.** v. echar una carrera; correr de prisa.
rack, 1. n. (cooking) pesebre m.; (clothing) colgador m. **2.** v. atormentar.
racket, n. (noise) ruido m.; (tennis) raqueta f.; (graft) fraude organizado.
radar, n. radar m.
radiance, n. brillo m.
radiant, a. radiante.
radiate, v. irradiar.
radiation, n. irradiación f.
radiator, n. calorífero m.; (auto.) radiador m.
radical, a. & n. radical m.
radio, n. radio m. or f. r. **station,** estación radiodifusora.
radioactive, a. radioactivo.
radish, n. rábano m.
radium, n. radio m.
radius, n. radio m.
raffle, 1. n. rifa, lotería f. **2.** v. rifar.
raft, n. balsa f.
rafter, n. viga f.
rag, n. trapo m.
ragamuffin, n. galopín m.
rage, 1. n. rabia f. **2.** v. rabiar.
ragged, a. andrajoso; desigual.
raid, n. (mil.) correría f.
rail, n. baranda f.; carril m. **by r.,** por ferrocarril.
railroad, n. ferrocarril m.
rain, n. lluvia f. **2.** v. llover.
rainbow, n. arco iris m.
raincoat, n. impermeable m.
rainfall, n. precipitación f.
rainy, a. lluvioso.
raise, n. aumento m. **2.** v. levantar, alzar; criar.
raisin, n. pasa f.
rake, 1. n. rastro m. **2.** v. rastrillar.
rally, 1. n. reunión f. **2.** v. reunirse.
ram, n. carnero m.
ramble, v. vagar.
ramp, n. rampa f.
rampart, n. terraplén m.
ranch, n. rancho m.
rancid, a. rancio.
rancor, n. rencor m.
random, a. fortuito. **at r.,** a la ventura.
range, 1. n. extensión f.; alcan-

ce m.; estufa; sierra f.; terreno de pasto. **2.** v. recorrer; extenderse.
rank, 1. a. espeso; rancio. **2.** n. fila f.; grado, rango m. **3.** v. clasificar.
ransack, v. saquear.
ransom, 1. n. rescate m. **2.** v. rescatar.
rap, 1. n. golpecito m. **2.** v. golpear.
rapid, a. rápido.
rapport, n. armonía f.
rapture, n. éxtasis m.
rare, a. raro.
rascal, n. pícaro, bribón m.
rash, 1. a. temerario. **2.** n. erupción f.
raspberry, n. frambuesa f.
rat, n. rata f.
rate, 1. n. velocidad; tasa f.; precio m.; (of exchange; of interest) tipo m. **at any r.,** de todos modos. **2.** v. valuar.
rather, adv. bastante; más bien, mejor dicho.
ratify, v. ratificar.
ratio, n. razón; proporción f.
ration, 1. n. ración f. **2.** v. racionar.
rational, a. racional.
rattle, 1. n. ruido m.; matraca f. **r. snake,** culebra de cascabel. **2.** v. matraquear; rechinar.
raucous, a. ronco.
ravage, v. pillar; destruir; asolar.
rave, v. delirar; entusiasmarse.
ravel, v. deshilar.
raven, n. cuervo m.
ravenous, a. voraz.
raw, a. crudo; verde.
ray, n. rayo m.
rayon, n. rayón m.
razor, n. navaja de afeitar. **r. blade,** hoja de afeitar.
reach, 1. n. alcance m. **2.** v. alcanzar.
react, v. reaccionar.
reaction, n. reacción f.
reactionary, 1. a. reaccionario. **2.** n. (pol.) retrógrado m.
read, v. leer.
reader, n. lector m.; libro de lectura.
readily, adv. fácilmente.
reading, n. lectura f.
ready, a. listo, preparado; dispuesto.
real, a. verdadero; real.
realist, n. realista m. & f.
reality, n. realidad f.
realization, n. comprensión; realización f.
realize, v. darse cuenta de; realizar.
really, adv. de veras; en realidad.
realm, n. reino; dominio m.
reap, v. segar, cosechar.
rear, 1. a. posterior. **2.** n. parte posterior. **3.** v. criar; levantar.
reason, 1. n. razón; causa f.; motivo m. **2.** v. razonar.

reasonable, a. razonable.
reassure, v. calmar, tranquilizar.
rebate, n. rebaja f.
rebel, 1. n. rebelde m. & f. **2.** v. rebelarse.
rebellion, n. rebelión f.
rebellious, a. rebelde.
rebirth, n. renacimiento m.
rebound, v. repercutir; resaltar.
rebuff, 1. n. repulsa f. **2.** v. rechazar.
rebuke, 1. n. reprensión f. **2.** v. reprender.
rebuttal, n. refutación f.
recalcitrant, a. recalcitrante.
recall, v. recordar; acordarse de; hacer volver.
recapitulate, v. recapitular.
recede, v. retroceder.
receipt, n. recibo m.; (com., pl.) ingresos m.pl.
receive, v. recibir.
receiver, n. receptor m.
recent, a. reciente.
recently, adv. recién.
receptacle, n. receptáculo m.
reception, n. acogida; recepción f.
receptionist, n. recepcionista m. & f.
receptive, a. receptivo.
recess, n. nicho; retiro; recreo m.
recipe, n. receta f.
recipient, n. receptor, recipiente m.
reciprocate, v. corresponder; reciprocar.
recite, v. recitar.
reckless, a. descuidado; imprudente.
reckon, v. contar; calcular.
reclaim, v. reformar; (leg.) reclamar.
recline, v. reclinar; recostar.
recognition, n. reconocimiento m.
recognize, v. reconocer.
recoil, 1. n. culatada f. **2.** v. recular.
recollect, v. recordar, acordarse de.
recommend, v. recomendar.
recommendation, n. recomendación f.
recompense, 1. n. recompensa f. **2.** v. recompensar.
reconcile, v. reconciliar.
recondition, v. reacondicionar.
reconsider, v. considerar de nuevo.
reconstruct, v. reconstruir.
record, 1. n. registro; (sports) record m. **phonograph r.,** disco m. **2.** v. registrar.
record player, n. tocadiscos m.
recount, v. relatar; contar.
recover, v. recobrar; restablecerse.
recovery, n. recobro m.; recuperación f.
recruit, 1. n. recluta m. **2.** v. reclutar.

rectangle, *n.* rectángulo *m.*

rectify, *v.* rectificar.

recuperate, *v.* recuperar.

recur, *v.* recurrir.

recycle, *v.* reciclar.

red, *a.* rojo; colorado.

redeem, *v.* redimir, rescatar.

redemption, *n.* redención *f.*

reduce, *v.* reducir.

reduction, *n.* reducción *f.*

reed, *n.* caña *f.*, (S.A.) bejuco *m.*

reef, *n.* arrecife, escollo *m.*

reel, 1. *n.* aspa *f.*, carrete *m.* 2. *v.* aspar.

refer, *v.* referir.

referee, *n.* árbitro *m.*

reference, *n.* referencia *f.*

refill, 1. *n.* relleno *m.* 2. *v.* rellenar.

refine, *n.* refinar.

refinement, *n.* refinamiento *m.*; cultura *f.*

reflect, *v.* reflejar; reflexionar.

reflection, *n.* reflejo *m.*; reflexión *f.*

reflex, *a.* reflejo.

reform, 1. *n.* reforma *f.* 2. *v.* reformar.

reformation, *n.* reformación *f.*

refractory, *a.* refractorio.

refrain, 1. *n.* estribillo *m.* 2. *v.* abstenerse.

refresh, *v.* refrescar.

refreshment, *n.* refresco *m.*

refrigerator, *n.* refrigerador *m.*

refuge, *n.* refugio *m.*

refugee, *n.* refugiado -da.

refund, 1. *n.* reembolso *m.* 2. *v.* reembolsar.

refusal, *n.* negativa *f.*

refuse, 1. *n.* basura *f.* 2. *v.* negarse, rehusar.

refute, *v.* refutar.

regain, *v.* recobrar.

regal, *a.* real.

regard, 1. *n.* aprecio; respeto *m.* with r. to, con respecto a. 2. *v.* considerar; estimar.

regarding, *prep.* en cuanto a, acerca de.

regardless (of), a pesar de.

regent, *n.* regente *m.*

regime, *n.* régimen *m.*

regiment, 1. *n.* regimiento *m.* 2. *v.* regimentar.

region, *n.* región *f.*

register, 1. *n.* registro *m.* cash r., caja registradora. 2. *v.* registrar; matricularse; (a letter) certificar.

registration, *n.* registro *m.*; matrícula *f.*

regret, 1. *n.* pena *f.* 2. *v.* sentir, lamentar.

regular, *a.* regular; ordinario.

regularity, *n.* regularidad *f.*

regulate, *v.* regular.

regulation, *n.* regulación *f.*

regulator, *n.* regulador *m.*

rehabilitate, *v.* rehabilitar.

rehearse, *v.* repasar; (theat.) ensayar.

reign, 1. *n.* reino, reinado *m.* 2. *v.* reinar.

reimburse, *v.* reembolsar.

rein, 1. *n.* rienda *f.* 2. *v.* refrenar.

reincarnation, *n.* reencarnación *f.*

reindeer, *n.* reno *m.*

reinforce, *v.* reforzar.

reinforcement, *n.* refuerzo *m.*; armadura *f.*

reiterate, *v.* reiterar.

reject, *v.* rechazar.

rejoice, *v.* regocijarse.

rejoin, *v.* reunirse con; replicar.

rejuvenate, *v.* rejuvenecer.

relapse, 1. *n.* recaída *f.* 2. *v.* recaer.

relate, *v.* relatar, contar; relacionar. r. to, llevarse bien con.

relation, *n.* relación *f.*; pariente *m.* & *f.*

relative, 1. *a.* relativo. 2. *n.* pariente *m.* & *f.*

relativity, *n.* relatividad *f.*

relax, *v.* descansar; relajar.

relay, 1. *n.* relevo *m.* 2. *v.* retransmitir.

release, 1. *n.* liberación *f.* 2. *v.* soltar.

relent, *v.* ceder.

relevant, *a.* pertinente.

reliability, *n.* veracidad *f.*

reliable, *a.* responsable; digno de confianza.

relic, *n.* reliquia *f.*

relief, *n.* alivio; (sculpture) relieve *m.*

relieve, *v.* aliviar.

religion, *n.* religión *f.*

religious, *a.* religioso.

relinquish, *v.* abandonar.

relish, 1. *n.* sabor; condimento *m.* 2. *v.* saborear.

reluctant, *a.* renuente.

rely, *v.* r. on, confiar en; contar con; depender de.

remain, *v.* (pl.) restos *m.pl.* 2. *v.* quedar, permanecer.

remainder, *n.* resto *m.*

remark, 1. *n.* observación *f.* 2. *v.* observar.

remarkable, *a.* notable.

remedial, *a.* reparador.

remedy, 1. *n.* remedio *m.* 2. *v.* remediar.

remember, *v.* acordarse de, recordar.

remembrance, *n.* recuerdo *m.*

remind, *v.* r. of, recordar.

reminisce, *v.* pensar en o hablar de cosas pasadas.

remiss, *a.* remiso; flojo.

remit, *v.* remitir.

remorse, *n.* remordimiento *m.*

remote, *a.* remoto.

removal, *n.* alejamiento *m.*; eliminación *f.*

remove, *v.* quitar; remover.

renaissance, *n.* renacimiento *m.*

rend, *v.* hacer pedazos; separar.

render, *v.* dar; rendir; (theat.) interpretar.

rendezvous, *n.* cita *f.*

rendition, *n.* interpretación, rendición *f.*

renege, *v.* renunciar.

renew, *v.* renovar.

renewal, *n.* renovación; (com.) prórroga *f.*

renounce, *v.* renunciar a.

renovate, *v.* renovar.

renown, *n.* renombre *m.*, fama *f.*

rent, 1. *n.* alquiler *m.* 2. *v.* arrendar, alquilar.

repair, 1. *n.* reparo *m.* 2. *v.* reparar.

repatriate, *v.* repatriar.

repay, *v.* pagar; devolver.

repeat, *v.* repetir.

repel, *v.* repeler, repulsar.

repent, *v.* arrepentirse.

repentance, *n.* arrepentimiento *m.*

repercussion, *n.* repercusión *f.*

repertoire, *n.* repertorio *m.*

repetition, *n.* repetición *f.*

replace, *v.* reemplazar.

replenish, *v.* rellenar; surtir de nuevo.

reply, 1. *n.* respuesta *f.* 2. *v.* replicar; contestar.

report, 1. *n.* informe *m.* 2. *v.* informar, contar; denunciar; presentarse.

reporter, *n.* repórter, reportero *m.*

repose, 1. *n.* reposo *m.* 2. *v.* reposar; reclinar.

reprehensible, *a.* reprensible.

represent, *v.* representar.

representation, *n.* representación *f.*

representative, 1. *a.* representativo. 2. *n.* representante *m.*

repress, *v.* reprimir.

reprimand, 1. *n.* regaño *m.* 2. *v.* regañar.

reprisal, *n.* represalia *f.*

reproach, 1. *n.* reproche *m.* 2. *v.* reprochar.

reproduce, *v.* reproducir.

reproduction, *n.* reproducción *f.*

reproof, *n.* censura *f.*

reprove, *v.* censurar, regañar.

reptile, *n.* reptil *m.*

republic, *n.* república *f.*

republican, *a.* & *n.* republicano -na.

repudiate, *v.* repudiar.

repulsive, *a.* repulsivo, repugnante.

reputation, *n.* reputación; fama *f.*

repute, 1. *n.* reputación *f.* 2. *v.* reputar.

request, 1. *n.* súplica *f.*, ruego *m.* 2. *v.* pedir; rogar, suplicar.

require, *v.* requerir; exigir.

requirement, *n.* requisito *m.*

requisite, 1. *a.* necesario. 2. *n.* requisito *m.*

requisition, *n.* requisición *f.*

rescind, *v.* rescindir, anular.

rescue, 1. *n.* rescate *m.* 2. *v.* rescatar.

research, *n.* investigación *f.*

resemble, *v.* parecerse a, asemejarse a.

resent, *v.* resentirse de.

reservation, *n.* reservación *f.*

reserve, 1. *n.* reserva *f.* **2.** *v.* reservar.

reservoir, *n* depósito; tanque *m.*

reside, *v.* residir, morar.

residence, *n.* residencia, morada *f.*

resident, *n.* residente *m. & f.*

residue, *n.* residuo *m.*

resign, *v.* dimitir; resignar.

resignation, *n.* dimisión, resignación *f.*

resist, *v.* resistir.

resistance, *n.* resistencia *f.*

resolute, *a.* resuelto.

resolution, *n.* resolución *f.*

resolve, *v.* resolver.

resonant, *a.* resonante.

resort, 1. *n.* recurso; expediente *m.* **summer r.,** lugar de veraneo. **2.** *v.* acudir, recurrir.

resound, *v.* resonar.

resource, *n.* recurso *m.*

respect, 1. *n.* respeto *m.* **with r. to,** con respecto a. **2.** *v.* respetar.

respectable, *a.* respetable.

respectful, *a.* respetuoso.

respective, *a.* respectivo.

respiration, *n.* respiración *f.*

respite, *n.* pausa, tregua *f.*

respond, *v.* responder.

response, *n.* respuesta *f.*

responsibility, *n.* responsabilidad *f.*

responsible, *a.* responsable.

responsive, *a.* respondiente, sensible.

rest, 1. *n.* descanso; reposo *m.;* (music) pausa *f.* **the r.,** el resto, lo demás; los demás. **2.** *v.* descansar; recostar.

restaurant, *n.* restaurante *m.*

restful, *a.* tranquilo.

restitution, *n.* restitución *f.*

restless, *a.* inquieto.

restoration, *n.* restauración *f.*

restore, *v.* restaurar.

restrain, *v.* refrenar.

restraint, *n.* limitación, restricción *f.*

restrict, *v.* restringir, limitar.

result, 1. *n.* resultado *m.* **2.** *v.* resultar.

resume, *v.* reasumir; empezar de nuevo.

resurgent, *a.* resurgente.

resurrect, *v.* resucitar.

retail, *n.* **at r.,** al por menor.

retain, *v.* retener.

retaliate, *v.* vengarse.

retard, *v.* retardar.

retention, *n.* retención *f.*

reticent, *a.* reticente.

retire, *v.* retirar.

retort, 1. *n.* réplica; (chem.) retorta *f.* **2.** *v.* replicar.

retreat, 1. *n.* retiro *m.;* (mil.) retirada, retreta *f.* **2.** *v.* retirarse.

retribution, *n.* retribución *f.*

retrieve, *v.* recobrar.

return, 1. *n.* vuelta *f.,* regreso; retorno *m.* **by r. mail,** a vuelta de correo. **2.** *v.* volver, regresar; devolver.

reunion, *n.* reunión *f.*

reveal, *v.* revelar.

revelation, *n.* revelación *f.*

revenge, *n.* venganza *f.* **to get r.,** vengarse.

revenue, *n.* renta *f.*

revere, *v.* reverenciar, venerar.

reverence, 1. *n.* reverencia *f.* **2.** *v.* reverenciar.

reverend, 1. *a.* reverendo. **2.** *n.* pastor *m.*

reverent, *a.* reverente.

reverse, 1. *a.* inverso. **2.** *n.* revés, inverso. **3.** *v.* invertir; revocar.

revert, *v.* revertir.

review, 1. *n.* repaso *m.;* revista *f.* **2.** *v.* repasar; revistar.

revise, *v.* revisar.

revision, *n.* revisión *f.*

revival, *n.* reavivamiento *m.*

revive, *v.* avivar; revivir.

revoke, *v.* revocar.

revolt, 1. *n.* rebelión *f.* **2.** *v.* rebelarse.

revolution, *n.* revolución *f.*

revolutionary, *a. & n.* revolucionario -ria.

revolve, *v.* girar; dar vueltas.

revolver, *n.* revólver *m.*

reward, 1. *n.* pago *m.;* recompensa *f.* **2.** *v.* recompensar.

rhetoric, *n.* retórica *f.*

rheumatism, *n.* reumatismo *m.*

rhinoceros, *n.* rinoceronte *m.*

rhyme, 1. *n.* rima *f.* **2.** *v.* rimar.

rhythm, *n.* ritmo *m.*

rhythmical, *a.* rítmico.

rib, *n.* costilla *f.*

ribbon, *n.* cinta *f.*

rice, *n.* arroz *m.*

rich, *a.* rico.

rid, *v.* librar. **get r. of,** deshacerse de, quitarse.

riddle, *n.* enigma, rompecabezas *m.*

ride, 1. *n.* paseo (a caballo o en coche) *m.* **2.** *v.* cabalgar; ir en coche.

ridge, *n.* cerro *m.;* arruga *f.;* (of a roof) caballete *m.*

ridicule, 1. *n.* ridículo *m.* **2.** *v.* ridiculizar.

ridiculous, *a.* ridículo.

rifle, 1. *n.* fusil *m.* **2.** *v.* robar.

rig, 1. *n.* aparejo *m.* **2.** *v.* aparejar.

right, 1. *a.* derecho; correcto. **to be r.,** tener razón. **2.** *adv.* bien, correctamente. **r. here,** etc., aquí mismo, etc. **all r.,** está bien, muy bien. **3.** *n.* derecho *m.;* justicia *f.* **to the r.,** a la derecha. **4.** *v.* corregir; enderezar.

righteous, *a.* justo.

rigid, *a.* rígido.

rigor, *n.* rigor *m.*

rigorous, *a.* riguroso.

rim, *n.* margen *m.* or *f.;* borde *m.*

ring, 1. *n.* anillo *m.;* sortija *f.;* círculo; campaneo *m.* **2.** *v.* cercar; sonar; tocar.

rinse, *v.* enjuagar, lavar.

riot, *n.* motín; alboroto *m.*

rip, 1. *n.* rasgadura *f.* **2.** *v.* rasgar; descoser.

ripe, *a.* maduro.

ripen, *v.* madurar.

ripoff, *n.* robo, atraco *m.*

ripple, 1. *n.* onda *f.* **2.** *v.* ondear.

rise, 1. *n.* subida *f.* **2.** *v.* ascender; levantarse; (moon) salir.

risk, 1. *n.* riesgo *m.* **2.** *v.* arriesgar.

rite, *n.* rito *m.*

ritual, *a. & n.* ritual *m.*

rival, 1. *n.* rival *m. & f.*

rivalry, *n.* rivalidad *f.*

river, *n.* río *m*

rivet, 1. *n.* remache, roblón *m.* **2.** *v.* remachar, roblar.

road, *n.* camino *m.;* carretera *f.*

roam, *v.* vagar.

roar, 1. *n.* rugido, bramido *m.* **2.** *v.* rugir, bramar.

roast, 1. *n.* asado *m.* **2.** *v.* asar.

rob, *v.* robar.

robber, *n.* ladrón -na.

robbery, *n.* robo *m.*

robe, *n.* manto *m.*

robin, *n.* petirrojo *m.*

robust, *a.* robusto.

rock, 1. *n.* roca *f.;* (music) rock *m.,* musica (de) rock *f.* **2.** *v.* mecer; oscilar.

rocker, *n.* mecedora *f.*

rocket, *n.* cohete *m.*

rocky, *a.* pedregoso.

rod, *n.* varilla *f.*

rodent, *n.* roedor *m.*

rogue, *n.* bribón, pícaro *m.*

roguish, *a.* pícaro.

role, *n.* papel *m.*

roll, 1. *n.* rollo *m.;* lista *f.;* panecillo *m.* **to call the r.,** pasar lista. **2.** *v.* rodar. **r. up,** enrollar.

roller, *n.* rodillo, cilindro *m.*

Roman, *a. & n.* romano -na.

romance, 1. *a.* romántico. **2.** *n.* romance *m.;* amorío *m.*

romantic, *a.* romántico.

romp, *v.* retozar; jugar.

roof, 1. *n.* techo *m.;* **2.** *v.* techar.

room, 1. *n.* cuarto *m.,* habitación *f.;* lugar *m.* **2.** *v.* alojarse.

roommate, *n.* compañero -ra de cuarto.

rooster, *n.* gallo *m.*

root, *n.* raíz *f.* **to take r.,** arraigar.

rope, *n.* cuerda, soga *f.*

rose, *n.* rosa *f.*

rosy, *a.* róseo, rosado.

rot, 1. *n.* putrefacción *f.* **2.** *v.* pudrirse.

rotary, *a.* giratorio; rotativo.

rotate, *v.* girar; alternar.

rotation, *n.* rotación *f.*

rotten, *a.* podrido.

rouge, *n.* colorete *m.*

rough, a. áspero; rudo; grosero; aproximado.

round, 1. a. rodondo. **r. trip,** viaje de ida y vuelta. 2. n. ronda f.; (boxing) asalto m.

rouse, v. despertar.

rout, 1. n. derrota f. 2. v. derrotar.

route, n. ruta, vía f.

routine, 1. a. rutinario. 2. n. rutina f.

rove, v. vagar.

rover, n. vagabundo -da.

row, 1. n. fila; pelea f. 2. v. (naut.) remar.

rowboat, n. bote de remos.

rowdy, a. alborotoso.

royal, a. real.

royalty, n. realeza f.; (pl.) regalías f.pl.

rub, v. frotar. **r. against,** rozar. **r. out,** borrar.

rubber, n. goma f.; caucho m.; (pl.) chanclos m.pl., zapatos de goma.

rubbish, n. basura f.; (nonsense) tonterías f.pl.

ruby, n. rubí m.

rudder, n. timón m.

ruddy, a. colorado.

rude, a. rudo; grosero; descortés.

rudiment, n. rudimento m.

rue, v. deplorar; lamentar.

ruffian, n. rufián, bandolero m.

ruffle, 1. n. volante fruncido. 2. v. fruncir; irritar.

rug, n. alfombra f.

rugged, a. áspero; robusto.

ruin, 1. n. ruina f. 2. v. arruinar.

ruinous, a. ruinoso.

rule, 1. n. regla f. **as a r.,** por regla general. 2. v. gobernar; mandar; rayar.

ruler, n. gobernante; soberano m.; regla f.

rum, n. ron m.

rumble, v. retumbar.

rumor, n. rumor m.

run, v. correr; hacer correr. **r. away,** escaparse. **r. into,** chocar con.

runner, n. corredor -ra; mensajero -ra.

rupture, 1. n. rotura; hernia f. 2. v. reventar.

rural, a. rural, campestre.

rush, 1. n. prisa f.; (bot.) junco m. 2. v. ir de prisa.

Russia, n. Rusia f.

Russian, a. & n. ruso -sa.

rust, 1. n. herrumbre m. 2. v. aherrumbrarse.

rustic, a. rústico.

rustle, 1. n. susurro m. 2. v. susurrar.

rusty, a. mohoso.

rut, n. surco m.

ruthless, a. cruel, inhumano.

rye, n. centeno m.

S

saber, n. sable m.

saber, n. sable m.

sable, n. cebellina f.

sabotage, n. sabotaje m.

sachet, n. perfumador m.

sack, 1. n. saco m. 2. v. (mil.) saquear.

sacred, a. sagrado, santo.

sacrifice, 1. n. sacrificio m. 2. v. sacrificar.

sacrilege, n. sacrilegio m.

sad, a. triste.

saddle, 1. n. silla de montar. 2. v. ensillar.

safe, 1. a. seguro; salvo. 2. n. caja de caudales.

safeguard, 1. n. salvaguardia m. 2. v. proteger, poner a salvo.

safety, n. seguridad, protección f.

safety pin, n. imperdible m.

sage, 1. a. sabio, sagaz. 2. n. sabio m.; (bot.) salvia f.

sail, 1. n. vela f.; paseo por mar. 2. v. navegar; embarcarse.

sailboat, n. barco de vela.

sailor, n. marinero m.

saint, n. santo -ta.

sake, n. **for the s. of,** por; por el bien de.

salad, n. ensalada f. **s. bowl,** ensaladera f.

salary, n. sueldo, salario m.

sale, n. venta f.

salesman, n. vendedor m.; viajante de comercio.

sales tax, impuesto sobre la venta.

saliva, n. saliva f.

salmon, n. salmón m.

salt, 1. n. sal f. 2. n. sal f. 3. v. salar.

salute, 1. n. saludo m. 2. v. saludar.

salvage, v. salvar; recobrar.

salvation, n. salvación; redención f.

salve, n. emplasto, ungüento m.

same, a. & pron. mismo. **it's all the s.,** lo mismo da.

sample, 1. n. muestra f. 2. v. probar.

sanatorium, n. sanatorio m.

sanctify, v. santificar.

sanction, 1. n. sanción f. 2. v. sancionar.

sanctity, n. santidad f.

sanctuary, n. santuario, asilo m.

sand, n. arena f.

sandal, n. sandalia f.

sandwich, n. sandwich m.

sandy, a. arenoso; (color) rufo.

sane, a. cuerdo; sano.

sanitary, a. higiénico, sanitario.

sanitation, n. saneamiento m.

sanity, n. cordura f.

sap, 1. n. savia f.; (coll.) estúpido, bobo m. 2. v. agotar.

sapphire, n. zafiro m.

sarcasm, n. sarcasmo m.

sardine, n. sardina f.

sash, n. cinta f.

satellite, n. satélite m.

satin, n. raso m.

satire, n. sátira f.

satisfaction, n. satisfacción; recompensa f.

satisfactory, a. satisfactorio.

satisfy, v. satisfacer. **be satisfied that . . .,** estar convencido de que.

saturate, v. saturar.

Saturday, n. sábado m.

sauce, n. salsa; compota f.

saucer, n. platillo m.

saucy, a. descarado, insolente.

sausage, n. salchicha f.

savage, a. & n. salvaje m.

save, 1. v. salvar; guardar; ahorrar, economizar. 2. prep. salvo, excepto.

savings, n. ahorros m.pl.

savior, n. salvador m.

savor, 1. n. sabor m. 2. v. saborear.

savory, a. sabroso.

saw, 1. n. sierra f. 2. v. aserrar.

say, v. decir; recitar.

saying, n. dicho, refrán m.

scaffold, n. andamio; (gallows) patíbulo m.

scald, v. escaldar.

scale, 1. n. escala f.; (of fish) escama f.; (pl.) balanza f. 2. v. escalar; escamar.

scalp, 1. n. pericráneo m. 2. v. escalpar.

scan, v. hojear, repasar; (poetry) escandir.

scandal, n. escándalo m.

scant, a. escaso.

scar, n. cicatriz f.

scarce, a. escaso; raro.

scarcely, adv. & conj. apenas.

scare, 1. n. susto m. 2. v. asustar. **s. away,** espantar.

scarf, n. pañueleta, bufanda f.

scarlet, a. escarlata f.

scatter, v. esparcir; dispersar.

scavenger, n. basurero m.

scenario, n. escenario m.

scene, n. vista f., paisaje m.; (theat.) escena f. **behind the scenes,** bajo cuerda.

scenery, n. paisaje m.; (theat.) decorado m.

scent, 1. n. olor, perfume; (sense) olfato m. 2. v. perfumar; (fig.) sospechar.

schedule, 1. n. programa, horario m. 2. v. fijar la hora para.

scheme, 1. n. proyecto; esquema m. 2. v. intrigar.

scholar, n. erudito; becado -da.

scholarship, n. beca; erudición f.

school, 1. n. escuela f.; colegio m.; (of fish) banco m. 2. v. enseñar.

sciatica, n. ciática f.

science, n. ciencia f.

science fiction, n. ciencia ficción f.

scientific, a. científico.

scientist, n. científico -ca.

scissors, n. tijeras f.pl.

scoff, v. mofarse, burlarse.

scold, v. regañar.

scoop, 1. n. cucharón m.; cucharada f. 2. v. s. out, recoger, sacar.

scope, n. alcance; campo m.

scorch, 1. n. tantos m.pl.; (music) partitura f. 2. v. marcar, hacer tantos.

scorn, 1. n. desprecio m. 2. v. despreciar.

scornful, a. desdeñoso.

Scotch, a. escocés.

Scotland, n. Escocia f.

scour, v. fregar, estregar.

scourge, n. azote m.; plaga f.

scout, 1. n. explorador m. 2. v. explorar, reconocer.

scramble, 1. n. ribatiña f. 2. v. bregar. scrambled eggs, huevos revueltos.

scrap, 1. n. migaja f.; pedacito m.; (coll.) riña f. s. metal, hierro viejo. s. paper, papel borrador. 2. v. desechar; (coll.) reñir.

scrape, 1. n. lío, apuro m. 2. v. rascar; (feet) restregar.

scratch, 1. n. rasguño m. 2. v. rasguñar; rayar.

scream, 1. n. grito, chillido m. 2. v. gritar, chillar.

screen, n. biombo m.; (for window) tela metálica; (movie) pantalla f.

screw, 1. n. tornillo m. 2. v. atornillar.

screwdriver, n. destornillador m.

scribble, v. hacer garabatos.

scroll, n. rúbrica f.; rollo de papel.

scrub, v. gregar, estregar.

scruple, n. escrúpulo m.

scrupulous, a. escrupuloso.

sculptor, n. escultor m.

sculpture, 1. n. escultura f. 2. v. esculpir.

scythe, n. guadaña f.

sea, n. mar m. or f.

seabed, n. lecho marino m.

seal, 1. n. sello m.; (animal) foca f. 2. v. sellar.

seam, n. costura f.

seaport, n. puerto de mar.

search, 1. n. registro m. in s. of, en busca de. 2. v. registrar. s. for, buscar.

seasick, a. mareado. to get s., marearse.

season, 1. n. estación; sazón, temporada f. 2. v. sazonar.

seasoning, n. condimento m.

seat, 1. n. asiento m.; residencia, sede f.; (theat.) localidad f. 2. v. sentar. be seated, sentarse.

second, 1. a. & n. segundo m. 2. v. apoyar, segundar.

secondary, a. secundario.

secret, a. & n. secreto m.

secretary, n. secretario -ria; (govt.) ministro m.; (furniture) papelera f.

sect, n. secta f.; partido m.

section, n. sección, parte f.

sectional, a. regional, local.

secular, a. secular.

secure, 1. a. seguro. 2. v. asegurar; obtener, conseguir; (fin.) garantizar.

security, n. seguridad; garantía f.

sedative, a. & n. sedativo m.

seduce, v. seducir.

see, v. ver; comprender. s. off, despedirse de. s. to, encargarse de.

seed, 1. n. semilla f. 2. v. sembrar.

seek, v. buscar. s. to, tratar de.

seem, v. parecer.

seep, v. colarse.

segment, n. segmento m.

segregate, v. segregar.

seize, v. agarrar; apoderarse de.

seldom, adv. rara vez.

select, 1. a. escogido, selecto. 2. v. elegir, seleccionar.

selection, n. selección f.

selective, a. escogedor.

selfish, a. egoísta.

selfishness, n. egoísmo m.

sell, v. vender.

semester, n. semestre m.

semicircle, n. semicírculo m.

senate, n. senado m.

senator, n. senador -ra.

send, v. mandar, enviar; (a wire) poner. s. away, despedir. s. back, devolver. s. for, mandar buscar. s. off, expedir. s. word, mandar recado.

senile, a. senil.

senior, a. mayor; más viejo. Sr., padre.

senior citizen, persona de edad.

sensation, n. sensación f.

sensational, a. sensacional.

sense, 1. n. sentido; juicio m. 2. v. percibir; sospechar.

sensible, a. sensato, razonable.

sensitive, a. sensible; sensitivo.

sensual, a. sensual.

sentence, 1. n. frase; (gram.) oración; (leg.) sentencia f. 2. v. condenar.

sentiment, n. sentimiento m.

sentimental, a. sentimental.

separate, 1. a. separado; suelto. 2. v. separar, dividir.

separation, n. separación f.

September, n. septiembre m.

sequence, n. serie f. in s., seguidos.

serenade, 1. n. serenata f. 2. v. dar serenata a.

serene, a. sereno; tranquilo.

sergeant, n. sargento m.

serial, a. en serie, de serie.

series, n. serie f.

serious, a. serio; grave.

sermon, n. sermón m.

serpent, n. serpiente f.

servant, n. criado -da; servidor -ra.

serve, v. servir.

service, 1. n. servicio m. at the s. of, a las órdenes de. to be of s., servir; ser útil. 2. v. (auto.) reparar.

session, n. sesión f.

set, 1. a. fijo. 2. n. colección f.; (of a game) juego; (mech.) aparato; (theat.) decorado m. 3. v. poner, colocar; fijar; (sun) ponerse. s. forth, exponer. s. off, s. out, salir. s. up, instalar; establecer.

settle, v. solucionar; arreglar; establecerse.

settlement, n. caserío; arreglo; acuerdo m.

settler, n. poblador -ra.

seven, a. & pron. siete.

seventeen, a. & pron. diecisiete.

seventh, a. séptimo.

seventy, a. & pron. setenta.

sever, v. desunir; romper.

several, a. & pron. varios.

severe, a. severo; grave.

severity, n. severidad f.

sew, v. coser.

sewer, n. cloaca f.

sex, n. sexo m.

sexism, n. sexismo m.

sexist, a. & n. sexista.

sexton, n. sacristán m.

sexual, a. sexual.

shabby, a. haraposo, desalineado.

shade, 1. n. sombra f.; tinte m.; (window) transparente m. 2. v. sombrear.

shadow, n. sombra f.

shady, a. sombroso; sospechoso.

shaft, n. columna; (mech.) asta f.

shake, v. sacudir; agitar; temblar. s. hands with, dar la mano a.

shallow, a. poco hondo; superficial.

shame, 1. n. vergüenza f. to be a s., ser una lástima. 2. v. avergonzar.

shameful, a. vergonzoso.

shampoo, n. champú m.

shape, 1. n. forma f.; estado m. 2. v. formar.

share, 1. n. parte; (stock) acción f. 2 v. compartir.

shark, n. tiburón m.

sharp, a. agudo; (blade) afilado.

sharpen, v. aguzar; afilar.

shatter, v. estrellar; hacer pedazos.

shave, 1. n. afeitada f. 2. v. afeitarse.

shawl, n. rebozo, chal m.

she, pron. ella f.

sheaf, n. gavilla f.

shear, v. cizallar.

shears, n. cizallas f.pl.

sheath, n. vaina f.

shed, 1. n. cobertizo m. 2. v. arrojar, quitarse.

sheep, n. oveja f.

sheet, *n.* sábana; (of paper) hoja *f.*

shelf, *n.* estante, *m.*, repisa *f.*

shell, 1. *n.* cáscara; (sea) concha *f.;* (mil.) proyectil *m.* 2. *v.* desgranar; bombardear.

shellac, *n.* laca *f.*

shelter, 1. *n.* albergue; refugio *m.* 2. *v.* albergar; amparar.

shepherd, *n.* pastor *m.*

sherry, *n.* jerez *m.*

shield, 1. *n.* escudo *m.* 2. *v.* amparar.

shift, 1. *n.* cambio; (work) turno *m.* 2. *v.* cambiar, mudar. s. for oneself, arreglárselas.

shine, 1. *n.* brillo, lustre *m.* 2. *v.* brillar; (shoes) lustrar.

shiny, *a.* brillante, lustroso.

ship, 1. *n.* barco *m.*, nave *f.* 2. *v.* embarcar; (com.) enviar.

shipment, *n.* envío, embarque *m.*

shirk, *v.* faltar a.

shirt, *n.* camisa *f.*

shiver, 1. *n.* temblor *m.* 2. *v.* temblar.

shock, 1. *n.* choque *m.* 2. *v.* chocar.

shoe, *n.* zapato *m.*

shoelace, *n.* lazo *m.;* cordón de zapato.

shoemaker, *n.* zapatero *m.*

shoot, *v.* tirar; (gun) disparar. s. away, s. off, salir disparado.

shop, *n.* tienda *f.*

shopping, *n.* to go s., hacer compras, ir de compras.

shore, *n.* orilla; playa *f.*

short, *a.* corto; breve; (in stature) pequeño, bajo. a s. time, poco tiempo. in s., en suma.

shortage, *n.* escasez; falta *f.*

shorten, *v.* acortar, abreviar.

shortly, *adv.* en breve, dentro de poco.

shorts, *n.* calzoncillos *m.pl.*

shot, *n.* tiro, disparo *m.*

shoulder, 1. *n.* hombro *m.* 2. *v.* asumir; cargar con.

shout, 1. *n.* grito *m.* 2. *v.* gritar.

shove, 1. *n.* empujón *m.* 2. *v.* empujar.

shovel, 1. *n.* pala *f.* 2. *v.* traspalar.

show, 1. *n.* ostentación *f.;* (theat.) función *f.;* espectáculo *m.* 2. *v.* enseñar, mostrar; verse. s. up, destacarse; (coll.) asomar.

shower, *n.* chubasco *m.;* (bath) ducha *f.*

shrapnel, *n.* metralla *f.*

shrewd, *a.* astuto.

shriek, 1. *n.* chillido *m.* 2. *v.* chillar.

shrill, *a.* chillón, agudo.

shrimp, *n.* camarón *m.*

shrine, *n.* santuario *m.*

shrink, *v.* encogerse, contraerse. s. from, huir de.

shroud, 1. *n.* mortaja *f.* 2. *v.* (fig.) ocultar.

shrub, *n.* arbusto *m.*

shudder, 1. *n.* estremecimiento *m.* 2. *v.* estremecerse.

shun, *v.* evitar, huir de.

shut, *v.* cerrar. s. in, encerrar. s. up, (coll.) callarse.

shutter, *n.* persiana *f.*

shy, *a.* tímido, vergonzoso.

sick, *a.* enfermo. s. of, aburrido de, cansado de.

sickness, *n.* enfermedad *f.*

side, 1. *n.* lado; partido *m.;* parte *f.;* (anat.) costado *m.* 2. *v.* s. with, ponerse del lado de.

sidewalk, *n.* acera, vereda *f.*

siege, *n.* asedio *m.*

sieve, *n.* cedazo *m.*

sift, *v.* cerner.

sigh, 1. *n.* suspiro *m.* 2. *v.* suspirar.

sight, 1. *n.* vista *f.;* punto de interés. to lose s. of, perder de vista. 2. *v.* divisar.

sign, 1. *n.* letrero; señal, seña *f.* 2. *v.* firmar. s. up, inscribirse.

signal, 1. *n.* señal *f.* 2. *v.* hacer señales.

signature, *n.* firma *f.*

significance, *n.* significación *f.*

significant, *a.* significativo.

signify, *v.* significar.

silence, 1. *n.* silencio *m.* 2. *v.* hacer callar.

silent, *a.* silencioso; callado.

silk, *n.* seda *f.*

silken, silky, *a.* sedoso.

sill, *n.* umbral de puerta *m.*, solera *f.*

silly, *a.* necio, tonto.

silo, *n.* silo *m.*

silver, *n.* plata *f.*

silverware, *n.* artículos de plata.

similar, *a.* semejante, parecido.

similarity, *n.* semejanza *f.*

simple, *a.* sencillo, simple.

simplicity, *n.* sencillez *f.*

simplify, *v.* simplificar.

simulate, *v.* simular.

simultaneous, *a.* simultáneo.

sin, 1. *n.* pecado *m.* 2. *v.* pecar.

since, 1. *adv.* desde entonces. 2. *prep.* desde. 3. *conj.* desde que; puesto que.

sincere, *a.* sincero.

sincerely, *adv.* sinceramente.

sincerity, *n.* sinceridad *f.*

sinew, *n.* tendón *m.*

sinful, *a.* pecador.

sing, *v.* cantar.

singe, *v.* chamuscar.

singer, *n.* cantante *m.* & *f.*

single, *a.* solo; (room) sencillo; (unmarried) soltero.

singular, *a.* & *n.* singular *m.*

sinister, *a.* siniestro.

sink, 1. *n.* fregadero *m.* 2. *v.* hundir; (fig.) abatir.

sinner, *n.* pecador -ra.

sinuous, *a.* sinuoso.

sinus, *n.* seno; hueco *m.*

sip, 1. *n.* sorbo *m.* 2. *v.* sorber.

siphon, *n.* sifón *m.*

sir, *title.* señor. ·

siren, *n.* sirena *f.*

sirloin, *n.* solomillo *m.*

sisal, *n.* henequén *m.*

sister, *n.* hermana *f.*

sister-in-law, *n.* cuñada *f.*

sit, *v.* sentarse; posar. be sitting, estar sentado. s. down, sentarse. s. up, incorporarse; quedar levantado.

site, *n.* sitio, local *m.*

sitting, *n.* sesión *f.*

situate, *v.* situar.

situation, *n.* situación *f.*

six, *a.* & *pron.* seis.

sixteen, *a.* & *pron.* dieciseis.

sixth, *a.* sexto.

sixty, *a.* & *pron.* sesenta.

size, 1. *n.* tamaño; (of shoe, etc.) número *m.*

sizing, *n.* aderezo *m.*

skate, 1. *n.* patín *m.* 2. *v.* patinar.

skateboard, *n.* monopatín *m.*

skein, *n.* madeja *f.*

skeleton, *n.* esqueleto *m.*

skeptic, *n.* escéptico -ca.

skeptical, *a.* escéptico.

sketch, 1. *n.* esbozo *m.* 2. *v.* esbozar.

ski, 1. *n.* esquí *m.* 2. *v.* esquiar.

skid, 1. *n.* resbalar. 2. *v.* varadera *f.*

skill, *n.* destreza, habilidad *f.*

skillful, *a.* diestro, hábil.

skim, *v.* rasar; (milk) desnatar. s. over, s. through, hojear.

skin, 1. *n.* piel; (of fruit) corteza *f.* 2. *v.* desollar.

skip, 1. *n.* brinco *m.* 2. *v.* brincar. s. over, pasar por alto.

skirmish, *n.* escaramuza *f.*

skirt, *n.* falda *f.*

skull, *n.* cráneo *m.*

skunk, *n.* zorrillo *m.*

sky, *n.* cielo *m.*

skylight, *n.* tragaluz *m.*

skyscraper, *n.* rascacielos *m.*

slab, *n.* tabla *f.*

slack, *a.* flojo; descuidado.

slacken, *v.* relajar.

slacks, *n.* pantalones flojos.

slam, 1. *n.* portazo *m.* 2. *v.* cerrar de golpe.

slander, 1. *n.* calumnia *f.* 2. *v.* calumniar.

slang, *n.* jerga *f.*

slant, 1. *n.* sesgo *m.* 2. *v.* sesgar.

slap, 1. *n.* bofetada, palmada *f.* 2. *v.* dar una bofetada.

slash, 1. *n.* cuchillada *f.* 2. *v.* acuchillar.

slat, 1. *n.* tablilla *f.* 2. *v.* lanzar.

slate, 1. *n.* pizarra *f.;* lista de candidatos. 2. *v.* destinar.

slaughter, 1. *n.* matanza *f.* 2. *v.* matar.

slave, *n.* esclavo -va.

slavery, *n.* esclavitud *f.*

Slavic, *a.* eslavo.

slay, *v.* matar, asesinar.

sled, *n.* trineo *m.*

sleek, *a.* liso.

sleep, 1. *n.* sueño *m.* to get much s., dormir mucho. 2. *v.* dormir.

sleeper, sleeping car, *n.* coche cama.

sleepy, *a.* soñoliento. **to be s.**, tener sueño.

sleet, 1. *n.* cellisca *f.* 2. *v.* cellisquear.

sleeve, *n.* manga *f.*

sleigh, *n.* trineo *m.*

slender, *a.* delgado.

slice, 1. *n.* rebanada; (of meat) tajada *f.* 2. *v.* rebanar; tajar.

slide, *v.* resbalar, deslizarse.

slide rule, *n.* regla de cálculo *f.*

slight, 1. *n.* desaire *m.* 2. *a.* pequeño; leve. 3. *v.* desairar.

slim, *a.* delgado.

slime, *n.* lama *f.*

sling, 1. *n.* honda *f.;* (med.) cabestrillo *m.* 2. *v.* tirar.

slink, *v.* escabullirse.

slip, 1. *n.* imprudencia; (garment) combinación *f.;* (of paper) trozo *m.;* ficha *f.* 2. *v.* resbalar; deslizar. **s. up**, equivocarse.

slipper, *n.* chinela *f.*

slippery, *a.* resbaloso.

slit, 1. *n.* abertura *f.* 2. *v.* cortar.

slogan, *n.* lema *m.*

slope, 1. *n.* declive *m.* 2. *v.* inclinarse.

sloppy, *a.* desaliñado, chapucero.

slot, *n.* ranura *f.*

slot machine, *n.* máquina de servicio automático *f.*

slouch, 1. *n.* patán *m.* 2. *v.* estar gacho.

slovenly, *a.* desaliñado.

slow, 1. *a.* lento; (watch) atrasado. 2. *v.* **s. down, s. up**, retardar; ir más despacio.

slowly, *adv.* despacio.

slowness, *n.* lentitud *f.*

sluggish, *a.* perezoso, inactivo.

slum, *n.* barrio bajo *m.*

slumber, *v.* dormitar.

slur, 1. *n.* estigma *m.* 2. *v.* menospreciar.

slush, *n.* fango *m.*

sly, *a.* taimado. **on the s.** a hurtadillas.

smack, 1. *n.* manotada *f.* 2. *v.* manotear.

small, *a.* pequeño.

smallpox, *n.* viruela *f.*

smart, 1. *a.* listo; elegante. 2. *v.* escocer.

smash, *v.* aplastar; hacer pedazos.

smear, 1. *n.* mancha; difamación *f.* 2. *v.* manchar; difamar.

smell, 1. *n.* olor; (sense) olfato *m.* 2. *v.* oler.

smelt, 1. *n.* eperlano *m.* 2. *v.* fundir.

smile, 1. *n.* sonrisa *f.* 2. *v.* sonreír.

smite, *v.* afligir; apenar.

smock, *n.* camisa de mujer *f.*

smoke, 1. *n.* humo *m.* 2. *v.* fumar; (food) ahumar.

smokestack, *n.* chimenea *f.*

smolder, *v.* arder sin llama.

smooth, 1. *a.* liso; suave; tranquilo. 2. *v.* alisar.

smother, *v.* sofocar.

smug, *a.* presumido.

smuggle, *v.* pasar de contrabando.

snack, *n.* bocadillo *m.*

snag, *n.* nudo *m.*, obstáculo *m.*

snail, *n.* caracol *m.*

snake, *n.* culebra, serpiente *f.*

snap, 1. *n.* trueno *m.* 2. *v.* tronar, romper.

snapshot, *n.* instantánea *f.*

snare, *n.* trampa *f.*

snarl, 1. *n.* gruñido *m.* 2. *v.* gruñir; (hair) enredar.

snatch, *v.* arrebatar.

sneak, *v.* ir, entrar; salir (etc.) a hurtadillas.

sneaker, *n.* sujeto ruin *m.*

sneer, 1. *n.* mofa *f.* 2. *v.* mofarse.

sneeze, 1. *n.* estornudo *m.* 2. *v.* estornudar.

snicker, *n.* risita *f.*

snob, *n.* esnob *m.*

snore, 1. *n.* ronquido *m.* 2. *v.* roncar.

snow, 1. *n.* nieve *f.* 2. *v.* nevar.

snowdrift, *n.* ventisquero *m.*

snub, *v.* desairar.

snug, *a.* abrigado y cómodo.

so, 1. *adv.* así; (also) también. **so as to**, para. **so that**, para que. **so . . . as**, tan . . . como. **so . . . that**, tan . . . que. 2. *conj.* así es que.

soak, *v.* empapar.

soap, 1. *n.* jabón *m.* 2. *v.* enjabonar.

soar, *v.* remontarse.

sob, 1. *n.* sollozo *m.* 2. *v.* sollozar.

sober, *a.* sobrio; pensativo.

sociable, *a.* sociable.

social, 1. *a.* social. 2. *n.* tertulia *f.*

socialism, *n.* socialismo *m.*

socialist, *a.* & *n.* socialista *m.*

society, *n.* sociedad; compañía *f.*

sociology, *n.* sociología *f.*

sock, 1. *n.* calcetín; puñetazo *m.* 2. *v.* dar un puñetazo a.

socket, *n.* cuenca *f.;* (elec.) enchufe *m.*

sod, *n.* césped *m.*

soda, *n.* soda; (chem.) sosa *f.*

sodium, *n.* sodio *m.*

sofa, *n.* sofá *m.*

soft, *a.* blando; fino; suave.

soft drink, *n.* bebida no alcohólica *m.*

soften, *v.* ablandar; suavizar.

soil, 1. *n.* suelo *m.;* tierra *f.* 2. *v.* ensuciar.

sojourn, *n.* morada *f.*, estancia *f.*

solace, 1. *n.* solaz *m.* 2. *v.* solazar.

solar, *a.* solar.

solar system, *n.* sistema solar *m.*

solder, 1. *v.* soldar. 2. *n.* soldadura *f.*

soldier, *n.* soldado *m.*

sole, 1. *n.* suela; (of foot) planta *f.;* (fish) lenguado *m.* 2. *a.* único.

solemn, *a.* solemne.

solemnity, *n.* solemnidad *f.*

solicit, *v.* solicitar.

solicitous, *a.* solícito.

solid, *a.* & *n.* sólido *m.*

solidify, *v.* solidificar.

solidity, *n.* solidez *f.*

solitary, *a.* solitario.

solitude, *n.* soledad *f.*

solo, *n.* solo *m.*

soloist, *n.* solista *m.*

soluble, *a.* soluble.

solution, *n.* solución *f.*

solve, *v.* solucionar; resolver.

solvent, *a.* solvente.

somber, *a.* sombrío.

some, *a.* & *pron.* algo (de), un poco (de); alguno; (pl.) algunos, unos.

somebody, **someone**, *pron.* alguien.

somehow, *adv.* de algún modo.

someone, *n.* alguien o alguno

somersault, *n.* salto mortal *m.*

something, *pron.* algo, alguna cosa.

sometime, *adv.* alguna vez.

sometimes, *adv.* a veces, algunas veces.

somewhat, *adv.* algo, un poco.

somewhere, *adv.* en (or a) alguna parte.

son, *n.* hijo *m.*

song, *n.* canción *f.*

son-in-law, *n.* yerno *m.*

soon, *adv.* pronto. **as s. as possible**, cuanto antes. **sooner or later**, tarde o temprano. **no sooner . . . than**, apenas . . . cuando.

soot, *n.* hollín *m.*

soothe, *v.* calmar.

soothingly, *adv.* tiernamente.

sophisticated, *a.* sofisticado.

sophomore, *n.* estudiante de segundo año *m.*

soprano, *n.* soprano *m.* & *f.*

sorcery, *n.* encantamiento *m.*

sordid, *a.* sórdido.

sore, 1. *n.* llaga *f.* 2. *a.* lastimado; (coll.) enojado. **to be s.**, doler.

sorority, *n.* hermandad de mujeres *f.*

sorrow, *n.* pesar, dolor *m.*, aflicción *f.*

sorrowful, *a.* doloroso; afligido.

sorry, *a.* **to be s.**, sentir, lamentar. **to be s. for**, compadecer.

sort, 1. *n.* tipo *m.;* clase, especie *f.* **s. of**, algo, un poco. 2. *v.* clasificar.

soul, *n.* alma *f.*

sound, 1. *a.* sano; razonable; firme. 2. *n.* sonido *m.* 3. *v.* sonar; parecer.

soup, *n.* sopa *f.*

sour, *a.* agrio; ácido; rancio.

source, *n.* fuente; causa *f.*

south, *n.* sur *m.*

South America, n. Sud América, América del Sur.
South American, a. & n. sudamericano -na.
southeast, n. sudeste m.
southern, a. meridional.
South Pole, n. polo sur m.
southwest, n. sudoeste m.
souvenir, n. recuerdo m.
sovereign, n. soberano m.
sovereignty, n. soberanía f.
Soviet Russia, n. Rusia Soviética f.
sow, 1. n. puerca f. 2. v. sembrar.
space, 1. n. espacio m. 2. v. espaciar.
space shuttle, n. vehículo que comunica a dos naves espaciales.
spacious, a. espacioso.
spade, 1. n. laya; (cards) espada f. 2. v. layar.
spaghetti, n. fideo m.
Spain, n. España f.
span, 1. n. tramo m. 2. v. extenderse sobre.
Spaniard, n. español -la.
Spanish, a. & n. español m.
spank, v. pegar.
spanking, n. tunda, zumba f.
spar, v. altercar.
spare, 1. a. de respuesto. 2. v. perdonar; ahorrar; prestar. **have . . . to s.,** tener . . . de sobra.
spark, n. chispa f.
sparkle, 1. n. destello m. 2. v. chispear. **sparkling wine,** vino espumoso.
spark plug, n. bujía f.
sparrow, n. gorrión m.
sparse, a. esparcido.
spasm, n. espasmo m.
spasmodic, a. espasmódico.
spatter, v. salpicar; manchar.
speak, v. hablar.
speaker, n. conferencista m. & f.
spear, n. lanza f.
special, a. especial. **s. delivery,** entrega inmediata, entrega urgente.
specialist, n. especialista m. & f.
specialty, n. especialidad f.
species, n. especie f.
specific, a. específico.
specify, v. especificar.
specimen, n. espécimen m.; muestra f.
spectacle, n. espectáculo m.; (pl.) lentes, anteojos m.pl.
spectacular, a. espectacular, aparatoso.
spectator, n. espectador -ra.
spectrum, n. espectro m.
speculate, v. especular.
speculation, n. especulación f.
speech, n. habla f.; lenguaje; discurso m. **part of s.,** parte de la oración.
speechless, a. mudo.
speed, 1. n. velocidad; rapidez

f. 2. v. **s. up,** acelerar, apresurar.
speedometer, n. velocímetro m.
speedy, a. veloz, rápido.
spell, 1. n. hechizo; rato; (med.) ataque m. 2. v. escribir; relevar.
spelling, n. ortografía f.
spend, v. gastar; (time) pasar.
spendthrift, n. pródigo; manirroto m.
sphere, n. esfera f.
spice, 1. n. especia f. 2. v. especiar.
spider, n. araña f.
spike, n. alcayata f.
spill, v. derramar.
spillway, n. vertedero m.
spin, v. hilar; girar.
spinach, n. espinaca f.
spine, n. espinazo m.
spinet, n. espineta m.
spinster, n. solterona f.
spiral, a. & n. espiral m.
spire, n. caracol m., espira f.
spirit, n. espíritu; ánimo m.
spiritual, a. espiritual.
spiritualism, n. espiritismo m.
spit, v. escupir.
spite, n. despecho m. **in s. of, a** pesar de.
splash, 1. n. salpicadura f. 2. v. salpicar.
splendid, a. espléndido.
splendor, n. esplendor m.
splice, 1. v. empalmar. 2. n. empalme m.
splint, n. tablilla f.
splinter, 1. n. astilla f. 2. v. astillar.
split, 1. n. división f. 2. v. dividir, romper en dos.
splurge, 1. v. fachendear. 2. n. fachenda f.
spoil, 1. n. (pl.) botín m. 2. v. echar a perder; (a child) mimar.
spoke, n. rayo (de rueda) m.
spokesman, n. interlocutor m.
sponge, n. esponja f.
sponsor, 1. n. patrocinador m. 2. v. patrocinar; costear.
spontaneity, n. espontaneidad f.
spontaneous, a. espontáneo.
spool, n. carrete m.
spoon, n. cuchara f.
spoonful, n. cucharada f.
sporadic, a. esporádico.
sport, n. deporte m.
sportsman, 1. a. deportivo. 2. n. deportista m.
spot, 1. n. mancha f.; lugar, punto m. 2. v. distinguir.
spouse, n. esposo (o esposa) m. or f.
spout, 1. n. chorro; (of teapot) pico m. 2. v. correr a chorro.
sprain, 1. n. torcedura f. 2. v. torcerse.
sprawl, v. tenderse.
spray, 1. n. rociada f. 2. v. rociar.
spread, 1. n. propagación; ex-

tensión; (for bed) colcha f. 2. v. propagar; extender.
spree, n. parranda f.
sprig, n. ramita f.
sprightly, a. garboso.
spring, n. resorte, muelle m.; (season) primavera f.; (of water) manantial m.
springboard, n. trampolín m.
sprinkle, v. rociar; (rain) lloviznar.
sprint, n. carrera f.
sprout, n. retoño m.
spry, a. ágil.
spun, a. hilado.
spur, 1. n. espuela f. **on the s. of the moment,** sin pensarlo. 2. v. espolear.
spurious, a. espurio.
spurn, v. rechazar, despreciar.
spurt, 1. n. chorro m.; esfuerzo supremo. 2. v. salir en chorro.
spy, 1. espía m. & f. 2. v. espiar.
squabble, 1. n. riña f. 2. v. reñir.
squad, n. escuadra f.
squadron, n. escuadrón m.
squalid, a. escuálido.
squall, n. borrasca f.
squalor, n. escualidez f.
squander, v. malgastar.
square, 1. a. cuadrado. 2. n. cuadrado m.; plaza f.
square dance, n. contradanza f.
squat, v. agacharse.
squeak, 1. n. chirrido m. 2. v. chirriar.
squeamish, a. escrupuloso.
squeeze, 1. n. apretón m. 2. v. apretar; (fruit) exprimir.
squirrel, n. ardilla f.
squirt, 1. n. chisguete m. 2. v. jeringar.
stab, 1. n. puñalada f. 2. v. apuñalar.
stability, n. estabilidad f.
stabilize, v. estabilizar.
stable, 1. a. estable, equilibrado. 2. n. caballeriza f.
stack, 1. n. pila f. 2. v. apilar.
stadium, n. estadio m.
staff, n. personal m. **editorial s.,** cuerpo de redacción. **general s.,** estado mayor.
stag, n. ciervo m.
stage, 1. n. etapa; (theat.) escena f. 2. v. representar.
stagflation, n. estagnación e inflación a la vez.
stagger, v. tambalear.
stagnant, a. estancado.
stagnate, v. estancarse.
stain, 1. n. mancha f. 2. v. manchar.
staircase, stairs, n. escalera f.
stake, n. estaca; (bet) apuesta f. **at s.,** en juego; en peligro.
stale, a. rancio.
stalemate, n. estancación f., tablas.
stalk, n. caña f.; (of flower) tallo m.
stall, 1. n. tenderete; (for

horse) pesebre *m.* 2. *v.* demorar; (motor) atascar.

stallion, *n.* garañón *m.*

stalwart, *a.* fornido.

stamina, *n.* vigor *m.*

stammer, *v.* tartamudear.

stamp, 1. *n.* sello *m.*, estampilla *f.* 2. *v.* sellar.

stampede, *n.* estampida *f.*

stand, 1. *n.* puesto *m.;* posición; (speaker's) tribuna; (furniture) mesita *f.* 2. *v.* estar; estar de pie; aguantar. **s. up,** pararse, levantarse.

standard, 1. *a.* normal, corriente. 2. *n.* norma *f.* **s. of living,** nivel de vida.

standardize, *v.* uniformar.

standing, *a.* fijo; establecido.

standpoint, *n.* punto de vista *m.*

staple, *n.* materia prima *f.*

star, *n.* estrella *f.*

starboard, *n.* estribor *m.*

starch, 1. *n.* almidón *m.;* (in diet) fécula *f.* 2. *v.* almidonar.

stare, *v.* mirar fijamente.

stark, 1. *a.* severo. 2. *adv.* completamente.

start, 1. *n.* susto; principio *m.* 2. *v.* comenzar, empezar; salir; poner en marcha; causar.

startle, *v.* asustar.

starvation, *n.* hambre *f.*

starve, *v.* morir de hambre.

state, 1. *n.* estado *m.* 2. *v.* declarar, decir.

statement, *n.* declaración *f.*

stateroom, *n.* camarote *m.*

statesman, *n.* estadista *m.*

static, *a.* estático. *n.* estática *f.*

station, *n.* estación *f.*

stationary, *a.* estacionario, fijo.

stationery, *n.* papel de escribir.

statistics, *n.* estadística *f.*

statue, *n.* estatua *f.*

stature, *n.* estatura *f.*

status, *n.* estado legal *m.*

statute, *n.* ley *f.*

staunch, *a.* fiel; constante.

stay, 1. *n.* estancia; vista *f.* 2. *v.* quedar, permanecer; parar; alojarse. **s. away,** ausentarse. **s. up,** velar.

steadfast, *a.* inmutable.

steady, 1. *a.* firme; permanente; regular. 2. *v.* sostener.

steak, *n.* biftec, bistec *m.*

steal, 1. *n.* plagio *m.* 2. *v.* robar. **s. away,** escabullirse.

stealth, *n.* cautela *f.*

steam, *n.* vapor *m.*

steamboat, steamer, steamship, *n.* vapor *m.*

steel, *n.* acero *m.* 2. *v.* **s. oneself,** fortalecerse.

steep, *a.* escarpado, empinado.

steeple, *n.* campanario *m.*

steer, 1. *n.* buey *m.* 2. *v.* guiar, manejar.

stellar, *a.* astral.

stem, 1. *n.* tallo *m.* 2. *v.* parar. **s. from,** emanar de.

stencil, 1. *n.* estarcidor. 2. *v.* estarcir.

stenographer, *n.* estenógrafo - fa.

stenography, *n.* taquigrafía *f.*

step, 1. *n.* paso *m.;* medida *f.;* (stairs) escalón *m.* 2. *v.* pisar. **s. back,** retirarse.

stepladder, *n.* escalera de mano *f.*

stereophonic, *a.* estereofónico.

stereotype, 1. *n.* estereotipo. 2 *v.* estereotipar.

sterile, *a.* estéril.

sterilize, *v.* esterilizar.

sterling, *a.* esterlina, genuino.

stern, 1. *n.* popa *f.* 2. *a.* duro, severo.

stethoscope, *n.* estetoscopio *m.*

stevedore, *n.* estibador *m.*

stew, 1. *n.* guisado *m.* 2. *v.* estofar.

steward, *n.* camarero.

stewardess, *n.* azafata *f.*, aeromoza *f.*

stick, 1. *n.* palo, bastón *m.* 2. *v.* pegar; (put) poner, meter.

sticky, *a.* pegajoso.

stiff, *a.* tieso; duro.

stiffness, *n.* tiesura *f.*

stifle, *v.* sofocar; (fig.) suprimir.

stigma, *n.* estigma *m.*

still, 1. *a.* quieto; silencioso. **to keep s.,** callarse. 2. *adv.* todavía, aún; no obstante. 3. *n.* alambique *m.*

stillborn, *a. & a.* nacido muerto *m.*

still life, *n.* naturaleza muerta *f.*

stillness, *n.* silencio *m.*

stilted, *a.* altisonante.

stimulant, *a. & n.* estimulante *m.*

stimulate, *v.* estimular.

stimulus, *n.* estímulo *m.*

sting, 1. *n.* picadura *f.* 2. *v.* picar.

stingy, *a.* tacaño.

stipulate, *v.* estipular.

stir, 1. *n.* conmoción *f.* 2. *v.* mover. **s. up,** conmover; suscitar.

stitch, 1. *n.* puntada *f.* 2. *v.* coser.

stock, *n.* surtido *f.;* raza *f.;* (finance) acciones. *f.pl.* **in s.,** en existencia. **to take s. in,** tener fe en.

stock exchange, *n.* bolsa *f.*

stockholder, *n.* corredor de bolsa *m.*

stocking, *n.* media *f.*

stockyard, *n.* corral de ganado *m.*

stodgy, *a.* pesado.

stoical, *a.* estoico.

stole, *n.* estola *f.*

stolid, *a.* impasible.

stomach, *n.* estómago *m.*

stone, *n.* piedra *f.*

stool, *n.* banquillo *m.*

stoop, *v.* encorvarse; (fig.) rebajarse.

stop, 1. *n.* parada *f.* **to put a s. to,** poner fin a. 2. *v.* parar; suspender; detener; impedir. **s. doing** (etc.), dejar de hacer (etc.).

stopgap, *n.* subterfugio *m.*

storage, *n.* almacenaje *m.*

store, 1. *n.* tienda; provisión *f.* **department s.,** almacén *m.* 2. *v.* guardar; almacenar.

storm, *n.* tempestad, tormenta *f.*

stormy, *a.* tempestuoso.

story, *n.* cuento; relato *m.;* historia *f.* **short s.,** cuento.

stout, *a.* corpulento.

stove, *n.* hornilla; estufa *f.*

straight, 1. *a.* recto; derecho. 2. *adv.* directamente.

straighten, *v.* enderezar. **s. out,** poner en orden.

straightforward, *a.* recto, sincero.

strain, 1. *n.* tensión *f.* 2. *v.* colar.

strainer, *n.* colador *m.*

strait, *n.* estrecho *m.*

strand, 1. *n.* hilo *m.* 2. *v.* **be stranded,** encallarse.

strange, *a.* extraño; raro.

stranger, *n.* extranjero -ra. forastero -ra; desconocido -da.

strangle, *v.* estrangular.

strap, *n.* correa *f.*

stratagem, *n.* estratagema *f.*

strategic, *a.* estratégico.

strategy, *n.* estrategia *f.*

stratosphere, *n.* estratosfera *f.*

straw, *n.* paja *f.*

strawberry, *n.* fresa *f.*

stray, 1. *a.* vagabundo. 2. *v.* extraviarse.

streak, 1. *n.* racha; raya *f.;* lado *m.* 2. *v.* rayar.

stream, *n.* corriente *f.*

street, *n.* calle *f.*

streetcar, *n.* tranvía *m.*

strength, *n.* fuerza *m.*

strengthen, *v.* reforzar.

strenuous, *a.* estrenuo.

streptococcus, *n.* estreptococo *m.*

stress, 1. *n.* tensión *f.;* énfasis *m.* 2. *v.* recalcar; acentuar.

stretch, 1. *n.* trecho *m.* **at one s.,** de un tirón. 2. *v.* tender; extender; estirarse.

stretcher, *n.* camilla *f.*

strew, *v.* esparcir.

stricken, *a.* agobiado.

strict, *a.* estricto; severo.

stride, 1. *n.* tranco *m.;* (fig., pl.) progresos. 2. *v.* andar a trancos.

strife, *n.* contienda *f.*

strike, 1. *n.* huelga *f.* 2. *v.* pegar; chocar con; (clock) dar.

string, *n.* cuerda *f.;* cordel *m.*

string bean, *n.* habichuela *f.*

stringent, *a.* estricto.

strip, 1. *n.* tira *f.* 2. despojar; desnudarse.

stripe, *n.* raya *f.;* (mil.) galón *m.*

strive, *v.* esforzarse.

stroke, n. golpe m.; (swimming) brazada f.; (med.) ataque m. **s. of luck,** suerte f.

stroll, 1. n. paseo m. 2. v. pasearse.

stroller, n. vagabundo m.

strong, a. fuerte.

stronghold, n. fortificación f.

structure, n. estructura f.

struggle, 1. n. lucha f. 2. v. luchar.

strut, 1. n. pavonada f. 2. v. pavonear.

stub, 1. n. cabo; (ticket) talón m. 2. v. **s. one's toe on,** tropezar con.

stubborn, a. testarudo.

stucco, 1. n. estuco. 2. v. estucar.

student, n. alumno -na, estudiante -ta.

studio, n. estudio m.

studious, a. aplicado; estudioso.

study, 1. n. estudio m. 2. v. estudiar.

stuff, 1. n. cosas f.pl. 2. v. llenar; rellenar.

stuffing, n. relleno m.

stumble, v. tropezar.

stump, n. tronco m.

stun, v. aturdir.

stunt, 1. n. suerte f. 2. v. impedir crecimiento.

stupendous, a. estupendo.

stupid, a. estúpido.

stupidity, n. estupidez f.

stupor, n. estupor m.

sturdy, a. robusto.

stutter, 1. v. tartamudear. 2. n. tartamudeo m.

sty, n. pocilga f.

style, n. estilo m.; moda f.

stylish, a. elegante; a la moda.

suave, a. afable, suave.

subconscious, a. subconsciente.

subdue, v. dominar.

subject, 1. a. sujeto. 2. n. tema m.; (of study) materia f.; (pol.) súbdito -ta; (gram.) sujeto m. 3. v. someter.

subjugate, v. sojuzgar, subjugar.

subjunctive, a. & n. subjuntivo m.

sublimate, v. sublimar.

sublime, a. sublime.

submarine, a. & n. submarino m.

submerge, v. sumergir.

submission, n. sumisión f.

submit, v. someter.

subnormal, a. subnormal.

subordinate, 1. a. & n. subordinado m. 2. v. subordinar.

subscribe, v. aprobar; abonarse.

subscription, n. abono m.

subsequent, a. subsiguiente.

subservient, a. servicial.

subside, v. apaciguarse.

subsidy, n. subvención f.

substance, n. substancia f.

substantial, a. substancial; considerable.

substitute, 1. a. substitutivo. 2. n. substituto m. 3. v. substituir.

substitution, n. substitución f.

subterfuge, n. subterfugio m.

subtle, a. sutil.

subtract, v. substraer.

suburb, n. suburbio m.; (pl.) afueras f.pl.

subversive, a. subversivo.

subway, n. metro m.

succeed, v. lograr, tener éxito; (in office) suceder a.

success, n. éxito m.

successful, a. próspero; afortunado.

succession, n. sucesión f.

successive, a. sucesivo.

successor, n. sucesor -ra; heredero -ra.

succor, 1. n. socorro m. 2. v. socorrer.

succumb, v. sucumbir.

such, a. tal.

suck, v. chupar.

suction, n. succión f.

sudden, a. repentino, súbito. **all of a s.,** de repente.

suds, n. jabonaduras f.

sue, v. demandar.

suffer, v. sufrir; padecer.

suffice, v. bastar.

sufficient, a. suficiente.

suffocate, v. sofocar.

sugar, n. azúcar m.

suggest, v. sugerir.

suggestion, n. sugerencia f.

suicide, n. suicidio m.; (person) suicida m. & f. **to commit s.,** suicidarse.

suit, 1. n. traje; (cards) palo; (law) pleito m. 2. v. convenir a.

suitable, a. apropiado; que conviene.

suitcase, n. maleta f.

suite, n. serie f., séquito m.

suitor, n. pretendiente m.

sullen, a. hosco.

sum, 1. n. suma f. 2. v. **s. up,** resumir.

summarize, v. resumir.

summary, n. resumen m.

summer, n. verano m.

summon, v. llamar; (law) citar.

summons, n. citación f.

sumptuous, a. suntuoso.

sun, 1. n. sol m. 2. v. tomar el sol.

sunburn, n. quemadura de sol.

sunburned, a. quemado por el sol.

Sunday, n. domingo m.

sunken, a. hundido.

sunny, a. asoleado. **s. day,** día de sol. **to be s.,** (weather) hacer sol.

sunshine, n. luz del sol.

superb, a. soberbio.

superficial, a. superficial.

superfluous, a. superfluo.

superhuman, a. sobrehumano.

superintendent, n. superinten-

dente m.; (of building) conserje m.; (of school) director general.

superior, a. & n. superior m.

superiority, n. superioridad f.

superlative, a. superlativo.

supernatural, a. sobrenatural.

supersede, v. reemplazar.

superstar, n. superstar m.

superstition, n. superstición f.

superstitious, a. supersticioso.

supervise, v. supervisar.

supper, n. cena f.

supplement, 1. n. suplemento m. 2. v. suplementar.

supply, 1. n. provisión f.; (com.) surtido m.; (econ.) existencia f. 2. v. suplir; proporcionar.

support, 1. n. sustento; apoyo m. 2. v. mantener; apoyar.

suppose, v. suponer. **be supposed to,** deber.

suppress, v. suprimir.

suppression, n. supresión f.

supreme, a. supremo.

sure, a. seguro, cierto. **for s.,** con seguridad. **to make s.,** asegurarse.

surety, n. garantía f.

surf, n. marejada f.

surface, n. superficie f.

surge, v. surgir.

surgeon, n. cirujano m.

surgery, n. cirugía f.

surmise, 1. n. conjetura f. 2. v. suponer.

surmount, v. vencer.

surname, n. apellido m.

surpass, v. superar.

surplus, a. & n. sobrante m.

surprise, 1. n. sorpresa 2. v. sorprender. **I am surprised . . . ,** me extraña . . .

surrender, 1. n. rendición f. 2. v. rendir.

surround, v. rodear, circundar.

surveillance, n. vigilancia f.

survey, 1. n. examen estudio m. 2. v. examinar, estudiar; (land) medir.

survival, n. supervivencia f.

survive, v. sobrevivir.

susceptible, a. susceptible.

suspect, v. sospechar.

suspend, v. suspender.

suspense, n. incertidumbre f. **in s.,** en suspenso.

suspension, n. suspensión f.

suspension bridge, n. puente colgante m.

suspicion, n. sospecha f.

suspicious, a. sospechoso.

sustain, v. sustentar; mantener.

swallow, 1. n. trago m.; (bird) golondrina f. 2. v. tragar.

swamp, 1. n. pantano m. 2. v. (fig.) abrumar.

swan, n. cisne m.

swap, 1. n. trueque m. 2. v. cambalachear.

swarm, n. enjambre m.

sway, 1. n. predominio m. 2. v. bambolearse; (fig.) influir en.

swear, v. jurar. **s. off**, renunciar a.

sweat, 1. sudor m. 2. v. sudar.

sweater, n. suéter m.

Swede, n. sueco -ca.

Sweden, n. Suecia f.

Swedish, a. sueco.

sweep, v. barrer.

sweet, 1. a. dulce; amable; simpático. 2. n. (pl.) dulces m.pl.

sweetheart, n. amante m.

sweetness, n. dulzura f.

swell, 1. a. (coll.) estupendo, excelente. 2. n. (mar.) oleada f. 3. v. hincharse; aumentar.

swelter, v. sofacar.

swift, a. rápido, veloz.

swim, 1. n. nadada f. 2. v. nadar.

swindle, 1. n. estafa. 2. v. estafar.

swine, n. puercos m.pl.

swing, 1. n. columpio m. **in full s.**, en plena actividad. 2. v. mecer; balancear.

swirl, 1. n. remolino m. 2. v. arremolinar.

Swiss, a. & n. suizo -za.

switch, 1. n. varilla f.; (elec.) llave f., conmutador m.; (railway) cambiavia m. 2. v. cambiar; trocar.

switchboard, n. cuadro conmutador m.

Switzerland, n. Suiza f.

sword, n. espada f.

syllable, n. sílaba f.

symbol, n. símbolo m.

sympathetic, a. compasivo. **to be s.**, tener simpatía.

sympathy, n. lástima; condolencia f.

symphony, n. sinfonía f.

symptom, n. síntoma m.

synchronize, v. sincronizar.

syndicate, n. sindicato m.

syndrome, n. sindroma m.

synonym, n. sinónimo m.

synthetic, a. sintético.

syringe, n. jeringa f.

syrup, n. almíbar; (cough) jarabe m.

system, n. sistema m.

systematic, a. sistemático.

T

tabernacle, n. tabernáculo m.

table, n. mesa; (list) tabla f.

tablespoon, n. cuchara f.

tablespoonful, n. cucharada f.

tablet, n. tableta; (med.) pastilla f.

tack, n. tachuela f.

tact, n. tacto m.

tag, n. etiqueta f., rótulo m.

tail, n. cola f., rabo m.

tailor, n. sastre m.

take, v. tomar; llevar. **t. away**, quitar. **t. off**, quitarse. **t. out**, sacar. **t. long**, tardar mucho.

tale, n. cuento m.

talent, n. talento m.

talk, 1. n. plática, habla f.; discurso m. 2. v. hablar.

talkative, a. locuaz.

tall, a. alto.

tame, 1. a. manso, domesticado. 2. v. domesticar.

tamper, v. **t. with**, entremeterse en.

tan, 1. a. color de arena. 2. v. curtir; tostar.

tangible, a. tangible.

tangle, 1. n. enredo m. 2. v. enredar.

tank, n. tanque m.

tap, 1. n. golpe ligero. 2. v. golpear ligeramente; decentar.

tape, n. cinta f.

tape recorder, n. magnetófono m.

tapestry, n. tapiz m.; tapicería f.

tar, 1. n. brea f. 2. v. embrear.

target, n. blanco m.

tarnish, 1. n. deslustre m. 2. v. deslustrar.

task, n. tarea f.

taste, 1. n. gusto; sabor m. 2. v. gustar; progar. **t. of**, saber a.

tasty, a. sabroso.

taut, a. tieso.

tavern, n. taberna f.

tax, 1. n. impuesto m. 2. v. imponer impuestos.

taxi, n. taxi, taxímetro m.

tea, n. té m.

teach, v. enseñar.

teacher, n. maestro -tra, profesor -ra.

team, n. equipo m.; pareja f.

tear, 1. n. rasgón m.; lágrima f. 2. v. rasgar, lacerar; separar.

tease, v. atormentar; embromar.

teaspoon, n. cucharita f.

technical, a. técnico.

technique, n. técnica f.

tedious, a. tedioso.

telegram, n. telegrama m.

telegraph, 1. telégrafo m. 2. v. telegrafiar.

telephone, 1. teléfono m. **t. book**, directorio telefónico. 2. v. telefonear; llamar por teléfono.

telescope, 1. n. telescopio m. 2. v. enchufar.

television, n. televisión f.

tell, v. decir; contar; distinguir.

temper, 1. n. temperamento, genio m. 2. v. templar.

temperament, n. temperamento m.

temperamental, a. sensible, emocional.

temperance, n. moderación; sobriedad f.

temperate, a. templado.

temperature, n. temperatura f.

tempest, n. tempestad f.

tempestuous, a. tempestuoso.

temple, n. templo m.

temporary, a. temporal, temporario.

tempt, v. tentar.

temptation, n. tentación f.

ten, a. & pron. diez.

tenant, n. inquilino -na.

tend, v. tender. **t. to**, atender.

tendency, n. tendencia f.

tender, 1. a. tierno. 2. v. ofrecer.

tenderness, n. ternura f.

tennis, n. tenis m.

tenor, n. tenor m.

tense, 1. a. tenso. 2. n. tiempo m.

tent, n. tienda, carpa f.

tenth, a. décimo.

term, 1. n. término; plazo m. 2. v. llamar.

terrace, n. terraza f.

terrible, a. terrible, espantoso.

territory, n. territorio m.

terror, n. terror, espanto m.

test, 1. n. prueba f.; examen m. 2. v. probar, examinar.

testament, n. testamento m.

testify, v. atestiguar, testificar.

testimony, n. testimonio m.

text, n. texto; tema m.

textile, 1. a. textil. 2. n. tejido m.

texture, n. textura f.; tejido m.

than, conj. que; de.

thank, v. agradecer, dar gracias; **thanks**, **th. you**, gracias.

thankful, a. agradecido; grato.

that, 1. a. ese, aquel. 2. dem. pron. ése, aquél; eso, aquello. 3. rel. pron. & conj. que.

the, art. el, la, los, las; lo.

theater, n. teatro m.

theft, n. robo m.

their, a. su.

theirs, pron. suyo, de ellos.

them, pron. ellos, ellas; los, las; les.

theme, n. tema m.; (mus.) motivo m.

themselves, pron. sí, sí mismos -as. **they th.**, ellos mismos, ellas mismas. **with th.**, consigo.

then, adv. entonces, después; pues.

thence, adv. de allí.

theology, n. teología f.

theory, n. teoría f.

there, adv. allí, allá, ahí. **there is**, **there are**, hay.

therefore, adv. por lo tanto, por consiguiente.

thermometer, n. termómetro m.

they, pron. ellos, ellas.

thick, a. espeso, grueso, denso; torpe.

thicken, v. espesar, condensar.

thief, n. ladrón -na.

thigh, n. muslo m.

thimble, n. dedal m.

thin, 1. a. delgado; raro; claro; escaso. 2. v. enrarecer; adelgazar.

thing, n. cosa f.

think, v. pensar; creer.

thinker, n. pensador -ra.

third, a. tercero.

Third World, n. Tercer Mundo m.

thirst, n. sed f.

thirsty, a. sediento. **to be th.**, tener sed.

thirteen, a. & pron. trece.

thirty, a. & pron. treinta.

this, 1. a. este. 2. pron. éste; esto.

thorough, a. completo; cuidadoso.

though, 1. adv. sin embargo. 2. conj. aunque. **as th.**, como si.

thought, n. pensamiento.

thoughtful, a. pensativo; considerado.

thousand, a. & pron. mil.

thread, n. hilo m.; (of screw) rosca f.

threat, n. amenaza f.

threaten, v. amenazar.

three, a. & pron. tres.

thrift, n. economía, frugalidad f.

thrill, 1. n. emoción f. 2. v. emocionar.

thrive, v. prosperar.

throat, n. garganta f.

throne, n. trono m.

through, 1. prep. por; a través de; por medio de. 2. a. continuo. **th. train**, tren directo. **to be th.**, haber terminado.

throughout, 1. prep. por todo, durante todo. 2. adv. en todas partes; completamente.

throw, 1. n. tiro m. 2. v. tirar, lanzar. **th. away**, arrojar. **th. out**, echar.

thrust, 1. n. lanzada f. 2. v. empujar.

thumb, n. pulgar m.

thunder, 1. n. trueno m. 2. v. tronar.

Thursday, n. jueves m.

thus, adv. así, de este modo.

thwart, v. frustrar.

ticket, 1. n. billete, boleto m. **t. window**, taquilla f. **round trip t.**, billete de ida y vuelta.

tickle, 1. n. cosquilla f. 2. v. hacer cosquillas a.

ticklish, a. cosquilloso.

tide, n. marea f.

tidy, 1. a. limpio, ordenado. 2. v. poner en orden.

tie, 1. n. corbata f.; lazo; (game) empate m. 2. v. atar; anudar.

tier, n. hilera f.

tiger, n. tigre m.

tight, a. apretado; tacaño.

tighten, v. estrechar, apretar.

tile, n. teja f., azulejo m.

till, 1. prep. hasta. 2. conj. hasta que. 3. n. cajón m. 4. v. cultivar, labrar.

tilt, 1. n. inclinación; justa f. 2. v. inclinar; justar.

timber, n. madera f.; (beam) madero m.

time, n. tiempo m.; vez f.; (of day) hora f.

timetable, n. horario, itinerario m.

timid, a. tímido.

timidity, n. timidez f.

tin, n. estaño m.; hojalata f. **t. can**, lata f.

tint, 1. n. tinte m. 2. v. teñir.

tiny, a. chiquito, pequeñito.

tip, 1. n. punta; propina f. 2. v. inclinar; dar propina a.

tire, 1. n. llanta, goma f., neumático m. 2. v. cansar.

tired, a. cansado.

tissue, n. tejido m. **t. paper**, papel de seda.

title, 1. n. título m. 2. v. titular.

to, prep. a; para.

toast, 1. n. tostada f.; (drink) brindis m. 2. v. tostar; brindar por.

tobacco, n. tabaco m.

today, adv. hoy.

toe, n. dedo del pie.

together, 1. a. juntos. 2. adv. juntamente.

toil, 1. n. trabajo m. 2. v. afanarse.

toilet, n. tocado; excusado, retrete m. **t. paper**, papel higiénico.

token, n. señal f.

tolerance, n. tolerancia f.

tolerate, v. tolerar.

tomato, n. tomate m.

tomb, n. tumba f.

tomorrow, adv. mañana. **day after t.**, pasado mañana.

ton, n. tonelada f.

tone, n. tono m.

tongue, n. lengua f.

tonic, n. tónico m.

tonight, adv. esta noche.

tonsil, n. amígdala f.

too, adv. también; demasiado. **t. much**, demasiado. **t. many**, demasiados.

tool, n. herramienta f.

tooth, n. diente m.; (back) muela f.

toothache, n. dolor de muela.

toothbrush, n. cepillo de dientes.

top, 1. n. parte de arriba. 2. v. cubrir; sobrepasar.

topic, n. tópico m.

topical, a. tópico.

torch, n. antorcha f.

torment, 1. n. tormento m. 2. v. atormentar.

torrent, n. torrente m.

torture, 1. n. tortura f. 2. v. torturar.

toss, v. tirar; agitar.

total, 1. a. total, entero. 2. n. total m.

totalitarian, a. totalitario.

touch, 1. n. tacto m. **in t.**, en comunicación. 2. v. tocar; conmover.

tough, a. tosco; tieso; fuerte.

tour, 1. n. viaje m., jira f. 2. v. viajar.

tourist, n. turista m. & f.

tournament, n. torneo m.

tow, 1. n. remolque m. 2. v. remolcar.

toward, prep. hacia.

towel, n. toalla f.

tower, n. torre f.

town, n. pueblo m.

toy, 1. n. juguete m. 2. v. jugar.

trace, 1. n. vestigio; rastro m. 2. v. trazar; rastrear; investigar.

track, 1. n. huella, pista f. **race t.**, hipódromo m. 2. v. rastrear.

tract, n. trecho, tracto; tratado m.

tractor, n. tractor m.

trade, 1. n. comercio, negocio; oficio; canje m. 2. v. comerciar, negociar; cambiar.

trader, n. comerciante m.

tradition, n. tradición f.

traditional, a. tradicional.

traffic, 1. n. tráfico m. 2. v. traficar.

tragedy, n. tragedia f.

tragic, a. trágico.

trail, 1. n. sendero; rastro m. 2. v. rastrear; arrastrar.

train, 1. n. tren m. 2. v. enseñar; disciplinar; (sport) entrenarse.

traitor, n. traidor m.

tramp, 1. n. caminata f.; vagabundo m. 2. v. patear.

tranquil, a. tranquilo.

tranquillity, n. tranquilidad f.

transaction, n. transacción f.

transfer, 1. n. traslado m.; boleto de transbordo. 2. v. trasladar, transferir.

transform, v. transformar.

transfusion, n. transfusión f.

transition, n. transición f.

translate, v. traducir.

translation, n. traducción f.

transmit, v. transmitir.

transparent, a. transparente.

transport, 1. n. transporte m., transportación f. 2. v. transportar.

transportation, n. transporte m.

transsexual, a. transexual.

transvestite, n. travesti m.

trap, 1. n. trampa f. 2. v. atrapar.

trash, n. desecho m.; basura f.

travel, 1. n. tráfico m.; (pl.) viajes m.pl. 2. v. viajar.

traveler, n. viajero -ra.

traveler's check, n. cheque de viaje m.

tray, n. bandeja f.

tread, 1. n. pisada f.; (of a tire) cubierta f. 2. v. pisar.

treason, n. traición f.

treasure, n. tesoro m.

treasurer, n. tesorero -ra.

treasury, n. tesorería f.

treat, v. tratar; convidar.

treatment, n. trato, tratamiento m.

treaty, n. tratado, pacto m.

tree, n. árbol m.

tremble, v. temblar.

tremendous, a. tremendo.

trench, n. foso m.; (mil.) trinchera f.

trend, 1. *n.* tendencia *f.* **2.** *v.* tender.

trespass, *v.* traspasar; violar.

triage, *n.* clasificación de los heridos después del combate.

trial, *n.* prueba *f.;* (leg.) proceso, juicio *m.*

triangle, *n.* triangulo *m.*

tribulation, *n.* tribulación *f.*

tributary, *a. & n.* tributario *m.*

tribute, *n.* tributo *m.*

trick, 1. *n.* engaño *m.;* maña *f.;* (cards) baza *f.* **2.** *v.* engañar.

trifle, 1. *n.* pequeñez *f.* **2.** *v.* juguetear.

trigger, *n.* gatillo *m.*

trim, 1. *a.* ajustado, acicalado. **2.** *n.* adorno *m.* **3.** *v.* adornar; ajustar; cortar un poco.

trinket, *n.* bagatela, chuchería *f.*

trip, 1. *n.* viaje *m.* **2.** *v.* tropezar.

triple, 1. *a.* triple **2.** *v.* triplicar.

trite, *a.* banal.

triumph, 1. *n.* triunfo *m.* **2.** *v.* triunfar.

triumphant, *a.* triunfante.

trivial, *a.* trivial.

trolley, *n.* tranvía *m.*

troop, *n.* tropa *f.*

trophy, *n.* trofeo *m.*

tropical, *a.* trópico.

tropics, *n.* trópico *m.*

trot, 1. *n.* trote *m.* **2.** *v.* trotar.

trouble, 1. *n.* apuro *m.;* congoja; aflicción *f.* **2.** *v.* molestar; afligir.

troublesome, *a.* penoso, molesto.

trough, *n.* artesa *f.*

trousers, *n.* pantalones, calzones *m.pl.*

trout, *n.* trucha *f.*

truce, *n.* tregua *f.*

truck, *n.* camión *m.*

true, *a.* verdadero; cierto, verdad.

trumpet, *n.* trompeta, trompa *f.*

trunk, *n.* baúl *m.;* (of a tree) tronco *m.*

trust, 1. *n.* confianza *f.* **2.** *v.* confiar.

trustworthy, *a.* digno de confianza.

truth, *n.* verdad *f.*

truthful, *a.* veraz.

try, 1. *n.* prueba *f.;* ensayo *m.* **2.** *v.* tratar; probar; ensayar; (leg.) juzgar. **t. on,** probarse.

T-shirt, *n.* camiseta *f.*

tub, *n.* tina *f.*

tube, *n.* tubo *m.*

tuberculosis, *n.* tuberculosis, tisis *f.*

tuck, 1. *n.* recogido *m.* **2.** *v.* recoger.

Tuesday, *n.* martes *m.*

tug, 1. *n.* tirada *f.;* (boat) remolcador *m.* **2.** *v.* tirar.

tuition, *n.* matrícula, colegiatura *f.*

tumble, 1. *n.* caída *f.* **2.** *v.* caer, tumbar; voltear.

tumult, *n.* tumulto, alboroto *m.*

tune, *n.* tono *m.;* melodía, canción *f.* **2.** *v.* templar.

tunnel, *n.* túnel *m.*

turf, *n.* césped *m.*

Turkey, *n.* Turquía *f.*

Turkish, *a.* turco.

turmoil, *n.* disturbio *m.*

turn, 1. *n.* vuelta *f.;* giro; turno *m.* **2.** *v.* volver, tornear, girar; transformar. **t. around,** volverse. **t. on,** encender; abrir. **t. off, t. out,** apagar.

turnip, *n.* nabo *m.*

turret, *n.* torrecilla *f.*

turtle, *n.* tortuga *f.*

tutor, 1. *n.* tutor *m.* **2.** *v.* enseñar.

twelve, *a. & pron.* doce.

twenty, *a. & pron.* veinte.

twice, *adv.* dos veces.

twig, *n.* varita, ramita *f.;* vástago *m.*

twilight, *n.* crepúsculo *m.*

twin, *n.* gemelo -la.

twine, 1. *n.* guita *f.* **2.** *v.* torcer.

twinkle, *v.* centellear.

twist, *v.* torcer.

two, *a. & pron.* dos.

type, 1. *n.* tipo *m.* **2.** *v.* escribir a máquina.

typewriter, *n.* máquina de escribir.

typhoid fever, fiebre tifoidea.

typical, *a.* típico.

typist, *n.* mecanógrafo -fa.

tyranny, *n.* tiranía *f.*

tyrant, *n.* tirano *m.*

U

udder, *n.* ubre *f.*

ugly, *a.* feo.

ulcer, *n.* úlcera *f.*

ulterior, *a.* ulterior.

ultimate, *a.* último.

umbrella, *n.* paraguas *m.* **sun u.,** quitasol *m.*

umpire, *n.* árbitro *m.*

unable, *a.* incapaz. **to be u.,** no poder.

unanimous, *a.* unánime.

uncertain, *a.* incierto, inseguro.

uncle, *n.* tío *m.*

unconscious, *a.* inconsciente; desmayado.

uncover, *v.* descubrir.

under, 1. *adv.* debajo, abajo. **2.** *prep.* bajo, debajo de.

underestimate, *v.* menospreciar, subestimar.

undergo, *v.* sufrir.

underground, *a.* subterráneo.

underline, *v.* subrayar.

underneath, 1. *adv.* por debajo. **2.** *prep.* debajo de.

undershirt, *n.* camiseta *f.*

understand, *v.* entender, comprender.

undertake, *v.* emprender.

underwear, *n.* ropa interior.

undo, *v.* deshacer; desatar.

undress, *v.* desnudar, desvestir.

uneasy, *a.* inquieto.

uneven, *a.* desigual.

unexpected, *a.* inesperado.

unfair, *a.* injusto.

unfit, *a.* incapaz; inadecuado.

unfold, *v.* desplegar; revelar.

unforgettable, *a.* inolvidable.

unfortunate, *a.* desafortunado, desgraciado.

unhappy, *a.* infeliz.

uniform, *a. & n.* uniforme *m.*

unify, *v.* unificar.

union, *n.* unión *f.* **labor u.,** sindicato de obreros.

unique, *a.* único.

unisex, *a.* unisex.

unit, *n.* unidad *f.*

unite, *v.* unir.

unity, *n.* unidad *f.*

universal, *a.* universal.

universe, *n.* universo *m.*

university, *n.* universidad *f.*

unleaded, *a.* sin plomo.

unless, *conj.* a menos que, si no es que.

unlike, *a.* disímil.

unload, *v.* descargar.

unlock, *v.* abrir.

untie, *v.* desatar, soltar.

until, 1. *prep.* hasta. **2.** *conj.* hasta que.

unusual, *a.* raro, inusitado.

up, 1. *adv.* arriba. **2.** *prep.* **u. the street,** *etc.* calle arriba, etc.

uphold, *v.* apoyar, defender.

upholster, *v.* entapizar.

upon, *prep.* sobre, encima de.

upper, *a.* superior.

upright, *a.* derecho, recto.

uproar, *n.* alboroto, tumulto *m.*

upset, 1. *n.* trastorno *m.* **2.** *v.* trastornar.

uptight, *a.* (psicológicamente) tenso, tieso.

upward, *adv.* hacia arriba.

urge, 1. *n.* deseo *m.* **2.** *v.* instar.

urgency, *n.* urgencia *f.*

urgent, *a.* urgente. **to be u.,** urgir.

us, *pron.* nosotros -as; nos.

use, 1. *n.* uso *m.* **2.** *v.* usar, emplear. **u. up,** gastar, agotar. **be used to,** ser acostumbrado a.

useful, *a.* útil.

useless, *a.* inútil.

usher, 1. *n.* acomodador *m.* **2.** *v.* introducir.

usual, *a.* usual.

utensil, *n.* utensilio *m.*

utmost, *a.* sumo, extremo.

utter, 1. *a.* completo. **2.** *v.* proferir; dar.

utterance, *n.* expresión *f.*

V

vacancy, *n.* vacante *f.*

vacant, *a.* desocupado, libre.

vacation, *n.* vacaciones *f.pl.*

vaccinate, *v.* vacunar.

vacuum, n. vacuo, vacío m. **v. cleaner,** aspirador m.

vagrant, n. vagabundo.

vague, a. vago.

vain, a. vano; vanidoso. **in v., en** vano.

valiant, a. valiente.

valid, a. válido.

valley, n. valle m.

valor, n. valor m., valentía f.

valuable, a. precioso. **to be v.,** valer mucho.

value, 1. n. valor, importe m. 2. v. valorar; estimar.

vandal, n. vándalo m.

vanish, v. desaparecer.

vanity, n. vanidad f. **v. case,** polvera f.

vanquish, v. vencer.

vapor, n. vapor m.

variation, n. variación f.

variety, n. variedad f.

various, a. varios, diversos.

varnish, 1. n. barniz m. 2. v. barnizar.

vary, v. variar; cambiar.

vase, n. vaso, jarrón m.

vasectomy, n. vasectomía f.

vassal, n. vasallo m.

vast, a. vasto.

vat, n. tina f., tanque m.

vault, n. bóveda f.

vegetable, 1. a. & n. vegetal m.; (pl.) legumbres, verduras f.pl.

vehement, a. vehemente.

vehicle, n. vehículo m.

veil, 1. n. velo m. 2. v. velar.

vein, n. vena f.

velocity, n. velocidad f.

velvet, n. terciopelo m.

vengeance, n. venganza f.

vent, n. apertura f.

ventilate, v. ventilar.

venture, n. ventura f.

verb, n. verbo m.

verbose, a. verboso.

verdict, n. veredicto, fallo m.

verge, n. borde m.

verify, v. verificar.

versatile, a. versátil.

verse, n. verso m.

version, n. versión f.

vertical, a. vertical.

very, 1. a. mismo. 2. adv. muy.

vessel, n. vasija f.; barco m.

vest, n. chaleco m.

veteran, a. & n. veterano -na.

veto, n. veto m.

vex, v. molestar.

via, prep. por la vía de; por.

viaduct, n. viaducto m.

vibrate, v. vibrar.

vibration, n. vibración f.

vice, n. vicio m.

vicinity, n. vecindad f.

vicious, a. vicioso.

victim, n. víctima f.

victor, n. vencedor m.

victorious, a. victorioso.

victory, n. victoria f.

videodisc, n. videodisco m.

videotape, n. vídeo m., magnetoscopio m.

view, 1. n. vista f. 2. v. ver.

vigil, n. vigilia, vela f.

vigilant, a. vigilante.

vigor, n. vigor m.

vile, a. vil, bajo.

village, n. aldea f.

villain, n. malvado m.

vindicate, v. vindicar.

vine, n. parra, vid f.

vinegar, n. vinagre m.

vintage, n. vendimia f.

violate, v. violar.

violation, n. violación f.

violence, n. violencia f.

violent, a. violento.

violin, n. violín m.

virgin, n. virgen f.

virile, a. viril.

virtual, a. virtual.

virtue, n. virtud f.

virtuous, a. virtuoso.

virus, n. virus m.

visa, n. visa f.

visible, a. visible.

vision, n. visión f.

visit, 1. n. visita f. 2. v. visitar.

visitor, n. visitante m. & f.

visual, a. visual.

vital, a. vital.

vitality, n. vitalidad f.

vitamin, n. vitamina f.

vivacious, a. vivaz.

vivid, a. vivo; gráfico.

vocabulary, n. vocabulario m.

vocal, a. vocal.

vogue, n. boga; moda f.

voice, 1. n. voz f. 2. v. expresar.

void, 1. a. vacío. 2. n. vacío m. 3. v. invalidar.

volume, n. volumen, tomo m.

voluntary, a. voluntario.

volunteer, 1. n. voluntario m. 2. v. ofrecerse.

vomit, v. vomitar.

vote, 1. n. voto m. 2. v. votar.

voter, n. votante m & f.

vouch, v. v. for, garantizar.

vow, 1. n. voto m. 2. v. jurar.

vowel, n. vocal f.

voyage, n. viaje m.

vulgar, a. vulgar; común.

vulnerable, a. vulnerable.

W

wade, v. vadear.

wag, v. menear.

wage, 1. n. (pl.) sueldo, salario m. 2. v. w. war, hacer guerra.

wagon, n. carreta f.

wail, 1. n. lamento, gemido m. 2. v. lamentar, gemir.

waist, n. cintura f.

wait, 1. n. espera f. 2. v. esperar. w. for, esperar. w. on, atender.

waiter, waitress, n. camarero -ra.

wake, v. w. up, despertar.

walk, 1. n. paseo m.; vuelta; caminata f.; modo de andar. 2. v. andar; caminar; ir a pie.

wall, n. pared; (outdoor) tapia; muralla f.

wallcovering, n. tapizado de pared m.

wallet, n. cartera f.

wallpaper, n. empapelado m.

walnut, n. nuez f.

waltz, n. vals m.

wander, v. vagar.

want, 1. n. necesidad f. 2. v. querer.

war, n. guerra f.

ward, 1. n. (pol.) barrio m.; (hospital) cuadra f. 2. v. w. off, parar.

wares, n. mercancías f.pl.

warlike, a. belicoso.

warm, 1. a. caliente; (fig.) caluroso. **to be w.,** tener calor; (weather) hacer calor. 2. v. calentar.

warmth, n. calor m.

warn, v. advertir.

warp, v. alabear.

warrant, v. justificar.

warrior, n. guerrero m.

warship, n. navío de guerra.

wash, v. lavar.

wasp, n. avispa f.

waste, 1. n. gasto m.; desechos m.pl. 2. v. gastar, perder.

watch, 1. n. reloj m.; (mil.) guardia f. 2. v. observar, mirar. w. for, esperar. w. out for, tener cuidado con. w. over, guardar; velar por.

watchful, a. desvelado.

watchmaker, n. relojero m.

watchman, n. sereno m.

water, 1. n. agua f. w. color, acuarela f. 2. v. aguar.

waterbed, n. cama de agua f.

waterfall, n. catarata f.

waterproof, a. impermeable.

wave, 1. n. onda; ola f. 2. v. ondear; agitar; hacer señas.

waver, v. vacilar.

wax, 1. n. cera f. 2. v. encerar.

way, n. camino; modo m., manera f. **in a w.,** hasta cierto punto. **a long w.,** muy lejos. **by the w.,** a propósito. **this w.,** por aquí. **that w.,** por allí. **which w.,** por dónde.

we, pron. nosotros -as.

weak, a. débil.

weaken, v. debilitar.

weakness, n. debilidad f.

wealth, n. riqueza f.

wealthy, a. rico.

weapon, n. arma f.

wear, 1. n. uso, desgaste m.; (clothes) ropa f. 2. v. usar, llevar. w. out, gastar; cansar.

weary, a. cansado, rendido.

weather, n. tiempo m.

weave, v. tejer.

weaver, n. tejedor -ra.

web, n. tela f.

wedding, n. boda f.

wedge, n. cuña f.

Wednesday, n. miércoles m.

weed, n. maleza f.

week, n. semana f. **w. end,** fin de semana.

weekday, n. día de trabajo.

weekly, a. semanal.

weep, v. llorar.

weigh, v. pesar.

weight, *n.* peso *m.*

weird, *a.* misterioso, sobrenatural.

welcome, 1. *a.* bienvenido. **you're w.,** de nada, no hay de qué. **2.** *n.* acogida, bienvenida *f.* **3.** *v.* acoger, recibir bien.

welfare, *n.* bienestar *m.*

well, 1. *a.* sano, bueno. **2.** *adv.* bien; pues. **3.** *n.* pozo *m.*

well-known, *a.* bien conocido.

west, *n.* oeste, occidente *m.*

western, *a.* occidental.

westward, *adv.* hacia el oeste.

wet, 1. *a.* mojado. **to get w.,** mojarse. **2.** *v.* mojar.

whale, *n.* ballena *f.*

what, 1. *a.* qué; cuál. **2.** *interrog. pron.* qué. **3.** *rel. pron.* lo que.

whatever, 1. *a.* cualquier. **2.** *pron.* lo que; todo lo que.

wheat, *n.* trigo *m.*

wheel, *n.* rueda *f.* **steering w.,** volante *m.*

when, 1. *adv.* cuándo. **2.** *conj.* cuando.

whenever, *conj.* siempre que, cuando quiera que.

where, 1. *adv.* dónde, adónde. **2.** *conj.* donde.

wherever, *conj.* dondequiera que, adondequiera que.

whether, *conj.* si.

which, 1. *a.* qué. **2.** *interrog. pron.* cuál. **3.** *rel. pron.* que; el cual; lo cual.

whichever, *a. & pron.* cualquiera que.

while, 1. *conj.* mientras; mientras que. **2.** *n.* rato *m.* **to be worth w.,** valer la pena.

whip, 1. *n.* látigo *m.* **2.** *v.* azotar.

whirl, *v.* girar.

whirlpool, *n.* vórtice *m.*

whirlwind, *n.* torbellino *m.*

whisk broom, *n.* escobilla *f.*

whisker, *n.* bigote *m.*

whiskey, *n.* whisky *m.*

whisper, 1. *n.* cuchicheo *m.* **2.** *v.* cuchichear.

whistle, 1. *n.* pito; silbido *m.* **2.** *v.* silbar.

white, 1. *a.* blanco. **2.** *n.* (of egg) clara *f.*

who, whom, 1. *interrog. pron.* quién. **2.** *rel. pron.* que; quien.

whoever, whomever, *pron.* quienquiera que.

whole, 1. *a.* entero. **the wh.,** todo el. **2.** *n.* totalidad *f.* **on the wh.,** por lo general.

wholesale, *n.* **at wh.,** al por mayor.

wholesome, *a.* sano, saludable.

wholly, *adv.* enteramente.

whose, 1. *interrog. adj.* de quién. **2.** *rel. adj.* cuyo.

why, *adv.* por qué; para qué.

wicked, *a.* malo, malvado.

wickedness, *n.* maldad *f.*

wide, 1. *a.* ancho; extenso. **2.** *adv.* **w. open,** abierto de par en par.

widen, *v.* ensanchar; extender.

widespread, *a.* extenso.

widow, *n.* viuda *f.*

widower, *n.* viudo *m.*

width, *n.* anchura *f.*

wield, *v.* manejar, empuñar.

wife, *n.* esposa, señora, mujer *f.*

wig, *n.* peluca *f.*

wild, *a.* salvaje; bárbaro.

wilderness, *n.* desierto *m.*

wildlife, *n.* fauna silvestre *f.*

will, 1. *n.* voluntad *f.;* testamento *m.* **2.** *v.* querer; determinar; (leg.) legar.

willful, *a.* voluntarioso; premeditado.

willing, *a.* **to be w.,** estar dispuesto.

willingly, *adv.* de buena gana.

wilt, *v.* marchitar.

win, *v.* ganar.

wind, 1. *n.* viento *m.* **2.** *v.* torcer; dar cuerda a.

window, *n.* ventana *f.;* (of car) ventanilla *f.*

windy, *a.* ventoso. **to be w.,** (weather) hacer viento.

wine, *n.* vino *m.*

wing, *n.* ala *f.;* (theat.) bastidor *m.*

wink, 1. *n.* guiño *m.* **2.** *v.* guiñar.

winner, *n.* ganador -ra.

winter, *n.* invierno *m.*

wipe, *v.* limpiar; (dry) secar. **w. out,** destruir.

wire, 1. *n.* alambre; hilo; telegrama *m.* **2.** *v.* telegrafiar.

wireless, *n.* telégrafo sin hilos.

wisdom, *n.* juicio *m.;* sabiduría *f.*

wise, *a.* sensato, juicioso; sabio.

wish, 1. *n.* deseo; voto *m.* **2.** *v.* desear; querer.

wit, *n.* ingenio *m.*, sal *f.*

witch, *n.* bruja *f.*

with, *prep.* con.

withdraw, *v.* retirar.

wither, *v.* marchitar.

withhold, *v.* retener, suspender.

within, 1. *adv.* dentro, por dentro. **2.** *prep.* dentro de; en.

without, 1. *adv.* fuera, por fuera. **2.** *prep.* sin.

witness, 1. *n.* testigo; testimonio *m.* **2.** *v.* presenciar; atestar.

witty, *a.* ingenioso, gracioso.

wizard, *n.* hechicero *m.*

woe, *n.* dolor *m.;* pena *f.*

wolf, *n.* lobo *m.*

woman, *n.* mujer *f.*

womb, *n.* entrañas *f.pl.,* matriz *f.*

wonder, 1. *n.* maravilla; admiración *f.* **for a w.,** por milagro. **no w.,** no es extraño. **2.** *v.* preguntarse; maravillarse.

wonderful, *a.* maravilloso; estupendo.

woo, *v.* cortejar.

wood, *n.* madera; (for fire) leña *f.*

wooden, *a.* de madera.

wool, *n.* lana *f.*

word, 1. *n.* palabra *f.* **the words** (of a song), la letra. **2.** *v.* expresar.

work, 1. *n.* trabajo *m.;* (of art) obra *f.* **2.** *v.* trabajar; obrar; funcionar.

worker, *n.* trabajador -ra; obrero -ra.

workman, *n.* obrero *m.*

world, *n.* mundo *m.* **w. war,** guerra mundial.

worldly, *a.* mundano.

worldwide, *a.* mundial.

worm, *n.* gusano *m.*

worn, *a.* usado. **w. out,** gastado, cansado, rendido.

worry, 1. *n.* preocupación *f.* **2.** *v.* preocupar.

worse, *a.* peor. **to get w.,** empeorar.

worship, 1. *n.* adoración *f.* **2.** *v.* adorar.

worst, *a.* peor.

worth, 1. *a.* **to be w.,** valer. **2.** *n.* valor *m.*

worthless, *a.* sin valor.

worthy, *a.* digno.

wound, 1. *n.* herida *f.* **2.** *v.* herir.

wrap, 1. *n.* (pl.) abrigos *m.pl.* **2.** *n.* envolver.

wrapping, *n.* cubierta *f.*

wrath, *n.* ira, cólera *f.*

wreath, *n.* guirnalda; corona *f.*

wreck, 1. *n.* ruina *f.;* accidente *m.* **2.** *v.* destrozar, arruinar.

wrench, *n.* llave *f.* **monkey w.,** llave inglesa.

wrestle, *v.* luchar.

wretched, *a.* miserable.

wring, *v.* retorcer.

wrinkle, 1. *n.* arruga *f.* **2.** *v.* arrugar.

wrist, *n.* muñeca *f.* **w. watch,** reloj de pulsera.

write, *v.* escribir. **w. down,** apuntar.

writer, *n.* escritor -ra.

writhe, *v.* contorcerse.

wrong, 1. *a.* equivocado; incorrecto. **to be w.,** equivocarse; no tener razón. **2.** *adv.* mal, incorrectamente. **3.** *n.* agravio *m.* **right and w.,** el bien y el mal. **4.** *v.* agraviar, ofender.

X, Y, Z

x-ray, *n.* rayo X *m.*

xylophone, *n.* xilófono *m.*

yacht, *n.* yate *m.*

yard, *n.* patio, corral *m.;* (measure) yarda *f.*

yarn, *n.* hilo.

yawn, 1. *n.* bostezo *m.* **2.** *v.* bostezar.

year, *n.* año *m.*

yearly, *a.* anual.

yearn, *v.* anhelar.
yell, 1. *n.* grito *m.* **2.** *v.* gritar.
yellow, *a.* amarillo.
yes, *adv.* sí.
yesterday, *adv.* ayer.
yet, *adv.* todavía, aún.
yield, *v.* producir; ceder.
yoke, *n.* yugo *m.*
yolk, *n.* yema *f.*
you, *pron.* usted, (pl.) ustedes; lo, la, los, las; le, les; (famil-iar) tú, (pl.) vosotros -as; ti; te, (pl.) os. **with y.,** contigo.
young, *a.* joven.
your, *a.* su; (familiar) tu; (pl.) vuestro.
yours, *pron.* suyo; (familiar) tuyo; (pl.) vuestro.
yourself, -selves, *pron.* sí; se; (familiar) ti; te. **with y.,** con-sigo; contigo. **you y.,** usted mismo, ustedes mismos; tú mismo, vosotros mismos.

youth, *n.* juventud *f.;* (person) joven *m.*
youthful, *a.* juvenil.
zap, *v.* desintegrar, aniquilar.
zeal, *n.* celo, fervor *m.*
zealous, *a.* celoso, fervoroso.
zero, *n.* cero *m.*
zest, *n.* gusto *m.*
zip code, *n.* número de distrito postal.
zone, *n.* zona *f.*
zoo, *n.* jardín zoológico.